UNIFORM
PROBATE CODE

NINTH EDITION

OFFICIAL 1990 TEXT

WITH COMMENTS

INCLUDING
REVISED ARTICLE II

[INTESTACY, WILLS AND DONATIVE
TRANSFERS (1990)]

AND
REVISED ARTICLE VI

[NONPROBATE TRANSFERS ON DEATH (1989)]

INDEX

ST. PAUL, MINN.
WEST PUBLISHING CO.

FOREWORD

This Ninth Edition, which replaces the Eighth Edition, contains the Official Text of the Uniform Probate Code, and includes the Uniform Durable Power of Attorney Act, incorporated by amendment of Part 5 of Article V in 1979, the Uniform Guardianship and Protective Proceedings Act, incorporated by amendment of Parts 1, 2, 3 and 4 of Article V in 1982, provisions relating to Succession Without Administration added in 1982 as sections 3–312 to 3–322, amendments to various sections of the Code in 1984, 1987, 1988 and 1989, the Official Text of the 1989 revision of Article VI, the Official Text of the 1990 revision of Article II, and Comments promulgated by the National Conference of Commissioners on Uniform State Laws through its Joint Editorial Board for the Uniform Probate Code. Note that Part 9, Subpart 1, of Revised Article II has also been adopted as the free-standing Uniform Statutory Rule Against Perpetuities. Note further that Parts 2 and 3 of Revised Article VI have also been adopted as the free-standing Uniform Multiple-Person Accounts Act and Uniform TOD Security Registration Act, respectively.

As an aid for those who wish to study the changes made by the amendments of 1984, 1987, 1988 and 1989 an Appendix is included for each, with additions indicated by underscore and deletions by strikeout. In addition, the Official Text and Comments of Article II as it existed prior to revision in 1990 are also set out in a separate Appendix, as are the Official Text and Comments of Article VI as it existed prior to revision in 1989. Further, the Official Text and Comments of Article V as originally approved in 1969 are similarly set out in a separate Appendix.

The Uniform Probate Code was approved by the National Conference of Commissioners on Uniform State Laws and by the American Bar Association in August, 1969.

The text is made available in this convenient and compact form for ready reference by members of the Bar, the Judiciary, Legislators, and Teachers and Students of the law.

For this Ninth Edition an expanded and up-to-date Index has been prepared by the publisher's Editorial Staff.

THE PUBLISHER

March, 1991

COMMITTEES

The Committee that acted for the National Conference of Commissioners on Uniform State Laws in preparing the Uniform Probate Code was as follows:

SPECIAL COMMITTEE ON UNIFORM PROBATE CODE

Tom Martin Davis, Houston, Texas, *Co-Chairman*
Charles Horowitz, Seattle, Washington, *Co-Chairman* (Deceased)
Sverre Roang, Janesville, Wisconsin, *Chairman* (1963–67)
Fred T. Hanson, McCook, Nebraska (Deceased)
James T. Harrison (Deceased)
Thomas L. Jones, Tuscaloosa, Alabama
Robert A. Lucas, Merrillville, Indiana
Miller Manier, Nashville, Tennessee (Deceased)
Bert McElroy, Tulsa, Oklahoma (Deceased)
Godfrey L. Munter, Washington, D.C.
J. William O'Brien, Burlington, Vermont
Russell W. Smith (Deceased)
Clarence A. Swainson (Deceased)
Allan D. Vestal, Iowa City, Iowa (Deceased)
Joe W. Worley, Kingsport, Tennessee
Robert R. Wright, Little Rock, Arkansas
C. P. Von Herzen, Los Angeles, California, *Chairman, Section B*

Ex-Officio

William J. Pierce, Ann Arbor, Michigan, *President, NCCUSL*
Albert E. Jenner, Jr., Chicago, Illinois, *Chairman, Executive Committee, NCCUSL* (Deceased)
Allison Dunham, Chicago, Illinois, *Executive Director, NCCUSL*

Reporters

Paul E. Basye, Burlingame, California
Richard W. Effland, Tempe, Arizona (Deceased)
William F. Fratcher, Columbia, Missouri
Edward C. Halbach, Jr., Berkeley, California
James B. MacDonald, Madison, Wisconsin
Eugene F. Scoles, Eugene, Oregon
Allan D. Vestal, Iowa City, Iowa (Deceased)
Harold G. Wren, Louisville, Kentucky
Richard V. Wellman, Athens, Georgia, *Chief Reporter*

COMMITTEES

JOINT EDITORIAL BOARD FOR UNIFORM PROBATE CODE

Conference Representatives:

Gravel, Clarke A., P.O. Box 369, 76 St. Paul St., Burlington, VT 05402

Langbein, John H., Yale Law School, 401A Yale Station, New Haven, CT 06520

Stein, Robert A., Univ. of Minnesota, School of Law, Minneapolis, MN 55455

American Bar Association Representatives:

Bruce, Jackson M., Jr., 28th Fl., 411 E. Wisconsin Ave., Milwaukee, WI 53202

Halbach, Edward C., Jr., Univ. of California, School of Law, Boalt Hall, Berkeley, CA 94720

Moore, Malcolm A., 2600 Century Sq., 1501 Fourth Ave., Seattle, WA 98101

American College of Trust and Estate Counsel Representatives:

Straus, J. Pennington, *Chairman,* Ste. 3600, 1600 Market St., Philadelphia, PA 19103

Collier, Charles A., Jr., Ste. 800, 1800 Avenue of the Stars, Los Angeles, CA 90067

Young, Raymond H., Ste. 1820, 60 State St., Boston, MA 02109

Durand, Harrison F., (Emeritus), 2nd Fl., 65 Livingston Ave., Roseland, NJ 07068

Spitler, Harley J., (Emeritus), 20th Fl., One Maritime Plaza, San Francisco, CA 94111

Liaison—Law School Teachers:

Fellows, Mary Louise, Univ. of Minnesota, School of Law, 338 Law Ctr., Minneapolis, MN 55455

Scoles, Eugene F., Univ. of Oregon, School of Law, 11th & Kincaid Ave., Eugene, OR 97403

Liaison—Probate Judges:

Wade, James R., Ste. 400, 360 S. Monroe St., Denver, CO 80209

COMMITTEES

Executive Director:

Wellman, Richard V., Univ. of Georgia, School of Law, Athens, GA
30602

Director of Research:

Waggoner, Lawrence W., Univ. of Michigan Law School, Hutchins
Hall, Ann Arbor, MI 48109

Joint Editorial Board for the Uniform Probate Code
676 North St. Clair Street, Suite 1700
Chicago, Illinois 60611
(312) 915–0195

*

1975 TECHNICAL AMENDMENTS

After approval and promulgation of the Uniform Probate Code in 1969, the National Conference of Commissioners on Uniform State Laws and The Real Property, Probate and Trust Law Section of the American Bar Association formed the Joint Editorial Board Composed of five Commissioners and five representatives of the Section. Since the Fall of 1971, the Board has monitored the legal literature concerning the Code, searched reports about the Code by various bar and legislative study committees and examined the eleven enactments to date of the Code, for ways of strengthening and improving the Code. As changes and corrections were considered and approved by the Board, the text was released for the guidance of others then known by the Board to be considering the Code in preparation for partial or total enactment. Consequently, when West Publishing Company published the 1974 Edition of the Code, it was able to include an Appendix of recommendations concerning changes as previously released by the Board, and fifteen of the thirty-one changes approved by the National Conference in 1975 were included in this Appendix. Several of these, plus others that were not released by the Board before the 1975 annual meeting of the National Conference in Quebec City, already have been incorporated into the Code in one or more of the eleven full enactments.

The thirty-one changes recently approved by the National Conference are aptly described as technical amendments for none reflect any pulling back from, or marked extension of, any of the principles or provisions of the Code. Nineteen of the thirty-one changes involve mere word changes or re-arrangements of the ordering of sentences that improve or clarify sections and eliminate gaps in, or inconsistencies between, sections. Three of the changes, including two relating to inheritance rights of children born out of wedlock, and one that restructures the Code's provision regarding renunciation of rights arising via intestate or testate succession, merely conform the Probate Code to more recent acts of the National Conference; e.g. the Uniform Parentage Act (1973) and the Uniform Disclaimer of Transfers By Will, Intestacy or Appointment Act (1973).

Of the remaining nine amendments, two affect the Elective Share of the Surviving Spouse, one by adding more explicit language to protect bona fide purchasers from a deceased spouse and clarifying the time limits for the elective share remedy, and the other by charging an electing spouse with renounced values made available to her/him by the decedent. Two other amendments reflect a slight change in the original position of the Code *vis a vis* inheritance rights of, from or through adopted children.

The remaining changes add minor new safeguards and remedies to the Code's system for probate of wills and administration of estates. For example, a "long-arm" provision is added which will permit the court of probate to give a personal judgment against one who, as applicant in an informal proceeding, commits fraud or perjury. The Code as originally approved facilitates remedies for wrongful conduct against one who accepts letters of administration; the change extends the same procedural efficiency to remedies against all applicants. Another example is a change that adds as a duty for any person who obtains probate of a will in informal proceedings without seeking appointment of a personal representative, that he give information of the probate to interested persons. Also, a small change in section 3–106 makes it clear that interested persons can be bound by a probate court order determining heirs or construing a will if notice of the proceeding as prescribed by the Code is given to all interested persons and if the estate has not been, and cannot now be, opened for administration. This fills a gap in the text as originally approved by supplying a convenient court proceeding for resolving title questions that may occur where no one acts to secure probate of a will or administration within the limitations period, as provided in the original text, of three years from death.

Overall, the amendments demonstrate that a shake-down period for the Code now has passed, and that identified defects have been corrected and needed improvements have been added. Undoubtedly, political and other local concerns will cause local changes and exclusions in future enactments modelled after the Code. Even so, the amendments, which show that considerable thought and effort already have been expended in national attempts to improve the Code, should serve to reduce the tendency of local draftsmen to make purely technical language and style changes.

1977, 1979, 1982, 1984, 1987, 1988, 1989 AND 1990 AMENDMENTS

For the Prefatory Note and Comments relating to the Uniform International Wills Act, approved in 1977, see Article II, Part 10.

For the Prefatory Note and Comments relating to the Uniform Durable Power of Attorney Act, approved in 1979, see Article V, Part 5.

For the Prefatory Note and Comments relating to the Uniform Guardianship and Protective Proceedings Act, approved in 1982, see Article V, Parts 1, 2, 3 and 4.

For the Prefatory Note and Comments relating to the provisions concerning Succession Without Administration, see Sections 3–312 to 3–322.

For the changes made by the 1984 amendment to Section 5–501, see Appendix II, infra.

For the changes made by the amendments of 1987 and Comments thereto, see Appendix I, infra.

For the changes made by the amendments of 1988, see Appendix III, infra.

For the changes made by the amendments of 1989 and Comments thereto, see Appendix IV, infra.

For the Prefatory Note and Comments relating to the 1989 Revision of Article VI, see said Article VI, infra. The Official Text and Comments of Pre-Revision Article VI are set out in Appendix V, infra.

For the Prefatory Note and Comments relating to the 1990 Revision of Article II, see said Article II, infra. The Official Text and Comments of Pre-Revision Article II are set out in Appendix VII, infra. Further, Appendix VI contains Pre-1990 Section 1–201 (General Definitions), said section having been revised in 1990 in conjunction with the approval of Revised Article II.

*

Acknowledgment

Official Text and Comments

Acknowledgment is gratefully made to the National Conference of Commissioners on Uniform State Laws for permission to reproduce the Official Text and Comments for the Uniform Probate Code.

THE PUBLISHER

*

UNIFORM PROBATE CODE

Official Text and Comments Approved by the National Conference of Commissioners on Uniform State Laws

---

ARTICLE, PART AND SECTION ANALYSIS

Article I
GENERAL PROVISIONS, DEFINITIONS AND PROBATE JURISDICTION OF COURT

Part 1
SHORT TITLE, CONSTRUCTION, GENERAL PROVISIONS

Part 2
DEFINITIONS

Part 3
SCOPE, JURISDICTION AND COURTS

Part 4
NOTICE, PARTIES AND REPRESENTATION IN ESTATE LITIGATION AND OTHER MATTERS

1

Article II

INTESTACY, WILLS, AND DONATIVE TRANSFERS (1990)

PART 1

INTESTATE SUCCESSION

PART 2

ELECTIVE SHARE OF SURVIVING SPOUSE

PART 3

SPOUSE AND CHILDREN UNPROVIDED FOR IN WILLS

PART 4

EXEMPT PROPERTY AND ALLOWANCES

PART 5

WILLS, WILL CONTRACTS, AND CUSTODY AND DEPOSIT OF WILLS

PART 6

RULES OF CONSTRUCTION APPLICABLE ONLY TO WILLS

PART 7

RULES OF CONSTRUCTION APPLICABLE TO DONATIVE DISPOSITIONS IN WILLS AND OTHER GOVERNING INSTRUMENTS

PART 8

GENERAL PROVISIONS CONCERNING PROBATE AND NONPROBATE TRANSFERS

PART 9

STATUTORY RULE AGAINST PERPETUITIES; HONORARY TRUSTS

Subpart 1.   Statutory Rule Against Perpetuities

Subpart 2.   [Honorary Trusts]

PART 10

UNIFORM INTERNATIONAL WILLS ACT [INTERNATIONAL WILL; INFORMATION REGISTRATION]

Article III

PROBATE OF WILLS AND ADMINISTRATION

Part 1

GENERAL PROVISIONS

Part 2

VENUE FOR PROBATE AND ADMINISTRATION; PRIORITY TO ADMINISTER; DEMAND FOR NOTICE

Part 3

INFORMAL PROBATE AND APPOINTMENT PROCEEDINGS; SUCCESSION WITHOUT ADMINISTRATION

SUCCESSION WITHOUT ADMINISTRATION

Part 4

FORMAL TESTACY AND APPOINTMENT PROCEEDINGS

Part 5

SUPERVISED ADMINISTRATION

Part 6

PERSONAL REPRESENTATIVE; APPOINTMENT, CONTROL AND TERMINATION OF AUTHORITY

Part 7

DUTIES AND POWERS OF PERSONAL REPRESENTATIVES

ARTICLE, PART AND SECTION ANALYSIS

9

ARTICLE, PART AND SECTION ANALYSIS

Part 4

PROTECTION OF PROPERTY OF PERSONS UNDER DISABILITY AND MINORS

Part 5

DURABLE POWER OF ATTORNEY

Article VI

NONPROBATE TRANSFERS ON DEATH (1989)

PART 1

PROVISIONS RELATING TO EFFECT OF DEATH

PART 2

MULTIPLE–PERSON ACCOUNTS

SUBPART 1

DEFINITIONS AND GENERAL PROVISIONS

SUBPART 2

OWNERSHIP AS BETWEEN PARTIES AND OTHERS

SUBPART 3

PROTECTION OF FINANCIAL INSTITUTIONS

ARTICLE, PART AND SECTION ANALYSIS

PART 3

UNIFORM TOD SECURITY REGISTRATION ACT

Article VII

TRUST ADMINISTRATION

Part 1

TRUST REGISTRATION

Part 2

JURISDICTION OF COURT CONCERNING TRUSTS

Part 3

DUTIES AND LIABILITIES OF TRUSTEES

Part 4

POWERS OF TRUSTEES

[GENERAL COMMENT ONLY]

Article VIII

EFFECTIVE DATE AND REPEALER

UNIFORM PROBATE CODE

Official Text and Comments Approved by the National Conference of Commissioners on Uniform State Laws

---

AN ACT

Relating to affairs of decedents, missing persons, protected persons, minors, incapacitated persons and certain others and constituting the Uniform Probate Code; consolidating and revising aspects of the law relating to wills and intestacy and the administration and distribution of estates of decedents, missing persons, protected persons, minors, incapacitated persons and certain others; ordering the powers and procedures of the Court concerned with the affairs of decedents and certain others; providing for the validity and effect of certain non-testamentary transfers, contracts and deposits which relate to death and appear to have testamentary effect; providing certain procedures to facilitate enforcement of testamentary and other trusts; making uniform the law with respect to decedents and certain others; and repealing inconsistent legislation.

COMMENT

The long title of the Code should be adapted to the constitutional, statutory requirements and practices of the enacting state. The concept of the Code is that the "affairs of decedents, missing persons, disabled persons, minors, and certain others" is a single subject of the law notwithstanding its many facets.

*

ARTICLE I

GENERAL PROVISIONS, DEFINITIONS AND PROBATE JURISDICTION OF COURT

PART 1

SHORT TITLE, CONSTRUCTION, GENERAL PROVISIONS

PART 2

DEFINITIONS

PART 3

SCOPE, JURISDICTION AND COURTS

PART 4

NOTICE, PARTIES AND REPRESENTATION IN ESTATE LITIGATION AND OTHER MATTERS

PART 1

SHORT TITLE, CONSTRUCTION, GENERAL PROVISIONS

Section 1–101. [Short Title.]

This Act shall be known and may be cited as the Uniform Probate Code.

Section 1–102. [Purposes; Rule of Construction.]

(a) This Code shall be liberally construed and applied to promote its underlying purposes and policies.

(b) The underlying purposes and policies of this Code are:

(1) to simplify and clarify the law concerning the affairs of decedents, missing persons, protected persons, minors and incapacitated persons;

(2) to discover and make effective the intent of a decedent in distribution of his property;

(3) to promote a speedy and efficient system for liquidating the estate of the decedent and making distribution to his successors;

(4) to facilitate use and enforcement of certain trusts;

(5) to make uniform the law among the various jurisdictions.

Section 1–103. [Supplementary General Principles of Law Applicable.]

Unless displaced by the particular provisions of this Code, the principles of law and equity supplement its provisions.

Section 1–104. [Severability.]

If any provision of this Code or the application thereof to any person or circumstances is held invalid, the invalidity shall not affect other provisions or applications of the Code which can be given effect without the invalid provision or application, and to this end the provisions of this Code are declared to be severable.

Section 1–105. [Construction Against Implied Repeal.]

This Code is a general act intended as a unified coverage of its subject matter and no part of it shall be deemed impliedly repealed by subsequent legislation if it can reasonably be avoided.

Section 1–106. [Effect of Fraud and Evasion.]

Whenever fraud has been perpetrated in connection with any proceeding or in any statement filed under this Code or if fraud is used to avoid or circumvent the provisions or purposes of this Code, any person injured thereby may obtain appropriate relief against the perpetrator of the fraud or restitution from any person (other than a bona fide purchaser) benefitting from the fraud, whether innocent or not. Any proceeding must be commenced within 2 years after the discovery of the fraud, but no proceeding may be brought against one not a perpetrator of the fraud later than 5 years after the time of commission of the fraud. This section has no bearing on remedies relating to fraud practiced on a decedent during his lifetime which affects the succession of his estate.

COMMENT

This is an overriding provision that provides an exception to the procedures and limitations provided in the Code. The remedy of a party wronged by fraud is intended to be supplementary to other protections provided in the Code and can be maintained outside the process of settlement of the estate. Thus, if a will which is known to be a forgery is probated informally, and the forgery is not discovered until after the period for contest has run, the defrauded heirs still could bring a fraud action under this section. Or if a will is fraudulently concealed after the testator's death and its existence not discovered until after the basic three year period (section 3–108) has elapsed, there still may be an action under this section. Similarly, a closing statement normally provides binding protection for the personal representative after six months from filing (section 3–1005). However, if there is fraudulent misrepresentation or concealment in the preparation of the claim, a later suit may be brought under this section against the personal representative for damages; or restitution may be obtained from those distributees who benefit by the fraud. In any case innocent purchasers for value are protected.

Any action under this section is subject to usual rules of res judicata; thus, if a forged will has been informally probated, an heir discovers the forgery, and then there is a formal proceeding under section 3–1001 of which the heir is given notice, followed by an order of complete settlement of the estate, the heir could not bring a subsequent action under section 1–106 but would be bound by the litigation in which the issue could have been raised. The usual rules for securing relief for fraud on a court would govern, however.

The final limitation in this section is designed to protect innocent distributees after a reasonable period of time. There is no limit (other than the 2 years from discovery of the fraud) against the wrongdoer. But there ought to be some limit after which innocent persons who have built up expectations in good faith cannot be deprived of the property by a restitution action.

The time of "discovery" of a fraud is a fact question to be determined in the individual case. In some situations persons may not actually know that a fraud has been perpetrated but have such strong suspicion and evidence that a court may conclude there has been a discovery of the fraud at that stage. On the other hand there is no duty to exercise reasonable care to discover fraud; the burden should not be on the heirs and devisees to check on the honesty of the other interested persons or the fiduciary.

Section 1–107. [Evidence as to Death or Status.]

In proceedings under this Code the rules of evidence in courts of general jurisdiction including any relating to simultaneous deaths, are applicable unless specifically displaced by the Code. In addition, the following rules relating to determination of death and status are applicable:

(1) a certified or authenticated copy of a death certificate purporting to be issued by an official or agency of the place where the death purportedly occurred is prima facie proof of the fact, place, date and time of death and the identity of the decedent;

(2) a certified or authenticated copy of any record or report of a governmental agency, domestic or foreign, that a person is missing, detained, dead, or alive is prima facie evidence of the status and of the dates, circumstances and places disclosed by the record or report;

(3) in the absence of prima facie evidence of death under (1) or (2) above, the fact of death may be established by clear and convincing evidence, including circumstantial evidence;

(4) a person whose death is not established under the preceding subparagraphs who is absent for a continuous period of 5 years, during which he has not been heard from, and whose absence is not satisfactorily explained after diligent search or inquiry is presumed to be dead. His death is presumed to have occurred at the end of the period unless there is sufficient evidence for determining that death occurred earlier.

As amended in 1987.

For material relating to the 1987 amendment, see Appendix I, infra.

COMMENT

Subsection (3) is inconsistent with Section 1 of Uniform Absence as Evidence of Death and Absentees' Property Act (1938).

Proceedings to secure protection of property interests of an absent person may be commenced as provided in 5–401.

The preliminary paragraph is designed to accommodate the Uniform Simultaneous Death Act, if it is a part of a state's law.

Section 1–108. [Acts by Holder of General Power.]

For the purpose of granting consent or approval with regard to the acts or accounts of a personal representative or trustee, including relief from liability or penalty for failure to post bond, to register a trust, or to perform other duties, and for purposes of consenting to modification or termination of a trust or to deviation from its terms, the sole holder or all co-holders of a presently exercisable general power of appointment, including one in the form of a power of amendment or revocation, are deemed to act for beneficiaries to the extent their interests (as objects, takers in default, or otherwise) are subject to the power.

COMMENT

The status of a holder of a general power in estate litigation is dealt with by section 1–403.

This section permits the settlor of a revocable trust to excuse the trustee from registering the trust so long as the power of revocation continues.

"General power," as used in this section, is intended to refer to the common law concept, rather than to tax or other statutory meanings. A general power, as used herein, is one which enables the power holder to draw absolute ownership to himself.

PART 2

DEFINITIONS

Section 1–201. General Definitions.

*The following is the text of section 1–201 as revised in
1990 in conjunction with the approval of Revised Article II
of the Code. See text of section 1–201 as it existed prior to
the 1990 revision in Appendix VI, infra.*

Subject to additional definitions contained in the subsequent
Articles that are applicable to specific Articles, parts, or sections,
and unless the context otherwise requires, in this Code:

(1) "Agent" includes an attorney-in-fact under a durable or
nondurable power of attorney, an individual authorized to make
decisions concerning another's health care, and an individual
authorized to make decisions for another under a natural death
act.

(2) "Application" means a written request to the Registrar for
an order of informal probate or appointment under Part 3 of
Article III.

(3) "Beneficiary," as it relates to a trust beneficiary, includes a
person who has any present or future interest, vested or contingent, and also includes the owner of an interest by assignment or
other transfer; as it relates to a charitable trust, includes any
person entitled to enforce the trust; as it relates to a "beneficiary
of a beneficiary designation," refers to a beneficiary of an insurance or annuity policy, of an account with POD designation, of a
security registered in beneficiary form (TOD), or of a pension,
profit-sharing, retirement, or similar benefit plan, or other nonprobate transfer at death; and, as it relates to a "beneficiary
designated in a governing instrument," includes a grantee of a
deed, a devisee, a trust beneficiary, a beneficiary of a beneficiary
designation, a donee, appointee, or taker in default of a power of
appointment, or a person in whose favor a power of attorney or a
power held in any individual, fiduciary, or representative capacity is exercised.

(4) "Beneficiary designation" refers to a governing instrument
naming a beneficiary of an insurance or annuity policy, of an
account with POD designation, of a security registered in beneficiary form (TOD), or of a pension, profit-sharing, retirement, or
similar benefit plan, or other nonprobate transfer at death.

22

(5) "Child" includes an individual entitled to take as a child under this Code by intestate succession from the parent whose relationship is involved and excludes a person who is only a stepchild, a foster child, a grandchild, or any more remote descendant.

(6) "Claims," in respect to estates of decedents and protected persons, includes liabilities of the decedent or protected person, whether arising in contract, in tort, or otherwise, and liabilities of the estate which arise at or after the death of the decedent or after the appointment of a conservator, including funeral expenses and expenses of administration. The term does not include estate or inheritance taxes, or demands or disputes regarding title of a decedent or protected person to specific assets alleged to be included in the estate.

(7) "Court" means the [. . . . . Court] or branch in this State having jurisdiction in matters relating to the affairs of decedents.

(8) "Conservator" means a person who is appointed by a Court to manage the estate of a protected person.

(9) "Descendant" of an individual means all of his [or her] descendants of all generations, with the relationship of parent and child at each generation being determined by the definition of child and parent contained in this Code.

(10) "Devise," when used as a noun, means a testamentary disposition of real or personal property and, when used as a verb, means to dispose of real or personal property by will.

(11) "Devisee" means a person designated in a will to receive a devise. In the case of a devise to an existing trust or trustee, or to a trustee on trust described by will, the trust or trustee is the devisee and the beneficiaries are not devisees.

(12) "Disability" means cause for a protective order as described in Section 5–401.

(13) "Distributee" means any person who has received property of a decedent from his [or her] personal representative other than as a creditor or purchaser. A testamentary trustee is a distributee only to the extent of distributed assets or increment thereto remaining in his [or her] hands. A beneficiary of a testamentary trust to whom the trustee has distributed property received from a personal representative is a distributee of the personal representative. For the purposes of this provision, "testamentary trustee" includes a trustee to whom assets are transferred by will, to the extent of the devised assets.

(14) "Estate" includes the property of the decedent, trust, or other person whose affairs are subject to this Code as originally constituted and as it exists from time to time during administration.

(15) "Exempt property" means that property of a decedent's estate which is described in Section 2–403.

(16) "Fiduciary" includes a personal representative, guardian, conservator, and trustee.

(17) "Foreign personal representative" means a personal representative appointed by another jurisdiction.

(18) "Formal proceedings" means proceedings conducted before a judge with notice to interested persons.

(19) "Governing instrument" means a deed, will, trust, insurance or annuity policy, account with POD designation, security registered in beneficiary form (TOD), pension, profit-sharing, retirement, or similar benefit plan, instrument creating or exercising a power of appointment or a power of attorney, or a donative, appointive, or nominative instrument of any other type.

(20) "Guardian" means a person who has qualified as a guardian of a minor or incapacitated person pursuant to testamentary or court appointment, but excludes one who is merely a guardian ad litem.

(21) "Heirs," except as controlled by Section 2–711, means persons, including the surviving spouse and the state, who are entitled under the statutes of intestate succession to the property of a decedent.

(22) "Incapacitated person" means an individual described in Section 5–103.

(23) "Informal proceedings" means those conducted without notice to interested persons by an officer of the Court acting as a registrar for probate of a will or appointment of a personal representative.

(24) "Interested person" includes heirs, devisees, children, spouses, creditors, beneficiaries, and any others having a property right in or claim against a trust estate or the estate of a decedent, ward, or protected person. It also includes persons having priority for appointment as personal representative, and other fiduciaries representing interested persons. The meaning as it relates to particular persons may vary from time to time and must be determined according to the particular purposes of, and matter involved in, any proceeding.

(25) "Issue" of a person means descendant as defined in subsection (9).

(26) "Joint tenants with the right of survivorship" and "community property with the right of survivorship" includes co-owners of property held under circumstances that entitle one or more to the whole of the property on the death of the other or others, but excludes forms of co-ownership registration in which the underlying ownership of each party is in proportion to that party's contribution.

(27) "Lease" includes an oil, gas, or other mineral lease.

(28) "Letters" includes letters testamentary, letters of guardianship, letters of administration, and letters of conservatorship.

(29) "Minor" means a person who is under [21] years of age.

(30) "Mortgage" means any conveyance, agreement, or arrangement in which property is encumbered or used as security.

(31) "Nonresident decedent" means a decedent who was domiciled in another jurisdiction at the time of his [or her] death.

(32) "Organization" means a corporation, business trust, estate, trust, partnership, joint venture, association, government or governmental subdivision or agency, or any other legal or commercial entity.

(33) "Parent" includes any person entitled to take, or who would be entitled to take if the child died without a will, as a parent under this Code by intestate succession from the child whose relationship is in question and excludes any person who is only a stepparent, foster parent, or grandparent.

(34) "Payor" means a trustee, insurer, business entity, employer, government, governmental agency or subdivision, or any other person authorized or obligated by law or a governing instrument to make payments.

(35) "Person" means an individual or an organization.

(36) "Personal representative" includes executor, administrator, successor personal representative, special administrator, and persons who perform substantially the same function under the law governing their status. "General personal representative" excludes special administrator.

(37) "Petition" means a written request to the Court for an order after notice.

(38) "Proceeding" includes action at law and suit in equity.

(39) "Property" includes both real and personal property or any interest therein and means anything that may be the subject of ownership.

(40) "Protected person" is as defined in Section 5–103.

(41) "Protective proceeding" means a proceeding described in Section 5–103.

(42) "Registrar" refers to the official of the Court designated to perform the functions of Registrar as provided in Section 1–307.

(43) "Security" includes any note, stock, treasury stock, bond, debenture, evidence of indebtedness, certificate of interest or participation in an oil, gas, or mining title or lease or in payments out of production under such a title or lease, collateral trust certificate, transferable share, voting trust certificate or, in general, any interest or instrument commonly known as a security, or any certificate of interest or participation, any temporary or interim certificate, receipt, or certificate of deposit for, or any warrant or right to subscribe to or purchase, any of the foregoing.

(44) "Settlement," in reference to a decedent's estate, includes the full process of administration, distribution, and closing.

(45) "Special administrator" means a personal representative as described by Sections 3–614 through 3–618.

(46) "State" means a state of the United States, the District of Columbia, the Commonwealth of Puerto Rico, or any territory or insular possession subject to the jurisdiction of the United States.

(47) "Successor personal representative" means a personal representative, other than a special administrator, who is appointed to succeed a previously appointed personal representative.

(48) "Successors" means persons, other than creditors, who are entitled to property of a decedent under his [or her] will or this Code.

(49) "Supervised administration" refers to the proceedings described in Article III, Part 5.

(50) "Survive," except for purposes of Part 3 of Article VI [Uniform TOD Security Registration Act], means that an individual has neither predeceased an event, including the death of another individual, nor is deemed to have predeceased an event under Section 2–104 or 2–702. The term includes its derivatives, such as "survives," "survived," "survivor," "surviving."

(51) "Testacy proceeding" means a proceeding to establish a will or determine intestacy.

(52) "Testator" includes an individual of either sex.

(53) "Trust" includes an express trust, private or charitable, with additions thereto, wherever and however created. The term also includes a trust created or determined by judgment or decree under which the trust is to be administered in the manner of an

express trust. The term excludes other constructive trusts and excludes resulting trusts, conservatorships, personal representatives, trust accounts as defined in Article VI, custodial arrangements pursuant to [each state should list its legislation, including that relating to [gifts] [transfers] to minors, dealing with special custodial situations], business trusts providing for certificates to be issued to beneficiaries, common trust funds, voting trusts, security arrangements, liquidation trusts, and trusts for the primary purpose of paying debts, dividends, interest, salaries, wages, profits, pensions, or employee benefits of any kind, and any arrangement under which a person is nominee or escrowee for another.

(54) "Trustee" includes an original, additional, or successor trustee, whether or not appointed or confirmed by court.

(55) "Ward" means an individual described in Section 5–103.

(56) "Will" includes codicil and any testamentary instrument that merely appoints an executor, revokes or revises another will, nominates a guardian, or expressly excludes or limits the right of an individual or class to succeed to property of the decedent passing by intestate succession.

[FOR ADOPTION IN COMMUNITY PROPERTY STATES]

[(57) "Separate property" (if necessary, to be defined locally in accordance with existing concept in adopting state).

(58) "Community property" (if necessary, to be defined locally in accordance with existing concept in adopting state).]

As revised in 1990.

COMMENT

Special definitions for Articles V and VI are contained in Sections 5–103, 6–201, and 6–301. Except as controlled by special definitions applicable to these particular Articles, or applicable to particular sections, the definitions in Section 1–201 apply to the entire Code.

PART 3

SCOPE, JURISDICTION AND COURTS

Section 1–301. [Territorial Application.]

Except as otherwise provided in this Code, this Code applies to (1) the affairs and estates of decedents, missing persons, and persons to be protected, domiciled in this state, (2) the property of nonresidents located in this state or property coming into the control of a fiduciary who is subject to the laws of this state, (3) incapacitated persons and minors in this state, (4) survivorship and related accounts in this state, and (5) trusts subject to administration in this state.

Section 1–302. [Subject Matter Jurisdiction.]

(a) To the full extent permitted by the constitution, the Court has jurisdiction over all subject matter relating to (1) estates of decedents, including construction of wills and determination of heirs and successors of decedents, and estates of protected persons; (2) protection of minors and incapacitated persons; and (3) trusts.

(b) The Court has full power to make orders, judgments and decrees and take all other action necessary and proper to administer justice in the matters which come before it.

(c) The Court has jurisdiction over protective proceedings and guardianship proceedings.

(d) If both guardianship and protective proceedings as to the same person are commenced or pending in the same court, the proceedings may be consolidated.

Section 1–303. [Venue; Multiple Proceedings; Transfer.]

(a) Where a proceeding under this Code could be maintained in more than one place in this state, the Court in which the proceeding is first commenced has the exclusive right to proceed.

(b) If proceedings concerning the same estate, protected person, ward, or trust are commenced in more than one Court of this state, the Court in which the proceeding was first commenced shall continue to hear the matter, and the other courts shall hold the matter in abeyance until the question of venue is decided, and if the ruling Court determines that venue is properly in another Court, it shall transfer the proceeding to the other Court.

28

(c) If a Court finds that in the interest of justice a proceeding or a file should be located in another Court of this state, the Court making the finding may transfer the proceeding or file to the other Court.

Section 1–304. [Practice in Court.]

Unless specifically provided to the contrary in this Code or unless inconsistent with its provisions, the rules of civil procedure including the rules concerning vacation of orders and appellate review govern formal proceedings under this Code.

Section 1–305. [Records and Certified Copies.]

The [Clerk of Court] shall keep a record for each decedent, ward, protected person or trust involved in any document which may be filed with the Court under this Code, including petitions and applications, demands for notices or bonds, trust registrations, and of any orders or responses relating thereto by the Registrar or Court, and establish and maintain a system for indexing, filing or recording which is sufficient to enable users of the records to obtain adequate information. Upon payment of the fees required by law the clerk must issue certified copies of any probated wills, letters issued to personal representatives, or any other record or paper filed or recorded. Certificates relating to probated wills must indicate whether the decedent was domiciled in this state and whether the probate was formal or informal. Certificates relating to letters must show the date of appointment.

Section 1–306. [Jury Trial.]

(a) If duly demanded, a party is entitled to trial by jury in [a formal testacy proceeding and] any proceeding in which any controverted question of fact arises as to which any party has a constitutional right to trial by jury.

(b) If there is no right to trial by jury under subsection (a) or the right is waived, the Court in its discretion may call a jury to decide any issue of fact, in which case the verdict is advisory only.

Section 1–307. [Registrar; Powers.]

The acts and orders which this Code specifies as performable by the Registrar may be performed either by a judge of the Court or by a person, including the clerk, designated by the Court by a written order filed and recorded in the office of the Court.

Section 1–308. [Appeals.]

Appellate review, including the right to appellate review, interlocutory appeal, provisions as to time, manner, notice, appeal bond, stays, scope of review, record on appeal, briefs, arguments and power of the appellate court, is governed by the rules applicable to the appeals to the [Supreme Court] in equity cases from the [court of general jurisdiction], except that in proceedings where jury trial has been had as a matter of right, the rules applicable to the scope of review in jury cases apply.

Section 1–309. [Qualifications of Judge.]

A judge of the Court must have the same qualifications as a judge of the [court of general jurisdiction.]

COMMENT

In Article VIII, Section 8–101 on transition from old law to new law provision is made for the continuation in service of a sitting judge not qualified for initial selection.

Section 1–310. [Oath or Affirmation on Filed Documents.]

Except as otherwise specifically provided in this Code or by rule, every document filed with the Court under this Code including applications, petitions, and demands for notice, shall be deemed to include an oath, affirmation, or statement to the effect that its representations are true as far as the person executing or filing it knows or is informed, and penalties for perjury may follow deliberate falsification therein.

PART 4

NOTICE, PARTIES AND REPRESENTATION IN ESTATE LITIGATION AND OTHER MATTERS

Section 1–401. [Notice; Method and Time of Giving.]

(a) If notice of a hearing on any petition is required and except for specific notice requirements as otherwise provided, the petitioner shall cause notice of the time and place of hearing of any petition to be given to any interested person or his attorney if he has appeared by attorney or requested that notice be sent to his attorney. Notice shall be given:

(1) by mailing a copy thereof at least 14 days before the time set for the hearing by certified, registered or ordinary first class mail addressed to the person being notified at the post office address given in his demand for notice, if any, or at his office or place of residence, if known;

(2) by delivering a copy thereof to the person being notified personally at least 14 days before the time set for the hearing; or

(3) if the address, or identity of any person is not known and cannot be ascertained with reasonable diligence, by publishing at least once a week for 3 consecutive weeks, a copy thereof in a newspaper having general circulation in the county where the hearing is to be held, the last publication of which is to be at least 10 days before the time set for the hearing.

(b) The Court for good cause shown may provide for a different method or time of giving notice for any hearing.

(c) Proof of the giving of notice shall be made on or before the hearing and filed in the proceeding.

Section 1–402. [Notice; Waiver.]

A person, including a guardian ad litem, conservator, or other fiduciary, may waive notice by a writing signed by him or his attorney and filed in the proceeding. A person for whom a guardianship or other protective order is sought, a ward, or a protected person may not waive notice.

COMMENT

The subject of appearance is covered by Section 1–304.

31

Section 1–403. [Pleadings; When Parties Bound by Others; Notice.]

In formal proceedings involving trusts or estates of decedents, minors, protected persons, or incapacitated persons, and in judicially supervised settlements, the following apply:

(1) Interests to be affected shall be described in pleadings which give reasonable information to owners by name or class, by reference to the instrument creating the interests, or in other appropriate manner.

(2) Persons are bound by orders binding others in the following cases:

(i) Orders binding the sole holder or all co-holders of a power of revocation or a presently exercisable general power of appointment, including one in the form of a power of amendment, bind other persons to the extent their interests (as objects, takers in default, or otherwise) are subject to the power.

(ii) To the extent there is no conflict of interest between them or among persons represented, orders binding a conservator bind the person whose estate he controls; orders binding a guardian bind the ward if no conservator of his estate has been appointed; orders binding a trustee bind beneficiaries of the trust in proceedings to probate a will establishing or adding to a trust, to review the acts or accounts of a prior fiduciary and in proceedings involving creditors or other third parties; and orders binding a personal representative bind persons interested in the undistributed assets of a decedent's estate in actions or proceedings by or against the estate. If there is no conflict of interest and no conservator or guardian has been appointed, a parent may represent his minor child.

(iii) An unborn or unascertained person who is not otherwise represented is bound by an order to the extent his interest is adequately represented by another party having a substantially identical interest in the proceeding.

(3) Notice is required as follows:

(i) Notice as prescribed by Section 1–401 shall be given to every interested person or to one who can bind an interested person as described in (2)(i) or (2)(ii) above. Notice may be given both to a person and to another who may bind him.

(ii) Notice is given to unborn or unascertained persons, who are not represented under (2)(i) or (2)(ii) above, by giving notice to all known persons whose interests in the proceedings are substantially identical to those of the unborn or unascertained persons.

(4) At any point in a proceeding, a court may appoint a guardian ad litem to represent the interest of a minor, an incapacitated, unborn, or unascertained person, or a person whose identity or address is unknown, if the Court determines that representation of the interest otherwise would be inadequate. If not precluded by conflict of interests, a guardian ad litem may be appointed to represent several persons or interests. The Court shall set out its reasons for appointing a guardian ad litem as a part of the record of the proceeding.

COMMENT

A general power, as used here and in Section 1–108, is one which enables the power holder to draw absolute ownership to himself. The section assumes a valid general power. If the validity of the power itself were in issue, the power holder could not represent others, as for example, the takers in default.

The general rules of civil procedure are applicable where not replaced by specific provision, see Section 1–304. Those rules would determine the mode of giving notice or serving process on a minor or the mode of notice in class suits involving large groups of persons made party to a suit.

*

ARTICLE II

INTESTACY, WILLS, AND DONATIVE TRANSFERS (1990)

PART 1

INTESTATE SUCCESSION

PART 2
ELECTIVE SHARE OF SURVIVING SPOUSE

PART 3
SPOUSE AND CHILDREN UNPROVIDED FOR IN WILLS

PART 4
EXEMPT PROPERTY AND ALLOWANCES

Historical Note

A Revised Article II of the Uniform Probate Code [Intestacy, Wills, and Donative Transfers (1990)] was approved by the National Conference of Commissioners on Uniform State Laws in 1990.

See text of prior Article II in Appendix VII, infra.

Note, also, that section 1–201 of the Code [General Definitions] was revised in conjunction with the revision of Article II. See said revised section 1–201, supra.

ADOPTION OF UNIFORM STATUTORY RULE AGAINST PERPETUITIES

Note that Part 9, Subpart 1 of Revised Article II has also been adopted as the free-standing Uniform Statutory Rule Against Perpetuities.

The Committee that acted for the National Conference of Commissioners on Uniform State Laws in preparing the Uniform Probate Code Article II—Intestacy, Wills, and Donative Transfers—(1990) was as follows:

RICHARD V. WELLMAN, University of Georgia, School of Law, Athens, GA 30602, *Chair*

FLORENCE NELSON CRISP, P.O. Box 7146, 119 West 3rd Street, Greenville, NC 27835

RICHARD E. FORD, 203 West Randolph Street, Lewisburg, WV 24901

CLARKE A. GRAVEL, P.O. Box 369, 76 St. Paul Street, Burlington,
VT 05402

JOHN H. LANGBEIN, Yale Law School, 401A Yale Station, New Haven,
CT 06520

ROBERT A. STEIN, University of Minnesota, School of Law, Minneapolis, MN 55455

OGLESBY H. YOUNG, Suite 800, Pacific Building, 520 S.W. Yamhill
Street, Portland, OR 97204

Review Committee

FRANK W. DAYKIN, 4745 Giles Way, Carson City, NV 89704, *Chair*

TIMOTHY J. CRONIN, JR., New England School of Law, 154 Stuart
Street, Boston, MA 02116

ALVIN J. MEIKLEJOHN, JR., Suite 1600, 1625 Broadway, Denver,

    CO 80202

Ex Officio

LAWRENCE J. BUGGE, P.O. Box 1497, 1 South Pinckney Street, Madison, WI 53701, *President, NCCUSL*

WILLIAM J. PIERCE, 1505 Roxbury Road, Ann Arbor, MI 48104, *Executive Director, NCCUSL*

WILLIAM S. ARNOLD, P.O. Drawer A, Crossett, AR 71635, *Chair, Division D*

Reporter

LAWRENCE W. WAGGONER, University of Michigan Law School, Hutchins

    Hall, Ann Arbor, MI 48109

Advisors

MARTIN D. BEGLEITER, *American Bar Association*

GAIL M. BECKMAN, *National Association of Women Lawyers*

Joint Editorial Board for Uniform Probate Code

National Conference Representatives:

CLARKE A. GRAVEL, P.O. Box 369, 76 St. Paul Street, Burlington,

    VT 05402

JOHN H. LANGBEIN, Yale Law School, 401A Yale Station, New Haven,

    CT 06520

ROBERT A. STEIN, University of Minnesota, School of Law,

    Minneapolis, MN 55455

American Bar Association Representatives:

JACKSON M. BRUCE, JR., 28th Floor, 411 East Wisconsin Avenue,

    Milwaukee, WI 53202

EDWARD C. HALBACH, JR., University of California, School of Law,

    Boalt Hall, Berkeley, CA 94720

MALCOLM A. MOORE, 2600 Century Square, 1501 Fourth Avenue,

    Seattle, WA 98101

The American College of Trust and Estate Counsel Representatives:

J. PENNINGTON STRAUS, Suite 3600, 1600 Market Street,

    Philadelphia, PA 19103, *Chair*

CHARLES A. COLLIER, JR., Suite 800, 1800 Avenue of the Stars,
   Los Angeles, CA 90067

RAYMOND H. YOUNG, Suite 1820, 60 State Street, Boston, MA
02109

Liaison—Law School Teachers:

EUGENE F. SCOLES, University of Oregon, School of Law, 11th
&

   Kincaid Avenue, Eugene, OR 97403

Liaison—Probate Judges:

JAMES R. WADE, Suite 400, 360 South Monroe Street, Denver,
   CO 80209

Executive Director:

RICHARD V. WELLMAN, University of Georgia, School of Law,
   Athens, GA 30602

Director of Research:

LAWRENCE W. WAGGONER, University of Michigan Law
School, Hutchins

   Hall, Ann Arbor, MI 48109

PREFATORY NOTE

The Uniform Probate Code was promulgated in 1969. In 1990,
Article II of the Code underwent significant revision. The 1990
revisions are the culmination of a systematic study of the Code
conducted by the Joint Editorial Board for the Uniform Probate
Code (JEB–UPC) and a special Drafting Committee to Revise Article II. The 1990 revisions concentrate on Article II, which is the
article that covers the substantive law of intestate succession;
spouse's elective share; omitted spouse and children; probate
exemptions and allowances; execution and revocation of wills;
will contracts; rules of construction; disclaimers; the effect of
homicide and divorce on succession rights; and the rule against
perpetuities and honorary trusts.

In the twenty or so years between the original promulgation of
the Code and the 1990 revisions, several developments occurred
that prompted the systematic round of review. Three themes were
sounded: (1) the decline of formalism in favor of intent-serving
policies; (2) the recognition that will substitutes and other inter-vivos transfers have so proliferated that they now constitute a major,
if not the major, form of wealth transmission; (3) the advent of the
multiple-marriage society, resulting in a significant fraction of the
population being married more than once and having stepchildren
and children by previous marriages and in the acceptance of a
partnership or marital-sharing theory of marriage.

The 1990 revisions respond to these themes. The multiple-marriage society and the partnership/marital-sharing theory are reflected in the revised elective-share provisions of Part 2. As the
General Comment to Part 2 explains, the revised elective share
grants the surviving spouse a right of election that implements the

partnership/marital-sharing theory by adjusting the elective share to the length of the marriage.

The children-of-previous-marriages and stepchildren phenomena are reflected most prominently in the revised rules on the spouse's share in intestacy.

The proliferation of will substitutes and other inter-vivos transfers is recognized, mainly, in measures tending to bring the law of probate and nonprobate transfers into greater unison. One aspect of this tendency is reflected in the restructuring of the rules of construction. Rules of construction are rules that supply presumptive meaning to donative dispositions. Part 6 of the pre–1990 Code contained several rules of construction that applied only to wills. Some of those rules of construction appropriately applied only to wills; provisions relating to lapse, testamentary exercise of a power of appointment, and ademption of a devise by satisfaction exemplify such rules of construction. Other rules of construction, however, properly apply to all forms of donative dispositions, not just wills; the provision relating to inclusion of adopted persons in class gift language exemplifies this type of rule of construction. The 1990 revisions divide pre–1990 Part 6 into two parts—Part 6, containing rules of construction for wills only; and Part 7, containing rules of construction for wills and other donative dispositions. A few new rules of construction are also added.

In addition to separating the rules of construction into two parts, and adding new rules of construction, the revocation-upon-divorce provision (section 2–804) is substantially revised so that divorce not only revokes devises, but also nonprobate beneficiary designations, in favor of the former spouse. Another feature of the 1990 revisions is a new section (section 2–503) that brings the execution formalities for wills more into line with those for nonprobate transfers.

The 1990 Article II revisions also respond to other modern trends. During the period from 1969 to 1990, many developments occurred in the case law and statutory law. Also, many specific topics in probate, estate, and future-interests law were examined in the scholarly literature. The influence of many of these developments is seen in the 1990 revisions of Article II.

PART 1

INTESTATE SUCCESSION

GENERAL COMMENT

The pre-1990 Code's basic pattern of intestate succession, contained in Part 1, was designed to provide suitable rules for the person of modest means who relies on the estate plan provided by law. The 1990 revisions are intended to further that purpose, by fine tuning the various sections and bringing them into line with developing public policy.

The principal features of the 1990 revisions are:

1. So-called negative wills are authorized, under which the decedent who dies intestate, in whole or in part, can by will disinherit a particular heir.

2. A surviving spouse receives the whole of the intestate estate, if the decedent left no surviving descendants and no parents or if the decedent's surviving descendants are also descendants of the surviving spouse and the surviving spouse has no descendants who are not descendants of the decedent. The surviving spouse receives the first $200,000 plus three-fourths of the balance if the decedent left no surviving descendants but a surviving parent. The surviving spouse receives the first $150,000 plus one-half of the balance of the intestate estate, if the decedent's surviving descendants are also descendants of the surviving spouse but the surviving spouse has one or more other descendants. The surviving spouse receives the first $100,000 plus one-half of the balance of the intestate estate, if the decedent has one or more surviving descendants who are not descendants of the surviving spouse.

3. A system of representation called per capita at each generation is adopted as a means of more faithfully carrying out the underlying premise of the pre-1990 UPC system of representation. Under the per-capita-at-each-generation system, all grandchildren (whose parent has predeceased the intestate) receive equal shares.

4. Although only a modest revision of the section dealing with the status of adopted children and children born of unmarried parents is made at this time, the question is under continuing review and further revisions may be presented in the future.

5. The section on advancements is revised so that it applies to partially intestate estates as well as to wholly intestate estates.

Section 2–101. Intestate Estate.

(a) Any part of a decedent's estate not effectively disposed of by will passes by intestate succession to the decedent's heirs as prescribed in this Code, except as modified by the decedent's will.

(b) A decedent by will may expressly exclude or limit the right of an individual or class to succeed to property of the decedent passing by intestate succession. If that individual or a member of that class survives the decedent, the share of the decedent's intestate estate to which that individual or class would have succeeded passes as if that individual or each member of that class had disclaimed his [or her] intestate share.

COMMENT

Purpose of Revision. The amendments to subsection (a) are stylistic, not substantive.

New subsection (b) authorizes the decedent, by will, to exclude or limit the right of an individual or class to share in the decedent's intestate estate, in effect disinheriting that individual or class. By specifically authorizing so-called negative wills, subsection (b) reverses the usually accepted common-law rule, which defeats a testator's intent for no sufficient reason. See Note, "The Intestate Claims of Heirs Excluded by Will: Should 'Negative Wills' Be Enforced?," 52 U.Chi.L.Rev. 177 (1985).

Whether or not in an individual case the decedent's will has excluded or limited the right of an individual or class to take a share of the decedent's intestate estate is a question of construction. A clear case would be one in which the decedent's will expressly states that an individual is to receive none of the decedent's estate. Examples would be testamentary language such as "my brother, Hector, is not to receive any of my property" or "Brother Hector is disinherited."

Another rather clear case would be one in which the will states that an individual is to receive only a nominal devise, such as "I devise $50.00 to my brother, Hector, and no more."

An individual need not be identified by name to be excluded. Thus, if brother Hector is the decedent's only brother, Hector could be identified by a term such as "my brother." A group or class of relatives (such as "my brothers and sisters") can also be excluded under this provision.

Subsection (b) establishes the consequence of a disinheritance—the share of the decedent's intestate estate to which the disinherited individual or class would have succeeded passes as if that individual or class had disclaimed the intestate share. Thus, if the decedent's will provides that brother Hector is to receive $50.00 and no more, Hector is entitled to the $50.00 devise (because Hector is *not* treated as having predeceased the decedent for purposes of *testate* succession), but the portion of the decedent's *intestate* estate to which Hector would have succeeded passes as if Hector had disclaimed his intestate share. The consequence of a disclaimer by Hector of his intestate share is governed by Section 2–801(d)(1), which provides that Hector's intestate share passes to Hector's descendants by representation.

Example: G died partially intestate. G is survived by brother Hector, Hector's 3 children (X, Y, and Z), and the child (V) of a deceased sister. G's will excluded Hector from sharing in G's intestate estate.

Solution: V takes half of G's intestate estate. X, Y, and Z split the other half, i.e., they take ⅙ each. Sections 2–103(3); 2–106; 2–801(d)(1). Had Hector not been excluded by G's will, the share to which Hector would have succeeded would have been ½. Under section 2–801(d)(1), that half, not the whole of G's intestate estate, is what passes to Hector's descendants by representation as if Hector had disclaimed his intestate share.

Note that if brother Hector had *actually* predeceased G, or was treated as if he predeceased G by reason of not surviving G by 120 hours (see section 2–104), then no consequence flows from Hector's disinheritance: V, X, Y, and Z would each take ¼ of G's intestate estate under sections 2–103(3) and 2–106.

Section 2–102.   Share of Spouse.

The intestate share of a decedent's surviving spouse is:

(1) the entire intestate estate if:

(i) no descendant or parent of the decedent survives the decedent; or

(ii) all of the decedent's surviving descendants are also descendants of the surviving spouse and there is no other descendant of the surviving spouse who survives the decedent;

(2) the first [$200,000], plus three-fourths of any balance of the intestate estate, if no descendant of the decedent survives the decedent, but a parent of the decedent survives the decedent;

(3) the first [$150,000], plus one-half of any balance of the intestate estate, if all of the decedent's surviving descendants are also descendants of the surviving spouse and the surviving spouse has one or more surviving descendants who are not descendants of the decedent;

(4) the first [$100,000], plus one-half of any balance of the intestate estate, if one or more of the decedent's surviving descendants are not descendants of the surviving spouse.

COMMENT

Purpose and Scope of Revisions. This section is revised to give the surviving spouse a larger share than the pre–1990 UPC. If the decedent leaves no surviving descendants and no surviving parent or if the decedent does leave surviving descendants but neither the decedent nor the surviving spouse has other descendants, the surviving spouse is entitled to all of the decedent's intestate estate.

If the decedent leaves no surviving descendants but does leave a surviving parent, the decedent's surviving spouse receives the first $200,000 plus three-fourths of the balance of the intestate estate.

If the decedent leaves surviving descendants and if the surviving spouse (but not the decedent) has other descendants, and thus the decedent's descendants are unlikely to be the *exclusive* beneficiaries of the surviving spouse's estate, the surviving spouse receives the first $150,-000 plus one-half of the balance of the intestate estate. The purpose is to assure the decedent's own descendants of a share in the decedent's intestate estate when the estate exceeds $150,000.

If the decedent has other descendants, the surviving spouse receives $100,000 plus one-half of the balance. In this type of case, the decedent's descendants who are not descendants of the surviving spouse are not natural objects of the bounty of the surviving spouse.

Note that in all the cases where the surviving spouse receives a lump sum plus a fraction of the balance, the lump sums must be understood to be in addition to the probate exemptions and allowances to which the surviving spouse is entitled under Part 4. These can add up to a minimum of $43,000.

Under the pre–1990 Code, the decedent's surviving spouse received the entire intestate estate only if there were neither surviving descendants nor parents. If there were surviving descendants, the descendants took one-half of the balance of the estate in excess of $50,000 (for example, $25,000 in a $100,000 estate). If there were no surviving descendants, but there was a surviving parent or parents, the parent or parents took that one-half of the balance in excess of $50,000.

References. The theory of this section is discussed in Waggoner, "Spousal Probate Rights in a Multiple–Marriage Society," 45 The Record of the Ass'n of the Bar of the City of New York 339, 344–48 (1990) (Mortimer H. Hess Memorial Lecture).

Empirical studies support the increase in the surviving spouse's intestate share, reflected in the revisions of this section. The studies have shown that testators in smaller estates (which intestate estates overwhelmingly tend to be) tend to devise their *entire* estates to their surviving spouses, even when the couple has children. See C. Shammas, M. Salmon & M. Bahlin, Inheritance in America from Colonial Times to the Present 184–85 (1987); M. Sussman, J. Cates & D. Smith, The Family and Inheritance (1970); Browder, "Recent Patterns of Testate Succession in the United States and England," 67 Mich.L.Rev. 1303, 1307–08 (1969); Dunham, "The Method, Process and Frequency of Wealth Transmission at Death," 30 U.Chi.L. Rev. 241, 252 (1963); Gibson, "Inheritance of Community Property in Texas—A Need for Reform," 47 Texas L.Rev. 359, 364–66 (1969); Price, "The Transmission of Wealth at Death in a Community Property Jurisdiction," 50 Wash.L.Rev. 277, 283, 311–17 (1975). See also Fellows, Simon & Rau, "Public Attitudes About Property Distribution at Death and Intestate Succession Laws in the United States," 1978 Am. B. F. Research J. 319, 355–68; Note, "A Comparison of Iowans' Dispositive Preferences with Selected Provisions of the Iowa and Uniform Probate Codes," 63 Iowa L.Rev. 1041, 1091–92 (1978).

Cross Reference. See Section 2–802 for the definition of spouse, which controls for purposes of intestate succession.

[ALTERNATIVE PROVISION FOR COMMUNITY PROPERTY STATES]

[Section 2–102A. Share of Spouse.

(a) The intestate share of a surviving spouse in separate property is:

(1) the entire intestate estate if:

(i) no descendant or parent of the decedent survives the decedent; or

45

(ii) all of the decedent's surviving descendants are also descendants of the surviving spouse and there is no other descendant of the surviving spouse who survives the decedent;

(2) the first [$200,000], plus three-fourths of any balance of the intestate estate, if no descendant of the decedent survives the decedent, but a parent of the decedent survives the decedent;

(3) the first [$150,000], plus one-half of any balance of the intestate estate, if all of the decedent's surviving descendants are also descendants of the surviving spouse and the surviving spouse has one or more surviving descendants who are not descendants of the decedent;

(4) the first [$100,000], plus one-half of any balance of the intestate estate, if one or more of the decedent's surviving descendants are not descendants of the surviving spouse.

(b) The one-half of community property belonging to the decedent passes to the [surviving spouse] as the intestate share.]

COMMENT

The brackets around the term "surviving spouse" in subsection (b) indicate that states are free to adopt a different scheme for the distribution of the decedent's half of the community property, as some community property states have done.

Section 2–103. Share of Heirs other than Surviving Spouse.

Any part of the intestate estate not passing to the decedent's surviving spouse under Section 2–102, or the entire intestate estate if there is no surviving spouse, passes in the following order to the individuals designated below who survive the decedent:

(1) to the decedent's descendants by representation;

(2) if there is no surviving descendant, to the decedent's parents equally if both survive, or to the surviving parent;

(3) if there is no surviving descendant or parent, to the descendants of the decedent's parents or either of them by representation;

(4) if there is no surviving descendant, parent, or descendant of a parent, but the decedent is survived by one or more grandparents or descendants of grandparents, half of the estate passes to the decedent's paternal grandparents equally if both survive, or to the surviving paternal grandparent, or to the descendants of the decedent's paternal grandparents or either of them if both are deceased, the descendants taking by representation; and the other half passes to the decedent's maternal relatives in the same manner; but if there is no surviving grandparent or descendant

of a grandparent on either the paternal or the maternal side, the entire estate passes to the decedent's relatives on the other side in the same manner as the half.

COMMENT

This section provides for inheritance by descendants of the decedent, parents and their descendants, and grandparents and collateral relatives descended from grandparents; in line with modern policy, it eliminates more remote relatives tracing through great-grandparents.

Purpose and Scope of Revisions. The revisions are stylistic and clarifying, not substantive. The pre-1990 version of this section contained the phrase "if they are all of the same degree of kinship to the decedent they take equally (etc.)." That language has been removed.

It was unnecessary and confusing because the system of representation in Section 2–106 gives equal shares if the decedent's descendants are all of the same degree of kinship to the decedent.

The word "descendants" replaces the word "issue" in this section and throughout the revisions of Article II. The term issue is a term of art having a biological connotation. Now that inheritance rights, in certain cases, are extended to adopted children, the term descendants is a more appropriate term.

Section 2–104. Requirement that Heir Survive Decedent for 120 Hours.

An individual who fails to survive the decedent by 120 hours is deemed to have predeceased the decedent for purposes of homestead allowance, exempt property, and intestate succession, and the decedent's heirs are determined accordingly. If it is not established by clear and convincing evidence that an individual who would otherwise be an heir survived the decedent by 120 hours, it is deemed that the individual failed to survive for the required period. This section is not to be applied if its application would result in a taking of intestate estate by the state under Section 2–105.

COMMENT

This section is a limited version of the type of clause frequently found in wills to take care of the common accident situation, in which several members of the same family are injured and die within a few days of one another. The Uniform Simultaneous Death Act provides only a partial solution, since it applies only if there is no proof that the parties died otherwise than simultaneously. (Section 2–702 recommends revi-sion of the Uniform Simultaneous Death Act.)

This section requires an heir to survive by five days in order to succeed to the decedent's intestate property; for a comparable provision as to wills and other governing instruments, see Section 2–702. This section avoids multiple administrations and in some instances prevents the property from passing to persons not desired by the decedent. The 120-hour period will not delay the administration of a decedent's estate because sections 3–302 and 3–307 prevent informal issuance of letters for a period of five days from death. The last sentence prevents the survivorship requirement from defeating inheritance by the last eligible relative of the intestate who survives him or her for any period.

In the case of a surviving spouse who survives the 120-hour period, the 120-hour requirement of survivorship does not disqualify the spouse's intestate share for the federal estate-tax marital deduction. See Int. Rev. Code § 2056(b)(3).

Section 2–105. No Taker.

If there is no taker under the provisions of this Article, the intestate estate passes to the [state].

Section 2–106. Representation.

(a) [Definitions.] In this section:

(1) "Deceased descendant," "deceased parent," or "deceased grandparent" means a descendant, parent, or grandparent who either predeceased the decedent or is deemed to have predeceased the decedent under Section 2–104.

(2) "Surviving descendant" means a descendant who neither predeceased the decedent nor is deemed to have predeceased the decedent under Section 2–104.

(b) [Decedent's Descendants.] If, under Section 2–103(1), a decedent's intestate estate or a part thereof passes "by representation" to the decedent's descendants, the estate or part thereof is divided into as many equal shares as there are (i) surviving descendants in the generation nearest to the decedent which contains one or more surviving descendants and (ii) deceased descendants in the same generation who left surviving descendants, if any. Each surviving descendant in the nearest generation is allocated one share. The remaining shares, if any, are combined and then divided in the same manner among the surviving descendants of the deceased descendants as if the surviving descendants who were allocated a share and their surviving descendants had predeceased the decedent.

(c) [Descendants of Parents or Grandparents.] If, under Section 2–103(3) or (4), a decedent's intestate estate or a part thereof passes "by representation" to the descendants of the decedent's deceased parents or either of them or to the descendants of the decedent's deceased paternal or maternal grandparents or either of them, the estate or part thereof is divided into as many equal shares as there are (i) surviving descendants in the generation nearest the deceased parents or either of them, or the deceased grandparents or either of them, that contains one or more surviving descendants and (ii) deceased descendants in the same generation who left surviving descendants, if any. Each surviving descendant in the nearest generation is allocated one share. The remaining shares, if any, are combined and then divided in the same manner among the surviving descendants of the deceased descendants as if the surviving descendants who were allocated a share and their surviving descendants had predeceased the decedent.

COMMENT

Purpose and Scope of Revisions. This section is revised to adopt the system of representation called per capita at each generation. The per-capita-at-each-generation system is more responsive to the underlying premise of the original UPC system, in that it always provides equal shares to those equally related; the pre-1990 UPC achieved this objective in most but not all cases. (See Variation 4, below, for an illustration of this point.) In addition, a recent survey of client preferences, conducted by Fellows of the American College of Trust and Estate Counsel, suggests that the per-capita-at-each-generation system of representation is preferred by most clients. See Young, "Meaning of 'Issue' and 'Descendants,'" 13 ACTEC Probate Notes 225 (1988). The survey results were striking: Of 761 responses, 541 (71.1%) chose the per-capita-at-each-generation system; 145 (19.1%) chose the per-stirpes system, and 70 (9.2%) chose the pre-1990 UPC system.

To illustrate the differences among the three systems, consider a family, in which G is the intestate. G has 3 children, A, B, and C. Child A has 3 children, U, V, and W. Child B has 1 child, X. Child C has 2 children, Y and Z. Consider four variations.

Variation 1: All three children survive G.

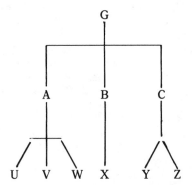

Solution: All three systems reach the same result: A, B, and C take 1/3 each.

Variation 2: One child, A, predeceases G; the other two survive G.

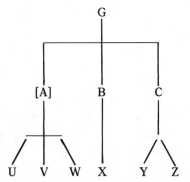

Solution: Again, all three systems reach the same result: B and C take 1/3 each; U, V, and W take 1/9 each.

Variation 3: All three children predecease G.

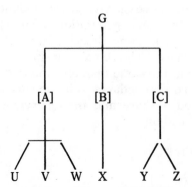

Solution: The pre-1990 UPC and the 1990 UPC systems reach the same result: U, V, W, X, Y, and Z take 1/6 each.

The per-stirpes system gives a different result: U, V, and W take 1/9 each; X takes 1/3; and Y and Z take 1/6 each.

Variation 4: Two of the three children, A and B predecease G; C survives G.

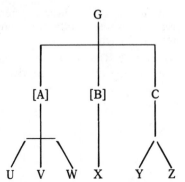

Solution: In this instance, the 1990 UPC system (per capita at each generation) departs from the pre–1990 UPC system. Under the 1990 UPC system, C takes 1/3 and the other two 1/3 shares are combined into a single share (amounting to 2/3 of the estate) and distributed as if C, Y and Z had predeceased G; the result is that U, V, W, and X take 1/6 each.

Although the pre–1990 UPC rejected the per-stirpes system, the

result reached under the pre–1990 UPC was aligned with the per-stirpes system in this instance: C would have taken 1/3, X would have taken 1/3, and U, V, and W would have taken 1/9 each.

The 1990 UPC system furthers the *purpose* of the pre–1990 UPC. The pre–1990 UPC system was premised on a desire to provide equality among those equally related. The pre–1990 UPC system failed to achieve that objective in this instance. The 1990 system (per-capita-at-each-generation) remedies that defect in the pre–1990 system.

Reference. Waggoner, "A Proposed Alternative to the Uniform Probate Code's System for Intestate Distribution among Descendants," 66 Nw. U.L. Rev. 626 (1971).

Effect of Disclaimer. By virtue of Section 2–801(d)(1), a disclaimer to effect a change in the division of an intestate's estate. To an heir cannot use a disclaimer to effect a change in the division of an intestate's estate. To illustrate this point, consider the following example:

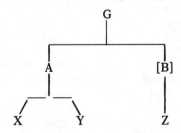

As it stands, G's intestate estate is divided into two equal parts: A takes half and B's child, Z, takes the other half. Suppose, however, that A files a disclaimer under Section 2–801. A cannot affect the basic division of G's intestate estate by this maneuver. Section 2–801(d)(1) provides that "the disclaimed interest devolves as if the disclaimant had predeceased the decedent, except that if by law or under the testamentary instrument the disclaimant's descendants would take the disclaimant's share by representation if the disclaimant actually predeceased the decedent, and if the disclaimant left descendants who survive the decedent, the disclaimed interest passes by representation to the disclaimant's descendants who survive the decedent." In this example, the "disclaimed interest" is A's share (½) of G's estate; thus the ½ interest renounced by A de- volves to A's children, X and Y, who take ¼ each.

If Section 2–801(d) had provided that G's "estate" is to be divided as if A predeceased G, A could have used his disclaimer to increase the share going to his children from ½ to ⅔ (⅓ for each child) and to decrease Z's share to ⅓. The careful wording of Section 2–801(d)(1), however, prevents A from manipulating the result by this method.

Section 2–107. Kindred of Half Blood.

Relatives of the half blood inherit the same share they would inherit if they were of the whole blood.

Section 2–108. Afterborn Heirs.

An individual in gestation at a particular time is treated as living at that time if the individual lives 120 hours or more after birth.

Section 2–109. Advancements.

(a) If an individual dies intestate as to all or a portion of his [or her] estate, property the decedent gave during the decedent's lifetime to an individual who, at the decedent's death, is an heir is treated as an advancement against the heir's intestate share only if (i) the decedent declared in a contemporaneous writing or the heir acknowledged in writing that the gift is an advancement or (ii) the decedent's contemporaneous writing or the heir's written acknowledgment otherwise indicates that the gift is to be taken into account in computing the division and distribution of the decedent's intestate estate.

(b) For purposes of subsection (a), property advanced is valued as of the time the heir came into possession or enjoyment of the property or as of the time of the decedent's death, whichever first occurs.

(c) If the recipient of the property fails to survive the decedent, the property is not taken into account in computing the division and distribution of the decedent's intestate estate, unless the decedent's contemporaneous writing provides otherwise.

COMMENT

Purpose of the Revisions. This section is revised so that an advancement can be taken into account with respect to the intestate portion of a partially intestate estate.

Other than these revisions, and a few stylistic and clarifying amendments, the original content of the section is maintained, under which the common law relating to advancements is altered by requiring written evidence of the intent that an inter-vivos gift be an advancement.

The statute is phrased in terms of the donee being an heir "at the decedent's death." The donee need be a prospective heir at the time of the gift. For example, if the intestate, G, made an inter-vivos gift intended to be an advancement to a grandchild at a time when the intestate's child who is the grandchild's parent is alive, the grandchild would not then be a prospective heir. Nevertheless, if G's intent that the gift be an advancement is contained in a written declaration or acknowledgment as provided in subsection (a), the gift is regarded as an advancement if G's child (who is the grandchild's parent) predeceases G, making the grandchild an heir.

To be an advancement, the gift need not be an outright gift; it can be in the form of a will substitute, such as designating the donee as the beneficiary of the intestate's life-insurance policy or the beneficiary of the remainder interest in a revocable inter-vivos trust.

Most inter-vivos transfers today are intended to be absolute gifts or are carefully integrated into a total estate plan. If the donor intends that any transfer during the donor's lifetime be deducted from the donee's share of his estate, the donor may either execute a will so providing or, if he or she intends to die

intestate, charge the gift as an advance by a writing within the present section.

This section applies to advances to the decedent's spouse and collaterals (such as nephews and nieces) as well as to descendants.

Computation of Shares—Hotchpot Method. This section does not specify the method of taking an advancement into account in distributing the decedent's intestate estate. That process, called the hotchpot method, is provided by the common law. The hotchpot method is illustrated by the following example.

Example: G died intestate, survived by his wife (W) and his three children (A, B, and C) by a prior marriage. G's probate estate is valued at $190,000. During his lifetime, G had advanced A $50,000 and B $10,000. G memorialized both gifts in a writing declaring his intent that they be advancements.

Solution. The first step in the hotchpot method is to add the value of the advancements to the value of G's probate estate. This combined figure is called the hotchpot estate.

In this case, G's hotchpot estate preliminarily comes to $250,000 (190,000 + $50,000 + $10,000). W's intestate share of a $250,000 estate under section 2–102(4) is $175,000 ($100,000 + ½ of $150,-000). The remaining $75,000 is divided equally among A, B, and C, or $25,000 each. This calculation reveals that A has received an advancement greater than the share to which he is entitled; A can retain the $50,000 advancement, but is not entitled to any additional amount. A and A's $50,000 advancement are therefore disregarded and the process is begun over.

Once A and A's $50,000 advancement are disregarded, G's revised hotchpot estate is $200,000 ($190,000 + $10,000). W's intestate share is $150,000 ($100,000 + ½ of $100,000). The remaining $50,000 is divided equally between B and C, or $25,000 each. From G's intestate estate, B receives $15,000 (B already having received $10,000 of his ultimate $25,000 share as an advancement); and C receives $25,000. The final division of G's probate estate is $150,000 to W, zero to A, $15,000 to B, and $25,000 to C.

Effect if Advancee Predeceases the Decedent; Disclaimer. If a decedent had made an advancement to a person who predeceased the decedent, the last sentence of Section 2–109 provides that the advancement is not taken into account in computing the intestate share of the recipient's descendants (unless the decedent's declaration provides otherwise). The rationale is that there is no guarantee that the recipient's descendants received the advanced property or its value from the recipient's estate.

To illustrate the application of the last sentence of Section 2–109, consider this case: During her lifetime, G had advanced $10,000 to her son, A. G died intestate, leaving a probate estate of $50,000. G was survived by her daughter, B, and by A's child, X. A predeceased G.

G's advancement to A is *disregarded*. G's $50,000 intestate estate is divided into two equal shares, half ($25,000) going to B and the other half ($25,000) going to A's child, X.

Now, suppose that A survived G. In this situation, of course, the advancement to A is taken into account in the division of G's intestate estate. Under the hotchpot method, illustrated above, G's hotchpot estate is $60,000 (probate estate of $50,000 plus advancement to A of $10,000). A takes half of this $60,000 amount, or $30,000, but is charged with already having received $10,000 of it. Consequently, A takes only a ⅖ share ($20,000) of G's intestate estate, and B takes the remaining ⅗ share ($30,000).

Note that A cannot use a disclaimer under Section 2–801 in effect to give his child, X, a larger share than A was entitled to. Under Section 2–801(d)(1), the effect of a disclaimer by A is that the disclaimant's "interest" devolves to A's descendants as if the disclaimant had predeceased the decedent. The "interest" that A renounced was a right to a ⅖ share of G's estate, not a ½ share. Consequently, A's ⅖ share ($20,000) passes to A's child, X.

Section 2–110. Debts to Decedent.

A debt owed to a decedent is not charged against the intestate share of any individual except the debtor. If the debtor fails to survive the decedent, the debt is not taken into account in computing the intestate share of the debtor's descendants.

COMMENT

Section 2–110 supplements Section 3–903, Right of Retainer.

Effect of Disclaimer. Section 2–801(d)(1) prevents a living debtor from using the combined effects of the last sentence of Section 2–110 and a disclaimer to avoid a set-off. Although Section 2–110 provides that, if the debtor actually fails to survive the decedent, the debt is not taken into account in computing the intestate share of the debtor's descendants, the same result is not produced when a living debtor disclaims. Section 2–801(d) provides that the "interest" disclaimed, not the decedent's estate as a whole, devolves as though the disclaimant predeceased the decedent. The "interest" disclaimed by a living debtor is the share the *debtor* would have taken had he or she not disclaimed—his or her intestate share minus the debt.

Section 2–111. Alienage.

No individual is disqualified to take as an heir because the individual or an individual through whom he [or she] claims is or has been an alien.

COMMENT

This section eliminates the ancient rule that an alien cannot acquire or transmit land by descent, a rule based on the feudal notions of the obligations of the tenant to the King. Although there never was a corresponding rule as to personalty, the present section is phrased in light of the basic premise of the Code that distinctions between real and personal property should be abolished.

[Section 2–112. Dower and Curtesy Abolished.

The estates of dower and curtesy are abolished.]

COMMENT

The provisions of this Code replace the common-law concepts of dower and curtesy and their statutory counterparts. Those estates provided both a share in intestacy and a protection against disinheritance.

In states that have previously abolished dower and curtesy, or where those states have never existed, the above section should be omitted.

Section 2–113. Individuals Related to Decedent Through Two Lines.

An individual who is related to the decedent through two lines of relationship is entitled to only a single share based on the relationship that would entitle the individual to the larger share.

COMMENT

This section prevents double inheritance. It has potential application in a case in which a deceased person's brother or sister marries the spouse of the decedent and adopts a child of the former marriage; if the adopting parent died thereafter leaving the child as a natural and adopted grandchild of its grandparents, this section prevents the child from taking as an heir from the grandparents in both capacities.

Section 2–114. Parent and Child Relationship.

(a) Except as provided in subsections (b) and (c), for purposes of intestate succession by, through, or from a person, an individual is the child of his [or her] natural parents, regardless of their marital status. The parent and child relationship may be established under [the Uniform Parentage Act] [applicable state law] [insert appropriate statutory reference].

(b) An adopted individual is the child of his [or her] adopting parent or parents and not of his [or her] natural parents, but adoption of a child by the spouse of either natural parent has no effect on (i) the relationship between the child and that natural parent or (ii) the right of the child or a descendant of the child to inherit from or through the other natural parent.

(c) Inheritance from or through a child by either natural parent or his [or her] kindred is precluded unless that natural parent has openly treated the child as his [or hers], and has not refused to support the child.

COMMENT

Subsection (a). Subsection (a) sets forth the general rule: For purposes of intestate succession, a child is the child of his or her natural parents, regardless of their marital status. In states that have enacted the Uniform Parentage Act (UPA), the parent and child relationship may be established under the UPA. Non-UPA states should insert a reference to its own statute or, if it has no statute on the question, should insert the phrase "applicable state law."

Subsection (b). Subsection (b) contains exceptions to the general rule of subsection (a). Subsection (b) states the rule that, for inheritance purposes, an adopted individual becomes part of the adopting family and is no longer part of the natural family.

The revision of subsection (b) affects only the exception from the rule pertaining to the adoption of an individual by that individual's stepparent. As revised, an individual who is adopted by his or her stepparent (the spouse of the custodial natural parent) becomes part of the adopting stepparent's family for inheritance purposes but also continues to be part of the family of the custodial natural parent. With respect to the noncustodial natural parent and that parent's family, however, a different rule is promulgated. The adopted individual and the adopted individual's descendants continue to have a right of inheritance from and through that noncustodial natural parent, but that noncustodial natural parent and that noncustodial natural parent's family do not have a right to inherit from or through the adopted individual.

Subsection (c). Subsection (c) is revised to provide that neither natural parent (nor that natural parent's kindred) can inherit from or through a child unless that natural parent, mother or father, has openly treated the child as his or hers and has not refused to support the child. Prior to the revision, that rule was applied only to the father.

PART 2

ELECTIVE SHARE OF SURVIVING SPOUSE

GENERAL COMMENT

The elective share of the surviving spouse is substantially revised. The revised elective share has been endorsed by the Assembly of the National Association of Women Lawyers (NAWL), on the unanimous recommendation of NAWL's Executive Board.

The main purpose of the revisions is to bring elective-share law into line with the contemporary view of marriage as an economic partnership. The economic partnership theory of marriage is already implemented under the equitable-distribution system applied in both the common-law and community-property states when a marriage ends in divorce. When a marriage ends in death, that theory is also already implemented under the community-property system and under the system promulgated in the Uniform Marital Property Act. In the common-law states, however, elective-share law has not caught up to the partnership theory of marriage.

The general effect of implementing the partnership theory in elective-share law is to increase the entitlement of a surviving spouse in a long-term marriage in cases in which the marital assets were disproportionately titled in the decedent's name; and to decrease or even eliminate the entitlement of a surviving spouse in a long-term marriage in cases in which the marital assets were more or less equally titled or disproportionately titled in the surviving spouse's name. A further general effect is to decrease or even eliminate the entitlement of a surviving spouse in a short-term, later-in-life marriage in which neither spouse contributed much, if anything, to the acquisition of the other's wealth, except that a special supplemental elective-share amount is provided in cases in which the surviving spouse would otherwise be left without sufficient funds for support.

The Partnership Theory of Marriage

The partnership theory of marriage, sometimes also called the marital-sharing theory, is stated in various ways. Sometimes it is thought of "as an expression of the presumed intent of husbands and wives to pool their fortunes on an equal basis, share and share alike." M. Glendon, The Transformation of Family Law 131 (1989). Under this approach, the economic rights of each spouse are seen as deriving from an unspoken marital bargain under which the partners agree that each is to enjoy a half interest in the fruits of the marriage, i.e., in the property normally acquired by and titled in the sole name of either partner during the marriage (other than in property acquired by gift or inheritance). A decedent who disinherits his or her surviving spouse is seen as having reneged on the bargain. Sometimes the theory is expressed in restitutionary terms, a return-of-contribution notion. Under this approach, the law grants each spouse an entitlement to compensation for non-monetary contributions to the marital enterprise, as "a recognition of the activity of one spouse in the home and to compen-

57

sate not only for this activity but for opportunities lost." Id.

No matter how the rationale is expressed, it is sometimes thought that the community-property system, including that version of community law promulgated in the Uniform Marital Property Act, recognizes the partnership theory, but that the common-law system denies it. In the ongoing marriage, it is true that the basic principle in the common-law (title-based) states is that marital status does not affect the ownership of property. The regime is one of separate property. Each spouse owns all that he or she earns. By contrast, in the community-property states, each spouse acquires an ownership interest in half the property the other earns during the marriage. By granting each spouse *upon acquisition* an immediate half interest in the earnings of the other, the community-property regimes directly recognize that the couple's enterprise is in essence collaborative.

The common-law states, however, also give effect or purport to give effect to the partnership theory when a marriage is dissolved by divorce. If the marriage ends in divorce, a spouse who sacrificed his or her financial-earning opportunities to contribute so-called domestic services to the marital enterprise (such as child-rearing and home-making) stands to be recompensed. All states now follow the equitable-distribution system upon divorce, under which "broad discretion [is given to] trial courts to assign to either spouse property acquired during the marriage, irrespective of title, taking into account the circumstances of the particular case and recognizing the value of the contributions of a nonworking spouse or homemaker to the acquisition of that property. Simply stated, the system of equitable distribution views marriage as essentially a shared enterprise or joint undertak-ing in the nature of a partnership to which both spouses contribute—directly and indirectly, financially and nonfinancially—the fruits of which are distributable at divorce." J. Gregory, The Law of Equitable Distribution ¶ 1.03, at p. 1–6 (1989).

The other situation in which spousal property rights figure prominently is disinheritance at death. The pre-1990 Uniform Probate Code, along with almost all other non-UPC common-law states, treats this as one of the few instances in American law where the decedent's testamentary freedom with respect to his or her title-based ownership interests must be curtailed. No matter what the decedent's intent, the pre-1990 Uniform Probate Code and almost all of the non-UPC common-law states recognize that the surviving spouse does have some claim to a portion of the decedent's estate. These statutes provide the spouse a so-called forced share. The forced share is expressed as an option that the survivor can elect or let lapse during the administration of the decedent's estate, hence in the UPC the forced share is termed the "elective" share.

Elective-share law in the common-law states, however, has not caught up to the partnership theory of marriage. Under typical American elective-share law, including the elective share provided by the pre-1990 Uniform Probate Code, a surviving spouse may claim a one-third share of the decedent's estate—not the 50 percent share of the couple's combined assets that the partnership theory would imply.

Long-term Marriages. To illustrate the discrepancy between the partnership theory and conventional elective-share law, consider first a long-term marriage, in which the couple's combined assets were accumulated mostly during the course of the marriage. The pre-1990

58

elective-share fraction of one-third of the decedent's estate plainly does not implement a partnership principle. The actual result depends on which spouse happens to die first and on how the property accumulated during the marriage was nominally titled.

Example 1—Long-term Marriage under Conventional Forced-share Law. Consider A and B, who were married in their twenties or early thirties; they never divorced, and A died at age, say 70, survived by B. For whatever reason, A left a will entirely disinheriting B.

Throughout their long life together, the couple managed to accumulate assets worth $600,000, marking them as a somewhat affluent but hardly wealthy couple.

Under conventional elective-share law, B's ultimate entitlement depends on the manner in which these $600,000 in assets were nominally titled as between them. B could end up much poorer or much richer than a 50/50 partnership principle would suggest. The reason is that under conventional elective-share law, B has a claim to one-third of A's "estate."

Marital Assets Disproportionately Titled in Decedent's Name; Conventional Elective-share Law Frequently Entitles Survivor to Less Than Equal Share of Marital Assets. If all the marital assets were titled in A's name, B's claim against A's estate would only be for $200,000—well below B's $300,000 entitlement produced by the partnership/marital-sharing principle.

If $500,000 of the marital assets were titled in A's name, B's claim against A's estate would still only be for $166,500 (⅓ of $500,000), which when combined with B's "own" $100,000 yields a $266,500 cut for B—still below the $300,000

figure produced by the partnership/marital-sharing principle.

Marital Assets Equally Titled; Conventional Elective-share Law Entitles Survivor to Disproportionately Large Share. If $300,000 of the marital assets were titled in A's name, B would still have a claim against A's estate for $100,000, which when combined with B's "own" $300,000 yields a $400,000 cut for B—well above the $300,000 amount to which the partnership/marital-sharing principle would lead.

Marital Assets Disproportionately Titled in Survivor's Name; Conventional Elective-share Law Entitles Survivor to Magnify the Disproportion. If only $200,000 were titled in A's name, B would still have a claim against A's estate for $66,667 (⅓ of $200,000), even though B was already overcompensated as judged by the partnership/marital-sharing theory.

Short-term, Later-in-Life Marriages. Short-term marriages, particularly the short-term marriage later in life, present different considerations. Because each spouse in this type of marriage typically comes into the marriage owning assets derived from a former marriage, the one-third fraction of the decedent's estate far exceeds a 50/50 division of assets acquired during the marriage.

Example 2—Short-term, Later-in-Life Marriage under Conventional Elective-share Law. Consider B and C. A year or so after A's death, B married C. Both B and C are in their seventies, and after five years of marriage, B dies survived by C. Both B and C have adult children and a few grandchildren by their prior marriages, and each naturally would prefer to leave most or all of his or her property to those children.

The value of the couple's combined assets is $600,000, $300,000 of which is titled in B's name (the decedent) and $300,000 of which is titled in C's name (the survivor).

For reasons that are not immediately apparent, conventional elective-share law gives the survivor, C, a right to claim one-third of B's estate, thereby shrinking B's estate (and hence the share of B's children by B's prior marriage to A) by $100,000 (reducing it to $200,000) while supplementing C's assets (which will likely go to C's children by C's prior marriage) by $100,000 (increasing their value to $400,000).

Conventional elective-share law, in other words, basically rewards the children of the remarried spouse who manages to outlive the other, arranging for those children a windfall share of one-third of the "loser's" estate. The "winning" spouse who chanced to survive gains a windfall, for this "winner" is unlikely to have made a contribution, monetary or otherwise, to the "loser's" wealth remotely worth one-third.

The Redesigned Elective Share

The redesigned elective share is intended to bring elective-share law into line with the partnership theory of marriage.

In the long-term marriage illustrated in Example 1, the effect of implementing a partnership theory is to increase the entitlement of the surviving spouse when the marital assets were disproportionately titled in the decedent's name; and to decrease or even eliminate the entitlement of the surviving spouse when the marital assets were more or less equally titled or disproportionately titled in the surviving spouse's name. Put differently, the effect is both to reward the surviving spouse who sacrificed his or her financial-earning opportunities in order to contribute so-called domestic services to the marital enterprise and to deny an additional windfall to the surviving spouse in whose name the fruits of a long-term marriage were mostly titled.

In the short-term, later-in-life marriage illustrated in Example 2, the effect of implementing a partnership theory is to decrease or even eliminate the entitlement of the surviving spouse because in such a marriage neither spouse is likely to have contributed much, if anything, to the acquisition of the other's wealth. Put differently, the effect is to deny a windfall to the survivor who contributed little to the decedent's wealth, and ultimately to deny a windfall to the survivor's children by a prior marriage at the expense of the decedent's children by a prior marriage. Bear in mind that in such a marriage, which produces no children, a decedent who disinherits or largely disinherits the surviving spouse may not be acting so much from malice or spite toward the surviving spouse, but from a natural instinct to want to leave most or all of his or her property to the children of his or her former, long-term marriage. In hardship cases, however, as explained later, a special supplemental elective-share amount is provided when the surviving spouse would otherwise be left without sufficient funds for support.

Specific Features of the Redesigned Elective Share

Because ease of administration and predictability of result are prized features of the probate system, the redesigned elective share implements the marital-partnership theory by means of a mechanically determined approximation system, which can be called an accrual-type elective share. Under the accrual-type elective share, there is no need to identify which of the couple's property was earned during the marriage and which was acquired prior to the marriage or acquired during the marriage by gift or inheritance. For further discussion of the reasons for choosing this method, see Waggoner, "Spousal Probate Rights in a Multiple-Marriage Society," 45 The Record of the Ass'n of the Bar of the City of New York 339 (1990) (Mortimer H. Hess Memorial Lecture); see also Langbein & Waggoner, "Redesigning the Spouse's Forced Share," 22 Real Prop. Prob. & Tr. J. 303 (1987).

Section 2–201(a)—The "Elective-share Percentage." Section 2–201(a) establishes the first step in the overall redesign of the elective share. Section 2–201(a) implements the accrual-type elective share by adjusting the surviving spouse's ultimate entitlement to the length of the marriage. The longer the marriage, the larger the "elective-share percentage." The sliding scale adjusts for the correspondingly greater contribution to the acquisition of the couple's marital property in a marriage of 15 years than in a marriage of 15 days. Specifically, the "elective-share percentage" starts low and increases annually according to a graduated schedule until it levels off at fifty percent. The schedule established in Section 2–201(a) starts by providing the surviving spouse, during the first year of marriage, a right to elect the "supplemental elective-share amount" only. (The supplemental-elective share amount is explained later.) After one year of marriage, the surviving spouse's "elective-share percentage" is three percent of the augmented estate and it increases with each additional year of marriage until it reaches the maximum 50 percent level after 15 years of marriage.

Section 2–202(b)—the "Augmented Estate." The elective-share percentage determined under Section 2–201(a) is applied to the value of the "augmented estate." As defined in Section 2–202(b), the "augmented estate" equals the value of the couple's *combined* assets, not merely to the value of the assets nominally titled in the decedent's name.

More specifically, the "augmented estate" is composed of the sum of four elements:

Subsection (b)(1)—the value of the decedent's net probate estate;

Subsection (b)(2)—the value of the decedent's "reclaimable estate," composed of will-substitute-type inter-vivos transfers made by the decedent to others than the surviving spouse during the marriage and property subject to a presently exercisable general power of appointment held by the decedent;

Subsection (b)(3)—the value property shifting to the surviving spouse by reason of the decedent's death, such as life insurance on the decedent's life payable to the surviving spouse as the beneficiary; and

Subsection (b)(4)—the value of the surviving spouse's assets at the decedent's death, plus any property that would have been in the surviving spouse's reclaimable estate under subsection (b)(2) had the surviving spouse predeceased the decedent.

Section 2–201(a)—the "Elective-share Amount." Section 2–201(a) requires the elective-share percentage to be applied to the augmented estate. This calculation yields the "elective-share amount"—the amount to which the surviving spouse is entitled. If the elective-share percentage were to be applied only to the *decedent's* assets, a surviving spouse who has already been overcompensated in terms of the way the couple's marital assets have been nominally titled would receive a further windfall under the elective-share system. The couple's marital assets, in other words, would not be equalized. By applying the elective-share percentage to the augmented estate (the couple's combined assets), the redesigned system denies any significance to the possibly fortuitous factor of how the spouses happened to have taken title to particular assets.

Section 2–207—Satisfying the Elective-share Amount. Section 2–207 determines how the elective-share amount is to be satisfied. Under Section 2–207, the decedent's net probate and reclaimable estates are liable to contribute to the satisfaction of the elective-share amount only to the extent the elective-share amount is not fully satisfied by the sum of the following amounts:

Subsection (a)(1)—amounts that pass or have passed from the decedent to the surviving spouse by testate or intestate succession;

Subsection (a)(2)—amounts included in the augmented estate under Section 2–202(b)(3), i.e., the value of property to which the surviving spouse succeeds by reason of the decedent's death;

Subsection (a)(3)—amounts that would have passed to the spouse but were disclaimed; and

Subsection (a)(4)—twice the elective-share percentage, under Section 2–201(a), of the survivor's owned or reclaimable assets as determined under Section 2–202(b)(4).

If the combined value of these amounts equals or exceeds the

elective-share amount, the surviving spouse is not entitled to any further amount from the decedent's probate estate or recipients of the decedent's reclaimable estate, unless the surviving spouse is entitled to a supplemental elective-share amount under Section 2–201(b).

Note that under Section 2–207(a)(4), the portion of the surviving spouse's assets that counts toward making up the elective-share amount is derived by applying a percentage to the survivor's assets equal to double the elective-share percentage. In a long-term marriage, the elective-share percentage will be 50%; thus, in such a marriage, all of the survivor's assets are counted toward making up the spouse's elective-share amount.

Example 3—15-Year or Longer Marriage under Redesigned Elective Share; Marital Assets Disproportionately Titled in Decedent's Name. A and B were married to each other more than 15 years. A died, survived by B. A's will left nothing to B, and no amounts shifted to B by reason of A's death. A made no transfers to others during the marriage and held no presently exercisable general power of appointment at death.

The augmented estate is the sum of the amounts described in Section 2–202(b):

(1) (A's net probate estate)	$400,000
(2) (A's reclaimable estate)	0
(3) (amounts shifting to B)	0
(4) (B's assets and reclaimables)	$200,000
Augmented Estate	$600,000

The elective-share percentage for a 15-year or longer marriage is 50%. This means that B's elective-share amount is $300,000 (50% of $600,000).

Under Section 2–207(a)(4), the percentage of B's assets that counts first toward making up B's entitlement is 100% (twice the elective-share percentage of 50%), or $200,000. B, therefore, is treated as already having received $200,000 of B's ultimate entitlement of $300,000. Section 2–207(b) makes A's net probate estate liable for the unsatisfied balance of the elective-share amount, $100,000, which is the amount needed to bring B's own $200,000 up to the $300,000 level.

Example 4—15–Year or Longer Marriage under Redesigned Elective Share; Marital Assets Disproportionately Titled in Survivor's Name. As in Example 3, A and B were married to each other more than 15 years. A died, survived by B. A's will left nothing to B, and no amounts shifted to B by reason of A's death. A made no transfers to others during the marriage and held no presently exercisable general power of appointment at death.

The augmented estate is the sum of the amounts described in Section 2–202(b):

(1) (A's net probate estate)	$200,000
(2) (A's reclaimable estate)	0
(3) (amounts shifting to B)	0
(4) (B'S assets and reclaimables)	$400,000
Augmented Estate	$600,000

The elective–share percentage for a 15–year or longer marriage is 50%. This means that B's elective–share amount is $300,000 (50% of $600,000).

Under Section 2–207(a)(4), the percentage of B's assets that counts first toward making up B's

entitlement is 100% (twice the elective–share percentage of 50%), or $400,000. B, therefore, is treated as already having received more than B's ultimate entitlement of $300,000. B has no claim on A's net probate estate.

In a marriage that has lasted less than 15 years, only a portion of the survivor's assets—not all—count toward making up the elective-share amount. This is because the elective-share percentage in these shorter-term marriages is less than 50% and, under Section 2–207(a)(4), the portion of the survivor's assets that count toward making up the elective-share amount is double the elective-share percentage.

To explain why this is appropriate requires further elaboration of the underlying theory of the redesigned system. The system avoids the tracing-to-source problem by applying an ever-increasing percentage to the couple's combined assets without regard to when or how those assets were acquired, rather than applying a constant percentage (50%) to an ever-growing accumulation of assets. By approximation, the redesigned system equates the elective-share percentage of the couple's combined assets with 50% of the couple's marital assets—assets subject to equalization under the partnership/marital-sharing theory. Thus, in a marriage that has endured long enough for the elective-share percentage to be 30%, Section 2–207(a)(4) in effect equates 30% of the couple's combined assets with 50% of those assets that were acquired during the marriage (other than by gift or inheritance). In the aggregate, Section 2–207(a)(4) equates 60% of the couple's combined assets with the assets acquired during the marriage (other than by gift or inheritance).

Example 5—Under 15–Year Marriage under the Redesigned Elective Share; Marital Assets Dis-

proportionately Titled in Decedent's Name. A and B were married to each other more than 5 but less than 6 years. A died, survived by B. A's will left nothing to B, and no amounts shifted to B by reason of A's death. A made no transfers to others during the marriage and held no presently exercisable general power of appointment at death.

The augmented estate is the sum of the amounts described in Section 2–202(b):

(1)	(A's net probate estate)	$400,000
(2)	(A's reclaimable estate)	0
(3)	(amounts shifting to B)	0
(4)	(B's assets and reclaimables)	$200,000
	Augmented Estate	$600,000

Under Section 2–201(a), the elective-share percentage for a 5-year marriage is 15%. This means that B's elective-share amount is $90,000 (15% of $600,000).

To say that B's entitlement is $90,000 presupposes (by approximation) that $180,000 of their $600,000 are marital assets—assets subject to equalization. Hence, B's entitlement is half of that amount, or $90,000. Exempted from equalization is the other $420,000 of their combined assets, some of which would have been A's individual or exempted property and the rest of which would have been B's individual or exempted property.

The redesigned system applies the same ratio to the asset mix of each spouse as it does to the couple's combined assets. To say that the elective-share percentage is 15% means that the combined assets are treated as being in a 30/70 ratio (30% marital, subject to equalization; 70% individual, exempted from equalization). This same ratio, in turn, governs the approximation of each spouse's mix of marital and individual property. Consequently, the redesigned system attributes 30% of A's $400,000 ($120,000) to marital property and the other 70% ($280,000) to individual property. And, the system does the same for B's $200,000, i.e., it treats 30% ($60,000) as marital property and 70% ($140,000) as individual property.

Accordingly, B is treated as already owning $60,000 of the $180,000 of marital property. Under Section 2–207(a)(4), $60,000 of B's $90,000 elective-share amount comes from B's own assets. Section 2–207(b) makes A's net probate estate liable for the unsatisfied balance—$30,000. (Remember that $120,000 of A's assets are attributed to marital property; thus, removing $30,000 of those $120,000 from A and adding that $30,000 to B's $60,000 in marital assets equalizes the aggregate $180,000 marital assets in a 50/50 split—$90,000 for A and $90,000 for B.)

The Support Theory

The partnership/marital-sharing theory is not the only driving force behind elective-share law. Another theoretical basis for elective-share law is that the spouses' mutual duties of support during their joint lifetimes should be continued in some form after death in favor of the survivor, as a claim on the decedent's estate. Current elective-share law implements this theory poorly. The fixed fraction, whether it is the typical one-third or some other fraction, disregards the survivor's actual need. A one-third share may be inadequate to the surviving spouse's needs, especially in a modest estate. On the other hand, in a very large estate, it may go far beyond the survivor's needs. In either a modest or a large estate, the survivor may or may not have ample independent means, and this factor, too, is disregarded in conventional elective-share law.

The redesigned elective share system implements the support theory by granting the survivor a supplemental elective-share amount related to the survivor's actual needs. In implementing a support rationale, the length of the marriage is quite irrelevant. Because the duty of support is founded upon status, it arises at the time of the marriage.

Section 2–201(b)—the "Supplemental Elective-share Amount." Section 2–201(b) is the provision that implements the support theory by providing a supplemental elective-share amount of $50,000. The $50,000 figure is bracketed to indicate that individual states may wish to select a higher or lower amount.

In making up this $50,000 amount, the surviving spouse's own titled-based ownership interests count first toward making up this supplemental amount; included in the survivor's assets for this purpose are amounts shifting to the survivor at the decedent's death and amounts owing to the survivor from the decedent's estate under the accrual-type elective-share apparatus discussed above, but excluded are (1) amounts going to the survivor under the Code's probate exemptions and allowances and (2) the survivor's Social Security benefits (and other governmental benefits, such as Medicare insurance coverage). If the survivor's assets are less than the $50,000 minimum, then the survivor is entitled to whatever additional portion of the decedent's estate is necessary, up to 100 percent of it, to bring the survivor's assets up to that minimum level. In the case of a late marriage, in which the survivor is perhaps aged in the mid-seventies, the minimum figure plus the probate exemptions and allowances (which under the Code amounts to a minimum of another $43,000) is pretty much on target—in conjunction with Social Security payments and other governmental benefits—to provide the survivor with a fairly adequate means of support.

Example   6—Supplemental Elective–share Amount. After A's death in Example 1, B married C. Five years later, B died, survived by C. B's will left nothing to C, and no amounts shifted to C by reason of B's death. B made no transfers to others during the marriage and held no presently exercisable general power of appointment at death.

The augmented estate is the sum of the amounts described in Section 2–202(b):

(1) (B's net probate estate)	$90,000
(2) (B's reclaimable estate)	0
(3) (amounts shifting to C)	0
(4) (C's assets and reclaimables)	$10,000
Augmented Estate	$100,000

The elective-share percentage for a 5–year marriage is 15%. This means that C's elective-share amount is $15,000 (15% of $100,000).

Solution under Redesigned Elective Share. Under Section 2–207(a)(4), $3,000 (30%) of C's assets count first toward making up C's elective-share amount; under

Section 2–207(b), the remaining $12,000 elective-share amount would come from B's net probate estate.

Application of Section 2–201(b) shows that C is entitled to a supplemental elective-share amount. The sum of the amounts described in Sections:

2–202(b)(3)	0
2–202(b)(4)	$10,000
2–207(a)(1)	0
Elective–share amount payable from decedent's probate estate under Section 2–207(b)	$12,000
Total	$22,000

The above calculation shows that C is entitled to a supplemental elective-share amount under Section 2–201(b) of $28,000 ($50,000 minus $22,000). The supplemental elective-share amount is payable entirely from B's net probate estate, as prescribed in Section 2–207(b).

The end result is that C is entitled to $40,000 ($12,000 + $28,000) by way of elective share from B's net probate estate (and reclaimable estate, had there been any). Forty thousand dollars is the amount necessary to bring C's $10,000 in assets up to $50,000.

Decedent's Reclaimable Estate

The pre–1990 Code made great strides toward preventing "fraud on the spouse's share." The problem of "fraud on the spouse's share" arises when the decedent seeks to evade the spouse's elective share by engaging in various kinds of nominal inter-vivos transfers. To render that type of behavior ineffective, the pre–1990 Code adopted the augmented-estate concept, which extended the elective-share entitlement to property that was the subject of specified types of inter-vivos transfer, such as revocable inter-vivos trusts.

In the redesign of the elective share, the augmented-estate concept has been strengthened. The pre–1990 Code left several loopholes ajar in the augmented estate—a notable one being life insurance the decedent buys, naming someone other than his or her surviving spouse as the beneficiary. With appropriate protection for the insurance company that pays off before receiving notice of an elective-share claim, the redesigned elective-share system includes these types of insurance policies in the augmented estate as part of the decedent's reclaimable estate under Section 2–202(b)(2).

Section 2–201. Elective Share.

(a) [Elective–Share Amount.] The surviving spouse of a decedent who dies domiciled in this State has a right of election, under the limitations and conditions stated in this Part, to take an elective-share amount equal to the value of the elective-share percentage of the augmented estate, determined by the length of time the spouse and the decedent were married to each other, in accordance with the following schedule:

If the decedent and the spouse were married to each other:	The elective-share percentage is:
Less than 1 year	Supplemental Amount Only.
1 year but less than 2 years	3% of the augmented estate.
2 years but less than 3 years	6% of the augmented estate.
3 years but less than 4 years	9% of the augmented estate.
4 years but less than 5 years	12% of the augmented estate.
5 years but less than 6 years	15% of the augmented estate.
6 years but less than 7 years	18% of the augmented estate.
7 years but less than 8 years	21% of the augmented estate.
8 years but less than 9 years	24% of the augmented estate.
9 years but less than 10 years	27% of the augmented estate.
10 years but less than 11 years	30% of the augmented estate.
11 years but less than 12 years	34% of the augmented estate.
12 years but less than 13 years	38% of the augmented estate.
13 years but less than 14 years	42% of the augmented estate.
14 years but less than 15 years	46% of the augmented estate.
15 years or more	50% of the augmented estate.

(b) [Supplemental Elective–Share Amount.] If the sum of the amounts described in Sections 2–202(b)(3) and (4), 2–207(a)(1) and (3), and that part of the elective-share amount payable from the decedent's probate and reclaimable estates under Sections 2–207(b) and (c) is less than [$50,000], the surviving spouse is entitled to a supplemental elective-share amount equal to [$50,000], minus the sum of the amounts described in those sections. The supplemental elective-share amount is payable from the decedent's probate estate and from recipients of the decedent's reclaimable estate in the order of priority set forth in Sections 2–207(b) and (c).

(c) [Non-Domiciliary.] The right, if any, of the surviving spouse of a decedent who dies domiciled outside this State to take an elective share in property in this State is governed by the law of the decedent's domicile at death.

COMMENT

Pre–1990 Provision. The pre–1990 provisions granted the surviving spouse a one-third share of the augmented estate. The one-third fraction was largely a carry over from common-law dower, under which a surviving widow had a one-third interest for life in her deceased husband's land.

Purpose and Scope of Revisions. The revision of this section is the first step in the overall plan of implementing a partnership or marital-sharing theory of marriage, with a support theory back-up.

Subsection (a). Subsection (a) implements the partnership theory by increasing the maximum elective-share percentage of the augmented estate to fifty percent, but by phasing that ultimate entitlement in so that it does not reach the maximum fifty-percent level until the marriage has lasted at least 15 years.

Subsection (b). Subsection (b) implements the support theory of the elective share by providing a [$50,000] supplemental elective-share amount, in case the surviving spouse's assets and other entitlements are below this figure.

Cross Reference. To have the right to an elective share under sub- section (a), the decedent's spouse must survive the decedent. Under Section 2-702(a), the requirement of survivorship is satisfied only if it can be established that the spouse survived the decedent by 120 hours.

Section 2-202. Augmented Estate.

(a) [Definitions.]

(1) In this section:

(i) "Bona fide purchaser" means a purchaser for value in good faith and without notice of an adverse claim. The notation of a state documentary fee on a recorded instrument pursuant to [insert appropriate reference] is prima facie evidence that the transfer described therein was made to a bona fide purchaser.

(ii) "Nonadverse party" means a person who does not have a substantial beneficial interest in the trust or other property arrangement that would be adversely affected by the exercise or nonexercise of the power that he [or she] possesses respecting the trust or other property arrangement. A person having a general power of appointment over property is deemed to have a beneficial interest in the property.

(iii) "Presently exercisable general power of appointment" means a power of appointment under which, at the time in question, the decedent by an exercise of the power could have created an interest, present or future, in himself [or herself] or his [or her] creditors.

(iv) "Probate estate" means property, whether real or personal, movable or immovable, wherever situated, that would pass by intestate succession if the decedent died without a valid will.

(v) "Right to income" includes a right to payments under an annuity or similar contractual arrangement.

(vi) "Value of property owned by the surviving spouse at the decedent's death" and "value of property to which the surviving spouse succeeds by reason of the decedent's death" include the commuted value of any present or future interest then held by the surviving spouse and the commuted value of amounts payable to the surviving spouse after the decedent's death under any trust, life insurance settlement option, annuity contract, public or private pension, disability compensation, death benefit or retirement plan, or any similar arrangement, exclusive of the federal Social Security system.

(2) In subsections (b)(2)(iii) and (iv), "transfer" includes an exercise or release of a power of appointment, but does not include a lapse of a power of appointment.

(b) [Property Included in Augmented Estate.] The augmented estate consists of the sum of:

(1) the value of the decedent's probate estate, reduced by funeral and administration expenses, homestead allowance, family allowances and exemptions, and enforceable claims;

(2) the value of the decedent's reclaimable estate. The decedent's reclaimable estate is composed of all property, whether real or personal, movable or immovable, wherever situated, not including in the decedent's probate estate, of any of the following types:

(i) property to the extent the passing of the principal thereof to or for the benefit of any person, other than the decedent's surviving spouse, was subject to a presently exercisable general power of appointment held by the decedent alone, if the decedent held that power immediately before his [or her] death or if and to the extent the decedent, while married to his [or her] surviving spouse and during the two-year period next preceding the decedent's death, released that power or exercised that power in favor of any person other than the decedent or the decedent's estate, spouse, or surviving spouse;

(ii) property, to the extent of the decedent's unilaterally severable interest therein, held by the decedent and any other person, except the decedent's surviving spouse, with right of survivorship, if the decedent held that interest immediately before his [or her] death or if and to the extent the decedent, while married to his [or her] surviving spouse and during the two-year period preceding the decedent's death, transferred that interest to any person other than the decedent's surviving spouse;

(iii) proceeds of insurance, including accidental death benefits, on the life of the decedent payable to any person other than the decedent's surviving spouse, if the decedent owned the insurance policy, had the power to change the beneficiary of the insurance policy, or the insurance policy was subject to a presently exercisable general power of appointment held by the decedent alone immediately before his [or her] death or if and to the extent the decedent, while married to his [or her] surviving spouse and during the two-year period next preceding the decedent's death, transferred that policy to any person other than the decedent's surviving spouse; and

(iv) property transferred by the decedent to any person other than a bona fide purchaser at any time during the decedent's marriage to the surviving spouse, to or for the benefit or any person, other than the decedent's surviving spouse, if the transfer is of any of the following types:

(A) any transfer to the extent that the decedent retained at the time of or during the two-year period next preceding his [or her] death the possession or enjoyment of, or right to income from, the property;

(B) any transfer to the extent that, at the time of or during the two-year period next preceding the decedent's death, the income or principal was subject to a power, exercisable by the decedent alone or in conjunction with any other person or exercisable by a nonadverse party, for the benefit of the decedent or the decedent's estate;

(C) any transfer of property, to the extent the decedent's contribution to it, as a percentage of the whole, was made within two years before the decedent's death, by which the property is held, at the time of or during the two-year period next preceding the decedent's death, by the decedent and another, other than the decedent's surviving spouse, with right of survivorship; or

(D) any transfer made to a donee within two years before the decedent's death to the extent that the aggregate transfers to any one donee in either of the years exceed $10,000.00;

(3) the value of property to which the surviving spouse succeeds by reason of the decedent's death, other than by homestead allowance, exempt property, family allowance, testate succession, or intestate succession, including the proceeds of insurance, including accidental death benefits, on the life of the decedent and benefits payable under a retirement plan in which the decedent was a participant, exclusive of the federal Social Security system; and

(4) the value of property owned by the surviving spouse at the decedent's death, reduced by enforceable claims against that property or that spouse, plus the value of amounts that would have been includible in the surviving spouse's reclaimable estate had the spouse predeceased the decedent. But amounts that would have been includible in the surviving spouse's reclaimable estate under subsection (b)(2)(iii) are not valued as if he [or she] were deceased.

(c) [Exclusions.] Any transfer or exercise or release of a power of appointment is excluded from the decedent's reclaimable estate (i) to the extent the decedent received adequate and full consideration in money or money's worth for the transfer, exercise, or release or (ii) if irrevocably made with the written consent or joinder of the surviving spouse.

(d) [Valuation.] Property is valued as of the decedent's death, but property irrevocably transferred during the two-year period next preceding the decedent's death which is included in the decedent's reclaimable estate under subsection (b)(2)(i), (ii), and (iv) is valued as of the time of the transfer. If the terms of more than one of the subparagraphs or sub-subparagraphs of subsection (b)(2) apply, the property is included in the augmented estate under the subparagraph or sub-subparagraph that yields the highest value. For the purposes of this subsection, an "irrevocable transfer of property" includes an irrevocable exercise or release of a power of appointment.

(e) [Protection of Payors and Other Third Parties.]

(1) Although under this section a payment, item of property, or other benefit is included in the decedent's reclaimable estate, a payor or other third party is not liable for having made a payment or transferred an item of property or other benefit to a beneficiary designated in a governing instrument, or for having taken any other action in good faith reliance on the validity of a governing instrument, upon request and satisfactory proof of the decedent's death, before the payor or other third party received written notice from the surviving spouse or spouse's representative of an intention to file a petition for the elective share or that a petition for the elective share has been filed. A payor or other third party is liable for payments made or other actions taken after the payor or other third party received written notice of an intention to file a petition for the elective share or that a petition for the elective share has been filed.

(2) The written notice of intention to file a petition for the elective share or that a petition for the elective share has been filed must be mailed to the payor's or other third party's main office or home by registered or certified mail, return receipt requested, or served upon the payor or other third party in the same manner as a summons in a civil action. Upon receipt of written notice of intention to file a petition for the elective share or that a petition for the elective share has been filed, a payor or other third party may pay any amount owed or transfer or deposit any item of property held by it to or with the court having jurisdiction of the probate proceedings relating to the decedent's

estate, or if no proceedings have been commenced, to or with the court having jurisdiction of probate proceedings relating to decedents' estates located in the county of the decedent's residence. The court shall hold the funds or item of property and, upon its determination under Section 2–205(d), shall order disbursement in accordance with the determination. If no petition is filed in the court within the specified time under Section 2–205(a) or, if filed, the demand for an elective share is withdrawn under Section 2–205(c), the court shall order disbursement to the designated beneficiary. Payments, transfers, or deposits made to or with the court discharge the payor or other third party from all claims for the value of amounts paid to or items of property transferred to or deposited with the Court.

(3) Upon petition to the probate court by the beneficiary designated in a governing instrument, the court may order that all or part of the property be paid to the beneficiary in an amount and subject to conditions consistent with this section.

(f) [Protection of Bona Fide Purchasers; Personal Liability of Recipient.]

(1) A person who purchases property from a recipient for value and without notice, or who receives a payment or other item of property in partial or full satisfaction of a legally enforceable obligation, is neither obligated under this Part to return the payment, item of property, or benefit nor is liable under this Part for the amount of the payment or the value of the item of property or benefit. But a person who, not for value, receives a payment, item of property, or any other benefit included in the decedent's reclaimable estate is obligated to return the payment, item of property, or benefit, or is personally liable for the amount of the payment or the value of the item of property or benefit, as provided in Section 2–207.

(2) If any section or part of any section of this Part is preempted by federal law with respect to a payment, an item of property, or any other benefit included in the decedent's reclaimable estate, a person who, not for value, receives the payment, item of property, or any other benefit is obligated to return that payment, item of property, or benefit, or is personally liable for the amount of that payment or the value of that item of property or benefit, as provided in Section 2–207, to the person who would have been entitled to it were that section or part of that section not preempted.

COMMENT

Under the pre–1990 and 1990 Code, the decedent's probate estate is first reduced by funeral and administration expenses, homestead allowance, family allowances and exemptions, and enforceable claims. The term "claims" is defined in Section 1–201 as including "liabilities of the decedent or protected person whether arising in contract, in tort, or otherwise, and liabilities of the estate which arise at or after the death of the decedent or after the appointment of a conservator, including funeral expenses and expenses of administration. The term does not include estate or inheritance taxes, or demands or disputes regarding title of a decedent or protected person to specific assets alleged to be included in the estate."

Purpose and Scope of Revisions. The revisions of this section implement a key component of the overall plan for redesigning the elective share, as described in the General Comment to Part 2. The elective-share percentage, determined by the length of the marriage under Section 2–201, is applied to the augmented estate. Under Section 2–202(b)(4), the augmented estate includes the value of property owned by the surviving spouse at the decedent's death plus the value of amounts that would have been includible in the surviving spouse's reclaimable estate had the spouse predeceased the decedent, reduced by enforceable claims against that property or that spouse. (Note that amounts that would have been includible in the surviving spouse's reclaimable estate under subsection (b)(2)(iii) are not valued as if he [or she] were deceased. Thus, if, at the decedent's death, the surviving spouse owns a $1 million life insurance policy on his or her life, payable to his or her sister, that policy would not be valued at its face value of $1 million, but rather could be valued under the method used in the federal estate tax under Treas. Reg. § 20.2031–8.)

The purpose of combining the estates and reclaimables of both spouses is to implement a partnership or marital-sharing theory. Under that theory, there is a fifty/fifty split of the property acquired by *both* spouses. Hence the redesigned elective share includes the survivor's net assets in the augmented-estate entity. (Under a different rationale, no longer appropriate under the redesigned system, the pre–1990 version of Section 2–202 also added the value of property owned by the surviving spouse, but only to the extent the owned property had been derived from the decedent. An incidental benefit of the redesigned system is that this tracing-to-source feature of the pre–1990 version is eliminated.)

Under the pre–1990 Code, the decedent's probate estate was also augmented by adding the value of specified inter-vivos transfers made by the decedent during the marriage. The purpose was to protect the surviving spouse against so-called "fraud on the spouse's share." The revisions of Section 2–202 not only continue but strengthen this feature of the pre–1990 Code by extending the spouse's elective-share entitlement to property the decedent owned in substance as well as in form. The general theory of revised Section 2–202(b)(2)(i) is that a decedent who, during life, alone had a power to make himself or herself the full technical owner of property was in substance the owner of that property for purposes of the elective share. Whether the decedent created that power or it was created by another, and whether that power was created before or after the marriage, are irrelevant. The only relevant criteria are whether the decedent held that power at (or immediately before) death or (while married and during the two-year period prior to the decedent's death) irrevocably exercised or released it. If

the decedent (during marriage) released or allowed such a power to
lapse at death, the decedent in effect
transferred the property subject to
the power to the persons who benefit from a nonexercise of the power.

Although the pre–1990 Code did
not include life insurance, annuities, etc., payable to other persons in
the augmented estate, the revisions
do include their value; this move
recognizes that such arrangements
could, under the pre–1990 Code,
have been used to deplete the estate
and reduce the spouse's elective-

share entitlement. Subsection (e)
provides protection to "payors" and
other third parties who made payments or took any other action before receiving written notice of the
spouse's intention to make an election under this Part or that an election has been made. The term "pay-
or" is defined in section 1–201 as
meaning "a trustee, insurer, business entity, employer, government,
governmental agency or subdivision, or any other person authorized
or obligated by law or a governing
instrument to make payments."

Section 2–203. Right of Election Personal to Surviving Spouse.

(a) [Surviving Spouse Must Be Living at Time of Election.] The
right of election may be exercised only by a surviving spouse who is
living when the petition for the elective share is filed in the court
under Section 2–205(a). If the election is not exercised by the
surviving spouse personally, it may be exercised on the surviving
spouse's behalf by his [or her] conservator, guardian, or agent
under the authority of a power of attorney.

(b) [Incapacitated Surviving Spouse.] If the election is exercised on behalf of a surviving spouse who is an incapacitated
person, that portion of the elective-share and supplemental elective-
share amounts due from the decedent's probate estate and recipients of the decedent's reclaimable estate under Sections 2–207(b)
and (c) must be placed in a custodial trust for the benefit of the
surviving spouse under the provisions of the [Enacting state] Uniform Custodial Trust Act, except as modified below. For the
purposes of this subsection, an election on behalf of a surviving
spouse by an agent under a durable power of attorney is presumed
to be on behalf of a surviving spouse who is an incapacitated
person. For purposes of the custodial trust established by this
subsection, (i) the electing guardian, conservator, or agent is the
custodial trustee, (ii) the surviving spouse is the beneficiary, (iii) the
custodial trust is deemed to have been created by the decedent
spouse by written transfer that takes effect at the decedent spouse's
death and that directs the custodial trustee to administer the custodial trust as for an incapacitated beneficiary.

(c) [Custodial Trust.] For the purposes of subsection (b), the
[Enacting state] Uniform Custodial Trust Act must be applied as if

74

Section 6(b) thereof were repealed and Sections 2(e), 9(b), and 17(a) were amended to read as follows:

(1) Neither an incapacitated beneficiary nor anyone acting on behalf of an incapacitated beneficiary has a power to terminate the custodial trust; but if the beneficiary regains capacity, the beneficiary then acquires the power to terminate the custodial trust by delivering to the custodial trustee a writing signed by the beneficiary declaring the termination. If not previously terminated, the custodial trust terminates on the death of the beneficiary.

(2) If the beneficiary is incapacitated, the custodial trustee shall expend so much or all of the custodial trust property as the custodial trustee considers advisable for the use and benefit of the beneficiary and individuals who were supported by the beneficiary when the beneficiary became incapacitated, or who are legally entitled to support by the beneficiary. Expenditures may be made in the manner, when, and to the extent that the custodial trustee determines suitable and proper, without court order but with regard to other support, income, and property of the beneficiary [exclusive of] [and] benefits of medical or other forms of assistance from any state or federal government or governmental agency for which the beneficiary must qualify on the basis of need.

(3) Upon the beneficiary's death, the remaining custodial trust property, in the following order: (i) under the residuary clause, if any, of the will of the beneficiary's predeceased spouse against whom the elective share was taken, as if that predeceased spouse died immediately after the beneficiary; or (ii) to that predeceased spouse's heirs under Section 2–711 of [this State's] Uniform Probate Code.

[STATES THAT HAVE NOT ADOPTED THE UNIFORM CUSTODIAL TRUST ACT SHOULD ADOPT THE FOLLOWING ALTERNATIVE SUBSECTION (B) AND NOT ADOPT SUBSECTION (B) OR (C) ABOVE]

[(b) [Incapacitated Surviving Spouse.] If the election is exercised on behalf of a surviving spouse who is an incapacitated person, the court must set aside that portion of the elective-share and supplemental elective-share amounts due from the decedent's probate estate and recipients of the decedent's reclaimable estate under Section 2–207(b) and (c) and must appoint a trustee to administer that property for the support of the surviving spouse. For the purposes of this subsection, an election on behalf of a surviving spouse by an agent under a durable power of attorney is presumed to be on behalf of a surviving spouse who is an incapaci-

tated person. The trustee must administer the trust in accordance
with the following terms and such additional terms as the court
determines appropriate:

(1) Expenditures of income and principal may be made in the
manner, when, and to the extent that the trustee determines
suitable and proper for the surviving spouse's support, without
court order but with regard to other support, income, and property of the surviving spouse [exclusive of] [and] benefits of medical
or other forms of assistance from any state or federal government
or governmental agency for which the surviving spouse must
qualify on the basis of need.

(2) During the surviving spouse's incapacity, neither the surviving spouse nor anyone acting on behalf of the surviving spouse
has a power to terminate the trust; but if the surviving spouse
regains capacity, the surviving spouse then acquires the power to
terminate the trust and acquire full ownership of the trust property free of trust, by delivering to the trustee a writing signed by the
surviving spouse declaring the termination.

(3) Upon the surviving spouse's death, the trustee shall transfer
the unexpended trust property in the following order: (i) under
the residuary clause, if any, of the will of the predeceased spouse
against whom the elective share was taken, as if that predeceased
spouse died immediately after the surviving spouse; or (ii) to that
predeceased spouse's heirs under Section 2-711.]

COMMENT

Subsection (a). Subsection (a) is revised to make it clear that the right of election may be exercised only by or on behalf of a living surviving spouse. If the election is not made by the surviving spouse personally, it can be made on behalf of the surviving spouse by the spouse's conservator, guardian, or agent. In any case, the surviving spouse must be alive when the election is made. The election cannot be made on behalf of a deceased surviving spouse.

Subsections (b) and (c). If the election is made on behalf of a sur-viving spouse who is an "incapaci-tated person," as defined in section 5-103(7), that portion of the elective-share and supplemental elective-share amounts which, un-der Section 2-207(b) and (c), are payable from the decedent's probate and reclaimable estates must go into a custodial trust under the Uniform Custodial Trust Act, as adjusted in subsection (c).

If the election is made on behalf of the surviving spouse by his or her guardian or conservator, the surviv-ing spouse is by definition an "inca-pacitated person." If the election is made by the surviving spouse's agent under a durable power of at-torney, the surviving spouse is pre-sumed to be an "incapacitated per-son"; the presumption is rebuttable.

The terms of the custodial trust are governed by the Uniform Custo-dial Trust Act, except as adjusted in subsection (c).

The custodial trustee is authorized to expend the custodial trust property for the use and benefit of the surviving spouse to the extent the custodial trustee considers it advisable. In determining the amounts, if any, to be expended for the spouse's benefit, the custodial trustee is directed to take into account the spouse's other support, income, and property; these items would include governmental benefits such as Social Security and Medicare.

Bracketed language in subsection (c)(2) (and in Alternative subsection (b)(1)) gives enacting states a choice as to whether governmental benefits for which the spouse must qualify on the basis of need, such as Medicaid, are also to be considered. If so, the enacting state should include the bracketed word "and" but not the bracketed phrase "exclusive of" in its enactment; if not, the enacting state should include the bracketed phrase "exclusive of" and not include the bracketed word "and" in its enactment.

At the surviving spouse's death, the remaining custodial trust property does not go to the surviving spouse's estate, but rather under the residuary clause of the will of the predeceased spouse whose probate and reclaimable estates were the source of the property in the custodial trust, as if the predeceased spouse died immediately after the surviving spouse. In the absence of a residuary clause, the property goes to the predeceased spouse's heirs. See Section 2–711.

Alternative Subsection (b). For states that have not enacted the Uniform Custodial Trust Act, an Alternative subsection (b) is provided under which the court must set aside that portion of the elective-share and supplemental elective-share amounts which, under Sections 2–207(b) and (c), are due from the decedent's probate and reclaimable estates and must appoint a trustee to administer that property for the support of the surviving spouse, in accordance with the terms set forth in Alternative subsection (b).

Planning for an Incapacitated Surviving Spouse Not Disrupted. Note that the portion of the elective-share or supplemental elective-share amounts that go into the custodial or support trust is that portion due from the decedent's probate and reclaimable estates under Section 2–207(b) and (c). These amounts constitute the involuntary transfers to the surviving spouse under the elective-share system. Amounts voluntarily transferred to the surviving spouse under the decedent's will, by intestacy, or by nonprobate transfer, if any, do not go into the custodial or support trust. Thus, estate planning measures deliberately established for a surviving spouse who is incapacitated are not disrupted. For example, the decedent's will might establish a trust that qualifies for or that can be elected as qualifying for the federal estate tax marital deduction. Although the value of the surviving spouse's interests in such a trust count toward satisfying the elective-share amount under Section 2–207(a)(1), the trust itself is not dismantled by virtue of Section 2–203(b) in order to force that property into the nonqualifying custodial or support trust.

Rationale. The approach of this section is based on a general expectation that most surviving spouses are, at the least, generally aware of an accept their decedents' overall estate plans are not antagonistic to them. Consequently, to elect the elective share, and not have the disposition of that part of it that is payable from the decedent's probate and reclaimable estates under Sections 2–207(b) and (c) governed by subsections (b) and (c), the surviving spouse must not be an incapacitated person. When the election is made by or on behalf of a surviving spouse who is not an incapacitated person, the surviving spouse has personally signified his or her opposition to the decedent's overall estate plan.

If the election is made on behalf of a surviving spouse who is an incapacitated person, subsections (b) and (c) control the disposition of that part of the elective-share amount or supplemental elective-share amount payable under Sections 2–207(b) and (c) from the decedent's probate and reclaimable estates. The purpose of subsections (b) and (c), generally speaking, is to assure that that part of the elective share is devoted to the personal economic benefit and needs of the surviving spouse, but not to the economic benefit of the surviving spouse's heirs or devisees.

Section 2–204. Waiver of Right to Elect and of Other Rights.

(a) The right of election of a surviving spouse and the rights of the surviving spouse to homestead allowance, exempt property, and family allowance, or any of them, may be waived, wholly or partially, before or after marriage, by a written contract, agreement, or waiver signed by the surviving spouse.

(b) A surviving spouse's waiver is not enforceable if the surviving spouse proves that:

(1) he [or she] did not execute the waiver voluntarily;

(2) the waiver was unconscionable when it was executed and, before execution of the waiver, he [or she]:

(i) was not provided a fair and reasonable disclosure of the property or financial obligations of the decedent;

(ii) did not voluntarily and expressly waive, in writing, any right to disclosure of the property or financial obligations of the decedent beyond the disclosure provided; and

(iii) did not have, or reasonably could not have had, an adequate knowledge of the property or financial obligations of the decedent.

(c) An issue of unconscionability of a waiver is for decision by the court as a matter of law.

(d) Unless it provides to the contrary, a waiver of "all rights," or equivalent language, in the property or estate of a present or prospective spouse or a complete property settlement entered into after or in anticipation of separation or divorce is a waiver of all rights of elective share, homestead allowance, exempt property, and family allowance by each spouse in the property of the other and a renunciation by each of all benefits that would otherwise pass to him [or her] from the other by intestate succession or by virtue of any will executed before the waiver or property settlement.

COMMENT

Apart from minor stylistic changes, this section is revised to incorporate the standards by which the validity of a premarital agreement is determined under the Uniform Premarital Agreement Act § 6.

The right to homestead allowance, exempt property and family allowance are conferred by the provisions of Part 4. The right to disclaim interests is recognized by Section 2–801.

The provisions of this section, permitting a spouse or prospective spouse to waive all statutory rights in the other spouse's property, seem desirable in view of the common desire of parties to second and later marriages to insure that property derived from the prior spouse passes at death to the joint children (or descendants) of the prior marriage instead of to the later spouse. The operation of a property settlement in anticipation of separation or divorce as a waiver and renunciation takes care of most situations arising when a spouse dies while a divorce suit is pending.

Section 2–205. Proceeding for Elective Share; Time Limit.

(a) Except as provided in subsection (b), the election must be made by filing in the court and mailing or delivering to the personal representative, if any, a petition for the elective share within nine months after the date of the decedent's death, or within six months after the probate of the decedent's will, whichever limitation later expires. The surviving spouse must give notice of the time and place set for hearing to persons interested in the estate and to the distributees and recipients of portions of the augmented estate whose interests will be adversely affected by the taking of the elective share. Except as provided in subsection (b), the decedent's reclaimable estate, described in Section 2–202(b)(2), is not included within the augmented estate for the purpose of computing the elective share, if the petition is filed more than nine months after the decedent's death.

(b) Within nine months after the decedent's death, the surviving spouse may petition the court for an extension of time for making an election. If, within nine months after the decedent's death, the spouse gives notice of the petition to all persons interested in the decedent's reclaimable estate, the court for cause shown by the surviving spouse may extend the time for election. If the court grants the spouse's petition for an extension, the decedent's reclaimable estate, described in Section 2–202(b)(2), is not excluded from the augmented estate for the purpose of computing the elective-share and supplemental elective-share amounts, if the spouse makes an election by filing in the court and mailing or delivering to the personal representative, if any, a petition for the elective share within the time allowed by the extension.

(c) The surviving spouse may withdraw his [or her] demand for an elective share at any time before entry of a final determination by the court.

(d) After notice and hearing, the court shall determine the elective-share and supplemental elective-share amounts, and shall order its payment from the assets of the augmented estate or by contribution as appears appropriate under Section 2-207. If it appears that a fund or property included in the augmented estate has not come into the possession of the personal representative, or has been distributed by the personal representative, the court nevertheless shall fix the liability of any person who has any interest in the fund or property or who has possession thereof, whether as trustee or otherwise. The proceeding may be maintained against fewer than all persons against whom relief could be sought, but no person is subject to contribution in any greater amount than he [or she] would have been under Section 2-207 had relief been secured against all persons subject to contribution.

(e) An order or judgment of the court may be enforced as necessary in suit for contribution or payment in other courts of this State or other jurisdictions.

COMMENT

This section is revised to coordinate the terminology with that used in revised section 2-202 and with the fact that an election can be made by a conservator, guardian, or agent on behalf of a surviving spouse, as provided in section 2-203(a).

Section 2-206. Effect of Election on Statutory Benefits.

If the right of election is exercised by or on behalf of the surviving spouse, the surviving spouse's homestead allowance, exempt property, and family allowance, if any, are not charged against but are in addition to the elective-share and supplemental elective-share amounts.

COMMENT

The title of this section is revised to correspond to the section's content.

The homestead, exempt property, and family allowances provided by Article II, Part 4, are not charged to the electing spouse as a part of the elective share. Consequently, these allowances may be distributed from the probate estate without reference to whether an elective share right is asserted.

Section 2–207. Charging Spouse with Owned Assets and Gifts Received; Liability of Others for Balance of Elective Share.

(a) [Elective–Share Amount Only.] In a proceeding for an elective share, the following are applied first to satisfy the elective-share amount and to reduce or eliminate any contributions due from the decedent's probate estate and recipients of the decedent's reclaimable estate:

(1) amounts included in the augmented estate which pass or have passed to the surviving spouse by testate or intestate succession;

(2) amounts included in the augmented estate under Section 2–202(b)(3);

(3) amounts included in the augmented estate which would have passed to the spouse but were disclaimed; and

(4) amounts included in the augmented estate under Section 2–202(b)(4) up to the applicable percentage thereof. For the purposes of this subsection, the "applicable percentage" is twice the elective-share percentage set forth in the schedule in Section 2–201(a) appropriate to the length of time the spouse and the decedent were married to each other.

(b) [Unsatisfied Balance of Elective–Share Amount; Supplemental Elective–Share Amount.] If, after the application of subsection (a), the elective-share amount is not fully satisfied or the surviving spouse is entitled to a supplemental elective-share amount, amounts included in the decedent's probate estate and that portion of the decedent's reclaimable estate other than amounts irrevocably transferred within two years before the decedent's death are applied first to satisfy the unsatisfied balance of the elective-share amount or the supplemental elective-share amount. The decedent's probate estate and that portion of the decedent's reclaimable estate are so applied that liability for the unsatisfied balance of the elective-share amount or for the supplemental elective-share amount is equitably apportioned among the recipients of the decedent's probate estate and that portion of the decedent's reclaimable estate in proportion to the value of their interests therein.

(c) [Unsatisfied Balance of Elective–Share and Supplemental Elective–Share Amounts.] If, after the application of subsections (a) and (b), the elective-share or supplemental elective-share amount is not fully satisfied, the remaining portion of the decedent's reclaimable estate is so applied that liability for the unsatisfied balance of the elective-share or supplemental elective-share amount is equitably apportioned among the recipients of that portion of the decedent's reclaimable estate in proportion to the value of their interests therein.

(d) [Liability of Recipients of Reclaimable Estate and Their Donees.] Only original recipients of the reclaimable estate described in Section 2–202(b)(2), and the donees of the recipients of the reclaimable estate to the extent the donees have the property or its proceeds, are liable to make a proportional contribution toward satisfaction of the surviving spouse's elective-share or supplemental elective-share amount. A person liable to make contribution may choose to give up the proportional part of the reclaimable estate or to pay the value of the amount for which he [or she] is liable.

COMMENT

Purpose and Scope of Revisions. Section 2–207, as revised, is an integral part of the overall redesign of the elective share. It establishes the priority to be used in determining the source of the elective-share amount.

Subsection (a). Subsection (a) applies only to the elective-share amount determined under Section 2–201(a), not to the supplemental elective-share amount determined under Section 2–201(b). Under subsection (a), the following are counted first toward satisfying the elective-share amount (to the extent they are included in the augmented estate):

(1) amounts that pass or have passed to the surviving spouse by testate or intestate succession;

(2) amounts included in the augmented estate under Section 2–202(b)(3), i.e., the value of property to which the surviving spouse succeeds by reason of the decedent's death (other than by homestead allowance, exempt property, family allowance, testate succession, or intestate succession), including the proceeds of insurance (including accidental death benefits) on the life of the decedent

and benefits payable under a retirement plan in which the decedent was a participant, exclusive of the Federal Social Security system.

(3) amounts that would have passed to the spouse but were disclaimed, the theory being that the spouse is not compelled to accept the benefits devised by the decedent, but if these benefits are rejected, the values involved are charged to the electing spouse as if the devises were accepted, and

(4) amounts included in the augmented estate under Section 2–202(b)(4) up to the applicable percentage thereof, the applicable percentage being twice the elective-share percentage as determined under Section 2–201(a). (The phrase "amounts included in the augmented estate under Section 2–202(b)(4)" refers to the value of property owned by the surviving spouse at the decedent's death, reduced by enforceable claims against that property or that spouse, plus the value of property that would have been includible in the spouse's reclaimable estate had the surviving spouse predeceased the decedent.)

If the combined value of these amounts equals or exceeds the elective-share amount, the surviving spouse is not entitled to any further amount from the decedent's probate estate or recipients of the decedent's reclaimable estate, unless the surviving spouse is entitled to a supplemental elective-share amount under Section 2–201(b).

Subsections (b) and (c). Subsections (b) and (c) apply to both the elective-share amount and the supplemental elective-share amount, if any. As to the elective-share amount determined under Section 2–201(a), the decedent's probate and reclaimable estates become liable only if and to the extent that the amounts described in subsection (a) are insufficient to satisfy the elective-share amount. The decedent's probate and reclaimable estates are fully liable for the supplemental elective-share amount determined under Section 2–201(b), if any.

Subsections (b) and (c) establish a layer of priority within the decedent's probate and reclaimable estates. The decedent's probate estate and that portion of the decedent's reclaimable estate that was not irrevocably transferred within two years before the decedent's death are liable first. Only if and to the extent that those amounts are insufficient does the remaining portion of the decedent's reclaimable estate become liable.

Note that the exempt property and allowances provided by Sections 2–401, 2–402, and 2–403 are not charged against, but are in addition to the elective-share and supplemental elective-share amounts.

PART 3

SPOUSE AND CHILDREN UNPROVIDED FOR IN WILLS

Section 2–301. Entitlement of Spouse; Premarital Will.

(a) If a testator's surviving spouse married the testator after the testator executed his [or her] will, the surviving spouse is entitled to receive, as an intestate share, no less than the value of the share of the estate he [or she] would have received if the testator had died intestate as to that portion of the testator's estate, if any, that neither is devised to a child of the testator who was born before the testator married the surviving spouse and who is not a child of the surviving spouse nor is devised or passes under Sections 2–603 or 2–604 to a descendant of such a child, unless:

(1) it appears from the will or other evidence that the will was made in contemplation of the testator's marriage to the surviving spouse;

(2) the will expresses the intention that it is to be effective notwithstanding any subsequent marriage; or

(3) the testator provided for the spouse by transfer outside the will and the intent that the transfer be in lieu of a testamentary provision is shown by the testator's statements or is reasonably inferred from the amount of the transfer or other evidence.

(b) In satisfying the share provided by this section, devises made by the will to the testator's surviving spouse, if any, are applied first, and other devises, other than a devise to a child of the testator who was born before the testator married the surviving spouse and who is not a child of the surviving spouse or a devise or substitute gift under Section 2–603 or 2–604 to a descendant of such a child, abate as provided in Section 3–902.

COMMENT

Purpose and Scope of the Revisions. This section applies only to a premarital will, a will executed prior to the testator's marriage to his or her surviving spouse. This section reflects the view that the intestate share of the spouse in that portion of the testator's estate not devised to certain of the testator's children (or that is not devised to their descendants or does not pass to their descendants under the anti-lapse statute) is what the testator would want the spouse to have if he or she had thought about the relationship of his or her old will to the new situation.

Under this section, a surviving spouse who married the testator after the testator executed his or her will may be entitled to a certain minimum amount of the testator's estate. The surviving spouse's entitlement under this section, if any, is granted automatically; it need

84

not be elected. If the surviving spouse exercises his or her right to take an elective share, amounts provided under this section count toward making up the elective-share amount by virtue of the language in subsection (a) stating that the amount provided by this section is treated as "an intestate share." Under Section 2–207(a)(1), amounts passing to the surviving spouse by intestate succession count first toward making up the spouse's elective-share amount.

Subsection (a). Subsection (a) is revised to make it clear that a surviving spouse who, by a premarital will, is devised less than the share of the testator's estate he or she would have received had the testator died intestate as to that part of the estate, if any, not devised to certain of the testator's children (or that is not devised to their descendants or does not pass to their descendants under the antilapse statute) is entitled to be brought up to that share. The pre–1990 version of Section 2–301 was titled *"Omitted* Spouse," and the section used phrases such as *"fails* to provide" and *"omitted* spouse." The implication of the title and these phrases was that the section was inapplicable if the person the decedent later married was a devisee in his or her premarital will. It was clear, however, from the underlying purpose of the section that this was not intended. The courts recognized this and refused to interpret the section that way, but in doing so they have been forced to say that a premarital will containing a devise to the person to whom the testator was married at death could still be found to "fail to provide" for the survivor *in the survivor's capacity as spouse.* See Estate of Christensen, 665 P.2d 646 (Utah 1982); Estate of Ganier, 418 So.2d 256 (Fla.1982); Note, "The Problem of the 'Un-omitted' Spouse Under Section 2–301 of the [Pre–1990] Uniform Probate Code," 52 U.Chi. L.Rev. 481 (1985).

By making the existence and amount of a premarital devise to the spouse irrelevant, the revisions of subsection (a) make the operation of the statute more purposive.

Subsection (a)(1), (2), and (3) Exceptions. The moving party has the burden of proof on the exceptions contained in subsections (a)(1), (2), and (3). For a case interpreting the language of subsection (a)(3), see Estate of Bartell, 776 P.2d 885 (Utah 1989). This section can be barred by a premarital agreement, marital agreement, or waiver as provided in Section 2–204.

Subsection (b). Subsection (b) is also revised to provide that any premarital devise to the surviving spouse is used first to satisfy the spouse's entitlement under this section, before any other devises suffer abatement. This revision is made necessary by the revision of subsection (a): If the existence or amount of a premarital devise to the surviving spouse is irrelevant, any such devise must be counted toward and not be in addition to the ultimate share to which the spouse is entitled. Normally, a devise in favor of the person whom the testator *later* marries will be a specific or general devise, not a residuary devise. The effect under the pre–1990 version of subsection (b) was that the surviving spouse could take the intestate share under Section 2–301, which in the pre–1990 version was satisfied out of the residue (under the rules of abatement in Section 3–902), *plus* the devise in his or her favor. The revision of subsection (b) prevents this "double dipping," so to speak.

Reference. The theory of this section is discussed in Waggoner, "Spousal Probate Rights in a Multiple–Marriage Society," 45 The Record of the Ass'n of the Bar of the City of New York 339, 365–68 (1990) (Mortimer H. Hess Memorial Lecture).

Section 2–302. Omitted Children.

(a) Except as provided in subsection (b), if a testator fails to provide in his [or her] will for any of his [or her] children born or adopted after the execution of the will, the omitted after-born or after-adopted child receives a share in the estate as follows:

(1) If the testator had no child living when he [or she] executed the will, an omitted after-born or after-adopted child receives a share in the estate equal in value to that which the child would have received had the testator died intestate, unless the will devised all or substantially all the estate to the other parent of the omitted child and that other parent survives the testator and is entitled to take under the will.

(2) If the testator had one or more children living when he [or she] executed the will, and the will devised property or an interest in property to one or more of the then-living children, an omitted after-born or after-adopted child is entitled to share in the testator's estate as follows:

(i) The portion of the testator's estate in which the omitted after-born or after-adopted child is entitled to share is limited to devises made to the testator's then-living children under the will.

(ii) The omitted after-born or after-adopted child is entitled to receive the share of the testator's estate, as limited in subparagraph (i), that the child would have received had the testator included all omitted after-born and after-adopted children with the children to whom devises were made under the will and had given an equal share of the estate to each child.

(iii) To the extent feasible, the interest granted an omitted after-born or after-adopted child under this section must be of the same character, whether equitable or legal, present or future, as that devised to the testator's then-living children under the will.

(iv) In satisfying a share provided by this paragraph, devises to the testator's children who were living when the will was executed abate ratably. In abating the devises of the then-living children, the court shall preserve to the maximum extent possible the character of the testamentary plan adopted by the testator.

(b) Neither subsection (a)(1) nor subsection (a)(2) applies if:

(1) it appears from the will that the omission was intentional; or

(2) the testator provided for the omitted after-born or after-adopted child by transfer outside the will and the intent that the transfer be in lieu of a testamentary provision is shown by the testator's statements or is reasonably inferred from the amount of the transfer or other evidence.

(c) If at the time of execution of the will the testator fails to provide in his [or her] will for a living child solely because he [or she] believes the child to be dead, the child receives a share in the estate equal in value to that which the child would have received had the testator died intestate.

(d) In satisfying a share provided by subsection (a)(1) or (c), devises made by the will abate under Section 3–902.

COMMENT

This section provides for both the case where a child was born or adopted after the execution of the will and not foreseen at the time and thus not provided for in the will, and the rare case where a testator omits one of his or her children because of the mistaken belief that the child is dead.

Basic Purposes and Scope of Revisions. This section is substantially revised. The revisions have two basic objectives. The first basic objective is to provide that a will that devised all or substantially all of the testator's estate to the other parent of the omitted child prevents an after-born or after-adopted child from taking an intestate share if none of the testator's children was living when he or she executed the will. (Under this rule, the other parent must survive the testator and be entitled to take under the will.)

Under the pre–1990 Code, such a will prevented the omitted child's entitlement only if the testator had one or more children living when he or she executed the will. The rationale for the revised rule is found in the empirical evidence (cited in the Comment to section 2–102) that suggests that even testators with children tend to devise their entire estates to their surviving spouses, especially in smaller estates. The testator's purpose is not to disinherit the children; rather, such a will evidences a purpose to trust the surviving parent to use the property for the benefit of the children, as appropriate. This attitude of trust of the surviving parent carries over to the case where none of the children have been born when the will is executed.

The second basic objective of the revisions is to provide that if the testator had children when he or she executed the will, and if the will made provision for one or more of the then-living children, an omitted after-born or after-adopted child does not take a full intestate share (which might be substantially larger or substantially smaller than given to the living children). Rather, the omitted after-born or after-adopted child participates on a pro rata basis in the property devised to the then-living children.

A more detailed description of the revised rules follows.

No Child Living When Will Executed. If the testator had no child living when he or she executed the will, subsection (a)(1) provides that an omitted after-born or after-adopted child receives the share he or she would have received had the testator died intestate, unless the will devised all or substantially all of the estate to the other parent of the omitted child. If the will did devise all or substantially all of the estate to the other parent of the omitted child, and if that other parent survives the testator and is entitled to take under the will, the omitted after-born or after-adopted child receives no share of the estate. In the case of an after-adopted child, the term "other parent" refers to the other adopting parent. (The other parent of the omitted child might survive the testator, but not be entitled to take under the will because, for example, that devise to the other parent was revoked under Section 2–803 or 2–804.)

One or More Children Living When Will Executed. If the testator had one or more children living when the will was executed, subsection (a)(2), which implements the second basic objective stated above, provides that an omitted after-born or after-adopted child only receives a share of the testator's estate if the testator's will devised property or an interest in property to one or more of the children living at the time the will was executed; if not, the omitted after-born or after-adopted child receives nothing.

Subsection (a)(2) is modelled on N.Y. Est. Powers & Trusts Law § 5–3.2. Subsection (a)(2) is illustrated by the following example.

Example. When G executed her will, she had two living children, A and B. Her will devised $7,500 to each child. After G executed her will, she had another child, C.

C is entitled to $5,000. $2,500 (⅓ of $7,500) of C's entitlement comes from A's $7,500 devise (reducing it to $5,000); and $2,500 (⅓ of $7,500) comes from B's $7,500 devise (reducing it to $5,000).

Variation. If G's will had devised $10,000 to A and $5,000 to B, C would be entitled to $5,000. $3,333 (⅓ of $10,000) of C's entitlement comes from A's $10,000 devise (reducing it to $6,667); and $1,667 (⅓ of $5,000) comes from B's $5,000 devise (reducing it to $3,333).

Subsection (b) Exceptions. To preclude operation of subsection (a)(1) or (a)(2), the testator's will need not make any provision, even nominal in amount, for a testator's present or future children; under subsection (b)(1), a simple recital in the will that the testator intends to make no provision for then living children or any the testator thereafter may have would be sufficient.

For a case applying the language of subsection (b)(2), in the context of the omitted spouse provision, see Estate of Bartell, 776 P.2d 885 (Utah 1989).

The moving party has the burden of proof on the elements of subsections (b)(1) and (b)(2).

Abatement Under Subsection (d). Under subsection (d) and Section 3–902, any intestate estate would first be applied to satisfy the intestate share of an omitted after-born or after-adopted child under subsection (a)(1) or (c).

PART 4

EXEMPT PROPERTY AND ALLOWANCES

GENERAL COMMENT

For decedents who die domiciled in this State, this part grants various allowances to the decedent's surviving spouse and certain children. The allowances have priority over unsecured creditors of the estate and persons to whom the estate may be devised by will. If there is a surviving spouse, all of the allowances described in this Part, which (as revised to adjust for inflation) total $25,000, plus whatever is allowed to the spouse for support during administration, normally pass to the spouse. If the surviving spouse and minor or dependent children live apart from one another, the minor or dependent children may receive some of the support allowance. If there is no surviving spouse, minor or dependent children become entitled to the homestead exemption of $15,000 and to support allowances. The exempt property section confers rights on the spouse, if any, or on all children, to $10,000 in certain chattels, or funds if the unencumbered value of chattels is below the $10,000 level. This provision is designed in part to relieve a personal representative of the duty to sell household chattels when there are children who will have them.

These family protection provisions supply the basis for the important small estate provisions of Article III, Part 12.

States adopting the Code may see fit to alter the dollar amounts suggested in these sections, or to vary the terms and conditions in other ways so as to accommodate existing traditions. Although creditors of estates would be aided somewhat if all family exemption provisions relating to probate estates were the same throughout the country, there is probably less need for uniformity of law regarding these provisions than for any of the other parts of this article. Still, it is quite important for all states to limit their homestead, support allowance and exempt property provisions, if any, so that they apply only to estates of decedents who were domiciliaries of the state.

Cross Reference. Notice that under Section 2–104 a spouse or child claiming under this Part must survive the decedent by 120 hours.

Section 2–401. Applicable Law.

This Part applies to the estate of a decedent who dies domiciled in this State. Rights to homestead allowance, exempt property, and family allowance for a decedent who dies not domiciled in this State are governed by the law of the decedent's domicile at death.

Section 2–402. Homestead Allowance.

A decedent's surviving spouse is entitled to a homestead allowance of [$15,000]. If there is no surviving spouse, each minor child and each dependent child of the decedent is entitled to a homestead allowance amounting to [$15,000] divided by the number of minor and dependent children of the decedent. The homestead allowance is exempt from and has priority over all claims against the estate. Homestead allowance is in addition to any share passing to the surviving spouse or minor or dependent child by the will of the decedent, unless otherwise provided, by intestate succession, or by way of elective share.

COMMENT

As originally adopted in 1969, the bracketed dollar amount was $5,000. To adjust for inflation, the bracketed amount was increased to $15,000 in 1990.

See Section 2–802 for the definition of "spouse," which controls in this Part. Also, see Section 2–104. Waiver of homestead is covered by Section 2–204. "Election" between a provision of a will and homestead is not required unless the will so provides.

A set dollar amount for homestead allowance was dictated by the desirability of having a certain level below which administration may be dispensed with or be handled summarily, without regard to the size of allowances under Section 2–404. The "small estate" line is controlled largely, though not entirely, by the size of the homestead allowance. This is because Part 12 of Article III dealing with small estates rests on the assumption that the only justification for keeping a decedent's assets from his creditors is to benefit the decedent's spouse and children.

Another reason for a set amount is related to the fact that homestead allowance may prefer a decedent's minor or dependent children over his or her other children. It was felt desirable to minimize the consequence of application of an arbitrary age line among children of the decedent.

[Section 2–402A. Constitutional Homestead.

The value of any constitutional right of homestead in the family home received by a surviving spouse or child must be charged against the spouse or child's homestead allowance to the extent the family home is part of the decedent's estate or would have been but for the homestead provision of the constitution.]

COMMENT

This optional section is designed for adoption only in states with a constitutional homestead provision. The value of the surviving spouse's constitutional right of homestead may be considerably less than the full value of the family home if the constitution gives him or her only a terminable life estate enjoyable in common with minor children.

SECTION 2–403. EXEMPT PROPERTY.

In addition to the homestead allowance, the decedent's surviving spouse is entitled from the estate to a value, not exceeding $10,000 in excess of any security interests therein, in household furniture, automobiles, furnishings, appliances, and personal effects. If there is no surviving spouse, the decedent's children are entitled jointly to the same value. If encumbered chattels are selected and the value in excess of security interests, plus that of other exempt property, is less than $10,000, or if there is not $10,000 worth of exempt property in the estate, the spouse or children are entitled to other assets of the estate, if any, to the extent necessary to make up the $10,000 value. Rights to exempt property and assets needed to make up a deficiency of exempt property have priority over all claims against the estate, but the right to any assets to make up a deficiency of exempt property abates as necessary to permit earlier payment of homestead allowance and family allowance. These rights are in addition to any benefit or share passing to the surviving spouse or children by the decedent's will, unless otherwise provided, by intestate succession, or by way of elective share.

COMMENT

As originally adopted in 1969, the dollar amount exempted was set at $3,500. To adjust for inflation, the amount was increased to $10,000 in 1990.

Unlike the exempt amount described in Sections 2–402 and 2–404, the exempt amount described in this section is available in a case in which the decedent left no spouse but left only adult children. The provision in this section that establishes priorities is required because of possible difference between beneficiaries of the exemptions described in this section and those described in Sections 2–402 and 2–404.

Section 2–204 covers waiver of exempt property rights. This section indicates that a decedent's will may put a spouse to an election with reference to exemptions, but that no election is presumed to be required.

Section 2–404. Family Allowance.

(a) In addition to the right to homestead allowance and exempt property, the decedent's surviving spouse and minor children whom the decedent was obligated to support and children who were in fact being supported by the decedent are entitled to a reasonable allowance in money out of the estate for their maintenance during the period of administration, which allowance may not continue for longer than one year if the estate is inadequate to discharge allowed claims. The allowance may be paid as a lump sum or in periodic installments. It is payable to the surviving spouse, if living, for the use of the surviving spouse and minor and dependent children; otherwise to the children, or persons having their care and custody. If a minor child or dependent child is not living with the surviving spouse, the allowance may be made partially to the child or his [or her] guardian or other person having the child's care and custody, and partially to the spouse, as their needs may appear. The family allowance is exempt from and has priority over all claims except the homestead allowance.

(b) The family allowance is not chargeable against any benefit or share passing to the surviving spouse or children by the will of the decedent, unless otherwise provided, by intestate succession or by way of elective share. The death of any person entitled to family allowance terminates the right to allowances not yet paid.

COMMENT

The allowance provided by this section does not qualify for the marital deduction under the federal estate tax because the interest is a non-deductible terminable interest. A broad code must be drafted to provide the best possible protection for the family in all cases, even though this may not provide desired tax advantages for certain larger estates. In the estates falling in the federal estate tax bracket where careful planning may be expected, it is important to the operation of formula clauses that the family allowance be clearly deductible or clearly non-deductible. With the section clearly creating a non-deductible interest, estate planners can create a plan that will operate with certainty. Finally, in order to facilitate administration of this allowance without court supervision it is necessary to provide a fairly simple and definite framework.

In determining the amount of the family allowance, account should be taken of both the previous standard of living and the nature of other resources available to the family to meet current living expenses until the estate can be administered and assets distributed. While the death of the principal income producer may necessitate some change in the standard of living, there must also be a period of adjustment. If the surviving spouse has a substantial income, this may be taken into account. Whether life insurance proceeds payable in a lump sum or periodic installments were intended by the decedent to be used for the period of adjustment or to be conserved as capital may be considered. A living trust may provide the needed income without resorting to the probate estate.

Obviously, need is relative to the circumstances, and what is reasonable must be decided on the basis of the facts of each individual case. Note, however, that under the next section the personal representative may not determine an allowance of more that $1500 per month for one year; a Court order would be necessary if a greater allowance is reasonably necessary.

Section 2–405. Source, Determination, and Documentation.

(a) If the estate is otherwise sufficient, property specifically devised may not be used to satisfy rights to homestead allowance or exempt property. Subject to this restriction, the surviving spouse, guardians of minor children, or children who are adults may select property of the estate as homestead allowance and exempt property.

The personal representative may make those selections if the surviving spouse, the children, or the guardians of the minor children are unable or fail to do so within a reasonable time or there is no guardian of a minor child. The personal representative may execute an instrument or deed of distribution to establish the ownership of property taken as homestead allowance or exempt property. The personal representative may determine the family allowance in a lump sum not exceeding $18,000 or periodic installments not exceeding $1,500 per month for one year, and may disburse funds of the estate in payment of the family allowance and any part of the homestead allowance payable in cash. The personal representative or an interested person aggrieved by any selection, determination, payment, proposed payment, or failure to act under this section may petition the court for appropriate relief, which may include a family allowance other than that which the personal representative determined or could have determined.

(b) If the right to an elective share is exercised on behalf of a surviving spouse who is an incapacitated person, the personal representative may add any unexpended portions payable under the homestead allowance, exempt property, and family allowance to the trust established under Section 2–203(b).

COMMENT

Scope and Purpose of Revision. As originally adopted in 1969, the maximum family allowance the personal representative was authorized to determine without court order was a lump sum of $6,000 or periodic installments of $500 per month for one year. To adjust for inflation, the amounts are increased to $18,000 and $1,500 respectively.

A new subsection (b) is added to provide for the case where the right to an elective share is exercised on behalf of a surviving spouse who is an incapacitated person. In that case, the personal representative is authorized to add any unexpended portions under the homestead allowance, exempt property, and family allowance to the custodial trust established by Section 2–203(b).

If Domiciliary Assets Insufficient. Note that a domiciliary personal representative can collect against out of state assets if domiciliary assets are insufficient.

Cross References. See Sections 3–902, 3–906, and 3–907.

WILLS, WILL CONTRACTS, AND CUSTODY AND DEPOSIT OF WILLS

GENERAL COMMENT

Part 5 of Article II is retitled to reflect the fact that it now includes the provisions on will contracts (pre–1990 section 2–701) and on custody and deposit of wills (pre–1990 sections 2–901 and 2–902).

Part 5 deals with capacity and formalities for execution and revocation of wills. The basic intent of the pre–1990 sections was to validate wills whenever possible. To that end, the minimum age for making wills was lowered to eighteen, formalities for a written and attested will were reduced, holographic wills written and signed by the testator were authorized, choice of law as to validity of execution was broadened, and revocation by operation of law was limited to divorce or annulment. In addition, the statute also provided for an optional method of execution with acknowledgment before a public officer (the self-proved will).

These measures have been retained, and the purpose of validating wills whenever possible has been strengthened by the addition of a new section, section 2–503, which allows a will to be upheld despite a harmless error in it execution.

Section 2–501. Who May Make Will.

An individual 18 or more years of age who is of sound mind may make a will.

COMMENT

This section states a uniform minimum age of eighteen for capacity to execute a will. "Minor" is defined in Section 1–201, and may involve an age different from that prescribed here.

Section 2–502. Execution; Witnessed Wills; Holographic Wills.

(a) Except as provided in subsection (b) and in Sections 2–503, 2–506, and 2–513, a will must be:

(1) in writing;

(2) signed by the testator or in the testator's name by some other individual in the testator's conscious presence and by the testator's direction; and

(3) signed by at least two individuals, each of whom signed within a reasonable time after he [or she] witnessed either the

94

signing of the will as described in paragraph (2) or the testator's acknowledgment of that signature or acknowledgment of the will.

(b) A will that does not comply with subsection (a) is valid as a holographic will, whether or not witnessed, if the signature and material portions of the document are in the testator's handwriting.

(c) Intent that the document constitute the testator's will can be established by extrinsic evidence, including, for holographic wills, portions of the document that are not in the testator's handwriting.

COMMENT

Scope and Purpose of Revision. Section 2–502 and pre–1990 Section 2–503 are combined to make room for new Section 2–503. Also, a cross reference to new Section 2–503 is added, and fairly minor clarifying revisions are made.

Subsection (a). Three formalities for execution of a witnessed will are imposed. Subsection (a)(1) requires the will to be in writing. Any reasonably permanent record is sufficient. A tape-recorded will has been held not to be "in writing." Estate of Reed, 672 P.2d 829 (Wyo. 1983).

Under subsection (a)(2), the testator must sign the will or some other individual must sign the testator's name in the testator's presence and by the testator's direction. If the latter procedure is followed, and someone else signs the testator's name, the so-called "conscious presence" test is codified, under which a signing is sufficient if it was done in the testator's conscious presence, i.e., within the range of the testator's senses such as hearing; the signing need not have occurred within the testator's line of sight. For application of the "conscious-presence" test, see Cunningham v. Cunningham, 80 Minn. 180, 83 N.W. 58 (1900) (conscious-presence requirement held satisfied where "the signing was within the sound of the testator's voice; he knew what was being done . . . "); Healy v. Bartless, 73 N.H. 110, 59 A. 617 (1904) (indi-viduals are in the decedent's conscious presence "whenever they are so near at hand that he is conscious of where they are and of what they are doing, through any of his senses, and where he can readily see them if he is so disposed."); Demaris' Estate, 166 Or. 36, 110 P.2d 571 (1941) ("[W]e do not believe that sight is the only test of presence. We are convinced that any of the senses that a testator possesses, which enable him to know whether another is near at hand and what he is doing, may be employed by him in determining whether [an individual is] in his [conscious] presence . . . ").

Under subsection (a)(3), at least two individuals must sign the will, each of whom witnessed at least one of the following: the signing of the will; the testator's acknowledgment of the signature; or the testator's acknowledgment of the will.

Signing may be by mark, nickname, or initials, subject to the general rules relating to that which constitutes a "signature." There is no requirement that the testator "publish" the document as his or her will, or that he or she request the witnesses to sign, or that the witnesses sign in the presence of the testator or of each other. The testator may sign the will outside the presence of the witnesses, if he or she later acknowledges to the witnesses that the signature is his or hers (or that his or her name was signed by another) or that the document is his or her will. An acknowledgment need not be expressly stated, but can be inferred from the testator's conduct. Norton v. Georgia Railroad Bank & Tr. Co., 248 Ga. 847, 285 S.E.2d 910 (1982). The witnesses must sign as witnesses (see, e.g., Mossler v. Johnson, 565 S.W.2d 952 (Tex. Civ. App. 1978)), and must sign within a reasonable time after having witnessed the signing or acknowledgment. There is, however, no requirement that the witnesses sign before the testator's death; in a given case, the reasonable-time requirement could be satisfied even if the witnesses sign after the testator's death.

There is no requirement that the testator's signature be at the end of the will; thus, if he or she writes his or her name in the body of the will and intends it to be his or her signature, this would satisfy the statute. See Estate of Siegel, 214 N.J. Super. 586, 520 A.2d 798 (App. Div. 1987).

A will that does not meet these requirements may be valid under subsection (b) as a holograph or under Section 2–503.

Subsection (b). This subsection authorizes holographic wills. It enables a testator to write his or her own will in handwriting. There need be no witnesses. The only requirement is that the signature and the material portions of the document be in the testator's handwriting.

By requiring only the "material portions of the document" to be in the testator's handwriting (rather than requiring, as some existing statutes do, that the will be "entirely" in the decedent's handwriting), a holograph may be valid even though immaterial parts such as date or introductory wording are printed, typed, or stamped.

A valid holograph can also be executed on a printed will form if the material portions of the document are handwritten. The fact, for example, that the will form contains printed language such as "I give, devise, and bequeath to _____" does not disqualify the document as a holographic will, as long as the testator fills out the remaining portion of the dispositive provision in his or her own hand.

Under subsection (c), testamentary intent can be shown by extrinsic evidence, including for holographic wills the printed, typed, or stamped portions of the form or document.

Section 2–503. Writings Intended as Wills, etc.

Although a document or writing added upon a document was not executed in compliance with Section 2–502, the document or writing is treated as if it had been executed in compliance with that section if the proponent of the document or writing establishes by clear and convincing evidence that the decedent intended the document or writing to constitute (i) the decedent's will, (ii) a partial or complete revocation of the will, (iii) an addition to or an alteration of the will, or (iv) a partial or complete revival of his [or her] formerly revoked will or of a formerly revoked portion of the will.

COMMENT

Purpose of New Section. By way of dispensing power, this new section allows the probate court to excuse a harmless error in complying with the formal requirements for executing or revoking a will. The measure accords with legislation in force in the Canadian province of Manitoba and in several Australian jurisdictions. The Uniform Laws Conference of Canada approved a comparable measure for the Canadian Uniform Wills Act in 1987.

Legislation of this sort was enacted in the state of South Australia in 1975. The experience there has been closely studied by a variety of law reform commissions and in the scholarly literature. See, e.g., Law Reform Commission of British Columbia, Report on the Making and Revocation of Wills (1981); New South Wales Law Reform Commission, Wills: Execution and Revocation (1986); Langbein, Excusing Harmless Errors in the Execution of Wills: A Report on Australia's Tranquil Revolution in Probate Law, 87 Colum. L. Rev. 1 (1987). A similar measure has been in effect in Israel since 1965 (see British Columbia Report, supra, at 44–46; Langbein, supra, at 48–51).

Consistent with the general trend of the revisions of the UPC, Section 2–503 unifies the law of probate and nonprobate transfers, extending to will formalities the harmless error principle that has long been applied to defective compliance with the formal requirements for nonprobate transfers. See, e.g., Annot., 19 A.L. R.2d 5 (1951) (life insurance beneficiary designations).

Evidence from South Australia suggests that the dispensing power will be applied mainly in two sorts of cases. See Langbein, supra, at 15–33. When the testator misunderstands the attestation requirements of Section 2–502(a) and neglects to obtain one or both witnesses, new Section 2–503 permits the proponents of the will to prove that the defective execution did not result from irresolution or from circumstances suggesting duress or trickery — in other words, that the defect was harmless to the purpose of the formality. The measure reduces the tension between holographic wills and the two-witness requirement for attested wills under Section 2–502(a). Ordinarily, the testator who attempts to make an attested will but blunders will still have achieved a level of formality that compares favorably with that permitted for holographic wills under the Code.

The other recurrent class of case in which the dispensing power has been invoked in South Australia entails alterations to a previously executed will. Sometimes the testator adds a clause, that is, the testator attempts to interpolate a defectively executed codicil. More frequently, the amendment has the character of a revision — the testator crosses out former text and inserts replacement terms. Lay persons do not always understand that the execution and revocation requirements of Section 2–502 call for fresh execution in order to modify a will; rather, lay persons often think that the original execution has continuing effect.

By placing the burden of proof upon the proponent of a defective instrument, and by requiring the proponent to discharge that burden by clear and convincing evidence (which courts at the trial and appellate levels are urged to police with rigor), Section 2–503 imposes procedural standards appropriate to the seriousness of the issue. Experience in Israel and South Australia strongly supports the view that a dispensing power like Section 2–503 will not breed litigation. Indeed, as an Israeli judge reported to the British Columbia Law Reform Commission, the dispensing power "actually prevents a great deal of unnecessary litigation," because it eliminates disputes about technical lapses and limits the zone of dispute to the functional question of whether the instrument correctly expresses the testator's intent. British Columbia Report, supra, at 46.

The larger the departure from Section 2–502 formality, the harder it will be to satisfy the court that the instrument reflects the testator's intent. Whereas the South Australian and Israeli courts lightly excuse breaches of the attestation requirements, they have never excused noncompliance with the requirement that a will be in writing, and they have been extremely reluctant to excuse noncompliance with the signature requirement. See Langbein, supra, at 23–29, 49–50. The main circumstance in which the South Australian courts have excused signature errors has been in the recurrent class of cases in which two wills are prepared for simultaneous execution by two testators,

typically husband and wife, and each mistakenly signs the will prepared for the other. E.g., Estate of Blakely, 32 S.A.S.R. 473 (1983). Recently, the New York Court of Appeals remedied such a case without aid of statute, simply on the ground "what has occurred is so obvious, and what was intended so clear." In re Snide, 52 N.Y.2d 193, 196, 418 N.E.2d 656, 657, 437 N.Y.S.2d 63, 64 (1981).

Section 2–503 means to retain the intent-serving benefits of Section 2–502 formality without inflicting intent-defeating outcomes in cases of harmless error.

Reference. The rule of this section is supported by the Restatement (Second) of Property (Donative Transfers) § 33.1 comment g (as approved by the American Law Institute at the 1990 annual meeting).

Section 2–504. Self–Proved Will.

(a) A will may be simultaneously executed, attested, and made self-proved, by acknowledgment thereof by the testator and affidavits of the witnesses, each made before an officer authorized to administer oaths under the laws of the state in which execution occurs and evidenced by the officer's certificate, under official seal, in substantially the following form:

I, _____, the testator, sign my name to this instrument this ____ day of _____, and being first duly sworn, do hereby declare to the undersigned authority that I sign and execute this instrument as my will and that I sign it willingly (or willingly direct another to sign for me), that I execute it as my free and voluntary act for the purposes therein expressed, and that I am eighteen years of age or older, of sound mind, and under no constraint or undue influence.

_____
Testator

We, _____, _____, the witnesses, sign our names to this instrument, being first duly sworn, and do hereby declare to the undersigned authority that the testator signs and executes this instrument as [his] [her] will and that [he] [she] signs it willingly (or willingly directs another to sign for [him] [her]), and that each of us, in the presence and hearing of the testator, hereby signs this will as witness to the testator's signing, and that to the best of our knowledge the testator is eighteen years of age or older, of sound mind, and under no constraint or undue influence.

_____
Witness

_____
Witness

The State of _____

County of _____

Subscribed, sworn to and acknowledged before me by _____, the testator, and subscribed and sworn to before me by _____, and _____, witness, this ____ day of _____.

(Seal)

(Signed)_____

_____
(Official capacity of officer)

(b) An attested will may be made self-proved at any time after its execution by the acknowledgment thereof by the testator and the affidavits of the witnesses, each made before an officer authorized to administer oaths under the laws of the state in which the acknowledgment occurs and evidenced by the officer's certificate, under the official seal, attached or annexed to the will in substantially the following form:

The State of _____

County of _____

We, _____, _____, and _____, the testator and the witnesses, respectively, whose names are signed to the attached or foregoing instrument, being first duly sworn, do hereby declare to the undersigned authority that the testator signed and executed the instrument as the testator's will and that [he] [she] had signed willingly (or willingly directed another to sign for [him] [her]), and that [he] [she] executed it as [his] [her] free and voluntary act for the purposes therein expressed, and that each of the witnesses, in the presence and hearing of the testator, signed the will as witness and that to the best of [his] [her] knowledge the testator

99

was at that time eighteen years or age or older, of sound mind, and under no constraint or undue influence.

_____
Testator

_____
Witness

_____
Witness

Subscribed, sworn to and acknowledged before me by _____, the testator, and subscribed and sworn to before me by _____, and _____, witnesses, this ___ of _____.

(Seal)

(Signed)_____

_____
(Official capacity of officer)

(c) A signature affixed to a self-proving affidavit attached to a will is considered a signature affixed to the will, if necessary to prove the will's due execution.

COMMENT

A self-proved will may be admitted to probate as provided in Sections 3–303, 3–405, and 3–406 without the testimony of any subscribing witness, but otherwise it is treated no differently from a will not self proved. Thus, a self-proved will may be contested (except in regard to signature requirements), revoked, or amended by a codicil in exactly the same fashion as a will not self proved. The procedural advantage of a self-proved will is limited to formal testacy proceedings because Section 3–303, which deals with informal probate, dispenses with the necessity of testimony of witnesses even though the instrument is not self proved under this section.

A new subsection (c) is added to counteract an unfortunate judicial interpretation of similar self-proving will provisions in a few states, under which a signature on the self-proving affidavit has been held not to constitute a signature on the will, resulting in invalidity of the will in cases where the testator or witnesses got confused and only signed on the self-proving affidavit. See Mann, Self-proving Affidavits and Formalism in Wills Adjudication, 63 Wash.U.L.Q. 39 (1985); Estate of Ricketts, 773 P.2d 93 (Wash. Ct. App. 1989).

Section 2–505. Who May Witness.

(a) An individual generally competent to be a witness may act as a witness to a will.

(b) The signing of a will by an interested witness does not invalidate the will or any provision of it.

COMMENT

This section carries forward the position of the pre–1990 Code. The position adopted simplifies the law relating to interested witnesses. Interest no longer disqualifies a person as a witness, nor does it invalidate or forfeit a gift under the will. Of course, the purpose of this change is not to foster use of interested witnesses, and attorneys will continue to use disinterested witnesses in execution of wills. But the rare and innocent use of a member of the testator's family on a home-drawn will is not penalized.

This approach does not increase appreciably the opportunity for fraud or undue influence. A substantial devise by will to a person who is one of the witnesses to the execution of the will is itself a suspicious circumstance, and the devise might be challenged on grounds of undue influence. The requirement of disinterested witnesses has not succeeded in preventing fraud and undue influence; and in most cases of undue influence, the influencer is careful not to sign as a witness, but to procure disinterested witnesses.

Under Section 3–406, an interested witness is competent to testify to prove execution of the will.

Section 2–506. Choice of Law as to Execution.

A written will is valid if executed in compliance with Section 2–502 or 2–503 or if its execution complies with the law at the time of execution of the place where the will is executed, or of the law of the place where at the time of execution or at the time of death the testator is domiciled, has a place of abode, or is a national.

COMMENT

This section permits probate of wills in this state under certain conditions even if they are not executed in accordance with the formalities of Section 2–502 or 2–503. Such wills must be in writing but otherwise are valid if they meet the requirements for execution of the law of the place where the will is executed (when it is executed in another state or country) or the law of testator's domicile, abode or nationality at either the time of execution or at the time of death. Thus, if testator is domiciled in state 1 and executes a typed will merely by signing it without witnesses in state 2 while on vacation there, the Court of this state would recognize the will as valid if the law of either state 1 or state 2 permits execution by signature alone. Or if a national of Mexico executes a written will in this state which does not meet the requirements of Section 2–502 but meets the requirements of Mexican law, the will would be recognized as validly executed under this section. The purpose of this section is to provide a wide opportunity for validation of expectations of testators.

Section 2–507. Revocation by Writing or by Act.

(a) A will or any part thereof is revoked:

(1) by executing a subsequent will that revokes the previous will or part expressly or by inconsistency; or

(2) by performing a revocatory act on the will, if the testator performed the act with the intent and for the purpose of revoking the will or part or if another individual performed the act in the testator's conscious presence and by the testator's direction. For purposes of this paragraph, "revocatory act on the will" includes burning , tearing, canceling, obliterating, or destroying the will or any part of it. A burning, tearing, or canceling is a "revocatory act on the will," whether or not the burn, tear, or cancellation touched any of the words on the will.

(b) If a subsequent will does not expressly revoke a previous will, the execution of the subsequent will wholly revokes the previous will by inconsistency if the testator intended the subsequent will to replace rather than supplement the previous will.

(c) The testator is presumed to have intended a subsequent will to replace rather than supplement a previous will if the subsequent will makes a complete disposition of the testator's estate. If this presumption arises and is not rebutted by clear and convincing evidence, the previous will is revoked; only the subsequent will is operative on the testator's death.

(d) The testator is presumed to have intended a subsequent will to supplement rather than replace a previous will if the subsequent will does not make a complete disposition of the testator's estate. If this presumption arises and is not rebutted by clear and convincing evidence, the subsequent will revokes the previous will only to the extent the subsequent will is inconsistent with the previous will; each will is fully operative on the testator's death to the extent they are not inconsistent.

COMMENT

Purpose and Scope of Revisions. Revocation of a will may be by either a subsequent will or an authorized act done to the document. Revocation by subsequent will cannot be effective unless the subsequent will is valid.

Revocation by Inconsistency. As originally promulgated, this section provided no standard by which the courts were to determine whether in a given case a subsequent will with no revocation clause revokes a prior will, wholly or partly, by inconsistency. Some courts seem to have been puzzled about the standard to be applied. New subsections (b), (c), and (d) codify the workable and common-sense standards set forth in the Restatement (Second) of Property (Donative Transfers) § 34.2 comment b (1991). Under these subsections, the question whether the subsequent will was intended to replace rather than supplement the previous will depends upon whether the second will makes a complete disposition of the testator's estate. If the second will does make a complete disposition of the testator's estate, a presumption arises that the second will was intended to replace the previous will. If the second will does not make a complete disposition of the testator's estate, a presumption arises that the second will was intended to supplement rather than replace the previous will. The rationale is that, when the second will does not make a complete disposition of the testator's estate, the second will is more in the nature of a codicil to the first will. This standard has been applied in the cases without the benefit of a statutory provision to this effect. E.g., Gilbert v. Gilbert, 652 S.W.2d 663 (Ky. Ct. App. 1983).

Example. Five years before her death, G executed a will (Will # 1), devising her antique desk to A; $20,000 to B; and the residue of her estate to C. Two years later, A died, and G executed another will (Will # 2), devising her antique desk to A's spouse, X; $10,000 to B; and the residue of her estate to C. Will # 2 neither expressly revoked Will # 1 nor made any other reference to it. G's net probate estate consisted of her antique desk (worth $10,000) and other property (worth $90,000). X, B, and C survived G by 120 hours.

Solution. Will # 2 was presumptively intended by G to replace Will # 1 because Will # 2 made a complete disposition of G's estate. Unless this presumption is rebutted by clear and convincing evidence, Will # 1 is wholly revoked; only Will # 2 is operative on G's death.

If, however, Will # 2 had not contained a residuary clause, and hence had not made a complete disposition of G's estate, "Will # 2" is more in the nature of a codicil to Will # 1, and the solution would be different. Now, Will # 2 would presumptively be treated as

having been intended to supplement rather than replace Will # 1. In the absence of evidence clearly and convincingly rebutting this presumption, Will # 1 would be revoked only to the extent Will # 2 is inconsistent with it; both wills would be operative on G's death, to the extent they are not inconsistent. As to the devise of the antique desk, Will # 2 is inconsistent with Will # 1, and the antique desk would go to X. There being no residuary clause in Will # 2, there is nothing in Will # 2 that is inconsistent with the residuary clause in Will # 1, and so the residue would go to C. The more difficult question relates to the cash devises in the two wills. The question whether they are inconsistent with one another is a question of interpretation in the individual case. Section 2–507 does not establish a presumption one way or the other on that question. If the court finds that the cash devises are inconsistent with one another, i.e., if the court finds that the cash devise in Will # 2 was intended to replace rather than supplement the cash devise in Will # 1, then B takes $10,000. But if the court finds that the cash devises are not inconsistent with one another, B would take $30,000.

Revocatory Act. In the case of an act of revocation done to the document, subsection (a)(2) is revised to provide that a burning, tearing, or canceling is a sufficient revocatory act even though the act does not touch any of the words on the will. This is consistent with cases on burning or tearing (e.g., White v. Casten, 46 N.C. 197 (1853) (burning); Crampton v. Osburn, 356 Mo. 125, 201 S.W.2d 336 (1947) (tearing)), but inconsistent with most, but not all, cases on cancellation (e.g., Yont v. Eads, 317 Mass. 232, 57 N.E.2d 531 (1944); Kronauge v. Stoecklein, 33 Ohio App.2d 229, 293

N.E.2d 320 (1972); Thompson v. Royall, 163 Va. 492, 175 S.E. 748 (1934); contra, Warner v. Warner's Estate, 37 Vt. 356 (1864)). By substantial authority, it is held that removal of the testator's signature—by, for example, lining it through, erasing or obliterating it, tearing or cutting it out of the document, or removing the entire signature page—constitutes a sufficient revocatory act to revoke the entire will. Board of Trustees of the University of Alabama v. Calhoun, 514 So.2d 895 (Ala.1987) and cases cited therein.

Subsection (a)(2) is also revised to codify the "conscious-presence" test. As revised, subsection (a)(2) provides that, if the testator does not perform the revocatory act, but directs another to perform the act, the act is a sufficient revocatory act if the other individual performs it in the testator's conscious presence. The act need not be performed in the testator's line of sight. See the Comment to Section 2–502 for a discussion of the "conscious-presence" test.

Revocatory Intent. To effect a revocation, a revocatory act must be accompanied by revocatory intent. Determining whether a revocatory act was accompanied by revocatory intent may involve exploration of extrinsic evidence, including the testator's statement as to intent.

Partial Revocation. This section specifically permits partial revocation.

Dependent Relative Revocation. Each court is free to apply its own doctrine of dependent relative revocation. See generally Palmer, "Dependent Relative Revocation and Its Relation to Relief for Mistake," 69 Mich.L.Rev. 989 (1971). Note, however, that dependent relative revocation should less often be necessary under the revised provisions of the Code. Dependent relative revocation is the law of second best, i.e., its application does not produce the result the testator actually intended, but is designed to come as close as possible to that intent. A precondition to the application of dependent relative revocation is, or should be, good evidence of the testator's actual intention; without that, the court has no basis for determining which of several outcomes comes the closest to that actual intention.

When there is good evidence of the testator's actual intention, however, the revised provisions of the Code would usually facilitate the effectuation of the result the testator actually intended. If, for example, the testator by revocatory act revokes a second will for the purpose of reviving a former will, the evidence necessary to establish the testator's intent to revive the former will should be sufficient under Section 2–509 to effect a revival of the former will, making the application of dependent relative revocation as to the second will unnecessary. If, by revocatory act, the testator revokes a will in conjunction with an effort to execute a new will, the evidence necessary to establish the testator's intention that the new will be valid should, in most cases, be sufficient under Section 2–503 to give effect to the new will, making the application of dependent relative revocation as to the old will unnecessary. If the testator lines out parts of a will or dispositive provision in conjunction with an effort to alter the will's terms, the evidence necessary to establish the testator's intention that the altered terms be valid should be sufficient under Section 2–503 to give effect to the will as altered, making dependent relative revocation as to the lined-out parts unnecessary.

Section 2–508. Revocation by Change of Circumstances.

Except as provided in Sections 2–803 and 2–804, a change of circumstances does not revoke a will or any part of it.

Section 2–509. Revival of Revoked Will.

(a) If a subsequent will that wholly revoked a previous will is thereafter revoked by a revocatory act under Section 2–507(a)(2), the previous will remains revoked unless it is revived. The previous will is revived if it is evident from the circumstances of the revocation of the subsequent will or from the testator's contemporary or subsequent declarations that the testator intended the previous will to take effect as executed.

(b) If a subsequent will that partly revoked a previous will is thereafter revoked by a revocatory act under Section 2–507(a)(2), a revoked part of the previous will is revived unless it is evident from the circumstances of the revocation of the subsequent will or from the testator's contemporary or subsequent declarations that the testator did not intend the revoked part to take effect as executed.

(c) If a subsequent will that revoked a previous will in whole or in part is thereafter revoked by another, later, will, the previous will remains revoked in whole or in part, unless it or its revoked part is revived. The previous will or its revoked part is revived to the extent it appears from the terms of the later will that the testator intended the previous will to take effect.

COMMENT

Purpose and Scope of Revisions. Although a will takes effect as a revoking instrument when it is executed, it takes effect as a dispositive instrument at death. Once revoked, therefore, a will is ineffective as a dispositive instrument unless it has been revived. This section covers the standards to be applied in determining whether a will (Will # 1) that was revoked by a subsequent will (Will # 2), either expressly or by inconsistency, has been revived by the revocation of the subsequent will, i.e., whether the revocation of Will # 2 (the revoking will) revives Will # 1 (the will that Will # 2 revoked).

As revised, this section is divided into three subsections. Subsections (a) and (b) cover the effect of revoking Will # 2 (the revoking will) by a revocatory act under Section 2–507(a)(2). Under subsection (a), if Will # 2 (the revoking will) wholly revoked Will # 1, the revocation of Will # 2 does not revive Will # 1 unless "it is evident from the circumstances of the revocation of [Will # 2] or from the testator's contemporary or subsequent declarations that the testator intended [Will # 1] to take effect as executed." This standard places the burden of persuasion on the proponent of Will # 1 to establish that the decedent's intention was that Will # 1 is to be his or her valid will. Testimony as to the testator's statements at the time he or she revokes Will # 2 or at a later date can be admitted. Indeed, all relevant evidence of intention is to be considered by the court on this question; the open-ended statutory language is not to be undermined by translating it into discrete subsidiary elements, all of which must be met, as the court did in Estate of Boysen, 309 N.W.2d 45 (Minn. 1981).

The pre–1990 version of this section did not distinguish between complete and partial revocation. Regardless of whether Will # 2 wholly or partly revoked Will # 1, the pre–1990 version presumed against revival of Will # 1 when Will # 2 was revoked by act.

As revised, this section properly treats the two situations as distinguishable. The presumption against revival imposed by subsection (a) is justified because where Will # 2 wholly revoked Will # 1, the testator understood or should have understood that Will # 1 had no continuing effect. Consequently, subsection (a) properly presumes that the testator's act of revoking Will # 2 was not accompanied by an intent to revive Will # 1.

Subsection (b) establishes the opposite presumption where Will # 2 (the revoking will) revoked Will # 1 only in part. In this case, the revocation of Will # 2 revives the revoked part or parts of Will # 1 unless "it is evident from the circumstances of the revocation of [Will # 2] or from the testator's contemporary or subsequent declarations that the testator did not intend the revoked part to take effect as executed." This standard places the burden of persuasion on the party arguing that the revoked part or parts of Will # 1 were not revived. The justification is that where Will # 2 only partly revoked Will # 1, Will # 2 is only a codicil to Will # 1, and the testator knows (or should know) that Will # 1 does have continuing effect. Consequently, subsection (b) properly presumes that the testator's act of revoking Will # 2 (the codicil) was accompanied by an intent to revive or reinstate the revoked parts of Will # 1.

Subsection (c) covers the effect on Will # 1 of revoking Will # 2 (the revoking will) by another, later, will (Will # 3). Will # 1 remains revoked except to the extent that Will # 3 shows an intent to have Will # 1 effective.

Section 2–510. Incorporation by Reference.

A writing in existence when a will is executed may be incorporated by reference if the language of the will manifests this intent and describes the writing sufficiently to permit its identification.

COMMENT

This section codifies the common-law doctrine of incorporation by reference, except that the sometimes troublesome requirement that the will refer to the document as being in existence when the will was executed has been eliminated.

Section 2–511. Testamentary Additions to Trusts.

(a) A will may validly devise property to the trustee of a trust established or to be established (i) during the testator's lifetime by the testator, by the testator and some other person, or by some other person, including a funded or unfunded life insurance trust, although the settlor has reserved any or all rights of ownership of the insurance contracts, or (ii) at the testator's death by the testator's devise to the trustee, if the trust is identified in the testator's will and its terms are set forth in a written instrument, other than a will, executed before, concurrently with, or after the execution of the testator's will or in another individual's will if that other individual has predeceased the testator, regardless of the existence, size, or character of the corpus of the trust. The devise is not invalid because the trust is amendable or revocable, or because the trust was amended after the execution of the will or the testator's death.

(b) Unless the testator's will provides otherwise, property devised to a trust described in subsection (a) is not held under a testamentary trust of the testator, but it becomes a part of the trust to which it is devised, and must be administered and disposed of in accordance with the provisions of the governing instrument setting forth the terms of the trust, including any amendments thereto made before or after the testator's death.

(c) Unless the testator's will provides otherwise, a revocation or termination of the trust before the testator's death causes the devise to lapse.

COMMENT

Purpose and Scope of Revisions. In addition to making a few stylistic changes, several substantive changes in this section are made.

As revised, it has been made clear that the "trust" need not have been established (funded with a trust res) during the decedent's lifetime, but can be established (funded with a res) by the devise itself. The pre-1990 version probably contemplated this result and reasonably could be so interpreted (because of the phrase "regardless of the *exist-ence* . . . of the corpus of the trust"). Indeed, a few cases have expressly stated that statutory language like the pre–1990 version of this section authorizes pour-over devises to unfunded trusts. E.g., Clymer v. Mayo, 473 N.E.2d 1084 (Mass. 1985); Trosch v. Maryland Nat'l Bank, 32 Md.App. 249, 359 A.2d 564

(1976). The authority of these pronouncements is problematic, however, because the trusts in these cases were so-called "unfunded" life-insurance trusts. An unfunded life-insurance trust is not a trust without a trust res; the trust res in an unfunded life-insurance trust is the contract right to the proceeds of the life-insurance policy conferred on the trustee by virtue of naming the trustee the beneficiary of the policy. See Gordon v. Portland Trust Bank, 201 Or. 648, 271 P.2d 653 (1954) ("[T]he [trustee as the] beneficiary [of the policy] is the owner of a promise to pay the proceeds at the death of the insured . . ."); Gurnett v. Mutual Life Ins. Co., 356 Ill. 612, 191 N.E. 250 (1934). Thus, the term "unfunded life-insurance trust" does not refer to an unfunded trust, but to a funded trust that has not received *additional* funding. For further indication of the problematic nature of the idea that the pre–1990 version of this section permits pour-over devises to unfunded trusts, see Estate of Daniels, 665 P.2d 594 (Colo. 1983) (pour-over devise failed; before signing the trust instrument, the decedent was advised by counsel that the "mere signing of the trust agreement would not activate it and that, before the trust could come into being, [the decedent] would have to fund it;" decedent then signed the trust agreement and returned it to counsel "to wait for further directions on it;" no further action was taken by the decedent prior to death; the decedent's will devised the residue of her estate to the trustee of the trust, but added that the residue should go elsewhere "if the trust created by said agreement is not in effect at my death.")

Additional revisions of this section are designed to remove obstacles to carrying out the decedent's intention that were contained in the pre–1990 version. These revisions allow the trust terms to be set forth in a written instrument executed after as well as before or concurrently with the execution of the will; require the devised property to be administered in accordance with the terms of the trust as amended after as well as before the decedent's death, even though the decedent's will does not so provide; and allow the decedent's will to provide that the devise is not to lapse even if the trust is revoked or terminated before the decedent's death.

Proposed Revision of Uniform Testamentary Additions to Trusts Act. The Joint Editorial Board for the Uniform Probate Code and the Drafting Committee to Revise Article II recommend that the freestanding Uniform Testamentary Additions to Trusts Act be revised in accordance with the revisions to UPC § 2–511.

Section 2–512. Events of Independent Significance.

A will may dispose of property by reference to acts and events that have significance apart from their effect upon the dispositions made by the will, whether they occur before or after the execution of the will or before or after the testator's death. The execution or revocation of another individual's will is such an event.

Section 2–513. Separate Writing Identifying Devise of Certain Types of Tangible Personal Property.

Whether or not the provisions relating to holographic wills apply, a will may refer to a written statement or list to dispose of items of tangible personal property not otherwise specifically disposed of by the will, other than money. To be admissible under this section as evidence of the intended disposition, the writing must be signed by the testator and must describe the items and the devisees with reasonable certainty. The writing may be referred to as one to be in existence at the time of the testator's death; it may be prepared before or after the execution of the will; it may be altered by the testator after its preparation; and it may be a writing that has no significance apart from its effect on the dispositions made by the will.

COMMENT

Purpose and Scope of Revision. As part of the broader policy of effectuating a testator's intent and of relaxing formalities of execution, this section permits a testator to refer in his or her will to a separate document disposing of tangible personalty other than money. The pre–1990 version precluded the disposition of "evidences of indebtedness, documents of title, and securities, and property used in a trade or business." These limitations are deleted in the revised version, partly to remove a source of confusion in the pre–1990 version, which arose because evidences of indebtedness, documents of title, and securities are not items of tangible personal property to begin with, and partly to permit the disposition of a broader range of items of tangible personal property.

The language "items of tangible personal property" does not require that the separate document specifically itemize each item of tangible personal property covered. The only requirement is that the document describe the items covered "with reasonable certainty." Consequently, a document referring to "all my tangible personal property other than money" or to "all my tangible personal property located in my office" or using similar catch-all type of language would normally be sufficient.

The separate document disposing of an item or items of tangible personal property may be prepared after execution of the will, so would not come within Section 2–510 on incorporation by reference. It may even be altered from time to time. The only requirement is that the document be signed by the testator. The pre-1990 version of this section

gave effect to an unsigned document if it was in the testator's handwriting. The revisions remove the language giving effect to such an unsigned document. The purpose is to prevent a mere handwritten draft from becoming effective without sufficient indication that the testator intended it to be effective. The signature requirement is designed to prevent mere drafts from becoming effective against the testator's wishes. An unsigned document could still be given effect under Section 2–503, however, if the proponent could carry the burden of proving by clear and convincing evidence that the testator intended the document to be effective.

The typical case covered by this section would be a list of personal effects and the persons whom the decedent desired to take specified items.

Sample Clause. Section 2–513 might be utilized by a clause in the decedent's will such as the following:

I might leave a written statement or list disposing of items of tangible personal property. If I do and if my written statement or list is found and is identified as such by my Personal Representative no later than 30 days after the probate of this will, then my written statement or list is to be given effect to the extent authorized by law and is to take precedence over any contrary devise or devises of the same item or items of property in this will.

Section 2–513 only authorizes disposition of tangible personal property "not otherwise specifically disposed of by the will." The sample clause above is consistent with this restriction. By providing that the written statement or list takes precedence over any contrary devise in the will, a contrary devise is made conditional upon the written statement or list not contradicting it; if the written statement or list does contradict a devise in the will, the will does not otherwise specifically dispose of the property.

If, however, the clause in the testator's will does not provide that the written statement or list is to take precedence over any contrary devise in the will (or contain a provision having similar effect), then the written statement or list is ineffective to the extent it purports to dispose of items of property that were otherwise specifically disposed of by the will.

Section 2–514. Contracts Concerning Succession.

A contract to make a will or devise, or not to revoke a will or devise, or to die intestate, if executed after the effective date of this Article, may be established only by (i) provisions of a will stating material provisions of the contract, (ii) an express reference in a will to a contract and extrinsic evidence proving the terms of the contract, or (iii) a writing signed by the decedent evidencing the contract. The execution of a joint will or mutual wills does not create a presumption of a contract not to revoke the will or wills.

COMMENT

Section Relocated. No substantive revision of this section is made, but the section is relocated and renumbered to make room for new Part 7.

The purpose of this section is to tighten the methods by which contracts concerning succession may be proved. Oral contracts not to revoke wills have given rise to much litigation in a number of states; and in many states if two persons execute a single document as their joint will, this gives rise to a presumption that the parties had contracted not to revoke the will except by consent of both.

This section requires that either the will must set forth the material

provisions of the contract, or the will must make express reference to the contract and extrinsic evidence prove the terms of the contract, or there must be a separate writing signed by the decedent evidencing the contract. Oral testimony regarding the contract is permitted if the will makes reference to the contract, but this provision of the statute is not intended to affect normal rules regarding admissibility of evidence.

This section does not preclude recovery in quantum meruit for the value of services rendered the testator.

Section 2–515. Deposit of Will with Court in Testator's Lifetime.

A will may be deposited by the testator or the testator's agent with any court for safekeeping, under rules of the court. The will must be sealed and kept confidential.   During the testator's lifetime, a deposited will must be delivered only to the testator or to a person authorized in writing signed by the testator to receive the will.   A conservator may be allowed to examine a deposited will of a protected testator under procedures designed to maintain the confidential character of the document to the extent possible, and to ensure that it will be resealed and kept on deposit after the examination.   Upon being informed of the testator's death, the court shall notify any person designated to receive the will and deliver it to that person on request; or the court may deliver the will to the appropriate court.

COMMENT

Many states already have statutes permitting deposit of wills during a testator's lifetime.   Most of these statutes have elaborate provisions governing purely administrative matters: how the will is to be enclosed in a sealed wrapper, what is to be endorsed on the wrapper, the form of receipt or certificate given to the testator, the fee to be charged, how the will is to be opened after testator's death and who is to be notified.   Under this section, details have been left to Court rule, except as other relevant statutes such as one governing fees may apply.

It is, of course, vital to maintain the confidential nature of deposited wills.   However, this obviously does not prevent the opening of the will after the death of the testator if necessary in order to determine the executor or other interested persons to be notified.   Nor should it prevent opening the will to microfilm for confidential record storage, for example.   These matters could again be regulated by Court rule.

The provision permitting examination of a will of a protected person by the conservator supplements Section 5–427.

Section 2–516.   Duty of Custodian of Will; Liability.

After the death of a testator and on request of an interested person, a person having custody of a will of the testator shall deliver it with reasonable promptness to a person able to secure its probate and if none is known, to an appropriate court.   A person who wilfully fails to deliver a will is liable to any person aggrieved for any damages that may be sustained by the failure.   A person who wilfully refuses or fails to deliver a will after being ordered by the court in a proceeding brought for the purpose of compelling delivery is subject to penalty for contempt of court.

COMMENT

In addition to a registrar or clerk, a person authorized to accept delivery of a will from a custodian may be a universal successor or other person authorized under the law of another nation to carry out the terms of a will.

Section 2–517. Penalty Clause for Contest.

A provision in a will purporting to penalize an interested person for contesting the will or instituting other proceedings relating to the estate is unenforceable if probable cause exists for instituting proceedings.

COMMENT

This section replicates Section 3–   905.

PART 6

RULES OF CONSTRUCTION APPLICABLE ONLY TO WILLS

GENERAL COMMENT

Parts 6 and 7 address a variety of construction problems that commonly occur in wills, trusts, and other types of governing instruments. All of the "rules" set forth in these parts yield to a finding of a contrary intention and are therefore rebuttable presumptions.

The rules of construction set forth in Part 6 apply only to wills. The rules of construction set forth in Part 7 apply to wills and other governing instruments making donative dispositions.

The sections in Part 6 deal with such problems as death before the testator (lapse), the inclusiveness of the will as to property of the testator, effect of failure of a gift in the will, change in form of securities specifically devised, ademption by reason of fire, sale and the like, exoneration, and exercise of a power of appointment by general language in the will.

Section 2–601. Scope.

In the absence of a finding of a contrary intention, the rules of construction in this Part control the construction of a will.

COMMENT

Purpose and Scope of Revisions. Common-law rules of construction yield to a finding of a contrary intention. The pre–1990 version of this section provided that the rules of construction in Part 6 yielded only to a "contrary intention indicated by the will." To align the statutory rules of construction in Part 6 with those established at common law, this section is revised so that the rules of construction yield to a "finding of a contrary intention." As revised, evidence extrinsic to the will as well as the content of the will itself is admissible for the purpose of rebutting the rules of construction in Part 6.

As originally promulgated, this section began with the sentence: "The intention of a testator as expressed in his will controls the legal effect of his dispositions." This sentence is removed primarily because it is inappropriate and unnecessary in a part of the Code containing rules of construction. The deletion of this sentence does not signify a retreat from the widely accepted proposition that a testator's intention controls the legal effect of his or her dispositions.

A further reason for deleting this sentence is that a possible, though unintended, reading of this sentence might be that it prevents the judicial adoption of a general reformation doctrine for wills, as approved by the American Law Institute in the Restatement (Second) of Property § 34.7 & comment d, illustration 11, and as advocated in Langbein & Waggoner, "Reformation of Wills on the Ground of Mistake: Change of Direction in American Law?," 130 U.Pa.L.Rev. 521 (1982). The striking of this sentence removes that possible impediment to the judicial adoption of a general reformation doctrine for wills as approved by the American Law Institute and as advocated in the Langbein–Waggoner article.

Cross Reference. See Section 8–101(b) for the application of the rules of construction in this Part to documents executed prior to the effective date of this Article.

Section 2–602. Will May Pass All Property and After–Acquired Property.

A will may provide for the passage of all property the testator owns at death and all property acquired by the estate after the testator's death.

COMMENT

Purpose and Scope of Revision. This section is revised to assure that, for example, a residuary clause in a will not only passes property owned at death that is not otherwise devised, even though the property was acquired by the testator after the will was executed, but also passes property acquired by a testator's estate after his or her death. This reverses a case like Braman Estate, 435 Pa. 573, 258 A.2d 492 (1969), where the court held that Mary's residuary devise to her sister Ruth "or her estate," which had passed to Ruth's estate where Ruth predeceased Mary by about a year, could not go to Ruth's residuary legatee. The court held that Ruth's will had no power to control the devolution of property acquired by Ruth's estate after her death; such property passed, instead, by intestate succession from Ruth. This section, applied to the Braman Estate case, would mean that the property acquired by Ruth's estate after her death would pass under her residuary clause.

The added language also makes it clear that items such as bonuses awarded to an employee after his or her death pass under his or her will.

Section 2–603. Antilapse; Deceased Devisee; Class Gifts.

(a) [**Definitions.**] In this section:

(1) "Alternative devise" means a devise that is expressly created by the will and, under the terms of the will, can take effect instead of another devise on the happening of one or more events, including survival of the testator or failure to survive the testator, whether an event is expressed in condition-precedent, condition-subsequent, or any other form. A residuary clause constitutes an alternative devise with respect to a nonresiduary devise only if the will specifically provides that, upon lapse or failure, the nonresiduary devise, or nonresiduary devises in general, pass under the residuary clause.

(2) "Class member" includes an individual who fails to survive the testator but who would have taken under a devise in the form of a class gift had he [or she] survived the testator.

(3) "Devise" includes an alternative devise, a devise in the form of a class gift, and an exercise of a power of appointment.

(4) "Devisee" includes (i) a class member if the devise is in the form of a class gift, (ii) the beneficiary of a trust but not the trustee, (iii) an individual or class member who was deceased at the time the testator executed his [or her] will as well as an individual or class member who was then living but who failed to survive the testator, and (iv) an appointee under a power of appointment exercised by the testator's will.

(5) "Stepchild" means a child of the surviving, deceased, or former spouse of the testator or of the donor of a power of appointment, and not of the testator or donor.

(6) "Surviving devisee" or "surviving descendant" means a devisee or a descendant who neither predeceased the testator nor is deemed to have predeceased the testator under Section 2–702.

(7) "Testator" includes the donee of a power of appointment if the power is exercised in the testator's will.

(b) [Substitute Gift.] If a devisee fails to survive the testator and is a grandparent, a descendant of a grandparent, or a stepchild of either the testator or the donor of a power of appointment exercised by the testator's will, the following apply:

(1) Except as provided in paragraph (4), if the devise is not in the form of a class gift and the deceased devisee leaves surviving descendants, a substitute gift is created in the devisee's surviving descendants. They take by representation the property to which the devisee would have been entitled had the devisee survived the testator.

(2) Except as provided in paragraph (4), if the devise is in the form of a class gift, other than a devise to "issue," "descendants," "heirs of the body," "heirs," "next of kin," "relatives," or "family," or a class described by language of similar import, a substitute gift is created in the deceased devisee or devisee's surviving descendants. The property to which the devisees would have been entitled had all of them survived the testator passes to the surviving devisees and the surviving descendants of the deceased devisees. Each surviving devisee takes the share to which he [or she] would have been entitled had the deceased devisees survived the testator. Each deceased devisee's surviving descendants who are substituted for the deceased devisee take by representation the share to which the deceased devisee would have been entitled had the deceased devisee survived the testator. For the purposes of this paragraph, "deceased devisee" means a class member who

failed to survive the testator and left one or more surviving descendants.

(3) For the purposes of Section 2–601, words of survivorship, such as in a devise to an individual "if he survives me," or in a devise to "my surviving children," are not, in the absence of additional evidence, a sufficient indication of an intent contrary to the application of this section.

(4) If the will creates an alternative devise with respect to a devise for which a substitute gift is created by paragraph (1) or (2), the substitute gift is superseded by the alternative devise only if an expressly designated devisee of the alternative devise is entitled to take under the will.

(5) Unless the language creating a power of appointment expressly excludes the substitution of the descendants of an appointee for the appointee, a surviving descendant of a deceased appointee of a power of appointment can be substituted for the appointee under this section, whether or not the descendant is an object of the power.

(c) [More Than One Substitute Gift; Which One Takes.] If, under subsection (b), substitute gifts are created and not superseded with respect to more than one devise and the devises are alternative devises, one to the other, the determination of which of the substitute gifts takes effect is resolved as follows:

(1) Except as provided in paragraph (2), the devised property passes under the primary substitute gift.

(2) If there is a younger-generation devise, the devised property passes under the younger-generation substitute gift and not under the primary substitute gift.

(3) In this subsection:

(i) "Primary devise" means the devise that would have taken effect had all the deceased devisees of the alternative devises who left surviving descendants survived the testator.

(ii) "Primary substitute gift" means the substitute gift created with respect to the primary devise.

(iii) "Younger-generation devise" means a devise that (A) is to a descendant of a devisee of the primary devise, (B) is an alternative devise with respect to the primary devise, (C) is a devise for which a substitute gift is created, and (D) would have taken effect had all the deceased devisees who left surviving descendants survived the testator except the deceased devisee or devisees of the primary devise.

(iv) "Younger-generation substitute gift" means the substitute gift created with respect to the younger-generation devise.

COMMENT

Purpose and Scope of Revised Section. Revised Section 2–603 is a comprehensive antilapse statute that resolves a variety of interpretive questions that have arisen under standard antilapse statutes, including the antilapse statute of the pre–1990 Code.

Theory of Lapse. A will transfers property at the testator's death, not when the will was executed. The common-law rule of lapse is predicated on this principle and on the notion that property cannot be transferred to a deceased individual. Under the rule of lapse, all devises are automatically and by law conditioned on survivorship of the testator. A devise to a devisee who predeceases the testator fails (lapses); the devised property does not pass to the devisee's estate, to be distributed according to the devisee's will or pass by intestate succession from the devisee. (Section 2–702 modifies the rule of lapse by presumptively conditioning devises on a 120–hour period of survival.)

"Antilapse" Statutes—Rationale of Section 2–603. Statutes such as Section 2–603 are commonly called "antilapse" statutes. An antilapse statute is remedial in nature, tending to preserve equality of treatment among different lines of succession. Although Section 2–603 is a rule of construction, and hence under Section 2–601 yields to a finding of a contrary intention, the remedial character of the statute means that it should be given the widest possible latitude to operate in considering whether in an individual case there is an indication of a contrary intent sufficiently convincing to defeat the statute.

The 120–hour Survivorship Period. In effect, the requirement of survival of the testator's death means survival of the 120–hour period following the testator's death. This is because, under Section 2–702(a), "an individual who is not established to have survived an event ... by 120 hours is deemed to have predeceased the event." As made clear by subsection (a)(6), for the purposes of Section 2–707, the "event" to which Section 2–702(a) relates is the testator's death.

General Rule of Section 2–603— Subsection (b). Subsection (b) states the general rule of Section 2–603. Subsection (b)(1) applies to individual devises; subsection (b)(2) applies to devises in class gift form. Together, they show that the "antilapse" label is somewhat misleading. Strictly speaking, these subsections do not reverse the common-law rule of lapse. They do not abrogate the law-imposed condition of survivorship, so that devised property passes to the estates of predeceasing devisees. Subsections (b)(1) and (b)(2) leave the law-imposed condition of survivorship intact, but modify the devolution of lapsed devises by providing a statutory substitute gift in the case of specified relatives. The statutory substitute gift is to the devisee's descendants who survive the testator by 120 hours; they take the property to which the devisee would have been entitled had the devisee survived the testator by 120 hours.

Class Gifts. In line with modern policy, subsection (b)(2) continues the pre–1990 Code's approach of expressly extending the antilapse protection to class gifts. Class gifts to "issue," "descendants," "heirs of the body," "heirs," "next of kin," "relatives," "family," or a class described by language of similar import are excluded, however, because antilapse protection is unnecessary in class gifts of these types. They already contain within themselves the idea of representation, under which

117

a deceased class member's descendants are substituted for him or her. See Sections 2–708, 2–709, 2–711.

"Void" Gifts. By virtue of subsection (a)(4), subsection (b) applies to the so-called "void" gift, where the devisee is dead at the time of execution of the will. Though contrary to some decisions, it seems likely that the testator would want the descendants of a person included, for example, in a class term but dead when the will is made to be treated like the descendants of another member of the class who was alive at the time the will was executed but who dies before the testator.

Protected Relatives. The specified relatives whose devises are protected by this section are the testator's grandparents and their descendants and the testator's stepchildren or, in the case of a testamentary exercise of a power of appointment, the testator's (donee's) or donor's grandparents and their descendants and the testator's or donor's stepchildren.

Section 2–603 extends the "antilapse" protection to devises to the testator's own stepchildren. The term "stepchild" is defined in subsection (a)(5). Antilapse protection is not extended to descendants of the testator's stepchildren or to stepchildren of any of the testator's relatives. As to the testator's own stepchildren, note that under Section 2–804 a devise to a stepchild might be revoked if the testator and the stepchild's adoptive or biological parent become divorced; the antilapse statute does not, of course, apply to a deceased stepchild's devise if it was revoked by Section 2–804. Subsections (b)(1) and (b)(2) give this result by providing that the substituted descendants take the property to which the deceased devisee or deceased class member would have been entitled if he or she had survived the testator. If a deceased

stepchild whose devise was revoked by Section 2–804 had survived the testator, that stepchild would not have been entitled to his or her devise, and so his or her descendants take nothing, either.

Other than stepchildren, devisees related to the testator by affinity are not protected by this section.

Section 2–603 Applicable to Testamentary Exercise of a Power of Appointment Where Appointee Fails to Survive the Testator. Subsections (a)(3), (4), (5), (7), and (b)(5) extend the protection of this section to appointees under a power of appointment exercised by the testator's will. The extension of the antilapse statue to powers of appointment is a step long overdue. The extension brings the statute into line with the Restatement (Second) of Property (Donative Transfers) § 18.6 (1986).

Section 2–603 Applicable to Beneficiaries of a Testamentary Trust Who Fail to Survive the Testator. Subsection (a)(4) clarifies the point that, despite the contrary definition of "devisee" in Section 1–201, the devisees to which Section 2–603 applies, in the case of a devise to a trustee in trust, are the beneficiaries of the trust, not the trustee.

Substituted Gift. The substitute gifts provided for by subsections (b)(1) and (b)(2) are to the deceased devisee's descendants. They include adopted persons and children of unmarried parents to the extent they would inherit from the devisee; see Sections 1–201 and 2–114.

The 120–hour survival requirement stated in Section 2–702 does not require descendants who would be substituted for their parent by this section to survive *their parent* by any set period.

The statutory substitute gift is divided among the devisee's descendants "by representation," a term defined in Section 2–709(b).

Section 2–603 Restricted to Wills.
Section 2–603 is applicable only
when a devisee of a will predeceases
the testator. It does not apply to
beneficiary designations in life-insurance policies, retirement plans,
or transfer-on-death accounts, nor
does it apply to inter-vivos trusts,
whether revocable or irrevocable.
See, however, Sections 2–706 and
2–707 for rules of construction applicable when the beneficiary of a
life-insurance policy, a retirement
plan, or a transfer-on-death account
predeceases the decedent or when
the beneficiary of a future interest
is not living when the interest is to
take effect in possession or enjoyment.

**Contrary Intention—the Ratio-
nale of Subsection (b)(3).** An antilapse statute is a rule of construction, designed to carry out presumed intention. In effect, Section
2–603 declares that when a testator
devises property "to A (a specified
relative)," the testator (if he or she
had thought further about it) is presumed to have wanted to add: "but
if A is not alive (120 hours after my
death), I devise the property in A's
stead to A's descendants (who survive me by 120 hours)."

Under Section 2–601, the rule of
Section 2–603 yields to a finding of
a contrary intention. A foolproof
means of expressing a contrary intention is to add to a devise the
phrase "and not to [the devisee's]
descendants." In the case of a power of appointment, the phrase "and
not to an appointee's descendants"
can be added by the donor of the
power in the document creating the
power of appointment, if the donor
does not want the antilapse statute
to apply to an appointment under a
power. Another method of expressing a contrary intention as to nonresiduary devises is to add to the residuary clause the phrase "including
all lapsed or failed devises." Another foolproof method of expressing a
contrary intention is to add a separate clause stating that all lapsed or
failed nonresiduary devises are to
pass under the residuary clause.
See Section 2–603(a)(1).

A much-litigated question is
whether mere words of survivorship—such as in a devise "to my
daughter, A, if A survives me" or "to
my surviving children"—*automatically* defeat the antilapse statute.
Lawyers who believe that the attachment of words of survivorship to a
devise is a foolproof method of defeating an antilapse statue are mistaken. The very fact that the question is litigated so frequently is itself
proof that the use of mere words of
survivorship is far from foolproof.
In addition, the results of the litigated cases are divided on the question. To be sure, many cases hold
that mere words of survivorship do
automatically defeat the antilapse
statute. E.g., Estate of Stroble, 6
Kan.App.2d 955, 636 P.2d 236
(1981); Annot., 63 A.L.R.2d 1172,
1186 (1959); Annot., 92 A.L.R. 846,
857 (1934). Other cases, however,
reach the opposite conclusion. E.g.,
Estate of Ulrikson, 290 N.W.2d 757
(Minn.1980) (residuary devise to testator's brother Melvin and sister Rodine, and "in the event that either
one of them shall predecease me,
then to the other surviving brother
or sister"; Melvin and Rodine predeceased testator, Melvin but not
Rodine leaving descendants who
survived testator; court held residue
passed to Melvin's descendants under antilapse statute); Detzel v. Nie-
berding, 7 Ohio Misc. 262, 219
N.E.2d 327 (P.Ct.1966) (devise of
$5,000 to sister "provided she be liv-
ing at the time of my death"; sister
predeceased testator; court held
$5,000 devise passed under antilapse
statute to sister's descendants);
Henderson v. Parker, 728 S.W.2d
768 (Tex.1987) (devise of all of testator's property "unto our surviving
children of this marriage"; two of
testator's children survived testator,

but one child, William, predeceased testator leaving descendants who survived testator; court held that share William would have taken passed to Williams's descendants under antilapse statute; words of survivorship found ineffective to counteract antilapse statute because court interpreted those words as merely restricting the devisees to those living at the time the will was executed); see also Restatement (Second) of Property (Donative Transfers) § 27.2 comment f, illustration 5; cf. id. § 27.1 comment e, illustration 6.

Subsection (b)(3) adopts the position that mere words of survivorship do not—by themselves, *in the absence of additional evidence*—lead to *automatic* defeat of the antilapse statute. As noted in French, "Antilapse Statutes Are Blunt Instruments: A Blueprint for Reform," 37 Hastings L.J. 335, 369 (1985), "courts have tended to accord too much significance to survival requirements when deciding whether to apply antilapse statutes."

A formalistic argument sometimes employed by courts adopting the view that words of survivorship automatically defeat the antilapse statute is that, when words of survivorship are used, there is nothing upon which the antilapse statute can operate; the devise itself, it is said, is eliminated by the devisee's having predeceased the testator. The language of subsections (b)(1) and (b)(2), however, nullify this formalistic argument by providing that the predeceased devisee's descendants take the property to which the devisee would have been entitled had the devisee survived the testator.

Another objection to applying the antilapse statute is that mere words of survivorship somehow establish a contrary intention. The argument is that attaching words of survivorship indicates that the testator thought about the matter and intentionally did not provide a substitute gift to the devisee's descendants. At best, this is an inference only, which may or may not accurately reflect the testator's actual intention. An equally plausible inference is that the words of survivorship are in the testator's will merely because the testator's lawyer used a will form with words of survivorship. The testator who went to lawyer X and ended up with a will containing devises with a survivorship requirement could by chance have gone to lawyer Y and ended up with a will containing devises with no survivorship requirement—with no different intent on the testator's part from one case to the other.

Even a lawyer's deliberate use of mere words of survivorship to defeat the antilapse statute does not guarantee that the lawyer's intention represents the client's intention. Any linkage between the lawyer's intention and the client's intention is speculative unless the lawyer discussed the matter with the client. Especially in the case of younger-generation devisees, such as the client's children or nieces and nephews, it cannot be assumed that all clients, on their own, have anticipated the possibility that the devisee will predecease the client and will have thought through who should take the devised property in case the never-anticipated event happens.

If, however, evidence establishes that the lawyer did discuss the question with the client, and that the client decided that, for example, if the client's child predeceases the client, the deceased child's children (the client's grandchildren) should not take the devise in place of the deceased child, then the combination of the words of survivorship and the extrinsic evidence of the client's intention would support a finding of a contrary intention under Section 2-601. See Example 1, below. For this reason, Sections 2–601 and 2–603 will not expose lawyers to malpractice liability for the amount that, in the absence of the finding of the contrary intention, would have passed under the antilapse statute to a deceased devisee's descendants. The success of a malpractice claim depends upon sufficient evidence of a client's intention and the lawyer's failure to carry out that intention. In a case in which there is evidence that the client did not want the antilapse statute to apply, that evidence would support a finding of a contrary intention under Section 2–601, thus preventing the client's intention from being defeated by Section 2–603 and protecting the lawyer from liability for the amount that, in the absence of the finding of a contrary intention, would have passed under the antilapse statute to a deceased devisee's descendants.

Any inference about actual intention to be drawn from mere words of survivorship is especially problematic in the case of will substitutes such as life insurance, where it is less likely that the insured had the assistance of a lawyer in drafting the beneficiary designation. Although Section 2–603 only applies to wills, a companion provision is Section 2–706, which applies to will substitutes, including life insurance. Section 2–706 also contains language similar to that in subsection (b)(3), directing that words of survivorship do not, in the absence of additional evidence, indicate an intent contrary to the application of this section. It would be anomalous to provide one rule for wills and a different rule for will substitutes.

The basic operation of Section 2–603 is illustrated in the following example:

Example 1. G's will devised "$10,000 to my surviving children." G had two children, A and B. A predeceased G, leaving a child, X, who survived G by 120 hours. B also survived G by 120 hours.

Solution: Under subsection (b)(2), X takes $5,000 and B takes $5,000. The substitute gift to A's descendant, X, is not defeated by the fact that the devise is a class gift nor, under subsection (b)(3), is it automatically defeated by the fact that the word "surviving" is used.

Note that subsection (b)(3) provides that words of survivorship are not by themselves to be taken as expressing a contrary intention for purposes of Section 2–601. Under Section 2–601, a finding of a contrary intention could appropriately be based on affirmative evidence that G deliberately used the words of survivorship to defeat the antilapse statute. In the case of such a finding, B would take the full $10,000 devise. Relevant evidence tending to support such a finding might be a pre-execution letter or memorandum to G from G's attorney stating that G's attorney used the word "surviving" for the purpose of assuring that if one of G's children were to predecease G, that child's descendants would not take the predeceased child's share under any statute or rule of law.

In the absence of persuasive evidence of a contrary intent, however, the antilapse statue, being remedial in nature, and tending to preserve equality among different lines of succession, should be given the widest possible chance to operate and should be defeated only by a finding of intention that *directly contradicts* the substitute gift created by the statute. Mere words of survivorship—by themselves—do not directly contradict the statutory substitute gift to the descendants of a deceased devisee. The common law of lapse already conditions all devises on survivorship (and Section 2–702 presumptively conditions all devises on survivorship by 120 hours). As noted above, the antilapse statute does not reverse the law-imposed requirement of survivorship in any strict sense; it merely alters the devolution of lapsed devises by substituting the deceased devisee's descendants in place of those who would otherwise take. Thus, mere words of survivorship merely *duplicate* the law-imposed survivorship requirement deriving from the rule of lapse, and do not contradict the statutory substitute gift created by subsection (b)(1) or (b)(2).

Subsection (b)(4). Under subsection (b)(4), a statutory substitute gift is superseded if the testator's will expressly provides for its own alternative devisee and if that alternative devisee is otherwise entitled to take under the terms of the will. For example, the statute's substitute gift would be superseded in the case of a devise "to A if A survives me; if not, to B," where B survived the testator but A predeceased the testator leaving descendants who survived the testator. Under subsection (b)(4), B, not A's descendants, would take. In the same example, however, it should be noted that A's descendants *would* take under the statute if B as well as A predeceased the testator.

Subsection (b)(4) is illustrated by the following examples:

Example 2. G's will devised "$10,-000 to my sister, S" and "the rest, residue, and remainder of my estate to X–Charity." S predeceased G, leaving a child, N, who survived G by 120 hours.

Solution: S's $10,000 devise goes to N, not to X–Charity. The residuary clause does not create an "alternative devise," as defined in subsection (a)(1), because neither it nor any other language in the will specifically provides that S's $10,000 devise or lapsed or failed devises in general pass under the residuary clause.

Example 3. Same facts as Example 2, except that G's residuary clause devised "the rest, residue, and remainder of my estate, including all failed and lapsed devises, to X–Charity."

Solution: S's $10,000 devise goes to X–Charity, not to N. Under subsection (b)(4), the substitute gift to N created by subsection (b)(1) is superseded. The residuary clause expressly creates an "alternative devise," as defined in subsection (a)(1), in favor of X–Charity and that alternative devisee, X–Charity, is otherwise entitled to take under the terms of the will.

Example 4. G's will devised "$10,-000 to my two children, A and B, or to the survivor of them." A predeceased G, leaving a child, X, who survived G by 120 hours. B also survived G by 120 hours.

Solution: B takes the full $10,-000. Because the takers of the $10,000 devise are both named and numbered ("my *two* children, *A* and *B*"), the devise is not in the form of a class gift. The substance of the devise is as if it read "half of $10,000 to A, but if A predeceases me, that half to B if B survives me and the other half of $10,000 to B, but if B predeceases me, that other half to A if A survives me." With respect to each half, A and B have alternative devises, one to the other. Subsection (b)(1) creates a substitute gift to A's descendant, X, with respect to A's alternative devise in each half. Under subsection (b)(4), however, that substitute gift to X with respect to each half is superseded by the alternative devise to B because the alternative devisee, B, survived G by 120 hours and is otherwise entitled to take under G's will.

Example 5. G's will devised "$10,-000 to my two children, A and B, or to the survivor of them." A and B predeceased G. A left a child, X, who survived G by 120 hours; B died childless.

Solution: X takes the full $10,-000. Because the devise itself is in the same form as the one in Example 4, the substance of the devise is as if it read "half of $10,-000 to A, but if A predeceases me, that half to B if B survives me and the other half of $10,000 to B, but if B predeceases me, that other half to A if A survives me." With respect to each half, A and B have alternative devises, one to the other. As in Example 4, subsection (b)(1) creates a substitute gift to A's descendant, X, with respect to A's alternative devise in each half. Unlike the situation in Example 4, however, neither substitute gift to X is superseded under subsection (b)(4) by the alternative devise to B because, in this case, the alternative devisee, B, failed to survive G by 120 hours and is therefore not entitled to take either half under G's will.

Note that the order of deaths as between A and B is irrelevant. The phrase "or to the survivor" does not mean the survivor as between them if they both predecease G; it refers to the one who survives G if one but not the other survives G.

Subsection (c). Subsection (c) is necessary because there can be cases in which subsections (b)(1) or (b)(2) create substitute gifts with respect to two or more alternative devises of the same property, and those substitute gifts are not superseded under the terms of subsection (b)(4). Subsection (c) provides the tie-breaking mechanism for such situations.

The initial step is to determine which of the alternative devises would take effect had all the devi-sees themselves survived the testator (by 120 hours). In subsection (c), this devise is called the "primary devise." Unless subsection (c)(2) applies, subsection (c)(1) provides that the devised property passes under substitute gift created with respect to the primary devise. This substitute gift is called the "primary substitute gift." Thus, the devised property goes to the descendants of the devisee or devisees of the primary devise.

Subsection (c)(2) provides an exception to this rule. Under subsection (c)(2), the devised property does not pass under the primary substitute gift if there is a "younger-generation devise"—defined as a devise that (A) is to a descendant of a devisee of the primary devise, (B) is an alternative devise with respect to the primary devise, (C) is a devise for which a substitute gift is created, and (D) would have taken effect had all the deceased devisees who left surviving descendants survived the testator except the deceased devisee or devisees of the primary devise. If there is a younger-generation devise, the devised property passes under the "younger-generation substitute gift"—defined as the substitute gift created with respect to the younger-generation devise.

Subsection (c) is illustrated by the following examples:

Example 6. G's will devised "$5,000 to my son, A, if he is living at my death; if not, to my daughter, B" and devised "$7,500 to my daughter, B, if she is living at my death; if not, to my son, A." A and B predeceased G, both leaving descendants who survived G by 120 hours.

Solution: A's descendants take the $5,000 devise as substitute takers for A, and B's descendants take the $7,500 devise as substitute takers for B. In the absence of a finding based on affirmative evidence such as described in the solution to Example 1, the mere words of survivorship do not by themselves indicate a contrary intent.

Both devises require application of subsection (c). In the case of both devises, the statute produces a substitute gift for the devise to A and for the devise to B, each devise being an alternative devise, one to the other. The question of which of the substitute gifts takes effect is resolved by determining which of the devisees themselves would take the devised property if both A and B had survived G by 120 hours.

With respect to the devise of $5,000, the primary devise is to A because A would have taken the devised property had both A and B survived G by 120 hours. Consequently, the primary substitute gift is to A's descendants and that substitute gift prevails over the substitute gift to B's descendants.

With respect to the devise of $7,500, the primary devise is to B because B would have taken the devised property had both A and B survived G by 120 hours, and so the substitute gift to B's descendants is the primary substitute gift and it prevails over the substitute gift to A's descendants.

Subsection (c)(2) is inapplicable because there is no younger-generation devise. Neither A nor B is a descendant of the other.

Example 7. G's will devised "$10,-000 to my son, A, if he is living at my death; if not, to A's children, X and Y." A and X predeceased G. A's child, Y, and X's children, M and N, survived G by 120 hours.

Solution: Half ($5,000) of the devise goes to Y. The other half ($5,000) goes to M and N. The disposition of the latter half re-quires application of subsection (c).

Subsection (b)(1) produces substitute gifts as to that half for the devise of that half to A and for the devise of that half to X, each of these devises being alternative devises, one to the other. The primary devise is to A. But there is also a younger-generation devise, the alternative devise to X, who is a descendant of A, would take if X but not A survived G by 120 hours, and for which there is a substitute gift. So, the younger-generation substitute gift, which is to X's descendants (M and N), prevails over the primary substitute gift, which is to A's descendants (Y, M, and N).

Example 8. Same facts as Example 5, except that both A and B predeceased the testator and both left descendants who survived the testator by 120 hours.

Solution: A's descendants take half ($5,000) and B's descendants take half ($5,000).

As to the half devised to A, subsection (b)(1) produces a substitute gift to A's descendants and a substitute gift to B's descendants (because the language "or to the survivor of them" created an alternative devise in B of A's half). As to the half devised to B, subsection (b)(1) produces a substitute gift to B's descendants and a substitute gift to A's descendants (because the language "or to the survivor of them" created an alternative devise in A of B's half). Thus, with respect to each half, resort must be had to subsection (c) to determine which substitute gift prevails.

Under subsection (c)(1), each half passes under the primary substitute gift. The primary devise as to A's half is to A and the primary devise as to B's half is to B because, if both A and B had survived G by 120 hours, A would have taken half ($5,000) and B would have taken half ($5,000). Neither A nor B is a descendant of the other, so subsection (c)(2) does not apply. Only if one were a descendant of the other would the other's descendants take it all, under the rule of subsection (c)(2).

Section 2–604. Failure of Testamentary Provision.

(a) Except as provided in Section 2–603, a devise, other than a residuary devise, that fails for any reason becomes a part of the residue.

(b) Except as provided in Section 2–603, if the residue is devised to two or more persons, the share of a residuary devisee that fails for any reason passes to the other residuary devisee, or to other residuary devisees in proportion to the interest of each in the remaining part of the residue.

COMMENT

This section applies only if Section 2–603 does not produce a substitute taker for a devisee who fails to survive the testator by 120 hours. There is also a special rule for disclaimers contained in Section 2–801; a disclaimed devise may be governed by either Section 2–603 or the present section, depending on the circumstances.

Section 2–605. Increase in Securities; Accessions.

(a) If a testator executes a will that devises securities and the testator then owned securities that meet the description in the will, the devise includes additional securities owned by the testator at death to the extent the additional securities were acquired by the testator after the will was executed as a result of the testator's ownership of the described securities and are securities of any of the following types:

(1) securities of the same organization acquired by reason of action initiated by the organization or any successor, related, or acquiring organization, excluding any acquired by exercise of purchase options;

(2) securities of another organization acquired as a result of a merger, consolidation, reorganization, or other distribution by the organization or any successor, related, or acquiring organization; or

(3) securities of the same organization acquired as a result of a plan of reinvestment.

(b) Distributions in cash before death with respect to a described security are not part of the devise.

COMMENT

Purpose and Scope of Revisions. The rule of subsection (a), as revised, relates to a devise of securities (such as a devise of 100 shares of XYZ Company), regardless of whether that devise is characterized as a general or specific devise. If the testator executes a will that makes a devise of securities and if the testator then owned securities that meet the description in the will, then the devisee is entitled not only to the described securities to the extent they are owned by the testator at death; the devisee is also entitled to any additional securities owned by the testator at death that were acquired by the testator during his or her lifetime after the will was executed and were acquired as a result of the testator's ownership of the described securities by reason of an action specified in subsections (a)(1), (a)(2), or (a)(3), such as the declaration of stock splits or stock dividends or spinoffs of a subsidiary.

The impetus for these revisions derives from the rule on stock splits enunciated by Bostwick v. Hurstel, 364 Mass. 282, 304 N.E.2d 186 (1973), and now codified in Massachusetts as to actions covered by subsections (a)(1) and (a)(2). Mass. Gen.Laws c. 191, § 1A(4).

Subsection (a) Not Exclusive. Subsection (a) is not exclusive, i.e., it is not to be understood as setting forth the only conditions under which additional securities of the types described in paragraphs (1), (2), and (3) are included in the devise. For example, the express terms of subsection (a) do not apply to a case in which the testator owned the described securities when he or she executed the will, but later sold (or otherwise disposed of) those securities, and then later purchased (or otherwise acquired) securities that meet the description in the will, following which additional securities of the type or types described in paragraphs (1), (2), or (3) are acquired as a result of the testator's ownership of the later-acquired securities. Nor do the express terms of subsection (a) apply to a similar (but less likely) case in which the testator did not own the described securities when he or she executed the will, but later purchased (or otherwise acquired) such securities. Subsection (a) does not preclude a court, in an appropriate case, from deciding that additional securities of the type described in paragraphs (1), (2), or (3) acquired as a result of the testator's ownership of the later-acquired securities pass under the devise in either of these two cases, or in other cases if appropriate.

Subsection (b) codifies existing law that distributions in cash, such as interest, accrued rent, or cash dividends declared and payable as of a record date before the testator's death, do not pass as a part of the devise. It makes no difference whether such cash distributions were paid before or after death. See Section 4 of the Revised Uniform Principal and Income Act.

Cross Reference. The term "organization" is defined in Section 1–201.

Section 2–606. **Nonademption of Specific Devises; Unpaid Proceeds of Sale, Condemnation, or Insurance; Sale by Conservator or Agent.**

(a) A specific devisee has a right to the specifically devised property in the testator's estate at death and:

(1) any balance of the purchase price, together with any security agreement, owing from a purchaser to the testator at death by reason of sale of the property;

(2) any amount of a condemnation award for the taking of the property unpaid at death;

(3) any proceeds unpaid at death on fire or casualty insurance on or other recovery for injury to the property;

(4) property owned by the testator at death and acquired as a result of foreclosure, or obtained in lieu of foreclosure, of the security interest for a specifically devised obligation;

(5) real or tangible personal property owned by the testator at death which the testator acquired as a replacement for specifically devised real or tangible personal property; and

(6) unless the facts and circumstances indicate that ademption of the devise was intended by the testator or ademption of the devise is consistent with the testator's manifested plan of distribution, the value of the specifically devised property to the extent the specifically devised property is not in the testator's estate at death and its value or its replacement is not covered by paragraphs (1) through (5).

(b) If specifically devised property is sold or mortgaged by a conservator or by an agent acting within the authority of a durable power of attorney for an incapacitated principal, or if a condemnation award, insurance proceeds, or recovery for injury to the property are paid to a conservator or to an agent acting within the authority of a durable power of attorney for an incapacitated principal, the specific devisee has the right to a general pecuniary devise equal to the net sale price, the amount of the unpaid loan, the condemnation award, the insurance proceeds, or the recovery.

(c) The right of a specific devisee under subsection (b) is reduced by any right the devisee has under subsection (a).

(d) For the purposes of the references in subsection (b) to a conservator, subsection (b) does not apply if after the sale, mortgage, condemnation, casualty, or recovery, it was adjudicated that the testator's incapacity ceased and the testator survived the adjudication by one year.

(e) For the purposes of the references in subsection (b) to an agent acting within the authority of a durable power of attorney for an incapacitated principal, (i) "incapacitated principal" means a principal who is an incapacitated person, (ii) no adjudication of incapacity before death is necessary, and (iii) the acts of an agent within the authority of a durable power of attorney are presumed to be for an incapacitated principal.

COMMENT

Purpose and Scope of Revisions. Under the "identity" theory followed by most courts, the common-law doctrine of ademption by extinction is that a specific devise is adeemed—rendered ineffective—if the specifically devised property is not owned by the testator at death. In applying the "identity" theory, courts do not inquire into the testator's intent to determine whether the testator's objective in disposing of the specifically devised property was to revoke the devise. The only thing that matters is that the property is no longer owned at death. The application of the "identity" theory of ademption has resulted in harsh results in a number of cases, where it was reasonable clear that the testator did not intend to revoke the devise. Notable examples include McGee v. McGee, 122 R.I. 837, 413 A.2d 72 (1980); Estate of Dungan, 31 Del.Ch. 551, 73 A.2d 776 (1950).

Recently, some courts have begun to break away from the "identity" theory and adopt instead the so-called "intent" theory. E.g., Estate of Austin, 113 Cal.App.3d 167, 169 Cal.Rptr. 648 (1980). The major import of the revisions of this section is to adopt the "intent" theory in subsections (a)(5) and (a)(6).

Subsection (a)(5) does not import a tracing principle into the question of ademption, but rather should be seen as a sensible "mere change in form" principle.

Example. G's will devised to X "my 1984 Ford." After she executed her will, she sold her 1984 Ford and bought a 1988 Buick; later, she sold the 1988 Buick and bought a 1993 Chrysler. She still owned the 1993 Chrysler when she died. Under subsection (a)(5), X takes the 1993 Chrysler.

Variation. If G had sold her 1984 Ford (or any of the replacement cars) and used the proceeds to buy shares in a mutual fund, which she owned at death, subsection (a)(5) does not give X the shares in the mutual fund. If G owned an automobile at death as a replacement for her 1984 Ford, however, X would be entitled to that automobile, even though it was bought with funds other than the proceeds of the sale of the 1984 Ford.

Subsection (a)(6) applies only to the extent the specifically devised property is not in the testator's estate at death and its value or its replacement is not covered by the provisions of paragraphs (1) through (5). In that event, subsection (a)(6) creates a mild presumption against ademption by extinction, imposing on the party claiming that an ademption has occurred the burden of establishing that the facts and circumstances indicate that ademption of the devise was intended by the testator or that ademption of the devise is consistent with the testator's manifested plan of distribution.

Example. G's will devised to his son, A, "that diamond ring I inherited from grandfather" and devised to his daughter, B, "that diamond brooch I inherited from grandmother." After G executed his will, a burglar entered his home and stole the diamond ring (but not the diamond brooch, as it was in G's safety deposit box at his bank).

Under subsection (a)(6), the party claiming that A's devise was adeemed would be unlikely to be able to establish that G intended A's devise to be adeemed or that ademption is consistent with G's manifested plan of distribution. In fact, G's equalizing devise to B affirmatively indicates that ademption is inconsistent with G's manifested plan of distribution. The likely result is that, under subsection (a)(6), A would be entitled to the value of the diamond ring.

Section 2–607. Nonexoneration.

A specific devise passes subject to any mortgage interest existing at the date of death, without right of exoneration, regardless of a general directive in the will to pay debts.

COMMENT

See Section 3–814 empowering the personal representative to pay an encumbrance under some circumstances; the last sentence of that section makes it clear that such payment does not increase the right of the specific devisee. The present section governs the substantive rights of the devisee. The common-law rule of exoneration of the specific devise is abolished by this section, and the contrary rule is adopted.

For the rule as to exempt property, see Section 2–403.

The rule of this section is not inconsistent with Section 2–606(b). If a conservator or agent for an incapacitated principal mortgages specifically devised property, Section 2–606(b) provides that the specific devisee is entitled to a pecuniary devise equal to the amount of the unpaid loan. Section 2–606(b) does not contradict this section, which provides that the specific devise passes subject to any mortgage interest existing at the date of death, without right of exoneration.

Section 2–608. Exercise of Power of Appointment.

In the absence of a requirement that a power of appointment be exercised by a reference, or by an express or specific reference, to the power, a general residuary clause in a will, or a will making general disposition of all of the testator's property, expresses an intention to exercise a power of appointment held by the testator only if (i) the power is a general power and the creating instrument does not contain a gift if the power is not exercised or (ii) the testator's will manifests an intention to include the property subject to the power.

COMMENT

General Residuary Clause. As revised, this section provides that a general residuary clause (such as "All the rest, residue, and remainder of my estate, I devise to . . ..") in the testator's will or a will making general disposition of all of the testator's property (such as "All of my estate, I devise to . . ..") expresses an intent to exercise a power of appointment held by the donee of the power only if one or the other of two circumstances or sets of circumstances are satisfied. One such circumstance (whether the power is general or nongeneral) is if the testator's will manifests an intention to include the property subject to the power. A simple example of a residuary clause that manifests such an intention is a so-called "blending" or "blanket-exercise" clause, such as "All the rest, residue, and remainder of my estate, including any property over which I have a power of appointment, I devise to . . .."

The other circumstance that expresses an intent to exercise a power by a general residuary clause or a will making general disposition of all of the testator's property is that the power is a *general* power *and* the instrument that created the power does not contain a gift over in the event the power is not exercised (a "gift in default"). In well planned estates, a general power of appointment will be accompanied by a gift in default. The gift-in-default clause is ordinarily expected to take effect; it is not merely an afterthought just in case the power is not exercised. The power is not expected to be exercised, and in fact is often conferred mainly to gain a tax benefit—the federal estate-tax marital deduction under section 2056(b)(5) of the Internal Revenue

Code or, now, inclusion of the property in the gross estate of a younger-generation beneficiary under Section 2041 of the Internal Revenue Code, in order to avoid the possibly higher rates imposed by the new federal generation-skipping tax. See Blattmachr & Pennell, "Adventures in Generation Skipping, Or How We Learned to Love the 'Delaware Tax Trap,' " 24 Real Prop.Prob. & Tr.J. 75 (1989). A general power should not be exercised in such a case without a clear expression of an intent to appoint.

In poorly planned estates, on the other hand, there may be no gift-in-default clause. In the absence of a gift-in-default clause, it seems better to let the property pass under the donee's will than force it to return to the donor's estate, for the reason that the donor died before the donee died and it seems better to avoid forcing a reopening of the donor's estate.

Cross Reference. See also Section 2–704 for a provision governing the meaning of a requirement that a power of appointment be exercised by a reference (or by an express or specific reference) to the power.

Section 2–609. Ademption by Satisfaction.

(a) Property a testator gave in his [or her] lifetime to a person is treated as a satisfaction of a devise in whole or in part, only if (i) the will provides for deduction of the gift, (ii) the testator declared in a contemporaneous writing that the gift is in satisfaction of the devise or that its value is to be deducted from the value of the devise, or (iii) the devisee acknowledged in writing that the gift is in satisfaction of the devise or that its value is to be deducted from the value of the devise.

(b) For purposes of partial satisfaction, property given during lifetime is valued as of the time the devisee came into possession or enjoyment of the property or at the testator's death, whichever occurs first.

(c) If the devisee fails to survive the testator, the gift is treated as a full or partial satisfaction of the devise, as appropriate, in applying Sections 2–603 and 2–604, unless the testator's contemporaneous writing provides otherwise.

COMMENT

Scope and Purpose of Revisions. In addition to minor stylistic changes, this section is revised to delete the requirement that the gift in satisfaction of a devise be made to the devisee. The purpose is to allow the testator to satisfy a devise to A by making a gift to B. Consider why this might be desirable. G's will made a $20,000 devise to his child, A. G was a widower. Shortly before his death, G in consultation with his lawyer decided to take advantage of the $10,000 annual gift tax exclusion and sent a check for $10,000 to A and another check for $10,000 to A's spouse, B. The checks were accompanied by a letter from G explaining that the gifts were made for tax purposes and were made in lieu of the $20,000 devise to A. The removal of the phrase "to that person" from the statute allows the $20,000 devise to be fully satisfied by the gifts to A and B.

This section parallels Section 2–109 on advancements and follows the same policy of requiring written evidence that lifetime gifts are to be taken into account in the distribution of an estate, whether testate or intestate. Although courts traditionally call this "ademption by satisfaction" when a will is involved, and "advancement" when the estate is intestate, the difference in terminology is not significant.

Some wills expressly provide for lifetime advances by a hotchpot clause. Where the will contains no such clause, this section requires either the testator to declare in writing that the gift is in satisfaction of the devise or its value is to be deducted from the value of the devise or the devisee to acknowledge the same in writing.

To be a gift in satisfaction, the gift need not be an outright gift; it can be in the form of a will substitute, such as designating the devisee as the beneficiary of the testator's life-insurance policy or the beneficiary of the remainder interest in a revocable inter-vivos trust.

Subsection (b) on value accords with Section 2–109 and applies if, for example, property such as stock is given. If the devise is specific, a gift of the specific property to the devisee during lifetime adeems the devise by extinction rather than by satisfaction, and this section would be inapplicable. Unlike the common law of satisfaction, however, specific devises are not excluded from the rule of this section. If, for example, the testator makes a devise of a specific item of property, and subsequently makes a gift of cash or other property to the devisee, accompanied by the requisite written intent that the gift satisfies the devise, the devise is satisfied under this section even if the subject of the specific devise is still in the testator's estate at death (and hence would not be adeemed under the doctrine of ademption by extinction).

Under subsection (c), if a devisee to whom a gift in satisfaction is made predeceases the testator and his or her descendants take under Section 2–603 or 2–604, they take the same devise as their ancestor would have taken had the ancestor survived the testator; if the devise is reduced by reason of this section as to the ancestor, it is automatically reduced as to the devisee's descendants. In this respect, the rule in testacy differs from that in intestacy; see Section 2–109(c).

131

RULES OF CONSTRUCTION APPLICABLE TO DONATIVE DISPOSITIONS IN WILLS AND OTHER GOVERNING INSTRUMENTS

GENERAL COMMENT

Part 7 contains rules of construction applicable to donative dispositions in wills, deeds, trusts, appointments, beneficiary designations, and so on. Like the rules of construction in Part 6 (which apply only to wills), the rules of construction in this Part yield to a finding of a contrary intention.

Some of the sections in Part 7 are revisions of sections contained in Part 6 of the pre-1990 Code. Although these sections originally applied only to wills, their restricted scope was inappropriate.

Some of the sections in Part 7 are new, having been added to the Code as desirable means of carrying out common intention.

Section 2–701. Scope.

In the absence of a finding of a contrary intention, the rules of construction in this Part control the construction of a governing instrument. The rules of construction in this Part apply to a governing instrument of any type, except as the application of a particular section is limited by its terms to a specific type or types of donative disposition or governing instrument.

COMMENT

The rules of construction in this Part apply to governing instruments of any type, except as the application of a particular section is limited by its terms to a specific type or types of donative disposition or governing instrument.

The term "governing instrument" is defined in Section 1–201 as "a deed, will, trust, insurance or annuity policy, account with POD designation, security registered in beneficiary form (TOD), pension, profit-sharing, retirement, or similar benefit plan, instrument creating or exercising a power of appointment or a power of attorney, or a donative, appointive, or nominative instrument of any other type."

Certain of the sections in this Part are limited in their application to donative dispositions or governing instruments of a certain type or types. Section 2–704, for example, applies only to a governing instrument creating a power of appointment. Section 2–706 applies only to governing instruments that are "beneficiary designations," a term defined in Section 1–201 as referring to "a governing instrument naming a beneficiary of an insurance or annuity policy, of an account with POD designation, of a security registered in beneficiary form (TOD), or of a pension, profit-sharing, retirement, or similar benefit plan, or other nonprobate transfer at death." Section 2–707 applies only to governing instruments creating a future interest under the terms of a trust.

Cross References. See the Comment to Section 2–601. See Section 8–101(b) for the application of the rules of construction in this Part to documents executed prior to the effective date of this Article.

Section 2–702. Requirement of Survival by 120 Hours.

(a) [Requirement of Survival by 120 Hours Under Probate Code.] For the purposes of this Code, except for purposes of Part 3 of Article VI [Uniform TOD Security Registration Act] and except as provided in subsection (d), an individual who is not established by clear and convincing evidence to have survived an event, including the death of another individual, by 120 hours is deemed to have predeceased the event.

(b) [Requirement of Survival by 120 Hours under Donative Provision of Governing Instrument.] Except as provided in subsection (d) and except for a security registered in beneficiary form (TOD) under Part 3 of Article VI [Uniform TOD Security Registration Act], for purposes of a donative provision of a governing instrument, an individual who is not established by clear and convincing evidence to have survived an event, including the death of another individual, by 120 hours is deemed to have predeceased the event.

(c) [Co-owners With Right of Survivorship; Requirement of Survival by 120 Hours.] Except as provided in subsection (d), if (i) it is not established by clear and convincing evidence that one of two co-owners with right of survivorship survived the other co-owner by 120 hours, one-half of the property passes as if one had survived by 120 hours and one-half as if the other had survived by 120 hours and (ii) there are more than two co-owners and it is not established by clear and convincing evidence that at least one of them survived the others by 120 hours, the property passes in the proportion that one bears to the whole number of co-owners. For the purposes of this subsection, "co-owners with right of survivorship" includes joint tenants, tenants by the entireties, and other co-owners of property or accounts held under circumstances that entitles one or more to the whole of the property or account on the death of the other or others.

(d) [Exceptions.] This section does not apply if:

(1) the governing instrument contains language dealing explicitly with simultaneous deaths or deaths in a common disaster and that language is operable under the facts of the case;

(2) the governing instrument expressly indicates that an individual is not required to survive an event, including the death of

133

another individual, by any specified period or expressly requires the individual to survive the event by a specified period;

(3) the imposition of a 120-hour requirement of survival would cause a nonvested property interest or a power of appointment to fail to qualify for validity under Section 2–901(a)(1), (b)(1), or (c)(1) or to become invalid under Section 2–901(a)(2), (b)(2), or (c)(2); or

(4) the application of this section to multiple governing instruments would result in an unintended failure or duplication of a disposition.

(e) [Protection of Payors and Other Third Parties.]

(1) A payor or other third party is not liable for having made a payment or transferred an item of property or any other benefit to a beneficiary designated in a governing instrument who, under this section, is not entitled to the payment or item of property, or for having taken any other action in good faith reliance on the beneficiary's apparent entitlement under the terms of the governing instrument, before the payor or other third party received written notice of a claimed lack of entitlement under this section. A payor or other third party is liable for a payment made or other action taken after the payor or other third party received written notice of a claimed lack of entitlement under this section.

(2) Written notice of a claimed lack of entitlement under paragraph (1) must be mailed to the payor's or other third party's main office or home by registered or certified mail, return receipt requested, or served upon the payor or other third party in the same manner as a summons in a civil action. Upon receipt of written notice of a claimed lack of entitlement under this section, a payor or other third party may pay any amount owed or transfer or deposit any item of property held by it to or with the court having jurisdiction of the probate proceedings relating to the decedent's estate, or if no proceedings have been commenced, to or with the court having jurisdiction of probate proceedings relating to decedents' estates located in the county of the decedent's residence. The court shall hold the funds or item of property and, upon its determination under this section, shall order disbursement in accordance with the determination. Payments, transfers, or deposits made to or with the court discharge the payor or other third party from all claims for the value of amounts paid to or items of property transferred to or deposited with the court.

(f) [Protection of Bona Fide Purchasers; Personal Liability of Recipient.]

(1) A person who purchases property for value and without notice, or who receives a payment or other item of property in partial or full satisfaction of a legally enforceable obligation, is neither obligated under this section to return the payment, item of property, or benefit nor is liable under this section for the amount of the payment or the value of the item of property or benefit. But a person who, not for value, receives a payment, item of property, or any other benefit to which the person is not entitled under this section is obligated to return the payment, item of property, or benefit, or is personally liable for the amount of the payment or the value of the item of property or benefit, to the person who is entitled to it under this section.

(2) If this section or any part of this section is preempted by federal law with respect to a payment, an item of property, or any other benefit covered by this section, a person who, not for value, receives the payment, item of property, or any other benefit to which the person is not entitled under this section is obligated to return the payment, item of property, or benefit, or is personally liable for the amount of the payment or the value of the item of property or benefit, to the person who would have been entitled to it were this section or part of this section not preempted.

COMMENT

Scope and Purpose of Revision. This section parallels Section 2–104, which requires an heir to survive the intestate by 120 hours in order to inherit.

The scope of this section is expanded to cover all donative dispositions and provisions of this Code that relate to a person surviving an event (including the death of another person). As expanded, this section imposes the 120-hour requirement of survival in the areas covered by the Uniform Simultaneous Death Act.

Note that subsection (d)(1) provides that the 120-hour requirement of survival is inapplicable if the governing instrument "contains language dealing explicitly with simultaneous deaths or deaths in a common disaster and that language is operable under the facts of the case." The application of this provision is illustrated by the following example.

Example. G died leaving a will devising her entire estate to her husband, H, adding that "in the event he dies before I do, at the same time that I do, or under circumstances as to make it doubtful who died first," my estate is to go to my brother Melvin. H died about 38 hours after G's death, both having died as a result of injuries sustained in an automobile accident.

Under subsection (b), G's estate passes under the alternative devise to Melvin because H's failure to survive G by 120 hours means that H is deemed to have predeceased G. The language in the governing instrument does not, under subsection (d)(1), nullify the provision that causes H, because of his failure to survive G by 120 hours, to be deemed to have predeceased G. Although the governing instrument does contain language dealing with simultaneous deaths, that language is not operable under the facts of the case because H did not die before G, at the same time as G, or under circumstances as to make it doubtful who died first.

Note that subsection (d)(4) provides that the 120-hour requirement of survival is inapplicable if "the application of this section to multiple governing instruments would result in an unintended failure or duplication of a disposition." The application of this provision is illustrated by the following example.

Example. Pursuant to a common plan, H and W executed mutual wills with reciprocal provisions. Their intention was that a $50,000 charitable devise would be made on the death of the survivor. To that end, H's will devised $50,000 to the charity if W predeceased him. W's will devised $50,000 to the charity if H predeceased her. Subsequently, H and W were involved in a common accident. W survived H by 48 hours.

Were it not for subsection (d)(4), not only would the charitable devise in W's will be effective, because H in fact predeceased W, but the charitable devise in H's will would also be effective, because W's failure to survive H by 120 hours would result in her being deemed to have predeceased H. Because this would result in an unintended duplication of the

$50,000 devise, subsection (d)(4) provides that the 120-hour requirement of survival is inapplicable. Thus, only the $50,000 charitable devise in W's will is effective.

Subsection (d)(4) also renders the 120-hour requirement of survival inapplicable had H and W died in circumstances in which it could not be established that either survived the other. In such a case, an appropriate result might be to give effect to the common plan by paying half of the intended $50,000 devise from H's estate and half from W's estate.

ERISA Preemption of State Law. The Employee Retirement Income Security Act of 1974 (ERISA) federalizes pension and employee benefit law. Section 514(a) of ERISA, 29 U.S.C. § 1144(a), provides that the provisions of Titles I and IV of ERISA "shall supersede any and all State laws insofar as they may now or hereafter relate to any employee benefit plan" governed by ERISA. See the Comment to Section 2–804 for a discussion of the ERISA preemption question.

Revision of Uniform Simultaneous Death Act. The Joint Editorial Board for the Uniform Probate Code and the Drafting Committee to Revise Article II recommend that the freestanding Uniform Simultaneous Death Act be revised in accordance with the revisions of this section.

Section 2–703. Choice of Law as to Meaning and Effect of Donative Dispositions.

The meaning and legal effect of a donative disposition is determined by the local law of the state selected by the transferor in the governing instrument, unless the application of that law is contrary to the provisions relating to the elective share described in Part 2, the provisions relating to exempt property and allowances described in Part 4, or any other public policy of this State otherwise applicable to the disposition.

COMMENT

Purpose and Scope of Revisions.
The scope of this section is expanded to cover all donative dispositions, not just testamentary transfers. As revised, this section enables a transferor to select the law of a particular state for purposes of interpreting his will or other donative disposition without regard to the location of property covered thereby. So long as local public policy is accommodated, the section should be accepted as necessary and desirable.

Cross Reference. Choice of law rules regarding formal validity of a will are in Section 2–506. See also Sections 3–202 and 3–408.

Section 2–704. Power of Appointment; Meaning of Specific Reference Requirement.

If a governing instrument creating a power of appointment expressly requires that the power be exercised by a reference, an express reference, or a specific reference, to the power or its source, it is presumed that the donor's intention, in requiring that the donee exercise the power by making reference to the particular power or to the creating instrument, was to prevent an inadvertent exercise of the power.

COMMENT

Rationale of New Section. In the creation of powers of appointment, it has become common estate-planning practice to require that the donee of the power can exercise the power only by making reference (or express or specific reference) to it. The question of whether the donee has made a sufficiently specific reference is much litigated. The precise question often is whether a so-called blanket-exercise clause (also called a blending clause)—a clause referring to "any property over which I have a power of appointment"—constitutes a sufficient reference to a particular power to exercise that power. E.g., First National Bank v. Walker, 607 S.W.2d 469 (Tenn. 1980), and cases cited therein.

Section 2–704 sets forth the presumption that the donor's purpose in imposing a reference requirement was to prevent an inadvertent exercise of the power by the donee. Under this section, mere use by the donee of a blanket-exercise clause would be ineffective to exercise the power because such a clause would not make a sufficient reference to the particular power. If, however, it could be shown that the donee had knowledge of and intended to exercise the power, the blanket-exercise clause would be sufficient to exercise the power, unless the presumption of this section is overcome. Under Section 2–701, the presumption of this section would be overcome if it could be shown that the donor's intention was not merely to prevent an inadvertent exercise of the power but was to prevent any exercise of the power, intentional or inadvertent, that failed to identify in explicit terms the specific power or the creating instrument.

Reference. See Langbein & Waggoner, "Reformation of Wills on the Ground of Mistake: Change of Direction in American Law?," 130

137

U.Pa.L.Rev. 521, 583 n.223 (1982), suggesting that a donee's will that omits a sufficiently specific reference to a particular power can be reformed to include the necessary reference if it can be shown by clear and convincing evidence that the omission was caused by a scrivener's mistake. This approach is not inconsistent with Section 2–704. See Sections 2–601 (and accompanying Comment); 2–701. See also Motes/Henes Trust v. Mote, 297 Ark. 380, 761 S.W.2d 938 (1988) (do-nee's intended exercise given effect despite use of blanket-exercise clause); In re Strobel, 149 Ariz. 213, 717 P.2d 892 (1986) (donee's intended exercise given effect despite defective reference to power).

Cross Reference. See Section 2–608 for a provision governing whether a general residuary clause in the donee's will exercises a power of appointment that does not require a reference (or an express or specific reference) by the donee of the power.

Section 2–705. Class Gifts Construed to Accord With Intestate Succession.

(a) Adopted individuals and individuals born out of wedlock, and their respective descendants if appropriate to the class, are included in class gifts and other terms of relationship in accordance with the rules for intestate succession. Terms of relationship that do not differentiate relationships by blood from those by affinity, such as "uncles," "aunts," "nieces," or "nephews", are construed to exclude relatives by affinity. Terms of relationship that do not differentiate relationships by the half blood from those by the whole blood, such as "brothers," "sisters," "nieces," or "nephews", are construed to include both types of relationships.

(b) In addition to the requirements of subsection (a), in construing a donative disposition by a transferor who is not the natural parent, an individual born to the natural parent is not considered the child of that parent unless the individual lived while a minor as a regular member of the household of that natural parent or of that parent's parent, brother, sister, spouse, or surviving spouse.

(c) In addition to the requirements of subsection (a), in construing a donative disposition by a transferor who is not the adopting parent, an adopted individual is not considered the child of the adopting parent unless the adopted individual lived while a minor, either before or after the adoption, as a regular member of the household of the adopting parent.

COMMENT

Purpose and Scope of Revisions. This section facilitates a modern construction of gifts that identify the recipient by reference to a relationship to someone; usually these gifts will be class gifts. The rules set forth in this section are rules of construction, which under Section

138

2-701 are controlling in the absence of a finding of a contrary intention. With two exceptions, Section 2-705 invokes the rules pertaining to intestate succession as rules of construction for interpreting terms of relationship in private instruments.

The pre-1990 version of this section applied only to devises contained in wills. As revised and relocated in Part 7, this section is freed of that former restriction; it now applies to all donative dispositions, as prescribed by Section 2-701.

Subsections (b) and (c) are based on Cal.Prob.Code § 6152. These subsections impose requirements for inclusion that are additional to the requirement of subsection (a). Put differently, a child must satisfy subsection (a) in all cases. In addition, if either subsection (b) or (c) applies, the child must also satisfy the requirements of that subsection to be included under the class gift or term of relationship.

The general theory of subsection (b) is that a transferor who is not the natural (biological) parent of a child would want the child to be included in a class gift as a child of the biological parent only if the child lived while a minor as a regular member of the household of that biological parent (or of specified relatives of that biological parent).

Example. G's will created a trust, income to G's son, A, for life, remainder in corpus to A's descendants who survive A, by representation. A fathered a child, X; A and X's mother, D, never married each other, and X never lived while a minor as a regular member of A's household or the household of A's parent, brother, sister, spouse, or surviving spouse. D later married E; D and E raised X as a member of their household.

Solution: Never having lived as a regular member of A's household or of the household of any of A's specified relatives, X would

not be included as a member of the class of A's descendants who take the corpus of G's trust on A's death.

If, however, D's parent had created a similar trust, income to D for life, remainder in corpus to D's descendants who survive D, by representation, X would be included as a member of the class of D's descendants who take the corpus of this trust on D's death.

Also, if A executed a will containing a devise to his children or designated his children as beneficiary of his life insurance policy, X would be included in the class.

Under Section 2-114, X would be A's child for purposes of intestate succession. Subsection (b) is inapplicable because the transferor, A, is the biological parent.

The general theory of subsection (c) is that a transferor who is not the adopting parent of an adopted child would want the child to be included in a class gift as a child of the adopting parent only if the child lived while a minor, either before or after the adoption, as a regular member of the household of that adopting parent.

Example. G's will created a trust, income to G's daughter, A, for life, remainder in corpus to A's descendants who survive A, by representation. A and A's husband adopted a 47-year old man, X, who never lived *while a minor* as a regular member of A's household.

Solution: Never having lived while a minor as a regular member of A's household, X would not be included as a member of the class of A's descendants who take the corpus of G's trust on A's death.

If, however, A executed a will containing a device to her children or designated her children as beneficiary of her life insurance policy, X would be included in the class. Under Section 2–114, X would be A's child for purposes of intestate succession. Subsection (c) is inapplicable because the transferor, A, is an adopting parent.

Reference. Halbach, "Issues About Issue," 48 Mo.L.Rev. 333 (1983).

Section 2–706. Life Insurance; Retirement Plan; Account With POD Designation; Transfer-on-Death Registration; Deceased Beneficiary.

(a) [Definitions.] In this section:

(1) "Alternative beneficiary designation" means a beneficiary designation that is expressly created by the governing instrument and, under the terms of the governing instrument, can take effect instead of another beneficiary designation on the happening of one or more events, including survival of the decedent or failure to survive the decedent, whether an event is expressed in condition-precedent, condition-subsequent, or any other form.

(2) "Beneficiary" means the beneficiary of a beneficiary designation and includes (i) a class member if the beneficiary designation is in the form of a class gift and (ii) an individual or class member who was deceased at the time the beneficiary designation was executed as well as an individual or class member who was then living but who failed to survive the decedent.

(3) "Beneficiary designation" includes an alternative beneficiary designation and a beneficiary designation in the form of a class gift.

(4) "Class member" includes an individual who fails to survive the decedent but who would have taken under a beneficiary designation in the form of a class gift had he [or she] survived the decedent.

(5) "Stepchild" means a child of the decedent's surviving, deceased, or former spouse, and not of the decedent.

(6) "Surviving beneficiary" or "surviving descendant" means a beneficiary or a descendant who neither predeceased the decedent nor is deemed to have predeceased the decedent under Section 2–702.

(b) [Substitute Gift.] If a beneficiary fails to survive the decedent and is a grandparent, a descendant of a grandparent, or a stepchild of the decedent, the following apply:

(1) Except as provided in paragraph (4), if the beneficiary designation is not in the form of a class gift and the deceased

140

beneficiary leaves surviving descendants, a substitute gift is created in the beneficiary's surviving descendants. They take by representation the property to which the beneficiary would have been entitled had the beneficiary survived the decedent.

(2) Except as provided in paragraph (4), if the beneficiary designation is in the form of a class gift, other than a beneficiary designation to "issue," "descendants," "heirs of the body," "heirs," "next of kin," "relatives," or "family," or a class described by language of similar import, a substitute gift is created in the deceased beneficiary or beneficiaries' surviving descendants. The property to which the beneficiaries would have been entitled had all of them survived the decedent passes to the surviving beneficiaries and the surviving descendants of the deceased beneficiaries. Each surviving beneficiary takes the share to which he [or she] would have been entitled had the deceased beneficiaries survived the decedent. Each deceased beneficiary's surviving descendants who are substituted for the deceased beneficiary take by representation the share to which the deceased beneficiary would have been entitled had the deceased beneficiary survived the decedent. For the purposes of this paragraph, "deceased beneficiary" means a class member who failed to survive the decedent and left one or more surviving descendants.

(3) For the purposes of Section 2–701, words of survivorship, such as in a beneficiary designation to an individual "if he survives me," or in a beneficiary designation to "my surviving children," are not, in the absence of additional evidence, a sufficient indication of an intent contrary to the application of this section.

(4) If a governing instrument creates an alternative beneficiary designation with respect to a beneficiary designation for which a substitute gift is created by paragraph (1) or (2), the substitute gift is superseded by the alternative beneficiary designation only if an expressly designated beneficiary of the alternative beneficiary designation is entitled to take.

(c) [More Than One Substitute Gift; Which One Takes.] If, under subsection (b), substitute gifts are created and not superseded with respect to more than one beneficiary designation and the beneficiary designations are alternative beneficiary designations, one to the other, the determination of which of the substitute gifts takes effect is resolved as follows:

(1) Except as provided in paragraph (2), the property passes under the primary substitute gift.

141

(2) If there is a younger-generation beneficiary designation, the property passes under the younger-generation substitute gift and not under the primary substitute gift.

(3) In this subsection:

(i) "Primary beneficiary designation" means the beneficiary designation that would have taken effect had all the deceased beneficiaries of the alternative beneficiary designations who left surviving descendants survived the decedent.

(ii) "Primary substitute gift" means the substitute gift created with respect to the primary beneficiary designation.

(iii) "Younger-generation beneficiary designation" means a beneficiary designation that (A) is to a descendant of a beneficiary of the primary beneficiary designation, (B) is an alternative beneficiary designation with respect to the primary beneficiary designation, (C) is a beneficiary designation for which a substitute gift is created, and (D) would have taken effect had all the deceased beneficiaries who left surviving descendants survived the decedent except the deceased beneficiary or beneficiaries of the primary beneficiary designation.

(iv) "Younger-generation substitute gift" means the substitute gift created with respect to the younger-generation beneficiary designation.

(d) [Protection of Payors.]

(1) A payor is protected from liability in making payments under the terms of the beneficiary designation until the payor has received written notice of a claim to a substitute gift under this section. Payment made before the receipt of written notice of a claim to a substitute gift under this section discharges the payor, but not the recipient, from all claims for the amounts paid. A payor is liable for a payment made after the payor has received written notice of the claim. A recipient is liable for a payment received, whether or not written notice of the claim is given.

(2) The written notice of the claim must be mailed to the payor's main office or home by registered or certified mail, return receipt requested, or served upon the payor in the same manner as a summons in a civil action. Upon receipt of written notice of the claim, a payor may pay any amount owed by it to the court having jurisdiction of the probate proceedings relating to the decedent's estate or, if no proceedings have been commenced, to the court having jurisdiction of probate proceedings relating to decedents' estates located in the county of the decedent's residence. The court shall hold the funds and, upon its

determination under this section, shall order disbursement in accordance with the determination. Payment made to the court discharges the payor from all claims for the amounts paid.

(e) [Protection of Bona Fide Purchasers; Personal Liability of Recipient.]

(1) A person who purchases property for value and without notice, or who receives a payment or other item of property in partial or full satisfaction of a legally enforceable obligation, is neither obligated under this section to return the payment, item of property, or benefit nor is liable under this section for the amount of the payment or the value of the item of property or benefit. But a person who, not for value, receives a payment, item of property, or any other benefit to which the person is not entitled under this section is obligated to return the payment, item of property, or benefit, or is personally liable for the amount of the payment or the value of the item of property or benefit, to the person who is entitled to it under this section.

(2) If this section or any part of this section is preempted by federal law with respect to a payment, an item of property, or any other benefit covered by this section, a person who, not for value, receives the payment, item of property, or any other benefit to which the person is not entitled under this section is obligated to return the payment, item of property, or benefit, or is personally liable for the amount of the payment or the value of the item of property or benefit, to the person who would have been entitled to it were this section or part of this section not preempted.

COMMENT

Purpose of New Section. This new section provides an antilapse statute for "beneficiary designations," a term defined in Section 1–201 as "a governing instrument naming a beneficiary of an insurance or annuity policy, of an account with POD designation, of a security registered in beneficiary form (TOD), or of a pension, profit-sharing, retirement, or similar benefit plan, or other nonprobate transfer at death."

The terms of this section parallel those of Section 2–603, except that the provisions relating to payor protection and personal liability of recipients have been added. The Comment to Section 2–603 contains an elaborate exposition of Section 2–603, together with the examples illustrating its application. That Comment should aid understanding of Section 2–706. For a discussion of the reasons why Section 2–706 should not be preempted by federal law with respect to retirement plans covered by ERISA, see the Comment to Section 2–804.

Section 2–707. Survivorship with Respect to Future Interests under Terms of Trust; Substitute Takers.

(a) [Definitions.] In this section:

(1) "Alternative future interest" means an expressly created future interest that can take effect in possession or enjoyment instead of another future interest on the happening of one or more events, including survival of an event or failure to survive an event, whether an event is expressed in condition-precedent, condition-subsequent, or any other form. A residuary clause in a will does not create an alternative future interest with respect to a future interest created in a nonresiduary devise in the will, whether or not the will specifically provides that lapsed or failed devises are to pass under the residuary clause.

(2) "Beneficiary" means the beneficiary of a future interest and includes a class member if the future interest is in the form of a class gift.

(3) "Class member" includes an individual who fails to survive the distribution date but who would have taken under a future interest in the form of a class gift had he [or she] survived the distribution date.

(4) "Distribution date," with respect to a future interest, means the time when the future interest is to take effect in possession or enjoyment. The distribution date need not occur at the beginning or end of a calendar day, but can occur at a time during the course of a day.

(5) "Future interest" includes an alternative future interest and a future interest in the form of a class gift.

(6) "Future interest under the terms of a trust" means a future interest that was created by a transfer creating a trust or to an existing trust or by an exercise of a power of appointment to an existing trust, directing the continuance of an existing trust, designating a beneficiary of an existing trust, or creating a trust.

(7) "Surviving beneficiary" or "surviving descendant" means a beneficiary or a descendant who neither predeceased the distribution date nor is deemed to have predeceased the distribution date under Section 2–702.

(b) [Survivorship Required; Substitute Gift.] A future interest under the terms of a trust is contingent on the beneficiary's surviving the distribution date. If a beneficiary of a future interest under the terms of a trust fails to survive the distribution date, the following apply:

(1) Except as provided in paragraph (4), if the future interest is not in the form of a class gift and the deceased beneficiary leaves surviving descendants, a substitute gift is created in the beneficiary's surviving descendants. They take by representation the property to which the beneficiary would have been entitled had the beneficiary survived the distribution date.

(2) Except as provided in paragraph (4), if the future interest is in the form of a class gift, other than a future interest to "issue," "descendants," "heirs of the body," "heirs," "next of kin," "relatives," or "family," or a class described by language of similar import, a substitute gift is created in the deceased beneficiary or beneficiaries' surviving descendants. The property to which the beneficiaries would have been entitled had all of them survived the distribution date passes to the surviving beneficiaries and the surviving descendants of the deceased beneficiaries. Each surviving beneficiary takes the share to which he [or she] would have been entitled had the deceased beneficiaries survived the distribution date. Each deceased beneficiary's surviving descendants who are substituted for the deceased beneficiary take by representation the share to which the deceased beneficiary would have been entitled had the deceased beneficiary survived the distribution date. For the purposes of this paragraph, "deceased beneficiary" means a class member who failed to survive the distribution date and left one or more surviving descendants.

(3) For the purposes of Section 2–701, words of survivorship attached to a future interest are not, in the absence of additional evidence, a sufficient indication of an intent contrary to the application of this section. Words of survivorship include words of survivorship that relate to the distribution date or to an earlier or an unspecified time, whether those words of survivorship are expressed in condition-precedent, condition-subsequent, or any other form.

(4) If a governing instrument creates an alternative future interest with respect to a future interest for which a substitute gift is created by paragraph (1) or (2), the substitute gift is superseded by the alternative future interest only if an expressly designated beneficiary of the alternative future interest is entitled to take in possession or enjoyment.

(c) [More Than One Substitute Gift; Which One Takes.] If, under subsection (b), substitute gifts are created and not superseded with respect to more than one future interest and the future interests are alternative future interests, one to the other, the determina-

145

tion of which of the substitute gifts takes effect is resolved as follows:

(1) Except as provided in paragraph (2), the property passes under the primary substitute gift.

(2) If there is a younger-generation future interest, the property passes under the younger-generation substitute gift and not under the primary substitute gift.

(3) In this subsection:

(i) "Primary future interest" means the future interest that would have taken effect had all the deceased beneficiaries of the alternative future interests who left surviving descendants survived the distribution date.

(ii) "Primary substitute gift" means the substitute gift created with respect to the primary future interest.

(iii) "Younger-generation future interest" means a future interest that (A) is to a descendant of a beneficiary of the primary future interest, (B) is an alternative future interest with respect to the primary future interest, (C) is a future interest for which a substitute gift is created, and (D) would have taken effect had all the deceased beneficiaries who left surviving descendants survived the distribution date except the deceased beneficiary or beneficiaries of the primary future interest.

(iv) "Younger-generation substitute gift" means the substitute gift created with respect to the younger-generation future interest.

(d) [If No Other Takers, Property Passes Under Residuary Clause or to Transferor's Heirs.] If, after the application of subsections (b) and (c), there is no surviving taker, the property passes in the following order:

(1) if the trust was created in a nonresiduary devise in the transferor's will or in a codicil to the transferor's will, the property passes under the residuary clause in the transferor's will; for purposes of this section, the residuary clause is treated as creating a future interest under the terms of a trust.

(2) if no taker is produced by the application of paragraph (1), the property passes to the transferor's heirs under Section 2–711.

COMMENT

Rationale of New Section. This new section applies only to future interests under the terms of a trust. For shorthand purposes, references in this Comment to the term "future interest" refer to a future interest under the terms of a trust.

The objective of this section is to project the antilapse idea into the area of future interests. The structure of this section substantially parallels the structure of the regular antilapse statute, Section 2–603, and the antilapse-type statute relating to beneficiary designations, Section 2–706. The rationale for restricting this section to future interests under the terms of a trust is that legal life estates in land, followed by indefeasibly vested remainder interests, are still created in some localities, often with respect to farmland. In such cases, the legal life tenant and the person holding the remainder interest can, together, give good title in the sale of the land. If the antilapse idea were injected into this type of situation, the ability of the parties to sell the land would be impaired if not destroyed because the antilapse idea would, in effect, create a contingent substitute remainder interest in the present and future descendants of the person holding the remainder interest.

Background. At common law, conditions of survivorship are not implied with respect to *future* interests (whether in trust or otherwise). For example, in the simple case of a trust, "income to husband, A, for life, remainder to daughter, B," B's interest is not defeated at common law if she predeceases A; B's interest would pass through her estate to her successors in interest (probably either her residuary legatees or heirs), who would become entitled to possession when A died. If any of B's successors in interest died before A, the interest held by that deceased successor in interest would likewise pass through his or her estate to his or her successors in interest; and so on.

The rationale for adopting a statutory provision reversing the common-law rule is to prevent cumbersome and costly distributions to and through the estates of deceased beneficiaries of future interests, who may have died long before the distribution date.

Subsection (b): Subsection (b) imposes a condition of survivorship on future interests to the distribution date—defined as the time when the future interest is to take effect in possession or enjoyment.

The 120–hour Survivorship Period. In effect, the requirement of survival of the distribution date means survival of the 120–hour period following the distribution date. This is because, under Section 2–702(a), "an individual who is not established to have survived an event ... by 120 hours is deemed to have predeceased the event." As made clear by subsection (a)(7), for the purposes of section 2–707, the "event" to which section 2–702(a) relates is the distribution date.

Note that the "distribution date" need not occur at the beginning or end of a calendar day, but can occur at a time during the course of a day, such as the time of death of an income beneficiary.

References in Section 2–707 and in this Comment to survival of the distribution date should be understood as referring to survival of the distribution date by 120 hours.

Ambiguous Survivorship Language. Subsection (b) serves another purpose. It resolves a frequently litigated question arising from ambiguous language of survivorship, such as in a trust, "income to A for life, remainder in corpus to my surviving children." Although some case law interprets the word "surviving" as merely requiring survival of the testator (e.g., Nass' Estate, 320 Pa. 380, 182 A. 401 (1936)), the predominant position at common law interprets "surviving" as requiring survival of the life tenant, A. Hawke v. Lodge, 9 Del. Ch. 146, 77 A. 1090 (1910); Restatement of Property § 251 (1940). The first sentence of subsection (b), in conjunction with paragraph (3), codifies the predominant common-law/Restatement position that survival relates to the distribution date.

The first sentence of subsection (b), in combination with paragraph (3), imposes a condition of survivorship to the distribution date (the time of possession or enjoyment) even when an express condition of survivorship to an earlier time has been imposed. Thus, in a trust like "income to A for life, remainder in corpus to B, but if B predeceases A, to B's children who survive B," the first sentence of subsection (b) combined with paragraph (3) requires B's children to survive (by 120 hours) the death of the income beneficiary, A.

Rule of Construction. Note that Section 2-707 is a rule of construction. It is qualified by the rule set forth in Section 2-701, and thus it yields to a finding of a contrary intention. Consequently, in trusts like "income to A for life, remainder in corpus to B whether or not B survives A," or "income to A for life, remainder in corpus to B or B's estate," this section would not apply and, should B predecease A, B's future interest would pass through B's estate to B's successors in interest, who would become entitled to possession or enjoyment at A's death.

Classification. Subsection (b) renders a future interest "contingent" on the beneficiary's survival of the distribution date. As a result, future interests are "nonvested" and subject to the Rule Against Perpetuities. To prevent an injustice from resulting because of this, the Uniform Statutory Rule Against Perpetuities, which has a wait-and-see element, is incorporated into the Code as Part 9.

Substitute Gifts. Section 2-707 not only imposes a condition of survivorship to the distribution date; like its antilapse counterparts, Sections 2-603 and 2-706, it provides substitute takers in cases of a beneficiary's failure to survive the distribution date.

The statutory substitute gift is divided among the devisee's descendants "by representation," a term defined in Section 2-709(b).

Subsection (b)(1)—Future Interests Not in the Form of a Class Gift: Subsection (b)(1) applies to non-class gifts, such as the "income to A for life, remainder in corpus to B" trust discussed above. If B predeceases A, subsection (b)(1) creates a substitute gift with respect to B's future interest; the substitute gift is to B's descendants who survive A.

Subsection (b)(2)—Class Gift Future Interests. Subsection (b)(2) applies to class gifts, such as in a trust "income to A for life, remainder in corpus to A's children." Suppose that A had two children, X and Y. X predeceases A; Y survives A. Subsection (b)(2) creates a substitute gift with respect to any of A's children who predecease A leaving descendants who survive A. Thus, if X left descendants who survived A, X's descendants would take X's share; if X left no descendants living at A's death, Y would take it all.

Subsection (b)(2) does not apply to future interests to classes such as "issue," "descendants," "heirs of the body," "heirs," "next of kin," "distributees," "relatives," "family," or the like. The reason is that these types of class gifts have their own internal systems of representation, and so the substitute gift provided by subsection (b)(1) would be out of place with respect to these types of future interests. The first sentence of subsection (a) and subsection (d) do apply, however. For example, suppose a nonresiduary devise "to A for life, remainder to A's issue, by representation." If A leaves issue surviving him, they take. But if A leaves no issue surviving him, the testator's residuary devisees are the takers.

Subsection (b)(4). Subsection (b)(4) provides that, if a governing instrument creates an alternative future interest with respect to a future interest for which a substitute gift is created by paragraph (1) or (2), the substitute gift is superseded by the alternative future interest only if an expressly designated beneficiary of the alternative future interest is entitled to take in possession or enjoyment. Consider, for example, a trust under the income is to be paid to A for life, remainder in corpus to B if B survives A, but if not to C if C survives A. If B predeceases A, leaving descendants who survive A, subsection (b)(1) creates a substitute gift to B's descendants. But, if C survives A, the alternative future interest in C supersedes the substitute gift to B's descendants. Upon A's death, the trust corpus passes to C.

Subsection (c). Subsection (c) is necessary because there can be cases in which subsections (b)(1) or (b)(2) create substitute gifts with respect to two or more alternative future interests, and those substitute gifts are not superseded under the terms of subsection (b)(4). Subsection (c) provides the tie-breaking mechanism for such situations.

The initial step is to determine which of the alternative future interests would take effect had all the beneficiaries themselves survived the distribution date (by 120 hours). In subsection (c), this future interest is called the "primary future interest." Unless subsection (c)(2) applies, subsection (c)(1) provides that the property passes under substitute gift created with respect to the primary future interest. This substitute gift is called the "primary substitute gift." Thus, the property goes to the descendants of the beneficiary or beneficiaries of the primary future interest.

Subsection (c)(2) provides an exception to this rule. Under subsection (c)(2), the property does not pass under the primary substitute gift if there is a "younger-generation future interest"—defined as a future interest that (A) is to a descendant of a beneficiary of the primary future interest, (B) is an alternative future interest with respect to the primary future interest, (C) is a future interest for which a substitute gift is created, and (D) would have taken effect had all the deceased beneficiaries who left surviving descendants survived the distribution date except the deceased beneficiary or beneficiaries of the primary future interest. If there is a younger-generation future interest, the property passes under the "younger-generation substitute gift"—defined as the substitute gift created with respect to the younger-generation future interest.

Subsection (d). Since it is possible that, after the application of subsections (b) and (c), there are no substitute gifts, a back-stop set of substitute takers is provided in subsection (d)—the transferor's residuary devisees or heirs. Note that the transferor's residuary clause is treated as creating a future interest and, as such, is subject to this section. Note also that the meaning of the back-stop gift to the transferor's heirs is governed by Section 2–711, under which the gift is to the transferor's heirs determined as if transferor died when A died. Thus there will always be a set of substitute takers, even if it turns out to be the State. If the transferor's surviving spouse has remarried after the transferor's death but before A's death, he or she would not be a taker under this provision.

Examples. The application of Section 2–707 is illustrated by the following examples. Note that, in each example, the "distribution date" is the time of the income beneficiary's death. Assume, in each example, that an individual who is described as having "survived" the

149

income beneficiary's death survived the income beneficiary's death by 120 hours or more.

Example 1. A nonresiduary devise in G's will created a trust, income to A for life, remainder in corpus to B if B survives A. G devised the residue of her estate to a charity. B predeceased A. At A's death, B's child, X, is living.

Solution: On A's death, the trust property goes to X, not to the charity. Because B's future interest is not in the form of a class gift, subsection (b)(1) applies, not (b)(2). Subsection (b)(1) creates a substitute gift with respect to B's future interest; the substitute gift is to B's child, X. Under subsection (b)(3), the words of survivorship attached to B's future interest ("to B if B survives A") do not indicate an intent contrary to the creation of that substitute gift. Nor, under subsection (b)(4), is that substitute gift superseded by an alternative future interest because, as defined in subsection (a)(1), G's residuary clause does not create an alternative future interest. In the normal lapse situation, a residuary clause does not supersede the substitute gift created by the antilapse statute, and the same analysis applies to this situation as well.

Example 2. Same as Example 1, except that B left no descendants who survived A.

Solution: Subsection (b)(1) does not create a substitute gift with respect to B's future interest because B left no descendants who survived A. This brings subsection (d) into operation, under which the trust property passes to the charity under G's residuary clause.

Example 3. G created an irrevocable inter-vivos trust, income to A for life, remainder in corpus to B if B survives A. B predeceased

A. At A's death, G and X, B's child, are living.

Solution: X takes the trust property. Because B's future interest is not in the form of a class gift, subsection (b)(1) applies, not (b)(2). Subsection (b)(1) creates a substitute gift with respect to B's future interest; the substitute gift is to B's child, X. Under subsection (b)(3), the words of survivorship ("to B if B survives A") do not indicate an intent contrary to the creation of that substitute gift. Nor, under subsection (b)(4), is the substitute gift superseded by an alternative future interest; G's reversion is not an alternative future interest as defined in subsection (a)(1) because it was not *expressly* created.

Example 4. G created an irrevocable inter-vivos trust, income to A for life, remainder in corpus to B if B survives A; if not, to C. B predeceased A. At A's death, C and B's child are living.

Solution: C takes the trust property. Because B's future interest is not in the form of a class gift, subsection (b)(1) applies, not (b)(2). Subsection (b)(1) creates a substitute gift with respect to B's future interest; the substitute gift is to B's child, X. Under subsection (b)(3), the words of survivorship ("to B if B survives A") do not indicate an intent contrary to the creation of that substitute gift. But, under subsection (b)(4), the substitute gift to B's child is superseded by the alternative future interest held by C because C, having survived A (by 120 hours), is entitled to take in possession or enjoyment.

Example 5. G created an irrevocable inter-vivos trust, income to A for life, remainder in corpus to B, but if B predeceases A, to the person B appoints by will. B predeceased A. B's will exercised his power of appointment in favor of

C. C survives A. B's child, X, also survives A.

Solution: B's appointee, C, takes the trust property, not B's child, X. Because B's future interest is not in the form of a class gift, subsection (b)(1) applies, not (b)(2). Subsection (b)(1) creates a substitute gift with respect to B's future interest; the substitute gift is to B's child, X. Under subsection (b)(3), the words of survivorship ("to B if B survives A") do not indicate an intent contrary to the creation of that substitute gift. But, under subsection (b)(4), the substitute gift to B's child is superseded by the alternative future interest held by C because C, having survived A (by 120 hours), is entitled to take in possession or enjoyment. Because C's future interest was created in "a" governing instrument (B's will), it counts as an "alternative future interest."

Example 6. G creates an irrevocable inter-vivos trust, income to A for life, remainder in corpus to A's children who survive A; if none, to B. A's children predecease A, leaving descendants, X and Y, who survive A. B also survives A.

Solution: On A's death, the trust property goes to B, not to X and Y. Because the future interest in A's children is in the form of a class gift, subsection (b)(2) applies, not (b)(1). Subsection (b)(2) creates a substitute gift with respect to the future interest in A's children; the substitute gift is to the descendants of A's children, X and Y. Under subsection (b)(3), the words of survivorship ("to A's children who survive A") do not indicate an intent contrary to the creation of that substitute gift. But, under subsection (b)(4), the alternative future interest to B supersedes the substitute gift to the descendants of A's children because B survived A.

Alternative Facts: One of A's children, J, survives A; A's other child, K, predeceases A, leaving descendants, X and Y, who survive A. B also survives A.

Solution: J takes half the trust property and X and Y split the other half. Although there is an alternative future interest (in B) and although B did survive A, the alternative future interest was conditioned on none of A's children surviving A. Because that condition was not satisfied, the expressly designated beneficiary of that alternative future interest, B, is not entitled to take in possession or enjoyment. Thus, the alternative future interest in B does not supersede the substitute gift to K's descendants, X and Y.

Example 7. G created an irrevocable inter-vivos trust, income to A for life, remainder in corpus to B if B survives A; if not, to C. B and C predecease A. At A's death, B's child and C's child are living.

Solution: Subsection (b)(1) produces substitute gifts with respect to B's future interest and with respect to C's future interest. B's future interest and C's future interest are alternative future interests, one to the other. B's future interest is expressly conditioned on B's surviving A. C's future interest is conditioned on B's predeceasing A and C's surviving A. The condition that C survive A does not arise from express language in G's trust but from the first sentence of subsection (b); that sentence makes C's future interest contingent on C's surviving A. Thus, because neither B nor C survived A, neither B nor C is entitled to take in possession or enjoyment. So, under subsection (b)(4), neither substitute gift, created with respect to the future interests in B and C, is superseded by an alternative future interest. Consequently, resort must be had to subsection (c) to break the tie to determine which substitute gift takes effect.

Under subsection (c), B is the beneficiary of the "primary future interest" because B would have been entitled to the trust property had both B and C survived A. Unless subsection (c)(2) applies, the trust property passes to B's child as the taker under the "primary substitute gift."

Subsection (c)(2) would only apply if C's future interest qualifies as a "younger-generation future interest." This depends upon whether C is a descendant of B, for C's future interest satisfies the other requirements necessary to make it a younger-generation future interest. If C was a descendant of B, the substitute gift to C's child would be a "younger-generation substitute gift" and would become effective instead of the "primary substitute gift" to B's descendants. But if C was not a descendant of B, the property would pass under the "primary substitute gift" to B's descendants.

Example 8. G created an irrevocable inter-vivos trust, income to A for life, remainder in corpus to A's children who survive A; if none, to B. All of A's children predecease A. X and Y, who are descendants of one or more of A's children, survive A. B predeceases A, leaving descendants, M and N, who survive A.

Solution: On A's death, the trust property passes to X and Y under the "primary substitute gift," unless B was a descendant of any of A's children.

Subsection (b)(2) produces substitute gifts with respect to A's children who predeceased A leaving descendants who survived A. Subsection (b)(1) creates a substitute gift with respect to B's future interest. A's children's future interest and B's future interest are alternative future interests, one to the other. A's children's future interest is expressly conditioned on surviving A. B's future interest is conditioned on none of A's children surviving A and on B's surviving A. The condition of survivorship as to B's future interest does not arise because of express language in G's trust but because of the first sentence of subsection (b); that sentence makes B's future interest contingent on B's surviving A. Thus, because none of A's children survived A, and because B did not survive A, none of A's children nor B is entitled to take in possession or enjoyment. So, under subsection (b)(4), neither substitute gift—i.e., neither the one created with respect to the future interest in A's children nor the one created with respect to the future interest in B—is superseded by an alternative future interest. Consequently, resort must be had to subsection (c) to break the tie to determine which substitute gift takes effect.

Under subsection (c), A's children are the beneficiaries of the "primary future interest" because they would have been entitled to the trust property had all of them and B survived A. Unless subsection (c)(2) applies, the trust property passes to X and Y as the takers under the "primary substitute gift." Subsection (c)(2) would only apply if B's future interest qualifies as a "younger-generation future interest." This depends upon whether B is a descendant of any of A's children, for B's future interest satisfies the other requirements necessary to make it a "younger-generation future interest." If B was a descendant of one of A's children, the substitute gift to B's children, M and N, would be a "younger-generation substitute gift" and would become effective instead of the "primary substitute gift" to X and Y. But if B was not a descendant of any of A's children, the property would pass under the "primary substitute gift" to X and Y.

Example 9. G's will devised property in trust, income to niece Lilly for life, corpus on Lilly's death to her children; should Lilly die without leaving children, the corpus shall be equally divided among my nephews and nieces then living, the child or children of nieces who may be deceased to take the share their mother would have been entitled to if living.

Lilly never had any children. G had 3 nephews and 2 nieces in addition to Lilly. All 3 nephews and both nieces predeceased Lilly. A child of one of the nephews survived Lilly. One of the nieces had 8 children, 7 of whom survived Lilly. The other niece had one child, who did not survive Lilly. (This example is based on the facts of Bomberger's Estate, 347 Pa. 465, 32 A.2d 729 (1943).)

Solution: The trust property goes to the 7 children of the nieces who survived Lilly. The substitute gifts created by subsection (b)(2) to the nephew's son or to the nieces' children are superseded under subsection (b)(4) because there is an alternative future interest (the "child or children of nieces who may be deceased") and expressly designated beneficiaries of that alternative future interest (the 7 children of the nieces) are living at Lilly's death and are entitled to take in possession or enjoyment.

Example 10. G devised the residue of his estate in trust, income to his wife, W, for life, remainder in corpus to their children, John and Florence; if either John or Florence should predecease W, leaving descendants, such descendants shall take the share their parent would have taken if living.

G's son, John, survived W. G's daughter, Florence, predeceased W. Florence never had any children. Florence's husband survived W. (This example is based on the facts of Matter of Kroos, 302 N.Y. 424, 99 N.E.2d 222 (1951).)

Solution: John, of course, takes his half of the trust property. Because Florence left no descendants who survived W, subsection (b)(1) does not create a substitute gift with respect to Florence's future interest in her half. Subsection (d)(1) is inapplicable because G's trust was not created in a nonresiduary devise or in a codicil to G's will. Subsection (d)(2) therefore becomes applicable, under which Florence's half goes to G's heirs determined as if G died when W died, i.e., John. See Section 2–711.

Section 2–708. Class Gifts to "Descendants," "Issue," or "Heirs of the Body"; Form of Distribution if None Specified.

If a class gift in favor of "descendants," "issue," or "heirs of the body" does not specify the manner in which the property is to be distributed among the class members, the property is distributed among the class members who are living when the interest is to take effect in possession or enjoyment, in such shares as they would receive, under the applicable law of intestate succession, if the designated ancestor had then died intestate owning the subject matter of the class gift.

Purpose of New Section. This new section tracks Restatement (1st) of Property § 303(1), and does not accept the position taken in Restatement (Second) of Property, Donative Transfers § 28.2 (1988), under which a per stirpes form of distribution is presumed, regardless of the form of distribution used in the applicable law of intestate succession.

Section 2–709. Representation; Per Capita at Each Generation; Per Stirpes.

(a) **[Definitions.]** In this section:

(1) "Deceased child" or "deceased descendant" means a child or a descendant who either predeceased the distribution date or is deemed to have predeceased the distribution date under Section 2–702.

(2) "Distribution date," with respect to an interest, means the time when the interest is to take effect in possession or enjoyment. The distribution date need not occur at the beginning or end of a calendar day, but can occur at a time during the course of a day.

(3) "Surviving ancestor," "surviving child," or "surviving descendant" means an ancestor, a child, or a descendant who neither predeceased the distribution date nor is deemed to have predeceased the distribution date under Section 2–702.

(b) **[Representation; Per Capita at Each Generation.]** If an applicable statute or a governing instrument calls for property to be distributed "by representation" or "per capita at each generation," the property is divided into as many equal shares as there are (i) surviving descendants in the generation nearest to the designated ancestor which contains one or more surviving descendants (ii) and deceased descendants in the same generation who left surviving descendants, if any. Each surviving descendant in the nearest generation is allocated one share. The remaining shares, if any, are combined and then divided in the same manner among the surviving descendants of the deceased descendants as if the surviving descendants who were allocated a share and their surviving descendants had predeceased the distribution date.

(c) **[Per Stirpes.]** If a governing instrument calls for property to be distributed "per stripes," the property is divided into as many equal shares as there are (i) surviving children of the designated ancestor and (ii) deceased children who left surviving descendants.

Each surviving child is allocated one share. The share of each deceased child with surviving descendants is divided in the same manner, with subdivision repeating at each succeeding generation until the property is fully allocated among surviving descendants.

(d) [Deceased Descendant With No Surviving Descendant Disregarded.] For the purposes of subsections (b) and (c), an individual who is deceased and left no surviving descendant is disregarded, and an individual who leaves a surviving ancestor who is a descendant of the designated ancestor is not entitled to a share.

COMMENT

Purpose of New Section. This new section provides statutory definitions of "representation," "per capita at each generation," and "per stirpes." Subsection (b) applies to both private instruments and to provisions of applicable statutory law (such as Sections 2–603, 2–706, and 2–707) that call for property to be divided "by representation." The system of representation employed is the same as that which is adopted in Section 2–106 for intestate succession.

Subsection (c)'s definition of "per stirpes" accords with the predominant understanding of the term.

Section 2–710. Worthier–Title Doctrine Abolished.

The doctrine of worthier title is abolished as a rule of law and as a rule of construction. Language in a governing instrument describing the beneficiaries of a donative disposition as the transferor's "heirs," "heirs at law," "next of kin," "distributees," "relatives," or "family," or language of similar import, does not create or presumptively create a reversionary interest in the transferor.

COMMENT

Purpose of New Section. This new section abolishes the doctrine of worthier title as a rule of law and as a rule of construction.

Cross Reference. See Section 2–711 for a rule of construction concerning the meaning of a donative disposition to the heirs, etc., of a designated person.

Section 2–711. Future Interests in "Heirs" and Like.

If an applicable statute or a governing instrument calls for a future distribution to or creates a future interest in a designated individual's "heirs," "heirs at law," "next of kin," "relatives," or "family," or language of similar import, the property passes to those persons, including the state under Section 2–105, and in such shares as would succeed to the designated individual's intestate estate

155

under the intestate succession law of the designated individual's domicile if the designated individual died when the donative disposition is to take effect in possession or enjoyment. If the designated individual's surviving spouse is living but is remarried at the time the interest is to take effect in possession or enjoyment, the surviving spouse is not an heir of the designated individual.

COMMENT

Purpose of New Section. This new section provides a statutory definition of "heirs," etc., when contained in a donative disposition or a statute (such as Section 2–707(h)).

Cross Reference. See Section 2–710, abolishing the doctrine of worthier title.

GENERAL PROVISIONS CONCERNING PROBATE AND NONPROBATE TRANSFERS

GENERAL COMMENT

Part 8 contains four general provisions that cut across probate and nonprobate transfers. Section 2–801 is the Uniform Disclaimer of Property Interests Act; this Act replaces the narrower Uniform Disclaimer of Transfers By Will, Intestacy or Appointment Act, which was incorporated into the pre–1990 Code. The broader disclaimer act is not appropriate, given the broadened scope of Article II in covering nonprobate as well as probate transfers.

Section 2–802 deals with the effect of divorce and separation on the right to elect against a will, exempt property and allowances, and an intestate share.

Section 2–803 spells out the legal consequence of intentional and felonious killing on the right of the killer to take as heir and under wills and revocable inter-vivos transfers, such as revocable trusts and life-insurance beneficiary designations.

Section 2–804 deals with the consequences of a divorce on the right of the former spouse (and relatives of the former spouse) to take under wills and revocable inter-vivos transfers, such as revocable trusts and life-insurance beneficiary designations.

Section 2–801. Disclaimer of Property Interests.

(a) [Right to Disclaim Interest in Property.] A person, or the representative of a person, to whom an interest in or with respect to property or an interest therein devolves by whatever means may disclaim it in whole or in part by delivering or filing a written disclaimer under this section. The right to disclaim exists notwithstanding (i) any limitation on the interest of the disclaimant in the nature of a spendthrift provision or similar restriction or (ii) any restriction or limitation on the right to disclaim contained in the governing instrument. For purposes of this subsection, the "representative of a person" includes a personal representative of a decedent, a conservator of a disabled person, a guardian of a minor or incapacitated person, and an agent acting on behalf of the person within the authority of a power of attorney.

(b) [Time of Disclaimer.] The following rules govern the time when a disclaimer must be filed or delivered:

(1) If the property or interest has devolved to the disclaimant under a testamentary instrument or by the laws of intestacy, the disclaimer must be filed, if of a present interest, not later than [nine] months after the death of the deceased owner or deceased donee of a power of appointment and, if of a future interest, not

157

later than [nine] months after the event determining that the taker of the property or interest is finally ascertained and his [or her] interest is indefeasibly vested. The disclaimer must be filed in the [probate] court of the county in which proceedings for the administration of the estate of the deceased owner or deceased donee of the power have been commenced. A copy of the disclaimer must be delivered in person or mailed by registered or certified mail, return receipt requested, to any personal representative or other fiduciary of the decedent or donee of the power.

(2) If a property or interest has devolved to the disclaimant under a nontestamentary instrument or contract, the disclaimer must be delivered or filed, if of a present interest, not later than [nine] months after the effective date of the nontestamentary instrument or contract and, if of a future interest, not later than [nine] months after the event determining that the taker of the property or interest is finally ascertained and his [or her] interest is indefeasibly vested. If the person entitled to disclaim does not know of the existence of the interest, the disclaimer must be delivered or filed not later than [nine] months after the person learns of the existence of the interest. The effective date of a revocable instrument or contract is the date on which the maker no longer has power to revoke it or to transfer to himself [or herself] or another the entire legal and equitable ownership of the interest. The disclaimer or a copy thereof must be delivered in person or mailed by registered or certified mail, return receipt requested, to the person who has legal title to or possession of the interest disclaimed.

(3) A surviving joint tenant [or tenant by the entireties] may disclaim as a separate interest any property or interest therein devolving to him [or her] by right of survivorship. A surviving joint tenant [or tenant by the entireties] may disclaim the entire interest in any property or interest therein that is the subject of a joint tenancy [or tenancy by the entireties] devolving to him [or her], if the joint tenancy [or tenancy by the entireties] was created by act of a deceased joint tenant [or tenant by the entireties], the survivor did not join in creating the joint tenancy [or tenancy by the entireties], and has not accepted a benefit under it.

(4) If real property or an interest therein is disclaimed, a copy of the disclaimer may be recorded in the office of the [Recorder of Deeds] of the county in which the property or interest disclaimed is located.[*]

[*] If Torrens system is in effect, add provisions to comply with local law.

(c) [Form of Disclaimer.] The disclaimer must (i) describe the property or interest disclaimed, (ii) declare the disclaimer and extent thereof, and (iii) be signed by the disclaimant.

(d) [Effect of Disclaimer.] The effects of a disclaimer are:

(1) If property or an interest therein devolves to a disclaimant under a testamentary instrument, under a power of appointment exercised by a testamentary instrument, or under the laws of intestacy, and the decedent has not provided for another disposition of that interest, should it be disclaimed, or of disclaimed, or failed interests in general, the disclaimed interest devolves as if the disclaimant had predeceased the decedent, but if by law or under the testamentary instrument the descendants of the disclaimant would take the disclaimant's share by representation were the disclaimant to predecease the decedent, then the disclaimed interest passes by representation to the descendants of the disclaimant who survive the decedent. A future interest that takes effect in possession or enjoyment after the termination of the estate or interest disclaimed takes effect as if the disclaimant had predeceased the decedent. A disclaimer relates back for all purposes to the date of death of the decedent.

(2) If property or an interest therein devolves to a disclaimant under a nontestamentary instrument or contract and the instrument or contract does not provide for another disposition of that interest, should it be disclaimed, or of disclaimed or failed interests in general, the disclaimed interest devolves as if the disclaimant has predeceased the effective date of the instrument or contract, but if by law or under the nontestamentary instrument or contract the descendants of the disclaimant would take the disclaimant's share by representation were the disclaimant to predecease the effective date of the instrument, then the disclaimed interest passes by representation to the descendants of the disclaimant who survive the effective date of the instrument. A disclaimer relates back for all purposes to that date. A future interest that takes effect in possession or enjoyment at or after the termination of the disclaimed interest takes effect as if the disclaimant had died before the effective date of the instrument or contract that transferred the disclaimed interest.

(3) The disclaimer or the written waiver of the right to disclaim is binding upon the disclaimant or person waiving and all persons claiming through or under either of them.

(e) [Waiver and Bar.] The right to disclaim property or an interest therein is barred by (i) an assignment, conveyance, encumbrance, pledge, or transfer of the property or interest, or a contract therefor, (ii) a written waiver of the right to disclaim, (iii) an

159

acceptance of the property or interest or a benefit under it or (iv) a sale of the property or interest under judicial sale made before the disclaimer is made.

(f) [Remedy Not Exclusive.] This section does not abridge the right of a person to waive, release, disclaim, or renounce property or an interest therein under any other statute.

(g) [Application.] An interest in property that exists on the effective date of this section as to which, if a present interest, the time for filing a disclaimer under this section has not expired or, if a future interest, the interest has not become indefeasibly vested or the taker finally ascertained, may be disclaimed within [nine] months after the effective date of this section.

COMMENT

Purpose and Scope of Revisions. This section brings into the Code the Uniform Disclaimer of Property Interests Act, replacing the prior incorporation of the Uniform Disclaimer of Transfers by Will, Intestacy or Appointment Act. The reason for incorporating the broader Act is that the scope of Article II has now been expanded to cover donative transfers not contained in wills.

Explanation of Revisions. Only three revisions of the Uniform Disclaimer of Property Interests Act are adopted at this time, though the Joint Editorial Board believes that this and the other Uniform Disclaimer Acts are in need of revision in other respects.

Subsection (a). Subsection (a) is revised in two respects. First, the right to disclaim is extended to a decedent through his or her personal representative. The Uniform Disclaimer of Property Interests Act does not authorize disclaimers on behalf of a deceased person. Second, the sentence authorizing a disclaimer despite a limitation or restriction in the governing instrument is clarified to leave no doubt that an explicit restriction or limitation on the right to disclaim in the governing instrument is ineffective.

Subsection (d). The third revision clarifies the effect of a disclaimer. The Uniform Disclaimer of Property Interests Act states that "it" shall devolve "as if the disclaimant had predeceased the decedent." Literally interpreted, the word "it" refers to "the disclaimed interest," not to the estate as a whole. (One of the changes above is to make this point unmistakable by replacing "it" with "the disclaimed interest.")

Unfortunately, even though the word "it" refers to the disclaimed interest, not to the estate as a whole, there is still a plausible interpretation of the phrase "the disclaimed interest devolves as if the disclaimant had predeceased the decedent" that does not produce the desired result. The desired result is to prevent an heir, for example, from using a disclaimer to effect a change in the division of an intestate's estate. To illustrate this point, consider the following example:

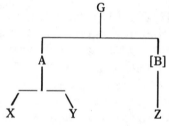

Under these facts, G's intestate estate is divided into two equal parts: A takes half and B's child, Z, takes the other half. Suppose, however, that A files a disclaimer. The desired effect of that disclaimer is to prevent A from affecting the basic division of G's intestate estate by this maneuver. If, however, the disclaimer statute merely provides that the "disclaimed interest" devolves as though the disclaimant (A) had predeceased the decedent, then A's one half interest would *not* pass *only* to X and Y, but to X, Y, *and Z*. To prevent this possible interpretation of that language, the "but if" phrase is added to (d)(1) and (d)(2). This added phrase explicitly provides that A's disclaimed interest passes to A's descendants, if A left any descendants.

Time Allowed for Filing Disclaimer. It should be noted that there may be a discrepancy between the time allowed for filing a disclaimer under this section (and under the freestanding Uniform Acts) and the time allowed for filing a qualified disclaimer under the Internal Revenue Code § 2518. Lawyers are cautioned to check both the state and federal disclaimer statutes before advising clients, especially with respect to disclaimers of future interests.

Section 2–802. Effect of Divorce, Annulment, and Decree of Separation.

(a) An individual who is divorced from the decedent or whose marriage to the decedent has been annulled is not a surviving spouse unless, by virtue of a subsequent marriage, he [or she] is married to the decedent at the time of death. A decree of separation that does not terminate the status of husband and wife is not a divorce for purposes of this section.

(b) For purposes of Parts 1, 2, 3, and 4 of this Article, and of Section 3–203, a surviving spouse does not include:

(1) an individual who obtains or consents to a final decree or judgment of divorce from the decedent or an annulment of their marriage, which decree or judgment is not recognized as valid in this State, unless subsequently they participate in a marriage ceremony purporting to marry each to the other or live together as husband and wife;

(2) an individual who, following an invalid decree or judgment of divorce or annulment obtained by the decedent, participates in a marriage ceremony with a third individual; or

(3) an individual who was a party to a valid proceeding concluded by an order purporting to terminate all marital property rights.

COMMENT

Clarifying Revision. The only substantive revision of this section is a clarifying revision of subsection (b)(2), making it clear that this subsection refers to an *invalid* decree of divorce or annulment.

Rationale. Although some existing statutes bar the surviving spouse for desertion or adultery, the present section requires some definitive legal act to bar the surviving spouse. Normally, this is divorce. Subsection (a) states an obvious proposition, but subsection (b) deals with the difficult problem of invalid divorce or annulment, which is particularly frequent as to foreign divorce decrees but may arise as to a local decree where there is some defect in jurisdiction; the basic principle underlying these provisions is estoppel against the surviving spouse. Where there is only a legal separation, rather than a divorce, succession patterns are not affected; but if the separation is accompanied by a complete property settlement, this may operate under Section 2–204 as a waiver or renunciation of benefits under a prior will and by intestate succession.

Cross Reference. See Section 2–804 for similar provisions relating to the effect of divorce to revoke devises and other revocable provisions to a former spouse.

Section 2–803. Effect of Homicide on Intestate Succession, Wills, Trusts, Joint Assets, Life Insurance, and Beneficiary Designations.

(a) [Definitions.] In this section:

(1) "Disposition or appointment of property" includes a transfer of an item of property or any other benefit to a beneficiary designated in a governing instrument.

(2) "Governing instrument" means a governing instrument executed by the decedent.

(3) "Revocable," with respect to a disposition, appointment, provision, or nomination, means one under which the decedent, at the time of or immediately before death, was alone empowered, by law or under the governing instrument, to cancel the designation, in favor of the killer, whether or not the decedent was then empowered to designate himself [or herself] in place of his [or her] killer and or the decedent then had capacity to exercise the power.

(b) [Forfeiture of Statutory Benefits.] An individual who feloniously and intentionally kills the decedent forfeits all benefits under this Article with respect to the decedent's estate, including an intestate share, an elective share, an omitted spouse's or child's share, a homestead allowance, exempt property, and a family allowance. If the decedent died intestate, the decedent's intestate estate passes as if the killer disclaimed his [or her] intestate share.

(c) [Revocation of Benefits Under Governing Instruments.] The felonious and intentional killing of the decedent:

(1) revokes any revocable (i) disposition or appointment of property made by the decedent to the killer in a governing instrument, (ii) provision in a governing instrument conferring a

general or nongeneral power of appointment on the killer, and (iii) nomination of the killer in a governing instrument, nominating or appointing the killer to serve in any fiduciary or representative capacity, including a personal representative, executor, trustee, or agent; and

(2) severs the interests of the decedent and killer in property held by them at the time of the killing as joint tenants with the right of survivorship [or as community property with the right of survivorship], transforming the interests of the decedent and killer into tenancies in common.

(d) [Effect of Severance.] A severance under subsection (c)(2) does not affect any third-party interest in property acquired for value and in good faith reliance on an apparent title by survivorship in the killer unless a writing declaring the severance has been noted, registered, filed, or recorded in records appropriate to the kind and location of the property which are relied upon, in the ordinary course of transactions involving such property, as evidence of ownership.

(e) [Effect of Revocation.] Provisions of a governing instrument that are not revoked by this section are given effect as if the killer disclaimed all revoked provisions or, in the case of a revoked nomination in a fiduciary or representative capacity, as if the killer predeceased the decedent.

(f) [Wrongful Acquisition of Property.] A wrongful acquisition of property or interest by a killer not covered by this section must be treated in accordance with the principle that a killer cannot profit from his [or her] wrong.

(g) [Felonious and Intentional Killing; How Determined.] After all right to appeal has been exhausted, a judgment of conviction establishing criminal accountability for the felonious and intentional killing of the decedent conclusively establishes the convicted individual as the decedent's killer for purposes of this section. In the absence of a conviction, the court, upon the petition of an interested person, must determine whether, under the preponderance of evidence standard, the individual would be found criminally accountable for the felonious and intentional killing of the decedent. If the court determines that, under that standard, the individual would be found criminally accountable for the felonious and intentional killing of the decedent, the determination conclusively establishes that individual as the decedent's killer for purposes of this section.

(h) [Protection of Payors and Other Third Parties.]

(1) A payor or other third party is not liable for having made a payment or transferred an item of property or any other benefit to a beneficiary designated in a governing instrument affected by an intentional and felonious killing, or for having taken any other action in good faith reliance on the validity of the governing instrument, upon request and satisfactory proof of the decedent's death, before the payor or other third party received written notice of a claimed forfeiture or revocation under this section. A payor or other third party is liable for a payment made or other action taken after the payor or other third party received written notice of a claimed forfeiture or revocation under this section.

(2) Written notice of a claimed forfeiture or revocation under paragraph (1) must be mailed to the payor's or other third party's main office or home by registered or certified mail, return receipt requested, or served upon the payor or other third party in the same manner as a summons in a civil action. Upon receipt of written notice of a claimed forfeiture or revocation under this section, a payor or other third party may pay any amount owed or transfer or deposit any item of property held by it to or with the court having jurisdiction of the probate proceedings relating to the decedent's estate, or if no proceedings have been commenced, to or with the court having jurisdiction of probate proceedings relating to decedents' estates located in the county of the decedent's residence. The court shall hold the funds or item of property and, upon its determination under this section, shall order disbursement in accordance with the determination. Payments, transfers, or deposits made to or with the court discharge the payor or other third party from all claims for the value of amounts paid to or items of property transferred to or deposited with the court.

(i) [Protection of Bona Fide Purchasers; Personal Liability of Recipient.]

(1) A person who purchases property for value and without notice, or who receives a payment or other item of property in partial or full satisfaction of a legally enforceable obligation, is neither obligated under this section to return the payment, item of property, or benefit nor is liable under this section for the amount of the payment or the value of the item of property or benefit. But a person who, not for value, receives a payment, item of property, or any other benefit to which the person is not entitled under this section is obligated to return the payment, item of property, or benefit, or is personally liable for the amount of the payment or the value of the item of property or benefit, to the person who is entitled to it under this section.

(2) If this section or any part of this section is preempted by federal law with respect to a payment, an item of property, or any other benefit covered by this section, a person who, not for value, receives the payment, item of property, or any other benefit to which the person is not entitled under this section is obligated to return the payment, item of property, or benefit, or is personally liable for the amount of the payment or the value of the item of property or benefit, to the person who would have been entitled to it were this section or part of this section not preempted.

COMMENT

Purpose and Scope of Revisions. This section is substantially revised. Although the revised version does make a few substantive changes in certain subsidiary rules (such as the treatment of multiple party accounts, etc.), it does not alter the main thrust of the pre–1990 version. The major change is that the revised version is more comprehensive than the pre–1990 version. The structure of the section is also changed so that it substantially parallels the structure of Section 2–804, which deals with the effect of divorce on revocable benefits to the former spouse.

The pre–1990 version of this section was bracketed to indicate that it may be omitted by an enacting state without difficulty. The revised version omits the brackets because the Joint Editorial Board/Article II Drafting Committee believes that uniformity is desirable on the question.

As in the pre–1990 version, this section is confined to felonious and intentional killing and excludes the accidental manslaughter killing. Subsection (g) leaves no doubt that, for purposes of this section, a killing can be "felonious and intentional," whether or not the killer has actually been convicted in a criminal prosecution. Under subsection (g), after all right to appeal has been exhausted, a judgment of conviction establishing criminal accountability for the felonious and intentional killing of the decedent conclusively establishes the convicted individual as the decedent's killer for purposes of this section. Acquittal, however, does not preclude the acquitted individual from being regarded as the decedent's killer for purposes of this section. This is because different considerations as well as a different burden of proof enter into the finding of criminal accountability in the criminal prosecution. Hence it is possible that the defendant on a murder charge may be found not guilty and acquitted, but if the same person claims as an heir, devisee, or beneficiary of a revocable beneficiary designation, etc. of the decedent, the probate court, upon the petition of an interested person, may find that, under a preponderance of the evidence standard, he or she would be found criminally accountable for the felonious and intentional killing of the decedent and thus be barred under this section from sharing in the affected property. In fact, in many of the cases arising under this section there may be no criminal prosecution because the killer has committed suicide.

It is now well accepted that the matter dealt with is not exclusively criminal in nature but is also a proper matter for probate courts. The concept that a wrongdoer may not profit by his or her own wrong is a civil concept, and the probate court is the proper forum to determine the effect of killing on succession to the decedent's property covered by this section. There are numerous situations where the same conduct gives rise to both criminal and civil consequences. A killing may result in criminal prosecution for murder and civil litigation by the decedent's family under wrongful death statutes. Another analogy exists in the tax field, where a taxpayer may be acquitted of tax fraud in a criminal prosecution but found to have committed the fraud in a civil proceeding.

The phrases "criminal accountability" and "criminally accountable" for the felonious and intentional killing of the decedent not only include criminal accountability as an actor or direct perpetrator, but also as an accomplice or co-conspirator.

Unlike the pre–1990 version, the revised version contains a subsection protecting payors who pay before receiving written notice of a claimed forfeiture or revocation under this section, and imposing personal liability on the recipient or killer.

The pre–1990 version's provision on the severance of joint tenancies and tenancies by the entirety also extended to "joint and multiple party accounts in banks, savings and loan associations, credit unions and other institutions, and any other form of co-ownership with survivorship incidents." Under subsection (c)(2) of the revised version, the severance applies only to "property held by [the decedent and killer] as joint tenants with the right of survivorship [or as community property with the right of survivorship]." The terms "joint tenants with the right of survivorship" and "community property with the right of survivorship" are defined in Section 1–201. That definition includes tenancies by the entirety, but excludes "forms of co-ownership registration in which the underlying ownership of each party is in proportion to that party's contribution." Under subsection (c)(1), any portion of the decedent's contribution to the co-ownership registration running in favor of the killer would be treated as a revocable and revoked disposition.

ERISA Preemption of State Law. The Employee Retirement Income Security Act of 1974 (ERISA) federalizes pension and employee benefit law. Section 514(a) of ERISA, 29 U.S.C. § 1144(a), provides that the provisions of Titles I and IV of ERISA "shall supersede any and all State laws insofar as they may now or hereafter relate to any employee benefit plan" governed by ERISA. See the Comment to Section 2–804 for a discussion of the ERISA preemption question.

Cross References. See Section 1–201 for definitions of "beneficiary designated in a governing instrument," "governing instrument," "joint tenants with the right of survivorship," "community property with the right of survivorship," and "payor."

Section 2–804.　Revocation of Probate and Nonprobate Transfers by Divorce; No Revocation by other Changes of Circumstances.

(a) [Definitions.] In this section:

(1) "Disposition or appointment of property" includes a transfer of an item of property or any other benefit to a beneficiary designated in a governing instrument.

(2) "Divorce or annulment" means any divorce or annulment, or any dissolution or declaration of invalidity of a marriage, that

would exclude the spouse as a surviving spouse within the meaning of Section 2–802. A decree of separation that does not terminate the status of husband and wife is not a divorce for purposes of this section.

(3) "Divorced individual" includes an individual whose marriage has been annulled.

(4) "Governing instrument" means a governing instrument executed by the divorced individual before the divorce or annulment of his [or her] marriage to his [or her] former spouse.

(5) "Relative of the divorced individual's former spouse" means an individual who is related to the divorced individual's former spouse by blood, adoption, or affinity and who, after the divorce or annulment, is not related to the divorced individual by blood, adoption, or affinity.

(6) "Revocable," with respect to a disposition, appointment, provision, or nomination, means one under which the divorced individual, at the time of the divorce or annulment, was alone empowered, by law or under the governing instrument, to cancel the designation in favor of his [or her] former spouse or former spouse's relative, whether or not the divorced individual was then empowered to designate himself [or herself] in place of his [or her] former spouse or in place of his [or her] former spouse's relative and whether or not the divorced individual then had the capacity to exercise the power.

(b) [Revocation Upon Divorce.] Except as provided by the express terms of a governing instrument, a court order, or a contract relating to the division of the marital estate made between the divorced individuals before or after the marriage, divorce, or annulment, the divorce or annulment of a marriage:

(1) revokes any revocable (i) disposition or appointment of property made by a divorced individual to his [or her] former spouse in a governing instrument and any disposition or appointment created by law or in a governing instrument to a relative of the divorced individual's former spouse, (ii) provision in a governing instrument conferring a general or nongeneral power of appointment on the divorced individual's former spouse or on a relative of the divorced individual's former spouse, and (iii) nomination in a governing instrument, nominating a divorced individual's former spouse or a relative of the divorced individual's former spouse to serve in any fiduciary or representative capacity, including a personal representative, executor, trustee, conservator, agent, or guardian; and

(2) severs the interests of the former spouses in property held by them at the time of the divorce or annulment as joint tenants with the right of survivorship [or as community property with the right of survivorship], transforming the interests of the former spouses into tenancies in common.

(c) [Effect of Severance.] A severance under subsection (b)(2) does not affect any third-party interest in property acquired for value and in good faith reliance on an apparent title by survivorship in the survivor of the former spouses unless a writing declaring the severance has been noted, registered, filed, or recorded in records appropriate to the kind and location of the property which are relied upon, in the ordinary course of transactions involving such property, as evidence of ownership.

(d) [Effect of Revocation.] Provisions of a governing instrument that are not revoked by this section are given effect as if the former spouse and relatives of the former spouse disclaimed the revoked provisions or, in the case of a revoked nomination in a fiduciary or representative capacity, as if the former spouse and relatives of the former spouse died immediately before the divorce or annulment.

(e) [Revival if Divorce Nullified.] Provisions revoked solely by this section are revived by the divorced individual's remarriage to the former spouse or by a nullification of the divorce or annulment.

(f) [No Revocation for Other Change of Circumstances.] No change of circumstances other than as described in this section and in Section 2–803 effects a revocation.

(g) [Protection of Payors and Other Third Parties.]

(1) A payor or other third party is not liable for having made a payment or transferred an item of property or any other benefit to a beneficiary designated in a governing instrument affected by a divorce, annulment, or remarriage, or for having taken any other action in good faith reliance on the validity of the governing instrument, before the payor or other third party received written notice of the divorce, annulment, or remarriage. A payor or other third party is liable for a payment made or other action taken after the payor or other third party received written notice of a claimed forfeiture or revocation under this section.

(2) Written notice of the divorce, annulment, or remarriage under subsection (g)(2) must be mailed to the payor's or other third party's main office or home by registered or certified mail, return receipt requested, or served upon the payor or other third party in the same manner as a summons in a civil action. Upon receipt of written notice of the divorce, annulment, or remarriage, a payor or other third party may pay any amount owed or

transfer or deposit any item of property held by it to or with the court having jurisdiction of the probate proceedings relating to the decedent's estate or, if no proceedings have been commenced, to or with the court having jurisdiction of probate proceedings relating to decedents' estates located in the county of the decedent's residence. The court shall hold the funds or item of property and, upon its determination under this section, shall order disbursement or transfer in accordance with the determination. Payments, transfers, or deposits made to or with the court discharge the payor or other third party from all claims for the value of amounts paid to or items of property transferred to or deposited with the court.

(h) [Protection of Bona Fide Purchasers; Personal Liability of Recipient.]

(1) A person who purchases property from a former spouse, relative of a former spouse, or any other person for value and without notice, or who receives from a former spouse, relative of a former spouse, or any other person a payment or other item of property in partial or full satisfaction of a legally enforceable obligation, is neither obligated under this section to return the payment, item of property, or benefit nor is liable under this section for the amount of the payment or the value of the item of property or benefit. But a former spouse, relative of a former spouse, or other person who, not for value, received a payment, item of property, or any other benefit to which that person is not entitled under this section is obligated to return the payment, item of property, or benefit, or is personally liable for the amount of the payment or the value of the item of property or benefit, to the person who is entitled to it under this section.

(2) If this section or any part of this section is preempted by federal law with respect to a payment, an item of property, or any other benefit covered by this section, a former spouse, relative of the former spouse, or any other person who, not for value, received a payment, item of property, or any other benefit to which that person is not entitled under this section is obligated to return that payment, item of property, or benefit, or is personally liable for the amount of the payment or the value of the item of property or benefit, to the person who would have been entitled to it were this section or part of this section not preempted.

COMMENT

Purpose and Scope of Revision. The revisions of this section, pre–1990 Section 2–508, intend to unify the law of probate and nonprobate transfers. As originally promulgated, pre–1990 Section 2–508 revoked a predivorce devise to the testator's former spouse. The revisions expand the section to cover "will substitutes" such as revocable inter-vivos trusts, life-insurance and retirement-plan beneficiary designations, transfer-on-death accounts, and other revocable dispositions to the former spouse that the divorced individual established before the divorce (or annulment). As revised, this section also effects a severance of the interests of the former spouses in property that they held at the time of the divorce (or annulment) as joint tenants with the right of survivorship; their co-ownership interests become tenancies in common.

As revised, this section is the most comprehensive provision of its kind, but many states have enacted piecemeal legislation tending in the same direction. For example, Michigan and Ohio have statutes transforming spousal joint tenancies in land into tenancies in common upon the spouses' divorce. Mich.Comp.Laws Ann. § 552.102; Ohio Rev.Code Ann. § 5302.20(c)(5). Ohio, Oklahoma, and Tennessee have recently enacted legislation effecting a revocation of provisions for the settlor's former spouse in revocable inter-vivos trusts. Ohio Rev.Code Ann. § 1339.62; Okla.Stat.Ann. tit. 60, § 175; Tenn.Code Ann. § 35–50–5115 (applies to revocable and irrevocable inter-vivos trusts). Statutes in Michigan, Ohio, Oklahoma, and Texas relate to the consequence of divorce on life–insurance and retirement–plan beneficiary designations. Mich.Comp.Laws Ann. § 552.101; Ohio Rev.Code Ann. § 1339.63; Okla.Stat.Ann. tit. 15, § 178; Tex.Fam.Code §§ 3.632–.633.

The courts have also come under increasing pressure to use statutory construction techniques to extend statutes like the pre–1990 version of Section 2–508 to various will substitutes. In Clymer v. Mayo, 393

Mass. 754, 473 N.E.2d 1084 (1985), the Massachusetts court held the statute applicable to a revocable inter–vivos trust, but restricted its "holding to the particular facts of this case—specifically the existence of a revocable pour–over trust funded entirely at the time of the decedent's death." 473 N.E.2d at 1093. The trust in that case was an unfunded life–insurance trust; the life insurance was employer–paid life insurance. In Miller v. First Nat'l Bank & Tr. Co., 637 P.2d 75 (Okla. 1981), the court also held such a statute to be applicable to an unfunded life–insurance trust. The testator's will devised the residue of his estate to the trustee of the life–insurance trust. Despite the absence of meaningful evidence of intent to incorporate, the court held that the pour–over devise incorporated the life–insurance trust into the will be reference, and thus was able to apply the revocation–upon–divorce statute. In Equitable Life Assurance Society v. Stitzel, 1 Pa.Fiduc.2d 316 (C.P.1981), however, the court held a statute similar to the pre–1990 version of Section 2–508 to be inapplicable to effect a revocation of a life–insurance beneficiary designation of the former spouse.

Revoking Benefits of the Former Spouse's Relatives. In several cases, including Clymer v. Mayo, 393 Mass. 754, 473 N.E.2d 1084 (1985), and Estate of Coffed, 46 N.Y.2d 514, 414 N.Y.S.2d 893, 387 N.E.2d 1209 (1979), the result of treating the former spouse as if he or she predeceased the testator was that a gift in the governing instrument was triggered in favor of relatives of the former spouse who, after the divorce, were no longer relatives of the testator. In the Massachusetts case, the former spouse's nieces and nephews ended up with an interest in the property. In the New York case, the winners included the former spouse's child by a prior marriage. For other cases to the same effect, see Porter v. Porter, 286 N.W.2d 649 (Iowa 1979); Bloom v. Selfon, 520 Pa. 519, 555 A.2d 75 (1989); Estate of Graef, 124 Wis.2d 25, 368 N.W.2d 633 (1985). Given that, during divorce process or in the aftermath of the divorce, the former spouse's relatives are likely to side with the former spouse, breaking down or weakening any former ties that may previously have developed between the transferor and the former spouse's relatives, seldom would the transferor have favored such a result. This section, therefore, also revokes these gifts.

Consequence of Revocation. The effect of revocation by this section is, of course, that the governing instrument is given effect as if the revoked provisions were removed or stricken therefrom at the time of the divorce or annulment. The remaining or unrevoked provisions of the governing instrument take effect as if the divorced individual's former spouse (and relatives of the former spouse) disclaimed the revoked provisions (see Section 2–801(d) for the effect of a disclaimer) or, in the case of a revoked nomination in a fiduciary or representative capacity, as if the former spouse and relatives of the former spouse died immediately before the divorce or annulment. If the divorced individual (or relative of the divorced individual) is the donee of an unexercised power of appointment that is revoked by this section, the gift–in–default clause, if any, is to take effect, to the extent that the gift–in–default clause is not itself revoked by this section.

ERISA Preemption of State Law. The Employee Retirement Income Security Act of 1974 (ERISA) federalizes pension and employee benefit law. Section 514(a) of ERISA, 29 U.S.C. § 1144(a), provides that the provisions of Titles I and IV of ERISA "shall supersede any and all State laws insofar as they may now or hereafter relate to any employee benefit plan" governed by ERISA.

ERISA's preemption clause is extraordinarily broad. ERISA Section 514(a) does not merely preempt state laws that conflict with specific provisions in ERISA. Section 514(a) preempts "any and all State laws" insofar as they "relate to" any ERISA–governed employee benefit plan.

A complex case law has arisen concerning the question of whether to apply ERISA Section 514(a) to preempt state law in circumstances in which ERISA supplies no substantive regulation. For example, until 1984, ERISA contained no authorization for the enforcement of state domestic relations decrees against pension accounts, but the federal courts were virtually unanimous in refusing to apply ERISA preemption against such state decrees. See, e.g., American Telephone & Telegraph Co. v. Merry, 592 F.2d 118 (2d Cir.1979). The Retirement Equity Act of 1984 amended ERISA to add Sections 206(d)(3) and 514(b)(7), confirming the judicially created exception for state domestic relations decrees.

The federal courts have been less certain about whether to defer to state probate law. In Board of Trustees of Western Conference of Teamsters Pension Trust Fund v. H.F. Johnson, Inc., 830 F.2d 1009 (9th Cir.1987), the court held that ERISA preempted the Montana nonclaim statute (which is Section 3–803 of the Uniform Probate Code). On the other hand, in Mendez–Bellido v. Board of Trustees, 709 F.Supp. 329 (E.D.N.Y.1989), the court applied the New York "slayer–rule" against an ERISA preemption claim, reasoning that "state laws prohibiting murderers from receiving death benefits are relatively uniform [and therefore] there is little threat of creating a 'patchwork scheme of regulations'" that ERISA sought to avoid.

It is to be hoped that the federal courts will continue to show sensitivity to the primary role of state law in the field of probate and nonprobate transfers. To the extent that the federal courts think themselves unable to craft exceptions to ERISA's preemption language, it is open to them to apply state law concepts as federal common law. Because the Uniform Probate Code contemplates multistate applicability, it is well suited to be the model for federal common law absorption.

Another avenue of reconciliation between ERISA preemption and the primacy of state law in this field is envisioned in subsection (h)(2) of this section. It imposes a personal liability for pension payments that pass to a former spouse or relative of a former spouse. This provision respects ERISA's concern that federal law govern the administration of the plan, while still preventing unjust enrichment that would result if an unintended beneficiary were to receive the pension benefits. Federal law has no interest in working a broader disruption of state probate and nonprobate transfer law than is required in the interest of smooth administration of pension and employee benefit plans.

Cross References. See Section 1–201 for definitions of "beneficiary designated in a governing instrument," "governing instrument," "joint tenants with the right of survivorship," "community property with the right of survivorship," and "payor."

References. The theory of this section is discussed in Waggoner "Spousal Probate Rights in a Multiple–Marriage Society," 45 The Record of the Ass'n of the Bar of the City of New York 339, 341–43 (1990) (Mortimer H. Hess Memorial Lecture). See also Langbein, "The Nonprobate Revolution and the Future of the Law of Succession," 97 Harv. L.Rev. 1108 (1984).

PART 9

STATUTORY RULE AGAINST PERPETUITIES; HONORARY TRUSTS

GENERAL COMMENT

Subpart 1 of this Part incorporates into the Code the Uniform Statutory Rule Against Perpetuities (USRAP or Uniform Statutory Rule) and Subpart 2 contains an optional section on honorary trusts and trusts for pets. Subpart 2 is under continuing review and, after appropriate study, might subsequently be revised to add provisions affecting certain types of commercial transactions respecting land, such as options in gross, that directly or indirectly restrain alienability.

In codifying Subparts 1 and 2, enacting states may deem it appropriate to locate them at some place other than in the probate code.

Subpart 1. Statutory Rule Against Perpetuities

GENERAL COMMENT

Simplified Wait–and–See/Deferred–Reformation Approach Adopted. The Uniform Statutory Rule reforms the common–law Rule Against Perpetuities (common–law Rule) by adding a simplified wait–and–see element and a deferred–reformation element.

Wait–and–see is a two–step strategy. Step One (Section 2–901(a)(1)) preserves the validating side of the common–law Rule. By satisfying the common–law Rule, a nonvested future interest in property is valid at the moment of its creation. Step Two (Section 2–901(a)(2)) is a salvage strategy for future interests that would have been invalid at common law. Rather than invalidating such interests at creation, wait–and–see allows a period of time, called the permissible vesting period, during which the nonvested interests are permitted to vest according to the trust's terms.

The traditional method of measuring the permissible vesting period has been by reference to lives in being at the creation of the interest (the measuring lives) plus 21 years. There are, however, various difficulties and costs associated with identifying and tracing a set of actual measuring lives to see which one is the survivor and when he or she dies. In addition, it has been documented that the use of actual measuring lives plus 21 years does not produce a period of time that self–adjusts to each disposition, extending dead–hand control no further than necessary in each case; rather, the use of actual measuring lives (plus 21 years) generates a permissible vesting period whose length almost always exceeds by some arbitrary margin the point of actual vesting in cases traditionally validated by the wait–and–see strategy. The actual–measuring–lives approach, therefore, performs a margin–of–safety function. Given this fact, and given the costs and difficulties associated with the actual–measuring–lives approach, the Uniform Statutory Rule forgoes the use of actual measuring lives and uses instead a permissible vesting period of a flat 90 years.

The philosophy behind the 90–year period is to fix a period of time

173

that approximates the average period of time that would traditionally be allowed by the wait–and–see doctrine. The flat–period–of–years method was not used as a means of increasing permissible dead–hand control by lengthening the permissible vesting period beyond its traditional boundaries. In fact, the 90–year period falls substantially short of the absolute maximum period of time that could theoretically be achieved under the common–law Rule itself, by the so–called "twelve–healthy–babies ploy"—a ploy that would average out to a period of about 115 years,[1] 25 years or 27.8% longer than the 90 years allowed by USRAP. The fact that the traditional period roughly averages out to a longish–sounding 90 years is a reflection of a quite different phenomenon: the dramatic increase in longevity that society as a whole has experienced in the course of the twentieth century.

The framers of the Uniform Statutory Rule derived the 90–year period as follows. The first point recognized was that if actual measuring lives were to have been used, the length of the permissible vesting period would, in the normal course of events, be governed by the life of the youngest measuring life. The second point recognized was that no matter what method is used to identify the measuring lives, the youngest measuring life, in standard trusts, is likely to be the transferor's youngest descendant living when the trust was created.[2] The 90–year period was premised on these propositions. Using four hypothetical families deemed to be representative of actual families, the framers of the Uniform Statutory Rule determined that, on average, the transfer-

or's youngest descendant in being at the transferor's death—assuming the transferor's death to occur between ages 60 and 90, which is when 73 percent of the population die—is about 6 years old. See Waggoner, "Perpetuities: A Progress Report on the Draft Uniform Statutory Rule Against Perpetuities," 20 U. Miami Inst. on Est. Plan. Ch. 7 at 7–17 (1986). The remaining life expectancy of a 6–year–old is about 69 years. The 69 years, plus the 21–year tack–on period, gives a permissible vesting period of 90 years.

Acceptance of the 90–year–period Approach under the Federal Generation–skipping Transfer Tax. Federal regulations, to be promulgated by the U.S. Treasury Department under the generation–skipping transfer tax, will accept the Uniform Statutory Rule's 90–year period as a valid approximation of the period that, on average, would be produced by lives in being plus 21 years. See Temp. Treas. Reg. § 26.2601–1(b)(1)(v)(B)(2) (as to be revised). When originally promulgated in 1988, this regulation was prepared without knowledge of the Uniform Statutory Rule Against Perpetuities, which had been promulgated in 1986; as first promulgated, the regulation only recognized a period measured by actual lives in being plus 21 years. After the 90–year approach of the Uniform Statutory Rule was brought to the attention of the U.S. Treasury Department, the Department issued a letter of intent to amend the regulation to treat the 90–year period as the equivalent of a lives–in–being–plus–21–years period. Letter from Michael J. Graetz, Deputy Assistant Secretary of the Treasury (Tax Policy), to Lawrence J. Bugge, President, National Con-

---

[1] Actuarially, the life expectancy of the longest living member of a group of twelve new–born babies is about 94 years; with the 21–year tack–on period, the "twelve–healthy–babies ploy" would produce, on average, a period of about 115 years (94 + 21).

[2] Under section 2–707, the descendants of a beneficiary of a future interest are presumptively made substitute beneficiaries, almost certainly making those descendants in being at the creation of the interest measuring lives, were measuring lives to have been used.

ference of Commissioners on Uniform State Laws (Nov. 16, 1990). For further discussion of the coordination of the federal generation–skipping transfer tax with the Uniform Statutory Rule, see the Comment to Section 2–901(e), infra, and the Comment to Section 1(e) of the Uniform Statutory Rule Against Perpetuities.

The 90–year Period Will Seldom be Used Up. Nearly all trusts (or other property arrangements) will terminate by their own terms long before the 90–year permissible vesting period expires, leaving the permissible vesting period to extend unused (and ignored) into the future long after the contingencies have been resolved and the property distributed. In the unlikely event that the contingencies have not been resolved by the expiration of the permissible vesting period, Section 2–903 requires the disposition to be reformed by the court so that all contingencies are resolved within the permissible period.

In effect, wait–and–see with deferred reformation operates similarly to a traditional perpetuity saving clause, which grants a margin–of–safety period measured by the lives of the transferor's descendants in being at the creation of the trust or other property arrangement (plus 21 years).

No New Learning Required. The Uniform Statutory Rule does not require the practicing bar to learn a new and unfamiliar set of perpetuity principles. The effect of the Uniform Statutory Rule on the planning and drafting of documents for clients should be distinguished from the effect on the resolution of actual or potential perpetuity–violation cases. The former affects many more practicing lawyers than the latter.

With respect to the planning and drafting end of the practice, the Uniform Statutory Rule requires no

modification of current practice and no new learning. *Lawyers can and should continue to use the same traditional perpetuity–saving/termination clause, using specified lives in being plus 21 years, they used before enactment.* Lawyers should not shift to a "later of" type clause that purports to operate upon the *later of* (A) 21 years after the death of the survivor of specified lives in being or (B) 90 years. As explained in more detail in the Comment to Section 2–901, such a clause is not effective. If such a "later of" clause is used in a trust that contains a violation of the common–law rule against perpetuities, Section 2–901(a), by itself, would render the clause ineffective, limit the maximum permissible vesting period to 90 years, and render the trust vulnerable to a reformation suit under Section 2–903. Section 2–901(e), however, saves documents using this type of clause from this fate. By limiting the effect of such clauses to the 21–year period following the death of the survivor of the specified lives, subsection (e) in effect transforms this type of clause into a traditional perpetuity–saving/termination clause, bringing the trust into compliance with the common–law rule against perpetuities and rendering it invulnerable to a reformation suit under Section 2–903.

Far fewer in number are those lawyers (and judges) who have an actual or potential perpetuity–violation case. An actual or potential perpetuity–violation case will arise very infrequently under the Uniform Statutory Rule. When such a case does arise, however, lawyers (or judges) involved in the case will find considerable guidance for its resolution in the detailed analysis contained in the commentary accompanying the Uniform Statutory Rule itself. In short, the detailed analysis in the commentary accompanying the Uniform Statutory Rule need not be part of the general learning required of lawyers in the drafting and planning of dispositive documents for their clients. The detailed analysis is supplied in the commentary for the assistance in the resolution of an actual violation. Only then need that detailed analysis be consulted and, in such a case, it will prove extremely helpful.

General References. Fellows, "Testing Perpetuity Reforms: A Study of Perpetuity Cases 1984–89," 25 Real Prop. Prob. & Tr. J. ___ (1990) (testing the various types of perpetuity reform measures and concluding, on the basis of empirical evidence, that the Uniform Statutory Rule is the best opportunity offered to date for a uniform perpe-

tuity law that efficiently and effectively achieves a fair balance between present and future property owners); Waggoner, "The Uniform Statutory Rule Against Perpetuities: Oregon Joins Up," 26 Willamette L. Rev. 259 (1990) (explaining the operation of the Uniform Statutory Rule); Waggoner, "The Uniform Statutory Rule Against Perpetuities: The Rationale of the 90–Year Waiting Period," 73 Cornell L. Rev. 157 (1988) (explaining the derivation of the 90–year period); Waggoner, "The Uniform Statutory Rule Against Perpetuities," 21 Real Prop., Prob. & Tr. J. 569 (1986) (explaining the theory and operation of the Uniform Statutory Rule).

Section 2–901. Statutory Rule Against Perpetuities.

(a) **[Validity of Nonvested Property Interest.]** A nonvested property interest is invalid unless:

(1) when the interest is created, it is certain to vest or terminate no later than 21 years after the death of an individual then alive; or

(2) the interest either vests or terminates within 90 years after its creation.

(b) **[Validity of General Power of Appointment Subject to a Condition Precedent.]** A general power of appointment not presently exercisable because of a condition precedent is invalid unless:

(1) when the power is created, the condition precedent is certain to be satisfied or becomes impossible to satisfy no later than 21 years after the death of an individual then alive; or

(2) the condition precedent either is satisfied or becomes impossible to satisfy within 90 years after its creation.

(c) **[Validity of Nongeneral or Testamentary Power of Appointment.]** A nongeneral power of appointment or a general testamentary power of appointment is invalid unless:

(1) when the power is created, it is certain to be irrevocably exercised or otherwise to terminate no later than 21 years after the death of an individual then alive; or

(2) the power is irrevocably exercised or otherwise terminates within 90 years after its creation.

176

(d) [Possibility of Post-death Child Disregarded.] In determining whether a nonvested property interest or a power of appointment is valid under subsection (a)(1), (b)(1), or (c)(1), the possibility that a child will be born to an individual after the individual's death is disregarded.

(e) [Effect of Certain "Later-of" Type Language.] If, in measuring a period from the creation of a trust or other property arrangement, language in a governing instrument (i) seeks to disallow the vesting or termination of any interest or trust beyond, (ii) seeks to postpone the vesting or termination of any interest or trust until, or (iii) seeks to operate in effect in any similar fashion upon, the later of (A) the expiration of a period of time not exceeding 21 years after the death of the survivor of specified lives in being at the creation of the trust or other property arrangement or (B) the expiration of a period of time that exceeds or might exceed 21 years after the death of the survivor of lives in being at the creation of the trust or other property arrangement, that language is inoperative to the extent it produces a period of time that exceeds 21 years after the death of the survivor of the specified lives.

COMMENT

Section 2–901 codifies the validating side of the common-law Rule and implements the wait-and-see feature of the Uniform Statutory Rule Against Perpetuities. As provided in Section 2–906, this section and the other sections in Subpart 1 of Part 9 supersede the common-law Rule Against Perpetuities (common-law Rule) in jurisdictions previously adhering to it (or repeals any statutory version or variation thereof previously in effect in the jurisdiction). The common-law Rule (or the statutory version or variation thereof) is replaced by the Statutory Rule in Section 2–901 and by the other provisions of Subpart 1 of Part 9.

Section 2–901(a) covers nonvested property interests, and will be the subsection most often applicable. Subsections (b) and (c) cover powers of appointment.

Paragraph (1) of subsections (a), (b), and (c) is a codified version of the validating side of the common-law Rule. In effect, paragraph (1) of these subsections provides that nonvested property interests and powers of appointment that are valid under the common-law Rule Against Perpetuities, including those that are rendered valid because of a perpetuity saving clause, continue to be valid under the Statutory Rule and can be declared so at their inceptions. This means that no new learning is required of competent estate planners: The practice of lawyers who competently draft trusts and other property arrangements for their clients is undisturbed.

Paragraph (2) of subsections (a), (b), and (c) establishes the wait-and-see rule. Paragraph (2) provides that an interest or a power of appointment that is not validated by paragraph (1), and hence would have been invalid under the common-law Rule, is given a second chance: Such an interest is valid if it does not actually remain in existence and nonvested when the 90-year permissible vesting period expires; such a power of appointment is valid if it ceases to be subject to a condition precedent or is no longer exercisable when the permissible 90-year period expires.

Subsection (d). The rule established in subsection (d) deserves a special comment. Subsection (d) declares that the possibility that a child will be born to an individual after the individual's death is to be disregarded. It is important to note that this rule applies only for the purpose of determining the validity of an interest (or a power of appointment) under paragraph (1) of subsection (a), (b), or (c). The rule of subsection (d) does not apply, for example, to questions such as whether a child who is born to an individual after the individual's death qualifies as a taker of a beneficial interest—as a member of a class or otherwise. Neither subsection (d), nor any other provision of Part 9, supersedes the widely accepted common-law principle, codified in Section 2–109, that a child in gestation (a child sometimes described as a child en ventre sa mere) who is later born alive (and, under Section 2–109, lives for 120 hours or more after birth) is regarded as alive during gestation.

The limited purpose of subsection (d) is to solve a perpetuity problem created by advances in medical science. The problem is illustrated by a case such as "to A for life, remainder to A's children who reach 21." When the common-law Rule was developing, the possibility was recognized, strictly speaking, that one or more of A's children might reach 21 more than 21 years after A's death. The possibility existed because A's wife (who might not be a life in being) might be pregnant when A died. If she was, and if the child was born viable a few months after A's death, the child could not reach his or her 21st birthday within 21 years after A's death. The device then invented to validate the inter-

est of A's children was to "extend" the allowable perpetuity period by tacking on a period of gestation, if needed. As a result, the common-law perpetuity period was comprised of three components: (1) a life in being (2) plus 21 years (3) plus a period of gestation, when needed. Today, thanks to sperm banks, frozen embryos, and even the possibility of artificially maintaining the body functions of a deceased pregnant woman long enough to develop the fetus to viability—advances in medical science unanticipated when the common-law Rule was in its developmental stages—having a pregnant wife at death is no longer the only way of having children after death. These medical developments, and undoubtedly others to come, make the mere addition of a period of gestation inadequate as a device to confer initial validity under Section 2–901(a)(1) on the interest of A's children in the above example. The rule of subsection (d), however, does insure the initial validity of the children's interest. Disregarding the possibility that children of A will be born after his death allows A to be the validating life. None of his children, under this assumption, can reach 21 more than 21 years after his death.

Note that subsection (d) subsumes not only the case of children conceived after death, but also the more conventional case of children in gestation at death. With subsection (d) in place, the third component of the common-law perpetuity period is unnecessary and has been jettisoned. The perpetuity period recognized in paragraph (1) of subsections (a), (b), and (c) has only two components: (1) a life in being (2) plus 21 years.

As to the legal status of conceived-after-death children, that question has not yet been resolved. For example, if in the above example A leaves sperm on deposit at a sperm bank and after A's death a woman (A's widow or another) becomes pregnant as a result of artificial insemination, the child or children produced thereby might not be included at all in the class gift. Cf. Restatement (Second) of Property (Donative Transfers) Introductory Note to Ch. 26 (1988). Without trying to predict how that question will be resolved in the future, the best way to handle the problem from the perpetuity perspective is the rule in subsection (d) requiring the possibility of post-death children to be disregarded.

Subsection (e)—Effect of Certain "Later-of" Type Language. Subsection (e) was added to the Uniform Statutory Rule in 1990. It primarily applies to a non-traditional type of "later of" clause (described below). Use of that type of clause might have produced unintended consequences, which are now rectified by the addition of subsection (e).

In general, perpetuity saving or termination clauses can be used in either of two ways. The predominant use of such clauses is as an override clause. That is, the clause is not an integral part of the dispositive terms of the trust, but operates independently of the dispositive terms; the clause provides that all interests must vest no later than at a specified time in the future, and sometimes also provides that the trust must then terminate, but only if any interest has not previously vested or if the trust has not previously terminated. The other use of such a clause is as an integral part of the dispositive terms of the trust; that is, the clause is the provision that directly regulates the duration of the trust. Traditional perpetuity saving or termination clauses do not use a "later of" approach; they mark off the maximum time of vesting or termination only by reference to a 21-year period following the death of the survivor of speci-

fied lives in being at the creation of the trust.

Subsection (e) applies to a non-traditional clause called a "later of " (or "longer of") clause. Such a clause might provide that the maximum time of vesting or termination of any interest or trust must occur no later than the later of (A) 21 years after the death of the survivor of specified lives in being at the creation of the trust or (B) 90 years after the creation of the trust.

Under the Uniform Statutory Rule as originally promulgated, this type of "later of" clause would not achieve a "later of" result. If used as an override clause in conjunction with a trust whose terms were, by themselves, valid under the common-law Rule against perpetuities (common-law Rule), the "later of" clause did no harm. The trust would be valid under the common-law Rule as codified in subsection (a)(1) because the clause itself would neither postpone the vesting of any interest nor extend the duration of the trust. But, if used either (1) as an override clause in conjunction with a trust whose terms were not valid under the common-law Rule or (2) as the provision that directly regulated the duration of the trust, the "later of" clause would not cure the perpetuity violation in case (1) and would create a perpetuity violation in case (2). In neither case would the clause qualify the trust for validity at common law under subsection (a)(1) because the clause would not guarantee that all interests will be certain to vest or terminate no later than 21 years after the death of an individual then alive. In any given case, 90 years can turn out to be longer than the period produced by the specified-lives-in-being-plus-21-years language.

Because the clause would fail to qualify the trust for validity under the common-law Rule of subsection (a)(1), the nonvested interests in the trust would be subject to the wait-and-see element of subsection (a)(2) and vulnerable to a reformation suit under Section 2–903. Under subsection (a)(2), an interest that is not valid at common law is invalid unless it actually vests or terminates within 90 years after its creation. Subsection (a)(2) does not grant such nonvested interests a permissible vesting period of either 90 years or a period of 21 years after the death of the survivor of specified lives in being. Subsection (a)(2) only grants such interest a period of 90 years in which to vest.

The operation of subsection (a), as outlined above, is also supported by perpetuity policy. If subsection (a) allowed a "later of" clause to achieve a "later of" result, it would authorize an improper use of the 90-year permissible vesting period of subsection (a)(2). The 90-year period of subsection (a)(2) is designed to approximate the period that, *on average*, would be produced by using actual lives in being plus 21 years. Because in any given case the period actually produced by lives in being plus 21 years can be shorter or longer than 90 years, an attempt to utilize a 90-year period in a "later of" clause improperly seeks to turn the 90-year *average* into a *minimum*.

Set against this background, the addition of subsection (e) is quite beneficial. Subsection (e) limits the effect of this type of "later of" language to 21 years after the death of the survivor of the specified lives, in effect transforming the clause into a traditional perpetuity saving/termination clause. By doing so, subsection (e) grants initial validity to the trust under the common-law Rule as codified in subsection (a)(1) and precludes a reformation suit under Section 2–903.

Note that subsection (e) covers variations of the "later of" clause described above, such as a clause that postpones vesting until the later or (A) *20* years after the death of the survivor of specified lives in being or (B) *89* years. Subsection (e) does not, however, apply to all dispositions that incorporate a "later of" approach. To come under subsection (e), the specified-lives prong must include a tack-on period of up to 21 years. Without a tack-on period, a "later of" disposition, unless valid at common law, comes under subsection (a)(2) and is given 90 years in which to vest. An example would be a disposition that creates an interest that is to vest upon "the later of the death of my widow or 30 years after my death."

Coordination of the Federal Generation-skipping Transfer Tax with the Uniform Statutory Rule. In 1990, the Treasury Department announced a decision to coordinate the tax regulations under the "grandfathering" provisions of the federal generation-skipping transfer tax with the Uniform Statutory Rule. Letter from Michael J. Graetz, Deputy Assistant Secretary of the Treasury (Tax Policy), to Lawrence J. Bugge, President, National Conference of Commissioners on Uniform State Laws (Nov. 16, 1990) (hereinafter *Treasury Letter*).

Section 1433(b)(2) of the Tax Reform Act of 1986 generally exempts ("grandfathers") trusts from the federal generation-skipping transfer tax that were irrevocable on September 25, 1985. This section adds, however, that the exemption shall apply "only to the extent that such transfer is not made out of corpus added to the trust after September 25, 1985." The provisions of Section 1433(b)(2) were first implemented by Temp. Treas. Reg. § 26.2601–1, promulgated by T.D. 8187 on March 14, 1988. Insofar as the Uniform Statutory Rule is concerned, a key feature of that temporary regulation is the concept that the statutory reference to "corpus added to the trust after September 25, 1985" not only covers actual post–9/25/85 transfers of new property or corpus to a grandfathered trust but "constructive" additions as well. Under the temporary regulation as first promulgated, a "constructive" addition occurs if, after 9/25/85, the donee of a nongeneral power of appointment exercises that power "in a manner that may postpone or suspend the vesting, absolute ownership or power of alienation of an interest in property for a period, measured from the date of creation of the trust, extending beyond any life in being at the date of creation of the trust plus a period of 21 years. If a power is exercised by creating another power it will be deemed to be exercised to whatever extent the second power may be exercised." Temp. Treas. Reg. § 26.2601–1(b)(1)(v)(B)(2) (1988).

Because the Uniform Statutory Rule was promulgated in 1986 and applies only prospectively, any "grandfathered" trust would have become irrevocable prior to the enactment of USRAP in any state. Nevertheless, the second sentence of Section 2–905(a) extends USRAP's wait-and-see approach to post-effective-date exercises of nongeneral powers even if the power itself was created prior to USRAP's effective date. Consequently, a post-USRAP-effective-date exercise of a nongeneral power of appointment created in a "grandfathered" trust could come under the provisions of the Uniform Statutory Rule.

The literal wording, then, of Temp. Treas. Reg. § 26.2601–1(b)(1)(v)(B)(2) (1988), as first promulgated, could have jeopardized the grandfathered status of an exempt trust if (1) the trust created a nongeneral power of appointment, (2) the donee exercised that nongeneral power, and (3) USRAP is the perpetuity law applicable

to the donee's exercise. This possibility arose not only because the donee's exercise itself might come under the 90–year permissible vesting period of subsection (a)(2) if it otherwise violated the common-law Rule and hence was not validated under subsection (a)(1). The possibility also arose in a less obvious way if the donee's exercise created another nongeneral power. The last sentence of the temporary regulation states that "if a power is exercised by creating another power it will be deemed to be exercised to whatever extent the second power may be exercised."

In late March 1990, the National Conference of Commissioners on Uniform State Laws (NCCUSL) and the Joint Editorial Board for the Uniform Probate Code (JEB-UPC) filed a formal request with the Treasury Department asking that measures be taken to coordinate the regulation with USRAP. By the Treasury Letter referred to above, the Treasury Department responded by stating that it "will amend the temporary regulations to accommodate the 90–year period under USRAP as originally promulgated [in 1986] or as amended [in 1990 by the addition of subsection (e)]." This should effectively remove the possibility of loss of grandfathered status under the Uniform Statutory Rule merely because the donee of a nongeneral power created in a grandfathered trust inadvertently exercises that power in violation of the common-law Rule or merely because the donee exercises that power by creating a second nongeneral power that might, in the future, be inadvertently exercised in violation of the common-law Rule.

The Treasury Letter states, however, that any effort by the donee of a nongeneral power in a grandfathered trust to obtain a "later of" specified-lives-in-being-plus-21-years or 90-years approach will be treated as a constructive addition, unless that effort is nullified by state law. As explained above, the Uniform Statutory Rule, as originally promulgated in 1986 or as amended in 1990 by the addition of subsection (e), nullifies any direct effort to obtain a "later of" approach by the use of a "later of" clause.

The Treasury Letter states that an indirect effort to obtain a "later of" approach would also be treated as a constructive addition that would bring grandfathered status to an end, unless the attempt to obtain the later-of approach is nullified by state law. The Treasury Letter indicates that an indirect effort to obtain a "later of" approach could arise if the donee of a nongeneral power successfully attempts to prolong the duration of a grandfathered trust by switching from a specified-lives-in-being-plus-21-years perpetuity period to a 90-year perpetuity period, or vice versa. Donees of nongeneral powers in grandfathered trusts would therefore be well advised to resist any temptation to wait until it becomes clear or reasonably predictable which perpetuity period will be longer and then make a switch to the longer period if the governing instrument creating the power utilized the shorter period. No such attempted switch and no constructive addition will occur if in each instance a traditional specified-lives-in-being-plus-21-years perpetuity saving clause is used.

Any such attempted switch is likely in any event to be nullified by state law and, if so, the attempted switch will not be treated as a constructive addition. For example, suppose that the original grandfathered trust contained a standard perpetuity saving clause declaring that all interests in the trust must vest no later than 21 years after the death of the survivor of specified lives in being. In exercising a non-general power created in that trust, any indirect effort by the donee to obtain a "later of" approach by adopting a 90-year perpetuity saving clause will likely be nullified by subsection (e). If that exercise occurs at a time when it has become clear or reasonably predictable that the 90-year period will prove longer, the donee's exercise would constitute language in a governing instrument that seeks to operate in effect to postpone the vesting of any interest until the later of the specified-lives-in-being-plus-21-years period or 90 years. Under subsection (e), "that language is inoperative to the extent it produces a period of time that exceeds 21 years after the death of the survivor of the specified lives."

Quite apart from subsection (e), the relation-back doctrine generally recognized in the exercise of nongeneral powers stands as a doctrine that could potentially be invoked to nullify an attempted switch from one perpetuity period to the other perpetuity period. Under that doctrine, interests created by the exercise of a nongeneral power are considered created by the donor of that power. See, e.g., Restatement (Second) of Property, Donative Transfers § 11.1 comment b (1986). As such, the maximum vesting period applicable to interests created by the exercise of a nongeneral power would apparently be covered by the perpetuity saving clause in the document that created the power, notwithstanding any different period the donee purports to adopt.

Reference. Section 2–901 is Section 1 of the Uniform Statutory Rule Against Perpetuities (Uniform Act). For further discussion of this section, with numerous examples illustrating its application, see the Official Comment to Section 1 of the Uniform Act.

Section 2–902. When Nonvested Property Interest or Power of Appointment Created.

(a) Except as provided in subsections (b) and (c) and in Section 2–905(a), the time of creation of a nonvested property interest or a power of appointment is determined under general principles of property law.

(b) For purposes of Subpart 1 of this Part, if there is a person who alone can exercise a power created by a governing instrument to become the unqualified beneficial owner of (i) a nonvested property interest or (ii) a property interest subject to a power of appointment described in Section 2–901(b) or (c), the nonvested property interest or power of appointment is created when the power to become the unqualified beneficial owner terminates. [For purposes of Subpart 1 of this Part, a joint power with respect to community property or to marital property under the Uniform Marital Property Act held by individuals married to each other is a power exercisable by one person alone.]

(c) For purposes of Subpart 1 of this Part, a nonvested property interest or a power of appointment arising from a transfer of property to a previously funded trust or other existing property arrangement is created when the nonvested property interest or power of appointment in the original contribution was created.

COMMENT

Section 2–902 defines the time when, for purposes of Subpart 1 of Part 9, a nonvested property interest or a power of appointment is created. The period of time allowed by Section 2–901 is measured from the time of creation of the nonvested property interest or power of appointment in question. Section 2–905, with certain exceptions, provides that Subpart 1 of Part 9 applies only to nonvested property interests and powers of appointment created on or after the effective date of Subpart 1 of Part 9.

Subsection (a). Subsection (a) provides that, with certain exceptions, the time of creation of nonvested property interests and powers of appointment is determined under general principles of property law. Because a will becomes effective as a dispositive instrument upon the decedent's death, not upon the execution of the will, general principles of property law determine that a nonvested property interest or a power of appointment created by will is created at the decedent's death. With respect to an inter-vivos transfer, an interest or power is created on the date the transfer becomes effective for purposes of property law generally, normally the date of delivery of the deed or the funding of the trust.

Nonvested Property Interests and Powers of Appointment Created by the Exercise of a Power of Appointment. If a nonvested property interest or a power of appointment was created by the testamentary or inter-vivos exercise of a power of appointment, general principles of property law adopt the "relation-back" doctrine. Under that doctrine, the appointed interests or powers are created when the power was created, not when it was exercised, if the exercised power was a nongeneral power or a general testamentary power. If the nonvested property interest or power of appointment was created by the exercise of a nongeneral or a testamentary power of appointment that was itself created by the exercise of a nongeneral or a testamentary power of appointment, the relation-back doctrine is applied twice and the nonvested property interest or power of appointment was created when the first power of appointment was created, not when the second power was created or exercised.

Example 1. G's will created a trust that provided for the income to go to G's son, A, for life, remainder to such of A's descendants as A shall by will appoint.

A died leaving a will that exercised his nongeneral power of appointment, providing that the trust is to continue beyond A's death, paying the income to A's daughter, X, for her lifetime, remainder in corpus to such of X's descendants as X shall by will appoint; in default of appointment, to X's descendants who survive X, by representation.

A's exercise of his nongeneral power of appointment gave a nongeneral power of appointment to X and a nonvested property interest to X's descendants. For purposes of Section 2-901, X's power of appointment and the nonvested property interest in X's descendants is deemed to have been "created" at G's death when A's nongeneral power of appointment was created, not at A's death when he exercised his power of appointment.

Suppose that X subsequently dies leaving a will that exercises her nongeneral power of appoint-

ment. For purposes of Section 2-901, any nonvested property interest or power of appointment created by an exercise of X's nongeneral power of appointment is deemed to have been "created" at G's death, not at A's death or at X's death.

If the exercised power was a presently exercisable general power, the relation-back doctrine is not followed; the time of creation of the appointed property interests or appointed powers is regarded as the time when the power was irrevocably exercised, not when the power was created.

Example 2. The same facts as Example 1, except that A's will exercised his nongeneral power of appointment by providing that the trust is to continue beyond A's death, paying the income to A's daughter, X, for her lifetime, remainder in corpus to such person or persons, including X, her estate, her creditors, and the creditors of her estate, as X shall appoint; in default of appointment, to X's descendants who survive X, by representation.

A's exercise of his nongeneral power of appointment gave a presently exercisable general power of appointment to X. For purposes of Section 2-901, any nonvested property interest or power of appointment created by an exercise of X's presently exercisable general power of appointment is deemed to be "created" when X irrevocably exercises her power of appointment, not when her power of appointment or A's power of appointment was created.

A's exercise of his nongeneral power also granted a nonvested property interest to X's descendants (under the gift-in-default clause). Were it not for the presently exercisable general power granted to X, the nonvested property interest in X's surviving descendants would, under the relation-back doctrine, be deemed "created" for purposes of Section 2–901 at the time of G's death. However, under Section 2–902(b), the fact that X is granted the presently exercisable general power postpones the time of creation of the nonvested property interest of X's descendants. Under Section 2–902(b), that nonvested property interest is deemed not to have been "created" for purposes of Section 2–901 at G's death but rather when X's presently exercisable general power "terminates." Consequently, the time of "creation" of the nonvested interest of X's descendants is postponed as of the time that X was granted the presently exercisable general power (upon A's death) and continues in abeyance until X's power terminates. X's power terminates by the first to happen of the following: X's irrevocable exercise of her power; X's release of her power; X's entering into a contract to exercise or not to exercise her power; X's dying without exercising her power; or any other action or nonaction that would have the effect of terminating her power.

Subsection (b). Subsection (b) provides that, if one person can exercise a power to become the unqualified beneficial owner of a nonvested property interest (or a property interest subject to a power of appointment described in Section 2–901(b) or 2–901(c)), the time of creation of the nonvested property interest (or the power of appointment) is postponed until the power to become the unqualified beneficial owner ceases to exist. This is in accord with existing common law. The standard example of the application of this subsection is a revocable inter-vivos trust. For perpetuity purposes, both at common law and under Subpart 1 of Part 9, the nonvested property interests and powers of appointment created in the trust are created when the power to revoke expires, usually at the settlor's death. For another example of the application of subsection (b), see the last paragraph of Example 2, above.

Subsection (c). Subsection (c) provides that nonvested property interests and powers of appointment arising out of transfers to a previously funded trust or other existing property arrangement are created when the nonvested property interest or power of appointment arising out of the original contribution was created. This avoids an administrative difficulty that can arise at common law when subsequent transfers are made to an existing irrevocable inter-vivos trust. Arguably, at common law, each transfer starts the period of the Rule running anew as to each transfer. The prospect of staggered periods is avoided by subsection (c). Subsection (c) is in accord with the saving-clause principle of wait-and-see embraced by Part 9. If the irrevocable inter-vivos trust had contained a saving clause, the perpetuity-period component of the clause would be measured by reference to lives in being when the original contribution to the trust was made, and the clause would cover subsequent contributions as well.

Reference. Section 2–902 is Section 2 of the Uniform Statutory Rule Against Perpetuities (Uniform Act). For further discussion of this section, with examples illustrating its application, see the Official Comment to Section 2 of the Uniform Act.

Section 2–903. Reformation.

Upon the petition of an interested person, a court shall reform a disposition in the manner that most closely approximates the transferor's manifested plan of distribution and is within the 90 years allowed by Section 2–901(a)(2), 2–901(b)(2), or 2–901(c)(2) if:

(1) a nonvested property interest or a power of appointment becomes invalid under Section 2–901 (statutory rule against perpetuities);

(2) a class gift is not but might become invalid under Section 2–901 (statutory rule against perpetuities) and the time has arrived when the share of any class member is to take effect in possession or enjoyment; or

(3) a nonvested property interest that is not validated by Section 2–901(a)(1) can vest but not within 90 years after its creation.

COMMENT

Section 2–903 implements the deferred-reformation feature of the Uniform Statutory Rule Against Perpetuities. Upon the petition of an interested person, the court is directed to reform a disposition within the limits of the allowable 90-year period, in the manner deemed by the court most closely to approximate the transferor's manifested plan of distribution, in any one of three circumstances. The "interested person" who would frequently bring the reformation suit would be the trustee.

Section 2–903 applies only to dispositions the validity of which is governed by the wait-and-see element of Section 2–901(a)(2), 2–901(b)(2), or 2–901(c)(2); it does not apply to dispositions that are initially valid under Section 2–901(a)(1), 2–901(b)(1), or 2–901(c)(1)—the codified version of the validating side of the common-law Rule.

Section 2–903 will seldom be applied. Of the fraction of trusts and other property arrangements that fail to meet the requirements for initial validity under the codified version of the validating side of the

common-law Rule, almost all of them will have been settled under their own terms long before any of the circumstances requisite to reformation under Section 2–903 arise.

If, against the odds, one of the circumstances requisite to reformation does arise, it will be found easier than perhaps anticipated to determine how best to reform the disposition. The court is given two criteria to work with: (i) the transferor's manifested plan of distribution, and (ii) the allowable 90-year period. Because governing instruments are where transferors manifest their plans of distribution, the imaginary horrible of courts being forced to probe the minds of long-dead transferors will not materialize.

Subsection (1). The theory of Section 2–903 is to defer the right to reformation until reformation becomes truly necessary. Thus, the basic rule of Section 2–903(1) is that the right to reformation does not arise until a nonvested property interest or a power of appointment becomes invalid; under Section 2–

901, this does not occur until the expiration of the 90-year permissible vesting period. This approach is more efficient than the "immediate cy pres" approach to perpetuity reform because it substantially reduces the number of reformation suits. It also is consistent with the saving-clause principle embraced by the Statutory Rule. Deferring the right to reformation until the permissible vesting period expires is the only way to grant every reasonable opportunity for the donor's disposition to work itself out without premature interference.

Subsection (2). Although, generally speaking, reformation is deferred until an invalidity has occurred, Section 2–903 grants an earlier right to reformation when it becomes necessary to do so or when there is no point in waiting the full 90-year period out. Thus subsection (2), which pertains to class gifts that are not yet but still might become invalid under the Statutory Rule, grants a right to reformation whenever the share of any class member whose share had vested within the permissible vesting period might otherwise have to wait out the remaining part of the 90 years before obtaining his or her share. Reformation under this subsection will seldom be needed, however, because of the common practice of structuring trusts to split into separate shares or separate trusts at the death of each income beneficiary, one such separate share or separate trust being created for each of the income beneficiary's then-living children; when this pattern is followed, the circumstances described in subsection (2) will not arise.

Subsection (3). Subsection (3) also grants a right to reformation before the 90-year permissible vesting period expires. The circumstances giving rise to the right to reformation under subsection (3) occurs if a nonvested property interest can vest but not before the 90-year period has expired. Though unlikely, such a case can theoretically arise. If it does, the interest—unless it terminates by its own terms earlier—is bound to become invalid under Section 2–901 eventually. There is no point in deferring the right to reformation until the inevitable happens. Section 2–903 provides for early reformation in such a case, just in case it arises.

Infectious Invalidity. Given the fact that this section makes reformation mandatory, not discretionary with the court, the common-law doctrine of infectious invalidity is superseded by this section. In a state in which the courts have been particularly zealous about applying the infectious-invalidity doctrine, however, an express codification of the abrogation of this doctrine might be thought desirable. If so, the above section could be made subsection (a), with the following new subsection (b) added:

(b) The common-law rule known as the doctrine of infectious invalidity is abolished.

Reference. Section 2–903 is Section 3 of the Uniform Statutory Rule Against Perpetuities (Uniform Act). For further discussion of this section, with examples illustrating its application, see the Official Comment to Section 3 of the Uniform Act.

Section 2–904. Exclusions from Statutory Rule Against Perpetuities.

Section 2–901 (statutory rule against perpetuities) does not apply to:

(1) a nonvested property interest or a power of appointment arising out of a nondonative transfer, except a nonvested property interest or a power of appointment arising out of (i) a premarital or postmarital agreement, (ii) a separation or divorce settlement, (iii) a spouse's election, (iv) a similar arrangement arising out of a prospective, existing, or previous marital relationship between the parties, (v) a contract to make or not to revoke a will or trust, (vi) a contract to exercise or not to exercise a power of appointment, (vii) a transfer in satisfaction of a duty of support, or (viii) a reciprocal transfer;

(2) a fiduciary's power relating to the administration or management of assets, including the power of a fiduciary to sell, lease, or mortgage property, and the power of a fiduciary to determine principal and income;

(3) a power to appoint a fiduciary;

(4) a discretionary power of a trustee to distribute principal before termination of a trust to a beneficiary having an indefeasibly vested interest in the income and principal;

(5) a nonvested property interest held by a charity, government, or governmental agency or subdivision, if the nonvested property interest is preceded by an interest held by another charity, government, or governmental agency or subdivision;

(6) a nonvested property interest in or a power of appointment with respect to a trust or other property arrangement forming part of a pension, profit-sharing, stock bonus, health, disability, death benefit, income deferral, or other current or deferred benefit plan for one or more employees, independent contractors, or their beneficiaries or spouses, to which contributions are made for the purpose of distributing to or for the benefit of the participants or their beneficiaries or spouses the property, income, or principal in the trust or other property arrangement, except a nonvested property interest or a power of appointment that is created by an election of a participant or a beneficiary or spouse; or

(7) a property interest, power of appointment, or arrangement that was not subject to the common-law rule against perpetuities or is excluded by another statute of this State.

COMMENT

This section lists the interests and powers that are excluded from the Statutory Rule Against Perpetuities. This section is in part declaratory of existing common law but in part not. Under subsection (7), all the exclusions from the common-law Rule recognized at common law and by statute in the state are preserved.

The major departure from existing common law comes in subsection (1). In line with long-standing scholarly commentary, subsection (1) excludes nondonative transfers from the Statutory Rule. The Rule Against Perpetuities is an inappropriate instrument of social policy to use as a control of such arrangements. The period of the Rule—a life in being plus 21 years—is suitable for donative transfers only, and this point applies with equal force to the 90-year allowable waiting period under the wait-and-see element of Section 2–901. That period, as noted, represents an approximation of the period of time that would be produced, on average, by tracing a set of actual measuring lives and adding a 21-year period following the death of the survivor.

Certain types of transactions—although in some sense supported by consideration, and hence arguably nondonative—arise out of a domestic situation, and should not be excluded from the Statutory Rule. To avoid uncertainty with respect to such transactions, subsection (1) lists and restores such transactions, such as premarital or postmarital agreements, contracts to make or not to revoke a will or trust, and so on, to the donative-transfers category that does not qualify for an exclusion.

Reference. Section 2–904 is Section 4 of the Uniform Statutory Rule Against Perpetuities (Uniform Act). For further discussion of this section, with examples illustrating its application, see the Official Comment to Section 4 of the Uniform Act.

Section 2–905. Prospective Application.

(a) Except as extended by subsection (b), Subpart 1 of this Part applies to a nonvested property interest or a power of appointment that is created on or after the effective date of Subpart 1 of this Part. For purposes of this section, a nonvested property interest or a power of appointment created by the exercise of a power of appointment is created when the power is irrevocably exercised or when a revocable exercise becomes irrevocable.

(b) If a nonvested property interest or a power of appointment was created before the effective date of Subpart 1 of this Part and is determined in a judicial proceeding, commenced on or after the effective date of Subpart 1 of this Part, to violate this State's rule against perpetuities as that rule existed before the effective date of Subpart 1 of this Part, a court upon the petition of an interested person may reform the disposition in the manner that most closely approximates the transferor's manifested plan of distribution and is within the limits of the rule against perpetuities applicable when the nonvested property interest or power of appointment was created.

COMMENT

Section 2–905 provides that, except for Section 2–905(b), this Part applies only to nonvested property interests or powers of appointment created on or after the effective date of this Subpart. The second sentence of subsection (a) establishes a special rule for nonvested property interests (and powers of appointment) created by the exercise of a power of appointment. The import of this special rule, which applies to the exercise of all types of powers of appointment (general testamentary powers and nongeneral powers as well as presently exercisable general powers), is that all the provisions of this Subpart except Section 2–905(b) apply if the donee of a power of appointment exercises the power on or after the effective date of this Subpart, whether the donee's exercise is revocable or irrevocable. In addition, all the provisions of Subpart 1 except Section 2–905(b) apply if the donee exercised the power before the effective date of this Subpart if (i) that pre-effective-date exercise was revocable and (ii) that revocable exercise becomes irrevocable on or after the effective date of this Subpart. The special rule, in other words, prevents the common-law doctrine of relation back from inappropriately shrinking the reach of this Subpart.

Although the Uniform Statutory Rule does not apply retroactively, Section 2–905(b) authorizes a court to exercise its equitable power of reform instruments that contain a violation of the state's former rule against perpetuities and to which the Uniform Statutory Rule does not apply because the offending property interest or power of appointment was created before the effective date of this Subpart. Courts are urged to consider reforming such dispositions by judicially inserting a perpetuity saving clause, because a perpetuity saving clause would probably have been used at the drafting stage of the disposition had it been drafted competently. To obviate any possibility of an inequitable exercise of the equitable power to reform, Section 2–905(b) limits the authority to reform to situations in which the violation of the former rule against perpetuities is determined in a judicial proceeding that is commenced on or after the effective date of this Subpart. The equitable power to reform would typically be exercised in the same judicial proceeding in which the invalidity is determined.

Reference. Section 2–905 is Section 5 of the Uniform Statutory Rule Against Perpetuities (Uniform Act). For further discussion of this section, with examples illustrating its application, see the Official Comment to Section 5 of the Uniform Act.

Section 2–906. [Supersession][Repeal].

Subpart 1 of this Part [supersedes the rule of the common law known as the rule against perpetuities][repeals (list statutes to be repealed)].

COMMENT

The first set of bracketed text is provided for states that follow the common-law Rule Against Perpetuities. The second set of bracketed text is provided for the repeal of statutory adoptions of the common-law Rule Against Perpetuities, statutory variations of the common-law Rule Against Perpetuities, or statutory prohibitions on the suspension of the power of alienation for more than a certain period. Some states may find it appropriate to enact both sets of bracketed text by joining them with the word "and." This would be appropriate in states having a statute that declares that the common-law Rule Against Perpetuities is in force in the state except as modified therein.

A cautionary note for states repealing listed statutes: If the statutes to be repealed contain exclusions from the rule against perpetuities, states should consider whether to repeal or retain those exclusions, in light of Section 2–904(7), which excludes from the Uniform Statutory Rule property interests, powers of appointment, and other arrangements "excluded by another statute of this State."

SUBPART 2.   [HONORARY TRUSTS]

GENERAL COMMENT

Subpart 2 contains an optional provision on honorary trusts and trusts for pets. If this optional provision is enacted, a new subsection (8) should be added to Section 2–904 to avoid an overlap or conflict between Subpart 1 of Part 9 (US-RAP) and Subpart 2 of Part 9. Subsection (8) makes it clear that Subpart 2 of Part 9 is the exclusive provision applicable to the property interests or arrangements subjected to a time limit by the provisions of Subpart 2. Subsection (8) states:

(8) a property interest or arrangement subjected to a time limit under Subpart 2 of Part 9.

Additionally, the "or" at the end of Section 2–904(6) should be removed and placed after Section 2–904(7).

[Optional provision for validating and limiting the duration of so-called honorary trusts and trusts for pets.]

[Section 2–907. Honorary Trusts; Trusts for Pets.

(a) [Honorary Trust.] A trust for a noncharitable corporation or unincorporated society or for a lawful noncharitable purpose may be performed by the trustee for [21] years but no longer, whether or not there is a beneficiary who can seek the trust's enforcement or termination and whether or not the terms of the trust contemplate a longer duration.

(b) [Trust for Pets.] Subject to this subsection, a trust for the care of a designated domestic or pet animal and the animal's offspring is valid. Except as expressly provided otherwise in the trust instrument:

(1) No portion of the principal or income may be converted to the use of the trustee or to any use other than for the benefit of a covered animal.

(2) The trust terminates at the earlier of [21] years after the trust was created or when no living animal is covered by the trust.

(3) Upon termination, the trustee shall transfer the unexpended trust property in the following order:

(i) as directed in the trust instrument;

(ii) if the trust was created in a nonresiduary clause in the transferor's will or in a codicil to the transferor's will, under the residuary clause in the transferor's will; and

(iii) if no taker is produced by the application of subparagraph (i) or (ii), to the transferor's heirs under Section 2-711.

(4) For the purposes of Section 2-707, the residuary clause is treated as creating a future interest under the terms of a trust.

(5) The intended use of the principal or income can be enforced by an individual designated for that purpose in the trust instrument or, if none, by an individual appointed by a court upon application to it by an individual.

(6) Except as ordered by the court or required by the trust instrument, no filing, report, registration, periodic accounting, separate maintenance of funds, appointment, or fee is required by reason of the existence of the fiduciary relationship of the trustee.

(7) A governing instrument must be liberally construed to bring the transfer within this section, to presume against the merely precatory or honorary nature of the disposition, and to carry out the general intent of the transferor. Extrinsic evidence is admissible in determining the transferor's intent.

(8) A court may reduce the amount of the property transferred, if it determines that that amount substantially exceeds the amount required for the intended use. The amount of the reduction, if any, passes as unexpended trust property under subsection (b)(3).

(9) If no trustee is designated or no designated trustee is willing or able to serve, a court shall name a trustee. A court may order the transfer of the property to another trustee, if required to assure that the intended use is carried out and if no successor trustee is designated in the trust instrument or if no designated successor trustee agrees to serve or is able to serve. A court may also make such other orders and determinations as shall be advisable to carry out the intent of the transferor and the purpose of this section.]

COMMENT

Subsection (a) of this section authorizes so-called honorary trusts and places a 21-year limit on their duration. The figure "21" is bracketed to indicate that an enacting state may select a different figure.

Subsection (b) provides more elaborate provisions for a particular type of honorary trust, the trust for the care of pets. Under subsection (b), a trust for the care of a designated domestic or pet animal and the animal's offspring is valid for a period of up to 21 years. Again, the figure "21" is bracketed to indicate that an enacting state may select a different figure.

The normal life span of some animal species exceeds 21 years. If a state would prefer to allow the trust to continue until the death of the animal, subsection (b) can easily be adapted to that purpose. If a state chooses to take this approach, it would probably be desirable not to allow the trust to continue for the lifetime of the animal's offspring. Appropriate adjustments for achieving this approach are to delete the phrase "and the animal's offspring" from the introductory portion of subsection (b) and to modify subsection (b)(2) to read: "The trust terminates at the death of the animal."

Subsection (b) meets a concern of many pet owners by providing them a means for leaving funds to be used for the pet's care.

PART 10

UNIFORM INTERNATIONAL WILLS ACT [INTERNATIONAL WILL; INFORMATION REGISTRATION]

The Board that acted for the National Conference of Commissioners on Uniform State Laws in preparing the Uniform International Wills Act was as follows:

JOINT EDITORIAL BOARD FOR UNIFORM PROBATE CODE

Conference Representatives:

CHARLES HOROWITZ, Supreme Court, Temple of Justice, Olympia, WA 98504, *Co-Chairman*

CLARKE A. GRAVEL, 109 South Winooski Avenue, Burlington, VT 05401

BERT MCELROY, 205 Denver Building, Tulsa, OK 74119

EUGENE F. SCOLES, University of Oregon, School of Law, Eugene, OR 97403

ALLAN D. VESTAL, University of Iowa, College of Law, Iowa City, IA 52242

DON J. MCCLENAHAN, 310 Simplot Building, Boise, ID 83/02, *Chairman, Division A, Ex Officio*

JAMES M. BUSH, 363 North First Avenue, Phoenix, AZ 85003, *President, Ex Officio*

RICHARD V. WELLMAN, University of Georgia, School of Law, Athens, GA 30602, *Reporter*

American Bar Association Representatives:

J. PENNINGTON STRAUS, 1719 Packard Building, Philadelphia, PA 19102, *Co-Chairman*

PETER J. BRENNAN, 111 West Monroe Street, Chicago, IL 60603

HARRISON F. DURAND, 250 Park Avenue, New York, NY 10017

J. THOMAS EUBANK, JR., 3000 One Shell Plaza, Houston, TX 77002

MALCOLM A. MOORE, 4200 Seattle First National Bank Building, Seattle, WA 98154

ADVISORS TO JOINT EDITORIAL BOARD
FOR UNIFORM PROBATE CODE

ROBERT E. DALTON, Department of State, Washington, DC 20520

RICHARD KEARNEY, Department of State, Washington, DC 20520

PREFATORY NOTE

Introduction

The purpose of the Washington Convention of 1973 concerning international wills is to provide testators with a way of making wills that will be valid as to form in all countries joining the Convention. As proposed by the Convention, the objective would be achieved through uniform local rules of form, rather than through local or international law that makes recognition of foreign wills turn on choice of law rules involving possible application of foreign law. The international will provisions, prepared for the National Conference of Commissioners on Uniform State Laws by the Joint Editorial Board for the Uniform Probate Code which has functioned as a special committee of the Conference for the project, should be enacted by all states, including those that have not accepted the Uniform Probate Code. To that end, this statute is framed both as a free-standing act and as an added part of the Uniform Probate Code. The bracketed headings and numbers fit the proposal into UPC; the others present the proposal as a free-standing act.

Uniform state enactment of these provisions will permit the Washington Convention of 1973 to be implemented through state legislation familiar to will draftsmen. Thus, local proof of foreign law and reliance on federal legislation regarding wills can be avoided when foreign wills come into our states to be implemented. Also, the citizens of all states will have a will form available that should greatly reduce perils of proof and risks of invalidity that attend proof of American wills abroad.

History of the International Will

Discussions about possible international accord on an acceptable form of will led the Governing Council of UNIDROIT (International Institute for the Unification of Private Law) in 1960 to appoint a small committee of experts from several countries to develop proposals. Following week-long meetings at the Institute's quarters in Rome in 1963, and on two occasions in 1965, the Institute published and circulated a Draft Convention of December 1966 with an annexed uniform law that would be required to be enacted locally by those countries agreeing to the convention. The package and accompanying explanations were reviewed in this country by the Secretary of State's Advisory Committee on Private International Law. In turn, it referred the proposal to a special committee of American probate specialists drawn from member of NCCUSL's Special Committee on the Uniform Probate Code and its advisers and reporters. The resulting reports and recommendations were affirmative and urged the State Department to cooperate in continuing efforts to develop the 1966 Draft Convention, and to endeavor to interest other countries in the subject.

Encouraged by support for the project from this country and several others, UNIDROIT served as host for a 1971 meeting in Rome of an expanded group that included some of the original panel of experts and others from several countries that were not represented in the early drafting sessions. The result of this meeting was a revised draft of the proposed convention and annexed uniform law and this, in turn, was the subject of study and discussion by many more persons in this country. In mid–1973, the proposal from UNIDROIT was discussed in a joint program of the Real Property Probate and Trust Law Section, and the Section of International Law at the American Bar Association's annual meeting held that year in Washington, D.C. By late 1973, the list of published, scholarly discussions of the International Will proposals included Fratcher, "The Uniform Probate Code and the International Will", 66 Mich.L.Rev. 469 (1968); Wellman, "Recent Unidroit Drafts on the International Will", 6 The International Lawyer 205 (1973); and Wellman, "Proposed International Convention Concerning Wills", 8/4 Real Property, Probate and Trust Journal 622 (1973).

In October 1973, pursuant to a commitment made earlier to UNIDROIT representatives that it would provide leadership for the international will proposal if sufficient interest from other countries became evident, the United States served as host for the diplomatic Conference on Wills which met in Washington from October 10 to 26, 1973. 42 governments were represented by delegations, 6 by observers. The United States delegation of 8 persons plus 2 Congressional advisers and 2 staff advisers, was headed by Ambassador Richard D. Kearney, Chairman of the Secretary of State's Advisory Committee on Private International Law who also was selected president of the Conference. The result of the Conference was the Convention of October 26, 1973 Providing a Uniform Law on the Form of an International Will, an appended Annex, Uniform Law on the Form of an International Will, and a Resolution recommending establishment of state assisted systems for the safekeeping and discovery of wills. These three documents are reproduced at the end of these preliminary comments.

A more detailed account of the UNIDROIT project and the 1973 Convention, together with recommendations regarding United States implementation of the Convention, appears in Nadelmann, "The Formal Validity of Wills and the Washington Convention 1973 Providing the Form of an International Will", XXII The American Journal of Comparative Law, 365 (1974).

Description of the Proposal

The 1973 Convention obligates countries becoming parties to make the annexed uniform law a part of their local law. The proposed uniform law contemplates the involvement in will executions under this law of a state recognized expert who is referred to throughout the proposals as the "authorized person". Hence, the local law called for by the Convention must designate authorized persons, and prescribe the formalities for an international will and the role of authorized persons relating thereto. The Convention binds parties to respect the authority of another party's authorized persons and this obligation, coupled with local enactment of the common statute prescribing the role of such persons and according finality to their certificates regarding due execution of wills, assures recognition of international wills under local law in all countries joining the Convention.

The Convention and the annexed uniform law deal only with the formal validity of wills. Thus, the proposal is entirely neutral in relation to local laws dealing with revocation of wills, or those defining the scope of testamentary power, or regulating the probate, interpretation, and construction of wills, and the administration of decedents' estates. The proposal describes a highly formal mode of will execution; one that is sufficiently protective against imposition and mistake to command international approval as being safe enough. However, failure to meet the requirements of an international will does not necessarily result in invalidity, for the mode of execution described for an international will does not pre-empt or exclude other standards of testamentary validity.

The details of the prescribed mode of execution reflect a blend of common and civil law elements. Two attesting witnesses are required in the tradition of the English Statute of Wills of 1837 and its American counterparts. The authorized person whose participation in the ceremony of execution is required, and whose certificate makes the will self-proved, plays a role not unlike that of the civil law notary, though he is not required to retain custody of the will as is customary with European notaries.

The question of who should be given state recognition as authorized persons was resolved by designation of all licensed attorneys. The reasons for this can be seen in the observations about the role of Kurt H. Nadelmann, writing in The American Journal of Comparative Law:

The duties imposed by the Uniform Law upon the person doing the certifying go beyond legalization of signatures, the domain of the notary public. At least paralegal training is a necessity. Abroad, in countries with the law trained notary, the designation is likely to go to this class or at least to include it. Similarly, in countries with a closely supervised class of solicitors, their designation may be expected.

Attorneys are subject to training and licensing requirements everywhere in this country. The degree to which they are supervised after qualification varies considerably from state to state, but the trend is definitely in the direction of more rather than less supervision. Designation of attorneys in the uniform law permits a state to bring the statute into its local law books without undue delay.

Roles for Federal and State Law in Relation to International Will

Several alternatives are available for arranging federal and state laws on the subject of international wills. The 1973 Convention obligates nations becoming parties to introduce the annexed uniform law into their local law, and to recognize the authority, *vis a vis* will executions and certificates relating to wills, of persons designated as authorized by other parties to the Convention. But, the Convention includes a clause for federal states that may be used by the United States as it moves, through the process of Senate Advice and Consent, to accept the international compact. Through it, the federal government may limit the areas in this country to which the Convention will be applicable. Thus, Article XIV of the 1973 Convention provides:

1. If a state has two or more territorial units in which different systems of law apply in relation to matters respecting the form of wills, it may at the time of signature, ratification, or accession, declare that this Convention shall extend to all its territorial units or only to one or more of them, and may modify its declaration by submitting another declaration at any time.

2. These declarations shall be notified to the Depositary Government and shall state expressly the territorial units to which the Convention applies.

One alternative would be for the federal government to refrain from use of Article XIV and to accept the Convention as applicable to all areas of the country. The obligation to introduce the uniform law into local law then could be met by passage of a federal statute incorporating the uniform law and designating authorized persons who can assist testators desiring to use the international format, possibly leaving it open for state legislatures, if they wish, to designate other or additional groups of authorized persons. As to constitutionality, the federal statute on wills could be rested on the power of the federal government to bind the states by treaty and to implement a treaty obligation to bring agreed upon rules into local law by any appropriate method. Missouri v. Holland, 252 U.S. 416 (1920); Nadelmann, "The Formal Validity of Wills and the Washington Convention 1973 Providing the Form of An International Will", XXII The Am. Jn'l of Comp.L. 365, 375 (1974). Prof. Nadelmann favors this approach, arguing that new risks of invalidity of wills would arise if the treaty were limited so as to be applicable only in designated areas of the country, presumably those where state enactment of the uniform law already had occurred.

One disadvantage of this approach is that it would place a potentially important method for validating wills in federal statutes where probate practitioners, long accustomed to finding the statutes pertinent to their specialty in state compilations, simply would not discover it. Another, of course, relates to more generalized concerns that would attend any move by the federal government into an area of law traditionally reserved to the states.

Alternatively, the federal government might accept the Convention and uniform law as applicable throughout the land, so that international wills executed with the aid of authorized persons of other countries would be good anywhere in this country, but refrain from any designation of authorized persons, other than possibly of some minimum federal cadre, or of those who could function within the District of Columbia, leaving the selection of more useful groups of authorized persons entirely to the states. One result would be to greatly narrow the advantage of international wills to American testators who wanted to execute their instruments at home. In probable consequence, there would be pressure on state legislatures to enact the uniform law so as to make the advantages of the system available to local testators. Assuming some state legislatures respond to the pressure affirmatively and others negatively, a crazyquilt pattern of international will states would develop, leading possibly to some of the confusion and risk of illegality feared by Prof. Nadelmann. On the other hand, since execution of an international will involves use of an authorized person who derives authority from (on this assumption) state legislation, it seem somewhat unlikely that testators in states which have not designated authorized persons will be led to believe that they can make an international will unless they go to a state where authorized persons have been designated. Hence, the confusion may not be as great as if the Convention were inapplicable to portions of the country.

Finally, the federal government might use Article XIV as suggested earlier, and designate some but not all states as areas of the country in which the Convention applied. This seems the least desirable of all alternatives because it subjects international wills from abroad to the risk of non-recognition in some states, and offers the risk of confusion of American testators regarding the areas of the country where they can execute a will that will be received outside this country as an international will.

Under any of the approaches, the desirability of widespread enactment of state statutes embodying the uniform law and designating authorized persons, seems clear, as does the necessity for this project of the National Conference of Commissioners on Uniform State Laws.

Style

In preparing the International Will proposal, the special committee, after considerable discussion and consideration of alternatives, decided to stick as closely as possible to the wording of the Annex to the Convention of October 26, 1973. The Convention and its Annex were written in the English, French, Russian and Spanish languages, each version, as declared by Article XVI of the Convention, being equally authentic. Not surprisingly, the English version of the Annex has a style that is somewhat different than that to which the National Conference is accustomed. Nonetheless, from the view of those using languages other than English who may be reviewing our state statutes on the International Will to see if they adhere to the Annex, it is more important to stick with the agreed formulations than it is to re-style these expressions to suit our traditions. However, some changes from the Annex were made in the interests of clarity, and because some of the language of the Annex is plainly inappropriate in a local enactment. These changes are explained in the Comments.

Will Registration

A bracketed section 10[2–1010], is included in the International Will proposal to aid survivors in locating international and other wills that have been kept secret by testators during their lives. Differing from the section 2–901 of the Uniform Probate Code and the many existing statutes from which section 2–901 was derived which constitute the probate court as an agency for the safekeeping of wills deposited by living testators, the bracketed proposal is for a system of registering certain minimum information about wills, including where the instrument will be kept pending the death of the testator. It can be separated or omitted from the rest of the Act.

This provision for a state will registration system is derived from recommendations by the Council of Europe for common market countries. These recommendations were urged on the group that assembled in Rome in 1971, and were received with interest by representatives of United Kingdom, Canada and United States, where will–making laws and customs have not included any officially sanctioned system for safekeeping of wills or for locating information about wills, other than occasional statutes providing for ante–mortem deposit of wills with probate courts. Interest was expressed also by the notaries from civil law countries who have traditionally aided will–making both by formalizing execution and by being the source thereafter of official certificates about wills, the originals of which are retained with the official records of the notary and carefully protected and regulated by settled customs of the profession. All recognized that acceptance of the international will would tend to increase the frequency with which owners of property in several different countries relied on a single will to control all of their properties. This prospect, plus increasing mobility of persons between countries, indicates that new methods for safekeeping and locating wills after death should be developed. The Resolution adopted as the final act of the 1973 Conference on Wills shows that the problem also attracted the interest and attention of that assembly.

Apart from problems of wills that may have effect in more than one country, Americans are moving from state to state with increasing frequency. As the international will statute becomes enacted in most if not all states, our laws will tend to induce persons to rely on a single will as sufficient even though they may own land in two or more states, and to refrain from making new wills when they change domicile from one state to another. The spread of the Uniform Probate Code, tending as it does to give wills the same meaning and procedural status in all states, will have a similar effect.

General enactment of the will registration section should lead to development of new state and interstate systems to meet the predictable needs of testators and survivors that will follow as the law of wills is detached from provincial restraints. It is offered with the international will provisions because both meet obvious needs of the times.

Documents from 1973 Convention

Three documents representing the work of the 1973 Convention are reproduced here for the convenience of members of the Conference.

CONVENTION PROVIDING A UNIFORM LAW ON THE FORM OF AN INTERNATIONAL WILL

The States signatory to the present Convention,

DESIRING to provide to a greater extent for the respecting of last wills by establishing an additional form of will hereinafter to be called an "international will" which, if employed, would dispense to some extent with the search for the applicable law;

HAVE RESOLVED to conclude a Convention for this purpose and have agreed upon the following provisions:

Article I 1. Each Contracting Party undertakes that not later than six months after the date of entry into force of this Convention in respect of that Party it shall introduce into its law the rules regarding an international will set out in the Annex to this Convention.

2. Each Contracting Party may introduce the provisions of the Annex into its law either by reproducing the actual text, or by translating it into its official language or languages.

3. Each Contracting Party may introduce into its law such further provisions as are necessary to give the provisions of the Annex full effect in its territory.

4. Each Contracting Party shall submit to the Depositary Government the text of the rules introduced into its national law in order to implement the provisions of this Convention.

Article II 1. Each Contracting Party shall implement the provisions of the Annex in its law, within the period provided for in the preceding article, by designating the persons who, in its territory, shall be authorized to act in connection with international wills. It may also designate as a person authorized to act with regard to its nationals its diplomatic or consular agents abroad insofar as the local law does not prohibit it.

2. The Party shall notify such designation, as well as any modifications thereof, to the Depositary Government.

Article III The capacity of the authorized person to act in connection with an international will, if conferred in accordance with the law of a Contracting Party, shall be recognized in the territory of the other Contracting Parties.

Article IV The effectiveness of the certificate provided for in Article 10 of the Annex shall be recognized in the territories of all Contracting Parties.

Article V 1. The conditions requisite to acting as a witness of an international will shall be governed by the law under which the authorized person was designated. The same rule shall apply as regards an interpreter who is called upon to act.

2. Nonetheless no one shall be disqualified to act as a witness of an international will solely because he is an alien.

Article VI 1. The signature of the testator, of the authorized person, and of the witnesses to an international will, whether on the will or on the certificate, shall be exempt from any legalization or like formality.

2. Nonetheless, the competent authorities of any Contracting Party may, if necessary, satisfy themselves as to the authenticity of the signature of the authorized person.

Article VII The safekeeping of an international will shall be governed by the law under which the authorized person was designated.

Article VIII No reservation shall be admitted to this Convention or to its Annex.

Article IX 1. The present Convention shall be open for signature at Washington from October 26, 1973, until December 31, 1974.

2. The Convention shall be subject to ratification.

3. Instruments of ratification shall be deposited with the Government of the United States of America, which shall be the Depositary Government.

Article X 1. The Convention shall be open indefinitely for accession.

2. Instruments of accession shall be deposited with the Depositary Government.

Article XI 1. The present Convention shall enter into force six months after the date of deposit of the fifth instrument of ratification or accession with the Depositary Government.

2. In the case of each State which ratifies this Convention or accedes to it after the fifth instrument of ratification or accession has been deposited, this Convention shall enter into force six months after the deposit of its own instrument of ratification or accession.

Article XII 1. Any Contracting Party may denounce this Convention by written notification to the Depositary Government.

2. Such denunciation shall take effect twelve months from the date on which the Depositary Government has received the notification, but such denunciation shall not affect the validity of any will made during the period that the Convention was in effect for the denouncing State.

Article XIII 1. Any State may, when it deposits its instrument of ratification or accession or at any time thereafter, declare, by a notice addressed to the Depositary Government, that this Convention shall apply to all or part of the territories for the international relations of which it is responsible.

2. Such declaration shall have effect six months after the date on which the Depositary Government shall have received notice thereof or, if at the end of such period the Convention has not yet come into force, from the date of its entry into force.

3. Each Contracting Party which has made a declaration in accordance with paragraph 1 of this Article may, in accordance

with Article XII, denounce this Convention in relation to all or part
of the territories concerned.

Article XIV 1. If a State has two or more territorial units in
which different systems of law apply in relation to matters respecting the form of wills, it may at the time of signature, ratification,
or accession, declare that this Convention shall extend to all its
territorial units or only to one or more of them, and may modify
its declaration by submitting another declaration at any time.

2. These declarations shall be notified to the Depositary
Government and shall state expressly the territorial units to which
the Convention applies.

Article XV If a Contracting Party has two or more territorial
units in which different systems of law apply in relation to matters
respecting the form of wills, any reference to the internal law of
the place where the will is made or to the law under which the
authorized person has been appointed to act in connection with
international wills shall be construed in accordance with the constitutional system of the Party concerned.

Article XVI 1. The original of the present Convention, in the
English, French, Russian and Spanish languages, each version
being equally authentic, shall be deposited with the Government of
the United States of America, which shall transmit certified copies
thereof to each of the signatory and acceding States and to the
International Institute for the Unification of Private Law.

2. The Depositary Government shall give notice to the signatory
and acceding States, and to the International Institute for the
Unification of Private Law, of:

(a) any signature;

(b) the deposit of any instrument of ratification or accession;

(c) any date on which this Convention enters into force in
accordance with Article XI;

(d) any communication received in accordance with Article
I, paragraph 4;

(e) any notice received in accordance with Article II, paragraph 2;

(f) any declaration received in accordance with Article XIII,
paragraph 2, and the date on which such declaration takes
effect;

(g) any denunciation received in accordance with Article
XII, paragraph 1, or Article XIII, paragraph 3, and the date on
which the denunciation takes effect;

(h) any declaration received in accordance with Article XIV,
paragraph 2, and the date on which the declaration takes
effect.

IN WITNESS WHEREOF, the undersigned Plenipotentiaries, being duly authorized to that effect, have signed the present Convention.

DONE at Washington this twenty–sixth day of October, one
thousand nine hundred and seventy–three.

Annex

UNIFORM LAW ON THE FORM OF AN INTERNATIONAL WILL

Article 1 1. A will shall be valid as regards form, irrespective particularly of the place where it is made, of the location of the assets and of the nationality, domicile or residence of the testator, if it is made in the form of an international will complying with the provisions set out in Articles 2 to 5 hereinafter.

2. The invalidity of the will as an international will shall not affect its formal validity as a will of another kind.

Article 2 This law shall not apply to the form of testamentary dispositions made by two or more persons in one instrument.

Article 3 1. The will shall be made in writing.

2. It need not be written by the testator himself.

3. It may be written in any language, by hand or by any other means.

Article 4 1. The testator shall declare in the presence of two witnesses and of a person authorized to act in connection with international wills that the document is his will and that he knows the contents thereof.

2. The testator need not inform the witnesses, or the authorized person, of the contents of the will.

Article 5 1. In the presence of the witnesses and of the authorized person, the testator shall sign the will or, if he has previously signed it, shall acknowledge his signature.

2. When the testator is unable to sign, he shall indicate the reason therefor to the authorized person who shall make note of this on the will. Moreover, the testator may be authorized by the law under which the authorized person was designated to direct another person to sign on his behalf.

3. The witnesses and the authorized person shall there and then attest the will by signing in the presence of the testator.

Article 6 1. The signatures shall be placed at the end of the will.

2. If the will consists of several sheets, each sheet shall be signed by the testator or, if he is unable to sign, by the person signing on his behalf or, if there is no such person, by the authorized person. In addition, each sheet shall be numbered.

Article 7 1. The date of the will shall be the date of its signature by the authorized person.

2. This date shall be noted at the end of the will by the authorized person.

Article 8 In the absence of any mandatory rule pertaining to the safekeeping of the will, the authorized person shall ask the testator whether he wishes to make a declaration concerning the safekeeping of his will. If so and at the express request of the testator the place where he intends to have his will kept shall be mentioned in the certificate provided for in Article 9.

Article 9   The authorized person shall attach to the will a certificate in the form prescribed in Article 10 establishing that the obligations of this law have been complied with.

Article 10   The certificate drawn up by the authorized person shall be in the following form or in a substantially similar form:

CERTIFICATE

(Convention of October 26, 1973)

1. I, _____ (name, address and capacity), a person authorized to act in connection with international wills
2. Certify that on _____ (date) at _____ (place)
3. (testator) _____ (name, address, date and place of birth) in my presence and that of the witnesses
4. (a) _____ (name, address, date and place of birth)
   (b) _____ (name, address, date and place of birth) has declared that the attached document is his will and that he knows the contents thereof.
5.   I furthermore certify that:
6. (a) in my presence and in that of the witnesses
       (1) the testator has signed the will or has acknowledged his signature previously affixed.
       *(2) following a declaration of the testator stating that he was unable to sign his will for the following reason _____
       —I have mentioned this declaration on the will
       *—the signature has been affixed by _____
       (name, address)
7. (b) the witnesses and I have signed the will;
8. *(c)each page of the will has been signed by _____ and numbered;
9. (d) I have satisfied myself as to the identity of the testator and of the witnesses as designated above;
10. (e) the witnesses met the conditions requisite to act as such according to the law under which I am acting;
11. *(f) the testator has requested me to include the following statement concerning the safekeeping of his will:

_____

_____

*To be completed if appropriate

12. PLACE
13. DATE
14. SIGNATURE and, if necessary, SEAL

Article 11   The authorized person shall keep a copy of the certificate and deliver another to the testator.

Article 12   In the absence of evidence to the contrary, the certificate of the authorized person shall be conclusive of the formal validity of the instrument as a will under this Law.

Article 13   The absence or irregularity of a certificate shall not affect the formal validity of a will under this Law.

Article 14   The international will shall be subject to the ordinary rules of revocation of wills.

Article 15 In interpreting and applying the provisions of this law, regard shall be had to its international origin and to the need for uniformity in its interpretation.

RESOLUTION

The Conference

Considering the importance of measures to permit the safeguarding of wills and to find them after the death of the testator;

Emphasizing the special interest in such measures with respect to the international will, which is often made by the testator far from his home;

RECOMMENDS to the States that participated in the present Conference

—that they establish an internal system, centralized or not, to facilitate the safekeeping, search and discovery of an international will as well as the accompanying certificate, for example, along the lines of the Convention on the Establishment of a Scheme of Registration of Wills, concluded at Basel on May 16, 1972;

—that they facilitate the international exchange of information in these matters and, to this effect, that they designate in each state an authority or a service to handle such exchanges.

NUMBERING SECTIONS OF ACT

The Uniform International Wills Act may be adopted as a separate act or as part of the Uniform Probate Code. If adopted as a separate act, the unbracketed section numbers would govern. If adopted as part of the Probate Code, i.e., as Part 10 of Article 2, the section numbers in brackets would govern.

Section 1. [2–1001.] [Definitions.]

In this Act: [Part:]

(1) "International will" means a will executed in conformity with sections 2 [2–1002] through 5 [2–1005].

(2) "Authorized person" and "person authorized to act in connection with international wills" mean a person who by section 9 [2–1009], or by the laws of the United States including members of the diplomatic and consular service of the United States designated by Foreign Service Regulations, is empowered to supervise the execution of international wills.

COMMENT

The term "international will" connotes only that a will has been executed in conformity with this act. It does not indicate that the will was

205

planned for implementation in more than one country, or that it relates to an estate that has or may have international implications. Thus, it will be entirely appropriate to use an "international will" whenever a will is desired.

The reference in subsection (2) to persons who derive their authority to act from federal law, including Foreign Service Regulations, anticipates that the United States will become a party to the 1973 Convention, and that Congress, pursuant to the obligation of the Convention, will enact the annexed uniform law and include therein some designation, possibly of a cadre only, of authorized persons. See the discussion under "Roles for Federal and State Law in Relation to International Will", in the Prefatory Note, *supra*. If all states enact similar laws and designate all attorneys as authorized persons, the need for testators to resort to those designated by federal law may be minimal. It seems desirable, nonetheless, to associate whoever may be designated by federal law as suitable authorized persons for purposes of implementing state enactments of the uniform act. The resulting "borrowing" of those designated federally should minimize any difficulties that might arise from variances in the details of execution of international wills that may develop in the state and federal enactment process.

In the Explanatory Report of the 1973 Convention prepared by Mr. Jean–Pierre Plantard, Deputy Secretary–General of the International Institute for the Unification of Private Law (UNIDROIT) as published by the Institute in 1974, the following paragraphs that are relevant to this section appear:

"The Uniform Law gives no definition of the term will. The preamble of the Convention also uses the expression 'last wills'. The material contents of the document are of little importance as the Uniform Law governs only its form. There is, therefore, nothing to prevent this form being used to register last wishes that do not involve the naming of an heir and which in some legal systems are called by a special name, such as 'Kodizill' in Austrian Law (ABGB § 553).

"Although it is given the qualification 'international', the will dealt with by the Uniform Law can easily be used for a situation without any international element, for example, by a testator disposing in his own country of his assets, all of which are situated in that same country. The adjective 'international', therefore, only indicates what was had in mind at the time when this new will was conceived. Moreover, it would have been practically impossible to define a satisfactory sphere of application, had one intended to restrict its use to certain situations with an international element. Such an element could only be assessed by reference to several factors (nationality, residence, domicile of the testator, place where the will was drawn up, place where the assets are situated) and, moreover, these might vary considerably between when the will was drawn up and the beginning of the inheritance proceedings.

"Use of the international will should, therefore, be open to all testators who decide they want to use it. Nothing should prevent it from competing with the traditional forms if it offers advantages of convenience and simplicity over the other forms and guarantees the necessary certainty."

Section 2. [2–1002.] [International Will; Validity.]

(a) A will shall be valid as regards form, irrespective particularly of the place where it is made, of the location of the assets and of the nationality, domicile, or residence of the testator, if it is made in the form of an international will complying with the requirements of this Act.   [Part.]

(b) The invalidity of the will as an international will shall not affect its formal validity as a will of another kind.

(c) This Act [Part] shall not apply to the form of testamentary dispositions made by two or more persons in one instrument.

COMMENT

This section combines what appears in Articles 1 and 2 of the Annex into a single section.   Except for the reference to later sections, the first sentence is identical to Article 1, section 1 of the Annex, the second sentence is identical to Article 1, section 2, and the third is identical to Article 2.

Mr. Plantard's commentary that is pertinent to this section is as follows:

"The Uniform Law is intended to be introduced into the legal system of each Contracting State.   Article 1, therefore, introduces into the internal law of each Contracting State the new, basic principle according to which the international will is valid irrespective of the country in which it was made, the nationality, domicile or residence of the testator and the place where the assets forming the estate are located.

"The scope of the Uniform Law is thus defined in the first sentence. As was mentioned above, the idea behind it was to establish a new type of will, the form of which would be the same in all countries. The Law obviously does not affect the subsistence of all the other forms of will known under each national law . . .

"Some of the provisions relating to form laid down by the Uniform Law are considered essential.   Violation of these provisions is sanctioned by the invalidity of the will as an international will.   These are: that the will must be made in writing, the presence of two witnesses and of the authorised person, signature by the testator and by the persons involved (witnesses and authorised person) and the prohibition of joint wills.   The other formalities, such as the position of the signature and date, the delivery and form of the certificate, are laid down for reasons of convenience and uniformity but do not affect the validity of the international will.

"Lastly, even when the international will is declared invalid because one of the essential provisions contained in Articles 2 to 5 has not been observed, it is not necessarily deprived of all effect.   Paragraph 2 of Article 1 specifies that it may still be valid as a will of another kind, if it conforms with the requirements of the applicable national law. Thus, for example, a will written, dated and signed by the testator but handed over to an authorised person in the absence of witnesses or without the signature of the witnesses and the authorised person could quite easily be considered a valid holograph will.   Similarly, an international will produced in the presence of a person who is not duly authorised might be valid as a will witnessed in accordance with Common law rules.

"However, in these circumstances, one could no longer speak of an international will and the validity of the document would have to be assessed on the basis of the rules of internal law or of private international law.

"A joint will cannot be drawn up in the form of an international will. This is the meaning of Article 2 of the Uniform Law which does not give an opinion as to whether this prohibition on joint wills, which exists in many legal systems, is connected with its form or its substance.

"A will made in this international form by several people together in the same document would, therefore, be invalid as an international will but could possibly be valid as another kind of will, in accordance with Article 1, paragraph 2 of the Uniform Law.

"The terminology used in Article 2 is in harmony with that used in Article 4 of The Hague Convention on the Conflicts of Laws Relating to the Form of Testamentary Dispositions."

Section 3. [2–1003.] [International Will; Requirements.]

(a) The will shall be made in writing. It need not be written by the testator himself. It may be written in any language, by hand or by any other means.

(b) The testator shall declare in the presence of two witnesses and of a person authorized to act in connection with international wills that the document is his will and that he knows the contents thereof. The testator need not inform the witnesses, or the authorized person, of the contents of the will.

(c) In the presence of the witnesses, and of the authorized person, the testator shall sign the will or, if he has previously signed it, shall acknowledge his signature.

(d) When the testator is unable to sign, the absence of his signature does not affect the validity of the international will if the testator indicates the reason for his inability to sign and the authorized person makes note thereof on the will. In these cases, it is permissible for any other person present, including the authorized person or one of the witnesses, at the direction of the testator to sign the testator's name for him, if the authorized person makes note of this also on the will, but it is not required that any person sign the testator's name for him.

(e) The witnesses and the authorized person shall there and then attest the will by signing in the presence of the testator.

COMMENT

The five subsections of this section correspond in content to Articles 3 through 5 of the Annex to the 1973 Convention. Article 1, section 1 makes it clear that compliance with all requirements listed in Articles 3 through 5 is necessary in order to achieve an international will. As re-organized for enactment in the United States, all mandatory requirements have been grouped in this section. Except for subsection (d), each of the sentences in the subsections corresponds exactly with a sentence in the Annex. Subsection (d), derived from Article 5, section 2 of the Annex, was re-worded for the sake of clarity.

Mr. Plantard's comments on the requirements are as follows:

"Paragraph 1 of Article 3 lays down an essential condition for a will's validity as an international will: it must be made in writing.

"The Uniform Law does not explain what is meant by 'writing'. This is a word of everyday language which, in the opinion of the Law's authors, does not call for any definition but which covers any form of expression made by signs on a durable substance.

"Paragraphs 2 and 3 show the very liberal approach of the draft.

"Under paragraph 2, the will does not necessarily have to be written by the testator himself. This provision marks a moving away from the holograph will toward the other types of will: the public will or the mystic will and especially the Common law will. The latter, which is often very long, is only in exceptional cases written in the hand of the testator, who is virtually obliged to use a lawyer, in order to use the technical formulae necessary to give effect to his wishes. This is all the more so as wills frequently involve inter vivos family arrangements, and fiscal considerations play a very important part in this matter.

"This provision also allows for the will of illiterate persons, or persons who, for some other reason, cannot write themselves, for example paralysed or blind persons.

"According to paragraph 3 a will may be written in any language. This provision is in contrast with the rules accepted in various countries as regards public wills. It will be noted that the Uniform Law does not even require the will to be written in a language known by the testator. The latter is, therefore, quite free to choose according to whichever suits him best: it is to be expected that he will usually choose his own language but, if he thinks it is better, he will sometimes also choose the language of the place where the will is drawn up or that of the place where the will is mainly to be carried out. The important point is that he have full knowledge of the contents of his will, as is guaranteed by Articles 4 and 10.

"Lastly, a will may be written by hand or by any other method. This provision is the corollary of paragraph 2. What is mainly had in mind is a typewriter, especially in the case of a will drawn up by a lawyer advising the testator.

"The liberal nature of the principles set out in Article 3 calls for certain guarantees on the other hand. These are provided by the presence of three persons, already referred to in the context of Articles III and V of the Convention, that is to say, the authorised person and the two witnesses. It is evident that these three persons must all be simultaneously present with the testator during the carrying out of the formalities laid down in Articles 4 and 5.

"Paragraph 1 of Article 4 requires, first of all, that the testator declare, in the presence of these persons, that the document produced by him is his will and that he knows the contents thereof. The word 'declares' covers any unequivocal expression of intention, by way of words as well as by gestures or signs, as, for example, in the case of a testator who is dumb. This declaration must be made on pain of the international will being invalid. This is justified by the fact that the will produced by the testator might have been materially drawn up by a person other than the testator and even, in theory, in a language which is not his own.

"Paragraph 2 of the article specifies that this declaration is sufficient: the testator does not need to 'inform' the witnesses or the authorised person 'of the contents of the will'. This rule makes the international will differ from the public will and brings it closer to the other types of will: the holograph will and especially the mystic will and the Common law will.

"The testator can, of course, always ask for the will to be read, a precaution which can be particularly useful if the testator is unable to read himself. The paragraph under consideration does not in any way prohibit this; it only aims at ensuring respect for secrecy, if the testator should so wish. The international will can therefore be a secret will without being a closed will.

"The declaration made by the testator under Article 4 is not sufficient: under Article 5, paragraph 1, he must also sign his will. However, the authors of the Uniform Law presumed that, in certain cases, the testator might already have signed the document forming his will before producing it. To require a second signature would be evidence of an exaggerated formalism and a will containing two signatures by the testator would be rather strange. That is why the same paragraph provides that, when he has already signed the will, the testator can merely acknowledge it. This acknowledgement is completely informal and is normally done by a simple declaration in the presence of the authorised person and witnesses.

"The Uniform Law does not explain what is meant by 'signature'. This is once more a word drawn from everyday language, the meaning of which is usually the same in the various legal systems. The presence of the authorised person, who will necessarily be a practising lawyer will certainly guarantee that there is a genuine signature correctly affixed.

"Paragraph 2 was designed to give persons incapable of signing the possibility of making an international will. All they have to do is indicate their incapacity and the reason therefore to the authorised person. The authorised person must then note this declaration on the will which will then be valid, even though it has not been signed by the testator. Indication of the reason for incapacity is an additional guarantee as it can be checked. The certificate drawn up by the authorised person in the form prescribed in Article 10 again reproduces this declaration.

"The authors of the Uniform Law were also conscious of the fact that in some legal systems—for example, English law—persons who are incapable of signing can name someone to sign in their place. Although this procedure is completely unknown to other systems in which a signature is exclusively personal, it was accepted that the testator can ask another person to sign in his name, if this is permitted under the law from which the authorised person derives his authority. This amounts to nothing more than giving satisfaction to the practice of certain legal systems, as the authorised person must, in any case, indicate on the will that the testator declared that he could not sign, and give the reason therefor. This indication is sufficient to make the will valid. There will, therefore simply be a signature affixed by a third person instead of that of the testator. Although there is nothing stipulating this in the Uniform Law, one can expect the authorised person to explain the source of this signature on the document, all the more so as the signature of this substitute for the testator must also appear on the other pages of the will, by virtue of Article 6.

"This method over which there were some differences of opinion at the Diplomatic Conference, should not however interfere in any way with the legal systems which do not admit a signature in the name of someone else. Besides, its use is limited to the legal systems which admit it already and it is now implicitly accepted by the others when they recognise the validity of a foreign document drawn up according to this method. However, this situation can be expected to arise but rarely, as an international will made by a person who is incapable of signing it will certainly be a rare event.

"Lastly, Article 5 requires that the witnesses and authorised person also sign the will there and then in the presence of the testator. By using the words 'attest the will by signing', when only the word 'sign' had been used when referring to the testator, the authors of the Uniform Law intended to make a distinction between the person acknowledging the contents of a document and those who have only to affix their signature in order to certify their participation and presence.

"In conclusion, the international will will normally contain four signatures: that of the testator, that of the authorised person and those of the two witnesses. The signature of the testator might be missing: in this case, the will must contain a note made by the authorised person indicating that the testator was incapable of signing, adding his reason. All these signatures and notes must be made on pain of invalidity. Finally, if the signature of the testator is missing, the will could contain the signature of a person designated by the testator to sign in his name, in addition to the above-mentioned note made by the authorised person."

Section 4. [2–1004.] [International Will; Other Points of Form.]

(a) The signatures shall be placed at the end of the will. If the will consists of several sheets, each sheet will be signed by the testator or, if he is unable to sign, by the person signing on his behalf or, if there is no such person, by the authorized person. In addition, each sheet shall be numbered.

(b) The date of the will shall be the date of its signature by the authorized person. That date shall be noted at the end of the will by the authorized person.

(c) The authorized person shall ask the testator whether he wishes to make a declaration concerning the safekeeping of his will. If so and at the express request of the testator the place where he intends to have his will kept shall be mentioned in the certificate provided for in Section 5.

(d) A will executed in compliance with Section 3 shall not be invalid merely because it does not comply with this section.

COMMENT

Mr. Plantard's commentary about Articles 6, 7 and 8 of the Annex [*supra*] relate to subsections (a), (b) and (c) respectively of this section. Subsections (a) and (b) are identical to Articles 6 and 7; subsection (c) is the same as Article 8 of the Annex except that the prefatory language "In the absence of any mandatory rule pertaining to the safekeeping of the will . . . " has been deleted because it is inappropriate for inclusion in a local statute designed for enactment by a state that has had no tradition or familiarity with mandatory rules regarding the safekeeping of the wills. Subsection (d) embodies the sense of Article 1, section 1 of the Annex which states that compliance with Articles 2 to 5 is necessary and so indicates that compliance with the remaining articles prescribing formal steps is not necessary.

Mr. Plantard's commentary is as follows:

"The provisions of Article 6 and those of the following articles are not imposed on pain of invalidity. They are nevertheless compulsory legal provisions which can involve sanctions, for example, the professional, civil and even criminal liability of the authorised person, according to the provisions of the law from which he derives his authority.

"The first paragraph, to guarantee a uniform presentation for international wills, simply indicates that signatures shall be placed at the end of international wills, that is, at the end of the text.

"Paragraph 2 provides for the frequent case in which the will consists of several sheets. Each sheet has to be signed by the testator, to guarantee its authenticity and to avoid substitutions. The use of the word 'signed' seems to imply that the signature must be in the same form as that at the end of the will. However, in the legal systems which merely require that the individual sheets be paraphed, usually by means of initials, this would certainly have the same value as signature, as a signature itself could simply consist of initials.

"The need for a signature on each sheet, for the purpose of authentifying each such sheet, led to the introduction of a special system for the case when the testator is incapable of signing. In this case it will generally be the authorised person who will sign each sheet in his place, unless, in accordance with Article 5, paragraph 2, the testator has designated another person to sign in his name. In this case, it will of course be this person who will sign each sheet.

"Lastly, it is prescribed that the sheets shall be numbered. Although no further details are given on this subject, it will in practice be up to the authorised person to check if they have already been numbered and, if not, to number them or ask the testator to do so.

"The aim of this provision is obviously to guarantee the orderliness of the document and to avoid losses, subtractions or substitutions.

"The date is an essential element of the will and its importance is quite clear in the case of successive wills. Paragraph 1 of Article 7 indicates that the date of the will in the case of an international will is the date on which it was signed by the authorised person, this being the last of the formalities prescribed by the Uniform Law on pain of invalidity (Article 5, paragraph 3). It is therefore, from the moment of this signature that the international will is valid.

"Paragraph 2 stipulates that the date shall be noted at the end of the will by the authorised person. Although this is compulsory for the authorised person, this formality is not sanctioned by the invalidity of the will which, as is the case in many legal systems such as English,

German and Austrian law, remains fully valid even if it is not dated or is wrongly dated. The date will then have to be proved by some other means. It can happen that the will has two dates, that of its drawing up and the date on which it was signed by the authorised person as a result of which it became an international will. Evidently only this last date is to be taken into consideration.

"During the preparatory work it had been intended to organise the safekeeping of the international will and to entrust its care to the authorised person. This plan caused serious difficulties both for the countries which do not have the notary as he is known in Civil law systems and for the countries in which wills must be deposited with a public authority, as is the case, for example, in the Federal Republic of Germany, where wills must be deposited with a court.

"The authors of the Uniform Law therefore abandoned the idea of introducing a unified system for the safekeeping of international wills. However, where a legal system already has rules on this subject, these rules of course also apply to the international will as well as to other types of will. Finally, the Washington Conference adopted, at the same time as the Convention, a resolution recommending States, in particular, to organise a system facilitating the safekeeping of international wills (see the commentary on this resolution, at the end of this Report). It should lastly be underlined that States desiring to give testators an additional guarantee as regards the international will will organise its safekeeping by providing, for exam-

ple, that it shall be deposited with the authorised person or with a public officer. Complementary legislation of this kind could be admitted within the framework of paragraph 3 of Article 1 of the Convention, as was mentioned in our commentary on that article.

"These considerations explain why Article 8 starts by stipulating that it only applies 'in the absence of any mandatory rule pertaining to the safekeeping of the will'. If there happens to be such a rule in the national law from which the authorised person derives his authority this rule shall govern the safekeeping of the will. If there is no such rule, Article 8 requires the authorised person to ask the testator whether he wishes to make a declaration in this regard. In this way, the authors of the Uniform Law sought to reconcile the advantage of exact information so as to facilitate the discovery of the will after the death of the testator, on the one hand, and respect for the secrecy which the testator may want as regards the place where his will is kept, on the other hand. The testator is therefore quite free to make or not to make a declaration in this regard, but his attention is nevertheless drawn to the possibility left open to him, and particular to the opportunity he has, if he expressly asks for it, to have the details he thinks appropriate in this regard mentioned on the certificate provided for in Article 9. It will thus be easier to find the will again at the proper time, by means of the certificate made out in three copies, one of which remains in the hands of the authorised person."

Section 5. [2–1005.] [International Will; Certificate.]

The authorized person shall attach to the will a certificate to be signed by him establishing that the requirements of this Act [Part] for valid execution of an international will have been complied with. The authorized person shall keep a copy of the certificate and deliver another to the testator. The certificate shall be substantially in the following form:

CERTIFICATE

(Convention of October 26, 1973)

1. I, _____ (name, address and capacity), a person authorized to act in connection with international wills
2. Certify that on _____ (date) at _____ (place)
3. (testator _____
   (name, address, date and place of birth) in my presence and that of the witnesses
4. (a) _____ (name, address, date and place of birth)
   (b) _____ (name, address, date and place of birth)
   has declared that the attached document is his will and that he knows the contents thereof.
5. I furthermore certify that:
6. (a) in my presence and in that of the witnesses
   (1) the testator has signed the will or has acknowledged his signature previously affixed.
   * following a declaration of the testator stating that he
   (2) was unable to sign his will for the following reason _____, I have mentioned this declaration on the will
   * and the signature has been affixed by _____ (name and address)
7. (b) the witnesses and I have signed the will;
8. * (c) each page of the will has been signed by _____ and numbered;
9. (d) I have satisfied myself as to the identity of the testator and of the witnesses as designated above;
10. (e) the witnesses met the conditions requisite to act as such according to the law under which I am acting;
11. * (f) the testator has requested me to include the following statement concerning the safekeeping of his will:
12. PLACE OF EXECUTION
13. DATE
14. SIGNATURE and, if necessary, SEAL

* to be completed if appropriate

COMMENT

This section embodies the content of Articles 9, 10 and 11 of the Annex with only minor, clarifying changes. Those familiar with the pre-proved will authorized by Uniform Probate Code § 2–504 should be comfortable with sections 5 and 6 of this act. Indeed, inclusion of these provisions in the Annex was the result of a concession by those familiar with civil law approaches to problems of execution and proof of wills, to the English speaking countries where will ceremonies are divided between those occurring as testator acts, and those occurring later when the will is probated. Further, since English and Canadian practices reduce post-mortem probate procedures down to little more than the presentation of the will to an appropriate registry and so, approach civil law customs, the concession was largely to accommodate American states where post-mortem probate procedures are very involved. Thus, the primary purpose of the certificate, which provides conclusive proof of the formal validity of the will, is to put wills executed before a civil law notary and wills executed in the American tradition on a par; with the certificate, both are good without question insofar as formal requirements are concerned.

It should be noted that Article III of the Convention binds countries becoming parties to recognize the capacity of an authorized person to act in relation to an international will, as conferred by the law of another country that is a party. This means that an international will coming into one of our states that has enacted the uniform law will be entirely good under local law, and that the certificate from abroad will provide conclusive proof of its validity.

May an international will be contested? The answer is clearly affirmative as to contests based on lack of capacity, fraud, undue influence, revocation or ineffectiveness based on the contents of the will or substantive restraints on testamentary power. Contests based on failure to follow mandatory requirements of execution are not precluded because the next section provides

that the certificate is conclusive only "in the absence of evidence to the contrary". However, the Convention becomes relevant when one asks whether a probate court may require additional proof of the genuineness of signatures by testators and witnesses. It provides:

Article VI 1. The signature of the testator, of the authorized person, and of the witnesses to an international will, whether on the will or on the certificate, shall be exempt from any legalization or like formality.

2. Nonetheless, the competent authorities of any Contracting Party may, if necessary, satisfy themselves as to the authenticity of the signature of the authorized person. Presumably, the prohibition against legalization would not preclude additional proof of genuineness if evidence tending to show forgery is introduced, but without contrary proof, the certificate proves the will.

Mr. Plantard's commentary on the articles of the Annex that are pertinent to section 5, are as follows:

"This provision specifies that the authorised person must attach to the international will a certificate drawn up in accordance with the form set out in Article 10, establishing that the Uniform Law's provisions have been complied with. The term 'joint au testament' means that the certificate must be added to the will, that is, fixed thereto. The English text which uses the work 'attach' is perfectly clear on this point. Furthermore, it results from Article 11 that the certificate must be made out in three copies. This document, the contents of which are detailed in Article 10, is proof that the formalities required for the validity of the international will have been complied with. It also reveals the identity of the persons who participated in drawing up the document and may, in addition, contain a declaration by the testator as to the place where he intends his will to be kept. It should be stressed that the certificate is drawn up under the entire responsibility of the authorised person who is the only person to sign it.

"Article 10 sets out the form for the certificate. The authorised person must abide by it, in accordance with the provisions of Article 10 itself, laying down this or a substantially similar form. This last phrase could not be taken as authorising him to depart from this form: it only serves to allow for small changes of detail which might be useful in the interests of improving its comprehensibility or presentation, for example, the omission of the particulars marked with an asterisk indicating that they are to be completed where appropriate when in fact they do not need to be completed and thus become useless.

"Including the form of a certificate in one of the articles of a Uniform Law is unusual. Normally these appear in the annexes to Conventions. However, in this way, the authors of the Uniform Law underlined the importance of the certificate and its contents. Moreover, the Uniform Law already forms the Annex to the Convention itself.

"The 14 particulars indicated on the certificate are numbered. These numbers must be reproduced on each certificate, so as to facilitate its reading, especially when the reader speaks a foreign language, as they will help him to find the relevant details more easily: the name of the authorised person and the testator, addresses, etc.

"The certificate contains all the elements necessary for the identification of the authorised person, testator and witnesses. It expressly mentions all the formalities which have to be carried out in accordance with the provisions of the Uniform Law. Furthermore, the certificate contains all the information required for the will's registration according to the system introduced by the Council of Europe Convention on the Establishment of a Scheme of Registration of Wills, signed at Basle on 16 May 1972.

"The authorised person must keep a copy of the certificate and deliver one to the testator. Seeing that another copy has to be attached to the will in accordance with Article 9, it may be deduced that the authorised person must make out altogether three copies of the certificate. These cannot be simple copies but have to be three signed originals. This provision is useful for a number of reasons. The fact that the testator keeps a copy of the certificate is a useful reminder for him, especially when his will is being kept by the authorised person or deposited with someone designated by national law. Moreover, discovery of the certificate among the testators' papers will inform his heirs of the existence of a will and will enable them to find it more easily. The fact that the authorised person keeps a copy of the certificate enables him to inform the heirs as well, if necessary. Lastly, the fact that there are several copies of the certificate is a guarantee against changes being made to one of them and even, to a certain extent, against certain changes to the will itself, for example as regards its date."

Section 6. [2–1006.] [International Will; Effect of Certificate.]

In the absence of evidence to the contrary, the certificate of the authorized person shall be conclusive of the formal validity of the instrument as a will under this Act. [Part.] The absence or irregularity of a certificate shall not affect the formal validity of a will under this Act. [Part.]

COMMENT

This section, which corresponds to Articles 11 and 12 of the Annex, must be read with the definition of "authorized person" in section 1, and Articles III and IV of the 1973 Convention which will become binding on all states if and when the United States joins that treaty. Articles III and IV of the Convention provide:

Article III The capacity of the authorized person to act in connection with an international will, if conferred in accordance with the law of a Contracting Party, shall be recognized in the territory of the other Contracting Parties.

Article IV The effectiveness of the certificate provided for in Article 10 of the Annex shall be recognized in the territories of all Contracting Parties.

In effect, the state enacting this law will be recognizing certificates by authorized persons designated, not only by this state, but by the United States and other parties to the 1973 Convention. Once the identity of one making a certificate on an international will is established, the will may be proved without more, assuming the presence of the recommended form of certificate. Article IX (3) of the 1973 Convention constitutes the United States as the Depositary under the Convention, and Article II obligates each country joining the Convention to notify the Depositary Government of the persons designated by its law as authorized to act in connection with international wills. Hence, persons interested in local probate of an international will from another country will be enabled to determine from the Department of State whether the official making the cer-

tificate in which they are interested had the requisite authority.

In this connection, it should be noted that under Article II of the Convention, each contracting country may designate its diplomatic or consular representatives abroad as authorized persons insofar as the local law does not prohibit it. Since the Uniform Act will be the law locally, and since it does not prohibit persons designated by foreign states that are parties to the Convention from acting locally in respect to international wills, there should be a considerable amount of latitude in selecting authorized persons to assist with wills and a correlative reduction in the chances of local nonrecognition of an authorized person from abroad. Also, it should be noted that the Uniform Act does not restrict the persons which it constitutes as authorized persons in relation to the places where they can so function. This supports the view that local law as embodied in this statute should not be construed as restrictive in relation to local activities concerning international wills of foreign diplomatic and consular representatives who are resident here.

The certificate requires the authorized person to state that the witnesses had the requisite capacity. If the authorized person derives his authority from the law of a state other than that where he is acting, it would be advisable to have the certificate identify the applicable law.

The Uniform Act is silent in regard to methods of meeting local probate requirements contemplating deposit of the original will with the court. Section 3–409 of the Uniform Probate Code, or its counterpart in a state that has not adopted the uniform law on the point, becomes pertinent. The last sentence of UPC 3–409 provides:

A will from a place which does not provide for probate of a will after death, may be proved for probate in this state by a duly authenticated certificate of its legal custodian that the copy introduced is a true copy and that the will has become effective under the law of the other place.

One final matter warrants mention. Implicit in local proof of an instrument by means of authentication provided by a foreign official, is the problem of proving the authority of the official. The traditional, exceedingly formalistic, method of accomplishing this has been through what has been known as "legalization", a process that involves a number of certificates. The capacity of the official who authenticates the signature of the party to the document, if derived from his status as a county official, is proved by the certificate of a high county official. In turn, the county official's status is proved by the certificate of the area's secretary of state, whose status is established by another and so on until, ultimately, the Department of State certifies to the identity of the highest state official in a format that will be persuasive to the receiving country's foreign relations representative.

Article VI of the 1973 Convention forbids legalization of the signature of testators and witnesses. It provides:

1. The signature of the testator, of the authorized person, and of the witnesses to an international will, whether on the will or on the certificate, shall be exempt from any legalization or like formality.

2. Nonetheless, the competent authorities of any Contracting Party may, if necessary, satisfy themselves as to the authenticity of the signature of the authorized person.

Thus, it would appear that if the United States, as contracting party, satisfies itself that the signature of a foreign authorized person is authentic, and so indicates to those interested in local probate of the document, the local court, though presumably able to receive and to act upon evidence to the contrary, cannot reject an international will for lack of proof. This is not to say, of course, that the authenticity of the signature of the foreign authorized person must be shown through the aid of the State Department; plainly, the point may be implied from the face of the document unless and until challenged.

Mr. Plantard's commentary on this portion of the uniform law is as follows:

"Article 12 states that the certificate is conclusive of the formal validity of the international will. It is therefore a kind of proof supplied in advance.

"This provision is only really understandable in those legal systems, like the United States, where a will can only take effect after it has been subjected to a preliminary procedure of verification ('Probate') designed to check on its validity. The mere presentation of the certificate should suffice to satisfy the requirements of this procedure.

"However, the certificate is not always irrefutable as proof, as is indicated by the words 'in the absence of evidence to the contrary'. If it is challenged, then the ensuing litigation will be solved in accordance with the legal procedure applicable in the Contracting State where the will and certificate are presented.

"The principle set out in Article 13 is already implied by Article 1, as only the provisions of Articles 2 to 5 are prescribed on pain of invalidity. Besides, it is perfectly logical that the absence of or irregularities in a certificate should not affect the formal validity of the will, as the certificate is a document serving essentially for purposes of proof drawn up by the authorized person, without the testator taking any part either in drawing it up or in checking it. This provision is in perfect harmony with Article 12 which by the terms 'in the absence of evidence to the contrary' means that one can challenge what is stated in the certificate.

"In consideration of the fact that the authorized person will be a practising lawyer officially designated by each Contracting State, it is difficult to imagine him omitting or neglecting to draw up the certificate provided for by the national law to which he is subject. Besides, he would lay himself open to an action based on his professional and civil liability. He could even expose himself to sanctions laid down by his national law.

"However, the international will subsists, even if, by some quirk, the certificate which is a means of proof but not necessarily the only one, should be missing, be incomplete or contain particulars which are manifestly erroneous. In these undoubtedly very rare circumstances, proof that the formalities prescribed on pain of invalidity have been carried out will have to be produced in accordance with the legal procedures applicable in each State which has adopted the Uniform Law."

Section 7. [2–1007.] [International Will; Revocation.]

The international will shall be subject to the ordinary rules of revocation of wills.

COMMENT

Mr. Plantard's commentary on this portion of the uniform law is as follows:

"The authors of the Uniform Law did not intend to deal with the subject of the revocation of wills. There is indeed no reason why the international will should be submitted to a regime different from that of other kinds of wills. Article 14 therefore merely gives expression to this idea. Whether or not there has been revocation—for example, by a subsequent will—is to be assessed in accordance with the law of each State which has adopted the Uniform Law, by virtue of Article 14. Besides, this is a question mainly concerning rules of substance which would thus overstep the scope of the Uniform Law."

Section 8. [2–1008.] [Source and Construction.]

Sections 1 [2–1001] through 7 [2–1007] derive from Annex to Convention of October 26, 1973, Providing a Uniform Law on the Form of an International Will. In interpreting and applying this Act [Part], regard shall be had to its international origin and to the need for uniformity in its interpretation.

COMMENT

Mr. Plantard's commentary on this portion of the uniform law is as follows:

"This Article contains a provision which is to be found in a similar form in several conventions or draft Uniform Laws. It seeks to avoid practising lawyers interpreting the Uniform Law solely in terms of the principles of their respective internal law, as this would prejudice the international unification being sought after. It requests judges to take the international character of the Uniform Law into consideration and to work towards elaborating a sort of common caselaw, taking account of the foreign legal systems which provided the foundation for the Uniform Law and the decisions handed down on the same text by the courts of other countries. The effort toward unification must not be limited to just bringing about the Law's adoption, but should be carried on into the process of putting it into operation."

Section 9. [2-1009.] [Persons Authorized to Act in Relation to International Will; Eligibility; Recognition by Authorizing Agency.]

Individuals who have been admitted to practice law before the courts of this state and who are in good standing as active law practitioners in this state, are hereby declared to be authorized persons in relation to international wills.

COMMENT

The subject of who should be designated to be authorized persons under the Uniform Law is discussed under the heading "Description of the Proposal" in the Prefatory Note.

The first draft of the Uniform Law presented to the National Conference at its 1975 meeting in Quebec City included provision for a special new licensing procedure through which others than attorneys might become qualified. The ensuing discussion resulted in rejection of this approach in favor of the simpler approach of section 9. Among other difficulties with the special licensee approach, representatives of the State Department expressed concern about the attendant burden on the U.S. as Depositary Government, of receiving, keeping up to date, and interpreting to foreign governments the results of fifty different state licensing systems.

[Section 10. [2-1010.] [International Will Information Registration.]

The [Secretary of State] shall establish a registry system by which authorized persons may register in a central information center, information regarding the execution of international wills, keeping that information in strictest confidence until the death of the maker and then making it available to any person desiring information about any will who presents a death certificate or other satisfactory evidence of the testator's death to the center. Information that may be received, preserved in confidence until death, and reported as indicated is limited to the name, social-security or any other individual-identifying number established by law, address, and date and place of birth of the testator, and the intended place of deposit or safekeeping of the instrument pending the death of the maker. The [Secretary of State], at the request of the authorized person, may cause the information it receives about execution of any international will to be transmitted to the registry system of another jurisdiction as identified by the testator, if that other system adheres to rules protecting the confidentiality of the information similar to those established in this state.]

COMMENT

The relevance of this optional, bracketed section to the other sections constituting the uniform law concerning international wills is explained in the Prefatory Note. Also, Mr. Plantard's observations regarding the Resolution attached to the 1973 Convention are pertinent. He writes:

"The Resolution adopted by the Washington Conference and annexed to its Final Act encourages States which adopt the Uniform Law to make additional provisions for the registering and safekeeping of the international will. The authors of the Uniform Law considered that it was not possible to lay down uniform rules on this subject on account of the differences in tradition and outlook, but several times, both during the preparatory work and during the final diplomatic phase, they underlined the importance of States making such provisions.

"The Resolution recommends organising a system enabling . . . 'the safekeeping, search and discovery of an international will as well as the accompanying certificate' . . .

"Indeed lawyers know that many wills are never carried out because the very existence of the will itself remains unknown or because the will is never found or is never pro-

duced. It would be quite possible to organise a register or index which would enable one to know after the death of a person whether he had drawn up a will. Some countries have already done something in this field, for example, Quebec, Spain, the Federal Republic of Germany, where this service is connected with the Registry of Births, Marriages and Deaths. Such a system could perfectly well be fashioned so as to ensure respect for the legitimate wish of testators to keep the very existence of their will secret.

"The Washington Conference also underlined that there is already an International Convention on this subject, namely the Council of Europe Convention on the Establishment of a Scheme of Registration of Wills, concluded at Basle on 16 May 1972, to which States which are not members of the Council of Europe may accede.

"In this Convention the Contracting States simply undertake to create an internal system for registering wills. The Convention stipulates the categories of will which should be registered, in terms which include the international will. Apart from national bodies in charge of registration, the Convention also provides for the designation by each Contracting State of a national body which must remain in contact with the national bodies of other States and communicate registrations and any information asked for. The Convention specifies that registration must remain secret during the life of the testator. This system, which will come into force between a number of European States in the near future, interested the authors of the Convention, even if they do not accede to it. The last paragraph of the Resolution follows the pattern of the Basle Convention by recommending, in the interests of facilitating an international exchange of information on this matter, the designation in each State of authorities or services to handle such exchanges.

"As for the organisation of the safekeeping of international wills, the resolution merely underlies the importance of this, without making any specific suggestions in this regard. This problem has already been discussed in connection with Article 8 of the Uniform Law.

"The Council of Europe Convention on the Establishment of a Scheme of Registration of Wills of May 16, 1972 and related documents were available to the reporter and provided the guidelines for section 10 of this Act."

ARTICLE III

PROBATE OF WILLS AND ADMINISTRATION

PART 1

GENERAL PROVISIONS

PART 2

VENUE FOR PROBATE AND ADMINISTRATION; PRIORITY TO ADMINISTER; DEMAND FOR NOTICE

PART 3

INFORMAL PROBATE AND APPOINTMENT PROCEEDINGS; SUCCESSION WITHOUT ADMINISTRATION

PART 11

COMPROMISE OF CONTROVERSIES

PART 12

COLLECTION OF PERSONAL PROPERTY BY AFFIDAVIT AND SUMMARY ADMINISTRATION PROCEDURE FOR SMALL ESTATES

GENERAL COMMENT

The provisions of this Article describe the Flexible System of Administration of Decedents' Estates. Designed to be applicable to both intestate and testate estates and to provide persons interested in decedents' estates with as little or as much by way of procedural and adjudicative safeguards as may be suitable under varying circumstances, this system is the heart of the Uniform Probate Code.

The organization and detail of the system here described may be expressed in varying ways and some states may see fit to reframe parts of this Article to better accommodate local institutions. Variations in language from state to state can be tolerated without loss of the essential purposes of procedural uniformity and flexibility, *if* the following essential characteristics are carefully protected in the redrafting process:

(1) Post-mortem probate of a will must occur to make a will effective and appointment of a personal representative by a public official after the decedent's death is required in order to create the duties and powers attending the office of personal representative. Neither are compelled, however, but are left to be obtained by persons having an interest in the consequence of probate or appointment. Estates descend at death to successors identified by any probated will, or to heirs if no will is probated, subject to rights which may be implemented through administration.

(2) Two methods of securing probate of wills which include a non-adjudicative determination

227

(informal probate) on the one hand, and a judicial determination after notice to all interested persons (formal probate) on the other, are provided.

(3) Two methods of securing appointment of a personal representative which include appointment without notice and without final adjudication of matters relevant to priority for appointment (informal appointment), on the one hand, and appointment by judicial order after notice to interested persons (formal appointment) on the other, are provided.

(4) A five day waiting period from death preventing informal probate or informal appointment of any but a special administrator is required.

(5) Probate of a will by informal or formal proceedings or an adjudication of intestacy may occur without any attendant requirement of appointment of a personal representative.

(6) One judicial, in rem, proceeding encompassing formal probate of any wills (or a determination after notice that the decedent left no will), appointment of a personal representative and complete settlement of an estate under continuing supervision of the Court (supervised administration) is provided for testators and persons interested in a decedent's estate, whether testate or intestate, who desire to use it.

(7) Unless supervised administration is sought and ordered, persons interested in estates (including personal representatives, whether appointed informally or after notice) may use an "in and out" relationship to the Court so that any question or assumption relating to the estate, including the status of an estate as testate or intestate, matters relating to one or more claims, disputed titles, accounts of personal representa-

tives, and distribution, may be resolved or established by adjudication after notice without necessarily subjecting the estate to the necessity of judicial orders in regard to other or further questions or assumptions.

(8) The status of a decedent in regard to whether he left a valid will or died intestate must be resolved by adjudication after notice in proceedings commenced within three years after his death. If not so resolved, any will probated informally becomes final, and if there is no such probate, the status of the decedent as intestate is finally determined, by a statute of limitations which bars probate and appointment unless requested within three years after death.

(9) Personal representatives appointed informally or after notice, and whether supervised or not, have statutory powers enabling them to collect, protect, sell, distribute and otherwise handle all steps in administration without further order of the Court, except that supervised personal representatives may be subjected to special restrictions on power as endorsed on their letters.

(10) Purchasers from personal representatives and from distributees of personal representatives are protected so that adjudications regarding the testacy status of a decedent or any other question going to the propriety of a sale are not required in order to protect purchasers.

(11) Provisions protecting a personal representative who distributes without adjudication are included to make nonadjudicated settlements feasible.

(12) Statutes of limitation bar creditors of the decedent who fail to present claims within four months after legal advertising of the administration and unsecured

claims not previously barred by non-claim statutes are barred after three years from the decedent's death.

Overall, the system accepts the premise that the Court's role in regard to probate and administration, and its relationship to personal representatives who derive their power from public appointment, is wholly passive until some interested person invokes its power to secure resolution of a matter. The state, through the Court, should provide remedies which are suitable and efficient to protect any and all rights regarding succession, but should refrain from intruding into family affairs unless relief is requested, and limit its relief to that sought.

PART 1

GENERAL PROVISIONS

Section 3-101. [Devolution of Estate at Death; Restrictions.]

The power of a person to leave property by will, and the rights of creditors, devisees, and heirs to his property are subject to the restrictions and limitations contained in this Code to facilitate the prompt settlement of estates. Upon the death of a person, his real and personal property devolves to the persons to whom it is devised by his last will or to those indicated as substitutes for them in cases involving lapse, renunciation, or other circumstances affecting the devolution of testate estate, or in the absence of testamentary disposition, to his heirs, or to those indicated as substitutes for them in cases involving renunciation or other circumstances affecting devolution of intestate estates, subject to homestead allowance, exempt property and family allowance, to rights of creditors, elective share of the surviving spouse, and to administration.

ALTERNATIVE SECTION FOR COMMUNITY PROPERTY STATES

[Section 3-101A. [Devolution of Estate at Death; Restrictions.]

The power of a person to leave property by will, and the rights of creditors, devisees, and heirs to his property are subject to the restrictions and limitations contained in this Code to facilitate the prompt settlement of estates. Upon the death of a person, his separate property devolves to the persons to whom it is devised by his last will, or to those indicated as substitutes for them in cases involving lapse, renunciation or other circumstances affecting the devolution of testate estates, or in the absence of testamentary disposition to his heirs, or to those indicated as substitutes for them in cases involving renunciation or other circumstances affecting the devolution of intestate estates, and upon the death of a husband or wife, the decedent's share of their community property devolves to the persons to whom it is devised by his last will, or in the absence of testamentary disposition, to his heirs, but all of their community property which is under the management and control of the decedent is subject to his debts and administration, and that portion of their community property which is not under the management and control of the decedent but which is necessary to carry out the provisions of his will is subject to administration; but the devolu-

230

tion of all the above described property is subject to rights to homestead allowance, exempt property and family allowances, to renunciation, to rights of creditors, [elective share of the surviving spouse] and to administration.]

COMMENT

In its present form, this section will not fit existing concepts concerning community property in all states recognizing community ownership. States differ in respect to how much testamentary power a decedent has over the community. Also, some changes of language may be necessary to reflect differing views concerning what estate is subject to "separate" and "community" debts. The reference to certain family rights is not intended to suggest that such rights relate to the survivor's interest in any community property. Rather, the assumption is that such rights relate only to property passing from the decedent at his death; e.g., his half of community property and his separate property.

Section 3–102. [Necessity of Order of Probate For Will.]

Except as provided in Section 3–1201, to be effective to prove the transfer of any property or to nominate an executor, a will must be declared to be valid by an order of informal probate by the Registrar, or an adjudication of probate by the Court, except that a duly executed and unrevoked will which has not been probated may be admitted as evidence of a devise if (1) no Court proceeding concerning the succession or administration of the estate has occurred, and (2) either the devisee or his successors and assigns possessed the property devised in accordance with the provisions of the will, or the property devised was not possessed or claimed by anyone by virtue of the decedent's title during the time period for testacy proceedings.

COMMENT

The basic idea of this section follows Section 85 of the Model Probate Code. The exception referring to Section 3–1201 relates to affidavit procedures which are authorized for collection of estates worth less than $5,000.

Section 3–107 and various sections in Parts 3 and 4 of this Article make it clear that a will may be probated without appointment of a personal representative, including any nominated by the will.

The requirement of probate stated here and the limitations on probate provided in 3–108 mean that questions as to testacy may be eliminated simply by the running of time. Under these sections, an informally probated will cannot be questioned after the later of three years from the decedent's death or one year from the probate whether or not an executor was appointed, or, if an executor was appointed, without regard to whether the estate has been distributed. If the decedent is believed to have died without a will, the running of three years from

231

death bars probate of a late-discovered will and so makes the assumption of intestacy conclusive.

The exceptions to the section (other than the exception relevant to small estates) are not intended to accommodate cases of late-discovered wills. Rather, they are designed to make the probate requirement inapplicable where circumstances led survivors of a decedent to believe that there was no point to probating a will of which they may have had knowledge. If any will was probated within three years of death, or if letters of administration were issued in this period, the exceptions to the section are inapplicable. If there has been no proceeding in probate, persons seeking to establish title by an unprobated will must show, with *reference to the estate they claim,* either that it has been possessed by those to whom it was devised or that it has been unknown to the decedent's heirs or devisees and not possessed by any.

It is to be noted, also, that devisees who are able to claim under one of the exceptions to this section may not obtain probate of the will or administration of the estate to assist them in their efforts to obtain the estate in question. The exceptions are to a rule which bars admission of a will into evidence, rather than to the section barring late probate and late appointment of personal representatives. Still, the exceptions should serve to prevent two "hard" cases which can be imagined readily. In one, a surviving spouse fails to seek probate of a will, giving her the entire estate of the decedent because she is informed or believes that all of her husband's property was held by them jointly, with right of survivorship. Later, it is discovered that she was mistaken as to the nature of her husband's title. The other case involves a devisee who sees no point to securing probate of a will in his favor because he is unaware of any estate. Subsequently, valuable rights of the decedent are discovered.

Section 3–103. [Necessity of Appointment For Administration.]

Except as otherwise provided in Article IV, to acquire the powers and undertake the duties and liabilities of a personal representative of a decedent, a person must be appointed by order of the Court or Registrar, qualify and be issued letters. Administration of an estate is commenced by the issuance of letters.

COMMENT

This section makes it clear that appointment by a public official is required before one can acquire the status of personal representative. "Qualification" is dealt with in Section 3–601. "Letters" are the subject of Section 1–305. Section 3–701 is also related, since it deals with the time of accrual of duties and powers of personal representatives.

See 3–108 for the time limit on requests for appointment of personal representatives.

In Article IV, Sections 4–204 and 4–205 permit a personal representative from another state to obtain the powers of one appointed locally by filing evidence of his authority with a local Court.

Section 3–104. [Claims Against Decedent; Necessity of Administration.]

No proceeding to enforce a claim against the estate of a decedent or his successors may be revived or commenced before the appointment of a personal representative. After the appointment and until distribution, all proceedings and actions to enforce a claim against the estate are governed by the procedure prescribed by this Article. After distribution a creditor whose claim has not been barred may recover from the distributees as provided in Section 3–1004 or from a former personal representative individually liable as provided in Section 3–1005. This section has no application to a proceeding by a secured creditor of the decedent to enforce his right to his security except as to any deficiency judgment which might be sought therein.

COMMENT

This and sections of Part 8, Article III, are designed to force creditors of decedents to assert their claims against duly appointed personal representatives. Creditors of a decedent are interested persons who may seek the appointment of a personal representative (Section 3–301). If no appointment is granted to another within 45 days after the decedent's death, a creditor may be eligible to be appointed if other persons with priority decline to serve or are ineligible (Section 3–203). But, if a personal representative has been appointed and has closed the estate under circumstances which leave a creditor's claim unbarred, the creditor is permitted to enforce his claims against distributees, as well as against the personal representative if any duty owed to creditors under 3–807 or 3–1003 has been breached. The methods for closing estates are outlined in Sections 3–1001 through 3–1003. Termination of appointment under Sections 3–608 et seq. may occur though the estate is *not* closed and so may be irrelevant to the question of whether creditors may pursue distributees.

Section 3–105. [Proceedings Affecting Devolution and Administration; Jurisdiction of Subject Matter.]

Persons interested in decedents' estates may apply to the Registrar for determination in the informal proceedings provided in this Article, and may petition the Court for orders in formal proceedings within the Court's jurisdiction including but not limited to those described in this Article. The Court has exclusive jurisdiction of formal proceedings to determine how decedents' estates subject to the laws of this state are to be administered, expended and distributed. The Court has concurrent jurisdiction of any other action or proceeding concerning a succession or to which an estate, through a personal representative, may be a party, including actions to determine title to property alleged to belong to the estate, and of any action or proceeding in which property distributed by a personal representative or its value is sought to be subjected to rights of creditors or successors of the decedent.

COMMENT

This and other sections of Article III contemplate a non-judicial officer who will act on informal application and a judge who will hear and decide formal petitions. See Section 1–307 which permits the judge to perform or delegate the functions of the Registrar. *However, the primary purpose of Article III is to describe functions to be performed by various public officials, rather than to prescribe how these responsibilities should be assigned within a given state or county.* Hence, any of several alternatives to the organizational scheme assumed for purposes of this draft would be acceptable.

For example, a state might assign responsibility for maintenance of probate files and records, and for receiving and acting upon informal applications, to existing, limited power probate offices. Responsibility for hearing and deciding formal petitions would then be assigned to the court of general jurisdiction of each county or district.

If separate courts or offices are not feasible, it may be preferable to concentrate authority for allocating responsibility respecting formal and informal proceedings in the judge. To do so helps fix responsibility for the total operation of the office. This is the assumption of this draft.

It will be up to each adopting state to select the organizational arrangement which best meets its needs.

If the office with jurisdiction to hear and decide formal petitions is the county or district court of general jurisdiction, there will be little basis for objection to the broad statement of concurrent jurisdiction of this section. However, if a more specialized "estates" court is used, there may be pressure to prevent it from hearing negligence and other actions involving jury trials, even though it may be given unlimited power to decide other cases to which a personal representative is a party. A system for certifying matters involving jury trials to the general trial court could be provided, although the alternative of permitting the estates court to empanel juries where necessary might not be unworkable. In any event, the jurisdiction of the "estates" or "probate" court in regard to negligence litigation would only be concurrent with that of the general trial court. The important point is that the estates court, whatever it is called, should have unlimited power to hear and finally dispose of all matters relevant to determination of the extent of the decedent's estate and of the claims against it. The jury trial question is peripheral.

See the comment to the next section regarding adjustments which might be made in the Code by a state with a single court of general jurisdiction for each county or district.

Section 3–106. [Proceedings Within the Exclusive Jurisdiction of Court; Service; Jurisdiction Over Persons.]

In proceedings within the exclusive jurisdiction of the Court where notice is required by this Code or by rule, and in proceedings to construe probated wills or determine heirs which concern estates that have not been and cannot now be open for administration, interested persons may be bound by the orders of the Court in respect to property in or subject to the laws of this state by notice in conformity with Section 1–401. An order is binding as to all who are given notice of the proceeding though less than all interested persons are notified.

COMMENT

The language in this and the preceding section which divides matters coming before the probate court between those within the court's "exclusive" jurisdiction and those within its "concurrent" jurisdiction would be inappropriate if probate matters were assigned to a branch of a single court of general jurisdiction. The Code could be adjusted to an assumption of a single court in various ways. Any adjusted version should contain a provision permitting the court to hear and settle certain kinds of matters after notice as provided in 1–401. It might be suitable to combine the second sentence of 3–105 and 3–106 into a single section as follows:

"The Court may hear and determine formal proceedings involving administration and distribution of decedents' estates after notice to interested persons in conformity with Section 1–401. Persons notified are bound though less than all interested persons may have been given notice."

An adjusted version also might provide:

"Subject to general rules concerning the proper location of civil litigation and jurisdiction of persons, the Court (meaning the probate division) may hear and determine any other controversy concerning a succession or to which an estate through a personal representative, may be a party."

The propriety of this sort of statement would depend upon whether questions of docketing and assignment, including the division of matters between coordinate branches of the Court, should be dealt with by legislation.

The Joint Editorial Board, in 1975, recommended the addition after "rule", of the language "and in proceedings to construe probated wills or determine heirs which concern estates that have not been and cannot now be opened for administration." This addition, coupled with the exceptions to the limitations provisions in Section 3–108 that permit proceedings to construe wills and to determine heirs of intestates to be commenced more than three years after death, clarifies the purpose of the draftsmen to offer a probate proceeding to aid the determination of rights of inheritance of estates that were not opened for administration within the time permitted by Section 3–108.

Section 3–107. [Scope of Proceedings; Proceedings Independent; Exception.]

Unless supervised administration as described in Part 5 is involved, (1) each proceeding before the Court or Registrar is independent of any other proceeding involving the same estate; (2) petitions for formal orders of the Court may combine various requests for relief in a single proceeding if the orders sought may be finally granted without delay. Except as required for proceedings which are particularly described by other sections of this Article, no petition is defective because it fails to embrace all matters which might then be the subject of a final order; (3) proceedings for probate of wills or adjudications of no will may be combined with proceedings for appointment of personal representatives; and (4) a proceeding for appointment of a personal representative is concluded by an order making or declining the appointment.

COMMENT

This section and others in Article III describe a system of administration of decedents' estates which gives interested persons control of whether matters relating to estates will become occasions for judicial orders. Sections 3–501 through 3–505 describe supervised administration, a judicial proceeding which is continuous throughout administration. It corresponds with the theory of administration of decedents' estates which prevails in many states. See, section 62, Model Probate Code. If supervised administration is not requested, persons interested in an estate may use combinations of the formal proceedings (order by judge after notice to persons concerned with the relief sought), informal proceedings (request for the limited response that nonjudicial personnel of the probate court are authorized to make in response to verified application) and filings provided in the remaining Parts of Article III to secure authority and protection needed to administer the estate. Nothing except self-interest will compel resort to the judge. When resort to the judge is necessary or desirable to resolve a dispute or to gain protection, the scope of the proceeding if not otherwise prescribed by the Code is framed by the petition. The securing of necessary jurisdiction over interested persons in a formal proceeding is facilitated by Sections 3–106 and 3–602. 3–201 locates venue for all proceedings at the place where the first proceeding occurred.

Section 3–108. [Probate, Testacy and Appointment Proceedings; Ultimate Time Limit.]

No informal probate or appointment proceeding or formal testacy or appointment proceeding, other than a proceeding to probate a will previously probated at the testator's domicile and appointment proceedings relating to an estate in which there has been a prior appointment, may be commenced more than 3 years after the decedent's death, except (1) if a previous proceeding was dismissed because of doubt about the fact of the decedent's death, appropriate probate, appointment or testacy proceedings may be maintained at any time thereafter upon a finding that the decedent's death occurred prior to the initiation of the previous proceeding and the applicant or petitioner has not delayed unduly in initiating the subsequent proceeding; (2) appropriate probate, appointment or testacy proceedings may be maintained in relation to the estate of an absent, disappeared or missing person for whose estate a conservator has been appointed, at any time within three years after the conservator becomes able to establish the death of the protected person; and (3) a proceeding to contest an informally probated will and to secure appointment of the person with legal priority for appointment in the event the contest is successful, may be commenced within the later of twelve months from the informal probate or three years from the decedent's death; and (4) if no proceeding concerning the succession or administration of the estate has occurred within 3 years after decedent's death, a formal testacy proceeding may be commenced at any time thereafter for the sole purpose of establishing a devise of property which the devisee or his successors and assigns possessed in accordance with the will or property which was not possessed or claimed by anyone by virtue of the decedent's title during the 3–year period, and the order of the Court shall be limited to that property. These limitations do not apply to proceedings to construe probated wills or determine heirs of an intestate. In cases under (1) or (2) above, the date on which a testacy or appointment proceeding is properly commenced shall be deemed to be the date of the decedent's death for purposes of other limitations provisions of this Code which relate to the date of death.

As amended in 1987.

For material relating to the 1987 amendment, see Appendix I, infra.

COMMENT

This section establishes a basic limitation period of three years within which it may be determined whether a decedent left a will and to commence administration of his estate. But, an exception assures that heirs will have at least one year after an informal probate to initiate a contest and to secure administration of the estate as intestate.

If no will is probated within three years from death, the section has the effect of making the assumption of intestacy final. If a will has been informally probated within the period, the section has the effect of making the informal probate conclusive after three years or within twelve months from informal probate, if later. Heirs or devisees can protect themselves against change within the three years of assumption concerning whether the decedent left a will or died intestate by bringing a formal proceeding shortening the period to that described in Sections 3–412 and 3–413.

A personal representative who has been appointed under an assumption concerning testacy which may be reversed in the three-year period if there has been no formal proceeding, is protected by Section 3–703. It relieves a personal representative of liability for surcharge for certain distributions made pursuant to an informally probated will, or under authority of informally issued letters of administration. Distributees who receive an estate distributed before the three-year period expires where there has been no formal determination accelerating the time for certainty, remain potentially liable to persons determined to be entitled by formal proceedings instituted within the basic period under Sections 3–909 and 3–1006.

Purchasers from personal representatives and distributees may be protected without regard to whether the three-year period has run. See Sections 3–715 and 3–910.

All creditors' claims are barred after three years from death. See Section 3–803(a)(2). Because of this, and since any possibility that letters may be issued at any time would be seen as a "cloud" on the title of heirs or devisees otherwise secure under 3–101, the three year statute

of limitations applies to bar appointment of a personal representative after the basic period has passed. Section 83 of the Model Probate Code barred probate and administration after five years, and other statutes imposing time limits on these proceedings are cited at pp. 307–310 of Model Probate Code. A qualification covers the situation where a closed administration is sought to be re-opened to administer after discovered assets. See Section 3–1008. If there has been no probate or appointment within three years, and if either exception to Section 3–102 applies, devisees under a late-discovered will may use a will to establish their title. But, they may not secure probate of the will, nor may they obtain appointment of a personal representative. The same pattern applies to heirs who, in a case where there has been no administration discover assets after the three year period has run. Such persons will not be able to protect purchasers with the ease of those interested in an estate where a personal representative has been appointed.

The basic premise underlying all of these time provisions is that interested persons who want to assume the risks implicit in the three-year period of limitations should be provided legitimate means by which they can do so. At the same time, parties should be afforded ample opportunity for earlier protection if they want it.

Section 3–109. [Statutes of Limitation on Decedent's Cause of Action.]

No statute of limitation running on a cause of action belonging to a decedent which had not been barred as of the date of his death, shall apply to bar a cause of action surviving the decedent's death sooner than four months after death. A cause of action which, but for this section, would have been barred less than four months after death, is barred after four months unless tolled.

PART 2

VENUE FOR PROBATE AND ADMINISTRATION; PRIORITY TO ADMINISTER; DEMAND FOR NOTICE

Section 3–201. [Venue for First and Subsequent Estate Proceedings; Location of Property.]

(a) Venue for the first informal or formal testacy or appointment proceedings after a decedent's death is:

(1) in the [county] where the decedent had his domicile at the time of his death; or

(2) if the decedent was not domiciled in this state, in any [county] where property of the decedent was located at the time of his death.

(b) Venue for all subsequent proceedings within the exclusive jurisdiction of the Court is in the place where the initial proceeding occurred, unless the initial proceeding has been transferred as provided in Section 1–303 or (c) of this section.

(c) If the first proceeding was informal, on application of an interested person and after notice to the proponent in the first proceeding, the Court, upon finding that venue is elsewhere, may transfer the proceeding and the file to the other court.

(d) For the purpose of aiding determinations concerning location of assets which may be relevant in cases involving non-domiciliaries, a debt, other than one evidenced by investment or commercial paper or other instrument in favor of a non-domiciliary is located where the debtor resides or, if the debtor is a person other than an individual, at the place where it has its principal office. Commercial paper, investment paper and other instruments are located where the instrument is. An interest in property held in trust is located where the trustee may be sued.

COMMENT

Sections 1–303 and 3–201 cover the subject of venue for estate proceedings. Sections 3–202, 3–301, 3–303 and 3–309 also may be relevant.

Provisions for transfer of venue appear in Section 1–303.

The interplay of these several sections may be illustrated best by examples.

(1) A formal probate or appointment proceeding is initiated in A County. Interested persons who believe that venue is in B County rather than A County must raise their question about venue in A County, because 1–303 gives the Court in which the proceeding is first commenced authority to resolve dis-

putes over venue. If the Court in A County erroneously determines that it has venue, the remedy is by appeal.

(2) An informal probate or appointment application is filed and granted without notice in A County. If interested persons wish to challenge the registrar's determination of venue, they may not simply file a formal proceeding in the county of their choice and thus force the proponent in the prior proceeding to debate the question of venue in their county. 3–201(b) locates the venue of any subsequent proceeding where the first proceeding occurred. The function of (b) is obvious when one thinks of subsequent proceedings as those which relate to claims, or accounts, or to efforts to control a personal representative. It is less obvious when it seems to locate the forum for squabbles over venue at the place accepting the first informal application. Still, the applicant seeking an informal order must be careful about the statements he makes in his application because he may be charged with perjury under Section 1–310 if he is deliberately inaccurate. Moreover, the registrar must be satisfied that the allegations in the application support a finding of venue. 3–201(c) provides a remedy for one who is upset about the venue-locating impact of a prior order in an informal proceeding and who does not wish to engage in full litigation about venue in the forum chosen by the other interested person unless he is forced to do so. Using it, he may succeed in getting the A County Court to transfer the proceedings to the county of his choice. He would be well advised to initiate formal proceedings if he gets the chance, for if he relies on informal proceedings, he, too, may be "bumped" if the judge in B County agrees with some movant that venue was not in B County.

(3) If the decedent's domicile was not in the state, venue is proper under 3–201 and 1–303 in any county where he had assets.

One contemplating starting administration because of the presence of local assets should have several other sections of the Code in mind. First, by use of the recognition provisions in Article IV, it may be possible to avoid administration in any state other than that in which the decedent was domiciled. Second, Section 3–203 may apply to give priority for local appointment to the representative appointed at domicile. Third, under Section 3–309, informal appointment proceedings in this state will be dismissed if it is known that a personal representative has been previously appointed at domicile.

Section 3–202. [Appointment or Testacy Proceedings; Conflicting Claim of Domicile in Another State.]

If conflicting claims as to the domicile of a decedent are made in a formal testacy or appointment proceeding commenced in this state, and in a testacy or appointment proceeding after notice pending at the same time in another state, the Court of this state must stay, dismiss, or permit suitable amendment in, the proceeding here unless it is determined that the local proceeding was commenced before the proceeding elsewhere. The determination of domicile in the proceeding first commenced must be accepted as determinative in the proceeding in this state.

COMMENT

This section is designed to reduce the possibility that conflicting findings of domicile in two or more states may result in inconsistent administration and distribution of parts of the same estate. Section 3–408 dealing with the effect of adjudications in other states concerning testacy supports the same general purpose to use domiciliary law to unify succession of property located in different states.

Whether testate or intestate, succession should follow the presumed wishes of the decedent whenever possible. Unless a decedent leaves a separate will for the portion of his estate located in each different state, it is highly unlikely that he would want different portions of his estate subject to different rules simply because courts reach conflicting conclusions concerning his domicile. It is pointless to debate whether he would prefer one or the other of the conflicting rules, when the paramount inference is that the decedent would prefer that his estate be unified under either rule rather than wasted in litigation.

The section adds very little to existing law. If a previous estate proceeding in State A has determined that the decedent was a domiciliary of A, persons who were personally before the court in A would be precluded by the principles of *res judicata* or collateral estoppel (and full faith and credit) from relitigating the issue of domicile in a later proceeding in State B. Probably, it would not matter in this setting that domicile was a jurisdictional fact. Stoll v. Gottlieb, 59 S.Ct. 134, 305 U.S. 165, 83 L.Ed. 104 (1938). Even if the parties to a present proceeding were not personally before the court in an earlier proceeding in State A involving the same decedent, the prior judgment would be binding as to property subject to the power of the courts in A, on persons to whom due notice of the proceeding was given. Riley v. New York Trust Co., 62 S.Ct. 608, 315 U.S. 343, 86 L.Ed. 885 (1942); Mullane v. Central Hanover Bank and Trust Co., 70 S.Ct. 652, 339 U.S. 306, 94 L.Ed. 865 (1950).

Where a court learns that parties before it are also parties to previously initiated litigation involving a common question, traditional judicial reluctance to deciding unnecessary questions, as well as considerations of comity, are likely to lead it to delay the local proceedings to await the result in the other court. A somewhat more troublesome question is involved when one of the parties before the local court manifests a determination not to appear personally in the prior initiated proceedings so that he can preserve his ability to litigate contested points in a more friendly, or convenient, forum. But, the need to preserve all possible advantages available to particular litigants should be subordinated to the decedent's probable wish that his estate not be wasted in unnecessary litigation. Thus, the section requires that the local claimant either initiate litigation in the forum of his choice before litigation is started somewhere else, or accept the necessity of contesting unwanted views concerning the decedent's domicile offered in litigation pending elsewhere.

It is to be noted, in this connection, that the local suitor always will have a chance to contest the question of domicile in the other state. His locally initiated proceedings may proceed to a valid judgment accepting his theory of the case unless parties who would oppose him appear and defend on the theory that the domicile question is currently being litigated elsewhere. If

241

the litigation in the other state has proceeded to judgment, Section 3–408 rather than the instant section will govern. If this section applies, it will mean that the foreign proceedings are still pending, so that the local person's contention concerning domicile can be made therein even though until the defense of litigation elsewhere is offered in the local proceedings, he may not have been notified of the foreign proceeding.

Section 3–203. [Priority Among Persons Seeking Appointment as Personal Representative.]

(a) Whether the proceedings are formal or informal, persons who are not disqualified have priority for appointment in the following order:

(1) the person with priority as determined by a probated will including a person nominated by a power conferred in a will;

(2) the surviving spouse of the decedent who is a devisee of the decedent;

(3) other devisees of the decedent;

(4) the surviving spouse of the decedent;

(5) other heirs of the decedent;

(6) 45 days after the death of the decedent, any creditor.

(b) An objection to an appointment can be made only in formal proceedings. In case of objection the priorities stated in (a) apply except that

(1) if the estate appears to be more than adequate to meet exemptions and costs of administration but inadequate to discharge anticipated unsecured claims, the Court, on petition of creditors, may appoint any qualified person;

(2) in case of objection to appointment of a person other than one whose priority is determined by will by an heir or devisee appearing to have a substantial interest in the estate, the Court may appoint a person who is acceptable to heirs and devisees whose interests in the estate appear to be worth in total more than half of the probable distributable value, or, in default of this accord any suitable person.

(c) A person entitled to letters under (2) through (5) of (a) above, and a person aged [18] and over who would be entitled to letters but for his age, may nominate a qualified person to act as personal representative. Any person aged [18] and over may renounce his right to nominate or to an appointment by appropriate writing filed with the Court. When two or more persons share a priority, those of them who do not renounce must concur in nominating another to act for them, or in applying for appointment.

(d) Conservators of the estates of protected persons, or if there is no conservator, any guardian except a guardian ad litem of a minor or incapacitated person, may exercise the same right to nominate, to object to another's appointment, or to participate in determining the preference of a majority in interest of the heirs and devisees that the protected person or ward would have if qualified for appointment.

(e) Appointment of one who does not have priority, including priority resulting from renunciation or nomination determined pursuant to this section, may be made only in formal proceedings. Before appointing one without priority, the Court must determine that those having priority, although given notice of the proceedings, have failed to request appointment or to nominate another for appointment, and that administration is necessary.

(f) No person is qualified to serve as a personal representative who is:

(1) under the age of [21];

(2) a person whom the Court finds unsuitable in formal proceedings.

(g) A personal representative appointed by a court of the decedent's domicile has priority over all other persons except where the decedent's will nominates different persons to be personal representative in this state and in the state of domicile. The domiciliary personal representative may nominate another, who shall have the same priority as the domiciliary personal representative.

(h) This section governs priority for appointment of a successor personal representative but does not apply to the selection of a special administrator.

COMMENT

The priorities applicable to informal proceedings are applicable to formal proceedings. However, if the proceedings are formal, a person with a substantial interest may object to the selection of one having priority other than because of will provisions. The provision for majority approval which is triggered by such a protest can be handled in a formal proceeding since all interested persons will be before the court, and a judge capable of handling discretionary matters, will be involved.

In considering this section as it relates to a devise to a trustee for various beneficiaries, it is to be noted that "interested persons" is defined by 1–201(20) to include fiduciaries. Also, 1–403(2) and 3–912 show a purpose to make trustees serve as representatives of all beneficiaries. The provision in (d) is consistent.

If a state's statutes recognize a public administrator or public trustee as the appropriate agency to seek administration of estates in which the state may have an interest, it would be appropriate to indicate in this section the circumstances under which such an officer may seek administration. If no officer is recognized locally, the state could claim as heir by virtue of 2–105.

Subsection (g) was inserted in connection with the decision to abandon the effort to describe ancillary administration in Article IV. Other provisions in Article III which are relevant to administration of assets in a state other than that of the decedent's domicile are 1–301 (territorial effect), 3–201 (venue), 3–308 (informal appointment for non-resident decedent delayed 30 days), 3–309 (no informal appointment here if a representative has been appointed at domicile), 3–815 (duty of personal representative where administration is more than one state) and 4–201 to 4–205 (local recognition of foreign personal representatives).

The meaning of "spouse" is determined by Section 2–802.

Section 3–204. [Demand for Notice of Order or Filing Concerning Decedent's Estate.]

Any person desiring notice of any order or filing pertaining to a decedent's estate in which he has a financial or property interest, may file a demand for notice with the Court at any time after the death of the decedent stating the name of the decedent, the nature of his interest in the estate, and the demandant's address or that of his attorney. The clerk shall mail a copy of the demand to the personal representative if one has been appointed. After filing of a demand, no order or filing to which the demand relates shall be made or accepted without notice as prescribed in Section 1–401 to the demandant or his attorney. The validity of an order which is issued or filing which is accepted without compliance with this requirement shall not be affected by the error, but the petitioner receiving the order or the person making the filing may be liable for any damage caused by the absence of notice. The requirement of notice arising from a demand under this provision may be waived in writing by the demandant and shall cease upon the termination of his interest in the estate.

COMMENT

The notice required as the result of demand under this section is regulated as far as time and manner requirements are concerned by Section 1–401.

This section would apply to any order which might be made in a supervised administration proceeding.

PART 3

INFORMAL PROBATE AND APPOINTMENT PROCEEDINGS; SUCCESSION WITHOUT ADMINISTRATION

Section 3–301. [Informal Probate or Appointment Proceedings; Application; Contents.]

(a) Applications for informal probate or informal appointment shall be directed to the Registrar, and verified by the applicant to be accurate and complete to the best of his knowledge and belief as to the following information:

(1) Every application for informal probate of a will or for informal appointment of a personal representative, other than a special or successor representative, shall contain the following:

(i) a statement of the interest of the applicant;

(ii) the name, and date of death of the decedent, his age, and the county and state of his domicile at the time of death, and the names and addresses of the spouse, children, heirs and devisees and the ages of any who are minors so far as known or ascertainable with reasonable diligence by the applicant;

(iii) if the decedent was not domiciled in the state at the time of his death, a statement showing venue;

(iv) a statement identifying and indicating the address of any personal representative of the decedent appointed in this state or elsewhere whose appointment has not been terminated;

(v) a statement indicating whether the applicant has received a demand for notice, or is aware of any demand for notice of any probate or appointment proceeding concerning the decedent that may have been filed in this state or elsewhere; and

(vi) that the time limit for informal probate or appointment as provided in this Article has not expired either because 3 years or less have passed since the decedent's death, or, if more than 3 years from death have passed, circumstances as described by Section 3–108 authorizing tardy probate or appointment have occurred.

(2) An application for informal probate of a will shall state the following in addition to the statements required by (1):

(i) that the original of the decedent's last will is in the possession of the court, or accompanies the application, or that an authenticated copy of a will probated in another jurisdiction accompanies the application;

(ii) that the applicant, to the best of his knowledge, believes the will to have been validly executed;

(iii) that after the exercise of reasonable diligence, the applicant is unaware of any instrument revoking the will, and that the applicant believes that the instrument which is the subject of the application is the decedent's last will.

(3) An application for informal appointment of a personal representative to administer an estate under a will shall describe the will by date of execution and state the time and place of probate or the pending application or petition for probate. The application for appointment shall adopt the statements in the application or petition for probate and state the name, address and priority for appointment of the person whose appointment is sought.

(4) An application for informal appointment of an administrator in intestacy shall state in addition to the statements required by (1):

(i) that after the exercise of reasonable diligence, the applicant is unaware of any unrevoked testamentary instrument relating to property having a situs in this state under Section 1–301, or, a statement why any such instrument of which he may be aware is not being probated;

(ii) the priority of the person whose appointment is sought and the names of any other persons having a prior or equal right to the appointment under Section 3–203.

(5) An application for appointment of a personal representative to succeed a personal representative appointed under a different testacy status shall refer to the order in the most recent testacy proceeding, state the name and address of the person whose appointment is sought and of the person whose appointment will be terminated if the application is granted, and describe the priority of the applicant.

(6) An application for appointment of a personal representative to succeed a personal representative who has tendered a resignation as provided in 3–610(c), or whose appointment has been terminated by death or removal, shall adopt the statements in the application or petition which led to the appointment of the person being succeeded except as specifically changed or corrected, state the name and address of the person who seeks appointment as successor, and describe the priority of the applicant.

(b) By verifying an application for informal probate, or informal appointment, the applicant submits personally to the jurisdiction of the court in any proceeding for relief from fraud relating to the application, or for perjury, that may be instituted against him.

COMMENT

Forcing one who seeks informal probate or informal appointment to make oath before a public official concerning the details required of applications should deter persons who might otherwise misuse the no-notice feature of informal proceedings. The application is available as a part of the public record. If deliberately false representation is made, remedies for fraud will be available to injured persons without specified time limit (see Article I). The section is believed to provide important safeguards that may extend well beyond those presently available under supervised administration for persons damaged by deliberate wrongdoing.

Section 1–310 deals with verification.

In 1975, the Joint Editorial Board recommended the addition of subsection (b) to reflect an improvement accomplished in the first enactment in Idaho. The addition, which is a form of long-arm provision that affects everyone who acts as an applicant in informal proceedings, in conjunction with Section 1–106 provides a remedy in the court of probate against anyone who might make known misstatements in an application. The addition is not needed in the case of an applicant who becomes a personal representative as a result of his application for the implied consent provided in Section 3–602 would cover the matter. Also, the requirement that the applicant state that time limits on informal probate and appointment have not run, formerly appearing as (iv) under paragraph (2) was expanded to refer to informal appointment and moved into (1). Correcting an oversight in the original text, this change coordinates the statements required in an application with the limitations provisions of Section 3–108.

Section 3–302. [Informal Probate; Duty of Registrar; Effect of Informal Probate.]

Upon receipt of an application requesting informal probate of a will, the Registrar, upon making the findings required by Section 3–303 shall issue a written statement of informal probate if at least 120 hours have elapsed since the decedent's death. Informal probate is conclusive as to all persons until superseded by an order in a formal testacy proceeding. No defect in the application or procedure relating thereto which leads to informal probate of a will renders the probate void.

COMMENT

Model Probate Code Sections 68 and 70 contemplate probate by judicial order as the only method of validating a will. This "umbrella" section and the sections it refers to describe an alternative procedure called "informal probate". It is a statement of probate by the Registrar. A succeeding section describes cases in which informal pro-

bate is to be denied. "Informal probate" is subjected to safeguards
which seem appropriate to a transaction which has the effect of making a will operative and which *may*
be the only official reaction concerning its validity. "Informal pro-

bate", it is hoped, will serve to keep
the simple will which generates no
controversy from becoming involved in *truly* judicial proceedings.
The procedure is very much like
"probate in common form" as it is
known in England and some states.

Section 3-303. [Informal Probate; Proof and Findings Required.]

(a) In an informal proceeding for original probate of a will, the Registrar shall determine whether:

(1) the application is complete;

(2) the applicant has made oath or affirmation that the statements contained in the application are true to the best of his knowledge and belief;

(3) the applicant appears from the application to be an interested person as defined in Section 1-201(20);

(4) on the basis of the statements in the application, venue is proper;

(5) an original, duly executed and apparently unrevoked will is in the Registrar's possession;

(6) any notice required by Section 3-204 has been given and that the application is not within Section 3-304; and

(7) it appears from the application that the time limit for original probate has not expired.

(b) The application shall be denied if it indicates that a personal representative has been appointed in another [county] of this state or except as provided in subsection (d) below, if it appears that this or another will of the decedent has been the subject of a previous probate order.

(c) A will which appears to have the required signatures and which contains an attestation clause showing that requirements of execution under Section 2-502, 2-503 or 2-506 have been met shall be probated without further proof. In other cases, the Registrar may assume execution if the will appears to have been properly executed, or he may accept a sworn statement or affidavit of any person having knowledge of the circumstances of execution, whether or not the person was a witness to the will.

(d) Informal probate of a will which has been previously probated elsewhere may be granted at any time upon written application by any interested person, together with deposit of an authenticated copy of the will and of the statement probating it from the office or court where it was first probated.

(e) A will from a place which does not provide for probate of a will after death and which is not eligible for probate under subsection (a) above, may be probated in this state upon receipt by the Registrar of a duly authenticated copy of the will and a duly authenticated certificate of its legal custodian that the copy filed is a true copy and that the will has become operative under the law of the other place.

COMMENT

The purpose of this section is to permit informal probate of a will which, from a simple attestation clause, appears to have been executed properly. It is not necessary that the will be notarized as is the case with "pre-proved" wills in some states. If a will is "pre-proved" as provided in Article II, it will, of course, "appear" to be well executed and include the recital necessary for easy probate here. If the instrument does not contain a proper recital by attesting witnesses, it may be probated informally on the strength of an affidavit by a person who can say what occurred at the time of execution.

Except where probate or its equivalent has occurred previously in another state, informal probate is available only where an original will exists and is available to be filed. Lost or destroyed wills must be established in formal proceedings. See Section 3–402. Under Section 3–401, pendency of formal testacy proceedings blocks informal probate or appointment proceedings.

Section 3–304. [Informal Probate; Unavailable in Certain Cases.]

Applications for informal probate which relate to one or more of a known series of testamentary instruments (other than a will and one or more codicils thereto), the latest of which does not expressly revoke the earlier, shall be declined.

As amended in 1987.

For material relating to the 1987 amendment, see Appendix I, infra.

COMMENT

The Registrar handles the informal proceeding, but is required to decline applications in certain cases where circumstances suggest that formal probate would provide desirable safeguards.

Section 3–305. [Informal Probate; Registrar Not Satisfied.]

If the Registrar is not satisfied that a will is entitled to be probated in informal proceedings because of failure to meet the requirements of Sections 3–303 and 3–304 or any other reason, he may decline the application. A declination of informal probate is not an adjudication and does not preclude formal probate proceedings.

COMMENT

The purpose of this section is to recognize that the Registrar should have some authority to deny probate to an instrument even though all stated statutory requirements may be said to have been met. Denial of an application for informal probate cannot be appealed. Rather, the proponent may initiate a formal proceeding so that the matter may be brought before the judge in the normal way for contested matters.

Section 3–306. [Informal Probate; Notice Requirements.]

[*] The moving party must give notice as described by Section 1–401 of his application for informal probate to any person demanding it pursuant to Section 3–204, and to any personal representative of the decedent whose appointment has not been terminated. No other notice of informal probate is required.

[(b) If an informal probate is granted, within 30 days thereafter the applicant shall give written information of the probate to the heirs and devisees. The information shall include the name and address of the applicant, the name and location of the court granting the informal probate, and the date of the probate. The information shall be delivered or sent by ordinary mail to each of the heirs and devisees whose address is reasonably available to the applicant. No duty to give information is incurred if a personal representative is appointed who is required to give the written information required by Section 3–705. An applicant's failure to give information as required by this section is a breach of his duty to the heirs and devisees but does not affect the validity of the probate.]

* This paragraph becomes (a) if optional subsection (b) is accepted.

COMMENT

This provision assumes that there will be a single office within each county or other area of jurisdiction of the probate court which can be checked for demands for notice relating to estates in that area. If there are or may be several registrars within a given area, provision would need to be made so that information concerning demands for notice might be obtained from the chief registrar's place of business.

In 1975, the Joint Editorial Board recommended the addition, as a bracketed, optional provision, of subsection (b). The recommendation was derived from a provision added to the Code in Idaho at the time of original enactment. The Board viewed the addition as interesting, possibly worthwhile, and worth being brought to the attention of enacting states as an optional addition. The Board views the informational notice required by Section 3–705 to be of more importance in preventing injustices under the Code, because the opening of an estate via appointment of a personal representative instantly gives the estate representative powers over estate assets that can be used wrongfully and to the possible detriment of interested persons. Hence, the 3–705 duty is a part of the recommended Code, rather than a bracketed, optional provision. By contrast, the informal probate of a will that is not accompanied or followed by appointment of a personal representative only serves to shift the burden of making the next move to disinterested heirs who, inter alia, may initiate a Section 3–401 formal testacy proceeding to contest the will at any time within the limitations prescribed by Section 3–108.

Section 3–307. [Informal Appointment Proceedings; Delay in Order; Duty of Registrar; Effect of Appointment.]

(a) Upon receipt of an application for informal appointment of a personal representative other than a special administrator as provided in Section 3–614, if at least 120 hours have elapsed since the decedent's death, the Registrar, after making the findings required by Section 3–308, shall appoint the applicant subject to qualification and acceptance; provided, that if the decedent was a non-resident, the Registrar shall delay the order of appointment until 30 days have elapsed since death unless the personal representative appointed at the decedent's domicile is the applicant, or unless the decedent's will directs that his estate be subject to the laws of this state.

(b) The status of personal representative and the powers and duties pertaining to the office are fully established by informal appointment. An appointment, and the office of personal representative created thereby, is subject to termination as provided in Sections 3–608 through 3–612, but is not subject to retroactive vacation.

COMMENT

Section 3–703 describes the duty of a personal representative and the protection available to one who acts under letters issued in informal proceedings. The provision requiring a delay of 30 days from death before appointment of a personal representative for a non-resident decedent is new. It is designed to permit the first appointment to be at the decedent's domicile. See Section 3–203.

Section 3–308. [Informal Appointment Proceedings; Proof and Findings Required.]

(a) In informal appointment proceedings, the Registrar must determine whether:

(1) the application for informal appointment of a personal representative is complete;

(2) the applicant has made oath or affirmation that the statements contained in the application are true to the best of his knowledge and belief;

(3) the applicant appears from the application to be an interested person as defined in Section 1–201(20);

(4) on the basis of the statements in the application, venue is proper;

(5) any will to which the requested appointment relates has been formally or informally probated; but this requirement does not apply to the appointment of a special administrator;

(6) any notice required by Section 3–204 has been given;

(7) from the statements in the application, the person whose appointment is sought has priority entitling him to the appointment.

(b) Unless Section 3–612 controls, the application must be denied if it indicates that a personal representative who has not filed a written statement of resignation as provided in Section 3–610(c) has been appointed in this or another [county] of this state, that (unless the applicant is the domiciliary personal representative or his nominee) the decedent was not domiciled in this state and that a personal representative whose appointment has not been terminated has been appointed by a Court in the state of domicile, or that other requirements of this section have not been met.

COMMENT

Sections 3–614 and 3–615 make it clear that a special administrator may be appointed to conserve the estate during any period of delay in probate of a will. Even though the will has not been approved, Section 3–614 gives priority for appointment as special administrator to the person nominated by the will which has been offered for probate. Section 3–203 governs priorities for appointment. Under it, one or more of the same class may receive priority through agreement of the others.

The last sentence of the section is designed to prevent informal appointment of a personal representative in this state when a personal representative has been previously appointed at the decedent's domicile. Sections 4–204 and 4–205 may make local appointment unnecessary. Appointment in formal proceedings is possible, however.

Section 3–309. [Informal Appointment Proceedings; Registrar Not Satisfied.]

If the Registrar is not satisfied that a requested informal appointment of a personal representative should be made because of failure to meet the requirements of Sections 3–307 and 3–308, or for any other reason, he may decline the application. A declination of informal appointment is not an adjudication and does not preclude appointment in formal proceedings.

COMMENT

Authority to decline an application for appointment is conferred on the Registrar. Appointment of a personal representative confers broad powers over the assets of a decedent's estate. The process of declining a requested appointment for unclassified reasons should be one which a registrar can use quickly and informally.

Section 3–310. [Informal Appointment Proceedings; Notice Requirements.]

The moving party must give notice as described by Section 1–401 of his intention to seek an appointment informally: (1) to any person demanding it pursuant to Section 3–204; and (2) to any person having a prior or equal right to appointment not waived in writing and filed with the Court. No other notice of an informal appointment proceeding is required.

Section 3–311. [Informal Appointment Unavailable in Certain Cases.]

If an application for informal appointment indicates the existence of a possible unrevoked testamentary instrument which may relate to property subject to the laws of this state, and which is not filed for probate in this court, the Registrar shall decline the application.

SUCCESSION WITHOUT ADMINISTRATION

The Committee that acted for the National Conference of Commissioners on Uniform State Laws in preparing the Uniform Succession Without Administration Act was as follows:

EUGENE F. SCOLES, University of Illinois, College of Law, Champaign, IL 61820. *Chairman*

ALLISON DUNHAM, 900 East Harrison Avenue, Pomona, CA 91767

CLARKE A. GRAVEL, 109 South Winooski Avenue, P.O. Box 1049, Burlington, VT 05402

CHARLES HOROWITZ, 2000 IBM Building, Seattle, WA 98101

BEN R. MILLER, SR., 3125 McCarroll Drive, Baton Rouge, LA 70809

RICHARD V. WELLMAN, University of Georgia, School of Law, Athens, GA 30602

M. KING HILL, JR., Sixth Floor, 100 Light Street, Baltimore, MD 21202, *President (Member Ex Officio)*

CARLYLE C. RING, JR., 710 Ring Building, Washington, DC 20036, *Chairman, Executive Committee*

WILLIAM J. PIERCE, University of Michigan, School of Law, Ann Arbor, MI 48109, *Executive Director*

ELMER R. OETTINGER, 58 Oakwood Drive, Chapel Hill, NC 27514, *Chairman, Division F (Member Ex Officio)*

Review Committee

HAROLD E. READ, JR., One State Street, Hartford, CT 06103, *Chairman*

BERNARD HELLRING, 1180 Raymond Boulevard, Newark, NJ 07102

ALLAN D. VESTAL, University of Iowa, College of Law, Iowa City, IA 52242

Advisors to Special Committee
on Uniform Succession Without Administration Act

American Bar Association:

EDWARD B. BENJAMIN, JR.

Joint Editorial Board for Uniform Probate Code:

HARRISON F. DURAND

J. THOMAS EUBANK

EDWARD C. HALBACH, JR.

MALCOLM A. MOORE

HARLEY J. SPITLER

ROBERT A. STEIN

J. PENNINGTON STRAUS

PREFATORY NOTE

This amendment to the Uniform Probate Code is an alternative to other methods of administering a decedent's estate. The Uniform Probate Code otherwise provides procedures for informal administration, formal administration and supervised administration. This amendment adds another alternative to the system of flexible administration provided by the Uniform Probate Code and permits the heirs of an intestate or residuary devisees of a testator to accept the estate assets without administration by assuming responsibility for discharging those obligations that normally would be discharged by the personal representative.

The concept of succession without administration is drawn from the civil law and is a variation of the method which is followed largely on the Continent in Europe, in Louisiana and in Quebec.

This proposed amendment contains cross-references to the procedures in the Uniform Probate Code and particularly implements the policies and concepts reflected in Sections 1–102, 3–101 and

3–109. These sections of the Uniform Probate Code provide in part:

SECTION 1–102. [Purposes; Rule of Construction.]

(a) This Code shall be liberally construed and applied to promote its underlying purposes and policies.

(b) The underlying purposes and policies of this Code are:

(1) to simplify and clarify the law concerning the affairs of decedents, missing persons, protected persons, minors and incapacitated persons;

(2) to discover and make effective the intent of a decedent in the distribution of his property;

(3) to promote a speedy and efficient system for liquidating the estate of the decedent and making distribution to his successors;

* * * * * * * * * *

SECTION 3–101. [Devolution of Estate at Death; Restrictions.]

The power of a person to leave property by will, and the rights of creditors, devisees, and heirs to his property are subject to the restrictions and limitations contained in this Code to facilitate the prompt settlement of estates. Upon the death of a person, his real and personal property devolves to the persons to whom it is devised by his last will or to those indicated as substitutes for them in cases involving lapse, renunciation, or other circumstances affecting the devolution of testate estate, or in the absence of testamentary disposition, to his heirs, or to those indicated as substitutes for them in cases involving renunciation or other circumstances affecting devolution of intestate estates, subject to homestead allowance, exempt property and family allowance, to rights of creditors, elective share of the surviving spouse, and to administration.

SECTION 3–901. [Successors' Rights if No Administration.]

In the absence of administration, the heirs and devisees are entitled to the estate in accordance with the terms of a probated will or the laws of intestate succession. Devisees may establish title by the probated will to devised property. Persons entitled to property by homestead allowance, exemption or intestacy may establish title thereto by proof of the decedent's ownership, his death, and their relationship to the decedent. Successors take subject to all charges incident to administration, including the claims of creditors and allowances of surviving spouse and dependent children, and subject to the rights of others resulting from abatement, retainer, advancement, and ademption.

Section 3–312. [Universal Succession; In General.]

The heirs of an intestate or the residuary devisees under a will, excluding minors and incapacitated, protected, or unascertained persons, may become universal successors to the decedent's estate by assuming personal liability for (1) taxes, (2) debts of the dece-

255

dent, (3) claims against the decedent or the estate, and (4) distributions due other heirs, devisees, and persons entitled to property of the decedent as provided in Sections 3–313 through 3–322.

COMMENT

This section states the general policy of the Act to permit heirs or residuary legatees to take possession, control and title to a decedent's estate by assuming a personal obligation to pay taxes, debts, claims and distributions due to others entitled to share in the decedent's property by qualifying under the statute. Although the surviving spouse most often will be an heir or residuary devisee, he or she may also be a person otherwise entitled to property of the decedent as when a forced share is claimed.

This Act does not contemplate that assignees of heirs or residuary devisees will have standing to apply for universal succession since this involves undertaking responsibility for obligations of the decedent. Of course, after the statement of universal succession has been issued, persons may assign their beneficial interests as any other asset.

The Act excludes incapacitated and unascertained persons as universal successors because of the need for successors to deal with the property for various purposes. The procedure permits competent heirs and residuary devisees to proceed even where there are some others incompetent or unascertained. If any unascertained or incompetent heir or devisee wishes, they may require bonding or if unprotected they may force the estate into administration. Subsequent sections permit the conservator, guardian ad litem or other fiduciary of unascertained or incompetent heirs or devisees to object. The universal successors' obligations may be enforced by appropriate remedy. In Louisiana the procedure is available even though there are incompetent heirs for whom a tutor or guardian is appointed to act.

In restricting universal succession to competent heirs and residuary legatees, the act makes them responsible to incompetent heirs and legatees. This restriction is deemed appropriate to avoid the problems in dealing with the estate assets vested in an incompetent. This is a variation from the Louisiana practice. The procedure also contemplates that all competent heirs and residuary devisees join and does not permit only part of the heirs to petition for succession without administration. This position means that succession without administration is essentially a consent procedure available when family members are in agreement.

This Act contemplates that known competent successors may proceed under it. Although all competent heirs are required to join in the informal process, the possibility of an unknown heir is not treated as jurisdictional. An unknown heir who appeared would be able to establish his or her rights as in administration unless barred by adjudication, estoppel or lapse of time.

Section 3–313. [Universal Succession; Application; Contents.]

(a) An application to become universal successors by the heirs of an intestate or the residuary devisees under a will must be directed to the [Registrar], signed by each applicant, and verified to be accurate and complete to the best of the applicant's knowledge and belief as follows:

(1) An application by heirs of an intestate must contain the statements required by Section 3–301(a)(1) and (4)(i) and state that the applicants constitute all the heirs other than minors and incapacitated, protected, or unascertained persons.

(2) An application by residuary devisees under a will must be combined with a petition for informal probate if the will has not been admitted to probate in this State and must contain the statements required by Section 3–301(a)(1) and (2). If the will has been probated in this State, an application by residuary devisees must contain the statements required by Section 3–301(a)(2)(iii). An application by residuary devisees must state that the applicants constitute the residuary devisees of the decedent other than any minors and incapacitated, protected, or unascertained persons. If the estate is partially intestate, all of the heirs other than minors and incapacitated, protected, or unascertained persons must join as applicants.

(b) The application must state whether letters of administration are outstanding, whether a petition for appointment of a personal representative of the decedent is pending in any court of this State, and that the applicants waive their right to seek appointment of a personal representative.

(c) The application may describe in general terms the assets of the estate and must state that the applicants accept responsibility for the estate and assume personal liability for (1) taxes, (2) debts of the decedent, (3) claims against the decedent or the estate and (4) distributions due other heirs, devisees, and persons entitled to property of the decedent as provided in Sections 3–316 through 3–322.

COMMENT

This section spells out in detail the form and requirements for application to the Registrar to become universal successors. The section requires the applicants to inform the Registrar whether the appointment of a personal representative has occurred or is pending in order to assure any administration is terminated before the application can be granted. The section requires applicants to waive their right to seek the appointment of a personal representative. The appointment of an executor would preclude or postpone universal succession by application for appointment unless the executor's appointment is avoided because of lack of interest in the estate. See Sections 3–611, 3–912.

The statements in the application are verified by signing and filing and deemed to be under oath as provided in Section 1–310. Like

other informal proceedings under
the U.P.C., false statements constitute fraud (U.P.C. 1–106).

Even though the presence of residuary devisees would seem to preclude partial intestacy (U.P.C. 2–605,
2–606), the last sentence of 3–313(a)
regarding partial intestacy warns all
parties that if there is a partial intestacy, the heirs must join. It avoids
problems of determining whether
the residuary takers are in all instances true residuary legatees, e.g.,
if a testator provides: "Lastly, I
give ½ and only ½ of the rest of my
estate to A." (cf. U.P.C. 2–603).

Section 3–313(c) provides that a
general description of the assets
may be included appropriate to the
assets in the estate and adequate to
inform the parties and the Registrar
of the nature of the estate involved.

In the event an heir or residuary
devisee were to disclaim prior to
acceptance of the succession, those
who would take in place of the disclaimant would be the successors
who could apply to become universal successors. The disclaimant

could not become a universal successor as to the disclaimed interest
and would not be subject to liability
as a universal successor.

Trustees of testamentary trusts
have standing as devisees. If the
trustee is a pecuniary devisee or a
specific devisee other than a residuary devisee, he would administer
the trust upon receipt of the assets
from the universal successors and
as a devisee could enforce distribution from the universal successors.

The trustee who is a residuary legatee has standing to qualify as a
universal successor by acceptance
of the decedent's assets, then to discharge the obligations of the universal successor, and finally to administer the residue under the trust
without appointment of a personal
representative. The will would be
probated in any event. The residuary trustee could choose to insist on
appointment of a personal representative and not seek universal succession. Neither alternative could
alter the provisions of the residuary
trust.

Section 3–314. [Universal Succession; Proof and Findings Required.]

(a) The [Registrar] shall grant the application if:

(1) the application is complete in accordance with Section 3–313;

(2) all necessary persons have joined and have verified that the statements contained therein are true, to the best knowledge and belief of each;

(3) venue is proper;

(4) any notice required by Section 3–204 has been given or waived;

(5) the time limit for original probate or appointment proceedings has not expired and the applicants claim under a will;

(6) the application requests informal probate of a will, the application and findings conform with Sections 3–301(a)(2) and 3–303(a)(c)(d) and (e) so the will is admitted to probate; and

(7) none of the applicants is a minor or an incapacitated or protected person.

(b) The [Registrar] shall deny the application if letters of administration are outstanding.

(c) Except as provided in Section 3–322, the [Registrar] shall deny the application if any creditor, heir, or devisee who is qualified by Section 3–605 to demand bond files an objection.

COMMENT

This section outlines the substantive requirements for universal succession and is the guideline to the Registrar for approval of the application. As in U.P.C. 3–303, review of the filed documents is all that is required, with the Registrar expected to determine whether to approve on the basis of information available to the Registrar. There is very little discretion in the Registrar except that if something appears lacking in the application, the Registrar would be able to request additional information. The analogy to U.P.C. 3–303 is rather direct and the authority of the Registrar is somewhat more limited because there is no parallel section to U.P.C. 3–305 as there is in probate. (See also U.P.C. 3–309.)

Section 3–314(a)(5) requires that the application for universal succession under a will be made before the time limit for original probate has expired. Against the background of U.P.C. 3–108 which limits administration proceedings after three years except for proof of heirship or will construction, the heirs could take possession of property and prove their title without the universal succession provisions.

The review of the application by the Registrar essentially is a clerical matter to determine if the application exhibits the appropriate circumstance for succession without administration. Hence, if there are letters of administration outstanding, the application must be denied under Section 3–314(b). Even though a disinterested executor under a will should not be able to preclude those interested in the estate from settling the estate without administration, coordination of the Registrar's action with the process of the probate court is imperative to protect the parties and the public. Consequently, any outstanding letters must be terminated before succession without administration is approved. Under the Uniform Probate Code, those with property interests in the estate are viewed as "interested persons" (U.P.C. 1–201(2)) and may initiate either informal (U.P.C. 3–105) or formal proceedings (U.P.C. 3–401); also the agreement of those interested in the estate is binding on the personal representative (U.P.C. 3–912, 3–1101). These provisions appear adequate to preclude the personal representative who has no other interest in the estate from frustrating those interested from utilizing succession without administration.

There is need for coordination with other process within the probate court when a petition for letters is pending (i.e., not withdrawn) as when letters were outstanding. The appropriateness of the appointment of the personal representative, i.e., whether administration was necessary, could be determined on an objection to the appointment under U.P.C. Sections 3–414(b); cf., 3–608 to 3–612. If the appointment of a personal representative is denied, then the application for universal succession without administration could be approved in appropriate cases.

Section 3–314 does not require prior notice unless requested under U.P.C. 3–204. Information to other heirs and devisees is provided after approval of the application. See Section 3–319.

If, after universal succession is approved, a creditor or devisee were not paid or secured, in addition to suing the successor directly, the creditor or devisee could move for appointment of a personal representative to administer the estate properly. This pressure on the universal successors to perform seems desirable. In view of the availability of informal administration and other flexible alternatives under the U.P.C., if any person properly moves for appointment of a personal representative, succession without administration should be foreclosed or terminated.

Section 3–315. [Universal Succession; Duty of Registrar; Effect of Statement of Universal Succession.]

Upon receipt of an application under Section 3–313, if at least 120 hours have elapsed since the decedent's death, the [Registrar], upon granting the application, shall issue a written statement of universal succession describing the estate as set forth in the application and stating that the applicants (i) are the universal successors to the assets of the estate as provided in Section 3–312, (ii) have assumed liability for the obligations of the decedent, and (iii) have acquired the powers and liabilities of universal successors. The statement of universal succession is evidence of the universal successors' title to the assets of the estate. Upon its issuance, the powers and liabilities of universal successors provided in Sections 3–316 through 3–322 attach and are assumed by the applicants.

COMMENT

This section provides for a written statement issued by the Registrar evidencing the right and power of the universal successors to deal with the property of the decedent and serves as an instrument of distribution to them. Although the application for universal succession may be filed anytime after death, within the time limit for original probate, the Registrar may not act before 120 hours have elapsed since the testator's death. This period parallels provisions for other informal proceedings under the U.P.C., e.g., §§ 2–601, 3–302, 3–307.

Section 3–316. [Universal Succession; Universal Successors' Powers.]

Upon the [Registrar's] issuance of a statement of universal succession:

(1) Universal successors have full power of ownership to deal with the assets of the estate subject to the limitations and liabili-

ties in this [Act]. The universal successors shall proceed expeditiously to settle and distribute the estate without adjudication but if necessary may invoke the jurisdiction of the court to resolve questions concerning the estate.

(2) Universal successors have the same powers as distributees from a personal representative under Sections 3–908 and 3–909 and third persons with whom they deal are protected as provided in Section 3–910.

(3) For purposes of collecting assets in another state whose law does not provide for universal succession, universal successors have the same standing and power as personal representatives or distributees in this State.

COMMENT

This section is the substantive provision (1) declaring the successors to be distributees and (2) to have the powers of owners so far as dealing with the estate assets subject to the obligations to others.

Details concerning the status of distributees under U.P.C. 3–908 and the power to deal with property are provided in U.P.C. 3–910.

Although one state cannot control the law of another, the universal successor should be recognized in other states as having the standing of either a foreign personal representative or a distributee of the claim to local assets. Paragraph (3) attempts to remove any limitation of this state in such a case.

Section 3–317. [Universal Succession; Universal Successors' Liability to Creditors, Other Heirs, Devisees and Persons Entitled to Decedent's Property; Liability of Other Persons Entitled to Property.]

(a) In the proportions and subject to limits expressed in Section 3–321, universal successors assume all liabilities of the decedent that were not discharged by reason of death and liability for all taxes, claims against the decedent or the estate, and charges properly incurred after death for the preservation of the estate, to the extent those items, if duly presented, would be valid claims against the decedent's estate.

(b) In the proportions and subject to the limits expressed in Section 3–321, universal successors are personally liable to other heirs, devisees, and persons entitled to property of the decedent for the assets or amounts that would be due those heirs, were the estate administered, but no allowance having priority over devisees may be claimed for attorney's fees or charges for preservation of the estate in excess of reasonable amounts properly incurred.

(c) Universal successors are entitled to their interests in the estate as heirs or devisees subject to priority and abatement pursuant to Section 3–902 and to agreement pursuant to Section 3–912.

(d) Other heirs, devisees, and persons to whom assets have been distributed have the same powers and liabilities as distributees under Sections 3–908, 3–909, and 3–910.

(e) Absent breach of fiduciary obligations or express undertaking, a fiduciary's liability is limited to the assets received by the fiduciary.

COMMENT

The purpose of succession without administration is not to alter the relative property interests of the parties but only to facilitate the family's expeditious settlement of the estate. Consistent with this, the liability arising from the assumption of obligations is stated explicitly here to assist in understanding the coupling of power and liability. Subsection (b) includes an abatement reference that recognizes the possible adjustment that may be necessary by reason of excess claims under U.P.C. 3–902.

In succession without administration, there being no personal representative's notice to creditors, the short non-claim period under U.P.C. Section 3–803(a)(1) does not apply and creditors are subject to the statutes of limitations and the limitation of three years on decedent's creditors when no notice is published under U.P.C. Section 3–803(a)(2). The general statutes of limitation are suspended for four months following the decedent's death but resume thereafter under U.P.C. Section 3–802. The assumption of liability by the universal successors upon the issuance of the Statement of Universal Succession is deemed to be by operation of law and does not operate to extend or renew any statute of limitations that had begun to run against the decedent. The result is that creditors are barred by the general statutes of limitation or 3 years whichever is the shorter.

The obligation of the universal successors to other heirs, devisees and distributees is based on the promise to perform in return for the direct distribution of property and any limitation or laches begins to run on issuance of the statement of universal succession unless otherwise extended by action or assurance of the universal successor.

It should be noted that this statute does not deal with the consequences or obligations that arise under either federal or state tax laws. The universal successors will be subject to obligations for the return and payment of both income and estate taxes in many situations depending upon the tax law and the circumstances of the decedent and the estate. These tax consequences should be determined before electing to utilize succession without administration.

Section 3-318. [Universal Succession; Universal Successors' Submission to Jurisdiction; When Heirs or Devisees May Not Seek Administration.]

(a) Upon issuance of the statement of universal succession, the universal successors become subject to the personal jurisdiction of the courts of this state in any proceeding that may be instituted relating to the estate or to any liability assumed by them.

(b) Any heir or devisee who voluntarily joins in an application under Section 3-313 may not subsequently seek appointment of a personal representative.

COMMENT

This section imposes jurisdiction over the universal successors and bars them from seeking appointment as personal representative.

Section 3-319. [Universal Succession; Duty of Universal Successors; Information to Heirs and Devisees.]

Not later than thirty days after issuance of the statement of universal succession, each universal successor shall inform the heirs and devisees who did not join in the application of the succession without administration. The information must be delivered or be sent by ordinary mail to each of the heirs and devisees whose address is reasonably available to the universal successors. The information must include the names and addresses of the universal successors, indicate that it is being sent to persons who have or may have some interest in the estate, and describe the court where the application and statement of universal succession has been filed. The failure of a universal successor to give this information is a breach of duty to the persons concerned but does not affect the validity of the approval of succession without administration or the powers or liabilities of the universal successors. A universal successor may inform other persons of the succession without administration by delivery or by ordinary first class mail.

COMMENT

The problem of residuary legatees or some of the heirs moving for universal succession without the knowledge of others interested in the estate is similar to that of informal administration. By this provision those devisees and heirs who do not participate in the application are informed of the application and its approval and may move to pro-

tect any interest that they perceive.
The provision parallels U.P.C. Section 3-705.

Section 3-320. [Universal Succession; Universal Successors' Liability For Restitution to Estate.]

If a personal representative is subsequently appointed, universal successors are personally liable for restitution of any property of the estate to which they are not entitled as heirs or devisees of the decedent and their liability is the same as a distributee under Section 3-909, subject to the provisions of Sections 3-317 and 3-321 and the limitations of Section 3-1006.

COMMENT

The liability of universal successors for restitution in the event a personal representative is appointed is spelled out in this section and keyed to the parallel sections in the U.P.C.

Section 3-321. [Universal Succession; Liability of Universal Successors for Claims, Expenses, Intestate Shares and Devises.]

The liability of universal successors is subject to any defenses that would have been available to the decedent. Other than liability arising from fraud, conversion, or other wrongful conduct of a universal successor, the personal liability of each universal successor to any creditor, claimant, other heir, devisee, or person entitled to decedent's property may not exceed the proportion of the claim that the universal successor's share bears to the share of all heirs and residuary devisees.

COMMENT

This is the primary provision for the successor's liability to creditors and others. The theory is that the universal successors as a group are liable in full to the creditors but that none have a greater liability than in proportion to the share of the estate received. Under the U.P.C., since informal administration is available with limited liability for the personal representative, the analogy to the Louisiana system would be to accept full responsibility for debts and claims if succession without administration is desired but to choose informal administration if protection of the inventory is desired.

This definition of liability assumes, first, that the devisees and heirs are subject to the usual priorities for creditors and devisees and abatement for them in §§ 3-316, 3-317. Second, it is assumed that if a creditor or a subsequently appointed personal representative were to proceed against the successors, having jurisdiction by submission, § 3–318, the liability would be on a theory of contribution by the successors with the burden on each universal successor to prove his or her own share of the estate and liability against that share.

Third, it is also assumed that, a creditor who is unprotected or unsecured under § 3–322, can object to universal succession under § 3–314(c) and if the creditor does not object, payments by the successors, like those by the decedent when alive, will be recognized as good without any theory of preferring creditors. Thus, until a creditor takes action to require adminis-

tration, that creditor should be bound by the successors' non-fraudulent prior payment to other creditors. If a creditor suspects insolvency, he can put the estate into administration and after the appointment of a personal representative would have the usual priority as to remaining assets. This would be subject to the theory of fraud, i.e., a knowing and conscious design on the part of the successors to ignore the priority of the decedent's creditors to the harm of a creditor. This would constitute fraud that would defeat the limits on successor's liability otherwise available under the statute.

Section 3–322. [Universal Succession; Remedies of Creditors, Other Heirs, Devisees or Persons Entitled to Decedent's Property.]

In addition to remedies otherwise provided by law, any creditor, heir, devisee, or person entitled to decedent's property qualified under Section 3–605, may demand bond of universal successors. If the demand for bond precedes the granting of an application for universal succession, it must be treated as an objection under Section 3–314(c) unless it is withdrawn, the claim satisfied, or the applicants post bond in an amount sufficient to protect the demandant. If the demand for bond follows the granting of an application for universal succession, the universal successors, within 10 days after notice of the demand, upon satisfying the claim or posting bond sufficient to protect the demandant, may disqualify the demandant from seeking administration of the estate.

COMMENT

This section provides necessary protection to creditors and other heirs, devisees or persons entitled to distribution. Any person to whom a universal successor is obligated could pursue any available remedy, e.g., a proceeding to collect a debt or to secure specific performance. By this section, any creditor or oth-

er heir, devisee or person entitled to distribution may also demand protection and, if it is not forthcoming, put the estate into administration. This seems adequate to coerce performance from universal successors while assuring creditors their historical preference and other beneficiaries of the estate their rights.

PART 4

FORMAL TESTACY AND APPOINTMENT PROCEEDINGS

Section 3–401. [Formal Testacy Proceedings; Nature; When Commenced.]

A formal testacy proceeding is litigation to determine whether a decedent left a valid will. A formal testacy proceeding may be commenced by an interested person filing a petition as described in Section 3–402(a) in which he requests that the Court, after notice and hearing, enter an order probating a will, or a petition to set aside an informal probate of a will or to prevent informal probate of a will which is the subject of a pending application, or a petition in accordance with Section 3–402(b) for an order that the decedent died intestate.

A petition may seek formal probate of a will without regard to whether the same or a conflicting will has been informally probated. A formal testacy proceeding may, but need not, involve a request for appointment of a personal representative.

During the pendency of a formal testacy proceeding, the Registrar shall not act upon any application for informal probate of any will of the decedent or any application for informal appointment of a personal representative of the decedent.

Unless a petition in a formal testacy proceeding also requests confirmation of the previous informal appointment, a previously appointed personal representative, after receipt of notice of the commencement of a formal probate proceeding, must refrain from exercising his power to make any further distribution of the estate during the pendency of the formal proceeding. A petitioner who seeks the appointment of a different personal representative in a formal proceeding also may request an order restraining the acting personal representative from exercising any of the powers of his office and requesting the appointment of a special administrator. In the absence of a request, or if the request is denied, the commencement of a formal proceeding has no effect on the powers and duties of a previously appointed personal representative other than those relating to distribution.

COMMENT

The word "testacy" is used to refer to the general status of a decedent in regard to wills. Thus, it embraces the possibility that he left no will, any question of which of sever-

266

al instruments is his valid will, and the possibility that he died intestate as to a part of his estate, and testate as to the balance. See Section 1–201(44).

The formal proceedings described by this section may be: (i) an original proceeding to secure "solemn form" probate of a will; (ii) a proceeding to secure "solemn form" probate to corroborate a previous informal probate; (iii) a proceeding to block a pending application for informal probate, or to prevent an informal application from occurring thereafter; (iv) a proceeding to contradict a previous order of informal probate; (v) a proceeding to secure a declaratory judgment of intestacy and a determination of heirs in a case where no will has been offered. If a pending informal application for probate is blocked by a formal proceeding, the applicant may withdraw his application and avoid the obligation of going forward with prima facie proof of due execution. See Section 3–407. The petitioner in the formal proceedings

may be content to let matters stop there, or he can frame his petition, or amend, so that he may secure an adjudication of intestacy which would prevent further activity concerning the will.

If a personal representative has been appointed prior to the commencement of a formal testacy proceeding, the petitioner must request confirmation of the appointment to indicate that he does not want the testacy proceeding to have any effect on the duties of the personal representative, or refrain from seeking confirmation, in which case, the proceeding suspends the distributive power of the previously appointed representative. If nothing else is requested or decided in respect to the personal representative, his distributive powers are restored at the completion of the proceeding, with Section 3–703 directing him to abide by the will. "Distribute" and "distribution" do not include payment of claims. See 1–201(10), 3–807 and 3–902.

Section 3–402. [Formal Testacy or Appointment Proceedings; Petition; Contents.]

(a) Petitions for formal probate of a will, or for adjudication of intestacy with or without request for appointment of a personal representative, must be directed to the Court, request a judicial order after notice and hearing and contain further statements as indicated in this section. A petition for formal probate of a will

(1) requests an order as to the testacy of the decedent in relation to a particular instrument which may or may not have been informally probated and determining the heirs,

(2) contains the statements required for informal applications as stated in the six subparagraphs under Section 3–301(a)(1), the statements required by subparagraphs (ii) and (iii) of Section 3–301(a)(2), and

(3) states whether the original of the last will of the decedent is in the possession of the Court or accompanies the petition.

If the original will is neither in the possession of the Court nor accompanies the petition and no authenticated copy of a will probated in another jurisdiction accompanies the petition, the petition also must state the contents of the will, and indicate that it is lost, destroyed, or otherwise unavailable.

(b) A petition for adjudication of intestacy and appointment of an administrator in intestacy must request a judicial finding and order that the decedent left no will and determining the heirs, contain the statements required by (1) and (4) of Section 3–301(a) and indicate whether supervised administration is sought. A petition may request an order determining intestacy and heirs without requesting the appointment of an administrator, in which case, the statements required by subparagraph (ii) of Section 3–301(a)(4) above may be omitted.

COMMENT

If a petitioner seeks an adjudication that a decedent died intestate, he is required also to obtain a finding of heirship. A formal proceeding which is to be effective on all interested persons must follow reasonable notice to such persons. It seems desirable to force the proceedings through a formal determination of heirship because the finding will bolster the order, as well as preclude later questions that might arise at the time of distribution.

Unless an order of supervised administration is sought, there will be little occasion for a formal order concerning appointment of a personal representative which does not also adjudicate the testacy status of the decedent. If a formal order of appointment is sought because of disagreement over who should serve, Section 3–414 describes the appropriate procedure.

The words "otherwise unavailable" in the last paragraph of subsection (a) are not intended to be read restrictively.

Section 1–310 expresses the verification requirement which applies to all documents filed with the Courts.

Section 3–403. [Formal Testacy Proceedings; Notice of Hearing on Petition.]

(a) Upon commencement of a formal testacy proceeding, the Court shall fix a time and place of hearing. Notice shall be given in the manner prescribed by Section 1–401 by the petitioner to the persons herein enumerated and to any additional person who has filed a demand for notice under Section 3–204 of this Code.

Notice shall be given to the following persons: the surviving spouse, children, and other heirs of the decedent, the devisees and executors named in any will that is being, or has been, probated, or offered for informal or formal probate in the [county,] or that is known by the petitioner to have been probated, or offered for informal or formal probate elsewhere, and any personal representative of the decedent whose appointment has not been terminated.

Notice may be given to other persons. In addition, the petitioner shall give notice by publication to all unknown persons and to all known persons whose addresses are unknown who have any interest in the matters being litigated.

(b) If it appears by the petition or otherwise that the fact of the death of the alleged decedent may be in doubt, or on the written demand of any interested person, a copy of the notice of the hearing on said petition shall be sent by registered mail to the alleged decedent at his last known address. The Court shall direct the petitioner to report the results of, or make and report back concerning, a reasonably diligent search for the alleged decedent in any manner that may seem advisable, including any or all of the following methods:

(1) by inserting in one or more suitable periodicals a notice requesting information from any person having knowledge of the whereabouts of the alleged decedent;

(2) by notifying law enforcement officials and public welfare agencies in appropriate locations of the disappearance of the alleged decedent;

(3) by engaging the services of an investigator.

The costs of any search so directed shall be paid by the petitioner if there is no administration or by the estate of the decedent in case there is administration.

COMMENT

Provisions governing the time and manner of notice required by this section and other sections in the Code are contained in 1–401.

The provisions concerning search for the alleged decedent are derived from Model Probate Code, Section 71.

Testacy proceedings involve adjudications that no will exists. Unknown wills as well as any which are brought to the attention of the Court are affected. Persons with potential interests under unknown wills have the notice afforded by death and by publication. Notice requirements extend also to persons named in a will that is known to the petitioners to exist, irrespective of whether it has been probated or offered for formal or informal probate, if their position may be affected adversely by granting of the petition. But, a rigid statutory requirement relating to such persons might cause undue difficulty. Hence, the statute merely provides that the petitioner may notify other persons.

It would not be inconsistent with this section for the Court to adopt rules designed to make petitioners exercise reasonable diligence in searching for as yet undiscovered wills.

Section 3–106 provides that an order is valid as to those given notice, though less than all interested persons were given notice. Section 3–1001(b) provides a means of extending a testacy order to previously unnotified persons in connection with a formal closing.

Section 3–404. [Formal Testacy Proceedings; Written Objections to Probate.]

Any party to a formal proceeding who opposes the probate of a will for any reason shall state in his pleadings his objections to probate of the will.

COMMENT

Model Probate Code section 72 requires a contestant to file written objections to any will he would oppose. The provision prevents potential confusion as to who must file what pleading that can arise from the notion that the probate of a will is in rem. The petition for probate of a revoking will is sufficient warning to proponents of the revoked will.

Section 3–405. [Formal Testacy Proceedings; Uncontested Cases; Hearings and Proof.]

If a petition in a testacy proceeding is unopposed, the Court may order probate or intestacy on the strength of the pleadings if satisfied that the conditions of Section 3–409 have been met, or conduct a hearing in open court and require proof of the matters necessary to support the order sought. If evidence concerning execution of the will is necessary, the affidavit or testimony of one of any attesting witnesses to the instrument is sufficient. If the affidavit or testimony of an attesting witness is not available, execution of the will may be proved by other evidence or affidavit.

COMMENT

For various reasons, attorneys handling estates may want interested persons to be gathered for a hearing before the Court on the formal allowance of the will. The Court is not required to conduct a hearing, however.

If no hearing is required, uncontested formal probates can be completed on the strength of the pleadings. There is no good reason for summoning attestors when no interested person wants to force the production of evidence on a formal probate. Moreover, there seems to be no valid distinction between litigation to establish a will, and other civil litigation, in respect to whether the court may enter judgment on the pleadings.

Section 3–406. [Formal Testacy Proceedings; Contested Cases; Testimony of Attesting Witnesses.]

(a) If evidence concerning execution of an attested will which is not self-proved is necessary in contested cases, the testimony of at

270

least one of the attesting witnesses, if within the state, competent and able to testify, is required. Due execution of an attested or unattested will may be proved by other evidence.

(b) If the will is self-proved, compliance with signature requirements for execution is conclusively presumed and other requirements of execution are presumed subject to rebuttal without the testimony of any witness upon filing the will and the acknowledgment and affidavits annexed or attached thereto, unless there is proof of fraud or forgery affecting the acknowledgment or affidavit.

COMMENT

Model Probate Code section 76, combined with section 77, substantially unchanged. The self-proved will is described in Article II. See Section 2–504. The "conclusive presumption" described here would foreclose questions like whether the witnesses signed in the presence of the testator. It would not preclude proof of undue influence, lack of testamentary capacity, revocation or any relevant proof that the testator was unaware of the contents of the document. The balance of the section is derived from Model Probate Code sections 76 and 77.

Section 3–407. [Formal Testacy Proceedings; Burdens in Contested Cases.]

In contested cases, petitioners who seek to establish intestacy have the burden of establishing prima facie proof of death, venue, and heirship. Proponents of a will have the burden of establishing prima facie proof of due execution in all cases, and, if they are also petitioners, prima facie proof of death and venue. Contestants of a will have the burden of establishing lack of testamentary intent or capacity, undue influence, fraud, duress, mistake or revocation. Parties have the ultimate burden of persuasion as to matters with respect to which they have the initial burden of proof. If a will is opposed by the petition for probate of a later will revoking the former, it shall be determined first whether the later will is entitled to probate, and if a will is opposed by a petition for a declaration of intestacy, it shall be determined first whether the will is entitled to probate.

COMMENT

This section is designed to clarify the law by stating what is believed to be a fairly standard approach to questions concerning burdens of going forward with evidence in will contest cases.

Section 3–408. [Formal Testacy Proceedings; Will Construction; Effect of Final Order in Another Jurisdiction.]

A final order of a court of another state determining testacy, the validity or construction of a will, made in a proceeding involving notice to and an opportunity for contest by all interested persons must be accepted as determinative by the courts of this state if it includes, or is based upon, a finding that the decedent was domiciled at his death in the state where the order was made.

COMMENT

This section is designed to extend the effect of final orders of another jurisdiction of the United States. It should not be read to restrict the obligation of the local court to respect the judgment of another court when parties who were personally before the other court also are personally before the local court. An "authenticated copy" includes copies properly certified under the full faith and credit statute. If conflicting claims of domicile are made in proceedings which are commenced in different jurisdictions, Section 3–202 applies. This section is framed to apply where a formal proceeding elsewhere has been previously concluded. Hence, if a local proceeding is concluded before formal proceedings at domicile are concluded, local law will control.

Informal proceedings by which a will is probated or a personal representative is appointed are not proceedings which must be respected by a local court under either Section 3–202 or this section.

Nothing in this section bears on questions of what assets are included in a decedent's estate.

This section adds nothing to existing law as applied to cases where the parties before the local court were also personally before the foreign court, or where the property involved was subject to the power of the foreign court. It extends present law so that, for some purposes, the law of another state may become binding in regard to due execution or revocation of wills controlling local land, and to questions concerning the meaning of ambiguous words in wills involving local land. But, choice of law rules frequently produce a similar result. See § 240 Restatement of the Law, Second: Conflict of Laws, p. 73, Proposed Official Draft III, 1969.

This section may be easier to justify than familiar choice of law rules, for its application is limited to instances where the protesting party has had notice of, and an opportunity to participate in, previous litigation resolving the question he now seeks to raise.

Section 3–409. [Formal Testacy Proceedings; Order; Foreign Will.]

After the time required for any notice has expired, upon proof of notice, and after any hearing that may be necessary, if the Court finds that the testator is dead, venue is proper and that the proceeding was commenced within the limitation prescribed by Section

3–108, it shall determine the decedent's domicile at death, his heirs and his state of testacy. Any will found to be valid and unrevoked shall be formally probated. Termination of any previous informal appointment of a personal representative, which may be appropriate in view of the relief requested and findings, is governed by Section 3–612. The petition shall be dismissed or appropriate amendment allowed if the court is not satisfied that the alleged decedent is dead. A will from a place which does not provide for probate of a will after death, may be proved for probate in this state by a duly authenticated certificate of its legal custodian that the copy introduced is a true copy and that the will has become effective under the law of the other place.

COMMENT

Model Probate Code section 80(a), slightly changed. If the court is not satisfied that the alleged decedent is dead, it may permit amendment of the proceeding so that it would become a proceeding to protect the estate of a missing and therefore "disabled" person. See Article V of this Code.

Section 3–410. [Formal Testacy Proceedings; Probate of More Than One Instrument.]

If two or more instruments are offered for probate before a final order is entered in a formal testacy proceeding, more than one instrument may be probated if neither expressly revokes the other or contains provisions which work a total revocation by implication. If more than one instrument is probated, the order shall indicate what provisions control in respect to the nomination of an executor, if any. The order may, but need not, indicate how any provisions of a particular instrument are affected by the other instrument. After a final order in a testacy proceeding has been entered, no petition for probate of any other instrument of the decedent may be entertained, except incident to a petition to vacate or modify a previous probate order and subject to the time limits of Section 3–412.

COMMENT

Except as otherwise provided in Section 3–412, an order in a formal testacy proceeding serves to end the time within which it is possible to probate after-discovered wills, or to give effect to late-discovered facts concerning heirship. Determination of heirs is not barred by the three year limitation but a judicial determination of heirs is conclusive unless the order may be vacated.

This section authorizes a court to engage in some construction of wills incident to determining whether a will is entitled to probate. It seems desirable to leave the extent

of this power to the sound discre- cial probate, they may be subject to
tion of the court. If wills are not construction at any time. See Sec-
construed in connection with a judi- tion 3–108.

Section 3–411. [Formal Testacy Proceedings; Partial Intestacy.]

If it becomes evident in the course of a formal testacy proceeding
that, though one or more instruments are entitled to be probated,
the decedent's estate is or may be partially intestate, the Court shall
enter an order to that effect.

Section 3–412. [Formal Testacy Proceedings; Effect of Order; Vacation.]

Subject to appeal and subject to vacation as provided herein and
in Section 3–413, a formal testacy order under Sections 3–409 to
3–411, including an order that the decedent left no valid will and
determining heirs, is final as to all persons with respect to all issues
concerning the decedent's estate that the court considered or might
have considered incident to its rendition relevant to the question of
whether the decedent left a valid will, and to the determination of
heirs, except that:

(1) The court shall entertain a petition for modification or
vacation of its order and probate of another will of the decedent
if it is shown that the proponents of the later-offered will were
unaware of its existence at the time of the earlier proceeding or
were unaware of the earlier proceeding and were given no notice
thereof, except by publication.

(2) If intestacy of all or part of the estate has been ordered, the
determination of heirs of the decedent may be reconsidered if it
is shown that one or more persons were omitted from the
determination and it is also shown that the persons were unaware
of their relationship to the decedent, were unaware of his death
or were given no notice of any proceeding concerning his estate,
except by publication.

(3) A petition for vacation under either (1) or (2) above must be
filed prior to the earlier of the following time limits:

(i) If a personal representative has been appointed for the
estate, the time of entry of any order approving final distribution of the estate, or, if the estate is closed by statement, 6
months after the filing of the closing statement.

(ii) Whether or not a personal representative has been appointed for the estate of the decedent, the time prescribed by

274

Section 3–108 when it is no longer possible to initiate an original proceeding to probate a will of the decedent.

(iii) 12 months after the entry of the order sought to be vacated.

(4) The order originally rendered in the testacy proceeding may be modified or vacated, if appropriate under the circumstances, by the order of probate of the later-offered will or the order redetermining heirs.

(5) The finding of the fact of death is conclusive as to the alleged decedent only if notice of the hearing on the petition in the formal testacy proceeding was sent by registered or certified mail addressed to the alleged decedent at his last known address and the court finds that a search under Section 3–403(b) was made.

If the alleged decedent is not dead, even if notice was sent and search was made, he may recover estate assets in the hands of the personal representative. In addition to any remedies available to the alleged decedent by reason of any fraud or intentional wrongdoing, the alleged decedent may recover any estate or its proceeds from distributees that is in their hands, or the value of distributions received by them, to the extent that any recovery from distributees is equitable in view of all of the circumstances.

COMMENT

The provisions barring proof of late-discovered wills is derived in part from section 81 of Model Probate Code. The same section is the source of the provisions of (5) above. The provisions permitting vacation of an order determining heirs on certain conditions reflect the effort to offer parallel possibilities for adjudications in testate and intestate estates. See Section 3–401. An objective is to make it possible to handle an intestate estate exactly as a testate estate may be handled. If this is achieved, some of the pressure on persons to make wills may be relieved.

If an alleged decedent turns out to have been alive, heirs and distributees are liable to restore the "estate or its proceeds". If neither can be identified through the normal process of tracing assets, their liability depends upon the circumstances. The liability of distributees to claimants whose claims have not been barred, or to persons shown to be entitled to distribution when a formal proceeding changes a previous assumption informally established which guided an earlier distribution, is different. See Sections 3–909 and 3–1004.

Section 3–413. [Formal Testacy Proceedings; Vacation of Order For Other Cause.]

For good cause shown, an order in a formal testacy proceeding may be modified or vacated within the time allowed for appeal.

COMMENT

See Sections 1–304 and 1–308.

Section 3–414. [Formal Proceedings Concerning Appointment of Personal Representative.]

(a) A formal proceeding for adjudication regarding the priority or qualification of one who is an applicant for appointment as personal representative, or of one who previously has been appointed personal representative in informal proceedings, if an issue concerning the testacy of the decedent is or may be involved, is governed by Section 3–402, as well as by this section. In other cases, the petition shall contain or adopt the statements required by Section 3–301(1) and describe the question relating to priority or qualification of the personal representative which is to be resolved. If the proceeding precedes any appointment of a personal representative, it shall stay any pending informal appointment proceedings as well as any commenced thereafter. If the proceeding is commenced after appointment, the previously appointed personal representative, after receipt of notice thereof, shall refrain from exercising any power of administration except as necessary to preserve the estate or unless the Court orders otherwise.

(b) After notice to interested persons, including all persons interested in the administration of the estate as successors under the applicable assumption concerning testacy, any previously appointed personal representative and any person having or claiming priority for appointment as personal representative, the Court shall determine who is entitled to appointment under Section 3–203, make a proper appointment and, if appropriate, terminate any prior appointment found to have been improper as provided in cases of removal under Section 3–611.

COMMENT

A petition raising a controversy concerning the priority or qualifications of a personal representative may be combined with a petition in a formal testacy proceeding. However, it is not necessary to petition formally for the appointment of a personal representative as a part of a formal testacy proceeding. A personal representative may be appointed on informal application either before or after formal proceedings which establish whether the de-cedent died testate or intestate or no appointment may be desired. See Sections 3–107, 3–301(a)(3), (4) and 3–307. Furthermore, procedures for securing the appointment of a new personal representative after a previous assumption as to testacy has been changed are provided by Section 3–612. These may be informal, or related to pending formal proceedings concerning testacy. A formal order relating to appointment may be desired when there is a dispute concerning priority or qualification to serve but no dispute concerning testacy. It is important to distinguish formal proceedings concerning appointment from "supervised administration". The former includes any proceeding after notice involving a request for an appointment. The latter originates in a "formal proceeding" and may be requested in addition to a ruling concerning testacy or priority or qualifications of a personal representative, but is descriptive of a special proceeding with a different scope and purpose than those concerned merely with establishing the bases for an administration. In other words, a personal representative appointed in a "formal" proceeding may or may not be "supervised".

Another point should be noted. The Court may not immediately issue letters even though a formal proceeding seeking appointment is involved and results in an order authorizing appointment. Rather, Section 3–601 et seq. control the subject of qualification. Section 1–305 deals with letters.

PART 5

SUPERVISED ADMINISTRATION

Section 3–501. [Supervised Administration; Nature of Proceeding.]

Supervised administration is a single in rem proceeding to secure complete administration and settlement of a decedent's estate under the continuing authority of the Court which extends until entry of an order approving distribution of the estate and discharging the personal representative or other order terminating the proceeding. A supervised personal representative is responsible to the Court, as well as to the interested parties, and is subject to directions concerning the estate made by the Court on its own motion or on the motion of any interested party. Except as otherwise provided in this Part, or as otherwise ordered by the Court, a supervised personal representative has the same duties and powers as a personal representative who is not supervised.

COMMENT

This and the following sections of this Part describe an optional procedure for settling an estate in one continuous proceeding in the Court. The proceeding is characterized as "in rem" to align it with the concepts described by the Model Probate Code. See Section 62, M.P.C. In cases where supervised administration is not requested or ordered, no compulsion other than self-interest exists to compel use of a formal testacy proceeding to secure an adjudication of a will or no will, because informal probate or appointment of an administrator in intestacy may be used. Similarly, unless administration is supervised, there is no compulsion other than self-interest to use a formal closing proceeding. Thus, even though an estate administration may be begun by use of a *formal* testacy proceeding which may involve an order concerning who is to be appointed personal representative, the proceeding is over when the order concerning testacy and appointment is entered. See Section 3–107. Supervised administration, therefore, is appropriate when an interested person desires assurance that the essential steps regarding opening and closing of an estate will be adjudicated. See the Comment following the next section.

Section 3–502. [Supervised Administration; Petition; Order.]

A petition for supervised administration may be filed by any interested person or by a personal representative at any time or the prayer for supervised administration may be joined with a petition in a testacy or appointment proceeding. If the testacy of the decedent and the priority and qualification of any personal representative have not been adjudicated previously, the petition for supervised administration shall include the matters required of a petition in a formal testacy proceeding and the notice requirements and procedures applicable to a formal testacy proceeding apply. If not previously adjudicated, the Court shall adjudicate the testacy of the decedent and questions relating to the priority and qualifications of the personal representative in any case involving a request for supervised administration, even though the request for supervised administration may be denied. After notice to interested persons, the Court shall order supervised administration of a decedent's estate: (1) if the decedent's will directs supervised administration, it shall be ordered unless the Court finds that circumstances bearing on the need for supervised administration have changed since the execution of the will and that there is no necessity for supervised administration; (2) if the decedent's will directs unsupervised administration, supervised administration shall be ordered only upon a finding that it is necessary for protection of persons interested in the estate; or (3) in other cases if the Court finds that supervised administration is necessary under the circumstances.

COMMENT

The expressed wishes of a testator regarding supervised administration should bear upon, but not control, the question of whether supervised administration will be ordered. This section is designed to achieve a fair balance between the wishes of the decedent, and the interests of successors in regard to supervised administration.

Since supervised administration normally will result in an adjudicated distribution of the estate, the issue of will or no will must be adjudicated. This section achieves this by forcing a petition for supervised administration to include matters necessary to put the issue of testacy before the Court. It is possible, however, that supervised administration will be requested because administrative complexities warranting it develop after the issue of will or no will has been resolved

in a previously concluded formal testacy proceeding.

It should be noted that supervised administration, though it compels a judicial settlement of an estate, is not the only route to obtaining judicial review and settlement at the close of an administration. The procedures described in Sections 3–1101 and 3–1102 are available for use by or against personal representatives who are not supervised. Also efficient remedies for breach of duty by a personal representative who is not supervised are available under Part 6 of this Article. Finally, each personal representative consents to jurisdiction of the Court as invoked by mailed notice of any proceeding relating to the estate which may be initiated by an interested person. Also, persons interested in the estate may be subjected to orders of the Court following mailed notices made in proceedings initiated by the personal representative. In combination, these possibilities mean that supervised administration will be valuable principally to persons who see some advantage in a single judicial proceeding which will produce adjudications on all major points involved in an estate settlement.

Section 3–503. [Supervised Administration; Effect on Other Proceedings.]

(a) The pendency of a proceeding for supervised administration of a decedent's estate stays action on any informal application then pending or thereafter filed.

(b) If a will has been previously probated in informal proceedings, the effect of the filing of a petition for supervised administration is as provided for formal testacy proceedings by Section 3–401.

(c) After he has received notice of the filing of a petition for supervised administration, a personal representative who has been appointed previously shall not exercise his power to distribute any estate. The filing of the petition does not affect his other powers and duties unless the Court restricts the exercise of any of them pending full hearing on the petition.

COMMENT

The duties and powers of personal representative are described in Part 7 of this Article. The ability of a personal representative to create a good title in a purchaser of estate assets is not hampered by the fact that the personal representative may breach a duty created by statute, court order or other circumstances in making the sale. See Section 3–715. However, formal proceedings against a personal representative may involve requests for qualification of the power normally possessed by personal representatives which, if granted, would subject the personal representative to the penalties for contempt of Court if he disregarded the restriction. See Section 3–607. If a proceeding also involved a demand that particular real estate be kept in the estate pending determination of a petitioner's claim thereto, notice of the pendency of the proceeding could be recorded as is usual under the jurisdiction's system for the lis pendens concept.

The word "restricts" in the last sentence is intended to negate the idea that a judicial order specially qualifying the powers and duties of a personal representative is a restraining order in the usual sense. The section means simply that some supervised personal representatives may receive the same powers and duties as ordinary personal representatives, except that they must obtain a Court order before paying claimants or distributing, while others may receive a more restricted set of powers. Section 3–607 governs petitions which seek to limit the power of a personal representative.

Section 3–504. [Supervised Administration; Powers of Personal Representative.]

Unless restricted by the Court, a supervised personal representative has, without interim orders approving exercise of a power, all powers of personal representatives under this Code, but he shall not exercise his power to make any distribution of the estate without prior order of the Court. Any other restriction on the power of a personal representative which may be ordered by the Court must be endorsed on his letters of appointment and, unless so endorsed, is ineffective as to persons dealing in good faith with the personal representative.

COMMENT

This section provides authority to issue letters showing restrictions of power of supervised administrators. In general, persons dealing with personal representatives are not bound to inquire concerning the authority of a personal representative, and are not affected by provisions in a will or judicial order unless they know of it. But, it is expected that persons dealing with personal representatives will want to see the personal representative's letters, and this section has the practical effect of requiring them to do so. No provision is made for noting restrictions in letters except in the case of supervised representatives. See Section 3–715.

Section 3–505. [Supervised Administration; Interim Orders; Distribution and Closing Orders.]

Unless otherwise ordered by the Court, supervised administration is terminated by order in accordance with time restrictions, notices and contents of orders prescribed for proceedings under Section 3–1001. Interim orders approving or directing partial distributions or granting other relief may be issued by the Court at any time during the pendency of a supervised administration on the application of the personal representative or any interested person.

COMMENT

Since supervised administration is a single proceeding, the notice requirement contained in 3–106 relates to the notice of institution of the proceedings which is described with particularity by Section 3–502. The above section makes it clear that an additional notice is required for a closing order. It was discussed whether provision for notice of interim orders should be included. It was decided to leave the point to be covered by court order or rule. There was a suggestion for a rule as follows: "Unless otherwise required by order, notice of interim orders in supervised administration need be given only to interested persons who request notice of all orders entered in the proceeding." 1–402 permits any person to waive notice by a writing filed in the proceeding.

A demand for notice under Section 3–204 would entitle any interested person to notice of any interim order which might be made in the course of supervised administration.

PART 6

PERSONAL REPRESENTATIVE; APPOINTMENT, CONTROL AND TERMINATION OF AUTHORITY

Section 3–601. [Qualification.]

Prior to receiving letters, a personal representative shall qualify by filing with the appointing Court any required bond and a statement of acceptance of the duties of the office.

COMMENT

This and related sections of this Part describe details and conditions of appointment which apply to all personal representatives without regard to whether the appointment proceeding involved is formal or informal, or whether the personal representative is supervised. Section 1–305 authorizes issuance of copies of letters and prescribes their content. The section should be read with Section 3–504 which directs endorsement on letters of any restrictions of power of a supervised administrator.

Section 3–602. [Acceptance of Appointment; Consent to Jurisdiction.]

By accepting appointment, a personal representative submits personally to the jurisdiction of the Court in any proceeding relating to the estate that may be instituted by any interested person. Notice of any proceeding shall be delivered to the personal representative, or mailed to him by ordinary first class mail at his address as listed in the application or petition for appointment or as thereafter reported to the Court and to his address as then known to the petitioner.

COMMENT

Except for personal representatives appointed pursuant to Section 3–502, appointees are not deemed to be "officers" of the appointing court or to be parties in one continuous judicial proceeding that extends until final settlement. See Section 3–107. Yet, it is desirable to continue present patterns which prevent a personal representative who might make himself unavailable to service within the state from affecting the power of the appointing court to enter valid orders affecting him. See Michigan Trust Co. v. Ferry, 33 S.Ct. 550, 228 U.S. 346, 57 L.Ed. 867 (1912). The concept employed to accomplish this is that of requiring each appointee to consent in advance to the personal jurisdiction of the Court in any proceeding relating to the estate that may be instituted against him. The section requires that he be given notice of any such proceeding, which, when considered in the light of the responsibility he

has undertaken, should make the
procedure sufficient to meet the requirements of due process.

Section 3–603. [Bond Not Required Without Court Order, Exceptions.]

No bond is required of a personal representative appointed in informal proceedings, except (1) upon the appointment of a special administrator; (2) when an executor or other personal representative is appointed to administer an estate under a will containing an express requirement of bond or (3) when bond is required under Section 3–605. Bond may be required by court order at the time of appointment of a personal representative appointed in any formal proceeding except that bond is not required of a personal representative appointed in formal proceedings if the will relieves the personal representative of bond, unless bond has been requested by an interested party and the Court is satisfied that it is desirable. Bond required by any will may be dispensed with in formal proceedings upon determination by the Court that it is not necessary. No bond is required of any personal representative who, pursuant to statute, has deposited cash or collateral with an agency of this state to secure performance of his duties.

COMMENT

This section must be read with the next three sections. The purpose of these provisions is to move away from the idea that bond always should be required of a probate fiduciary, or required unless a will excuses it. Also, it is designed to keep the registrar acting pursuant to applications in informal proceedings, from passing judgment in each case on the need for bond. The point is that the court and registrar are not responsible for seeing that personal representatives perform as they are supposed to perform. Rather, performance is coerced by the remedies available to interested persons. Interested persons are protected by their ability to demand prior notice of informal proceedings (Section 3–204), to contest a requested appointment by use of a formal testacy proceeding or by use of a formal proceeding seeking the

appointment of another person. Section 3–105 gives general authority to the court in a formal proceeding to make appropriate orders as desirable incident to estate administration. This should be sufficient to make it clear that an informal application may be blocked by a formal petition which disputes the matters stated in the petition. Furthermore, an interested person has the remedies provided in Sections 3–605 and 3–607. Finally, interested persons have assurance under this Code that their rights in respect to the values of a decedent's estate cannot be terminated without a judicial order after notice or before the passage of three years from the decedent's death.

It is believed that the total package of protection thus afforded may represent more real protection than a blanket requirement of bond. Surely, it permits a reduction in the procedures which must occur in un- complicated estates where interested persons are perfectly willing to trust each other and the fiduciary.

Section 3–604. [Bond Amount; Security; Procedure; Reduction.]

If bond is required and the provisions of the will or order do not specify the amount, unless stated in his application or petition, the person qualifying shall file a statement under oath with the Registrar indicating his best estimate of the value of the personal estate of the decedent and of the income expected from the personal and real estate during the next year, and he shall execute and file a bond with the Registrar, or give other suitable security, in an amount not less than the estimate. The Registrar shall determine that the bond is duly executed by a corporate surety, or one or more individual sureties whose performance is secured by pledge of personal property, mortgage on real property or other adequate security. The Registrar may permit the amount of the bond to be reduced by the value of assets of the estate deposited with a domestic financial institution (as defined in Section 6–101) in a manner that prevents their unauthorized disposition. On petition of the personal representative or another interested person the Court may excuse a requirement of bond, increase or reduce the amount of the bond, release sureties, or permit the substitution of another bond with the same or different sureties.

COMMENT

This section permits estimates of value needed to fix the amount of required bond to be filed when it becomes necessary. A consequence of this procedure is that estimates of value of estates no longer need appear in the petitions and applications which will attend every ad- ministered estate. Hence, a measure of privacy that is not possible under most existing procedures may be achieved. A co-signature arrangement might constitute adequate security within the meaning of this section.

Section 3–605. [Demand For Bond by Interested Person.]

Any person apparently having an interest in the estate worth in excess of [$1000], or any creditor having a claim in excess of [$1000], may make a written demand that a personal representative give bond. The demand must be filed with the Registrar and a copy mailed to the personal representative, if appointment and qualification have occurred. Thereupon, bond is required, but the requirement ceases if the person demanding bond ceases to be interested

285

in the estate, or if bond is excused as provided in Section 3–603 or 3–604. After he has received notice and until the filing of the bond or cessation of the requirement of bond, the personal representative shall refrain from exercising any powers of his office except as necessary to preserve the estate. Failure of the personal representative to meet a requirement of bond by giving suitable bond within 30 days after receipt of notice is cause for his removal and appointment of a successor personal representative.

COMMENT

The demand for bond described in this section may be made in a petition or application for appointment of a personal representative, or may be made after a personal representative has been appointed. The mechanism for compelling bond is designed to function without unnecessary judicial involvement. If demand for bond is made in a formal proceeding, the judge can determine the amount of bond to be required with due consideration for all circumstances. If demand is not made in formal proceedings, methods for computing the amount of bond are provided by statute so that the demand can be complied with without resort to judicial proceedings. The information which a personal representative is required by Section 3–705 to give each beneficiary includes a statement concerning whether bond has been required.

Section 3–606. [Terms and Conditions of Bonds.]

(a) The following requirements and provisions apply to any bond required by this Part:

(1) Bonds shall name the [state] as obligee for the benefit of the persons interested in the estate and shall be conditioned upon the faithful discharge by the fiduciary of all duties according to law.

(2) Unless otherwise provided by the terms of the approved bond, sureties are jointly and severally liable with the personal representative and with each other. The address of sureties shall be stated in the bond.

(3) By executing an approved bond of a personal representative, the surety consents to the jurisdiction of the probate court which issued letters to the primary obligor in any proceedings pertaining to the fiduciary duties of the personal representative and naming the surety as a party. Notice of any proceeding shall be delivered to the surety or mailed to him by registered or certified mail at his address as listed with the court where the bond is filed and to his address as then known to the petitioner.

(4) On petition of a successor personal representative, any other personal representative of the same decedent, or any interested person, a proceeding in the Court may be initiated against a

surety for breach of the obligation of the bond of the personal representative.

(5) The bond of the personal representative is not void after the first recovery but may be proceeded against from time to time until the whole penalty is exhausted.

(b) No action or proceeding may be commenced against the surety on any matter as to which an action or proceeding against the primary obligor is barred by adjudication or limitation.

COMMENT

Paragraph (2) is based, in part, on Section 109 of the Model Probate Code. Paragraph (3) is derived from Section 118 of the Model Probate Code.

Section 3–607. [Order Restraining Personal Representative.]

(a) On petition of any person who appears to have an interest in the estate, the Court by temporary order may restrain a personal representative from performing specified acts of administration, disbursement, or distribution, or exercise of any powers or discharge of any duties of his office, or make any other order to secure proper performance of his duty, if it appears to the Court that the personal representative otherwise may take some action which would jeopardize unreasonably the interest of the applicant or of some other interested person. Persons with whom the personal representative may transact business may be made parties.

(b) The matter shall be set for hearing within 10 days unless the parties otherwise agree. Notice as the Court directs shall be given to the personal representative and his attorney of record, if any, and to any other parties named defendant in the petition.

COMMENT

Cf. Section 3–401 which provides for a restraining order against a previously appointed personal representative incident to a formal testacy proceeding. The above section describes a remedy which is available for any cause against a previously appointed personal representative, whether appointed formally or informally.

This remedy, in combination with the safeguards relating to the process for appointment of a personal representative, permit "control" of a personal representative that is believed to be equal, if not superior to that presently available with respect to "supervised" personal representatives appointed by inferior courts. The request for a restraining order may mark the beginning of a new proceeding but the personal representative, by the consent provided in Section 3–602, is practically in

the position of one who, on motion,
may be cited to appear before a
judge.

Section 3–608. [Termination of Appointment; General.]

Termination of appointment of a personal representative occurs
as indicated in Sections 3–609 to 3–612, inclusive. Termination
ends the right and power pertaining to the office of personal
representative as conferred by this Code or any will, except that a
personal representative, at any time prior to distribution or until
restrained or enjoined by court order, may perform acts necessary
to protect the estate and may deliver the assets to a successor
representative. Termination does not discharge a personal representative from liability for transactions or omissions occurring
before termination, or relieve him of the duty to preserve assets
subject to his control, to account therefor and to deliver the assets.
Termination does not affect the jurisdiction of the Court over the
personal representative, but terminates his authority to represent
the estate in any pending or future proceeding.

COMMENT

"Termination", as defined by this
and succeeding provisions, provides
definiteness respecting when the
powers of a personal representative
(who may or may not be discharged
by court order) terminate.

It is to be noted that this section
does not relate to jurisdiction over
the estate in proceedings which may
have been commenced against the
personal representative prior to ter-

mination. In such cases, a substitution of successor or special representative should occur if the plain-
tiff desires to maintain his action
against the estate.

It is important to note that "termination" is not "discharge". However, an order of the Court entered
under 3–1001 or 3–1002 both terminates the appointment of, and discharges, a personal representative.

Section 3–609. [Termination of Appointment; Death or Disability.]

The death of a personal representative or the appointment of a
conservator for the estate of a personal representative, terminates
his appointment. Until appointment and qualification of a successor or special representative to replace the deceased or protected
representative, the representative of the estate of the deceased or
protected personal representative, if any, has the duty to protect the
estate possessed and being administered by his decedent or ward at
the time his appointment terminates, has the power to perform acts
necessary for protection and shall account for and deliver the estate

assets to a successor or special personal representative upon his appointment and qualification.

COMMENT

See Section 3–718, which establishes the rule that a surviving co-executor may exercise all powers incident to the office unless the will provides otherwise. Read together, this section and Section 3–718 mean that the representative of a deceased co-representative would not have any duty or authority in relation to the office held by his decedent.

Section 3–610. [Termination of Appointment; Voluntary.]

(a) An appointment of a personal representative terminates as provided in Section 3–1003, one year after the filing of a closing statement.

(b) An order closing an estate as provided in Section 3–1001 or 3–1002 terminates an appointment of a personal representative.

(c) A personal representative may resign his position by filing a written statement of resignation with the Registrar after he has given at least 15 days written notice to the persons known to be interested in the estate. If no one applies or petitions for appointment of a successor representative within the time indicated in the notice, the filed statement of resignation is ineffective as a termination of appointment and in any event is effective only upon the appointment and qualification of a successor representative and delivery of the assets to him.

COMMENT

Subparagraph (c) above provides a procedure for resignation by a personal representative which may occur without judicial assistance.

Section 3–611. [Termination of Appointment by Removal; Cause; Procedure.]

(a) A person interested in the estate may petition for removal of a personal representative for cause at any time. Upon filing of the petition, the Court shall fix a time and place for hearing. Notice shall be given by the petitioner to the personal representative, and to other persons as the Court may order. Except as otherwise ordered as provided in Section 3–607, after receipt of notice of removal proceedings, the personal representative shall not act except to account, to correct maladministration or preserve the estate. If removal is ordered, the Court also shall direct by order the disposition of the assets remaining in the name of, or under the control of, the personal representative being removed.

289

(b) Cause for removal exists when removal would be in the best interests of the estate, or if it is shown that a personal representative or the person seeking his appointment intentionally misrepresented material facts in the proceedings leading to his appointment, or that the personal representative has disregarded an order of the Court, has become incapable of discharging the duties of his office, or has mismanaged the estate or failed to perform any duty pertaining to the office. Unless the decedent's will directs otherwise, a personal representative appointed at the decedent's domicile, incident to securing appointment of himself or his nominee as ancillary personal representative, may obtain removal of another who was appointed personal representative in this state to administer local assets.

COMMENT

Thought was given to qualifying (a) above so that no formal removal proceedings could be commenced until after a set period from entry of any previous order reflecting judicial consideration of the qualifications of the personal representative. It was decided, however, that the matter should be left to the judgment of interested persons and the Court.

Section 3–612. [Termination of Appointment; Change of Testacy Status.]

Except as otherwise ordered in formal proceedings, the probate of a will subsequent to the appointment of a personal representative in intestacy or under a will which is superseded by formal probate of another will, or the vacation of an informal probate of a will subsequent to the appointment of the personal representative thereunder, does not terminate the appointment of the personal representative although his powers may be reduced as provided in Section 3–401. Termination occurs upon appointment in informal or formal appointment proceedings of a person entitled to appointment under the later assumption concerning testacy. If no request for new appointment is made within 30 days after expiration of time for appeal from the order in formal testacy proceedings, or from the informal probate, changing the assumption concerning testacy, the previously appointed personal representative upon request may be appointed personal representative under the subsequently probated will, or as in intestacy as the case may be.

COMMENT

This section and Section 3–401 describe the relationship between formal or informal proceedings which change a previous assumption concerning the testacy of the decedent, and a previously appointed personal representative. The basic assumption of both sections is that an appointment, with attendant powers of management, is separable from the basis of appointment; i.e., intestate or testate?; what will is the last will? Hence, a previously appointed personal representative continues to serve in spite of formal or informal proceedings that may give another a prior right to serve as personal representative. But, if the testacy status is changed in formal proceedings, the petitioner also may request appointment of the person who would be entitled to serve if his assumption concerning the decedent's will prevails. Provision is made for a situation where all interested persons are content to allow a previously appointed personal representative to continue to serve even though another has a prior right because of a change relating to the decedent's will. It is not necessary for the continuing representative to seek reappointment under the new assumption for Section 3–703 is broad enough to require him to administer the estate as intestate, or under a later probated will, if either status is established after he was appointed. Under Section 3–403, notice of a formal testacy proceeding is required to be given to any previously appointed personal representative. Hence, the testacy status cannot be changed without notice to a previously appointed personal representative.

Section 3–613. [Successor Personal Representative.]

Parts 3 and 4 of this Article govern proceedings for appointment of a personal representative to succeed one whose appointment has been terminated. After appointment and qualification, a successor personal representative may be substituted in all actions and proceedings to which the former personal representative was a party, and no notice, process or claim which was given or served upon the former personal representative need be given to or served upon the successor in order to preserve any position or right the person giving the notice or filing the claim may thereby have obtained or preserved with reference to the former personal representative. Except as otherwise ordered by the Court, the successor personal representative has the powers and duties in respect to the continued administration which the former personal representative would have had if his appointment had not been terminated.

Section 3–614. [Special Administrator; Appointment.]

A special administrator may be appointed:

(1) informally by the Registrar on the application of any interested person when necessary to protect the estate of a decedent prior to the appointment of a general personal representative or if a prior appointment has been terminated as provided in Section 3–609;

(2) in a formal proceeding by order of the Court on the petition of any interested person and finding, after notice and hearing, that

appointment is necessary to preserve the estate or to secure its proper administration including its administration in circumstances where a general personal representative cannot or should not act. If it appears to the Court that an emergency exists, appointment may be ordered without notice.

COMMENT

The appointment of a special administrator other than one appointed pending original appointment of a general personal representative must be handled by the Court. Appointment of a special administrator would enable the estate to participate in a transaction which the general personal representative could not, or should not, handle because of conflict of interest. If a need arises because of temporary absence or anticipated incapacity for delegation of the authority of a personal representative, the problem may be handled without judicial intervention by use of the delegation powers granted to personal representatives by Section 3–715(21).

Section 3–615. [Special Administrator; Who May Be Appointed.]

(a) If a special administrator is to be appointed pending the probate of a will which is the subject of a pending application or petition for probate, the person named executor in the will shall be appointed if available, and qualified.

(b) In other cases, any proper person may be appointed special administrator.

COMMENT

In some areas of the country, particularly where wills cannot be probated without full notice and hearing, appointment of special administrators pending probate is sought almost routinely. The provisions of this Code concerning informal probate should reduce the number of cases in which a fiduciary will need to be appointed pending probate of a will. Nonetheless, there will be instances where contests begin before probate and where it may be necessary to appoint a special administrator. The objective of this section is to reduce the likelihood that contestants will be encouraged to file contests as early as possible simply to gain some advantage via having a person who is sympathetic to their cause appointed special administrator. Most will contests are not successful. Hence, it seems reasonable to prefer the named executor as special administrator where he is otherwise qualified.

Section 3–616. [Special Administrator; Appointed Informally; Powers and Duties.]

A special administrator appointed by the Registrar in informal proceedings pursuant to Section 3–614(1) has the duty to collect and manage the assets of the estate, to preserve them, to account therefor and to deliver them to the general personal representative upon his qualification. The special administrator has the power of a personal representative under the Code necessary to perform his duties.

Section 3–617. [Special Administrator; Formal Proceedings; Power and Duties.]

A special administrator appointed by order of the Court in any formal proceeding has the power of a general personal representative except as limited in the appointment and duties as prescribed in the order. The appointment may be for a specified time, to perform particular acts or on other terms as the Court may direct.

Section 3–618. [Termination of Appointment; Special Administrator.]

The appointment of a special administrator terminates in accordance with the provisions of the order of appointment or on the appointment of a general personal representative. In other cases, the appointment of a special administrator is subject to termination as provided in Sections 3–608 through 3–611.

PART 7

DUTIES AND POWERS OF PERSONAL REPRESENTATIVES

Section 3–701. [Time of Accrual of Duties and Powers.]

The duties and powers of a personal representative commence upon his appointment. The powers of a personal representative relate back in time to give acts by the person appointed which are beneficial to the estate occurring prior to appointment the same effect as those occurring thereafter. Prior to appointment, a person named executor in a will may carry out written instructions of the decedent relating to his body, funeral and burial arrangements. A personal representative may ratify and accept acts on behalf of the estate done by others where the acts would have been proper for a personal representative.

COMMENT

This section codifies the doctrine that the authority of a personal representative relates back to death from the moment it arises. It also makes it clear that authority of a personal representative stems from his appointment. The sentence concerning ratification is designed to eliminate technical questions that might arise concerning the validity of acts done by others prior to appointment. Section 3–715(21) relates to delegation of authority after appointment. The third sentence accepts an idea found in the Illinois Probate Act, § 79 [S.H.A. ch. 3, § 79].

Section 3–702. [Priority Among Different Letters.]

A person to whom general letters are issued first has exclusive authority under the letters until his appointment is terminated or modified. If, through error, general letters are afterwards issued to another, the first appointed representative may recover any property of the estate in the hands of the representative subsequently appointed, but the acts of the latter done in good faith before notice of the first letters are not void for want of validity of appointment.

COMMENT

The qualification relating to "modification" of an appointment is intended to refer to the change that may occur in respect to the exclusive authority of one with letters upon later appointment of a co-representative or of a special administrator. The sentence concerning erroneous dual appointment is derived from recent New York legislation. See Section 704, Surrogate's Court Procedure Act [McKinney's SCPA 704].

Erroneous appointment of a second personal representative is possible if formal proceedings after notice are employed. It might be desirable for a state to promulgate a system whereby a notation of letters issued by each county probate office would be relayed to a central record keeping office which, in turn could indicate to any other office whether letters for a particular decedent, perhaps identified by social security number, had been issued previously. The problem can arise even though notice to known interested persons and by publication is involved.

Section 3–703. [General Duties; Relation and Liability to Persons Interested in Estate; Standing to Sue.]

(a) A personal representative is a fiduciary who shall observe the standards of care applicable to trustees as described by Section 7–302. A personal representative is under a duty to settle and distribute the estate of the decedent in accordance with the terms of any probated and effective will and this Code, and as expeditiously and efficiently as is consistent with the best interests of the estate. He shall use the authority conferred upon him by this Code, the terms of the will, if any, and any order in proceedings to which he is party for the best interests of successors to the estate.

(b) A personal representative shall not be surcharged for acts of administration or distribution if the conduct in question was authorized at the time. Subject to other obligations of administration, an informally probated will is authority to administer and distribute the estate according to its terms. An order of appointment of a personal representative, whether issued in informal or formal proceedings, is authority to distribute apparently intestate assets to the heirs of the decedent if, at the time of distribution, the personal representative is not aware of a pending testacy proceeding, a proceeding to vacate an order entered in an earlier testacy proceeding, a formal proceeding questioning his appointment or fitness to continue, or a supervised administration proceeding. Nothing in this section affects the duty of the personal representative to administer and distribute the estate in accordance with the rights of claimants, the surviving spouse, any minor and dependent children and any pretermitted child of the decedent as described elsewhere in this Code.

(c) Except as to proceedings which do not survive the death of the decedent, a personal representative of a decedent domiciled in this state at his death has the same standing to sue and be sued in the courts of this state and the courts of any other jurisdiction as his decedent had immediately prior to death.

COMMENT

This and the next section are especially important sections for they state the basic theory underlying the duties and powers of personal representatives. Whether or not a personal representative is supervised, this section applies to describe the relationship he bears to interested parties. If a supervised representative is appointed, or if supervision of a previously appointed personal representative is ordered, an additional obligation to the court is created. See Section 3–501.

The fundamental responsibility is that of a trustee. Unlike many trustees, a personal representative's authority is derived from appointment by the public agency known as the Court. But, the Code also makes it clear that the personal representative, in spite of the source of his authority, is to proceed with the administration, settlement and distribution of the estate by use of statutory powers and in accordance with statutory directions. See Sections 3–107 and 3–704. Subsection (b) is particularly important, for it ties the question of personal liability for administrative or distributive acts to the question of whether the act was "authorized at the time". Thus, a personal representative may rely upon and be protected by a will which has been probated without adjudication or an order appointing him to administer which is issued in no-notice proceedings even though proceedings occurring later may change the assumption as to whether the decedent died testate or intestate. See Section 3–302 concerning the status of a will probated without notice and Section 3–102 concerning the ineffectiveness of an unprobated will. However, it does *not* follow from the fact that the personal representative distributed under authority that the distributees may not be liable to restore the property or values received if the assumption concerning testacy is later changed. See Sections 3–909 and 3–1004. Thus, a distribution may be "authorized at the time" within the meaning of this section, but be "improper" under the latter section.

Paragraph (c) is designed to reduce or eliminate differences in the amenability to suit of personal representatives appointed under this Code and under traditional assumptions. Also, the subsection states that so far as the law of the appointing forum is concerned, personal representatives are subject to suit in other jurisdictions. It, together with various provisions of Article IV, are designed to eliminate many of the present reasons for ancillary administrations.

Section 3–704. [Personal Representative to Proceed Without Court Order; Exception.]

A personal representative shall proceed expeditiously with the settlement and distribution of a decedent's estate and, except as otherwise specified or ordered in regard to a supervised personal representative, do so without adjudication, order, or direction of the Court, but he may invoke the jurisdiction of the Court, in proceedings authorized by this Code, to resolve questions concerning the estate or its administration.

COMMENT

This section is intended to confer authority on the personal representative to initiate a proceeding at any time when it is necessary to resolve a question relating to administration. Section 3–105 grants broad subject matter jurisdiction to the probate court which covers a proceeding initiated for any purpose other than those covered by more explicit provisions dealing with testacy proceedings, proceedings for supervised administration, proceedings concerning disputed claims and proceedings to close estates.

Section 3–705. [Duty of Personal Representative; Information to Heirs and Devisees.]

Not later than 30 days after his appointment every personal representative, except any special administrator, shall give information of his appointment to the heirs and devisees, including, if there has been no formal testacy proceeding and if the personal representative was appointed on the assumption that the decedent died intestate, the devisees in any will mentioned in the application for appointment of a personal representative. The information shall be delivered or sent by ordinary mail to each of the heirs and devisees whose address is reasonably available to the personal representative. The duty does not extend to require information to persons who have been adjudicated in a prior formal testacy proceeding to have no interest in the estate. The information shall include the name and address of the personal representative, indicate that it is being sent to persons who have or may have some interest in the estate being administered, indicate whether bond has been filed, and describe the court where papers relating to the estate are on file. The information shall state that the estate is being administered by the personal representative under the [State] Probate Code without supervision by the Court but that recipients are entitled to information regarding the administration from the personal representative and can petition the Court in any matter relating to the estate, including distribution of assets and expenses of administration. The personal representative's failure to give this information is a breach of his duty to the persons concerned but does not affect the validity of his appointment, his powers or other duties. A personal representative may inform other persons of his appointment by delivery or ordinary first class mail.

As amended in 1987.

For material relating to the 1987 amendment, see Appendix I, infra.

COMMENT

This section requires the personal representative to inform persons who appear to have an interest in the estate as it is being administered, of his appointment. Also, it requires the personal representative to give notice to persons who appear to be disinherited by the assumption concerning testacy under which the personal representative was appointed. The communication involved is not to be confused with the notice requirements relating to litigation. The duty applies even though there may have been a prior testacy proceeding after notice, except that persons who have been adjudicated to be without interest in the estate are excluded. The rights, if any, of persons in regard to estates cannot be cut off completely except by the running of the three year statute of limitations provided in Section 3–108, or by a formal judicial proceeding which will include full notice to all interested persons. The interests of some persons may be shifted from rights to specific property of the decedent to the proceeds from sale thereof, or to rights to values re-ceived by distributees. However, such a shift of protected interest from one thing to another, or to funds or obligations, is not new in relation to trust beneficiaries. A personal representative may initiate formal proceedings to determine whether persons, other than those appearing to have interests, may be interested in the estate, under Section 3–401 or, in connection with a formal closing, as provided by Section 3–1001.

No information or notice is required by this section if no personal representative is appointed.

In any circumstance in which a fiduciary accounting is to be prepared, preparation of an accounting in conformity with the Uniform Principles and Model Account Formats promulgated by the National Fiduciary Accounting Project shall be considered as an appropriate manner of presenting a fiduciary account. See ALI–ABA Monograph, Whitman, Brown and Kramer, Fiduciary Accounting Guide (2nd edition 1990).

Section 3–706. [Duty of Personal Representative; Inventory and Appraisement.]

Within 3 months after his appointment, a personal representative, who is not a special administrator or a successor to another representative who has previously discharged this duty, shall prepare and file or mail an inventory of property owned by the decedent at the time of his death, listing it with reasonable detail, and indicating as to each listed item, its fair market value as of the date of the decedent's death, and the type and amount of any encumbrance that may exist with reference to any item.

The personal representative shall send a copy of the inventory to interested persons who request it. He may also file the original of the inventory with the court.

COMMENT

This and the following sections eliminate the practice now required by many probate statutes under which the judge is involved in the selection of appraisers. If the personal representative breaches his duty concerning the inventory, he may be removed. Section 3–611. Or, an interested person seeking to surcharge a personal representative for losses incurred as a result of his administration might be able to take advantage of any breach of duty concerning inventory. The section provides two ways in which a personal representative may handle an inventory. If the personal representative elects to send copies to all interested persons who request it, information concerning the assets of the estate need not become a part of the records of the probate court. The alternative procedure is to file the inventory with the court. This procedure would be indicated in estates with large numbers of interested persons, where the burden of sending copies to all would be substantial. The Court's role in respect to the second alternative is simply to receive and file the inventory with the file relating to the estate. See 3–204, which permits any interested person to demand notice of any document relating to an estate which may be filed with the Court.

In 1975, the Joint Editorial Board recommended elimination of the word "or" that separated the language dealing with the duty to send a copy of the inventory to interested persons requesting it, from the final part of the paragraph dealing with filing of the original. The purpose of the change was to prevent a literal interpretation of the original text that would have permitted a personal representative who filed the original inventory with the court to avoid compliance with requests for copies from interested persons.

Section 3–707. [Employment of Appraisers.]

The personal representative may employ a qualified and disinterested appraiser to assist him in ascertaining the fair market value as of the date of the decedent's death of any asset the value of which may be subject to reasonable doubt. Different persons may be employed to appraise different kinds of assets included in the estate. The names and addresses of any appraiser shall be indicated on the inventory with the item or items he appraised.

Section 3–708. [Duty of Personal Representative; Supplementary Inventory.]

If any property not included in the original inventory comes to the knowledge of a personal representative or if the personal representative learns that the value or description indicated in the original inventory for any item is erroneous or misleading, he shall make a supplementary inventory or appraisement showing the market value as of the date of the decedent's death of the new item or the revised market value or descriptions, and the appraisers or other data relied upon, if any, and file it with the Court if the original inventory was filed, or furnish copies thereof or information thereof to persons interested in the new information.

Section 3-709. [Duty of Personal Representative; Possession of Estate.]

Except as otherwise provided by a decedent's will, every personal representative has a right to, and shall take possession or control of, the decedent's property, except that any real property or tangible personal property may be left with or surrendered to the person presumptively entitled thereto unless or until, in the judgment of the personal representative, possession of the property by him will be necessary for purposes of administration. The request by a personal representative for delivery of any property possessed by an heir or devisee is conclusive evidence, in any action against the heir or devisee for possession thereof, that the possession of the property by the personal representative is necessary for purposes of administration. The personal representative shall pay taxes on, and take all steps reasonably necessary for the management, protection and preservation of, the estate in his possession. He may maintain an action to recover possession of property or to determine the title thereto.

COMMENT

Section 3-101 provides for the devolution of title on death. Section 3-711 defines the status of the personal representative with reference to "title" and "power" in a way that should make it unnecessary to discuss the "title" to decedent's assets which his personal representative acquires. This section deals with the personal representative's duty and right to possess assets. It proceeds from the assumption that it is desirable whenever possible to avoid disruption of possession of the decedent's assets by his devisees or heirs. But, if the personal representative decides that possession of an asset is necessary or desirable for purposes of administration, his judgment is made conclusive in any action for possession that he may need to institute against an heir or devisee. It may be possible for an heir or devisee to question the judgment of the personal representative in later action for surcharge for breach of fiduciary duty, but this possibility should not interfere with the personal representative's administrative authority as it relates to possession of the estate.

This Code follows the Model Probate Code in regard to partnership interests. In the introduction to the Model Probate Code, the following appears at p. 22:

"No provisions for the administration of partnership estates when a partner dies have been included. Several states have statutes providing that unless the surviving partner files a bond with the probate court, the personal representative of the deceased partner may administer the partnership estate upon giving an additional bond. Kan.Gen. Stat. (Supp.1943) §§ 59-1001 to 59-1005; Mo.Rev.Stat.Ann. (1942) §§ 81 to 93 [V.A.M.S. §§ 473.220 to 473.230]. In these states the administration of partnership estates upon the death of a partner is brought more or less completely under the jurisdiction of the probate court. While the provisions afford security to parties in interest, they have caused complications in the settlement of partnership estates and have produced much litigation. Woener, Administration (3rd ed., 1923) §§ 128 to 130; annotation, 121 A.L.R. 860. These statutes have been held to be inconsistent with section 37 of the Uniform Partnership Act providing for winding up by the surviving partner. Davis v. Hutchinson (C.C.A. 9th, 1929) 36 F.(2d) 309. Hence the Model Probate Code contains no provision regarding partnership property except for inclusion in the inventory of the decedent's proportionate share of any partnership. See § 120. However, it is suggested that the Uniform Partnership Act should be included in the statutes of the states which have not already enacted it."

Section 3–710. [Power to Avoid Transfers.]

The property liable for the payment of unsecured debts of a decedent includes all property transferred by him by any means which is in law void or voidable as against his creditors, and subject to prior liens, the right to recover this property, so far as necessary for the payment of unsecured debts of the decedent, is exclusively in the personal representative.

COMMENT

Model Probate Code section 125, with additions. See, also, Section 6–201, which saves creditors' rights in regard to non-testimentary transfers effective at death.

Section 3–711. [Powers of Personal Representatives; In General.]

Until termination of his appointment a personal representative has the same power over the title to property of the estate that an absolute owner would have, in trust however, for the benefit of the creditors and others interested in the estate. This power may be exercised without notice, hearing, or order of court.

COMMENT

The personal representative is given the broadest possible "power over title". He receives a *"power"*, rather than title, because the power concept eases the succession of assets which are not possessed by the personal representative. Thus, if the power is unexercised prior to its termination, its lapse clears the title of devisees and heirs. Purchasers from devisees or heirs who are "distributees" may be protected also by Section 3–910. The power over title of an absolute owner is conceived to embrace all possible transactions which might result in a conveyance or encumbrance of assets, or in a change of rights of possession. The relationship of the personal representative to the estate is that of a trustee. Hence, personal creditors or successors of a personal representative cannot avail themselves of his title to any greater extent than is true generally of creditors and successors of trustees. Interested persons who are apprehensive of possible misuse of power by a personal representative may secure themselves by use of the devices implicit in the several sections of Parts 1 and 3 of this Article. See especially Sections 3-501, 3-605, 3-607 and 3-611.

Section 3-712. [Improper Exercise of Power; Breach of Fiduciary Duty.]

If the exercise of power concerning the estate is improper, the personal representative is liable to interested persons for damage or loss resulting from breach of his fiduciary duty to the same extent as a trustee of an express trust. The rights of purchasers and others dealing with a personal representative shall be determined as provided in Sections 3-713 and 3-714.

COMMENT

An interested person has two principal remedies to forestall a personal representative from committing a breach of fiduciary duty. (1) Under Section 3-607 he may apply to the Court for an order restraining the personal representative from performing any specified act or from exercising any power in the course of administration. (2) Under Section 3-611 he may petition the Court for an order removing the personal representative.

Evidence of a proceeding, or order, restraining a personal representative from selling, leasing, encumbering or otherwise affecting title to real property subject to administration, if properly recorded under the laws of this state, would be effective to prevent a purchaser from acquiring a marketable title under the usual rules relating to recordation of real property titles.

In addition Sections 1-302 and 3-105 authorize joinder of third persons who may be involved in contemplated transactions with a personal representative in proceedings to restrain a personal representative under Section 3-607.

Section 3-713. [Sale, Encumbrance or Transaction Involving Conflict of Interest; Voidable; Exceptions.]

Any sale or encumbrance to the personal representative, his spouse, agent or attorney, or any corporation or trust in which he has a substantial beneficial interest, or any transaction which is affected by a substantial conflict of interest on the part of the personal representative, is voidable by any person interested in the estate except one who has consented after fair disclosure, unless

(1) the will or a contract entered into by the decedent expressly authorized the transaction; or

(2) the transaction is approved by the Court after notice to interested persons.

COMMENT

If a personal representative violates the duty against self-dealing described by this section, a voidable title to assets sold results. Other breaches of duty relating to sales of assets will not cloud titles except as to purchasers with actual knowledge of the breach. See Section 3–714. The principles of bona fide purchase would protect a purchaser for value without notice of defect in the seller's title arising from conflict of interest.

Section 3–714. [Persons Dealing with Personal Representative; Protection.]

A person who in good faith either assists a personal representative or deals with him for value is protected as if the personal representative properly exercised his power. The fact that a person knowingly deals with a personal representative does not alone require the person to inquire into the existence of a power or the propriety of its exercise. Except for restrictions on powers of supervised personal representatives which are endorsed on letters as provided in Section 3–504, no provision in any will or order of court purporting to limit the power of a personal representative is effective except as to persons with actual knowledge thereof. A person is not bound to see to the proper application of estate assets paid or delivered to a personal representative. The protection here expressed extends to instances in which some procedural irregularity or jurisdictional defect occurred in proceedings leading to the issuance of letters, including a case in which the alleged decedent is found to be alive. The protection here expressed is not by substitution for that provided by comparable provisions of the laws relating to commercial transactions and laws simplifying transfers of securities by fiduciaries.

COMMENT

This section qualifies the effect of a provision in a will which purports to prohibit sale of property by a personal representative. The provisions of a will may prescribe the duties of a personal representative and subject him to surcharge or other remedies of interested persons if he disregards them. See Section 3–703. But, the will's prohibition is not relevant to the rights of a purchaser unless he had actual knowledge of its terms. Interested persons who want to prevent a personal representative from having the power described here must use the procedures described in Sections 3–501 to 3–505. Each state will need to identify the relation between this section and other statutory provisions creating liens on estate assets for inheritance and other taxes.

The section cannot control whether a purchaser takes free of the lien of unpaid federal estate taxes. Hence, purchasers from personal representatives appointed pursuant to this Code will have to satisfy themselves concerning whether estate taxes are paid, and if not paid, whether the tax lien follows the property they are acquiring. See Section 6234, Internal Revenue Code [26 U.S.C.A. § 6324].

The impact of formal recording systems beyond the usual probate procedure depends upon the particular statute. In states in which the recording system provides for recording wills as muniments of title, statutory adaptation should be made to provide that recording of wills should be postponed until the validity has been established by probate or limitation. Statutory limitation to this effect should be added to statutes which do not so provide to avoid conflict with power of the personal representative during administration. The purpose of the Code is to make the deed or instrument of distribution the usual muniment of title. See Section 3–907, 3–908, 3–910. However, this is not available when no administration has occurred and in that event reliance upon general recording statutes must be had.

If a state continues to permit wills to be recorded as muniments of title, the above section would need to be qualified to give effect to the notice from recording.

Section 3–715. [Transactions Authorized for Personal Representatives; Exceptions.]

Except as restricted or otherwise provided by the will or by an order in a formal proceeding and subject to the priorities stated in Section 3–902, a personal representative, acting reasonably for the benefit of the interested persons, may properly:

(1) retain assets owned by the decedent pending distribution or liquidation including those in which the representative is personally interested or which are otherwise improper for trust investment;

(2) receive assets from fiduciaries, or other sources;

(3) perform, compromise or refuse performance of the decedent's contracts that continue as obligations of the estate, as he may determine under the circumstances. In performing enforceable contracts by the decedent to convey or lease land, the personal representative, among other possible courses of action, may:

(i) execute and deliver a deed of conveyance for cash payment of all sums remaining due or the purchaser's note for the sum remaining due secured by a mortgage or deed of trust on the land; or

(ii) deliver a deed in escrow with directions that the proceeds, when paid in accordance with the escrow agreement, be paid to the successors of the decedent, as designated in the escrow agreement;

(4) satisfy written charitable pledges of the decedent irrespective of whether the pledges constituted binding obligations of the decedent or were properly presented as claims, if in the judgment of the personal representative the decedent would have wanted the pledges completed under the circumstances;

(5) if funds are not needed to meet debts and expenses currently payable and are not immediately distributable, deposit or invest liquid assets of the estate, including moneys received from the sale of other assets, in federally insured interest-bearing accounts, readily marketable secured loan arrangements or other prudent investments which would be reasonable for use by trustees generally;

(6) acquire or dispose of an asset, including land in this or another state, for cash or on credit, at public or private sale; and manage, develop, improve, exchange, partition, change the character of, or abandon an estate asset;

(7) make ordinary or extraordinary repairs or alterations in buildings or other structures, demolish any improvements, raze existing or erect new party walls or buildings;

(8) subdivide, develop or dedicate land to public use; make or obtain the vacation of plats and adjust boundaries; or adjust differences in valuation on exchange or partition by giving or receiving considerations; or dedicate easements to public use without consideration;

(9) enter for any purpose into a lease as lessor or lessee, with or without option to purchase or renew, for a term within or extending beyond the period of administration;

(10) enter into a lease or arrangement for exploration and removal of minerals or other natural resources or enter into a pooling or unitization agreement;

(11) abandon property when, in the opinion of the personal representative, it is valueless, or is so encumbered, or is in condition that it is of no benefit to the state;

(12) vote stocks or other securities in person or by general or limited proxy;

(13) pay calls, assessments, and other sums chargeable or accruing against or on account of securities, unless barred by the provisions relating to claims;

(14) hold a security in the name of a nominee or in other form without disclosure of the interest of the estate but the personal representative is liable for any act of the nominee in connection with the security so held;

(15) insure the assets of the estate against damage, loss and liability and himself against liability as to third persons;

(16) borrow money with or without security to be repaid from the estate assets or otherwise; and advance money for the protection of the estate;

(17) effect a fair and reasonable compromise with any debtor or obligor, or extend, renew or in any manner modify the terms of any obligation owing to the estate. If the personal representative holds a mortgage, pledge or other lien upon property of another person, he may, in lieu of foreclosure, accept a conveyance or transfer of encumbered assets from the owner thereof in satisfaction of the indebtedness secured by lien;

(18) pay taxes, assessments, compensation of the personal representative, and other expenses incident to the administration of the estate;

(19) sell or exercise stock subscription or conversion rights; consent, directly or through a committee or other agent, to the reorganization, consolidation, merger, dissolution, or liquidation of a corporation or other business enterprise;

(20) allocate items of income or expense to either estate income or principal, as permitted or provided by law;

(21) employ persons, including attorneys, auditors, investment advisors, or agents, even if they are associated with the personal representative, to advise or assist the personal representative in the performance of his administrative duties; act without independent investigation upon their recommendations; and instead of acting personally, employ one or more agents to perform any act of administration, whether or not discretionary;

(22) prosecute or defend claims, or proceedings in any jurisdiction for the protection of the estate and of the personal representative in the performance of his duties;

(23) sell, mortgage, or lease any real or personal property of the estate or any interest therein for cash, credit, or for part cash and part credit, and with or without security for unpaid balances;

(24) continue any unincorporated business or venture in which the decedent was engaged at the time of his death (i) in the same business form for a period of not more than 4 months from the date of appointment of a general personal representative if continuation is a reasonable means of preserving the value of the business including good will, (ii) in the same business form for any additional period of time that may be approved by order of the Court in a formal proceeding to which the persons interested in the estate are

parties; or (iii) throughout the period of administration if the business is incorporated by the personal representative and if none of the probable distributees of the business who are competent adults object to its incorporation and retention in the estate;

(25) incorporate any business or venture in which the decedent was engaged at the time of his death;

(26) provide for exoneration of the personal representative from personal liability in any contract entered into on behalf of the estate;

(27) satisfy and settle claims and distribute the estate as provided in this Code.

COMMENT

This section accepts the assumption of the Uniform Trustee's Powers Act that it is desirable to equip fiduciaries with the authority required for the prudent handling of assets and extends it to personal representatives. The section requires that a personal representative act reasonably and for the benefit of the interested person. Subject to this and to the other qualifications described by the preliminary statement, the enumerated transactions are made authorized transactions for personal representatives. Sub-paragraphs (27) and (18) support the other provisions of the Code, particularly Section 3–704, which contemplates that personal representatives will proceed with all of the business of administration without court orders.

In part, sub-paragraph (4) involves a substantive question of whether noncontractual charitable pledges of a decedent can be honored by his personal representative. It is believed, however, that it is not desirable from a practical standpoint to make much turn on whether a charitable pledge is, or is not, contractual. Pledges are rarely made the subject of claims. The effect of subparagraph (4) is to permit the personal representative to discharge pledges where he believes the decedent would have wanted him to do so without exposing himself to surcharge. The holder of a contractual pledge may, of course, pursue the remedies of a creditor. If a pledge provides that the obligation ceases on the death of the pledgor, no personal representative would be safe in assuming that the decedent would want the pledge completed under the circumstances.

Subsection (3) is not intended to affect the right to performance or to damages of any person who contracted with the decedent. To do so would constitute an unreasonable interference with private rights. The intention of the subsection is simply to give a personal representative who is obligated to carry out a decedent's contracts the same alternatives in regard to the contractual duties which the decedent had prior to his death.

Section 3–716. [Powers and Duties of Successor Personal Representative.]

A successor personal representative has the same power and duty as the original personal representative to complete the administra-

tion and distribution of the estate, as expeditiously as possible, but
he shall not exercise any power expressly made personal to the
executor named in the will.

Section 3–717. [Co-representatives; When Joint Action Required.]

If two or more persons are appointed co-representatives and
unless the will provides otherwise, the concurrence of all is required on all acts connected with the administration and distribution of the estate. This restriction does not apply when any co-representative receives and receipts for property due the estate, when
the concurrence of all cannot readily be obtained in the time
reasonably available for emergency action necessary to preserve the
estate, or when a co-representative has been delegated to act for the
others. Persons dealing with a co-representative if actually unaware that another has been appointed to serve with him or if
advised by the personal representative with whom they deal that he
has authority to act alone for any of the reasons mentioned herein,
are as fully protected as if the person with whom they dealt had
been the sole personal representative.

COMMENT

With certain qualifications, this section is designed to compel co-representatives to agree on all matters relating to administration when circumstances permit. Delegation by one to another representative is a form of concurrence in acts that may result from the delegation. A co-representative who abdicates his responsibility to co-administer the estate by a blanket delegation breaches his duty to interested persons as described by Section 3–703. Section 3–715 (21) authorizes some limited delegations, which are reasonable and for the benefit of interested persons.

Section 3–718. [Powers of Surviving Personal Representative.]

Unless the terms of the will otherwise provide, every power
exercisable by personal co-representatives may be exercised by the
one or more remaining after the appointment of one or more is
terminated, and if one of 2 or more nominated as co-executors is
not appointed, those appointed may exercise all the powers incident
to the office.

COMMENT

Source, Model Probate Code section 102. This section applies where one of two or more co-repretion sentatives dies, becomes disabled or is removed. In regard to co-executors, it is based on the assumption that the decedent would not consider the powers of his fiduciaries to be personal, or to be suspended if one or more could not function. In regard to co-administrators in intestacy, it is based on the idea that the reason for appointing more than one ceases on the death or disability of either of them.

Section 3–719. [Compensation of Personal Representative.]

A personal representative is entitled to reasonable compensation for his services. If a will provides for compensation of the personal representative and there is no contract with the decedent regarding compensation, he may renounce the provision before qualifying and be entitled to reasonable compensation. A personal representative also may renounce his right to all or any part of the compensation. A written renunciation of fee may be filed with the Court.

COMMENT

This section has no bearing on the question of whether a personal representative who also serves as attorney for the estate may receive compensation in both capacities. If a will provision concerning a fee is framed as a condition on the nomination as personal representative, it could not be renounced.

Section 3–720. [Expenses in Estate Litigation.]

If any personal representative or person nominated as personal representative defends or prosecutes any proceeding in good faith, whether successful or not he is entitled to receive from the estate his necessary expenses and disbursements including reasonable attorneys' fees incurred.

COMMENT

Litigation prosecuted by a personal representative for the primary purpose of enhancing his prospects for compensation would not be in good faith.

A personal representative is a fiduciary for successors of the estate (Section 3–703). Though the will naming him may not yet be probated, the priority for appointment conferred by Section 3–203 on one named executor in a probated will means that the person named has an interest, as a fiduciary, in seeking the probate of the will. Hence, he is an interested person within the meaning of Sections 3–301 and 3–401. Section 3–912 gives the successors of an estate control over the executor, provided all are competent adults. So, if all persons possibly interested in the probate of a will, including trustees of any trusts created thereby, concur in directing the named executor to refrain from efforts to probate the instrument, he would lose standing to proceed. All of these observations apply with equal force to the case where the named executor of one instrument

seeks to contest the probate of another instrument. Thus, the Code
changes the idea followed in some
jurisdictions that an executor lacks
standing to contest other wills
which, if valid, would supersede the
will naming him, and standing to
oppose other contests that may be
mounted against the instrument
nominating him.

Section 3–721. [Proceedings for Review of Employment of Agents and Compensation of Personal Representatives and Employees of Estate.]

After notice to all interested persons or on petition of an interested person or on appropriate motion if administration is supervised,
the propriety of employment of any person by a personal representative including any attorney, auditor, investment advisor or other
specialized agent or assistant, the reasonableness of the compensation of any person so employed, or the reasonableness of the
compensation determined by the personal representative for his
own services, may be reviewed by the Court. Any person who has
received excessive compensation from an estate for services rendered may be ordered to make appropriate refunds.

COMMENT

In view of the broad jurisdiction
conferred on the probate court by
Section 3–105, description of the
special proceeding authorized by
this section might be unnecessary.
But, the Code's theory that personal
representatives may fix their own
fees *and* those of estate attorneys
marks an important departure from
much existing practice under which
fees are determined by the court in
the first instance. Hence, it seemed
wise to emphasize that any interested person can get judicial review of
fees if he desires it. Also, if excessive fees have been paid, this section
provides a quick and efficient remedy.

PART 8

CREDITORS' CLAIMS

GENERAL COMMENT

The need for uniformity of law regarding creditors' claims against estates is especially strong. Commercial and consumer credit depends upon efficient collection procedures. The cost of credit is pushed up by the cost of credit life insurance which becomes a practical necessity for lenders unwilling to bear the expense of understanding or using the cumbersome and provincial collection procedures found in 50 codes of probate.

The sections which follow facilitate collection of claims against decedents in several ways. First, a simple written statement mailed to the personal representative is a sufficient "claim." Allowance of claims is handled by the personal representative and is assumed if a claimant is not advised of disallowance. Also, a personal representative may pay any just claims without presentation and at any time, if he is willing to assume risks which will be minimal in many cases. The period of uncertainty regarding possible claims is only four months from first publication. This should expedite settlement and distribution of estates.

Section 3–801. [Notice to Creditors.]

(a) Unless notice has already been given under this section, a personal representative upon appointment [may] [shall] publish a notice to creditors once a week for three successive weeks in a newspaper of general circulation in the [county] announcing the appointment and the personal representative's address and notifying creditors of the estate to present their claims within four months after the date of the first publication of the notice or be forever barred.

(b) A personal representative may give written notice by mail or other delivery to a creditor, notifying the creditor to present his [or her] claim within four months after the published notice, if given as provided in subsection (a), or within 60 days after the mailing or other delivery of the notice, whichever is later, or be forever barred. Written notice must be the notice described in subsection (a) above or a similar notice.

(c) The personal representative is not liable to a creditor or to a successor of the decedent for giving or failing to give notice under this section.

As amended in 1989.

For material relating to the 1989 amendment, see Appendix IV, infra.

COMMENT

Section 3–1203, relating to small estates, contains an important qualification on the duty created by this section.

In 1989, the Joint Editorial Board recommended replacement of the word "shall" with "[may] [shall]" in (a) to signal its approval of a choice between mandatory publication and optional publication of notice to creditors to be made by the legislature in an enacting state. Publication of notice to creditors is quite expensive in some populous areas of the country and, if *Tulsa Professional Collection Services v. Pope,* 108 S.Ct. 1340, 485 U.S. 478 (1988) applies to this code, is useless except to bar unknown creditors. Even if *Pope* does not apply, personal representatives for estates involving successors willing to assume the risk of unbarred claims should have (and have had under the code as a practical consequence of absence of court supervision and mandatory closings) the option of failing to publish.

Additional discussion of the impact of *Pope* on the Code appears in the Comment to Section 3–803, infra.

If a state elects to make publication of notice to creditors a duty for personal representatives, failure to advertise for claims would involve a breach of duty on the part of the personal representative. If, as a result of such breach, a claim is later asserted against a distributee under Section 3–1004, the personal representative may be liable to the distributee for costs related to discharge of the claim and the recovery of contribution from other distributees. The protection afforded personal representatives under Section 3–1003 would not be available, for that section applies only if the personal representative truthfully recites that the time limit for presentation of claims has expired.

Putting aside *Pope* case concerns regarding state action under this code, it might be appropriate, by legislation, to channel publications through the personnel of the probate court. See Section 1–401. If notices are controlled by a centralized authority, some assurance could be gained against publication in newspapers of small circulation. Also, the form of notices could be made uniform and certain efficiencies could be achieved. For example, it would be compatible with this section for the Court to publish a single notice each day or each week listing the names of personal representatives appointed since the last publication, with addresses and dates of non-claim.

Section 3–802. [Statutes of Limitations.]

(a) Unless an estate is insolvent, the personal representative, with the consent of all successors whose interests would be affected, may waive any defense of limitations available to the estate. If the defense is not waived, no claim barred by a statute of limitations at the time of the decedent's death may be allowed or paid.

(b) The running of a statute of limitations measured from an event other than death or the giving of notice to creditors is suspended for four months after the decedent's death, but resumes thereafter as to claims not barred by other sections.

(c) For purposes of a statute of limitations, the presentation of a claim pursuant to Section 3–804 is equivalent to commencement of a proceeding on the claim.

As amended in 1989.

For material relating to the 1989 amendment, see Appendix IV, infra.

COMMENT

This section means that four months is added to the normal period of limitations by reason of a debtor's death before a debt is barred. It implies also that after the expiration of four months from death, the normal statute of limitations may run and bar a claim even though the non-claim provisions of Section 3–803 have not been triggered. Hence, the non-claim and limitation provisions of Section 3–803 are not mutually exclusive.

It should be noted that under Sections 3–803 and 3–804 it is possible for a claim to be barred by the process of claim, disallowance and failure by the creditor to commence a proceeding to enforce his claim prior to the end of the four month suspension period. Thus, the regular statute of limitations applicable during the debtor's lifetime, the non-claim provisions of Sections 3–803 and 3–804, and the three-year limitation of Section 3–803 all have potential application to a claim. The first of the three to accomplish a bar controls.

In 1975, the Joint Editorial Board recommended a change that makes it clear that only those successors who would be affected thereby, must agree to a waiver of a defense of limitations available to an estate. As the original text stood, the section appeared to require the consent of "all successors," even though this would include some who, under the rules of abatement, could not possibly be affected by allowance and payment of the claim in question.

In 1989, in connection with other amendments recommended in sequel to *Tulsa Professional Collection Services v. Pope*, 108 S.Ct. 1340, 485 U.S. 478 (1988), the Joint Editorial Board recommended the splitting out, into Subsections (b) and (c), of the last two sentences of what formerly was a four-sentence section. The first two sentences now appear as Subsection (a). The rearrangement aids understanding that the section deals with three separable ideas. No other change in language is involved, and the timing of the changes to coincide with *Pope* case amendments is purely coincidental.

Section 3–803. [Limitations on Presentation of Claims.]

(a) All claims against a decedent's estate which arose before the death of the decedent, including claims of the state and any subdivision thereof, whether due or to become due, absolute or contingent, liquidated or unliquidated, founded on contract, tort, or other legal basis, if not barred earlier by another statute of limitations or non-claim statute, are barred against the estate, the personal representative, and the heirs and devisees of the decedent, unless presented within the earlier of the following:

(1) one year after the decedent's death; or

(2) the time provided by Section 3–801(b) for creditors who are given actual notice, and within the time provided in 3–801(a) for all creditors barred by publication.

(b) A claim described in subsection (a) which is barred by the non-claim statute of the decedent's domicile before the giving of notice to creditors in this State is barred in this State.

(c) All claims against a decedent's estate which arise at or after the death of the decedent, including claims of the state and any subdivision thereof, whether due or to become due, absolute or contingent, liquidated or unliquidated, founded on contract, tort, or other legal basis, are barred against the estate, the personal representative, and the heirs and devisees of the decedent, unless presented as follows:

(1) a claim based on a contract with the personal representative, within four months after performance by the personal representative is due; or

(2) any other claim, within the later of four months after it arises, or the time specified in subsection (a)(1).

(d) Nothing in this section affects or prevents:

(1) any proceeding to enforce any mortgage, pledge, or other lien upon property of the estate;

(2) to the limits of the insurance protection only, any proceeding to establish liability of the decedent or the personal representative for which he is protected by liability insurance; or

(3) collection of compensation for services rendered and reimbursement for expenses advanced by the personal representative or by the attorney or accountant for the personal representative of the estate.

As amended in 1989.

For material relating to the 1989 amendment, see Appendix IV, infra.

COMMENT

There was some disagreement among the Reporters over whether a short period of limitations, or of non-claim, should be provided for claims arising at or after death. Sub-paragraph (b) was finally inserted because most felt it was desirable to accelerate the time when unadjudicated distributions would be final. The time limits stated would not, of course, affect any personal liability in contract, tort, or by statute, of the personal representative. Under Section 3–808 a personal representative is not liable on transactions entered into on behalf of the estate unless he agrees to be personally liable or unless he breaches a duty by making the contract. Creditors of the estate and not of the personal representative thus face a special limitation that runs four months after performance is due from the personal representative. Tort claims normally will involve casualty insurance of the decedent or of the personal representative, and so will fall within the exception of subparagraph (d). If a personal representative is personally at fault in respect to a tort claim arising after the decedent's death, his personal liability would not be affected by the running of the special short period provided here.

In 1989, the Joint Editorial Board recommended amendments to Subsection (a). The change in (1) shortens the ultimate limitations period on claims against a decedent from 3 years after death to 1 year after death. Corresponding amendments were recommended for Sections 3–1003(a)(1) and 3–1006. The new one-year from death limitation (which applies without regard to whether or when an estate is opened for administration) is designed to prevent concerns stemming from the possible applicability to this Code of *Tulsa Professional Collection Services v. Pope*, 108 S.Ct. 1340, 485 U.S. 478 (1988) from unduly prolonging estate settlements and closings.

Subsection (a)(2), by reference to 3–801(a) and 3–801(b), adds an additional method of barring a prospective claimant of whom the personal representative is aware. The new bar is available when it is appropriate, under all of the circumstances, to send a mailed warning to one or more known claimants who have not presented claims that the recipient's claim will be barred if not presented within 60 days from the notice. This optional, mailed notice, described in accompanying new text in Section 3–801(b), is designed to enhance the ability of personal representatives to protect distributees against pass-through liability (under Section 3–1004) to possibly unbarred claimants. Personal representatives acting in the best in-

terests of successors to the estate (see Section 3–703(a) and the definition of "successors" in Section 1–201(42)) may determine that successors are willing to assume risks (i) that *Pope,* supra, will be held to apply to this Code in spite of absence of any significant contact between an agency of the state and the acts of a personal representative operating independently of court supervision; and (ii) that a possibly unbarred claim is valid and will be pursued by its owner against estate distributees in time to avoid bar via the earliest to run of its own limitation period (which, under Section 3–802(b), resumes running four months after death), or the one-year from death limitation now provided by § 3–803(a)(1). If publication of notice as provided in Section 3–801 has occurred and if *Pope* either is inapplicable to this Code or is applicable but the late-arising claim in question is judged to have been unknown to the personal representative and unlikely to have been discovered by reasonable effort, an earlier, four months from first publication bar will apply.

The Joint Editorial Board recognized that the new bar running one year after death may be used by some sets of successors to avoid payment of claims against their decedents of which they are aware. Successors who are willing to delay receipt and enjoyment of inheritances may consider waiting out the non-claim period running from death simply to avoid any public record of an administration that might alert known and unknown creditors to pursue their claims. The scenario was deemed to be unlikely, however, for unpaid creditors of a decedent are interested persons (Section 1–201(20)) who are qualified to force the opening of an estate for purposes of presenting and enforcing claims. Further, successors who delay opening an administration will suffer from lack of proof of title to estate assets and attendant inability to enjoy their inheritances. Finally, the odds that holders of important claims against the decedent will need help in learning of the death and proper place of administration is rather small. Any benefit to such claimants of additional procedures designed to compel administrations and to locate and warn claimants of an impending non-claim bar, is quite likely to be heavily outweighed by the costs such procedures would impose on all estates, the vast majority of which are routinely applied to quick payment of the decedents' bills and distributed without any creditor controversy.

Note that the new bar described by Section 3–801(b) and Section 3–803(a)(2) is the earlier of one year from death or the period described by reference to § 3–801(b) and § 3–801(a) in § 3–803(a)(2). If publication of notice is made under § 3–801(a), and the personal representative thereafter gives actual notice to a known creditor, when is the creditor barred? If the actual notice is given less than 60 days prior to the expiration of the four months from first publication period, the claim will not be barred four months after first publication because the actual notice given by § 3–801(b) advises the creditor that it has no less than 60 days to present the claim. It is as if the personal representative gave the claimant a written waiver of any benefit the estate may have had by reason of the four month bar following published notice. (c.f., the ability of a personal representative, under § 3–802 to change claims from allowed to disallowed, and vice versa, and the 60 day period given by § 3–806(a) within which a claimant may contest a disallowance). The period ending with the running of 60 days from actual notice replaces the four month from

publication period as the "time for original presentation" referred to in Section 3–806(a).

Note, too, that if there is no publication of notice as provided in Section 3–801(a), the giving of actual notice to known creditors establishes separate, 60 days from time of notice, non-claim periods for those so notified. The failure to publish also means that no general non-claim period, other than the one year period running from death, will be working for the estate. If an actual notice to a creditor is given before notice by publication is given, a question arises as to whether the 60 day period from actual notice, or the longer, four-month from publication applies. Subsections 3–801(a) and (b), which are pulled into Section 3–803(a)(2) by reference, make no distinction between actual notices given before publication and those given after publication. Hence, it would seem that the later time bar would control in either case. This reading also fits more satisfactorily with Section 3–806(a) and other code language referring in various contexts to "the time limit prescribed in § 3–803."

The proviso, formerly appended to 3–803(a)(1), regarding the effect in this state of the prior running of a non-claim statute of the decedent's domicile, has been restated as 3–803(b), and former subsections (b) and (c) have been redesignated as (c) and (d). The relocation of the proviso was made to improve the style of the section. No change of meaning is intended.

The second paragraph of the original comment has been deleted because of inconsistency with amended § 3–803(a).

The 1989 changes recommended by the Joint Editorial Board relating to former § 3–803(b) now designated as 3–803(c) are unrelated to the *Pope* case problem. The original text failed to describe a satisfactory non-claim period for claims arising at or after the decedent's death other than claims based on contract. The four months "after [any other claim] arises" period worked unjustly as to tort claims stemming from accidents causing the decedent's death by snuffing out claims too quickly, sometimes before an estate had been opened. The language added by the 1989 amendment assures such claimants against any bar working prior to the later of one year after death or four months from the time the claim arises.

The other change affecting what is now § 3–803(d) is the addition of a third class of items which are not barred by any time bar running from death, publication of notice to creditors, or any actual notice given to an estate creditor. The addition resembles a modification to the Code as enacted in Arizona.

Section 3–804. [Manner of Presentation of Claims.]

Claims against a decedent's estate may be presented as follows:

(1) The claimant may deliver or mail to the personal representative a written statement of the claim indicating its basis, the name and address of the claimant, and the amount claimed, or may file a written statement of the claim, in the form prescribed by rule, with the clerk of the Court. The claim is deemed presented on the first to occur of receipt of the written statement of claim by the personal representative, or the filing of the claim with the Court. If a claim is not yet due, the date when it will become due shall be stated. If the claim is contingent or unliquidated, the nature of the uncertainty shall be stated. If the claim is secured, the security shall be described. Failure to describe correctly the security, the nature of any uncertainty, and the due date of a claim not yet due does not invalidate the presentation made.

(2) The claimant may commence a proceeding against the personal representative in any Court where the personal representative may be subjected to jurisdiction, to obtain payment of his claim against the estate, but the commencement of the proceeding must occur within the time limited for presenting the claim. No presentation of claim is required in regard to matters claimed in proceedings against the decedent which were pending at the time of his death.

(3) If a claim is presented under subsection (1), no proceeding thereon may be commenced more than 60 days after the personal representative has failed a notice of disallowance; but, in the case of a claim which is not presently due or which is contingent or unliquidated, the personal representative may consent to an extension of the 60–day period, or to avoid injustice the Court, on petition, may order an extension of the 60–day period, but in no

event shall the extension run beyond the applicable statute of limitations.

COMMENT

The filing of a claim with the probate court under (2) of this section does not serve to initiate a proceeding concerning the claim. Rather, it serves merely to protect the claimant who may anticipate some need for evidence to show that his claim is not barred. The probate court acts simply as a depository of the statement of claim, as is true of its responsibility for an inventory filed with it under Section 3-706.

In reading this section it is important to remember that a regular statute of limitation may run to bar a claim before the non-claim provisions run. See Section 3-802.

Section 3-805. [Classification of Claims.]

(a) If the applicable assets of the estate are insufficient to pay all claims in full, the personal representative shall make payment in the following order:

(1) costs and expenses of administration;

(2) reasonable funeral expenses;

(3) debts and taxes with preference under federal law;

(4) reasonable and necessary medical and hospital expenses of the last illness of the decedent, including compensation of persons attending him;

(5) debts and taxes with preference under other laws of this state;

(6) all other claims.

(b) No preference shall be given in the payment of any claim over any other claim of the same class, and a claim due and payable shall not be entitled to a preference over claims not due.

COMMENT

In 1975, the Joint Editorial Board recommended the separation of funeral expenses from the items now accorded fourth priority. Under federal law, funeral expenses, but not debts incurred by the decedent can be given priority over claims of the United States.

Section 3-806. [Allowance of Claims.]

(a) As to claims presented in the manner described in Section 3-804 within the time limit prescribed in 3-803, the personal representative may mail a notice to any claimant stating that the claim has been disallowed. If, after allowing or disallowing a claim, the personal representative changes his decision concerning the claim, he shall notify the claimant. The personal representative may not change a disallowance of a claim after the time for the claimant to file a petition for allowance or to commence a proceeding on the claim has run and the claim has been barred. Every claim which is disallowed in whole or in part by the personal representative is barred so far as not allowed unless the claimant files a petition for allowance in the Court or commences a proceeding against the personal representative not later than 60 days after the mailing of the notice of disallowance or partial allowance if the notice warns the claimant of the impending bar. Failure of the personal representative to mail notice to a claimant of action on his claim for 60 days after the time for original presentation of the claim has expired has the effect of a notice of allowance.

(b) After allowing or disallowing a claim the personal representative may change the allowance or disallowance as hereafter provided. The personal representative may prior to payment change the allowance to a disallowance in whole or in part, but not after allowance by a court order or judgment or an order directing payment of the claim. He shall notify the claimant of the change to disallowance, and the disallowed claim is then subject to bar as provided in subsection (a). The personal representative may change a disallowance to an allowance, in whole or in part, until it is barred under subsection (a); after it is barred, it may be allowed and paid only if the estate is solvent and all successors whose interests would be affected consent.

(c) Upon the petition of the personal representative or of a claimant in a proceeding for the purpose, the Court may allow in whole or in part any claim or claims presented to the personal representative or filed with the clerk of the Court in due time and not barred by subsection (a) of this section. Notice in this proceeding shall be given to the claimant, the personal representative and those other persons interested in the estate as the Court may direct by order entered at the time the proceeding is commenced.

(d) A judgment in a proceeding in another court against a personal representative to enforce a claim against a decedent's estate is an allowance of the claim.

(e) Unless otherwise provided in any judgment in another court entered against the personal representative, allowed claims bear interest at the legal rate for the period commencing 60 days after the time for original presentation of the claim has expired unless based on a contract making a provision for interest, in which case they bear interest in accordance with that provision.

As amended in 1987.

For material relating to the 1987 amendment, see Appendix I, infra.

Section 3–807. [Payment of Claims.]

(a) Upon the expiration of the earlier of the time limitations provided in Section 3–803 for the presentation of claims, the personal representative shall proceed to pay the claims allowed against the estate in the order of priority prescribed, after making provision for homestead, family and support allowances, for claims already presented that have not yet been allowed or whose allowance has been appealed, and for unbarred claims that may yet be presented, including costs and expenses of administration. By petition to the Court in a proceeding for the purpose, or by appropriate motion if the administration is supervised, a claimant whose claim has been allowed but not paid may secure an order directing the personal representative to pay the claim to the extent funds of the estate are available to pay it.

(b) The personal representative at any time may pay any just claim that has not been barred, with or without formal presentation, but is personally liable to any other claimant whose claim is allowed and who is injured by its payment if:

(1) payment was made before the expiration of the time limit stated in subsection (a) and the personal representative failed to require the payee to give adequate security for the refund of any of the payment necessary to pay other claimants; or

(2) payment was made, due to negligence or willful fault of the personal representative, in such manner as to deprive the injured claimant of priority.

As amended in 1989.

For material relating to the 1989 amendment, see Appendix IV, infra.

COMMENT

As recommended for amendment in 1989 by the Joint Editorial Board, the section directs the personal representative to pay allowed claims at the earlier of one year from death or the expiration of 4 months from first publication. This interpretation reflects that distribution need not be delayed further on account of creditors' claims once a time bar running from death or publication has run, for known creditors who have failed to present claims by such time may have received an actual notice leading to a bar 60 days thereafter and in any event can and should be the occasion for withholding or the making of other provision by the personal representative to cover the possibility of later presentation and allowance of such claims. Distribution would also be appropriate whenever competent and solvent distributees expressly agree to indemnify the estate for any claims remaining unbarred and undischarged after the distribution.

Section 3–808. [Individual Liability of Personal Representative.]

(a) Unless otherwise provided in the contract, a personal representative is not individually liable on a contract properly entered into in his fiduciary capacity in the course of administration of the estate unless he fails to reveal his representative capacity and identify the estate in the contract.

(b) A personal representative is individually liable for obligations arising from ownership or control of the estate or for torts committed in the course of administration of the estate only if he is personally at fault.

(c) Claims based on contracts entered into by a personal representative in his fiduciary capacity, on obligations arising from ownership or control of the estate or on torts committed in the course of estate administration may be asserted against the estate by proceeding against the personal representative in his fiduciary capacity, whether or not the personal representative is individually liable therefor.

(d) Issues of liability as between the estate and the personal representative individually may be determined in a proceeding for accounting, surcharge or indemnification or other appropriate proceeding.

COMMENT

In the absence of statute an executor, administrator or a trustee is personally liable on contracts entered into in his fiduciary capacity unless he expressly excludes personal liability in the contract. He is commonly personally liable for obligations stemming from ownership or possession of the property (e.g., taxes) and for torts committed by servants employed in the management of the property. The claimant ordinarily can reach the estate only after exhausting his remedies against the fiduciary as an individual and then only to the extent that the fiduciary is entitled to indemnity from the property. This and the following sections are designed to make the estate a quasi-corporation for purposes of such liabilities. The personal representative would be personally liable only if an agent for a corporation would be under the same circumstances, and the claimant has a direct remedy against the quasi-corporate property.

Section 3–809. [Secured Claims.]

Payment of a secured claim is upon the basis of the amount allowed if the creditor surrenders his security; otherwise payment is upon the basis of one of the following:

(1) if the creditor exhausts his security before receiving payment, [unless precluded by other law] upon the amount of the claim allowed less the fair value of the security; or

(2) if the creditor does not have the right to exhaust his security or has not done so, upon the amount of the claim allowed less the value of the security determined by converting it into money according to the terms of the agreement pursuant to which the security was delivered to the creditor, or by the creditor and personal representative by agreement, arbitration, compromise or litigation.

Section 3–810. [Claims Not Due and Contingent or Unliquidated Claims.]

(a) If a claim which will become due at a future time or a contingent or unliquidated claim becomes due or certain before the distribution of the estate, and if the claim has been allowed or established by a proceeding, it is paid in the same manner as presently due and absolute claims of the same class.

(b) In other cases the personal representative or, on petition of the personal representative or the claimant in a special proceeding for the purpose, the Court may provide for payment as follows:

(1) if the claimant consents, he may be paid the present or agreed value of the claim, taking any uncertainty into account;

(2) arrangement for future payment, or possible payment, on the happening of the contingency or on liquidation may be made by creating a trust, giving a mortgage, obtaining a bond or security from a distributee, or otherwise.

Section 3–811. [Counterclaims.]

In allowing a claim the personal representative may deduct any counterclaim which the estate has against the claimant. In determining a claim against an estate a Court shall reduce the amount allowed by the amount of any counterclaims and, if the counterclaims exceed the claim, render a judgment against the claimant in the amount of the excess. A counterclaim, liquidated or unliquidated, may arise from a transaction other than that upon which the claim is based. A counterclaim may give rise to relief exceeding in amount or different in kind from that sought in the claim.

Section 3–812. [Execution and Levies Prohibited.]

No execution may issue upon nor may any levy be made against any property of the estate under any judgment against a decedent or a personal representative, but this section shall not be construed to prevent the enforcement of mortgages, pledges or liens upon real or personal property in an appropriate proceeding.

Section 3–813. [Compromise of Claims.]

When a claim against the estate has been presented in any manner, the personal representative may, if it appears for the best interest of the estate, compromise the claim, whether due or not due, absolute or contingent, liquidated or unliquidated.

Section 3–814. [Encumbered Assets.]

If any assets of the estate are encumbered by mortgage, pledge, lien, or other security interest, the personal representative may pay the encumbrance or any part thereof, renew or extend any obligation secured by the encumbrance or convey or transfer the assets to the creditor in satisfaction of his lien, in whole or in part, whether or not the holder of the encumbrance has presented a claim, if it appears to be for the best interest of the estate. Payment of an encumbrance does not increase the share of the distributee entitled to the encumbered assets unless the distributee is entitled to exoneration.

COMMENT

Section 2–609 establishes a rule of construction against exoneration. Thus, unless the will indicates to the contrary, a specific devisee of mortgaged property takes subject to the lien without right to have other assets applied to discharge the secured obligation.

In 1975, the Joint Editorial Board recommended substitution of the word "presented", in the first sentence, for the word "filed" in the original text. The change aligns this section with Section 3–804, which describes several methods, including mailing or delivery to the personal representative, as methods of protecting a claim against nonclaim provisions of the Code.

Section 3–815. [Administration in More Than One State; Duty of Personal Representative.]

(a) All assets of estates being administered in this state are subject to all claims, allowances and charges existing or established against the personal representative wherever appointed.

(b) If the estate either in this state or as a whole is insufficient to cover all family exemptions and allowances determined by the law of the decedent's domicile, prior charges and claims, after satisfaction of the exemptions, allowances and charges, each claimant whose claim has been allowed either in this state or elsewhere in

323

administrations of which the personal representative is aware, is entitled to receive payment of an equal proportion of his claim. If a preference or security in regard to a claim is allowed in another jurisdiction but not in this state, the creditor so benefited is to receive dividends from local assets only upon the balance of his claim after deducting the amount of the benefit.

(c) In case the family exemptions and allowances, prior charges and claims of the entire estate exceed the total value of the portions of the estate being administered separately and this state is not the state of the decedent's last domicile, the claims allowed in this state shall be paid their proportion if local assets are adequate for the purpose, and the balance of local assets shall be transferred to the domiciliary personal representative. If local assets are not sufficient to pay all claims allowed in this state the amount to which they are entitled, local assets shall be marshalled so that each claim allowed in this state is paid its proportion as far as possible, after taking into account all dividends on claims allowed in this state from assets in other jurisdictions.

COMMENT

Under Section 3–803(a)(1), if a local (property only) administration is commenced and proceeds to advertisement for claims before non-claim statutes have run at domicile, claimants may prove claims in the local administration at any time before the local non-claim period expires. Section 3–815 has the effect of subjecting all assets of the decedent, wherever they may be located and administered, to claims properly presented in any local administration. It is necessary, however, that the personal representative of any portion of the estate be aware of other administrations in order for him to become responsible for claims and charges established against other administrations.

Section 3–816. [Final Distribution to Domiciliary Representative.]

The estate of a non-resident decedent being administered by a personal representative appointed in this state shall, if there is a personal representative of the decedent's domicile willing to receive it, be distributed to the domiciliary personal representative for the benefit of the successors of the decedent unless (1) by virtue of the decedent's will, if any, and applicable choice of law rules, the successors are identified pursuant to the local law of this state without reference to the local law of the decedent's domicile; (2) the personal representative of this state, after reasonable inquiry, is unaware of the existence or identity of a domiciliary personal representative; or (3) the Court orders otherwise in a proceeding for a closing order under Section 3–1001 or incident to the closing of a supervised administration. In other cases, distribution of the estate of a decedent shall be made in accordance with the other Parts of this Article.

PART 9

SPECIAL PROVISIONS RELATING TO DISTRIBUTION

Section 3–901. [Successors' Rights if No Administration.]

In the absence of administration, the heirs and devisees are entitled to the estate in accordance with the terms of a probated will or the laws of intestate succession. Devisees may establish title by the probated will to devised property. Persons entitled to property by homestead allowance, exemption or intestacy may establish title thereto by proof of the decedent's ownership, his death, and their relationship to the decedent. Successors take subject to all charges incident to administration, including the claims of creditors and allowances of surviving spouse and dependent children, and subject to the rights of others resulting from abatement, retainer, advancement, and ademption.

COMMENT

Title to a decedent's property passes to his heirs and devisees at the time of his death. See Section 3–101. This section adds little to Section 3–101 except to indicate how successors may establish record title in the absence of administration.

Section 3–902. [Distribution; Order in Which Assets Appropriated; Abatement.]

(a) Except as provided in subsection (b) and except as provided in connection with the share of the surviving spouse who elects to take an elective share, shares of distributees abate, without any preference or priority as between real and personal property, in the following order: (1) property not disposed of by the will; (2) residuary devises; (3) general devises; (4) specific devises. For purposes of abatement, a general devise charged on any specific property or fund is a specific devise to the extent of the value of the property on which it is charged, and upon the failure or insufficiency of the property on which it is charged, a general devise to the extent of the failure or insufficiency. Abatement within each classification is in proportion to the amounts of property each of the beneficiaries would have received if full distribution of the property had been made in accordance with the terms of the will.

(b) If the will expresses an order of abatement, or if the testamentary plan or the express or implied purpose of the devise would be defeated by the order of abatement stated in subsection (a), the shares of the distributees abate as may be found necessary to give effect to the intention of the testator.

(c) If the subject of a preferred devise is sold or used incident to administration, abatement shall be achieved by appropriate adjustments in, or contribution from, other interests in the remaining assets.

COMMENT

A testator may determine the order in which the assets of his estate are applied to the payment of his debts. If he does not, then the provisions of this section express rules which may be regarded as approximating what testators generally want. The statutory order of abatement is designed to aid in resolving doubts concerning the intention of a particular testator, rather than to defeat his purpose. Hence, subsection (b) directs that consideration be given to the purpose of a testator. This may be revealed in many ways. Thus, it is commonly held that, even in the absence of statute, general legacies to a wife, or to persons with respect to which the testator is in loco parentis, are to be preferred to other legacies in the same class because this accords with the probable purpose of the legacies.

[Section 3–902A. [Distribution; Order in Which Assets Appropriated; Abatement.]

(addendum for adoption in community property states)

[(a) and (b) as above.]

(c) If an estate of a decedent consists partly of separate property and partly of community property, the debts and expenses of administration shall be apportioned and charged against the different kinds of property in proportion to the relative value thereof.

[(d) same as (c) in common law state.]]

COMMENT

(c) is suggested for inclusion in Section 3–902 in a community property state. Its inclusion causes (c) as drafted for common law states to be redesignated (d). As is the case with other insertions suggested in the Code for community property states, the specific language of this draft is to be taken as illustrative of coverage that is desirable.

Section 3–903. [Right of Retainer.]

The amount of a non-contingent indebtedness of a successor to the estate if due, or its present value if not due, shall be offset against the successor's interest; but the successor has the benefit of any defense which would be available to him in a direct proceeding for recovery of the debt.

Section 3–904. [Interest on General Pecuniary Devise.]

General pecuniary devises bear interest at the legal rate beginning one year after the first appointment of a personal representative until payment, unless a contrary intent is indicated by the will.

COMMENT

Unlike the common law, this section provides that a general pecuniary devisee's right to interest begins one year from the time when administration was commenced, rather than one year from death. The rule provided here is similar to the common law rule in that the right to interest for delayed payment does not depend on whether the estate in fact realized income during the period of delay. The section is consistent with Section 5(b) of the Revised Uniform Principal and Income Act which allocates realized net income of an estate between various categories of successors.

Section 3–905. [Penalty Clause for Contest.]

A provision in a will purporting to penalize any interested person for contesting the will or instituting other proceedings relating to the estate is unenforceable if probable cause exists for instituting proceedings.

Section 3–906. [Distribution in Kind; Valuation; Method.]

(a) Unless a contrary intention is indicated by the will, the distributable assets of a decedent's estate shall be distributed in kind to the extent possible through application of the following provisions:

(1) A specific devisee is entitled to distribution of the thing devised to him, and a spouse or child who has selected particular assets of an estate as provided in Section 2–402 shall receive the items selected.

(2) Any homestead or family allowance or devise of a stated sum of money may be satisfied in kind provided

(i) the person entitled to the payment has not demanded payment in cash;

(ii) the property distributed in kind is valued at fair market value as of the date of its distribution, and

(iii) no residuary devisee has requested that the asset in question remain a part of the residue of the estate.

(3) For the purpose of valuation under paragraph (2) securities regularly traded on recognized exchanges, if distributed in kind, are valued at the price for the last sale of like securities traded on the business day prior to distribution, or if there was no sale on

that day, at the median between amounts bid and offered at the close of that day. Assets consisting of sums owed the decedent or the estate by solvent debtors as to which there is no known dispute or defense are valued at the sum due with accrued interest or discounted to the date of distribution. For assets which do not have readily ascertainable values, a valuation as of a date not more than 30 days prior to the date of distribution, if otherwise reasonable, controls. For purposes of facilitating distribution, the personal representative may ascertain the value of the assets as of the time of the proposed distribution in any reasonable way, including the employment of qualified appraisers, even if the assets may have been previously appraised.

(4) The residuary estate shall be distributed in any equitable manner.

(b) After the probable charges against the estate are known, the personal representative may mail or deliver a proposal for distribution to all persons who have a right to object to the proposed distribution. The right of any distributee to object to the proposed distribution on the basis of the kind or value of asset he is to receive, if not waived earlier in writing, terminates if he fails to object in writing received by the personal representative within 30 days after mailing or delivery of the proposal.

As amended in 1987.

For material relating to the 1987 amendment, see Appendix I, infra.

COMMENT

This section establishes a preference for distribution in kind. It directs a personal representative to make distribution in kind whenever feasible and to convert assets to cash only where there is a special reason for doing so. It provides a reasonable means for determining value of assets distributed in kind. It is implicit in Sections 3–101, 3–901 and this section that each residuary beneficiary's basic right is to his proportionate share of each asset constituting the residue.

Section 3–907. [Distribution in Kind; Evidence.]

If distribution in kind is made, the personal representative shall execute an instrument or deed of distribution assigning, transferring or releasing the assets to the distributee as evidence of the distributee's title to the property.

COMMENT

This and sections following should be read with Section 3–709 which permits the personal representative to leave certain assets of a decedent's estate in the possession of the person presumptively entitled thereto. The "release" contemplated by this section would be used as evidence that the personal representative had determined that he would not need to disturb the possession of an heir or devisee for purposes of administration.

Under Section 3–711, a personal representative's relationship to assets of the estate is described as the "same power over the title to property of the estate as an absolute owner would have." A personal representative may, however, acquire a full title to estate assets, as in the case where particular items are conveyed to the personal representative by sellers, transfer agents or others. The language of Section 3–907 is designed to cover instances where the instrument of distribution operates as a transfer, as well as those in which its operation is more like a release.

Section 3–908. [Distribution; Right or Title of Distributee.]

Proof that a distributee has received an instrument or deed of distribution of assets in kind, or payment in distribution, from a personal representative, is conclusive evidence that the distributee has succeeded to the interest of the estate in the distributed assets, as against all persons interested in the estate, except that the personal representative may recover the assets or their value if the distribution was improper.

COMMENT

The purpose of this section is to channel controversies which may arise among successors of a decedent because of improper distributions through the personal representative who made the distribution, or a successor personal representative. Section 3–108 does not bar appointment proceedings initiated to secure appointment of a personal representative to correct an erroneous distribution made by a prior representative. But see Section 3–1006.

Section 3–909. [Improper Distribution; Liability of Distributee.]

Unless the distribution or payment no longer can be questioned because of adjudication, estoppel, or limitation, a distributee of property improperly distributed or paid, or a claimant who was improperly paid, is liable to return the property improperly received and its income since distribution if he has the property. If he does not have the property, then he is liable to return the value as of the date of disposition of the property improperly received and its income and gain received by him.

COMMENT

The term "improperly" as used in this section must be read in light of Section 3–703 and the manifest purpose of this and other sections of the Code to shift questions concerning the propriety of various distributions from the fiduciary to the distributees in order to prevent every administration from becoming an adjudicated matter. Thus, a distribution may be "authorized at the time" as contemplated by Section 3–703, and still be "improper" under this section. Section 3–703 is designed to permit a personal representative to distribute without risk in some cases, even though there has been no adjudication. When an unadjudicated distribution has occurred, the rights of persons to show that the basis for the distribution (e.g., an informally probated will, or informally issued letters of administration) is incorrect, or that the basis was improperly applied (erroneous interpretation, for example) is preserved against distributees by this section.

The definition of "distributee" to include the trustee and beneficiary of a testamentary trust in 1–201(10) is important in allocating liabilities that may arise under Sections 3–909 and 3–910 on improper distribution by the personal representative under an informally probated will. The provisions of 3–909 and 3–910 are based on the theory that liability follows the property and the fiduciary is absolved from liability by reliance upon the informally probated will.

Section 3–910. [Purchasers from Distributees Protected.]

If property distributed in kind or a security interest therein is acquired for value by a purchaser from or lender to a distributee who has received an instrument or deed of distribution from the personal representative, or is so acquired by a purchaser from or lender to a transferee from such distributee, the purchaser or lender takes title free of rights of any interested person in the estate and incurs no personal liability to the estate, or to any interested person, whether or not the distribution was proper or supported by court order or the authority of the personal representative was terminated before execution of the instrument or deed. This section protects a purchaser from or lender to a distributee who, as personal representative, has executed a deed of distribution to himself, as well as a purchaser from or lender to any other distributee or his transferee. To be protected under this provision, a purchaser or lender need not inquire whether a personal representative acted properly in making the distribution in kind, even if the personal representative and the distributee are the same person, or whether the authority of the personal representative had terminated before the distribution. Any recorded instrument described in this section on which a state documentary fee is noted pursuant to [insert appropriate reference] shall be prima facie evidence that such transfer was made for value.

COMMENT

The words "instrument or deed of distribution" are explained in Section 3–907. The effect of this section may be to make an instrument or deed of distribution a very desirable link in a chain of title involving succession of land. Cf. Section 3–901.

In 1975, the Joint Editorial Board recommended additions that strengthen the protection extended by this section to bona fide purchasers from distributees. The additional language was derived from recommendations evolved with respect to the Colorado version of the Code by probate and title authorities who agreed on language to relieve title assurers of doubts they had identified in relation to some cases.

Section 3–911. [Partition for Purpose of Distribution.]

When two or more heirs or devisees are entitled to distribution of undivided interests in any real or personal property of the estate, the personal representative or one or more of the heirs or devisees may petition the Court prior to the formal or informal closing of the estate, to make partition. After notice to the interested heirs or devisees, the Court shall partition the property in the same manner as provided by the law for civil actions of partition. The Court may direct the personal representative to sell any property which cannot be partitioned without prejudice to the owners and which cannot conveniently be allotted to any one party.

COMMENT

Ordinarily heirs or devisees desiring partition of a decedent's property will resolve the issue by agreement without resort to the courts. (See Section 3–912.) If court determination is necessary, the court with jurisdiction to administer the estate has jurisdiction to partition the property.

Section 3–912. [Private Agreements Among Successors to Decedent Binding on Personal Representative.]

Subject to the rights of creditors and taxing authorities, competent successors may agree among themselves to alter the interests, shares, or amounts to which they are entitled under the will of the decedent, or under the laws of intestacy, in any way that they provide in a written contract executed by all who are affected by its provisions. The personal representative shall abide by the terms of the agreement subject to his obligation to administer the estate for the benefit of creditors, to pay all taxes and costs of administration, and to carry out the responsibilities of his office for the benefit of any successors of the decedent who are not parties. Personal representatives of decedents' estates are not required to see to the performance of trusts if the trustee thereof is another person who is willing to accept the trust. Accordingly, trustees of a testamentary trust are successors for the purposes of this section. Nothing herein relieves trustees of any duties owed to beneficiaries of trusts.

COMMENT

It may be asserted that this section is only a restatement of the obvious and should be omitted. Its purpose, however, is to make it clear that the successors to an estate have residual control over the way it is to be distributed. Hence, they may compel a personal representative to administer and distribute as they may agree and direct. Successors should compare the consequences and possible advantages of careful use of the power to renounce as described by Section 2–801 with the effect of agreement under this section. The most obvious difference is that an agreement among successors under this section would involve transfers by some participants to the extent it changed the pattern of distribution from that otherwise applicable.

Differing from a pattern that is familiar in many states, this Code does not subject testamentary trusts and trustees to special statutory provisions, or supervisory jurisdiction. A testamentary trustee is treated as a devisee with special duties which are of no particular concern to the personal representative. Article VII contains optional procedures extending the safeguards available to personal representatives to trustees of both inter vivos and testamentary trusts.

Section 3–913. [Distributions to Trustee.]

(a) Before distributing to a trustee, the personal representative may require that the trust be registered if the state in which it is to be administered provides for registration and that the trustee inform the beneficiaries as provided in Section 7–303.

(b) If the trust instrument does not excuse the trustee from giving bond, the personal representative may petition the appropriate Court to require that the trustee post bond if he apprehends that distribution might jeopardize the interests of persons who are not able to protect themselves, and he may withhold distribution until the Court has acted.

(c) No inference of negligence on the part of the personal representative shall be drawn from his failure to exercise the authority conferred by subsections (a) and (b).

COMMENT

This section is concerned with the fiduciary responsibility of the executor to beneficiaries of trusts to which he may deliver. Normally, the trustee represents beneficiaries in matters involving third persons, including prior fiduciaries. Yet, the executor may apprehend that delivery to the trustee may involve risks for the safety of the fund and for him. For example, he may be anxious to see that there is no equivocation about the devisee's willingness to accept the trust, and no problem of preserving evidence of the acceptance. He may have doubts about the integrity of the trustee, or about his ability to function satisfactorily. The testator's selection of the trustee may have been based on facts which are still current, or which are of doubtful relevance at the time of distribution. If the risks relate to the question of the trustee's intention to handle the fund without profit for himself, a conflict of interest problem is involved. If the risk relates to the ability of the trustee to manage prudently, a more troublesome question is posed for the executor. Is he, as executor, not bound to act in the best interests of the beneficiaries?

In many instances involving doubts of this sort, the executor probably will want the protection of a Court order. Sections 3–1001 and 3–1002 provide ample authority for an appropriate proceeding in the Court which issued the executor's letters.

In other cases, however, the executor may believe that he may be adequately protected if the acceptance of the trust by the devisee is unequivocal, or if the trustee is bonded. The purpose of this section is to make it clear that it is proper for the executor to require the trustee to register the trust and to notify beneficiaries before receiving distribution. Also, the section complements Section 7–304 by providing that the personal representative may petition an appropriate court to require that the trustee be bonded.

Status of testamentary trustees under the Uniform Probate Code. Under the Uniform Probate Code, the testamentary trustee by construction would be considered a devisee, distributee, and successor to whom title passes at time of the testator's death even though the will must be probated to prove the transfer. The informally probated will is conclusive until set aside and the personal representative may distribute to the trustee under the informally probated will or settlement agreement and the title of the trustee as distributee represented by the instrument or deed of distribution is conclusive until set aside on showing that it is improper. Should the informally probated will be set aside or the distribution to the trustee be shown to be improper, the trustee as distributee would be liable for value received but purchasers for value from the trustee as distributee under an instrument of distribution would be protected. Section 1–201's definition of "distributee" limits the distributee liability of the trustee and substitutes that of the trust beneficiaries to the extent of distributions by the trustee.

As a distributee as defined by 1–201, the testamentary trustee or beneficiary of a testamentary trust is liable to claimants like other distributees, would have the right of contribution from other distributees of the decedent's estate and would be protected by the same time limitations as other distributees (3–1006).

Incident to his standing as a distributee of the decedent's estate, the testamentary trustee would be an interested party who could petition for an order of complete settlement by the personal representative or for an order terminating testate administration. He also could appropriately receive the personal representative's account and distribution under a closing statement. As distributee he could represent his beneficiaries in compromise settlements in the decedent's estate which would be binding upon him and his beneficiaries. See Section 3–912.

The general fiduciary responsibilities of the testamentary trustee are not altered by the Uniform Probate Code and the trustee continues to have the duty to collect and reduce to possession within a reasonable time the assets of the trust estate including the enforcement of any claims on behalf of the trust against prior fiduciaries, including the personal representative, and third parties.

[Section 3–914. [Disposition of Unclaimed Assets.]

(a) If an heir, devisee or claimant cannot be found, the personal representative shall distribute the share of the missing person to his conservator, if any, otherwise to the [state treasurer] to become a part of the [state escheat fund].

(b) The money received by [state treasurer] shall be paid to the person entitled on proof of his right thereto or, if the [state treasurer] refuses or fails to pay, the person may petition the Court which appointed the personal representative, whereupon the Court upon notice to the [state treasurer] may determine the person entitled to the money and order the [treasurer] to pay it to him. No interest is allowed thereon and the heir, devisee or claimant shall pay all costs and expenses incident to the proceeding. If no petition is made to the [court] within 8 years after payment to the [state treasurer], the right of recovery is barred.]

COMMENT

The foregoing section is bracketed to indicate that the National Conference does not urge the specific content as set forth above over recent comprehensive legislation on the subject which may have been enacted in an adopting state.

This section applies when it is believed that a claimant, heir or distributee exists but he cannot be located. See 2–105.

Section 3–915. [Distribution to Person Under Disability.]

(a) A personal representative may discharge his obligation to distribute to any person under legal disability by distributing in a manner expressly provided in the will.

(b) Unless contrary to an express provision in the will, the personal representative may discharge his obligation to distribute to a minor or person under other disability as authorized by Section 5–101 or any other statute. If the personal representative knows that a conservator has been appointed or that a proceeding for appointment of a conservator is pending, the personal representative is authorized to distribute only to the conservator.

(c) If the heir or devisee is under disability other than minority, the personal representative is authorized to distribute to:

335

(1) an attorney in fact who has authority under a power of attorney to receive property for that person; or

(2) the spouse, parent or other close relative with whom the person under disability resides if the distribution is of amounts not exceeding [$10,000] a year, or property not exceeding [$10,-000] in value, unless the court authorizes a larger amount or greater value.

Persons receiving money or property for the disabled person are obligated to apply the money or property to the support of that person, but may not pay themselves except by way of reimbursement for out-of-pocket expenses for goods and services necessary for the support of the disabled person. Excess sums must be preserved for future support of the disabled person. The personal representative is not responsible for the proper application of money or property distributed pursuant to this subsection.

As amended in 1987.

For material relating to the 1987 amendment, see Appendix I, infra.

COMMENT

Section 5–103 is especially important as a possible source of authority for a valid discharge for payment or distribution made on behalf of a minor.

Section 3–916. [Apportionment of Estate Taxes.]

(a) For purposes of this section:

(1) "estate" means the gross estate of a decedent as determined for the purpose of federal estate tax and the estate tax payable to this state;

(2) "person" means any individual, partnership, association, joint stock company, corporation, government, political subdivision, governmental agency, or local governmental agency;

(3) "person interested in the estate" means any person entitled to receive, or who has received, from a decedent or by reason of the death of a decedent any property or interest therein included in the decedent's estate. It includes a personal representative, conservator, and trustee;

(4) "state" means any state, territory, or possession of the United States, the District of Columbia, and the Commonwealth of Puerto Rico;

(5) "tax" means the federal estate tax and the additional inheritance tax imposed by _____ and interest and penalties imposed in addition to the tax;

(6) "fiduciary" means personal representative or trustee.

(b) Except as provided in subsection (i) and, unless the will otherwise provides, the tax shall be apportioned among all persons interested in the estate. The apportionment is to be made in the proportion that the value of the interest of each person interested in the estate bears to the total value of the interests of all persons interested in the estate. The values used in determining the tax are to be used for that purpose. If the decedent's will directs a method of apportionment of tax different from the method described in this Code, the method described in the will controls.

(c)(1) The Court in which venue lies for the administration of the estate of a decedent, on petition for the purpose may determine the apportionment of the tax.

(2) If the Court finds that it is inequitable to apportion interest and penalties in the manner provided in subsection (b), because of special circumstances, it may direct apportionment thereof in the manner it finds equitable.

(3) If the Court finds that the assessment of penalties and interest assessed in relation to the tax is due to delay caused by the negligence of the fiduciary, the Court may charge him with the amount of the assessed penalties and interest.

(4) In any action to recover from any person interested in the estate the amount of the tax apportioned to the person in accordance with this Code the determination of the Court in respect thereto shall be prima facie correct.

(d)(1) The personal representative or other person in possession of the property of the decedent required to pay the tax may withhold from any property distributable to any person interested in the estate, upon its distribution to him, the amount of tax attributable to his interest. If the property in possession of the personal representative or other person required to pay the tax and distributable to any person interested in the estate is insufficient to satisfy the proportionate amount of the tax determined to be due from the person, the personal representative or other person required to pay the tax may recover the deficiency from the person interested in the estate. If the property is not in the possession of the personal representative or the other person required to pay the tax, the personal representative or the other person required to pay the tax may recover from any person interested in the estate the amount of the tax apportioned to the person in accordance with this Act.

(2) If property held by the personal representative is distributed prior to final apportionment of the tax, the distributee shall

337

provide a bond or other security for the apportionment liability in the form and amount prescribed by the personal representative.

(e)(1) In making an apportionment, allowances shall be made for any exemptions granted, any classification made of persons interested in the estate and for any deductions and credits allowed by the law imposing the tax.

(2) Any exemption or deduction allowed by reason of the relationship of any person to the decedent or by reason of the purposes of the gift inures to the benefit of the person bearing such relationship or receiving the gift; but if an interest is subject to a prior present interest which is not allowable as a deduction, the tax apportionable against the present interest shall be paid from principal.

(3) Any deduction for property previously taxed and any credit for gift taxes or death taxes of a foreign country paid by the decedent or his estate inures to the proportionate benefit of all persons liable to apportionment.

(4) Any credit for inheritance, succession or estate taxes or taxes in the nature thereof applicable to property or interests includable in the estate, inures to the benefit of the persons or interests chargeable with the payment thereof to the extent proportionately that the credit reduces the tax.

(5) To the extent that property passing to or in trust for a surviving spouse or any charitable, public or similar purpose is not an allowable deduction for purposes of the tax solely by reason of an inheritance tax or other death tax imposed upon and deductible from the property, the property is not included in the computation provided for in subsection (b) hereof, and to that extent no apportionment is made against the property. The sentence immediately preceding does not apply to any case if the result would be to deprive the estate of a deduction otherwise allowable under Section 2053(d) of the Internal Revenue Code of 1954, as amended, of the United States, relating to deduction for state death taxes on transfers for public, charitable, or religious uses.

(f) No interest in income and no estate for years or for life or other temporary interest in any property or fund is subject to apportionment as between the temporary interest and the remainder. The tax on the temporary interest and the tax, if any, on the remainder is chargeable against the corpus of the property or funds subject to the temporary interest and remainder.

(g) Neither the personal representative nor other person required to pay the tax is under any duty to institute any action to recover from any person interested in the estate the amount of the tax apportioned to the person until the expiration of the 3 months next following final determination of the tax. A personal representative or other person required to pay the tax who institutes the action within a reasonable time after the 3 months' period is not subject to any liability or surcharge because any portion of the tax apportioned to any person interested in the estate was collectible at a time following the death of the decedent but thereafter became uncollectible. If the personal representative or other person required to pay the tax cannot collect from any person interested in the estate the amount of the tax apportioned to the person, the amount not recoverable shall be equitably apportioned among the other persons interested in the estate who are subject to apportionment.

(h) A personal representative acting in another state or a person required to pay the tax domiciled in another state may institute an action in the courts of this state and may recover a proportionate amount of the federal estate tax, of an estate tax payable to another state or of a death duty due by a decedent's estate to another state, from a person interested in the estate who is either domiciled in this state or who owns property in this state subject to attachment or execution. For the purposes of the action the determination of apportionment by the Court having jurisdiction of the administration of the decedent's estate in the other state is prima facie correct.

(i) If the liabilities of persons interested in the estate as prescribed by this act differ from those which result under the Federal Estate tax law, the liabilities imposed by the federal law will control and the balance of this Section shall apply as if the resulting liabilities had been prescribed herein.

COMMENT

Section 3–916 copies the Uniform   Estate Tax Apportionment Act.

PART 10

CLOSING ESTATES

Section 3–1001. [Formal Proceedings Terminating Administration; Testate or Intestate; Order of General Protection.]

(a) A personal representative or any interested person may petition for an order of complete settlement of the estate. The personal representative may petition at any time, and any other interested person may petition after one year from the appointment of the original personal representative except that no petition under this section may be entertained until the time for presenting claims which arose prior to the death of the decedent has expired. The petition may request the Court to determine testacy, if not previously determined, to consider the final account or compel or approve an accounting and distribution, to construe any will or determine heirs and adjudicate the final settlement and distribution of the estate. After notice to all interested persons and hearing the Court may enter an order or orders, on appropriate conditions, determining the persons entitled to distribution of the estate, and, as circumstances require, approving settlement and directing or approving distribution of the estate and discharging the personal representative from further claim or demand of any interested person.

(b) If one or more heirs or devisees were omitted as parties in, or were not given notice of, a previous formal testacy proceeding, the Court, on proper petition for an order of complete settlement of the estate under this section, and after notice to the omitted or unnotified persons and other interested parties determined to be interested on the assumption that the previous order concerning testacy is conclusive as to those given notice of the earlier proceeding, may determine testacy as it affects the omitted persons and confirm or alter the previous order of testacy as it affects all interested persons as appropriate in the light of the new proofs. In the absence of objection by an omitted or unnotified person, evidence received in the original testacy proceeding shall constitute prima facie proof of due execution of any will previously admitted to probate, or of the fact that the decedent left no valid will if the prior proceedings determined this fact.

COMMENT

Subsection (b) is derived from § 64(b) of the Illinois Probate Act (1967) [S.H.A. ch. 3, § 64(b)]. Section 3–106 specifies that an order is binding as to all who are given notice even though less than all interested persons were notified. This section provides a method of curing an oversight in regard to notice which may come to light before the estate is finally settled. If the person who failed to receive notice of the earlier proceeding succeeds in obtaining entry of a different order from that previously made, others who received notice of the earlier proceeding may be benefitted. Still, they are not entitled to notice of the curative proceeding, nor should they be permitted to appear.

See, also, Comment following section 3–1002.

Section 3–1002. [Formal Proceedings Terminating Testate Administration; Order Construing Will Without Adjudicating Testacy.]

A personal representative administering an estate under an informally probated will or any devisee under an informally probated will may petition for an order of settlement of the estate which will not adjudicate the testacy status of the decedent. The personal representative may petition at any time, and a devisee may petition after one year, from the appointment of the original personal representative, except that no petition under this section may be entertained until the time for presenting claims which arose prior to the death of the decedent has expired. The petition may request the Court to consider the final account or compel or approve an accounting and distribution, to construe the will and adjudicate final settlement and distribution of the estate. After notice to all devisees and the personal representative and hearing, the Court may enter an order or orders, on appropriate conditions, determining the persons entitled to distribution of the estate under the will, and, as circumstances require, approving settlement and directing or approving distribution of the estate and discharging the personal representative from further claim or demand of any devisee who is a party to the proceeding and those he represents. If it appears that a part of the estate is intestate, the proceedings shall be dismissed or amendments made to meet the provisions of Section 3–1001.

COMMENT

Section 3–1002 permits a final determination of the rights between each other and against the personal representative of the devisees under a will when there has been no formal proceeding in regard to testacy. Hence, the heirs in intestacy need not be made parties. Section 3–1001 permits a final determination of the rights between each other and against the personal representative of all persons interested in an estate. If supervised administration is used, Section 3–505 directs that the estate be closed by use of procedures like those described in Section 3–1001. Of course, testacy will have been adjudicated before time for the closing proceeding if supervised administration is used.

Section 3–1003. [Closing Estates; By Sworn Statement of Personal Representative.]

(a) Unless prohibited by order of the Court and except for estates being administered in supervised administration proceedings, a personal representative may close an estate by filing with the court no earlier than six months after the date of original appointment of a general personal representative for the estate, a verified statement stating that the personal representatives or a previous personal representative, has:

(1) determined that the time limited for presentation of creditors' claims has expired.

(2) fully administered the estate of the decedent by making payment, settlement, or other disposition of all claims that were presented, expenses of administration and estate, inheritance and other death taxes, except as specified in the statement, and that the assets of the estate have been distributed to the persons entitled. If any claims remain undischarged, the statement must state whether the personal representative has distributed the estate subject to possible liability with the agreement of the distributees or state in detail other arrangements that have been made to accommodate outstanding liabilities; and

(3) sent a copy of the statement to all distributees of the estate and to all creditors or other claimants of whom the personal representative is aware whose claims are neither paid nor barred and has furnished a full account in writing of the personal representative's administration to the distributees whose interests are affected thereby.

(b) If no proceedings involving the personal representative are pending in the Court one year after the closing statement is filed, the appointment of the personal representative terminates.

As amended in 1989.

For material relating to the 1989 amendment, see Appendix IV, infra.

COMMENT

The Code uses "termination" to refer to events which end a personal representative's authority. See Sections 3–608, et seq. The word "closing" refers to circumstances which support the conclusions that the affairs of the estate either are, or have been alleged to have been, wound up. If the affairs of the personal representative are reviewed and adjudicated under either Sections 3–1001 or 3–1002, the judicial conclusion that the estate is wound up serves also to terminate the personal representative's authority. See Section 3–610(b). On the other hand, a "closing" statement under 3–1003 is only an affirmation by the personal representative that he believes the affairs of the estate to be completed. The statement is significant because it reflects that assets have been distributed. Any creditor whose claim has not been barred and who has not been paid is permitted by Section 3–1004 to assert his claim against distributees. The personal representative is also still fully subject to suit under Sections 3–602 and 3–608, for his authority is not "terminated" under Section 3–610(a) until one year after a closing statement is filed. Even if his authority is "terminated," he remains liable to suit unless protected by limitation or unless an adjudication settling his accounts is the reason for "termination". See Sections 3–1005 and 3–608.

From a slightly different viewpoint, a personal representative may obtain a complete discharge of his fiduciary obligations through a judicial proceeding after notice. Sections 3–1001 and 3–1002 describe two proceedings which enable a personal representative to gain protection from all persons or from devisees only. A personal representative who neither obtains a judicial

order of protection nor files a closing statement, is protected by 3–703 in regard to acts or distributions which were authorized when done but which become doubtful thereafter because of a change in testacy status. On the other questions, the personal representative who does not take any of the steps described by the Code to gain more protection, has no protection against later claims of breach of his fiduciary obligation other than any arising from consent or waiver of individual distributees who may have bound themselves by receipts given to the personal representative.

This section increases the prospects of full discharge of a personal representative who uses the closing statement route over those of a personal representative who relies on receipts. Full protection follows from the running of the six months limitations period described in 3–1005. But, 3–1005's protection does not prevent distributees from claiming lack of full disclosure. Hence, it offers little more protection than a receipt. Still, it may be useful to decrease the likelihood of later claim of non-disclosure. Its more significant function, however, is to provide a means for terminating the office of personal representative in a way that will be obvious to third persons.

In 1989 the Joint Editorial Board recommended changing subparagraph (a)(1) to make the time reference correspond to changes recommended for Section 3–803.

Section 3–1004. [Liability of Distributees to Claimants.]

After assets of an estate have been distributed and subject to Section 3–1006, an undischarged claim not barred may be prosecuted in a proceeding against one or more distributees. No distributee shall be liable to claimants for amounts received as exempt property, homestead or family allowances, or for amounts in excess of the value of his distribution as of the time of distribution. As between distributees, each shall bear the cost of satisfaction of unbarred claims as if the claim had been satisfied in the course of administration. Any distributee who shall have failed to notify other distributees of the demand made upon him by the claimant in sufficient time to permit them to join in any proceeding in which the claim was asserted against him loses his right of contribution against other distributees.

COMMENT

This section creates a ceiling on the liability of a distributee of "the value of his distribution" as of the time of distribution. The section indicates that each distributee is liable for all that a claimant may prove to be due, provided the claim does not exceed the value of the defendant's distribution from the estate. But, each distributee may preserve a right of contribution against other distributees. The risk of insolvency of one or more, but less than all distributees is on the distributee rather than on the claimant.

In 1975, the Joint Editorial Board recommended the addition, after "claimants for amounts" in the second sentence, of "received as exempt property, homestead or family allowances, or for amounts . . ." The purpose of the addition was to prevent unpaid creditors of a decedent from attempting to enforce their claims against a spouse or child who had received a distribution of exempt values.

Section 3–1005. [Limitations on Proceedings Against Personal Representative.]

Unless previously barred by adjudication and except as provided in the closing statement, the rights of successors and of creditors whose claims have not otherwise been barred against the personal representative for breach of fiduciary duty are barred unless a proceeding to assert the same is commenced within 6 months after the filing of the closing statement. The rights thus barred do not include rights to recover from a personal representative for fraud, misrepresentation, or inadequate disclosure related to the settlement of the decedent's estate.

COMMENT

This and the preceding section make it clear that a claimant whose claim has not been barred may have alternative remedies when an estate has been distributed subject to his claim. Under this section, he has six months to prosecute an action against the personal representative if the latter breached any duty to the claimant. For example, the personal representative may be liable to a creditor if he violated the provisions of Section 3–807. The preceding section describes the fundamental liability of the distributees to unbarred claimants to the extent of the value received. The last sentence emphasizes that a personal representative who fails to disclose matters relevant to his liability in his closing statement and in the account of administration he furnished to distributees, gains no protection from the period described here. A personal representative may, however, use Section 3–1001, or, where appropriate, 3–1002 to secure greater protection.

Section 3–1006. [Limitations on Actions and Proceedings Against Distributees.]

Unless previously adjudicated in a formal testacy proceeding or in a proceeding settling the accounts of a personal representative or otherwise barred, the claim of a claimant to recover from a distributee who is liable to pay the claim, and the right of an heir or devisee, or of a successor personal representative acting in their behalf, to recover property improperly distributed or its value from any distributee is forever barred at the later of three years after the decedent's death or one year after the time of its distribution thereof, but all claims of creditors of the decedent, are barred one year after the decedent's death. This section does not bar an action to recover property or value received as a result of fraud.

Amended in 1989.

For material relating to the 1989 amendment, see Appendix IV, infra.

COMMENT

This section describes an ultimate time limit for recovery by creditors, heirs and devisees of a decedent from distributees. It is to be noted: (1) Section 3–108 imposes a general limit of three years from death on one who must set aside an informal probate in order to establish his rights, or who must secure probate of a late-discovered will after an estate has been administered as intestate. Hence the time limit of 3–108 may bar one who would claim as an heir or devisee sooner than this section, although it would never cause a bar prior to three years from the decedent's death. (2) This section would not bar recovery by a supposed decedent whose estate has been probated. See Section 3–412. (3) The limitation of this section ends the possibility of appointment of a personal representative to correct an erroneous distribution as

mentioned in Sections 3–1005 and 3–1008. If there have been no adjudications under Section 3–409, or possibly 3–1001 or 3–1002, estate of the decedent which is discovered after administration has been closed may be the subject of different distribution than that attending the estate originally administered.

The last sentence excepting actions or suits to recover property kept from one by the fraud of another may be unnecessary in view of the blanket provision concerning fraud in Article I. See Section 1–106.

In 1989, the Joint Editorial Board recommended changing the section so as to separate proceedings involving claims by claimants barred one year after decedent's death by Section 3–803(a)(1), and other proceed-

345

ings by unbarred claimants or by omitted heirs or devisees.

Section 3-1007. [Certificate Discharging Liens Securing Fiduciary Performance.]

After his appointment has terminated, the personal representative, his sureties, or any successor of either, upon the filing of a verified application showing, so far as is known by the applicant, that no action concerning the estate is pending in any court, is entitled to receive a certificate from the Registrar that the personal representative appears to have fully administered the estate in question. The certificate evidences discharge of any lien on any property given to secure the obligation of the personal representative in lieu of bond or any surety, but does not preclude action against the personal representative or the surety.

COMMENT

This section does not affect the liability of the personal representative, or of any surety, but merely permits a release of security given by a personal representative, or his surety, when, from the passage of time and other conditions, it seems highly unlikely that there will be any liability remaining undischarged. See Section 3-607.

Section 3-1008. [Subsequent Administration.]

If other property of the estate is discovered after an estate has been settled and the personal representative discharged or after one year after a closing statement has been filed, the Court upon petition of any interested person and upon notice as it directs may appoint the same or a successor personal representative to administer the subsequently discovered estate. If a new appointment is made, unless the Court orders otherwise, the provisions of this Code apply as appropriate; but no claim previously barred may be asserted in the subsequent administration.

COMMENT

This section is consistent with Section 3-108 which provides a general period of limitations of three years from death for appointment proceedings, but makes appropriate exception for subsequent administrations.

346

PART 11

COMPROMISE OF CONTROVERSIES

Section 3–1101. [Effect of Approval of Agreements Involving Trusts, Inalienable Interests, or Interests of Third Persons.]

A compromise of any controversy as to admission to probate of any instrument offered for formal probate as the will of a decedent, the construction, validity, or effect of any probated will, the rights or interests in the estate of the decedent, of any successor, or the administration of the estate, if approved in a formal proceeding in the Court for that purpose, is binding on all the parties thereto including those unborn, unascertained or who could not be located. An approved compromise is binding even though it may affect a trust or an inalienable interest. A compromise does not impair the rights of creditors or of taxing authorities who are not parties to it.

Section 3–1102. [Procedure for Securing Court Approval of Compromise.]

The procedure for securing court approval of a compromise is as follows:

(1) The terms of the compromise shall be set forth in an agreement in writing which shall be executed by all competent persons and parents acting for any minor child having beneficial interests or having claims which will or may be affected by the compromise. Execution is not required by any person whose identity cannot be ascertained or whose whereabouts is unknown and cannot reasonably be ascertained.

(2) Any interested person, including the personal representative or a trustee, then may submit the agreement to the Court for its approval and for execution by the personal representative, the trustee of every affected testamentary trust, and other fiduciaries and representatives.

(3) After notice to all interested persons or their representatives, including the personal representative of the estate and all affected trustees of trusts, the Court, if it finds that the contest or controversy is in good faith and that the effect of the agreement upon the interests of persons represented by fiduciaries or other representatives is just and reasonable, shall make an order approving the agreement and directing all fiduciaries subject to its

jurisdiction to execute the agreement. Minor children represented only by their parents may be bound only if their parents join with other competent persons in execution of the compromise. Upon the making of the order and the execution of the agreement, all further disposition of the estate is in accordance with the terms of the agreement.

COMMENT

This section and the one preceding it outline a procedure which may be initiated by competent parties having beneficial interests in a decedent's estate as a means of resolving controversy concerning the estate. If all competent persons with beneficial interests or claims which might be affected by the proposal and parents *properly* representing interests of their children concur, a settlement scheme differing from that otherwise governing the devolution may be substituted. The procedure for securing representation of minors and unknown or missing persons with interests must be followed. See Section 1–403. The ultimate control of the question of whether the substitute proposal shall be accepted is with the court which must find: "that the contest or controversy is in good faith and that the effect of the agreement upon the interests of parties represented by fiduciaries is just and reasonable."

The thrust of the procedure is to put the authority for initiating settlement proposals with the persons who have beneficial interests in the estate, and to prevent executors and testamentary trustees from vetoing any such proposal. The only reason for approving a scheme of devolution which differs from that framed by the testator or the statutes governing intestacy is to prevent dissipation of the estate in wasteful litigation. Because executors and trustees may have an interest in fees and commissions which they might earn through efforts to carry out testator's intention, the judgment of the court is substituted for that of such fiduciaries in appropriate cases. A controversy which the court may find to be in good faith, as well as concurrence of all beneficially interested and competent persons and parent-representatives provide prerequisites which should prevent the procedure from being abused. Thus, the procedure does not threaten the planning of a testator who plans and drafts with sufficient clarity and completeness to eliminate the possibility of good faith controversy concerning the meaning and legality of his plan.

See Section 1–403 for rules governing representatives and appointment of guardians ad litem.

These sections are modeled after Section 93 of the Model Probate Code. Comparable legislative provisions have proved quite useful in Michigan. See M.C.L.A. §§ 702.45–702.49.

PART 12

COLLECTION OF PERSONAL PROPERTY BY AFFIDAVIT AND SUMMARY ADMINISTRATION PROCEDURE FOR SMALL ESTATES

GENERAL COMMENT

The four sections which follow include two designed to facilitate transfer of small estates without use of a personal representative, and two designed to simplify the duties of a personal representative, who is appointed to handle a small estate.

The Flexible System of Administration described by earlier portions of Article III lends itself well to situations involving small estates. Letters may be obtained quickly without notice or judicial involvement. Immediately, the personal representative is in a position to distribute to successors whose deeds or transfers will protect purchasers. This route accommodates the need for quick and inexpensive transfers of land of small value as well as other assets. Consequently, it was unnecessary to frame complex provisions extending the affidavit procedures to land.

Indeed, transfers via letters of administration may prove to be less troublesome than use of the affidavit procedure. Still, it seemed desirable to provide a quick collection mechanism which avoids all necessity to visit the probate court. For one thing, unpredictable local variations in probate practice may produce situations where the alternative procedure will be very useful. For another, the provision of alternatives is in line with the overall philosophy of Article III to provide maximum flexibility.

Figures gleaned from a recent authoritative report of a major survey of probated estates in Cleveland, Ohio, demonstrate that more than one-half of all estates in probate had a gross value of less than $15,000. This means that the principal measure of the relevance of any legislation dealing with probate procedures is to be found in its impact on very small and moderate sized estates. Here is the area where probate affects most people.

Section 3–1201. [Collection of Personal Property by Affidavit.]

(a) Thirty days after the death of a decedent, any person indebted to the decedent or having possession of tangible personal property or an instrument evidencing a debt, obligation, stock or chose in action belonging to the decedent shall make payment of the indebtedness or deliver the tangible personal property or an instrument evidencing a debt, obligation, stock or chose in action to a person claiming to be the successor of the decedent upon being presented an affidavit made by or on behalf of the successor stating that:

(1) the value of the entire estate, wherever located, less liens and encumbrances, does not exceed $5,000;

(2) 30 days have elapsed since the death of the decedent;

(3) no application or petition for the appointment of a personal representative is pending or has been granted in any jurisdiction; and

(4) the claiming successor is entitled to payment or delivery of the property.

(b) A transfer agent of any security shall change the registered ownership on the books of a corporation from the decedent to the successor or successors upon the presentation of an affidavit as provided in subsection (a).

COMMENT

This section provides for an easy method for collecting the personal property of a decedent by affidavit prior to any formal disposition. Existing legislation generally permits the surviving widow or children to collect wages and other small amounts of liquid funds. Section 3-1201 goes further in that it allows the collection of personal property as well as money and permits any devisee or heir to make the collection. Since the appointment of a personal representative may be obtained easily under the Code, it is unnecessary to make the provisions regarding small estates applicable to realty.

Section 3-1202. [Effect of Affidavit.]

The person paying, delivering, transferring, or issuing personal property or the evidence thereof pursuant to affidavit is discharged and released to the same extent as if he dealt with a personal representative of the decedent. He is not required to see to the application of the personal property or evidence thereof or to inquire into the truth of any statement in the affidavit. If any person to whom an affidavit is delivered refuses to pay, deliver, transfer, or issue any personal property or evidence thereof, it may be recovered or its payment, delivery, transfer, or issuance compelled upon proof of their right in a proceeding brought for the purpose by or on behalf of the persons entitled thereto. Any person to whom payment, delivery, transfer or issuance is made is answerable and accountable therefor to any personal representative of the estate or to any other person having a superior right.

COMMENT

Sections 3-1201 and 3-1202 apply to any personal property located in this state whether or not the decedent died domiciled in this state, to any successor to personal property located in this state whether or not a resident of this state, and, to the extent that the laws of this state may control the succession to personal property, to personal property wherever located of a decedent who died domiciled in this state.

Section 3-1203. [Small Estates; Summary Administration Procedure.]

If it appears from the inventory and appraisal that the value of the entire estate, less liens and encumbrances, does not exceed homestead allowance, exempt property, family allowance, costs and expenses of administration, reasonable funeral expenses, and reasonable and necessary medical and hospital expenses of the last illness of the decedent, the personal representative, without giving notice to creditors, may immediately disburse and distribute the estate to the persons entitled thereto and file a closing statement as provided in Section 3-1204.

COMMENT

This section makes it possible for the personal representative to make a summary distribution of a small estate without the necessity of giving notice to creditors. Since the probate estate of many decedents will not exceed the amount specified in the statute, this section will prove useful in many estates.

Section 3-1204. [Small Estates; Closing by Sworn Statement of Personal Representative.]

(a) Unless prohibited by order of the Court and except for estates being administered by supervised personal representatives, a personal representative may close an estate administered under the summary procedures of Section 3-1203 by filing with the Court, at any time after disbursement and distribution of the estate, a verified statement stating that:

(1) to the best knowledge of the personal representative, the value of the entire estate, less liens and encumbrances, did not exceed homestead allowance, exempt property, family allowance, costs and expenses of administration, reasonable funeral expenses, and reasonable, necessary medical and hospital expenses of the last illness of the decedent;

(2) the personal representative has fully administered the estate by disbursing and distributing it to the persons entitled thereto; and

(3) the personal representative has sent a copy of the closing statement to all distributees of the estate and to all creditors or other claimants of whom he is aware whose claims are neither paid nor barred and has furnished a full account in writing of his administration to the distributees whose interests are affected.

351

(b) If no actions or proceedings involving the personal representative are pending in the Court one year after the closing statement is filed, the appointment of the personal representative terminates.

(c) A closing statement filed under this section has the same effect as one filed under Section 3–1003.

COMMENT

The personal representative may elect to close the estate under Section 3–1002 in order to secure the greater protection offered by that procedure.

The remedies for fraudulent statement provided in Section 1–106 of course would apply to any intentional misstatements by a personal representative.

ARTICLE IV

FOREIGN PERSONAL REPRESENTATIVES; ANCILLARY ADMINISTRATION

PART 1

DEFINITIONS

PART 2

POWERS OF FOREIGN PERSONAL REPRESENTATIVES

PART 3

JURISDICTION OVER FOREIGN REPRESENTATIVES

PART 4

JUDGMENTS AND PERSONAL REPRESENTATIVE

GENERAL COMMENT

This Article concerns the law applicable in estate problems which involve more than a single state. It covers the powers and responsibilities in the adopting state of personal representatives appointed in other states.

Some provisions of the Code covering local appointment of personal representatives for non-residents appear in Article III. These include the following: 3–201 (venue), 3–202 (resolution of conflicting claims regarding domicile), 3–203 (priority as personal representative of representative previously appointed at domicile), 3–307(a) (30 days delay required before appointment of a local representative for a non-resident), 3–803(a) (claims barred by

353

non-claim at domicile before local administration commenced are barred locally) and 3–815 (duty of personal representative in regard to claims where estate is being administered in more than one state). See also 3–308, 3–611(a) and 3–816. Also, see Section 4–207.

The recognition provisions contained in Article IV and the various provisions of Article III which relate to administration of estates of non-residents are designed to coerce respect for domiciliary procedures and administrative acts to the extent possible.

The first part of Article IV contains some definitions of particular relevance to estates located in two or more states.

The second part of Article IV deals with the powers of foreign personal representatives in a jurisdiction adopting the Uniform Probate Code. There are different types of power which may be exercised. First, a foreign personal representative has the power under Section 4–201 to receive payments of debts owed to the decedent or to accept delivery of property belonging to the decedent. The foreign personal representative provides an affidavit indicating the date of death of the non-resident decedent, that no local administration has been commenced and that the foreign personal representative is entitled to payment or delivery. Payment under this provision can be made any time more than 60 days after the death of the decedent. When made in good faith the payment operates as a discharge of the debtor. A protection for local creditors of the decedent is provided in Section 4–203, under which local debtors of the non-resident decedent can be notified of the claims which local creditors have against the estate. This notification will prevent payment under this provision.

A second type of power is provided in Sections 4–204 to 4–206. Under these provisions a foreign personal representative can file with the appropriate court a copy of his appointment and official bond if he has one. Upon so filing, the foreign personal representative has all of the powers of a personal representative appointed by the local court. This would be all of the powers provided for in an unsupervised administration as provided in Article III of the Code.

The third type of power which may be obtained by a foreign personal representative is conferred by the priority the domiciliary personal representative enjoys in respect to local appointment. This is covered by Section 3–203. Also, see Section 3.611(b).

Part 3 provides for power in the local court over foreign personal representatives who act locally. If a local or ancillary administration has been started, provisions in Article III subject the appointee to the power of the court. See Section 3–602. In Part 3 of this Article, it is provided that a foreign personal representative submits himself to the jurisdiction of the local court by filing a copy of his appointment to get the powers provided in Section 4–205 or by doing any act which would give the state jurisdiction over him as an individual. In addition, the collection of funds as provided in Section 4–201 gives the court quasi-in-rem jurisdiction over the foreign personal representative to the extent of the funds collected.

Finally, Section 4–303 provides that the foreign personal representative is subject to the jurisdiction of the local court "to the same extent that his decedent was subject to jurisdiction immediately prior to death." This is similar to the typical non-resident motorist provision that provides for jurisdiction over the personal representative of a deceased non-resident motorist, see Note, 44 Iowa L.Rev. 384 (1959). It is, however, a much broader provision. Section 4–304 provides for the mechanical steps to be taken in serving the foreign personal representatives.

Part 4 of the Article deals with the res judicata effect to be given adjudications for or against a foreign personal representative. Any such adjudication is to be conclusive on a local personal representative "unless it resulted from fraud or collusion . . . to the prejudice of the estate." This provision must be read with Section 3–408 which deals with certain out-of-state findings concerning a decedent's estate.

PART 1

DEFINITIONS

Section 4–101. [Definitions.]

In this Article

(1) "local administration" means administration by a personal representative appointed in this state pursuant to appointment proceedings described in Article III.

(2) "local personal representative" includes any personal representative appointed in this state pursuant to appointment proceedings described in Article III and excludes foreign personal representatives who acquire the power of a local personal representative pursuant to Section 4–205.

(3) "resident creditor" means a person domiciled in, or doing business in this state, who is, or could be, a claimant against an estate of a non-resident decedent.

COMMENT

Section 1–201 includes definitions of "foreign personal representative", "personal representative" and "non-resident decedent".

PART 2

POWERS OF FOREIGN PERSONAL REPRESENTATIVES

Section 4–201. [Payment of Debt and Delivery of Property to Domiciliary Foreign Personal Representative Without Local Administration.]

At any time after the expiration of sixty days from the death of a nonresident decedent, any person indebted to the estate of the nonresident decedent or having possession or control of personal property, or of an instrument evidencing a debt, obligation, stock or chose in action belonging to the estate of the nonresident decedent may pay the debt, deliver the personal property, or the instrument evidencing the debt, obligation, stock or chose in action, to the domiciliary foreign personal representative of the nonresident decedent upon being presented with proof of his appointment and an affidavit made by or on behalf of the representative stating:

(1) the date of the death of the nonresident decedent,

(2) that no local administration, or application or petition therefor, is pending in this state,

(3) that the domiciliary foreign personal representative is entitled to payment or delivery.

COMMENT

Section 3–201(d) refers to the location of tangible personal estate and intangible personal estate which may be evidenced by an instrument. The instant section includes both categories. Transfer of securities is not covered by this section since that is adequately covered by Section 3 of the Uniform Act for Simplification of Fiduciary Security Transfers.

Section 4–202. [Payment or Delivery Discharges.]

Payment or delivery made in good faith on the basis of the proof of authority and affidavit releases the debtor or person having possession of the personal property to the same extent as if payment or delivery had been made to a local personal representative.

Section 4–203. [Resident Creditor Notice.]

Payment or delivery under Section 4–201 may not be made if a resident creditor of the nonresident decedent has notified the debtor of the nonresident decedent or the person having possession of the personal property belonging to the nonresident decedent that the debt should not be paid nor the property delivered to the domiciliary foreign personal representative.

COMMENT

Similar to provision in Colorado Revised Statute, 153–6–9.

Section 4–204. [Proof of Authority–Bond.]

If no local administration or application or petition therefor is pending in this state, a domiciliary foreign personal representative may file with a Court in this State in a [county] in which property belonging to the decedent is located, authenticated copies of his appointment and of any official bond he has given.

Section 4–205. [Powers.]

A domiciliary foreign personal representative who has complied with Section 4–204 may exercise as to assets in this state all powers of a local personal representative and may maintain actions and proceedings in this state subject to any conditions imposed upon nonresident parties generally.

Section 4–206. [Power of Representatives in Transition.]

The power of a domiciliary foreign personal representative under Section 4–201 or 4–205 shall be exercised only if there is no administration or application therefor pending in this state. An application or petition for local administration of the estate terminates the power of the foreign personal representative to act under Section 4–205, but the local Court may allow the foreign personal representative to exercise limited powers to preserve the estate. No person who, before receiving actual notice of a pending local administration, has changed his position in reliance upon the powers of a foreign personal representative shall be prejudiced by reason of the application or petition for, or grant of, local administration. The local personal representative is subject to all duties and obligations which have accrued by virtue of the exercise of the powers by the foreign personal representative and may be substituted for him in any action or proceedings in this state.

Section 4–207. [Ancillary and Other Local Administrations; Provisions Governing.]

In respect to a nonresident decedent, the provisions of Article III of this Code govern (1) proceedings, if any, in a Court of this state for probate of the will, appointment, removal, supervision, and discharge of the local personal representative, and any other order concerning the estate; and (2) the status, powers, duties and liabilities of any local personal representative and the rights of claimants, purchasers, distributees and others in regard to a local administration.

COMMENT

The purpose of this section is to direct attention to Article III for sections controlling local probates and administrations. See in particular, 1-301, 3-201, 3-202, 3-203, 3-307(a), 3-308, 3-611(b), 3-803(a), 3-815 and 3-816.

PART 3

JURISDICTION OVER FOREIGN REPRESENTATIVES

Section 4-301. [Jurisdiction by Act of Foreign Personal Representative.]

A foreign personal representative submits personally to the jurisdiction of the Courts of this state in any proceeding relating to the estate by (1) filing authenticated copies of his appointment as provided in Section 4-204, (2) receiving payment of money or taking delivery of personal property under Section 4-201, or (3) doing any act as a personal representative in this state which would have given the state jurisdiction over him as an individual. Jurisdiction under (2) is limited to the money or value of personal property collected.

COMMENT

The words "courts of this state" are sufficient under federal legislation to include a federal court having jurisdiction in the adopting state.

A foreign personal representative appointed at the decedent's domicile has priority for appointment in any local administration proceeding. See Section 3-203(g). Once appointed, a local personal representative remains subject to the jurisdiction of the appointing court under Section 3-602.

In 1975, the Joint Editorial Board recommended substitution of the word "personally" for "himself", in the preliminary language of the first sentence. Also, language restricting the submission to jurisdiction to cases involving the estate was added in 1975.

Section 4-302. [Jurisdiction by Act of Decedent.]

In addition to jurisdiction conferred by Section 4-301, a foreign personal representative is subject to the jurisdiction of the courts of this state to the same extent that his decedent was subject to jurisdiction immediately prior to death.

Section 4-303. [Service on Foreign Personal Representative.]

(a) Service of process may be made upon the foreign personal representative by registered or certified mail, addressed to his last reasonably ascertainable address, requesting a return receipt signed by addressee only. Notice by ordinary first class mail is sufficient if registered or certified mail service to the addressee is unavailable.

Service may be made upon a foreign personal representative in the manner in which service could have been made under other laws of this state on either the foreign personal representative or his decedent immediately prior to death.

(b) If service is made upon a foreign personal representative as provided in subsection (a), he shall be allowed at least [30] days within which to appear or respond.

COMMENT

The provision for ordinary mail as a substitute for registered or certified mail is provided because, under the present postal regulations, registered mail may not be available to reach certain addresses, 39 C.F.R. Sec. 51.3(c), and also certified mail may not be available as a process for service because of the method of delivery used, 39 C.F.R. Sec. 58.5(c) (rural delivery) and (d) (star route delivery.)

PART 4

JUDGMENTS AND PERSONAL REPRESENTATIVE

Section 4-401. [Effect of Adjudication For or Against Personal Representative.]

An adjudication rendered in any jurisdiction in favor of or against any personal representative of the estate is as binding on the local personal representative as if he were a party to the adjudication.

COMMENT

Adapted from Uniform Ancillary Administration of Estates Act, Section 8.

ARTICLE V

PROTECTION OF PERSONS UNDER DISABILITY AND THEIR PROPERTY

PART 1

GENERAL PROVISIONS AND DEFINITIONS

PART 2

GUARDIANS OF MINORS

PART 3

GUARDIANS OF INCAPACITATED PERSONS

Section

PART 4

PROTECTION OF PROPERTY OF PERSONS UNDER DISABILITY AND MINORS

PART 5

DURABLE POWER OF ATTORNEY

Historical Note

See text and comments of Article V as originally approved in 1969 in Appendix VIII, infra.

Adoption of Uniform Guardianship and Protective Proceedings Act

In 1982, the National Conference of Commissioners on Uniform State Laws adopted the Uniform Guardianship and Protective Proceedings Act. The Act was designed to be either a separate, free-standing act or to be integrated into the Uniform Probate Code by amendments to Article V, Parts 1, 2, 3 and 4 thereof (see Prefatory Note, infra).

The Committee that acted for the National Conference of Commissioners on Uniform State Laws in preparing the **Uniform Guardianship and Protective Proceedings Act** was as follows:

CLARKE A. GRAVEL, P.O. Box 1049, Burlington, VT 05402, *Chairman*

DONALD J. DUFFORD, P.O. Box 2188, Grand Junction, CO 81502

THOMAS L. JONES, University of Alabama, School of Law, P.O. Box 5557, University, AL 35486

THOMAS H. NEEDHAM, Superior Court, 250 Benefit Street, Providence, RI 02903

JOAN G. POULOS, 523 G Street, Davis, CA 95616

ROBERT C. ROBINSON, 4 Moulton Street, Portland, ME 04112

RICHARD V. WELLMAN, University of Georgia, School of Law, Athens, GA 30602

JOHN C. DEACON, P.O. Box 1245, Jonesboro, AR 72401, *President: 1979–1981 (Member Ex Officio)*

M. KING HILL, JR., Sixth Floor, 100 Light Street, Baltimore, MD 21202, *President: 1981–1983 (Member Ex Officio)*

CARLYLE C. RING, JR., 308 Monticello Boulevard, Alexandria, VA 22305, *Chairman, Executive Committee*

WILLIAM J. PIERCE, UNIVERSITY OF MICHIGAN, SCHOOL OF LAW, ANN ARBOR, MI 48109, *Executive Director*

EDWARD F. LOWRY, JR., Suite 1650, 3300 North Central Avenue, Phoenix, AZ 85012, *Chairman, Division A (Member Ex Officio)*

Review Committee

RICHARD E. FORD, 203 West Randolph Street, Lewisburg, WV 24901, *Chairman*

ROBINSON O. EVERETT, 450 E Street, N.W., Washington, DC 20442

HENRY M. GRETHER, JR., University of Nebraska, College of Law, Lincoln, NE 68583

PREFATORY NOTE

The Uniform Guardianship and Protective Proceedings Act is the product of a continuing review and study of laws in the area of probate matters by the National Conference of Commissioners on Uniform State Laws. In 1969, the National Conference adopted and promulgated the Uniform Probate Code. Since that time, various amendments and additions to the Uniform Probate Code have been adopted and promulgated.

Article V, Parts 1, 2, 3, and 4 of the original Uniform Probate Code cover guardianships for minors, guardianships for reasons other than minority, and protective proceedings seeking court-appointed conservators or other protective orders for the estate concerns of minors, adult incompetents, absentees and others. The following new provisions expand and extend Article V, Parts 1, 2, 3, and 4 of the original Uniform Probate Code to include the concept of "limited guardianships."

The impetus for adding a "limited guardianship" concept to the guardianship and conservator provisions of the Uniform Probate Code grew out of the recommendations of an American Bar Association project, the ABA Commission on the Mentally Disabled, which, in relation to guardianship other than for minors, recommended that state laws be changed to avoid an asserted "overkill" implicit in standard guardianship proceedings. In part, this occurs, it was asserted, because a finding of non compos mentis or incompetence has been the traditional threshold for the appointment of a guardian. As a result, in consequence of the appointment of a guardian, all personal and legal autonomy is stripped from the ward and vested in the appointing court and guardian. The call for "limited guardianship" was a call for more sensitive procedures and for appointments fashioned so that the authority of the protector would intrude only to the degree necessary on the liberties and prerogatives of the protected person. In short, rather than permitting an all-or-none status, there should be an intermediate status available to the courts through which the protected person will have personal liberties and prerogatives restricted only to the extent necessary under the circumstances. The court should be admonished to look for a least-restrictive protection approach.

For a time, spokesmen for the Uniform Probate Code took the position that the formulations approved by the National Conference in 1969 should not be classified with "typical" guardianship legislation, and that Article V met the objectives of advocates of "limited guardianship." In particular, it was pointed out that appointment of a guardian of the person under the 1969 UPC (Art. V, Part 3) involves elaborate personal notices (1969 UPC § 5–303), and avoids a determination of "incompetence" because of a new standard describing an "incapacitated person" (1969 UPC § 5–101[1]). Further, it was noted that a UPC guardian, who has not gained the powers of a conservator (1969 UPC, Art. V, Part 4) has very limited authority over a ward's estate (see 1969 UPC § 5–312), meaning that a common, historic reason for guardianship proceedings has been removed. A "protective proceeding" pursuant to 1969 UPC, Art. V, Part 4, through which a court appointee having broad powers over the estate of another may be obtained, does not involve any restriction or finding regarding the legal capacity of a protected person (1969 UPC § 5–408[5]). Also, great flexibility regarding the precise dimension of a protective

366

order or the legal authority of a conservator is provided by explicit statutory language (1969 UPC §§ 5–408, 5–409, & 5–426).

Nonetheless, Idaho, the first state to adopt the Uniform Probate Code, and other states acting in response to requests by followers of the ABA Commission's work, have been enacting new "limited guardianship" statutes. In Idaho, the new limited guardianship legislation was enacted without specific repeal of the provisions of the Uniform Probate Code that were already part of their statutory law. Other states were enacting rather short statutes that adopted the least-intrusive or least-restrictive concept of limited guardianship in skeleton form without further elaboration. These, and other similar instances of confusion, overlap and other problems born of hasty legislative acceptance of limited guardianship language demonstrated that the National Conference of Commissioners on Uniform State Laws should adjust its formulations on guardianship to include explicit language relative to the concept of "limited guardianships." The concept of "limited guardianships" certainly is consistent with the general policy considerations upon which the Uniform Probate Code, Article V, had been based in 1969. In addition, by making limited-guardianship concepts more explicit in the act, it was and is believed that some confusion could be eliminated and that this act could replace skeleton-type acts to make the concept workable.

The clearest and most explicit statements incorporating the "limited guardianship" philosophy of a least-intrusive approach to guardianships and protective proceedings are in §§ 5–306(a), 5–306(c) and 5–407(a) of the 1982 Uniform Probate Code. However, other language that appeared previously as Uniform Probate Code, Article V, Parts 1, 2, 3, and 4 has been reviewed, altered to achieve greater internal consistency and adjusted to accommodate the "limited guardianship" concept more clearly.

Indeed, the new work by the National Conference of Commissioners on Uniform State Laws of Article V of the Uniform Probate Code has resulted in two free-standing acts. These acts extend the Uniform Probate Code formulations, but each act has been designed to be enacted as a separate act should a state legislature wish to do so. The first of these, the Uniform Durable Power of Attorney Act, was completed and promulgated in 1979, and has been well received as an improved version of what was originally included as UPC Article V, Part 5. The second step has resulted in the Uniform Guardianship and Protective Proceedings Act.

In addition to the Commissioners on Uniform State Laws who worked on drafting this Uniform Guardianship and Protective Proceedings Act, the work and valuable contributions on the project of American Bar Association liaison persons, Messrs. Rodney N. Houghton, of Newark, New Jersey, and Russell E. Webb, III, of Idaho Falls, Idaho, is gratefully acknowledged.

PART 1

GENERAL PROVISIONS AND DEFINITIONS

Section 5–101. [Facility of Payment or Delivery.]

(a) Any person under a duty to pay or deliver money or personal property to a minor may perform the duty, in amounts not exceeding $5,000 a year, by paying or delivering the money or property to:

(1) the minor if 18 or more years of age or married;

(2) any person having the care and custody of the minor with whom the minor resides;

(3) a guardian of the minor; or

(4) a financial institution incident to a deposit in a state or federally insured savings account or certificate in the sole name of the minor with notice of the deposit to the minor.

(b) This section does not apply if the person making payment or delivery knows that a conservator has been appointed or proceedings for appointment of a conservator of the estate of the minor are pending.

(c) Persons, other than the minor or any financial institution, receiving money or property for a minor, are obligated to apply the money to the support and education of the minor, but may not pay themselves except by way of reimbursement for out-of-pocket expenses for goods and services necessary for the minor's support. Any excess sums must be preserved for future support and education of the minor and any balance not so used and any property received for the minor must be turned over to the minor when majority is attained. A person who pays or delivers money or property in accordance with provisions of this section is not responsible for the proper application thereof.

COMMENT

The source of this section is 1969 Uniform Probate Code (UPC) § 5–103.

Where a minor has only a small amount of property, it would be wasteful to require protective proceedings to deal with the property. This section makes it possible for other persons, possibly including a guardian, to handle the less compli-cated property affairs of the ward. Protective proceedings, including the possible establishment of a con-servatorship, should be sought where substantial property is in-volved.

This section does not go as far as many facility of payment provisions found in trust instruments, which usually permit application of sums

368

due a minor beneficiary to any expense or charge for the minor. It was felt that a grant of so large an area of discretion to any category of persons who might owe funds to a minor would be unwise. Nonetheless, the section as drafted should reduce the need for trust facility of payment provisions somewhat, while extending opportunities to insurance companies and other debtors to minors for relatively simple methods of gaining discharge.

The protection afforded by the section is unavailable if the person making payment or delivery knows that a conservator has been appointed for the minor's estate or knows that a proceeding seeking appointment of a conservator is pending. By way of contrast, the protection is available in spite of a payor's knowledge that a *guardian* for the minor has been appointed or may be appointed as a result of a pending proceeding. Guardianship proceedings affecting minors are described in Part 2 of this Article. A conservator for a minor comes into existence, if at all, incident to a protective proceeding as described in Part 4 of this Article. A guardian's powers, described in § 5–209, do not include the authority to *compel* payment of money due the ward, but include authority to receive payments made under the protection of this section. In contrast, a conservator has title to all assets of the minor's estate, except as otherwise provided in the case of a *limited* conservator. See § 5–419.

Section 5–102. [Delegation of Powers by Parent or Guardian.]

A parent or guardian of a minor or incapacitated person, by a properly executed power of attorney, may delegate to another person, for a period not exceeding 6 months, any power regarding care, custody or property of the minor child or ward, except the power to consent to marriage or adoption of a minor ward.

COMMENT

The source of this section is 1969 UPC § 5–104.

This section permits a temporary delegation of parental powers. For example, parents (or a guardian) of a minor plan to be out of the country for several months. They wish to empower a close relative (an uncle, e.g.) to take any necessary action regarding the child while they are away. Using this section, they could execute an appropriate power of attorney giving the uncle custody and power to consent. Then, if an emergency operation were required, the uncle could consent on behalf of the child; as a practical matter he would of course attempt to communicate with the parents before acting. The section is designed to reduce problems relating to consents for emergency treatment.

The problems touched by the section include some that would be eased but not eliminated if the jurisdiction has enacted the Model Health Care Consent Act. A guardian's authority over a ward, described in § 5–209 (guardians of minors) and § 5–309 (guardians of incapacitated persons), includes authority regarding the care, custody and control of the ward that goes well beyond consenting to health care.

In contrast to § 5–101, which relates only to certain business affairs of minors, this section is pertinent to the affairs of minors *and,* incapacitated persons for whom guardians have been appointed.

Section 5–103. [General Definitions.]

As used in Parts 1, 2, 3 and 4 of this Article:

(1) "Claims," in respect to a protected person, includes liabilities of the protected person, whether arising in contract, tort, or otherwise, and liabilities of the estate which arise at or after the appointment of a conservator, including expenses of administration.

(2) "Court" means the [_____] court.

(3) "Conservator" means a person who is appointed by a Court to manage the estate of a protected person and includes a limited conservator described in Section 5–419(a).

(4) "Disability" means cause for a protective order as described in Section 5–401.

(5) "Estate" includes the property of the person whose affairs are subject to this Article.

(6) "Guardian" means a person who has qualified as a guardian of a minor or incapacitated person pursuant to parental or spousal nomination or court appointment and includes a limited guardian as described in Sections 5–209(e) and 5–306(c), but excludes one who is merely a guardian ad litem.

(7) "Incapacitated person" means any person who is impaired by reason of mental illness, mental deficiency, physical illness or disability, advanced age, chronic use of drugs, chronic intoxication, or other cause (except minority) to the extent of lacking sufficient understanding or capacity to make or communicate responsible decisions.

(8) "Lease" includes an oil, gas, or other mineral lease.

(9) "Letters" includes letters of guardianship and letters of conservatorship.

(10) "Minor" means a person who is under [21] years of age.

(11) "Mortgage" means any conveyance, agreement, or arrangement in which property is used as collateral.

(12) "Organization" includes a corporation, business trust, estate, trust, partnership, association, 2 or more persons having a joint or common interest, government, governmental subdivision or agency, or any other legal entity.

(13) "Parent" includes any person entitled to take, or who would be entitled to take if the child died without a will, as a

parent by intestate succession from the child whose relationship is in question and excludes any person who is only a stepparent, foster parent, or grandparent.

(14) "Person" means an individual or an organization.

(15) "Petition" means a written request to the Court for an order after notice.

(16) "Proceeding" includes action at law and suit in equity.

(17) "Property" includes both real and personal property or any interest therein and means anything that may be the subject of ownership.

(18) "Protected person" means a minor or other person for whom a conservator has been appointed or other protective order has been made as provided in Sections 5–407 and 5–408.

(19) "Protective proceeding" means a proceeding under the provisions of Part 4 of this Article.

(20) "Security" includes any note, stock, treasury stock, bond, debenture, evidence of indebtedness, certificate of interest or participation in an oil, gas, or mining title or lease or in payments out of production under such a title or lease, collateral trust certificate, transferable share, voting trust certificate or, in general, any interest or instrument commonly known as a security, or any certificate of interest or participation, any temporary or interim certificate, receipt or certificate of deposit for, or any warrant or right to subscribe to or purchase any of the foregoing.

(21) "Visitor" means a person appointed in a guardianship or protective proceeding who is trained in law, nursing, or social work, is an officer, employee, or special appointee of the Court, and has no personal interest in the proceeding.

(22) "Ward" means a person for whom a guardian has been appointed. A "minor ward" is a minor for whom a guardian has been appointed solely because of minority.

COMMENT

The sources of this section are primarily 1969 UPC §§ 1–201 and 5–101.

In completing the definition of "court," an enacting jurisdiction should consider the power contemplated for the court described in § 1–302. Ideally, the tribunal designated should have the stature of a court of general jurisdiction. If constitutional allocations of subject matter jurisdiction of courts prevent use of a court of general jurisdiction as the court of guardianship, the court designated in § 5–103(2) should be staffed so as to generate community confidence in its ability to handle the formal and complicated proceedings contemplated by §§ 5–303 et seq. and 5–401 et seq. covering guardianship and protective proceedings. See § 1–309 option. Proceedings seeking appointment of a personal guardian for a minor without other disability as described in §§ 5-204 et seq. are somewhat less complicated, though formal in the sense that adjudications following notice and hearings are involved. The Act does not contemplate use in connection with guardianships and other protective proceedings of "summary" or "informal" proceedings of the sort utilized in decedent estate settlements for non-adjudicated probate of wills and appointment of personal representatives.

When read with § 5-407(d), the defined term "disability" plainly does not refer to lack of legal capacity, but only to the grounds described in warranting a protective proceeding as described in § 5-401.

The definition of "incapacitated person" supplies the substantive grounds for appointment of a guardian for reasons other than minority. See § 5-306(b).

The definition of "parent" is intended to include an adoptive parent, because an adoptive parent is eligible to inherit as a parent in intestate succession under the Uniform Probate Code and most statutes governing adoptions. The defined meaning of "parent" is especially significant when read with §§ 5-202 and 5-203 which prevent

the appointment of a guardian of a minor, other than a temporary guardian under § 5-204(b), for whom a parent still has custodial rights.

The terms "ward" and "protected person" help distinguish persons over whom another holds personal, custodial authority from those whose property, or some part thereof, has been ordered into a statutory trusteeship or otherwise subjected to a protective court order. A person for whom a guardian has been named and whose property is the subject of a conservatorship or other protective order is both a ward and a protected person. In this connection, note that § 5-423(a) gives a conservator of a minor for whom no parent or guardian has parental rights of custody and control the duties and powers of a guardian. This section also specifies that the parental authority thus conferred on a conservator of a minor does not prevent appointment of another as guardian. In contrast, the existence of any other person having the custodial authority of a parent, a guardian by appointment of any court, or a guardian arising by parental appointment under § 5-202 or as a result of parental or spousal appointment under § 5-301, blocks any court appointment of a guardian.

Section 5-104. [Request for Notice; Interested Person.]

Upon payment of any required fee, an interested person who desires to be notified before any order is made in a guardianship proceeding, including any proceeding subsequent to the appointment of a guardian under Section 5-312, or in a protective proceeding under Section 5-401, may file a request for notice with the clerk of the court in which the proceeding is pending. The clerk shall mail a copy of the request to the guardian and to the conservator if one has been appointed. A request is not effective unless it contains a statement showing the interest of the person making it and the address of that person or an attorney to whom notice is to be given. The request is effective only as to proceedings occurring after the filing. Any governmental agency paying or planning to pay benefits to the person to be protected is an interested person in protective proceedings.

COMMENT

The source of this section is 1969 UPC § 5–406, which has been extended by this section to permit a request for notice in guardianship proceedings.

This Article does not define "interest" or "interested person" as used in this section. The definition of "interested person" in § 1–201(20) is too narrow as a test of would-be participants in guardianship and protective proceedings for it points only to persons having a property interest in the estate of the respondent or a claim against the estate. If extended to guardianship proceedings, this test would preclude non-owner children from participating in a proceeding concerning their parent.

This Article contains special provisions, differing somewhat as between the three types of court proceedings it describes, regarding persons entitled to initiate a proceeding, persons entitled to notice of a proceeding, and persons who may intervene. Sections 5–206(a), 5–303(a), and 5–404(a), respectively, control the identity of petitioners in a guardianship-for-a-minor proceeding, a guardianship proceeding for an incapacitated person, and a protective proceeding. The notice provisions applicable to the three proceedings are in §§ 5–206(b), 5–304(a), and 5–405(a). Provisions governing intervenors in guardianships for incapacitated persons and protective proceedings are in §§ 5–303(d) and 5–406(e).

373

PART 2

GUARDIANS OF MINORS

Section 5–201. [Appointment and Status of Guardian of Minor.]

A person may become a guardian of a minor by parental appointment or upon appointment by the Court. The guardianship status continues until terminated, without regard to the location from time to time of the guardian or minor ward.

COMMENT

The source of this section is 1969 UPC § 5–201.

One purpose of this section is to establish that a guardian created by parental appointment under §§ 5–202 and 5–203, infra, has the same legal status, as a guardian by court appointment under § 5–204 and following sections. Another purpose is to declare that the relationship of guardian and ward continues even though both persons involved may move to another jurisdiction. Thus, this Article makes the guardian and ward status more like the parent/child status it replaces. This is in contrast to the older concept that the court of guardianship, acting through the guardian as its appointee, carries the principal responsibility for wards under its jurisdiction. The older concept is not satisfactory as applied to instances where the persons involved leave the jurisdiction of the appointing court.

Section 5–202. [Parental Appointment of Guardian for Minor.]

(a) The parent of an unmarried minor may appoint a guardian for the minor by will, or other writing signed by the parent and attested by at least 2 witnesses.

(b) Subject to the right of the minor under Section 5–203, if both parents are dead or incapacitated or the surviving parent has no parental rights or has been adjudged to be incapacitated, a parental appointment becomes effective when the guardian's acceptance is filed in the Court in which a nominating instrument is probated, or, in the case of a non-testamentary nominating instrument, in the Court at the place where the minor resides or is present. If both parents are dead, an effective appointment by the parent who died later has priority.

(c) A parental appointment effected by filing the guardian's acceptance under a will probated in the state of the testator's domicile is effective in this State.

(d) Upon acceptance of appointment, the guardian shall give written notice of acceptance to the minor and to the person having the minor's care or the minor's nearest adult relative.

COMMENT

Derived from 1969 UPC § 5–502, the section confers authority on a parent to *appoint* a guardian; no action by any court is required. Unlike its UPC predecessor, the section enables a parent to exercise the appointing authority by deed as well as by will. Both forms of appointment become effective only when the appointee files an acceptance in the appropriate court *and* the other conditions of the statute are met. These conditions are: (1) the minor involved has not previously filed an unwithdrawn written objection to the appointment as provided in § 5–203; and (2) both parents are dead or incapacitated as defined in § 5–103(7), or the surviving parent has been adjudged incapacitated or has surrendered or been deprived of parental rights. The existence of a guardian who has gained authority from a parental appointment precludes any other appointment of another guardian for the same minor. This result follows from § 5–209(a) which confers the powers and responsibilities of a parent on a guardian, and from § 5–204(a) which prevents appointment of a guardian for a minor over whom another has parental rights of custody. However, the authority of a guardian arising by parental authority may be terminated by objection of the ward if 14 or more years old as provided by § 5–203 or § 5–210.

The ability of a single custodial parent to appoint a guardian by deed as well as by will is especially important where local procedures for the probate of a will require advance notice to all interested persons and representation of all interested persons who are minors. The document making the appointment is not required to be filed in a public office but it would be desirable practice for it, or a conformed copy, to be attached to the written acceptance by the nominee when the latter document is filed in order to complete the appointment. Also, in cases where there is a prospect that the authority of the parental nominee may be challenged, it might be desirable to attach other documentation to the filed acceptance, including copies of death certificates or other documents tending to show that all parental rights of custody have been terminated. In this connection, it should be noted that guardians for minors, whether created by parental or court appointment, lack authority to sell or mortgage real or personal assets of the ward. See § 5–209. Hence, the tendency of title examiners and insurers to insist on public record documentation regarding every possible question concerning title may be disregarded as one considers the extent and form of documentation to accompany a guardian's acceptance under this section. Notice, however, that a conservator arising by court appointment in a protective proceeding as provided in Part 4 of this Article has full authority as a statutory trustee of all assets transferred by the appointment. Also, under § 5–423(a) a conservator of the estate of an unmarried minor as to whom no one has parental rights, has the authority of a guardian. However, a parent is not empowered to appoint a conservator by deed or will. A parent with assets to use for the purpose may, of course, establish a trust for a minor or anyone else, but a trustee's authority would not include authority over the person of the beneficiary like that available to a guardian.

The final sentence of the section was added to 1969 UPC § 5–202 in 1975 following a recommendation of the Joint Editorial Board for the Uniform Probate Code. In making the recommendation, the JEB–UPC signalled that it approved a safeguard added to the section at the time of its first enactment in Idaho. Section 1–401 governs the method and time requirements of a notice as required in this section.

Section 5–203. [Objection by Minor of Fourteen or Older to Parental Appointment.]

A minor 14 or more years of age who is the subject of a parental appointment may prevent the appointment or cause it to terminate by filing in the Court in which the nominating instrument is filed a written objection to the appointment before it is accepted or within 30 days after receiving notice of its acceptance. An objection may be withdrawn. An objection does not preclude appointment by the Court in a proper proceeding of the parental nominee or any other suitable person.

COMMENT

The source of this section is 1969 UPC § 5–203.

A written objection of a minor to a parental appointment prevents a later accepted appointment from becoming effective. However, if the objection is withdrawn before the filing of the guardian's acceptance, the effect of the objection is cancelled. An objection filed within 30 days following the filing of an acceptance terminates the appointment but does not invalidate acts done previously in reliance on the guardian's authority. See § 5–210. It may be questioned, however, whether a post-acceptance objection that serves to terminate the authority of a parental guardian may be withdrawn so as to re-instate the guardian's authority. Safe practice in such a case would dictate that those interested in establishing a legal guardianship petition the court for an appointment under § 5–204.

The final sentence in the section is not intended to imply that a court proceeding for appointment of a guardian is necessary or appropriate when there has been an effective parental appointment. It was inserted to indicate that a minor age 14 or more may not block a court appointment of one nominated as guardian by a parent even though the prospective ward is able to block or terminate a parental appointment that does not involve action by the court. In this connection, note that § 5–207, applicable to an appointment by the court, directs the court to respect the nomination of the prospective ward if 14 or more years of age. But, the court may conclude that appointment of the minor's nominee would be contrary to the best interest of the minor, clearing the way for appointment of a parental nominee or some other suitable person.

Section 5–204. [Court Appointment of Guardian of Minor; Conditions for Appointment.]

(a) The Court may appoint a guardian for an unmarried minor if all parental rights have been terminated or suspended by circumstances or prior Court order. A guardian appointed pursuant to Section 5–202 whose appointment has not been prevented or nullified under Section 5–203 has priority over any guardian who may be appointed by the Court, but the Court may proceed with another appointment upon a finding that the parental nominee has failed to accept the appointment within 30 days after notice of the guardianship proceeding.

(b) If necessary, and on appropriate petition or application, the Court may appoint a temporary guardian who shall have the full authority of a general guardian of a minor, but the authority of a temporary guardian may not last longer than 6 months. The appointment of a temporary guardian for a minor may occur even though the conditions described in subsection (a) have not been established.

COMMENT

The source of this section is 1969 UPC §§ 5–204 & 5–207(c).

This section and §§ 5–205 through 5–207 following cover proceedings to secure a court appointed guardian of a minor. Sections 5–208 through 5–212 are applicable to all guardians of minors who derive authority from parental appointment or court appointment as contemplated in this Part. Nothing in this Article is intended to deal with the status of a so-called natural guardian, with the authority of a parent over a child, or with authority over a child or children that may be conferred by other state laws.

The court is not authorized to appoint a guardian for one for whom a parent has custodial rights or for one who has a parental guardian. Two purposes are served by this restriction. First, it prevents use of guardianship proceedings as a weapon or tactic in a squabble between parents concerning child custody, thereby forcing these disputes to the court having jurisdiction over marital matters. Second, it establishes that a guardian by parental appointment is as completely endowed with authority as a guardian as one appointed by court order. A guardian by parental appointment may be replaced by one appointed by the court following removal in proceedings under § 5–212. If a court-appointed guardian comes into existence before a parental nomination is discovered or implemented by acceptance, it will be necessary to terminate the authority of the court-appointed guardian in order to clear the way for the parental nominee. See § 5–201. In this connection, the second sentence of § 5–204(a) may be invoked in appropriate cases by the proponent of the parental nomination. This would occur in proceedings incident to an application to the court for an order correcting the original appointment. Alternatively, the parental nominee may urge removal of the court-appointed guardian on the ground that the best interest of the minor as contemplated in § 5–212 would be served by termination of the prior appointment.

Subsection (b) gives the court having jurisdiction of guardianship matters important power regarding the welfare of a minor in the form of authority to appoint a temporary guardian in cases of necessity. The authority permits appointment of a temporary guardian even though one or both parents have parental authority. It is to be noted, however, that the appointment of a temporary guardian must be preceded by notice and hearing as required for appointment of any court appointed guardian. The authority might be particularly useful in a case where both parents have disappeared or simply departed without making adequate arrangements for their children. If the needs of minor children require the creation of guardianships before it is possible to prove the death of the parents, the subsection opens the way to appointment of one having parental authority for up to 6 months that does not require proof of the requirement of subsection (a) that "all

parental rights of custody have been terminated or suspended by circumstances ..."

In addition to guardians by parental appointment and court-appointed guardians, § 5–423(a) grants a conservator of the estate of a minor for whom no guardian or parent holds parental rights the powers of a guardian. The same section makes it clear that appointment of a conservator for the estate of a minor, even though it may create a form of guardianship authority over the minor, does not preclude court appointment of a guardian nor acceptance of a parental nomination. Thus, the statute enables persons interested in the affairs and welfare of a minor to secure a single authority competent to handle the personal and business needs of the minor. Alternatively, for cases where circumstances suggest that one person should be in charge of decisions regarding the minor's living conditions, health care, and education, and another in charge of management of the minor's property interests two appointments may be made.

Section 5–205. [Venue.]

The venue for guardianship proceedings for a minor is in the court at the place where the minor resides or is present at the time the proceedings are commenced.

COMMENT

The source of this section is 1969 UPC § 5–205. This section should be read with § 1–303 dealing with multiple venue proceedings and transfer of venue.

Section 5–206. [Procedure for Court-appointment of Guardian of Minor.]

(a) A minor or any person interested in the welfare of the minor may petition for appointment of a guardian.

(b) After the filing of a petition, the Court shall set a date for hearing, and the petitioner shall give notice of the time and place of hearing the petition in the manner prescribed by Section 1–401 to:

(1) the minor, if 14 or more years of age and not the petitioner;

(2) any person alleged to have had the principal care and custody of the minor during the 60 days preceding the filing of the petition; and

(3) any living parent of the minor.

(c) Upon hearing, if the Court finds that a qualified person seeks appointment, venue is proper, the required notices have been given, the conditions of Section 5–204(a) have been met, and the welfare and best interest of the minor will be served by the requested appointment, it shall make the appointment and issue letters. In other cases, the Court may dismiss the proceedings or make any other disposition of the matter that will serve the best interest of the minor.

(d) If the Court determines at any time in the proceeding that the interests of the minor are or may be inadequately represented, it may appoint an attorney to represent the minor, giving consideration to the preference of the minor if the minor is 14 or more years of age.

COMMENT

The source of this section is 1969 UPC § 5–207.

Subsection (a) is new. It is intended to qualify as a potential petitioner any person with a serious interest or concern for a minor's welfare, including a relative or a nonrelative having knowledge of the circumstances who completes a petition to the court, and any public official having official or personal concerns for the minor's welfare. If the court determines that the petitioner's concerns in the matter stem from interests that may not serve the welfare and best interest of the minor, it may dismiss the proceeding on the ground that the conditions for appointment as specified in subsection (b) have not been met.

The second sentence of subsection (b) may be interpreted to authorize an order directing that the petition be re-cast as a petition for a protective order under § 5–401. That authority is expressly conferred on the court by § 5–306 relating to a guardianship proceeding based on incapacity. The authority would be useful, for example, if the court determines that asset management is likely to be involved and that the person seeking appointment as guardian would be an appropriate person to serve as conservator with the power of a guardian. In these circumstances, two appointments could be avoided if the petitioner were willing to re-cast the petition as required by § 5–401.

Section 5–207. [Court Appointment of Guardian of Minor; Qualifications; Priority of Minor's Nominee.]

The Court may appoint as guardian any person whose appointment would be in the best interest of the minor. The Court shall appoint a person nominated by the minor, if the minor is 14 or more years of age, unless the Court finds the appointment contrary to the best interest of the minor.

COMMENT

The source of this section is 1969 UPC § 5–206.

Rather than provide for priorities among various classes of relatives, it was felt that the only priority should be for the person nominated by the minor. The important point is to locate someone whose appointment will be in the best interest of the minor. If there is contention among relatives over who should be named, it is not likely that a statutory priority keyed to degrees of kinship would help resolve the matter. For example, if the argument involved a squabble between relatives of the child's father and relatives of its mother, priority in terms of degrees of kinship would be useless.

Guardianships under this Article are not likely to be attractive positions for persons who are more interested in handling a minor's estate than in his or her personal well being. An order of a court having equity power is necessary if the guardian is to receive payment for services where there is no conservator for the minor's estate. Also, the powers of management of a ward's estate conferred on a guardian are restricted so that if a substantial estate is involved, a conservator will be needed to handle the financial matters.

Section 5–208. [Consent to Service by Acceptance of Appointment; Notice.]

By accepting a parental or court appointment as guardian, a guardian submits personally to the jurisdiction of the Court in any proceeding relating to the guardianship that may be instituted by any interested person. The petitioner shall cause notice of any proceeding to be delivered or mailed to the guardian at the guardian's address listed in the Court records and to the address then known to the petitioner. Letters of guardianship must indicate whether the guardian was appointed by court order or parental nomination.

COMMENT

The source of this section is 1969 UPC § 5–208.

The "long-arm" principle behind this section is well established. It seems desirable that the court in which acceptance is filed be able to serve its process on the guardian wherever he or she has moved. The continuing interest of that court in the welfare of the minor is ample to justify this provision. The consent to service is real rather than fictional in the guardianship situation, where the guardian acts voluntarily in filing acceptance. It is probable that the form of acceptance will expressly embody the provisions of this section, although the statute does not expressly require this.

Section 5-209. [Powers and Duties of Guardian of Minor.]

(a) A guardian of a minor ward has the powers and responsibilities of a parent regarding the ward's support, care, and education, but a guardian is not personally liable for the ward's expenses and is not liable to third persons by reason of the relationship for acts of the ward.

(b) In particular and without qualifying the foregoing, a guardian shall:

(1) become or remain personally acquainted with the ward and maintain sufficient contact with the ward to know of the ward's capacities, limitations, needs, opportunities, and physical and mental health;

(2) take reasonable care of the ward's personal effects and commence protective proceedings if necessary to protect other property of the ward;

(3) apply any available money of the ward to the ward's current needs for support, care, and education;

(4) conserve any excess money of the ward for the ward's future needs, but if a conservator has been appointed for the estate of the ward, the guardian, at least quarterly, shall pay to the conservator money of the ward to be conserved for the ward's future needs; and

(5) report the condition of the ward and of the ward's estate that has been subject to the guardian's possession or control, as ordered by the Court on petition of any person interested in the ward's welfare or as required by Court rule.

(c) A guardian may:

(1) receive money payable for the support of the ward to the ward's parent, guardian, or custodian under the terms of any statutory benefit or insurance system or any private contract, devise, trust, conservatorship, or custodianship, and money or property of the ward paid or delivered pursuant to Section 5-101;

(2) if consistent with the terms of any order by a court of competent jurisdiction relating to detention or commitment of

381

the ward, take custody of the person of the ward and establish the ward's place of abode within or without this State;

(3) if no conservator for the estate of the ward has been appointed, institute proceedings, including administrative proceedings, or take other appropriate action to compel the performance by any person of a duty to support the ward or to pay sums for the welfare of the ward;

(4) consent to medical or other professional care, treatment, or advice for the ward without liability by reason of the consent for injury to the ward resulting from the negligence or acts of third persons unless a parent would have been liable in the circumstances;

(5) consent to the marriage or adoption of the ward; and

(6) if reasonable under all of the circumstances, delegate to the ward certain responsibilities for decisions affecting the ward's well-being.

(d) A guardian is entitled to reasonable compensation for services as guardian and to reimbursement for room, board and clothing personally provided to the ward, but only as approved by order of the Court. If a conservator, other than the guardian or one who is affiliated with the guardian, has been appointed for the estate of the ward, reasonable compensation and reimbursement to the guardian may be approved and paid by the conservator without order of the Court controlling the guardian.

(e) In the interest of developing self-reliance on the part of a ward or for other good cause, the Court, at the time of appointment or later, on its own motion or on appropriate petition or motion of the minor or other interested person, may limit the powers of a guardian otherwise conferred by this section and thereby create a limited guardianship. Any limitation on the statutory power of a guardian of a minor must be endorsed on the guardian's letters or, in the case of a guardian by parental appointment, must be reflected in letters that are issued at the time any limitation is imposed. Following the same procedure, a limitation may be removed and appropriate letters issued.

COMMENT

This section, derived in part from 1969 UPC § 5–209, represents an expansion and reorganization of the UPC section. Subsection (a) specifies that the parental powers and responsibilities entailed in a guardianship are those concerned with the ward's "support, care, and education." These terms, when read with subsection (b), obviously refer to all kinds of considerations that should be weighed and implemented on behalf of the ward by one invested with legal authority to control the ward's activities.

Subsection (b)(1) is new. It reflects a consensus of the drafting committee that a person who accepts a guardianship for a minor should be forewarned by explicit statutory language that the position entails responsibilities to make and maintain personal contact with the ward.

The basic duties of a guardian are described in the mandates of subsection (b). Subsection (c) outlines optional authority that is extended to every guardian by the statute. Subsection (d), dealing with the delicate question of compensation for a guardian, requires that a guardian obtain approval from an independent conservator of the minor's estate or from the court before taking sums as compensation from funds of the minor that have been received by the guardian. In contrast to 1969 UPC § 5–312(a)(4) which permitted a guardian for an incapacitated person to take funds of the ward by way of reimbursement for personal funds previously expended for certain purposes, this section requires court approval before any guardian's claim for reimbursement can be satisfied otherwise than through a conservator. Note, however, that no advance court approval is required in order to permit a guardian to use available funds of the ward for the ward's current needs as provided in subsection (b)(3).

The powers of a guardian regarding property of the ward are quite limited. Note, also, that the section does not encourage a guardian to apply to the appointing court for additional property power. Rather, the provisions are designed to encourage use of a protective proceeding under § 5–401 if property powers beyond those statutorily available to a guardian are needed. In this connection, it may be observed

that subsection (c)(3), which contains one of the section's few references to use of the courts by a guardian, authorizes a guardian to institute proceedings to enforce a duty to support or pay money only if there is no conservator for the estate of the ward.

If the circumstances of a minor dictate that authority to control both person and property be obtained, protective proceedings under § 5–401 et seq. are indicated. Section 5–423(a) provides that a conservator for a minor as to whom no one has parental authority has the powers of a guardian as well as plenary power as a statutory trustee over the assets of the minor. In addition, as noted in the comment to § 5–204, the provisions of this Article enable interested persons to obtain appointment of the same or different persons as guardian and conservator for a minor even though § 5–423(a) makes it patently unnecessary to obtain two appointments in a case where a single person is to serve in both capacities.

Subsection (e) is new and extends the limited guardianship concept to guardians of minors by encouraging court orders limiting the already limited authority of a guardian. Using this provision, a court, at the time of appointment or on petition thereafter, might limit the authority of a guardian so that, for example, the guardian would not be able to direct the ward's religious training, or so that the guardian would be restricted in controlling the ward's place of abode by a condition that the ward's consent to any change of abode be given. The section provides that special restrictions of this sort may be removed or altered by further court order. Obviously, the drafters did not intend that the procedure for contracting and expanding special limitations on a guardian's power should be used to grant a

guardian greater powers than are
described in the section.

Section 5–210. [Termination of Appointment of Guardian; General.]

A guardian's authority and responsibility terminates upon the death, resignation, or removal of the guardian or upon the minor's death, adoption, marriage, or attainment of majority, but termination does not affect the guardian's liability for prior acts or the obligation to account for funds and assets of the ward. Resignation of a guardian does not terminate the guardianship until it has been approved by the Court. A parental appointment under an informally probated will terminates if the will is later denied probate in a formal proceeding.

COMMENT

The source of this section is 1969 UPC § 5–210.

The position taken in this section that termination of a guardian's authority and responsibility does not apply retroactively to nullify prior acts is intended to govern all forms of termination including termination by objection as described in § 5–203.

Any of various events, that may or may not appear from the records of the court that appointed a guardian may serve to terminate the guardi-

an's authority and responsibility. The extremely limited authority of a guardian over the ward's money and property tends to reduce instances when third persons may be jeopardized by an unknown termination of a guardian's authority. Principles protecting third persons who rely to their detriment on an apparent authority that has been terminated without their knowledge should govern the occasional cases in which a prior, unknown termination clouds the legality of a guardian's act.

Section 5–211. [Proceedings Subsequent to Appointment; Venue.]

(a) The Court at the place where the ward resides has concurrent jurisdiction with the Court that appointed the guardian or in which acceptance of a parental appointment was filed over resignation, removal, accounting, and other proceedings relating to the guardianship.

(b) If the Court at the place where the ward resides is neither the appointing court nor the court in which acceptance of appointment is filed, the court in which proceedings subsequent to appointment are commenced in all appropriate cases shall notify the other court, in this or another state, and after consultation with that court determine whether to retain jurisdiction or transfer the proceedings to the other court, whichever is in the best interest of the ward. A copy of any order accepting a resignation or removing a guardian must be sent to the appointing court or the court in which acceptance of appointment is filed.

COMMENT

The source of this section is 1969 UPC § 5–211 with the substitution of "parental appointment" for "testamentary appointment."

Under §§ 5–103(2) and 1–302, the Court is designated as the proper court to handle matters relating to guardianship. The present section is intended to give jurisdiction to the forum where the ward resides as well as to the one where appointment initiated. This provision has primary importance where the ward's residence has been moved from the appointing state. Because the Court where acceptance of appointment is filed may as a practical matter be the only forum in which jurisdiction over the person of the guardian may be obtained (by reason of § 5–208), that Court is given concurrent jurisdiction.

Section 5–212. [Resignation, Removal, and Other Post-appointment Proceedings.]

(a) Any person interested in the welfare of a ward or the ward, if 14 or more years of age, may petition for removal of a guardian on the ground that removal would be in the best interest of the ward or for any other order that is in the best interest of the ward. A guardian may petition for permission to resign. A petition for removal or for permission to resign may, but need not, include a request for appointment of a successor guardian.

(b) Notice of hearing on a petition for an order subsequent to appointment of a guardian must be given to the ward, the guardian, and any other person as ordered by the court.

(c) After notice and hearing on a petition for removal or for permission to resign, the Court may terminate the guardianship and make any further order that may be appropriate.

(d) If the Court determines at any time in the proceeding that the interest of the ward is or may be inadequately represented, it may appoint an attorney to represent the minor, giving consideration to the preference of the minor if the minor is 14 or more years of age.

COMMENT

The source of this section is 1969 UPC § 5–212. Subsection (a) of this section is identical to 1969 UPC § 5–212(a). Subsection (c) of this section also is identical to 1969 UPC § 5–212(b).

Subsection (b) of this section is new and identifies who must be given notice of any post-appointment proceedings affecting a guardianship. Section 1–401 describes methods and time requirements concerning notices required by this section. Section 1–402, which controls waiver of required notices, prevents waiver of notice by the ward. It would seem that a ward who is the petitioner in a post-appointment proceeding would not need to receive notice. However, a ward should be given notice of a petition initiated in the ward's name by a next friend.

PART 3

GUARDIANS OF INCAPACITATED PERSONS

Section 5–301. [Appointment of Guardian for Incapacitated Person by Will or Other Writing.]

(a) The parent of an unmarried incapacitated person may appoint by will, or other writing signed by the parent and attested by at least 2 witnesses, a guardian of the incapacitated person. If both parents are dead or the surviving parent is adjudged incapacitated, a parental appointment becomes effective when, after having given 7 days prior written notice of intention to do so to the incapacitated person and to the person having the care of the person or to the nearest adult relative, the guardian files acceptance of appointment in the court in which the will is [informally or formally] probated, or in the case of a non-testamentary nominating instrument, in the Court at the place where the incapacitated person resides or is present. The notice shall state that the appointment may be terminated by filing a written objection in the Court, as provided by subsection (d). If both parents are dead, an effective appointment by the parent who died later has priority.

(b) The spouse of a married incapacitated person may appoint by will, or other writing signed by the spouse and attested by at least 2 witnesses, a guardian of the incapacitated person. The appointment becomes effective when, after having given 7 days prior written notice of intention to do so to the incapacitated person and to the person having care of the incapacitated person or to the nearest adult relative, the guardian files acceptance of appointment in the Court in which the will is informally or formally probated or, in the case of non-testamentary nominating instrument, in the Court at the place where the incapacitated person resides or is present. The notice shall state that the appointment may be terminated by filing a written objection in the Court, as provided by subsection (d). An effective appointment by a spouse has priority over an appointment by a parent.

(c) An appointment effected by filing the guardian's acceptance under a will probated in the state of the decedent's domicile is effective in this State.

(d) Upon the filing in the Court in which the will was probated or, in the case of a non-testamentary nominating instrument, in the Court at the place where the incapacitated person resides or is present, of written objection to the appointment by the incapacitated person for whom a parental or spousal appointment of guardian has been made, the appointment is terminated. An objection does not prevent appointment by the Court in a proper proceeding of the parental or spousal nominee or any other suitable person upon an adjudication of incapacity in proceedings under the succeeding sections of this Part.

As amended in 1987.

For material relating to the 1987 amendment, see Appendix I, infra.

COMMENT

Derived from 1969 UPC § 5–301, this section confers authority on the spouse and a parent to appoint a guardian for an incapacitated person; no action by any court is required, but a condition of an effective parental or spousal appointment is that the appointee file an acceptance in an appropriate court. Such a filing does not initiate a court proceeding or require any response from the court. However, a parental or spousal guardian is entitled to a writing from the court showing that an acceptance has been filed and that a guardian's authority as provided by the statute (see § 1–305) appears to have been conferred.

The section differs from 1969 UPC § 5–301 only in that it authorizes a parental or spousal appointment to be made by a witnessed non-testamentary writing, as well as by will. This expansion is consistent with a parallel expansion of 1969 UPC § 5–202 by § 5–202 of this Article.

This section is modeled after § 5–202, but it differs from § 5–202 in several particulars. For one, it applies to guardians for persons who are incapacitated for reasons other than minority. See the definition of incapacity in § 5–103(7). Also, no advance written notice of intention to accept a parental appointment as a guardian for a minor under § 5–202 is required while 7 days' advance notice is required for completion of a parental or

spousal appointment under this section. Note, too, that termination by objection to an appointment under § 5–202 can be effected by virtue of § 5–203 only if the objection is filed within 30 days after the filing of the acceptance. In contrast, this section permits the ward to upset a parental or spousal appointment based on incapacity by written objection at any time.

Whether accomplished by deed or will, this section expressly provides that a parental appointment of a guardian based on the incapacity of a child cannot become effective until both parents are dead or the surviving parent has become incapacitated. Thus, a parent's appointing authority is limited to providing for a replacement of whatever authority might have been attached to the status of parent. A spousal appointment by will would be ambulatory and could not become effective until after the spouse's death. However, a spousal appointment by deed may become effective before the appointing spouse's death if the appointing instrument so provides and all other conditions of an effective appointment are met. Thus, a spouse of an incapacitated person is enabled to confer a guardian's authority over an incapacitated mate. The authority arising by spousal appointment may be helpful in cases where the appointing spouse plans to be absent, or in situations where some third person hesitates to respect the directions of an incompetent's spouse and insists on some form of guardianship paper.

The section provides several safeguards that attend the procedure. The case with which the authority available under this section may be ended by objection of the ward provides a safeguard against abuse of the procedure. For another safeguard, the absence of any adjudication of incapacity incident to a conferral of authority under the section means that a purported appointment is effective only if, upon challenge, it is determined by a court that the essential condition of incapacity existed when the appointment was accepted. Also, as noted earlier, the ward of a guardian who claims authority by virtue of the procedure described in this section may cause the authority to terminate by filing a written objection at any time.

It may be questioned whether a legislature should bother to provide for an authority as fragile as that contemplated by the section. The drafters of the Uniform Probate Code believed that the procedure would be particularly helpful to parents of children suffering from congenital or other defects who require some lifetime care arrangements. These parents may desire some legal assurance that persons of their choice will be able to continue monitoring the care arrangements for their children when they become unable to do so. Since the role to be played calls principally for personal concern for the welfare of the incapacitated person, a prima facie showing of legal authority will suffice in many cases and it will be unimportant that the overseer's legal authority is not impregnable.

See the Comment following § 5–202 for additional observations regarding the utility of appointments of guardians by deed.

Section 5–302. [Venue.]

The venue for guardianship proceedings for an incapacitated person is in the place where the incapacitated person resides or is present at the time the proceedings are commenced. If the incapacitated person is admitted to an institution pursuant to order of a court of competent jurisdiction, venue is also in the [county] in which that court is located.

COMMENT

This section is identical to 1969 UPC § 5–302 and introduces the procedure for securing a court appointment of a guardian for an incapacitated person described in §§ 5–302 through 5–308.

Except for the case in which the authority of a parental or spousal guardian for an incapacitated person may be questioned or ended, the powers of a court-appointed guardian are the same as those of a spousal or parental guardian. Sec-

tion 5–309 describes the powers. Perusal of § 5–309, of § 5–209 on which it is based, and of the Comments following § 5–209, is recommended. From these materials, it will be seen that most of the more traditional purposes of guardianships will not be served by the guardian's position described in this Article. Rather, a conservator, as described in Part 4 of this Article, will be much better equipped to handle financial affairs of an incapacitated person than a guardian.

Consequently, the new guardianship as described in this Article is likely to be much less widely used than traditional guardianship procedures. Counsellors will be well advised to determine, in all cases where a guardianship may be suggested whether a guardianship, as distinguished from a conservatorship, will serve any useful purpose. Alternative methods of obtaining health and care services, including consents to medical treatment available under the Model Health Care Consent Act or comparable legislation and authority for voluntary or involuntary diagnostic or protective custodies under modern mental health legislation should be given careful consideration. Also, volunteer or paid companions, or placements with public or private nursing homes or other limited or total care providers, may be possible without the interposition of a court-appointed guardian.

Section 5–303. [Procedure for Court-appointment of a Guardian of an Incapacitated Person.]

(a) An incapacitated person or any person interested in the welfare of the incapacitated person may petition for appointment of a guardian, limited or general.

(b) After the filing of a petition, the Court shall set a date for hearing on the issue of incapacity so that notices may be given as required by Section 5–304, and, unless the allegedly incapacitated person is represented by counsel, appoint an attorney to represent the person in the proceeding. The person so appointed may be granted the powers and duties of a guardian ad litem. The person alleged to be incapacitated must be examined by a physician or other qualified person appointed by the Court who shall submit a report in writing to the Court. The person alleged to be incapacitated also must be interviewed by a visitor sent by the Court. The visitor also shall interview the person who appears to have caused the petition to be filed and any person who is nominated to serve as guardian and visit the present place of abode of the person alleged to be incapacitated and the place it is proposed that the person will be detained or reside if the appointment is made and submit a report in writing to the Court. The Court may utilize the service of any public or charitable agency as an additional visitor to evaluate the condition of the allegedly incapacitated person and to make appropriate recommendations to the Court.

(c) A person alleged to be incapacitated is entitled to be present at the hearing in person. The person is entitled to be represented by counsel, to present evidence, to cross-examine witnesses, including the Court-appointed physician or other qualified person and any visitor [, and to trial by jury]. The issue may be determined at a closed hearing [or without a jury] if the person alleged to be incapacitated or counsel for the person so requests.

(d) Any person may apply for permission to participate in the proceeding, and the Court may grant the request, with or without hearing, upon determining that the best interest of the alleged incapacitated person will be served thereby. The Court may attach appropriate conditions to the permission.

COMMENT

The procedure described in this section involves three designations or appointments of persons as mandatory participants in a court-appointed guardianship proceeding based on incapacity. First, the respondent must be represented by counsel who also may be granted the powers and duties of a guardian ad litem and who may represent the respondent in all cases in which he or she lacks adequate counsel of choice. In context, the court probably should determine not only that private counsel is in the case, but that such counsel has been engaged by the respondent acting without undue pressure from others having some possible personal interest in the proceeding. Also, the court is required to designate a physician and a visitor to function as described. The roles of physician and visitor may be filled by a single person, provided the person has the requisite qualifications.

Mandatory participation by a visitor and physician (or other qualified person) is not mentioned in connection with guardianship proceedings based on minority. See § 5–206. These officials are mentioned in § 5–406 covering court proceedings seeking what has sometimes been called a "guardian of the estate" and is referred to in this Article as a conservator. However, in the protective proceedings described in § 5–406 the court has discretion concerning whether either or both of the functionaries should be involved.

Underlying the guardian ad litem, visitor and physician requirements in this section is the belief that an individual's liberty to select an abode, to receive or to refuse medical, psychiatric, vocational, or other therapy or attention should not be displaced by appointment of a guardian unless the appointment is clearly necessary. In order to properly evaluate the merits of a petition seeking appointment of a guardian, the court should have access to information regarding the respondent other than as provided by the petitioner and associated counsel. The precautionary procedures tend to reduce the risk that relatives of the respondent may use guardianship procedures to relieve themselves of burdensome but bearable responsibilities for care, or to prevent the respondent from dissipating assets they would like to inherit, or for other reasons that are not in the best interest of the respondent. Also, they are designed to increase the perceptions of the respondent available to the court and lessen the risk that honestly held but overly-narrow judgments regarding tolerable limits of eccentricity may cause the loss of an individual's liberty.

The mandatory features of a guardianship proceeding make the procedure somewhat more complex than a protective proceeding under § 5–401 et seq. seeking the appointment of a conservator. The differences may tend to discourage use of guardianships and so reduce the instances in which persons may be declared to be without legal capacity. Loss of control over one's property is serious, to be sure, but there are reasons why it may be viewed as less serious than suffering a judgment that one is legally incapacitated and must be placed under the care of a guardian. First, one's property can and should be made available for support of legal dependents. Also, court-directed management of one's property does not impede the personal liberty of the protected person nor prevent the acquisition and enjoyment of assets that may be acquired thereafter. Finally, the interposition of another's control of one's personal freedom is rarely necessary or justified in non-criminal settings. Alternative methods of protecting persons with little ability to care for themselves should be encouraged.

Section 5–304. [Notice in Guardianship Proceeding.]

(a) In a proceeding for the appointment of a guardian of an incapacitated person, and, if notice is required in a proceeding for appointment of a temporary guardian, notice of hearing must be given to each of the following:

(1) the person alleged to be incapacitated and spouse, or, if none, adult children, or if none, parents;

(2) any person who is serving as guardian, conservator, or who has the care and custody of the person alleged to be incapacitated;

(3) in case no other person is notified under paragraph (1), at least one of the nearest adult relatives, if any can be found; and

(4) any other person as directed by the Court.

(b) Notice of hearing on a petition for an order subsequent to appointment of a guardian must be given to the ward, the guardian and any other person as ordered by the Court.

(c) Notice must be served personally on the alleged incapacitated person. Notices to other persons as required by subsection (a)(1) must be served personally if the person to be notified can be found within the state. In all other cases, required notices must be given as provided in Section 1–401.

(d) The person alleged to be incapacitated may not waive notice.

COMMENT

This section is based on 1969 UPC § 5–309. Like the source section, it requires that notice of the proceeding be served personally on the person alleged to be incapacitated. This appears in subsection (c), which qualifies both subsections (a) and (b). Subsection (b) applies to proceedings subsequent to the institution of a guardianship as covered in § 5–312.

It may be noted that personal service is not necessary for the required notice to a minor age 14 or over under § 5–206 governing proceedings seeking a court-appointed guardian for a minor. In this connection, it should be observed that the instant section, rather than § 5–206, governs if the petition seeks to establish that a minor is incapacitated for reasons other than minority and so is in need of a guardian who will continue to serve in spite of the respondent's attainment of majority. See § 5–210 and compare § 5–310.

Section 5–305. [Who May Be Guardian; Priorities.]

(a) Any qualified person may be appointed guardian of an incapacitated person.

(b) Unless lack of qualification or other good cause dictates the contrary, the Court shall appoint a guardian in accordance with the incapacitated person's most recent nomination in a durable power of attorney.

(c) Except as provided in subsection (b), the following are entitled to consideration for appointment in the order listed:

(1) the spouse of the incapacitated person or a person nominated by will of a deceased spouse or by other writing signed by the spouse and attested by at least 2 witnesses;

(2) an adult child of the incapacitated person;

(3) a parent of the incapacitated person, or a person nominated by will of a deceased parent or by other writing signed by a parent and attested by at least two witnesses;

(4) any relative of the incapacitated person with whom the person has resided for more than 6 months prior to the filing of the petition; and

(5) a person nominated by the person who is caring for or paying for the care of the incapacitated person.

(d) With respect to persons having equal priority, the Court shall select the one it deems best qualified to serve. The Court, acting in the best interest of the incapacitated person, may pass over a person having priority and appoint a person having a lower priority or no priority.

COMMENT

Subsection (a) limits those who may act as guardians for incapacitated persons to "qualified" persons. "Qualified" in its application to "persons" is not defined in this Article, meaning that an appointing court has considerable discretion regarding the suitability of an individual to serve as guardian for a particular ward. In exercising this discretion, the court should give careful consideration to the needs of the ward and to the experience or other qualifications of the applicant to react sensitively and positively to the ward's needs.

Subsections (b) and (c) govern priorities among persons who may seek appointment. Unless good cause or lack of qualification dictates otherwise, priority is with one nominated in an unrevoked power

393

of attorney of the ward that remains effective though the ward has become incompetent since executing the power of attorney.

The source of this section is 1969 UPC § 5–311, which section also provided that a "suitable institution" might be appointed guardian. This suggestion was discussed thoroughly by the Uniform Law Commissioners for this Article and rejected. The reasoning for limiting appointments to "qualified persons" is that for a guardianship of the person, the needs, duties and responsibilities are so personal they should only be delegated to a person and not to an institution.

Section 5–306. [Findings; Order of Appointment.]

(a) The Court shall exercise the authority conferred in this Part so as to encourage the development of maximum self-reliance and independence of the incapacitated person and make appointive and other orders only to the extent necessitated by the incapacitated person's mental and adaptive limitations or other conditions warranting the procedure.

(b) The Court may appoint a guardian as requested if it is satisfied that the person for whom a guardian is sought is incapacitated and that the appointment is necessary or desirable as a means of providing continuing care and supervision of the person of the incapacitated person. The Court, on appropriate findings, may (i) treat the petition as one for a protective order under Section 5–401 and proceed accordingly, (ii) enter any other appropriate order, or (iii) dismiss the proceedings.

(c) The Court, at the time of appointment or later, on its own motion or on appropriate petition or motion of the incapacitated person or other interested person, may limit the powers of a guardian otherwise conferred by Parts 1, 2, 3 and 4 of this Article and thereby create a limited guardianship. Any limitation on the statutory power of a guardian of an incapacitated person must be endorsed on the guardian's letters or, in the case of a guardian by parental or spousal appointment, must be reflected in letters issued at the time any limitation is imposed. Following the same procedure, a limitation may be removed or modified and appropriate letters issued.

COMMENT

The purpose of subsections (a) and (c) is to remind an appointing court that a guardianship under this legislation should not confer more authority over the person of the ward than appears necessary to alleviate the problems caused by the ward's incapacity. This is a statement of the general principle underlying a "limited guardianship" concept. For example, if the principal reason for the guardianship is the ward's inability to comprehend a personal medical problem, the guardian's authority could be limited to making a judgment, after evaluation of all circumstances, concerning the advisability and form of treatment and to authorize actions necessary to carry out the decision. Or, if the ward's principal problem stems from memory lapses and associated wanderings, a guardian with authority limited to making arrangements for suitable security against this risk might be indicated. Subsection (c) facilitates use by the appointing court of a trial-and-error method to achieve a tailoring of the guardian's authority to changing needs and circumstances. Read with the last sentence of § 5–303(b) and with subsection (d) of § 5–303, the instant section authorizes use of any public or charitable agency that demonstrates interest and competence in evaluating the condition and needs of the ward in arriving at a decision regarding the appropriate powers of the guardian.

The section does not authorize enlargement of the powers of a guardian beyond those described in § 5–309 and related sections. Rather, limitations on a guardian's

§ 5–309 powers and duties may be imposed and removed. Thus, if the court determines that most of a respondent's demonstrated problems probably could be alleviated by the institution of an appropriate authority to manage the ward's property and make appropriate expenditures for the ward's well-being, the court should utilize subsection (b) to recast the proceedings so that a conservator, rather than a guardian, would be appointed. If the respondent's problems call for both a guardian and a conservator, subsection (b) authorizes the court to direct that the proceedings be recast to seek both forms of relief. In this connection, the case of an incapacitated person differs from that of a minor who needs both a personal guardian and a conservator. This difference is recognized in that the second sentence of § 5–423(a), which applies only to conservators of estates of unmarried minors, enables a minor's conservator, but not a conservator for an incapacitated person, to exercise the powers of a personal guardian.

Section 5–307. [Acceptance of Appointment; Consent to Jurisdiction.]

By accepting appointment, a guardian submits personally to the jurisdiction of the Court in any proceeding relating to the guardianship that may be instituted by any interested person. Notice of any proceeding must be delivered or mailed to the guardian at the address listed in the Court records and at the address as then known to the petitioner.

COMMENT

This section is comparable to §§ 5–208 and 5–412. These three sections are derived from 1969 UPC §§ 5–208, 5–305 and 5–413.

The "long-arm" principle behind this section is well established. It seems desirable that the court in which acceptance is filed be able to

serve its process on the guardian wherever he or she has moved. The continuing interest of that court in the welfare of the minor is ample to justify this provision. The consent to service is real rather than fictional in the guardianship situation, where the guardian acts voluntarily in filing acceptance. It is probable that the form of acceptance will expressly embody the provisions of this section, although the statute does not expressly require this.

The proceedings in this Article are flexible. The court should not appoint a guardian unless one is necessary or desirable for the care of the person. If it develops that the needs of the person who is alleged to be incapacitated are not those which would call for a guardian, the court may adjust the proceeding accordingly. By acceptance of the appointment, the guardian submits to the court's jurisdiction in much the same way as a personal representative.

Section 5–308. [Emergency Orders; Temporary Guardians.]

(a) If an incapacitated person has no guardian, an emergency exists, and no other person appears to have authority to act in the circumstances, on appropriate petition the Court may appoint a temporary guardian whose authority may not extend beyond [15 days] [the period of effectiveness of ex parte restraining orders], and who may exercise those powers granted in the order.

(b) If an appointed guardian is not effectively performing duties and the Court further finds that the welfare of the incapacitated person requires immediate action, it may appoint, with or without notice, a temporary guardian for the incapacitated person having the powers of a general guardian for a specified period not to exceed 6 months. The authority of any permanent guardian previously appointed by the Court is suspended as long as a temporary guardian has authority.

(c) The Court may remove a temporary guardian at any time. A temporary guardian shall make any report the Court requires. In other respects the provisions of Parts 1, 2, 3 and 4 of this Article concerning guardians apply to temporary guardians.

COMMENT

The source of this section generally is 1969 UPC § 5–310. However, subsection (a), while still requiring an "emergency" situation for its application, has been significantly revised as to the term of the appointment of this "temporary guardian." 1969 UPC § 5–310(a) permitted appointments of "temporary guardians" for "a specified period not to exceed 6 months." Subsection (a) offers alternative suggestions in bracketed language for permissible periods for appointment of "temporary guardians" in "emergencies."

Of course, it is recognized in providing for a shorter period of appointment that a court can renew the appointment for an additional period or additional periods according to the exigencies of the emergency.

The language "and no other person appears to have authority to act in the circumstances" has been added to subsection (a). The added language should aid in preventing the mere institution of a guardianship proceeding from upsetting an arrangement for care under a durable power of attorney, or for nullifying an opportunity to use legislation like the Model Health Care Consent Act to resolve a problem involving the care of a person who is unable to care for himself or herself.

Under subsection (b), the appointing court retains authority to act on petition or on its own motion to suspend a guardian's authority by appointing a temporary guardian. The necessary finding, which need not follow notice to interested persons, is that the welfare of the incapacitated person requires action and the appointed guardian is not acting effectively.

Section 5–309. [General Powers and Duties of Guardian.]

Except as limited pursuant to Section 5–306(c), a guardian of an incapacitated person is responsible for care, custody, and control of the ward, but is not liable to third persons by reason of that responsibility for acts of the ward. In particular and without qualifying the foregoing, a guardian has the same duties, powers and responsibilities as a guardian for a minor as described in Section 5–209(b), (c) and (d).

COMMENT

The reference to § 5–306 coordinates this section with the limited guardian concept. All guardians, however appointed, have the powers and duties of a guardian of a minor as provided in § 5–209, subsections (b), (c), and (d). As discussed in the Comment to § 5–209, these powers do not enable a guardian to deal with property matters of the ward. A protective order under § 5–401 et seq. is indicated when property management is needed. Though the legislation does not contemplate that the statutory authority of a guardian may be increased by court order, the court, at the time of appointment or on motion or petition thereafter, may limit the power of a guardian in any respect. The provisions of § 5–304(b) requiring advance notice of a proceeding regarding a guardian's power instituted subsequent to appointment would apply to a post-appointment proceeding to impose or remove restrictions on a guardian's authority.

The language regarding a guardian's liability to third persons for acts of the ward is based on a somewhat differently worded statement in 1969 UPC § 5–310. Both formulations are intended merely to prevent any attribution of liability to a guardian on account of a ward's acts that might be thought to follow from the guardian's legal control of the ward. Neither version is intended to exonerate a guardian from the consequences of his or her own negligence.

Section 5–310. [Termination of Guardianship for Incapacitated Person.]

The authority and responsibility of a guardian of an incapacitated person terminates upon the death of the guardian or ward, the determination of incapacity of the guardian, or upon removal or resignation as provided in Section 5–311. Testamentary appointment under an informally probated will terminates if the will is later denied probate in a formal proceeding. Termination does not affect a guardian's liability for prior acts or the obligation to account for funds and assets of the ward.

COMMENT

The source of this section is 1969 UPC § 5-306 as amended in 1975. The comparable section of this Article, § 5-210, dealing with termination of the authority of a guardian whose authority derives solely from a ward's minority, differs from the instant section in that a guardian of a minor automatically loses authority when the minor attains the age of majority. Under the instant section, an adjudication is necessary to establish that a ward's incapacity has ended otherwise than upon the ward's death.

The concept that a guardian's authority may be terminated even though the guardian remains liable for prior acts or unaccounted funds is a corollary of the proposition that a guardian's authority to act for the ward should end automatically and without court order in certain circumstances. A more primitive concept to the effect that a guardian's authority derived from a court order continues until the court orders otherwise generates unnecessary and excessive use of the courts. Nonetheless, the question of whether a person's incapacity exists or continues and whether a guardian is necessary to provide continuing care and supervision of the ward is too complex to be resolved automatically save in the instances enumerated in this section. If a court determines that a ward's incapacity or need for a guardian has ended, it may terminate the authority and make an appropriate, additional order regarding the guardian's liabilities for acts done or funds for which there has not been any accounting. The additional order might defer the determination regarding liabilities to a later time.

The penultimate sentence of this section should *not* be included in an enactment except in jurisdictions that have adopted the Uniform Probate Code or have similar legislation permitting the informal probate of wills.

Section 5-311. [Removal or Resignation of Guardian; Termination of Incapacity.]

(a) On petition of the ward or any person interested in the ward's welfare, the Court, after hearing, may remove a guardian if in the best interest of the ward. On petition of the guardian, the Court, after hearing, may accept a resignation.

(b) An order adjudicating incapacity may specify a minimum period, not exceeding six months, during which a petition for an adjudication that the ward is no longer incapacitated may not be filed without special leave. Subject to that restriction, the ward or any person interested in the welfare of the ward may petition for an order that the ward is no longer incapacitated and for termination of the guardianship. A request for an order may also be made informally to the Court and any person who knowingly interferes with transmission of the request may be adjudged guilty of contempt of court.

(c) Upon removal, resignation, or death of the guardian, or if the guardian is determined to be incapacitated, the Court may appoint a successor guardian and make any other appropriate order. Before appointing a successor guardian, or ordering that a ward's incapacity has terminated, the Court shall follow the same procedures to safeguard the rights of the ward that apply to a petition for appointment of a guardian.

As amended in 1987.

For material relating to the 1987 amendment, see Appendix I, infra.

COMMENT

The source of this section is 1969 UPC § 5–307.

The ward's incapacity is a question that usually may be reviewed at any time. However, provision is made for a discretionary restriction on review. In all review proceedings, the welfare of the ward is paramount.

The provisions of subsection (b) were designed to provide another protection against use of guardianship proceedings to secure a lock-up of a person who is not capable of looking out for his or her personal needs. If the safeguards imposed at the time of appointment fail to prevent an unnecessary guardianship, subsection (b) is intended to facilitate a ward's unaided or unassisted efforts to inform the court that an injustice has occurred as a result of the guardianship.

Section 5–312. [Proceedings Subsequent to Appointment; Venue.]

(a) The Court at the place where the ward resides has concurrent jurisdiction with the Court that appointed the guardian or in which acceptance of a parental or spousal appointment was filed over resignation, removal, accounting, and other proceedings relating to the guardianship, including proceedings to limit the authority previously conferred on a guardian or to remove limitations previously imposed.

(b) If the Court at the place where the ward resides is not the Court in which acceptance of appointment is filed, the Court in which proceedings subsequent to appointment are commenced, in all appropriate cases, shall notify the other Court, in this or another state, and after consultation with that Court determine whether to retain jurisdiction or transfer the proceedings to the other Court, whichever may be in the best interest of the ward. A copy of any order accepting a resignation, removing a guardian, or altering authority must be sent to the Court in which acceptance of appointment is filed.

COMMENT

The source of this section is 1969 UPC § 5–313. The source section has been expanded by the language in subsection (a) specifying that proceedings to alter the authority of the guardian, which may occur at any time subsequent to the original appointment of the guardian as provided in § 5–306(c), are included in the described concurrent jurisdiction.

The source section has been amended also to include recognition of appointments of guardians by non-testamentary written instruments executed by a parent or spouse.

PROTECTION OF PROPERTY OF PERSONS UNDER DISABILITY AND MINORS

Section 5–401. [Protective Proceedings.]

(a) Upon petition and after notice and hearing in accordance with the provisions of this Part, the Court may appoint a conservator or make any other protective order for cause as provided in this section.

(b) Appointment of a conservator or other protective order may be made in relation to the estate and affairs of a minor if the Court determines that a minor owns money or property requiring management or protection that cannot otherwise be provided or has or may have business affairs that may be jeopardized or prevented by minority, or that funds are needed for support and education and that protection is necessary or desirable to obtain or provide funds.

(c) Appointment of a conservator or other protective order may be made in relation to the estate and affairs of a person if the Court determines that (i) the person is unable to manage property and business affairs effectively for such reasons as mental illness, mental deficiency, physical illness or disability, chronic use of drugs, chronic intoxication, confinement, detention by a foreign power, or disappearance; and (ii) the person has property that will be wasted or dissipated unless property management is provided or money is needed for the support, care, and welfare of the person or those entitled to the person's support and that protection is necessary or desirable to obtain or provide money.

As amended in 1988.

For changes made by the 1988 amendment, see Appendix III, infra.

COMMENT

This is the basic section of this Part providing for protective proceedings for minors and disabled persons. "Protective proceeding" is a generic term used to describe proceedings to establish conservatorships and obtain protective orders. Persons who may be subjected to the proceedings described here include a broad category of persons who, for a variety of different reasons, may be unable to manage their own property.

Since the problems of property management are generally the same for minors and disabled persons, it was thought undesirable to treat these problems in two separate parts. Where there are differences, these have been separately treated in specific sections.

The Comment to § 5–306, supra, points up the different meanings of "incapacity" (warranting guardianship) and "disability."

The source of this section is 1969 UPC § 5–401.

Section 5–402. [Protective Proceedings; Jurisdiction of Business Affairs of Protected Persons.]

After the service of notice in a proceeding seeking the appointment of a conservator or other protective order and until termination of the proceeding, the Court in which the petition is filed has:

(1) exclusive jurisdiction to determine the need for a conservator or other protective order until the proceedings are terminated;

(2) exclusive jurisdiction to determine how the estate of the protected person which is subject to the laws of this State must be managed, expended, or distributed to or for the use of the protected person, the protected person's dependents, or other claimants; and

(3) concurrent jurisdiction to determine the validity of claims against the person or estate of the protected person and questions of title concerning any estate asset.

COMMENT

The source of this section is 1969 UPC § 5–402.

While the bulk of all judicial proceedings involving the conservator will be in the court supervising the conservatorship, third parties may bring suit against the conservator or the protected person on some matters in other courts. Claims against the conservator after appointment are dealt with by § 5–427.

Section 5–403. [Venue.]

Venue for proceedings under this Part is:

(1) in the Court at the place in this State where the person to be protected resides whether or not a guardian has been appointed in another place; or

(2) if the person to be protected does not reside in this State, in the Court at any place where property of the person is located.

COMMENT

The source of this section is 1969 UPC § 5–403.

Venue for protective proceedings lies in the county of residence (rather than domicile) or, in the case of a non-resident, where property of the protected person is located. Unitary management of the property is obtainable through easy transfer of proceedings (§ 1–303[b]) and easy collection of assets by foreign conservators (§ 5–430).

Section 5–404. [Original Petition for Appointment or Protective Order.]

(a) The person to be protected or any person who is interested in the estate, affairs, or welfare of the person, including a parent, guardian, custodian, or any person who would be adversely affected by lack of effective management of the person's property and business affairs may petition for the appointment of a conservator or for other appropriate protective order.

(b) The petition must set forth to the extent known the interest of the petitioner; the name, age, residence, and address of the person to be protected; the name and address of the guardian, if any; the name and address of the nearest relative known to the petitioner; a general statement of the person's property with an estimate of the value thereof, including any compensation, insurance, pension, or allowance to which the person is entitled; and the reason why appointment of a conservator or other protective order is necessary. If the appointment of a conservator is requested, the petition must also set forth the name and address of the person whose appointment is sought and the basis of the claim to priority for appointment.

COMMENT

The source of this section is 1969 UPC § 5–404 with some slight change of wording. For example, the word "business" has been inserted before "affairs" for clarification.

Section 5–405. [Notice.]

(a) On a petition for appointment of a conservator or other protective order, the requirements for notice described in Section 5–304 apply, but (i) if the person to be protected has disappeared or is otherwise situated so as to make personal service of notice impracticable, notice to the person must be given by publication as provided in Section 1–401, and (ii) if the person to be protected is a minor, the provisions of Section 5–206 also apply.

(b) Notice of hearing on a petition for an order subsequent to appointment of a conservator or other protective order must be given to the protected person, any conservator of the protected person's estate, and any other person as ordered by the Court.

COMMENT

The primary sections providing for notice in this Code are §§ 1–401 and 5–304. The source of this section is 1969 UPC § 5–405, but the provisions have been altered somewhat to make reference back to the primary notice provisions rather than repeating the requirements here again.

The provision relative to responding to requests for notice, which had been in 1969 UPC § 5–405, has been moved to and extended in § 5–104. This section intends to include responses to requests for notice through the provision for giving notice to other persons as ordered by the Court in subsection (b).

Section 5–406. [Procedure Concerning Hearing and Order on Original Petition.]

(a) Upon receipt of a petition for appointment of a conservator or other protective order because of minority, the Court shall set a date for hearing. If the Court determines at any time in the proceeding that the interests of the minor are or may be inadequately represented, it may appoint an attorney to represent the minor, giving consideration to the choice of the minor if 14 or more years of age. An attorney appointed by the Court to represent a minor may be granted the powers and duties of a guardian ad litem.

(b) Upon receipt of a petition for appointment of a conservator or other protective order for reasons other than minority, the Court shall set a date for hearing. Unless the person to be protected has chosen counsel, the Court shall appoint an attorney to represent the person who may be granted the powers and duties of a guardian ad litem. If the alleged disability is mental illness, mental deficiency, physical illness or disability, chronic use of drugs, or chronic intoxication, the Court may direct that the person to be protected be examined by a physician designated by the Court, preferably a physician who is not connected with any institution in which the person is a patient or is detained. The Court may send a visitor to interview the person to be protected. The visitor may be a guardian ad litem or an officer or employee of the Court.

(c) The Court may utilize, as an additional visitor, the service of any public or charitable agency to evaluate the condition of the person to be protected and make appropriate recommendations to the Court.

(d) The person to be protected is entitled to be present at the hearing in person. The person is entitled to be represented by counsel, to present evidence, to cross-examine witnesses, including any Court-appointed physician or other qualified person and any visitor [, and to trial by jury]. The issue may be determined at a closed hearing [or without a jury] if the person to be protected or counsel for the person so requests.

(e) Any person may apply for permission to participate in the proceeding and the Court may grant the request, with or without hearing, upon determining that the best interest of the person to be protected will be served thereby. The Court may attach appropriate conditions to the permission.

(f) After hearing, upon finding that a basis for the appointment of a conservator or other protective order has been established, the Court shall make an appointment or other appropriate protective order.

As amended in 1988.

For changes made by the 1988 amendment, see Appendix III, infra.

COMMENT

The section establishes a framework within which professionals, including the judge, attorney, and physician, if any, may be expected to exercise good judgment in regard to the minor or disabled person who is the subject of the proceeding. The National Conference accepts that it is desirable to rely on professionals rather than to attempt to draft detailed standards or conditions for appointment.

The source of subsections (a), (b), and (f) is 1969 UPC § 5–407. The phrase "if 14 or more years of age" has been changed for consistency within this Article.

Since there has not been any prior determination of incapacity, the person, for whom a protective order is sought, should be extended the same rights as any other person whose personal freedom may be restricted as a result of the proceedings. Subsection (d) expressly recognizes those rights. The hearing will be an open hearing, unless the protected person or counsel for the person requests a closed hearing.

Subsection (c) permits, but does not require, the court to utilize agencies, who may have a particular expertise, to aid in evaluating the person's condition when a protective order is sought. Subsection (e) permits a person, who might not otherwise be an "interested person," to request permission to participate in the proceeding. The court may or may not grant the permission and may attach conditions to the permission when granted. The court is given broad latitude in using public-interest agencies and in permitting persons, who do not otherwise qualify as "interested persons," in aiding the court to evaluate the case and in determining measures that will be in the best interest of the person for whom a protective order is sought. There are not any rights for these groups to participate in the proceedings—their involvement initially and the extent of their involvement is within the discretionary control of the court.

Section 5–407. [Permissible Court Orders.]

(a) The Court shall exercise the authority conferred in this Part to encourage the development of maximum self-reliance and independence of a protected person and make protective orders only to the extent necessitated by the protected person's mental and adaptive limitations and other conditions warranting the procedure.

(b) The Court has the following powers that may be exercised directly or through a conservator in respect to the estate and business affairs of a protected person:

(1) While a petition for appointment of a conservator or other protective order is pending and after preliminary hearing and without notice to others, the Court may preserve and apply the property of the person to be protected as may be required for the support of the person or dependents of the person.

(2) After hearing and upon determining that a basis for an appointment or other protective order exists with respect to a minor without other disability, the Court has all those powers over the estate and business affairs of the minor which are or may be necessary for the best interest of the minor and members of the minor's immediate family.

(3) After hearing and upon determining that a basis for an appointment or other protective order exists with respect to a person for reasons other than minority, the Court, for the benefit of the person and members of the person's immediate family, has all the powers over the estate and business affairs which the person could exercise if present and not under disability, except the power to make a will. Those powers include, but are not limited to, power to make gifts; to convey or release contingent and expectant interests in property, including marital property rights and any right of survivorship incident to joint tenancy or tenancy by the entirety; to exercise or release powers held by the protected person as trustee, personal representative, custodian for minors, conservator, or donee of a power of appointment; to enter into contracts; to create revocable or irrevocable trusts of property of the estate which may extend beyond the disability or life of the protected person; to exercise options of the protected person to purchase securities or other property; to exercise rights to elect options and change beneficiaries under insurance and annuity policies and to surrender the policies for their cash value; to exercise any right to an elective share in the estate of the person's deceased spouse and to renounce or disclaim any interest by testate or intestate succession or by inter vivos transfer.

(c) The Court may exercise or direct the exercise of the following powers only if satisfied, after notice and hearing, that it is in the best interest of the protected person, and that the person either is incapable of consenting or has consented to the proposed exercise of power:

(1) to exercise or release powers of appointment of which the protected person is donee;

(2) to renounce or disclaim interests;

(3) to make gifts in trust or otherwise exceeding 20 percent of any year's income of the estate; and

(4) to change beneficiaries under insurance and annuity policies.

(d) A determination that a basis for appointment of a conservator or other protective order exists has no effect on the capacity of the protected person.

COMMENT

The court which is supervising a conservatorship is given all the powers that the individual would have if the person were of full capacity. These powers are given to the court that is managing the protected person's property, because the exercise of these powers has important consequences with respect to the protected person's property.

The source of this section is 1969 UPC § 5–408. Subsection (a) has been added. It is the general admonition against an overly intrusive exercise of its authority by the court adopting the concept of a limited guardianship. The court should not assume any greater authority over the protected person than the capacity and ability of that person necessitates.

There is some change of wording to provide consistency in terminology throughout this Article. Subparagraph (d) has been shortened, but it does not reflect a substantive change.

Section 5–408. [Protective Arrangements and Single Transactions Authorized.]

(a) If it is established in a proper proceeding that a basis exists as described in Section 5–401 for affecting the property and business affairs of a person, the Court, without appointing a conservator, may authorize, direct or ratify any transaction necessary or desirable to achieve any security, service, or care arrangement meeting the foreseeable needs of the protected person. Protective arrangements include payment, delivery, deposit, or retention of funds or property; sale, mortgage, lease, or other transfer of property; entry into an annuity contract, a contract for life care, a deposit contract, or a contract for training and education; or addition to or establishment of a suitable trust.

(b) If it is established in a proper proceeding that a basis exists as described in Section 5–401 for affecting the property and business affairs of a person, the Court, without appointing a conservator, may authorize, direct, or ratify any contract, trust, or other transaction relating to the protected person's property and business affairs if the Court determines that the transaction is in the best interest of the protected person.

(c) Before approving a protective arrangement or other transaction under this section, the Court shall consider the interests of creditors and dependents of the protected person and, in view of the disability, whether the protected person needs the continuing protection of a conservator. The Court may appoint a special conservator to assist in the accomplishment of any protective arrangement or other transaction authorized under this section who shall have the authority conferred by the order and serve until discharged by order after report to the Court of all matters done pursuant to the order of appointment.

COMMENT

It is important that the provision be made for the approval of single transactions or the establishment of protective arrangements as alternatives to full conservatorship. Under present law, a guardianship often must be established simply to make possible a valid transfer of land or securities. This section, consistent with the concept of a limited conservatorship, eliminates the necessity of the establishment of long-term arrangements in this situation.

The source of this section is 1969 UPC § 5–409. There have been some slight changes in terms, but there is not any substantive change from the 1969 UPC.

Section 5–409. [Who May Be Appointed Conservator; Priorities.]

(a) The Court may appoint an individual or a corporation with general power to serve as trustee or conservator of the estate of a protected person. The following are entitled to consideration for appointment in the order listed:

(1) a conservator, guardian of property, or other like fiduciary appointed or recognized by an appropriate court of any other jurisdiction in which the protected person resides;

(2) an individual or corporation nominated by the protected person 14 or more years of age and of sufficient mental capacity to make an intelligent choice;

(3) the spouse of the protected person;

(4) an adult child of the protected person;

(5) a parent of the protected person, or a person nominated by the will of a deceased parent;

(6) any relative of the protected person who has resided with the protected person for more than 6 months before the filing of the petition; and

(7) a person nominated by one who is caring for or paying benefits to the protected person.

(b) A person in priorities (1), (3), (4), (5), or (6) may designate in writing a substitute to serve instead and thereby transfer the priority to the substitute. With respect to persons having equal priority, the Court shall select the one it deems best qualified to serve. The Court, acting in the best interest of the protected person, may pass over a person having priority and appoint a person having a lower priority or no priority.

COMMENT

A flexible system of priorities for appointment as conservator has been provided. A parent may name a conservator for minor children in a will if the parent deems this to be desirable.

The source of this section is 1969 UPC § 5–410. There has been some slight changes in wording, particularly in subsection (b), for clarity without any intent to change substance.

Section 5–410. [Bond.]

The Court may require a conservator to furnish a bond conditioned upon faithful discharge of all duties of the trust according to law, with sureties as it shall specify. Unless otherwise directed, the bond must be in the amount of the aggregate capital value of the property of the estate in the conservator's control, plus one year's estimated income, and minus the value of securities deposited under arrangements requiring an order of the Court for their removal and the value of any land which the fiduciary, by express limitation of power, lacks power to sell or convey without Court authorization. The Court, in lieu of sureties on a bond, may accept other collateral for the performance of the bond, including a pledge of securities or a mortgage of land.

COMMENT

The bond requirements for conservators in this section are somewhat more strict than the requirements for personal representatives under Article III, Part 6 of this Code.

The source of this section is 1969 UPC § 5–411. Some slight changes in words used, but there has not been any change in substance.

Section 5–411. [Terms and Requirements of Bonds.]

(a) The following requirements and provisions apply to any bond required under Section 5–410.

(1) Unless otherwise provided by the terms of the approved bond, sureties are jointly and severally liable with the conservator and with each other.

(2) By executing an approved bond of a conservator, the surety consents to the jurisdiction of the Court that issued letters to the primary obligor in any proceeding pertaining to the fiduciary duties of the conservator and naming the surety as a party respondent. Notice of any proceeding must be delivered to the surety or mailed by registered or certified mail to the address listed with the Court at the place where the bond is filed and to the address as then known to the petitioner.

(3) On petition of a successor conservator or any interested person, a proceeding may be initiated against a surety for breach of the obligation of the bond of the conservator.

(4) The bond of the conservator is not void after the first recovery but may be proceeded against from time to time until the whole penalty is exhausted.

(b) No proceeding may be commenced against the surety on any matter as to which an action or proceeding against the primary obligor is barred by adjudication or limitation.

COMMENT

The source of this section is 1969 UPC § 5–412. The word "respondent" has been substituted for "defendant" to be more accurate, perhaps. There is no substantive change in this section.

Section 5–412. [Effect of Acceptance of Appointment.]

By accepting appointment, a conservator submits personally to the jurisdiction of the Court in any proceeding relating to the estate which may be instituted by any interested person. Notice of any proceeding must be delivered to the conservator or mailed by registered or certified mail to the address as listed in the petition for appointment or as thereafter reported to the Court and to the address as then known to the petitioner.

COMMENT

The source of this section is 1969 UPC § 5–413 without substantive change.

Section 5–413. [Compensation and Expenses.]

If not otherwise compensated for services rendered, any visitor, attorney, physician, conservator, or special conservator appointed in a protective proceeding and any attorney whose services resulted in a protective order or in an order that was beneficial to a protected person's estate is entitled to reasonable compensation from the estate.

COMMENT

The source of this section is 1969 UPC § 5–414 without change.

Section 5–414. [Death, Resignation, or Removal of Conservator.]

The Court may remove a conservator for good cause, upon notice and hearing, or accept the resignation of a conservator. Upon the conservator's death, resignation, or removal, the Court may appoint another conservator. A conservator so appointed succeeds to the title and powers of the predecessor.

COMMENT

The source of this section is 1969 UPC § 5–415 without substantive change.

Section 5–415. [Petitions for Orders Subsequent to Appointment.]

(a) Any person interested in the welfare of a person for whom a conservator has been appointed may file a petition in the appointing court for an order:

(1) requiring bond or collateral or additional bond or collateral, or reducing bond;

(2) requiring an accounting for the administration of the trust;

(3) directing distribution;

(4) removing the conservator and appointing a temporary or successor conservator; or

(5) granting other appropriate relief.

(b) A conservator may petition the appointing court for instructions concerning fiduciary responsibility.

411

(c) Upon notice and hearing, the Court may give appropriate instructions or make any appropriate order.

COMMENT

Once a conservator has been appointed, the Court supervising the trust acts only upon the request of some moving party.

The source of this section is 1969 UPC § 5–416 without change.

Section 5–416. [General Duty of Conservator.]

A conservator, in relation to powers conferred by this Part, or implicit in the title acquired by virtue of the proceeding, shall act as a fiduciary and observe the standards of care applicable to trustees.

COMMENT

The source of this section is 1969 UPC § 5–417. The wording necessarily has been revised because 1969 UPC § 5–417 refers to the Standard of Care and Performance for trustees described in Article VII of the UPC. This section as revised adopts for conservators the standard of care and performance otherwise applicable to trustees in the enacting jurisdiction. If the enacting jurisdiction has enacted 1969 UPC § 7–302, or the standard of care and performance for trustees described in that section (i.e. the prudent-man rule) is otherwise the standard of the enacting jurisdiction, this section as revised will not effectuate any change in substance from 1969 UPC § 5–417.

Section 5–417. [Inventory and Records.]

(a) Within 90 days after appointment, each conservator shall prepare and file with the appointing Court a complete inventory of the estate subject to the conservatorship together with an oath or affirmation that the inventory is believed to be complete and accurate as far as information permits. The conservator shall provide a copy thereof to the protected person if practicable and the person has attained the age of 14 years and has sufficient mental capacity to understand the arrangement. A copy also shall be provided to any guardian or parent with whom the protected person resides.

(b) The conservator shall keep suitable records of the administration and exhibit the same on request of any interested person.

COMMENT

The source of this section is 1969 UPC § 5–418. There has not been any substantive change. In the second sentence, "if practicable" has been substituted for "if he can be located" and there has been some

slight change in sentence structure
for clarity.

Section 5–418. [Accounts.]

Each conservator shall account to the Court for administration of the trust not less than annually unless the Court directs otherwise, upon resignation or removal and at other times as the Court may direct. On termination of the protected person's minority or disability, a conservator shall account to the Court or to the formerly protected person or the successors of that person. Subject to appeal or vacation within the time permitted, an order after notice and hearing allowing an intermediate account of a conservator adjudicates as to liabilities concerning the matters considered in connection therewith; and an order, following notice and hearing, allowing a final account adjudicates as to all previously unsettled liabilities of the conservator to the protected person or the protected person's successors relating to the conservatorship. In connection with any account, the Court may require a conservator to submit to a physical check of the estate, to be made in any manner the Court specifies.

As amended in 1987.

For material relating to the 1987 amendment, see Appendix I, infra.

COMMENT

The persons who are to receive notice of intermediate and final accounts will be identified by court order as provided in § 5–405. Notice is given as described in § 1–401. In other respects, procedures applicable to accountings will be as provided by court rule.

The source of this section is 1969 UPC § 5–419 without substantive change.

Section 5–419. [Conservators; Title By Appointment.]

(a) The appointment of a conservator vests in the conservator title as trustee to all property, or to the part thereof specified in the order, of the protected person, presently held or thereafter acquired, including title to any property theretofore held for the protected person by custodians or attorneys-in-fact. An order specifying that only a part of the property of the protected person vests in the conservator creates a limited conservatorship.

(b) Except as otherwise provided herein, the interest of the protected person in property vested in a conservator by this section is not transferrable or assignable by the protected person. An attempted transfer or assignment by the protected person, though ineffective to affect property rights, may generate a claim for restitution or damages which, subject to presentation and allowance, may be satisfied as provided in Section 5–427.

(c) Neither property vested in a conservator by this section nor the interest of the protected person in that property is subject to levy, garnishment, or similar process other than an order issued in the protective proceeding made as provided in Section 5–427.

COMMENT

This section permits independent administration of the property of the protected person once the appointment of a conservator has been obtained. Any interested person may require the conservator to account in accordance with § 5–418. As a trustee, a conservator holds title to the property of the protected person. The appointment of a conservator is a serious matter and the court must select the fiduciary with great care. Once appointed, the conservator is free to carry on all fiduciary responsibilities. If the conservator defaults in these in any way, the conservator may be made to account to the court.

Unlike a situation involving appointment of a guardian, the appointment of a conservator has no bearing on the capacity of the disabled person to contract or engage in other transactions except insofar as the spendthrift provisions of subsections (b) and (c) of this section apply to property transactions.

The source of this section is 1969 UPC § 5–420 generally. The phrase "or to the part thereof specified in the order," in the first sentence and the second sentence of subsection (a) have been added adopting the concept of a limited guardianship.

The provision in 1969 UPC § 5–420, that the appointment of a conservator is not a transfer or alienation within the meaning of those terms as used in statutes or other legal instrument restraining transfer or alienation, has not been included in this section, because it is believed that the statement is unnecessary.

Subsection (b) provides a spendthrift effect for property of the protected person vested in the conservator. An attempt by the protected person to transfer or alienate property may nevertheless generate a claim for restitution. This subsection was not a part of 1969 UPC § 5–420, but several suggestions have been made that the spendthrift provisions should be incorporated. The concept is analogous to spendthrift trust provisions often included when the beneficiary is incapable of managing his or her own property. The concept is also consistent with a conservatorship arrangement for protecting the estate of an incapacitated person.

Subsection (c) is the involuntary side of the spendthrift effect (subparagraph [b] is the voluntary restraint), which is also analogous to the spendthrift trust provisions and it was not a part of 1969 UPC § 5–420.

Section 5–420. [Recording of Conservator's Letters.]

(a) Letters of conservatorship are evidence of transfer of all assets, or the part thereof specified in the letters, of a protected person to the conservator. An order terminating a conservatorship is evidence of transfer of all assets subjected to the conservatorship from the conservator to the protected person, or to successors of the person.

(b) Subject to the requirements of general statutes governing the filing or recordation of documents of title to land or other property, letters of conservatorship and orders terminating conservatorships, may be filed or recorded to give record notice of title as between the conservator and the protected person.

COMMENT

The source of this section is 1969 UPC § 5–421. The phrases "or the part thereof specified in the letters," in the first sentence and "subjected to the conservatorship" in the second sentence have been added to recognize the concept of a limited conservatorship.

Section 5–421. [Sale, Encumbrance, or Transaction Involving Conflict of Interest; Voidable; Exceptions.]

Any sale or encumbrance to a conservator, the spouse, agent, attorney of a conservator, or any corporation, trust, or other organization in which the conservator has a substantial beneficial interest, or any other transaction involving the estate being administered by the conservator which is affected by a substantial conflict between fiduciary and personal interests is voidable unless the transaction is approved by the Court after notice as directed by the Court.

COMMENT

The source of this section is 1969 UPC § 5–422. The phrase, "or any other transaction involving the estate being administered by the conservator which is affected by a substantial conflict between fiduciary and personal interests ..." has been substituted for the phrase, "or any transaction which is affected by a substantial conflict of interest ..." for clarity. The phrase, "notice as directed by the Court" is a revision of wording and recognizes that notice may be to persons or agencies other than "interested parties" at the direction of the court, but the phrase is not a substantive change from the provision in 1969 UPC § 5–422.

Section 5–422. [Persons Dealing With Conservators; Protection.]

(a) A person who in good faith either assists or deals with a conservator for value in any transaction other than those requiring a Court order as provided in Section 5–407 is protected as if the conservator properly exercised the power. The fact that a person knowingly deals with a conservator does not alone require the person to inquire into the existence of a power or the propriety of its exercise, but restrictions on powers of conservators which are endorsed on letters as provided in Section 5–425 are effective as to third persons. A person is not bound to see to the proper application of estate assets paid or delivered to a conservator.

(b) The protection expressed in this section extends to any procedural irregularity or jurisdictional defect occurred in proceedings leading to the issuance of letters and is not a substitution for protection provided by comparable provisions of the law relating to commercial transactions or to simplifying transfers of securities by fiduciaries.

COMMENT

The source of this section is 1969 UPC § 5–423 adopted without substantive change.

The section codifies the *b.f.p.* rule generally followed in transactions with fiduciaries. Nevertheless, any person dealing with a known conservator for another should examine the letters of appointment of the conservator for any limitations on the conservator's authority endorsed on the letters pursuant to § 5–425.

Section 5–423. [Powers of Conservator in Administration.]

(a) Subject to limitation provided in Section 5–425, a conservator has all of the powers conferred in this section and any additional powers conferred by law on trustees in this State. In addition, a conservator of the estate of an unmarried minor [under the age of 18 years], as to whom no one has parental rights, has the duties and powers of a guardian of a minor described in Section 5–209 until the minor attains [the age of 18 years] or marries, but the parental rights so conferred on a conservator do not preclude appointment of a guardian as provided in Part 2.

(b) A conservator without Court authorization or confirmation, may invest and reinvest funds of the estate as would a trustee.

(c) A conservator, acting reasonably in efforts to accomplish the purpose of the appointment, may act without Court authorization or confirmation, to

(1) collect, hold, and retain assets of the estate including land in another state, until judging that disposition of the assets should be made, and the assets may be retained even though they include an asset in which the conservator is personally interested;

(2) receive additions to the estate;

(3) continue or participate in the operation of any business or other enterprise;

(4) acquire an undivided interest in an estate asset in which the conservator, in any fiduciary capacity, holds an undivided interest;

(5) invest and reinvest estate assets in accordance with subsection (b);

(6) deposit estate funds in a state or federally insured financial institution, including one operated by the conservator;

(7) acquire or dispose of an estate asset, including land in another state, for cash or on credit, at public or private sale, and manage, develop, improve, exchange, partition, change the character of, or abandon an estate asset;

(8) make ordinary or extraordinary repairs or alterations in buildings or other structures; demolish any improvements; and raze existing or erect new party walls or buildings;

(9) subdivide, develop, or dedicate land to public use; make or obtain the vacation of plats and adjust boundaries; adjust differences in valuation or exchange or partition by giving or receiving considerations; and dedicate easements to public use without consideration;

(10) enter for any purpose into a lease as lessor or lessee with or without option to purchase or renew for a term within or extending beyond the term of the conservatorship;

(11) enter into a lease or arrangement for exploration and removal of minerals or other natural resources or enter into a pooling or unitization agreement;

(12) grant an option involving disposition of an estate asset and take an option for the acquisition of any asset;

(13) vote a security, in person or by general or limited proxy;

(14) pay calls, assessments, and any other sums chargeable or accruing against or on account of securities;

(15) sell or exercise stock-subscription or conversion rights;

(16) consent, directly or through a committee or other agent, to the reorganization, consolidation, merger, dissolution, or liquidation of a corporation or other business enterprise;

(17) hold a security in the name of a nominee or in other form without disclosure of the conservatorship so that title to the security may pass by delivery, but the conservator is liable for any act of the nominee in connection with the stock so held;

(18) insure the assets of the estate against damage or loss and the conservator against liability with respect to third persons;

(19) borrow money to be repaid from estate assets or otherwise; advance money for the protection of the estate or the protected person and for all expenses, losses, and liability sustained in the administration of the estate or because of the holding or ownership of any estate assets, for which the conservator has a lien on the estate as against the protected person for advances so made;

(20) pay or contest any claim; settle a claim by or against the estate or the protected person by compromise, arbitration, or otherwise; and release, in whole or in part, any claim belonging to the estate to the extent the claim is uncollectible;

(21) pay taxes, assessments, compensation of the conservator, and other expenses incurred in the collection, care, administration, and protection of the estate;

(22) allocate items of income or expense to either estate income or principal, as provided by law, including creation of reserves out of income for depreciation, obsolescence, or amortization, or for depletion in mineral or timber properties;

(23) pay any sum distributable to a protected person or dependent of the protected person by paying the sum to the distributee or by paying the sum for the use of the distributee to the guardian of the distributee, or, if none, to a relative or other person having custody of the distributee;

(24) employ persons, including attorneys, auditors, investment advisors, or agents, even though they are associated with the conservator, to advise or assist in the performance of administrative duties; act upon their recommendation without independent investigation; and instead of acting personally, employ one or more agents to perform any act of administration, whether or not discretionary;

(25) prosecute or defend actions, claims, or proceedings in any jurisdiction for the protection of estate assets and of the conservator in the performance of fiduciary duties; and

(26) execute and deliver all instruments that will accomplish or facilitate the exercise of the powers vested in the conservator.

COMMENT

The source of this section is 1969 UPC § 5–424. There have been some minor stylistic changes, but there has not been any substantive change.

Any limitations or enlargements of the powers provided in this section for the conservator must be endorsed on the conservator's letters of appointment as provided in § 5–425.

Section 5–424. [Distributive Duties and Powers of Conservator.]

(a) A conservator may expend or distribute income or principal of the estate without Court authorization or confirmation for the support, education, care, or benefit of the protected person and dependents in accordance with the following principles:

(1) The conservator shall consider recommendations relating to the appropriate standard of support, education, and benefit for the protected person or dependent made by a parent or guardian, if any. The conservator may not be surcharged for sums paid to persons or organizations furnishing support, education, or care to the protected person or a dependent pursuant to the recommendations of a parent or guardian of the protected person unless the conservator knows that the parent or guardian derives personal financial benefit therefrom, including relief from any personal duty of support or the recommendations are clearly not in the best interest of the protected person.

(2) The conservator shall expend or distribute sums reasonably necessary for the support, education, care, or benefit of the protected person and dependents with due regard to (i) the size of the estate, the probable duration of the conservatorship, and the likelihood that the protected person, at some future time, may be fully able to be wholly self-sufficient and able to manage business affairs and the estate; (ii) the accustomed standard of living of the protected person and dependents; and (iii) other funds or sources used for the support of the protected person.

(3) The conservator may expend funds of the estate for the support of persons legally dependent on the protected person and others who are members of the protected person's household who are unable to support themselves, and who are in need of support.

(4) Funds expended under this subsection may be paid by the conservator to any person, including the protected person, to reimburse for expenditures that the conservator might have made, or in advance for services to be rendered to the protected person if it is reasonable to expect the services will be performed and advance payments are customary or reasonably necessary under the circumstances.

419

(5) A conservator, in discharging the responsibilities conferred by Court order and this Part, shall implement the principles described in Section 5–407(a), to the extent possible.

(b) If the estate is ample to provide for the purposes implicit in the distributions authorized by the preceding subsections, a conservator for a protected person other than a minor has power to make gifts to charity and other objects as the protected person might have been expected to make, in amounts that do not exceed in total for any year 20 percent of the income from the estate.

(c) When a minor who has not been adjudged disabled under Section 5–401(c) attains majority, the conservator, after meeting all claims and expenses of administration, shall pay over and distribute all funds and properties to the formerly protected person as soon as possible.

(d) If satisfied that a protected person's disability, other than minority, has ceased, the conservator, after meeting all claims and expenses of administration, shall pay over and distribute all funds and properties to the formerly protected person as soon as possible.

(e) If a protected person dies, the conservator shall deliver to the Court for safekeeping any will of the deceased protected person which may have come into the conservator's possession, inform the executor or beneficiary named therein of the delivery, and retain the estate for delivery to a duly appointed personal representative of the decedent or other persons entitled thereto. If, 40 days after the death of the protected person, no other person has been appointed personal representative and no application or petition for appointment is before the Court, the conservator may apply to exercise the powers and duties of a personal representative in order to be able to proceed to administer and distribute the decedent's estate. Upon application for an order granting the powers of a personal representative to a conservator, after notice to any person nominated personal representative by any will of which the applicant is aware, the Court may grant the application upon determining that there is no objection and endorse the letters of the conservator to note that the formerly protected person is deceased and that the conservator has acquired all of the powers and duties of a personal representative. The making and entry of an order under this section has the effect of an order of appointment of a personal representative [as provided in Section 3–308 and Parts 6 through 10 of Article III], but the estate in the name of the conservator, after administration, may be distributed to the decedent's successors without prior re-transfer to the conservator as personal representative.

COMMENT

This section sets out those situations wherein the conservator may distribute property or disburse funds during the continuance of or on termination of the trust. Section 5–415(b) makes it clear that a conservator may seek instructions from the court on questions arising under this section. Subsection (e) is derived in part from § 11.80.150 Revised Code of Washington (RCWA 11.80.150).

The source of this section is 1969 UPC § 5–425. There have been some stylistic changes in the wording.

Wording has been added to paragraphs (a)(1) and (a)(2) to make it clear that those provisions apply to dependents of the protected person as well as to the protected person. The additions are consistent with provisions in paragraphs (a)(3) and (a)(4).

Paragraph (a)(5) has been added in this section. It is a cross reference to the admonition in § 5–407(a) reiterating the principle that the conservator should continually be conscious of the policies of this Article against an overly intrusive exercise of control over property of the protected person.

The term "prior" has been deleted before the word "claims" in subsection (c). "Prior claims" is ambiguous in 1969 UPC § 5–425(c).

In the bracketed portion of subsection (e), the reference should be to the relevant statutes of the enacting jurisdiction pertaining to appointment proceedings for personal representatives in decedents' estates.

Section 5–425. [Enlargement or Limitation of Powers of Conservator.]

Subject to the restrictions in Section 5–407(c), the Court may confer on a conservator at the time of appointment or later, in addition to the powers conferred by Sections 5–423 and 5–424, any power that the Court itself could exercise under Sections 5–407(b)(2) and 5–407(b)(3). The Court, at the time of appointment or later, may limit the powers of a conservator otherwise conferred by Sections 5–423 and 5–424 or previously conferred by the Court and may at any time remove or modify any limitation. If the Court limits any power conferred on the conservator by Section 5–423 or Section 5–424, or specifies, as provided in Section 5–419(a), that title to some but not all assets of the protected person vest in the conservator, the limitation or specification of assets subject to the conservatorship must be endorsed upon the letters of appointment.

COMMENT

This section makes it possible to appoint a fiduciary whose powers are limited to part of the estate or who may conduct important transactions, such as sales and mortgages of land, only with special court authorization. In the latter case, a conservator would be in much the same position of a guardian of property under the law currently in force in most states, but he would have title to the property. The purpose of giving conservators title as trustees is to ensure that the provisions for protection of third parties have full effect. The Veterans Administration may insist, when it is paying benefits to a minor or disabled person, that the letters of conservatorship limit powers to those of a guardian under the Uniform Veteran's Guardianship Act and require the conservator to file annual accounts.

The court may not only limit the powers of the conservator, but it may expand powers of the conservator so as to make it possible to act as the court itself might act.

The source of this section is 1969 UPC § 5-426. Although the UPC originally contemplated that limited conservatorships could be accommodated by application of the provisions of this section, the phrase "or specifies, as provided in Section 5-419(a), that title to some but not all assets of the protected person vest in the conservator, ..." has been added to the last sentence to make it explicit and clearer that there can be a conservatorship limited both in terms of powers of the conservator and as to the property to which it applies.

Section 5-426. [Preservation of Estate Plan; Right to Examine.]

In (i) investing the estate, (ii) selecting assets of the estate for distribution under subsections (a) and (b) of Section 5-424, and (iii) utilizing powers of revocation or withdrawal available for the support of the protected person and exercisable by the conservator or the Court, the conservator and the Court shall take into account any estate plan of the protected person known to them, including a will, any revocable trust of which the person is settlor, and any contract, transfer, or joint ownership arrangement originated by the protected person with provisions for payment or transfer of benefits or interests at the person's death to another or others. The conservator may examine the will of the protected person.

COMMENT

The source of this section is 1969 UPC § 5-427 with some minor stylistic changes.

Section 5-427. [Claims Against Protected Person; Enforcement.]

(a) A conservator may pay or secure from the estate claims against the estate or against the protected person arising before or after the conservatorship upon their presentation and allowance in accordance with the priorities stated in subsection (c). A claim may be presented by either of the following methods:

(1) The claimant may deliver or mail to the conservator a written statement of the claim indicating its basis, the name and mailing address of the claimant, and the amount claimed; or

(2) The claimant may file a written statement of the claim, in the form prescribed by rule, with the clerk of Court and deliver or mail a copy of the statement to the conservator.

(b) A claim is deemed presented on the first to occur of receipt of the written statement of claim by the conservator or the filing of the claim with the Court. A presented claim is allowed if it is not disallowed by written statement mailed by the conservator to the claimant within 60 days after its presentation. The presentation of a claim tolls any statute of limitation relating to the claim until 30 days after its disallowance.

(c) A claimant whose claim has not been paid may petition the [appropriate] Court for determination of the claim at any time before it is barred by the applicable statute of limitation and, upon due proof, procure an order for its allowance, payment, or security from the estate. If a proceeding is pending against a protected person at the time of appointment of a conservator or is initiated against the protected person thereafter, the moving party shall give notice of the proceeding to the conservator if the proceeding could result in creating a claim against the estate.

(d) If it appears that the estate in conservatorship is likely to be exhausted before all existing claims are paid, the conservator shall distribute the estate in money or in kind in payment of claims in the following order:

(1) costs and expenses of administration;

(2) claims of the federal or state government having priority under other laws;

(3) claims incurred by the conservator for care, maintenance, and education, previously provided to the protected person or the protected person's dependents;

(4) claims arising prior to the conservatorship;

(5) all other claims.

(e) No preference may be given in the payment of any claim over any other claim of the same class, and a claim due and payable is not entitled to a preference over claims not due; but if it appears that the assets of the conservatorship are adequate to meet all existing claims, the Court, acting in the best interest of the protected person, may order the conservator to give a mortgage or other security on the conservatorship estate to secure payment at some future date of any or all claims in class 5.

COMMENT

The source of subsections (a) and (b) is 1969 UPC § 5–428(a) and (b) with the addition of a provision in subsection (a) recognizing that a priority for claims is established in subsection (c).

The sources of subsection (c) are 1969 UPC §§ 3–805 and 5–428(c) generally. Since the priorities established in UPC § 3–805 apply to decedents' estates, the priorities established here for conservatorships are different. The establishment of preferences by categories of claims for conservatorships is new in this Article.

Section 5–428. [Personal Liability of Conservator.]

(a) Unless otherwise provided in the contract, a conservator is not personally liable on a contract properly entered into in fiduciary capacity in the course of administration of the estate unless the conservator fails to reveal the representative capacity and identify the estate in the contract.

(b) The conservator is personally liable for obligations arising from ownership or control of property of the estate or for torts committed in the course of administration of the estate only if personally at fault.

(c) Claims based on (i) contracts entered into by a conservator in fiduciary capacity, (ii) obligations arising from ownership or control of the estate, or (iii) torts committed in the course of administration of the estate, may be asserted against the estate by proceeding against the conservator in fiduciary capacity, whether or not the conservator is personally liable therefor.

(d) Any question of liability between the estate and the conservator personally may be determined in a proceeding for accounting, surcharge, or indemnification, or other appropriate proceeding or action.

COMMENT

The source of this section is 1969 UPC § 5–429 with some stylistic changes. There is not any change in substance.

Section 5–429. [Termination of Proceedings.]

The protected person, conservator, or any other interested person, may petition the Court to terminate the conservatorship. A protected person seeking termination is entitled to the same rights and procedures as in an original proceeding for a protective order. The Court, upon determining after notice and hearing that the minority or disability of the protected person has ceased, shall terminate the conservatorship. Upon termination, title to assets of the estate passes to the formerly protected person or to successors. The order of termination must provide for expenses of administration and direct the conservator to execute appropriate instruments to evidence the transfer.

COMMENT

Persons entitled to notice of a petition to terminate a conservatorship are identified by § 5–405.

Any interested person may seek the termination of a conservatorship if there is some question as to whether the trust is still needed. In some situations (e.g., the individual who returns after being missing) it may be perfectly clear that the person is no longer in need of a conservatorship.

An order terminating a conservatorship may be recorded as evidence of the transfer of title from the estate. See § 5–420.

The source of this section is 1969 UPC § 5–430 with some stylistic changes. The "personal representative" of the protected person has been deleted from specific enumeration in the first sentence because the "personal representative" also is covered by the term "other interested person".

Section 5–430. [Payment of Debt and Delivery of Property to Foreign Conservator without Local Proceedings.]

(a) Any person indebted to a protected person or having possession of property or of an instrument evidencing a debt, stock, or chose in action belonging to a protected person may pay or deliver it to a conservator, guardian of the estate, or other like fiduciary appointed by a court of the state of residence of the protected person upon being presented with proof of appointment and an affidavit made by or on behalf of the fiduciary stating:

(1) that no protective proceeding relating to the protected person is pending in this State; and

(2) that the foreign fiduciary is entitled to payment or to receive delivery.

(b) If the person to whom the affidavit is presented is not aware of any protective proceeding pending in this State, payment or delivery in response to the demand and affidavit discharges the debtor or possessor.

COMMENT

Section 5–409(a)(1) gives a foreign conservator or guardian of property, appointed in the jurisdiction in which the disabled person resides, first priority for appointment as conservator in this State. A

foreign conservator may easily obtain any property in this State and
take it to the residence of the protected person for management.

The source of this section is 1969
UPC § 5–431.

Section 5–431. [Foreign Conservator; Proof of Authority; Bond; Powers.]

If a conservator has not been appointed in this State and no petition in a protective proceeding is pending in this State, a conservator appointed in the state in which the protected person resides may file in a Court of this State in a [county] in which property belonging to the protected person is located, authenticated copies of letters of appointment and of any bond. Thereafter, the domiciliary foreign conservator may exercise as to assets in this State all powers of a conservator appointed in this State and may maintain actions and proceedings in this State subject to any conditions imposed upon non-resident parties generally.

COMMENT

The source of this section is 1969 UPC § 5–432 with some stylistic changes.

PART 5

DURABLE POWER OF ATTORNEY

Adoption of Uniform Durable Power of Attorney Act

Part 5 of Article V of the Uniform Probate Code was amended by the National Conference of Commissioners on Uniform State Laws in 1979. Sections 5–501 to 5–505, as enacted in 1979, are identical to sections 1 to 5 of the Uniform Durable Power of Attorney Act, also approved by the National Conference in 1979 as an alternative to Part 5 of Article V of the Uniform Probate Code. See Prefatory Note, infra.

The Board that acted for the National Conference of Commissioners on Uniform State Laws in preparing the Uniform Durable Power of Attorney Act was as follows:

JOINT EDITORIAL BOARD
FOR UNIFORM PROBATE CODE

Conference Representatives:

Charles Horowitz, Supreme Court, Temple of Justice, Olympia, WA 98504, *Co–Chairman*

Clarke A. Gravel, 109 South Winooski Avenue, Burlington, VT 05401

Robert A. Lucas, Suite 606, 1000 East 80th Place, Merrillville, IN 46410

Eugene F. Scoles, University of Oregon, School of Law, Eugene, OR 97403

Allan D. Vestal, University of Iowa, College of Law, Iowa City, IA 52242

Richard V. Wellman, University of Georgia, School of Law, Athens, GA 30602, *Reporter*

William E. Hogan, Cornell Law School, Ithaca, NY 14853, *Chairman, Division A, Ex Officio*

George C. Keely, 1600 Colorado National Building, 950 Seventeenth Street, Denver, CO 80202, *President, Ex Officio*

John C. Deacon, P.O. Box 1245, Jonesboro, AR 72401, *Chairman, Executive Committee, Ex Officio*

William J. Pierce, University of Michigan, School of Law, Ann Arbor, MI 48109, *Executive Director, Ex Officio*

American Bar Association Representatives:

J. Pennington Straus, 1719 Packard Building, Philadelphia, PA 19102, *Co–Chairman*

Peter J. Brennan, 111 West Monroe Street, Chicago, IL 60603

Harrison F. Durand, 250 Park Avenue, New York, NY 10017

J. Thomas Eubank, 3000 One Shell Plaza, Houston, TX 77002

Malcolm A. Moore, 4200 Seattle First National Bank Building, Seattle, WA 98154

PREFATORY NOTE

The National Conference included Sections 5–501 and 5–502 in Uniform Probate Code (1969) (1975) concerning powers of attorney to assist persons interested in establishing non-court regimes for the management of their affairs in the event of later incompetency or disability. The purpose was to recognize a form of senility insurance comparable to that available to relatively wealthy persons who use funded, revocable trusts for persons who are unwilling or unable to transfer assets as required to establish a trust.

The provisions included in the original UPC modify two principles that have controlled written powers of attorney. Section 5–501 (UPC (1969) (1975)), creating what has come to be known as a "durable power of attorney," permits a principal to create an agency in another that continues in spite of the principal's later loss of capacity to contract. The only requirement is that an instrument creating a durable power contain language showing that the principal intends the agency to remain effective in spite of his later incompetency.

Section 5–502 (UPC (1969) (1975)) alters the common law rule that a principal's death ends the authority of his agents and voids all acts occurring thereafter including any done in complete ignorance of the death. The new view, applicable to durable and nondurable, written powers of attorney, validates post-mortem exercise of authority by agents who act in good faith and without actual knowledge of the principal's death. The idea here was to encourage use of powers of attorney by removing a potential trap for agents in fact and third persons who decide to rely on a power at a time when they cannot be certain that the principal is then alive.

To the knowledge of the Joint Editorial Board for the Uniform Probate Code, the only statutes resembling the power of attorney sections of the UPC (1969) (1975) that had been enacted prior to the approval and promulgation of the Code were Sections 11–9.1 and 11–9.2 of Code of Virginia [1950]. Since then, a variety of UPC inspired statutes adjusting agency rules have been enacted in more than thirty states.

This [Act] [Section] originated in 1977 with a suggestion from within the National Conference that a new free-standing uniform act, designed to make powers of attorney more useful, would be welcome in many states. For states that have yet to adopt durable power legislation, this new National Conference product represents a respected, collective judgment, identifying the best of the ideas reflected in the recent flurry of new state laws on the subject; additional enactments of a new and improved uniform act should result. For other states that have acted already, this new act offers a reason to consider amendments, including elimination of restrictions that no longer appear necessary.

In the course of preparing this [Act] [Section], the Joint Editorial Board for the Uniform Probate Code, acting as a Special Committee on the new project, evolved what it considers to be improvements in §§ 5–501 and 5–502 of the 1969 and 1975 versions of the Code. In the main, the changes reflect stylistic matters. However, the idea reflected in Section 3(a)—that draftsmen of powers of attorney may wish to anticipate the appointment of a conservator or guardian for the principal—is new, and a brief explanation is in order.

When the Code was originally drafted, the dominant idea was that durable powers would be used as *alternatives* to court-oriented, protective procedures. Hence, the draftsmen merely provided that appointment of a conservator for a principal who had granted a durable power to another did not automatically revoke the agency; rather, it would be up to the court's appointee to determine whether revocation was appropriate. The provision was designed to discourage the institution of court proceedings by persons interested solely in ending an agent's authority. It later appeared sensible to adjust the durable power concept so that it may be used either as an alternative to a protective procedure, or as a designed supplement enabling nomination of the principal's choice for guardian to an appointing court and continuing to authorize efficient estate management under the direction of a court appointee.

The sponsoring committee considered and rejected the suggestion that the word "durable" be omitted from the title. While it is true that the act describes "durable" and "non-durable" powers of attorney, this is merely the result of use of language to accomplish a purpose of making both categories of power more reliable for use than formerly. In the case of non-durable powers, the act extends validity by the provisions in Section [4] [5–504] protecting agents in fact and third persons who rely in good faith on a power of attorney when, unknown to them, the principal is incompetent or deceased. The general purpose of the act is to alter common law rules that created traps for the unwary by voiding powers on the principal's incompetency or death. The act does not purport to deal with other aspects of powers of attorney, and a label that would result from dropping "durable" would be misleading to the extent that it suggested otherwise.

Section 5–501. [Definition.]

A durable power of attorney is a power of attorney by which a principal designates another his attorney in fact in writing and the writing contains the words "This power of attorney shall not be affected by subsequent disability or incapacity of the principal, or lapse of time," or "This power of attorney shall become effective upon the disability or incapacity of the principal," or similar words showing the intent of the principal that the authority conferred shall be exercisable notwithstanding the principal's subsequent disability or incapacity, and, unless it states a time of termination, notwithstanding the lapse of time since the execution of the instrument.

As amended in 1984.

For changes made by the 1984 amendment, see Appendix II, infra.

COMMENT

This section, derived from the first sentence of UPC 5–501 (1969) (1975), is a definitional section that supports use of the term "durable power of attorney" in the sections that follow. The second quoted expression was designed to emphasize that a durable power with postponed effectiveness is permitted. Some UPC critics have been bothered by the reference here to a later condition of "disability or incapacity," a circumstance that may be difficult to ascertain *if* it can be established without a court order. The answer, of course, is that draftsmen of durable powers are not limited in their choice of words to describe the later time when the principal wishes the authority of the agent in fact to become operative. For example, a durable power might be framed to confer authority commencing when two or more named persons, possibly including the principal's lawyer, physician or spouse, concur that the principal has become incapable of managing his affairs in a sensible and efficient manner and deliver a signed statement to that effect to the attorney in fact.

In this and following sections, it is assumed that the principal is competent when the power of attorney is signed. If this is not the case, nothing in this Act is intended to alter the result that would be reached under general principles of law.

Section 5–502. [Durable Power of Attorney Not Affected By Lapse of Time, Disability or Incapacity.]

All acts done by an attorney in fact pursuant to a durable power of attorney during any period of disability or incapacity of the principal have the same effect and inure to the benefit of and bind the principal and his successors in interest as if the principal were competent and not disabled. Unless the instrument states a time of termination, the power is exercisable notwithstanding the lapse of time since the execution of the instrument.

As amended in 1987.

For material relating to the 1987 amendment, see Appendix I, infra.

COMMENT

This section is derived from the second sentence of UPC 5–501 (1969) (1975) modified by deleting reference to the effect on a durable power of the principal's death, a matter that is now covered in Section [4] [5–504] which provides a single standard for durable and non-durable powers.

The words "any period of disability or incapacity of the principal" are intended to include periods during which the principal is legally incompetent, but are not intended to be limited to such periods. In the Uniform Probate Code, the word "disability" is defined, and the term "in-capacitated person" is defined. In the context of this section, however, the important point is that the terms embrace "legal incompetence," as well as less grievous disadvantages.

Section 5–503. [Relation of Attorney in Fact to Court-appointed Fiduciary.]

(a) If, following execution of a durable power of attorney, a court of the principal's domicile appoints a conservator, guardian of the estate, or other fiduciary charged with the management of all of the principal's property or all of his property except specified exclusions, the attorney in fact is accountable to the fiduciary as well as to the principal. The fiduciary has the same power to revoke or amend the power of attorney that the principal would have had if he were not disabled or incapacitated.

(b) A principal may nominate, by a durable power of attorney, the conservator, guardian of his estate, or guardian of his person for consideration by the court if protective proceedings for the principal's person or estate are thereafter commenced. The court shall make its appointment in accordance with the principal's most recent nomination in a durable power of attorney except for good cause or disqualification.

COMMENT

Subsection (a) closely resembles the last two sentences of UPC § 5–501 (1969) (1975); most of the changes are stylistic. One change going beyond style states that an agent in fact is accountable *both* to the principal and a conservator or guardian if a court has appointed a fiduciary; the earlier version described accountability only to the fiduciary.

As explained in the introductory comment, the purpose of subsection (b) is to emphasize that agencies under durable powers and guardians or conservators may co-exist. It is not the purpose of the act to encourage resort to court for a fiduciary appointment that should be largely unnecessary when an alternative regime has been provided via a durable power. Indeed, the best reason for permitting a principal to use a durable power to express his preference regarding any future court appointee charged with the care and protection of his person or estate may be to secure the authority of the attorney in fact against upset by arranging matters so that the likely appointee in any future protective proceedings will be the attorney in fact or another equally congenial to the principal and his plans. However, the evolution of a free-standing durable power act increases the prospects that UPC-type statutes covering protective proceedings will not apply when a protective proceeding is commenced for one who has created a durable power. This means that a court receiving a petition for a guardian or conservator may not be governed by

431

standards like those in UPC § 5–304 (personal guardians) and § 5–401(2) and related sections which are designed to deter unnecessary protective proceedings. Finally, attorneys and others may find various good uses for a regime in which a conservator directs exercise of an agent's authority under a durable power. For example, the combination would confer jurisdiction on the court handling the protective proceeding to approve or ratify a desirable transaction that might not be possible without the protection of a court order. The alternative of a declaratory judgment proceeding might be difficult or impossible in some states.

It is to be noted that the "fiduciary" described in subsection (a), to whom an attorney in fact under a durable power is accountable and who may revoke or amend the durable power, does not include a guardian of the person only. In subsection (b), however, the authority of a principal to nominate extends to a guardian of the person as well as to conservators and guardians of estates.

Discussion of this section in NCCUSL's Committee of the Whole involved the question of whether an agent's accountability, as described here, might be effectively countermanded by appropriate language in a power of attorney. The response was negative. The reference is to basic accountability like that owed by every fiduciary to his beneficiary and that distinguishes a fiduciary relationship from those involving gifts or general powers of appointment. The section is not intended to describe a particular form of accounting. Hence, the context differs from those involving statutory duties to account in court, or with specified frequency, where draftsmen of controlling instruments may be able to excuse statutory details relating to accountings without affecting the general principle of accountability.

Section 5–504. [Power of Attorney Not Revoked Until Notice.]

(a) The death of a principal who has executed a written power of attorney, durable or otherwise, does not revoke or terminate the agency as to the attorney in fact or other person, who, without actual knowledge of the death of the principal, acts in good faith under the power. Any action so taken, unless otherwise invalid or unenforceable, binds successors in interest of the principal.

(b) The disability or incapacity of a principal who has previously executed a written power of attorney that is not a durable power does not revoke or terminate the agency as to the attorney in fact or other person, who, without actual knowledge of the disability or incapacity of the principal, acts in good faith under the power. Any action so taken, unless otherwise invalid or unenforceable, binds the principal and his successors in interest.

COMMENT

UPC §§ 5–501 and 5–502 (1969) (1975) are flawed by different standards for durable and nondurable powers *vis a vis* the protection of an attorney in fact who purports to exercise a power after the principal has died. Section 5–501 (1969) (1975), applicable only to durable powers, expresses a most unsatisfactory standard; i.e. the attorney in fact is protected if the exercise occurs "during any period of uncertainty as to whether the principal is dead or alive ...." Section 5–502 (1969) (1975), applicable only to non-durable powers, protects the agent who "without actual knowledge of the death ... of the principal, acts in good faith under the power of attorney...." Section [4] [5–504](a) expresses as a single test the standard now contained in § 5–502 (1969) (1975).

Subsection (b), applicable only to nondurable powers that are controlled by the traditional view that a principal's loss of capacity ends the authority of his agents, embodies the substance of UPC § 5–502 (1969) (1975).

The discussion in the Committee of the Whole established that the language "or other person" in subsections (a) and (b) is intended to refer to persons who transact business with the attorney in fact under the authority conferred by the power. Consequently, persons in this category who act in good faith and without the actual knowledge described in the subsections are protected by the statute.

Also, there was discussion of possible conflict between the actual knowledge test here prescribed for protection of persons relying on the continuance of a power and constructive notice concepts under statutes governing the recording of instruments affecting real estate. The view was expressed in the Committee of the Whole that the recording statutes would continue to control since those statutes are specifically designed to encourage public recording of documents affecting land titles. It was also suggested that "good faith," as required by this section, might be lacking in the unlikely case of one who, without actual knowledge of the principal's death or incompetency, accepted a conveyance executed by an attorney in fact without checking the public record where he would have found an instrument disclosing the principal's death or incompetency. If so, there would be no conflict between this act and recording statutes.

It is to be noted, also, that this section deals only with the effect of a principal's death or incompetency as a revocation of a power of attorney; it does not relate to an express revocation of a power or to the expiration of a power according to its terms. Further, since a durable power is not revoked by incapacity, the section's coverage of revocation of powers of attorney by the principal's incapacity is restricted to powers that are not durable. The only effect of the Act on rules governing express revocations of powers of attorney is as described in Section [5] [5–505].

Section 5–505. [Proof of Continuance of Durable and Other Powers of Attorney by Affidavit.]

As to acts undertaken in good faith reliance thereon, an affidavit executed by the attorney in fact under a power of attorney, durable or otherwise, stating that he did not have at the time of exercise of the power actual knowledge of the termination of the power by revocation or of the principal's death, disability, or incapacity is

433

conclusive proof of the nonrevocation or nontermination of the power at that time. If the exercise of the power of attorney requires execution and delivery of any instrument that is recordable, the affidavit when authenticated for record is likewise recordable. This section does not affect any provision in a power of attorney for its termination by expiration of time or occurrence of an event other than express revocation or a change in the principal's capacity.

COMMENT

This section, embodying the substance and form of UPC 5–502(b) (1969) (1975), has been extended to apply to durable powers. It is unclear whether UPC 5–502(b) (1969) (1975) applies to durable powers. Affidavits protecting persons dealing with attorneys in fact extend the utility of powers of attorney and plainly should be available for use by all attorneys in fact.

The matters stated in an affidavit that are strengthened by this section are limited to the revocation of a power by the principal's voluntary act, his death, or, in the case of non-durable power, by his incompetence. With one possible exception, other matters, including circumstances made relevant by the terms of the instrument to the commencement of the agency or to its termination by other circumstances, are not covered. The exception concerns the case of a power created to begin on "incapacity." The affidavit of the agent in fact that all conditions necessary to the valid exercise of the power might be aided by the statute in relation to the fact of incapacity. An affidavit as to the existence or nonexistence of facts and circumstances not covered by this section nonetheless may be useful in establishing good faith reliance.

ARTICLE VI

NONPROBATE TRANSFERS ON DEATH (1989)

PART 1

PROVISIONS RELATING TO EFFECT OF DEATH

PART 2

MULTIPLE–PERSON ACCOUNTS

SUBPART 1

DEFINITIONS AND GENERAL PROVISIONS

SUBPART 2

OWNERSHIP AS BETWEEN PARTIES AND OTHERS

SUBPART 3

PROTECTION OF FINANCIAL INSTITUTIONS

PART 3

UNIFORM TOD SECURITY REGISTRATION ACT

Historical Note

A Revised Article VI of the Uniform Probate Code [Nonprobate Transfers on Death (1989)], was approved by the National Conference of Commissioners on Uniform State Laws in 1989.

See text of prior Article VI in Appendix V, infra.

Adoption of Uniform Multiple–Person Accounts Act and Uniform TOD Security Registration Act

Note that Parts 2 and 3 of Revised Article 6 have also been adopted as the free-standing Uniform Multiple–Person Accounts Act and Uniform TOD Security Registration Act, respectively.

The Committee that acted for the National Conference of Commissioners on Uniform State Laws in preparing the Uniform Probate Code Article VI—Nonprobate Transfers on Death—(1989) was as follows:

WILLIAM S. ARNOLD, P.O. Drawer A, Crossett, AR 71635, *Chairman*

JOHN H. DeMOULLY, Law Revision Commission, Suite D–2, 4000 Middlefield Road, Palo Alto, CA 94303, *Drafting Liaison*

CLARKE A. GRAVEL, P.O. Box 1049, 76 St. Paul Street, Burlington, VT 05402

MAURICE A. HARTNETT, III, Chambers, Court of Chancery, 45 The Green, Dover, DE 19901

WILLIAM E. KRETSCHMAR, P.O. Box 36, 211 West Main Street, Ashley, ND 58413

JOHN H. LANGBEIN, University of Chicago Law School, 1111 East 60th Street, Chicago, IL 60637

GODFREY L. MUNTER, Suite 400, 4801 Massachusetts Avenue, N.W., Washington, DC 20016

WILLIS E. SULLIVAN, III, P.O. Box 359, Boise, ID 83701

RICHARD V. WELLMAN, University of Georgia, School of Law, Athens, GA 30602

Review Committee

PREFATORY NOTE

This amendment of Uniform Probate Code Article VI (nonprobate transfers) replaces former Article VI with a revised article. Part 1 (provisions relating to effect of death) of the revised article is amended and relocated from former Part 2. Part 2 (multiple-person accounts) of the revised article is amended and relocated from former Part 1. Part 3 (Uniform TOD Security Registration Act) of the revised article is new. This reorganization allows for general provisions at the beginning of the article, and permits parts to be divided into subparts that group related provisions together.

Multiple-Person Accounts

The amendment of Part 2 (multiple-person accounts) of the revised article simplifies drafting and terminology. It consolidates treatment of POD accounts and trust accounts so that the same rules apply to both, since both types of account operate identically and serve the same function of passing property to a beneficiary at the death of the account owner. The amendment likewise eliminates references to "joint" accounts, since the statute treats joint tenancy accounts and tenancy in common accounts the same for all purposes other than survivorship. Other terminological and drafting simplifications and standardizations are made throughout the statute. Treatment of existing accounts is included.

The amendment makes a few substantive changes in rules previously established in the multiple-person account statute. The changes include recognition of checks issued by an account owner before death and presented for payment after death, revision of the creditor rights procedure to enable a survivor or beneficiary to spread the burden among survivors and beneficiaries of other accounts of the decedent and to provide a uniform one-year limitation period for creditors, and a provision that a financial institution must have received notice at the appropriate office and have had a reasonable time to act before it is charged with knowledge that any change in account circumstances has occurred. A provision is also added that on the death of a married person, beneficial ownership of the decedent's share in a survivorship account passes to the surviving spouse who is an account party in preference to other surviving account parties.

The amendment includes a number of important improvements designed to make multiple-person accounts more useful. An agency designation is authorized to enable an account owner to add another person to the account as a convenience in making withdrawals without creating any ownership or survivorship interest in the person identified as an agent. Optional statutory forms for multiple-person accounts are provided for the convenience and protection of financial institutions. Payment to a minor who is an account beneficiary is authorized pursuant to the Uniform Transfers to Minors Act. A provision is added to make clear that marital funds deposited in an account retain any community property incidents, and the law governing tenancy by the entireties is preserved where applicable.

The drafting committee believes that this amendment of the multiple-person account statute is a substantial improvement in an already successful law. This part of the Uniform Probate Code is one of the most broadly accepted, having been adopted either as part of the code or independently by over half the states. This amendment draws on useful improvements made by various states that have enacted the statute, and should make the statute even more attractive.

Uniform TOD Security Registration Act

The purpose of Part 3 (Uniform TOD Security Registration Act) of the revised article is to allow the owner of securities to register the title in transfer-on-death (TOD) form. Mutual fund shares and accounts maintained by brokers and others to reflect a customer's holdings of securities (so-called "street accounts") are also covered. The legislation enables an issuer, transfer agent, broker, or other such intermediary to transfer the securities directly to the designated transferee on the owner's death. Thus, TOD registration achieves for securities a certain parity with existing TOD and pay-on-death (POD) facilities for bank deposits and other assets passing at death outside the probate process.

The TOD registration under this part is designed to give the owner of securities who wishes to arrange for a nonprobate transfer at death an alternative to the frequently troublesome joint tenancy form of title. Because joint tenancy registration of securities normally entails a sharing of lifetime entitlement and control, it works satisfactorily only so long as the co-owners cooperate. Difficulties arise when co-owners fall into disagreement, or when one becomes afflicted or insolvent.

Use of the TOD registration form encouraged by this legislation has no effect on the registered owner's full control of the affected security during his or her lifetime. A TOD designation and any beneficiary interest arising under the designation ends whenever the registered asset is transferred, or whenever the owner otherwise complies with the issuer's conditions for changing the title form of the investment. The part recognizes, in Section 6–302, that co-owners with right of survivorship may be registered as owners together with a TOD beneficiary designated to take if the registration remains unchanged until the beneficiary survives the joint owners. In such a case, the survivor of the joint owners has full control of the asset and may change the registration form as he or she sees fit after the other's death.

Implementation of the part is wholly optional with issuers. The drafting committee received the benefit of considerable advice and assistance from representatives of the mutual fund and stock transfer industries during the course of its three years of preparatory work. Accordingly, it is believed that this part takes full account of the practical requirements for efficient transfer within the securities industry.

Section 6–303 invites application of the legislation to locally owned securities though the statute may not have been locally enacted, so long as the part or similar legislation is in force in a jurisdiction of the issuer or transfer agent. Thus, if the principal jurisdictions in which securities issuers and transfer agents are sited enact the measure, its benefits will become generally available to persons domiciled in states that do not at once enact the statute.

The legislation has been drafted as a separate part, hence not interpolated as an expansion of the former UPC Article VI, Part 1, treating bank accounts ("multiple-party accounts"). Securities merit a distinct statutory regime, because a different principle has governed concurrent ownership of securities. By virtue either of statute or of account terms (contract), multiple-party bank accounts allow any one cotenant to consume or transfer account balances. See R. Brown, The Law of Personal Property § 65, at 217 (2d ed. 1955); Langbein, The Nonprobate Revolution and the Future of the Law of Succession, 97 Harv.L.Rev. 1108, 1112 (1984). The rule for securities, however, has been the rule that applies to real property: all cotenants must act together in transferring the securities. This difference in the legal regime reflects differences in function among the types of assets. Multiple-party bank accounts typically arise as convenience accounts, to facilitate frequent small transactions, often on an agency basis (as when spouses or relatives share an account). Securities resemble real estate in that the values are typically large and the transactions relatively infrequent, which is why the legal regime requires the concurrence of all concurrent owners for transfers affecting such assets.

Recently, of course, this distinction between bank accounts and securities has begun to crumble. Banks are offering certificates of deposit of large value under the same account forms that were devised for low-value convenience accounts. Meanwhile, broker-age houses with their so-called cash management accounts and mutual funds with their money market accounts have rendered securities subject to small recurrent transactions. In the latest developments, even the line between real estate and bank accounts is becoming indistinct, as the "home equity line of credit" creates a check-writing conduit to real estate values.

Nevertheless, even though new forms of contract have rendered the boundaries between securities and bank accounts less firm, the distinction seems intuitively correct for statutory default rules. True co-owners of securities, like owners of realty, should act together in transferring the asset.

The joint bank account and the Totten trust originated in ambig-uous lifetime ownership forms, which required former UPC § 6–103 or comparable state legislation to clarity that an inter vivos transfer was not intended. In the securities field, by con-trast, we start with unambiguous lifetime ownership rules. The sole purpose of the present statute is to facilitate a nonprobate TOD mechanism as an option for those owners.

For a comprehensive discussion of the issues entailed in this legislation, see Wellman, Transfer-on-Death Securities Registration: A New Title Form, 21 Ga.L.Rev. 709 (1987).

PART 1

PROVISIONS RELATING TO EFFECT OF DEATH

§ 6–101. Nonprobate Transfers on Death.

(a) A provision for a nonprobate transfer on death in an insurance policy, contract of employment, bond, mortgage, promissory note, certificated or uncertificated security, account agreement, custodial agreement, deposit agreement, compensation plan, pension plan, individual retirement plan, employee benefit plan, trust, conveyance, deed of gift, marital property agreement, or other written instrument of a similar nature is nontestamentary. This subsection includes a written provision that:

(1) money or other benefits due to, controlled by, or owned by a decedent before death must be paid after the decedent's death to a person whom the decedent designates either in the instrument or in a separate writing, including a will, executed either before or at the same time as the instrument, or later;

(2) money due or to become due under the instrument ceases to be payable in the event of death of the promisee or the promisor before payment or demand; or

(3) any property controlled by or owned by the decedent before death which is the subject of the instrument passes to a person the decedent designates either in the instrument or in a separate writing, including a will, executed either before or at the same time as the instrument, or later.

(b) This section does not limit rights of creditors under other laws of this State.

COMMENT

This section is a revised version of former Section 6–201 of the original Uniform Probate Code, which authorized a variety of contractual arrangements that had sometimes been treated as testamentary in prior law. For example, most courts treated as testamentary a provision in a promissory note that if the payee died before making payment, the note should be paid to another named person; or a provision in a land contract that if the seller died before completing payment, the bal- ance should be canceled and the property should belong to the vendee. These provisions often occurred in family arrangements. The result of holding such provisions testamentary was usually to invalidate them because not executed in accordance with the statute of wills. On the other hand, the same courts for years upheld beneficiary designations in life insurance contracts. The drafters of the original Uniform Probate Code declared in the Comment that they were un-

441

able to identify policy reasons for continuing to treat these varied arrangements as testamentary. The drafters said that the benign experience with such familiar will substitutes as the revocable inter vivos trust, the multiple-party bank account, and United States government bonds payable on death to named beneficiaries all demonstrated that the evils envisioned if the statute of wills were not rigidly enforced simply do not materialize. The Comment also observed that because these provisions often are part of a business transaction and are evidenced by a writing, the danger of fraud is largely eliminated.

Because the modes of transfer authorized by an instrument under this section are declared to be nontestamentary, the instrument does not have to be executed in compliance with the formalities for wills prescribed under Section 2–502; nor does the instrument have to be probated, nor does the personal representative have any power or duty with respect to the assets.

The sole purpose of this section is to prevent the transfers authorized here from being treated as testamentary. This section does not invalidate other arrangements by negative implication. Thus, this section does not speak to the phenomenon of the oral trust to hold property at death for named persons, an arrangement already generally enforceable under trust law.

The reference to a "marital property agreement" in the introductory portion of subsection (a) of Section 6–101 includes an agreement made during marriage as well as a premarital contract.

The term "or other written instrument of a similar nature" in the introductory portion of subsection (a) replaces the former language "or any other written instrument effective as a contract, gift, conveyance or trust" in the original Section 6–201. The Supreme Court of Washington read that language to relieve against the delivery requirement of the law of deeds, a result that was not intended. *Estate of O'Brien v. Woodhouse,* 109 Wash.2d 913, 749 P.2d 154 (1988). The point was correctly decided in *First National Bank in Minot v. Bloom,* 264 N.W.2d 208, 212 (N.D.1978), in which the Supreme Court of North Dakota held that "nothing in [former Section 6–201] of the Uniform Probate Code . . . eliminates the necessity of delivery of a deed to effectuate a conveyance from one living person to another."

PART 2

MULTIPLE–PERSON ACCOUNTS

SUBPART 1

DEFINITIONS AND GENERAL PROVISIONS

§ 6–201. Definitions.

In this part:

(1) "Account" means a contract of deposit between a depositor and a financial institution, and includes a checking account, savings account, certificate of deposit, and share account.

(2) "Agent" means a person authorized to make account transactions for a party.

(3) "Beneficiary" means a person named as one to whom sums on deposit in an account are payable on request after death of all parties or for whom a party is named as trustee.

(4) "Financial institution" means an organization authorized to do business under state or federal laws relating to financial institutions, and includes a bank, trust company, savings bank, building and loan association, savings and loan company or association, and credit union.

(5) "Multiple-party account" means an account payable on request to one or more of two or more parties, whether or not a right of survivorship is mentioned.

(6) "Party" means a person who, by the terms of an account, has a present right, subject to request, to payment from the account other than as a beneficiary or agent.

(7) "Payment" of sums on deposit includes withdrawal, payment to a party or third person pursuant to check or other request, and a pledge of sums on deposit by a party, or a set-off, reduction, or other disposition of all or part of an account pursuant to a pledge.

(8) "POD designation" means the designation of (i) a beneficiary in an account payable on request to one party during the party's lifetime and on the party's death to one or more beneficiaries, or to one or more parties during their lifetimes and on death of all of them to one or more beneficiaries, or (ii) a beneficiary in an account in the name of one or more parties as trustee for one or more beneficiaries if the relationship is estab-

443

lished by the terms of the account and there is no subject of the trust other than the sums on deposit in the account, whether or not payment to the beneficiary is mentioned.

(9) "Receive," as it relates to notice to a financial institution, means receipt in the office or branch office of the financial institution in which the account is established, but if the terms of the account require notice at a particular place, in the place required.

(10) "Request" means a request for payment complying with all terms of the account, including special requirements concerning necessary signatures and regulations of the financial institution; but, for purposes of this part, if terms of the account condition payment on advance notice, a request for payment is treated as immediately effective and a notice of intent to withdraw is treated as a request for payment.

(11) "Sums on deposit" means the balance payable on an account, including interest and dividends earned, whether or not included in the current balance, and any deposit life insurance proceeds added to the account by reason of death of a party.

(12) "Terms of the account" includes the deposit agreement and other terms and conditions, including the form, of the contract of deposit.

COMMENT

This and the sections that follow are designed to reduce certain questions concerning many forms of multiple-person accounts (including the so-called Totten trust account). A "payable on death" designation and an "agency" designation are also authorized for both single-party and multiple-party accounts. The POD designation is a more direct means of achieving the same purpose as a Totten trust account; this part therefore discourages creation of a Totten trust account and treats existing Totten trust accounts as POD designations.

An agent (paragraph (2)) may not be a party. The agency designation must be signed by all parties, and the agent is the agent of all parties. See Section 6–205 (designation of agent).

A "beneficiary" of a party (paragraph (3)) may be either a POD beneficiary or the beneficiary of a Totten trust; the two types of designations in an account serve the same function and are treated the same under this part. See paragraph (8) ("POD designation" defined). The definition of "beneficiary" refers to a "person," who may be an individual, corporation, organization, or other legal entity. Section 1–201(29). Thus a church, trust company, family corporation, or other entity, as well as any individual, may be designated as a beneficiary.

The term "multiple-party account" (paragraph 5)) is used in this part in a broad sense to include any account having more than one owner with a present interest in the account. Thus an account may be a "multiple-party account" within the meaning of this part regardless of whether the terms of the account refer to it as "joint tenancy" or as "tenancy in common," regardless of whether the parties named are coupled by "or" or "and," and regardless of whether any reference is made to survivorship rights, whether expressly or by abbreviation such as JTWROS or JT TEN. Survivorship rights in a multiple-party account are determined by the terms of the account and by statute, and survivorship is not a necessary incident of a multiple-party account. See Section 6–212 (rights at death).

Under paragraph (6), a "party" is a person with a present right to payment from an account. Therefore, present owners of a multiple-party account are parties, as is the present owner of an account with a POD designation. The beneficiary of an account with a POD designation is not a party, but is entitled to payment only on the death of all parties. The trustee of a Totten trust is a party but the beneficiary is not. An agent with the right of withdrawal on behalf of a party is not itself a party. A person claiming on behalf of a party such as a guardian or conservator, or claiming the interest of a party such as a creditor, is not itself a party, and the right of such a person to payment is governed by general law other than this part.

Various signature requirements may be involved in order to meet the payment requirements of the account. A "request" (paragraph (10)) involves compliance with these requirements. A party is one to whom an account is presently payable without regard to whose signature may be required for a "request."

§ 6–202. Limitation on Scope of Part.

This part does not apply to (i) an account established for a partnership, joint venture, or other organization for a business purpose, (ii) an account controlled by one or more persons as an agent or trustee for a corporation, unincorporated association, or charitable or civic organization, or (iii) a fiduciary or trust account in which the relationship is established other than by the terms of the account.

COMMENT

This part applies to accounts in this State. Section 1–301(4).

The reference to a fiduciary or trust account in item (iii) includes a regular trust account under a testamentary trust or a trust agreement that has significance apart from the account, and a fiduciary account arising from a fiduciary relation such as attorney-client.

§ 6–203. Types of Account; Existing Accounts.

(a) An account may be for a single party or multiple parties. A multiple-party account may be with or without a right of survivorship between the parties. Subject to Section 6–212(c), either a single-party account or a multiple-party account may have a POD designation, an agency designation, or both.

(b) An account established before, on, or after the effective date of this part, whether in the form prescribed in Section 6–204 or in any other form, is either a single-party account or a multiple-party account, with or without right of survivorship, and with or without a POD designation or an agency designation, within the meaning of this part, and is governed by this part.

COMMENT

In the case of an account established before (or after) the effective date of this part that is not in substantially the form provided in Section 6–204, the account is governed by the provisions of this part applicable to the type of account that most nearly conforms to the depositor's intent. See Section 6–204 (forms).

Thus, a tenancy in common account established before or after the effective date of this part would be classified as a "multiple-party account" for purposes of this part. See Section 6–201(5) ("multiple-party account" defined). On death of a party there would not be a right of survivorship since the tenancy in common title would be treated as a multiple-party account without right of survivorship. See Section 6–212(c). It should be noted that a POD designation may not be made in a multiple-party account without right of survivorship. See Sections 6–201(8) ("POD designation" defined), 6–204 (forms), and 6–212 (rights at death).

Under this section, a Totten trust account established before, on, or after the effective date of this part is governed by the provisions of this part applicable to an account with a POD designation. See Section 6–201(8) ("POD designation" defined) and the Comment to Section 6–201.

§ 6–204. Forms.

(a) A contract of deposit that contains provisions in substantially the following form establishes the type of account provided, and the account is governed by the provisions of this part applicable to an account of that type:

UNIFORM SINGLE–OR MULTIPLE–PARTY ACCOUNT FORM

PARTIES [Name One or More Parties]:

_____   _____

OWNERSHIP [Select One And Initial]:
_____SINGLE–PARTY ACCOUNT
_____MULTIPLE–PARTY ACCOUNT
          Parties own account in proportion to net contributions unless there is clear and convincing evidence of a different intent.
RIGHTS AT DEATH [Select One And Initial]:
_____SINGLE–PARTY ACCOUNT
          At death of party, ownership passes as part of party's estate.

_____SINGLE–PARTY ACCOUNT WITH POD (PAY ON DEATH) DESIGNATION
[Name One Or More Beneficiaries]:

_____   _____

At death of party, ownership passes to POD beneficiaries and is not part of party's estate.
_____MULTIPLE–PARTY ACCOUNT WITH RIGHT OF SURVIVORSHIP
At death of party, ownership passes to surviving parties.
_____MULTIPLE–PARTY ACCOUNT WITH RIGHT OF SURVIVORSHIP AND POD (PAY ON DEATH) DESIGNATION
[Name One Or More Beneficiaries]:

_____   _____

At death of last surviving party, ownership passes to POD beneficiaries and is not part of last surviving party's estate.
_____MULTIPLE–PARTY ACCOUNT WITHOUT RIGHT OF SURVIVORSHIP
At death of party, deceased party's ownership passes as part of deceased party's estate.
AGENCY (POWER OF ATTORNEY) DESIGNATION [Optional]
Agents may make account transactions for parties but have no ownership or rights at death unless named as POD beneficiaries.
[To Add Agency Designation To Account, Name One Or More Agents]:

_____   _____

[Select One And Initial]:
_____ AGENCY DESIGNATION SURVIVES DISABILITY OR INCAPACITY OF PARTIES
_____ AGENCY DESIGNATION TERMINATES ON DISABILITY OR INCAPACITY OF PARTIES

(b) A contract of deposit that does not contain provisions in substantially the form provided in subsection (a) is governed by the provisions of this part applicable to the type of account that most nearly conforms to the depositor's intent.

COMMENT

This section provides short forms for single- and multiple-party accounts which, if used, bring the accounts within the terms of this part. A financial institution that uses the statutory form language in its accounts is protected in acting in reliance on the form of the account. See also Section 6–226 (discharge).

The forms provided in this section enable a person establishing a multiple-party account to state expressly in the account whether there are to be survivorship rights between the parties. The account forms permit greater flexibility than traditional account designations. It should be noted that no separate form is provided for a Totten trust account, since the POD designation serves the same function.

An account that is not substantially in the form provided in this section is nonetheless governed by this part. See Section 6–203 (types of account; existing accounts).

§ 6–205. Designation of Agent.

(a) By a writing signed by all parties, the parties may designate as agent of all parties on an account a person other than a party.

(b) Unless the terms of an agency designation provide that the authority of the agent terminates on disability or incapacity of a party, the agent's authority survives disability and incapacity. The agent may act for a disabled or incapacitated party until the authority of the agent is terminated.

(c) Death of the sole party or last surviving party terminates the authority of an agent.

COMMENT

An agent has no beneficial interest in the account. See Section 6–211 (ownership during lifetime). The agency relationship is governed by the general law of agency of the state, except to the extent this part provides express rules, including the rule that the agency survives the disability or incapacity of a party.

A financial institution may make payments at the direction of an agent notwithstanding disability, incapacity, or death of the party, subject to receipt of a stop notice. Section 6–226 (discharge); see also Section 6–224 (payment to designated agent).

The rule of subsection (b) applies to agency designations on all types of accounts, including nonsurvivorship as well as survivorship forms of multiple-party accounts.

§ 6–206. Applicability of Part.

The provisions of Subpart 2 concerning beneficial ownership as between parties or as between parties and beneficiaries apply only to controversies between those persons and their creditors and other successors, and do not apply to the right of those persons to payment as determined by the terms of the account. Subpart 3 governs the liability and set-off rights of financial institutions that make payments pursuant to it.

SUBPART 2

OWNERSHIP AS BETWEEN PARTIES AND OTHERS

§ 6–211. Ownership During Lifetime.

(a) In this section, "net contribution" of a party means the sum of all deposits to an account made by or for the party, less all payments from the account made to or for the party which have not been paid to or applied to the use of another party and a proportionate share of any charges deducted from the account, plus a proportionate share of any interest or dividends earned, whether or not included in the current balance. The term includes deposit life insurance proceeds added to the account by reason of death of the party whose net contribution is in question.

(b) During the lifetime of all parties, an account belongs to the parties in proportion to the net contribution of each to the sums on deposit, unless there is clear and convincing evidence of a different intent. As between parties married to each other, in the absence of proof otherwise, the net contribution of each is presumed to be an equal amount.

(c) A beneficiary in an account having a POD designation has no right to sums on deposit during the lifetime of any party.

(d) An agent in an account with an agency designation has no beneficial right to sums on deposit.

COMMENT

This section reflects the assumption that a person who deposits funds in an account normally does not intend to make an irrevocable gift of all or any part of the funds represented by the deposit. Rather, the person usually intends no present change of beneficial ownership. The section permits parties to accounts to be as definite, or as indefinite, as they wish in respect to the matter of how beneficial ownership should be apportioned between them.

The assumption that no present change of beneficial ownership is intended may be disproved by showing that a gift was intended. For example, under subsection (c) it is presumed that the beneficiary of a POD designation has no present ownership interest during lifetime. However, it is possible that in the case of a POD designation in trust form an irrevocable gift was intended.

It is important to note that the section is limited to ownership of an account while parties are alive.

Section 6–212 prescribes what happens to beneficial ownership on the death of a party.

The section does not undertake to describe the situation between parties if one party withdraws more than that party is then entitled to as against the other party. Sections 6–221 and 6–226 protect a financial institution in that circumstance without reference to whether a withdrawing party may be entitled to less than that party withdraws as against another party. Rights between parties in this situation are governed by general law other than this part.

"Net contribution" as defined by subsection (a) has no application to the financial institution-depositor relationship. Rather, it is relevant only to controversies that may arise between parties to a multiple-party account.

The last sentence of subsection (b) provides a clear rule concerning the amount of "net contribution" in a case where the actual amount cannot be established as between spouses. This part otherwise contains no provision dealing with a failure of proof. The omission is deliberate. The theory of these sections is that the basic relationship of the parties is that of individual ownership of values attributable to their respective deposits and withdrawals, and not equal and undivided ownership that would be an incident of joint tenancy.

In a state that recognizes tenancy by the entireties for personal property, this section would not change the rule that parties who are married to each other own their combined net contributions to an account as tenants by the entireties. See Section 6–216 (community property and tenancy by the entireties).

§ 6–212. Rights at Death.

(a) Except as otherwise provided in this section, on death of a party sums on deposit in a multiple-party account belong to the surviving party or parties. If two or more parties survive and one is the surviving spouse of the decedent, the amount to which the decedent, immediately before death, was beneficially entitled under Section 6–211 belongs to the surviving spouse. If two or more parties survive and none is the surviving spouse of the decedent, the amount to which the decedent, immediately before death, was beneficially entitled under Section 6–211 belongs to the surviving parties in equal shares, and augments the proportion to which each survivor, immediately before the decedent's death, was beneficially entitled under Section 6–211, and the right of survivorship continues between the surviving parties.

(b) In an account with a POD designation:

(1) On death of one of two or more parties, the rights in sums on deposit are governed by subsection (a).

(2) On death of the sole party or the last survivor of two or more parties, sums on deposit belong to the surviving beneficiary or beneficiaries. If two or more beneficiaries survive, sums on deposit belong to them in equal and undivided shares, and there is no right of survivorship in the event of death of a beneficiary thereafter. If no beneficiary survives, sums on deposit belong to the estate of the last surviving party.

(c) Sums on deposit in a single-party account without a POD designation, or in a multiple-party account that, by the terms of the account, is without right of survivorship, are not affected by death of a party, but the amount to which the decedent, immediately before death, was beneficially entitled under Section 6–211 is transferred as part of the decedent's estate. A POD designation in a multiple-party account without right of survivorship is ineffective. For purposes of this section, designation of an account as a tenancy in common establishes that the account is without right of survivorship.

(d) The ownership right of a surviving party or beneficiary, or of the decedent's estate, in sums on deposit is subject to requests for payment made by a party before the party's death, whether paid by the financial institution before or after death, or unpaid. The surviving party or beneficiary, or the decedent's estate, is liable to the payee of an unpaid request for payment. The liability is limited to a proportionate share of the amount transferred under this section, to the extent necessary to discharge the request for payment.

COMMENT

The effect of subsection (a) is to make an account payable to one or more of two or more parties a survivorship arrangement unless a non-survivorship arrangement is specified in the terms of the account. This rule applies to community property as well as other forms of marital property. See Section 6–216 (community property and tenancy by the entireties). The section also applies to various forms of multiple-party accounts that may be in use at the effective date of the legislation. See Sections 6–203 (type of account; existing accounts) and 6–204 (forms).

Subsection (b) applies to both POD and Totten trust beneficiaries. See Section 6–201(8) ("POD designation" defined). It accepts the New York view that an account opened by "A" in A's name as "trustee for B" usually is intended by A to be an informal will of any balance remaining on deposit at A's death.

§ 6–213. Alteration of Rights.

(a) Rights at death under Section 6–212 are determined by the type of account at the death of a party. The type of account may be altered by written notice given by a party to the financial institution to change the type of account or to stop or vary payment under the terms of the account. The notice must be signed by a party and received by the financial institution during the party's lifetime.

(b) A right of survivorship arising from the express terms of the account, Section 6–212, or a POD designation, may not be altered by will.

COMMENT

Under this section, rights of parties and beneficiaries are determined by the type of account at the time of death. It is to be noted that only a "party" may give notice blocking the provisions of Section 6–212 (rights at death). "Party" is defined by Section 6–201(6). Thus if there is an account with a POD designation in the name of A and B with C as beneficiary, C cannot change the right of survivorship be-

cause C has no present right to payment and hence is not a party.

§ 6–214. Accounts and Transfers Nontestamentary.

Except as provided in Part 2 of Article II (elective share of
surviving spouse) or as a consequence of, and to the extent directed
by, Section 6–215, a transfer resulting from the application of
Section 6–212 is effective by reason of the terms of the account
involved and this part and is not testamentary or subject to Articles
I through IV (estate administration).

COMMENT

The purpose of classifying the transactions contemplated by this part as nontestamentary is to bolster the explicit statement that their validity as effective modes of transfers on death is not to be determined by the requirements for wills. The section is consistent with Part 1 of Article VI (provisions relating to effect of death).

§ 6–215. Rights of Creditors and Others.

(a) If other assets of the estate are insufficient, a transfer resulting from a right of survivorship or POD designation under this part
is not effective against the estate of a deceased party to the extent
needed to pay claims against the estate and statutory allowances to
the surviving spouse and children.

(b) A surviving party or beneficiary who receives payment from
an account after death of a party is liable to account to the personal
representative of the decedent for a proportionate share of the
amount received to the extent necessary to discharge the claims and
allowances described in subsection (a) remaining unpaid after application of the decedent's estate. A proceeding to assert the liability may not be commenced unless the personal representative has
received a written demand by the surviving spouse, a creditor, a
child, or a person acting for a child of the decedent. The proceeding must be commenced within one year after death of the decedent.

(c) A surviving party or beneficiary against whom a proceeding
to account is brought may join as a party to the proceeding a
surviving party or beneficiary of any other account of the decedent.

(d) Sums recovered by the personal representative must be administered as part of the decedent's estate. This section does not
affect the protection from claims of the personal representative or
estate of a deceased party provided in Section 6–226 for a financial

institution that makes payment in accordance with the terms of the account.

COMMENT

The sections of this article authorize transfers on death that reduce the estate to which the surviving spouse, creditors, and minor children normally must look for protection against a decedent's gifts by will. Accordingly, this section provides a remedy to these classes of persons that assures them that multiple-person accounts cannot be used to reduce the essential protection they would be entitled to if such accounts were deemed to permit a special form of specific devise. This section provides a remedy for collection of amounts necessary to pay tax obligations incurred by the decedent during life, but not for death taxes. See Section 1–201(4) ("claims" defined). Apportionment and allocation of death taxes, and their collection, is governed by law other than this section.

Under this section a surviving spouse is automatically assured of some protection against a multiple-person account if the probate estate is insolvent; rights are limited, however, to sums needed for statutory allowances. The phrase "statutory allowances" includes the homestead allowance under Section 2–401, the family allowance under Section 2–403, and any allowance needed to make up the deficiency in exempt property under Section 2–402. In any case (including a solvent estate) the surviving spouse could proceed under Section 2–201 et seq. to claim an elective share in the account if the deposits by the decedent satisfy the requirements of Section 2–202 so that the account falls within the augmented net estate concept. In the latter situation the spouse is not proceeding as a creditor under this section.

Under subsection (b), a proceeding must be commenced within one year after the decedent's death. This limitation period corresponds to the long term self-executing statute of limitations applicable under the code to creditors' claims generally.

§ 6–216. Community Property and Tenancy by the Entireties.

(a) A deposit of community property in an account does not alter the community character of the property or community rights in the property, but a right of survivorship between parties married to each other arising from the express terms of the account or Section 6–212 may not be altered by will.

(b) This part does not affect the law governing tenancy by the entireties.

COMMENT

Section 6–216 does not affect or limit the right of the financial institution to make payments pursuant to Subpart 3 (protection of financial institutions) and the deposit agreement. See Section 6–206 (applicability of part). For this reason, Section 6–216 does not affect the definiteness and certainty that the financial institution must have in order to be induced to make payments from the account and, at the same time, the section preserves the rights of the parties, creditors, and successors that arise out of the nature of the funds in the account—community or separate, or tenancy by the entireties.

SUBPART 3

PROTECTION OF FINANCIAL INSTITUTIONS

§ 6–221. Authority of Financial Institution.

A financial institution may enter into a contract of deposit for a multiple-party account to the same extent it may enter into a contract of deposit for a single-party account, and may provide for a POD designation and an agency designation in either a single-party account or a multiple-party account. A financial institution need not inquire as to the source of a deposit to an account or as to the proposed application of a payment from an account.

COMMENT

The provisions of this subpart relate only to protection of a financial institution that makes payment as provided in the subpart. Nothing in this subpart affects the beneficial rights of persons to sums on deposit or paid out. Ownership as between parties, and others, is governed by Subpart 2. See Section 6–206 (applicability of part).

§ 6–222. Payment on Multiple-Party Account.

A financial institution, on request, may pay sums on deposit in a multiple-party account to:

(1) one or more of the parties, whether or not another party is disabled, incapacitated, or deceased when payment is requested and whether or not the party making the request survives another party; or

(2) the personal representative, if any, or, if there is none, the heirs or devisees of a deceased party if proof of death is presented to the financial institution showing that the deceased party was the survivor of all other persons named on the account either as a party or beneficiary, unless the account is without right of survivorship under Section 6–212.

COMMENT

A financial institution that makes payment on proper request under this section is protected unless the financial institution has received written notice not to. Section 6–226 (discharge). Paragraph (1) applies to both a multiple-party account with right of survivorship and a multiple-party account without right of survivorship (including an account in tenancy in common form). Paragraph (2) is limited to a multiple-party account with right of survivorship; payment to the personal representative or heirs or devisees of a deceased party to an account without right of survivorship is governed by the general law of the state relating to the authority of such persons to collect assets alleged to belong to a decedent.

§ 6–223. Payment on POD Designation.

A financial institution, on request, may pay sums on deposit in an account with a POD designation to:

(1) one or more of the parties, whether or not another party is disabled, incapacitated, or deceased when the payment is requested and whether or not a party survives another party;

(2) the beneficiary or beneficiaries, if proof of death is presented to the financial institution showing that the beneficiary or beneficiaries survived all persons named as parties; or

(3) the personal representative, if any, or, if there is none, the heirs or devisees of a deceased party, if proof of death is presented to the financial institution showing that the deceased party was the survivor of all other persons named on the account either as a party or beneficiary.

COMMENT

A financial institution that makes payment on proper request under this section is protected unless the financial institution has received written notice not to. Section 6–226 (discharge). Payment to the personal representative or heirs or devisees of a deceased beneficiary who would be entitled to payment under paragraph (2) is governed by the general law of the state relating to the authority of such persons to collect assets alleged to belong to a decedent.

§ 6–224. Payment to Designated Agent.

A financial institution, on request of an agent under an agency designation for an account, may pay to the agent sums on deposit in the account, whether or not a party is disabled, incapacitated, or deceased when the request is made or received, and whether or not the authority of the agent terminates on the disability or incapacity of a party.

COMMENT

This section is intended to protect a financial institution that makes a payment pursuant to an account with an agency designation even

455

though the agency may have terminated at the time of the payment due to disability, incapacity, or death of the principal. The protection does not apply if the financial institution has received notice under Section 6–226 not to make pay-

ment or that the agency has terminated. This section applies whether or not the agency survives the party's disability or incapacity under Section 6–205 (designation of agent).

§ 6–225. Payment to Minor.

If a financial institution is required or permitted to make payment pursuant to this part to a minor designated as a beneficiary, payment may be made pursuant to the Uniform Transfers to Minors Act.

COMMENT

Section 6–225 is intended to avoid the need for a guardianship or other protective proceeding in situations where the Uniform Transfers to Minors Act may be used.

§ 6–226. Discharge.

(a) Payment made pursuant to this part in accordance with the type of account discharges the financial institution from all claims for amounts so paid, whether or not the payment is consistent with the beneficial ownership of the account as between parties, beneficiaries, or their successors. Payment may be made whether or not a party, beneficiary, or agent is disabled, incapacitated, or deceased when payment is requested, received, or made.

(b) Protection under this section does not extend to payments made after a financial institution has received written notice from a party, or from the personal representative, surviving spouse, or heir or devisee of a deceased party, to the effect that payments in accordance with the terms of the account, including one having an agency designation, should not be permitted, and the financial institution has had a reasonable opportunity to act on it when the payment is made. Unless the notice is withdrawn by the person giving it, the successor of any deceased party must concur in a request for payment if the financial institution is to be protected under this section. Unless a financial institution has been served with process in an action or proceeding, no other notice or other information shown to have been available to the financial institution affects its right to protection under this section.

(c) A financial institution that receives written notice pursuant to this section or otherwise has reason to believe that a dispute exists as to the rights of the parties may refuse, without liability, to make payments in accordance with the terms of the account.

(d) Protection of a financial institution under this section does not affect the rights of parties in disputes between themselves or their successors concerning the beneficial ownership of sums on deposit in accounts or payments made from accounts.

COMMENT

The provision of subsection (a) protecting a financial institution for payments made after the death, disability, or incapacity of a party is a specific elaboration of the general protective provisions of this section and is drawn from Uniform Commercial Code Section 4–405.

Knowledge of disability, incapacity, or death of a party does not affect payment on request of an agent, whether or not the agent's authority survives disability or incapacity. See Section 6–224 (payment to designated agent). But under subsection (b), the financial institution may not make payments on request of an agent after it has received written notice not to, whether because the agency has terminated or otherwise.

§ 6–227. Set-Off.

Without qualifying any other statutory right to set-off or lien and subject to any contractual provision, if a party is indebted to a financial institution, the financial institution has a right to set-off against the account. The amount of the account subject to set-off is the proportion to which the party is, or immediately before death was, beneficially entitled under Section 6–211 or, in the absence of proof of that proportion, an equal share with all parties.

PART 3

UNIFORM TOD SECURITY REGISTRATION ACT

§ 6–301. Definitions.

In this part:

(1) "Beneficiary form" means a registration of a security which indicates the present owner of the security and the intention of the owner regarding the person who will become the owner of the security upon the death of the owner.

(2) "Register," including its derivatives, means to issue a certificate showing the ownership of a certificated security or, in the case of an uncertificated security, to initiate or transfer an account showing ownership of securities.

(3) "Registering entity" means a person who originates or transfers a security title by registration, and includes a broker maintaining security accounts for customers and a transfer agent or other person acting for or as an issuer of securities.

(4) "Security" means a share, participation, or other interest in property, in a business, or in an obligation of an enterprise or other issuer, and includes a certificated security, an uncertificated security, and a security account.

(5) "Security account" means (i) a reinvestment account associated with a security, a securities account with a broker, a cash balance in a brokerage account, cash, interest, earnings, or dividends earned or declared on a security in an account, a reinvestment account, or a brokerage account, whether or not credited to the account before the owner's death, or (ii) a cash balance or other property held for or due to the owner of a security as a replacement for or product of an account security, whether or not credited to the account before the owner's death.

COMMENT

"Security" is defined as provided in UCC § 8–102 and includes shares of mutual funds and other investment companies. The defined term "security account" is not intended to include securities held in the name of a bank or similar institution as nominee for the benefit of a trust.

"Survive" is not defined. No effort is made in this part to define survival as it is for purposes of intestate succession in UPC § 2–104 which requires survival by an heir of the ancestor for 120 hours. For purposes of this part, survive is used in its common law sense of outliving another for any time interval no matter how brief. The drafting committee sought to avoid imposition of a new and unfamiliar meaning of the term on intermediaries familiar with the meaning of "survive" in joint tenancy registrations.

§ 6–302. Registration in Beneficiary Form; Sole or Joint Tenancy Ownership.

Only individuals whose registration of a security shows sole ownership by one individual or multiple ownership by two or more with right of survivorship, rather than as tenants in common, may obtain registration in beneficiary form. Multiple owners of a security registered in beneficiary form hold as joint tenants with right of survivorship, as tenants by the entireties, or as owners of community property held in survivorship form, and not as tenants in common.

COMMENT

This section is designed to prevent co-owners from designating any death beneficiary other than one who is to take only upon survival of *all* co-owners. It coerces co-owning registrants to signal whether they hold as joint tenants with right of survivorship (JT TEN), as tenants by the entireties (T ENT), or as owners of community property. Also, it imposes survivorship on co-owners holding in a beneficiary form that fails to specify a survivorship form of holding. Tenancy in common and community property otherwise than in a survivorship setting is negated for registration in beneficiary form because persons desiring to signal independent death beneficiaries for each individual's fractional interest in a co-owned security normally will split their holding into separate registrations of the

number of units previously constituting their fractional share. Once divided, each can name his or her own choice of death beneficiary.

The term "individuals," as used in this section, limits those who may register as owner or co-owner of a security in beneficiary form to natural persons. However, the section does not restrict individuals using this ownership form as to their choice of death beneficiary. The definition of "beneficiary form" in Section 6–301 indicates that any "person" may be designated beneficiary in a registration in beneficiary form. "Person" is defined so that a church, trust company, family corporation, or other entity, as well as any individual, may be designated as a beneficiary. Section 1–201(29).

§ 6–303. Registration in Beneficiary Form; Applicable Law.

A security may be registered in beneficiary form if the form is authorized by this or a similar statute of the state of organization of the issuer or registering entity, the location of the registering entity's principal office, the office of its transfer agent or its office making the registration, or by this or a similar statute of the law of the state listed as the owner's address at the time of registration. A registration governed by the law of a jurisdiction in which this or similar legislation is not in force or was not in force when a registration in beneficiary form was made is nevertheless presumed to be valid and authorized as a matter of contract law.

COMMENT

This section encourages registrations in beneficiary form to be made whenever a state with which either of the parties to a registration has contact has enacted this or a similar statute. Thus, a registration in beneficiary form of X Company shares might rely on an enactment of this Act in X Company's state of incorporation, or in the state of incorporation of X Company's transfer agent. Or, an enactment by the state of the issuer's principal office, the transfer agent's principal office, or of the issuer's office making the registration also would validate the registration. An enactment of the state of the registering owner's address at time of registration also might be used for validation purposes.

The last sentence of this section is designed, as is UPC § 6–101, to establish a statutory presumption that a general principle of law is available to achieve a result like that made possible by this part.

§ 6–304. Origination of Registration in Beneficiary Form.

A security, whether evidenced by certificate or account, is registered in beneficiary form when the registration includes a designation of a beneficiary to take the ownership at the death of the owner or the deaths of all multiple owners.

COMMENT

As noted above in commentary to Section 6–302, this part places no restriction on who may be designated beneficiary in a registration in beneficiary form.

§ 6–305. Form of Registration in Beneficiary Form.

Registration in beneficiary form may be shown by the words "transfer on death" or the abbreviation "TOD," or by the words "pay on death" or the abbreviation "POD," after the name of the registered owner and before the name of a beneficiary.

COMMENT

The abbreviation POD is included for use without regard for whether the subject is a money claim against an issuer, such as its own note or bond for money loaned, or is a claim to securities evidenced by conventional title documentation. The use of POD in a registration in beneficiary form of shares in an investment company should not be taken as a signal that the investment is to be sold or redeemed on the owner's death so that the sums realized may be "paid" to the death beneficiary. Rather, only a transfer on death, not a liquidation on death, is indicated. The committee would have used only the abbreviation

TOD except for the familiarity, rooted in experience with certificates of deposit and other deposit accounts in banks, with the abbreviation POD as signalling a valid nonprobate death benefit or transfer on death.

§ 6–306. Effect of Registration in Beneficiary Form.

The designation of a TOD beneficiary on a registration in beneficiary form has no effect on ownership until the owner's death. A registration of a security in beneficiary form may be canceled or changed at any time by the sole owner or all then surviving owners without the consent of the beneficiary.

COMMENT

This section simply affirms the right of a sole owner, or the right of all multiple owners, to end a TOD beneficiary registration without the assent of the beneficiary. The section says nothing about how a TOD beneficiary designation may be canceled, meaning that the registering entity's terms and conditions, if any,

may be relevant. See Section 6–310. If the terms and conditions have nothing on the point, cancellation of a beneficiary designation presumably would be effected by a reregistration showing a different beneficiary or omitting reference to a TOD beneficiary.

§ 6–307. Ownership on Death of Owner.

On death of a sole owner or the last to die of all multiple owners, ownership of securities registered in beneficiary form passes to the beneficiary or beneficiaries who survive all owners. On proof of death of all owners and compliance with any applicable requirements of the registering entity, a security registered in beneficiary form may be reregistered in the name of the beneficiary or beneficiaries who survive the death of all owners. Until division of the security after the death of all owners, multiple beneficiaries surviving the death of all owners hold their interests as tenants in common. If no beneficiary survives the death of all owners, the security belongs to the estate of the deceased sole owner or the estate of the last to die of all multiple owners.

COMMENT

Even though multiple owners holding in the beneficiary form here authorized hold with right of survivorship, no survivorship rights attend the positions of multiple benefi-

ciaries who become entitled to securities by reason of having survived the sole owner or the last to die of multiple owners. Issuers (and registering entities) who decide to accept registrations in beneficiary form involving more than one primary beneficiary also should provide by rule whether fractional shares will be registered in the names of surviving beneficiaries where the number of shares held by the deceased owner does not divide without remnant among the survivors. If fractional shares are not desired, the issuer may wish to provide for sale of odd shares and division of proceeds, for an uneven distribution with the first or last named to receive the odd share, or for other resolution. Section 6–308 deals with whether intermediaries have any obligation to offer beneficiary registrations of any sort; Section 6–310 enables issuers to adopt terms and conditions controlling the details of applications for registrations they decide to accept and procedures for implementing such registrations after an owner's death.

The reference to surviving, multiple TOD beneficiaries as tenants in common is not intended to suggest that a registration form specifying unequal shares, such as "TOD A (20%), B (30%), C (50%)," would be improper. Though not included in the beneficiary forms described for illustrative purposes in Section 6–310, the part enables a registering entity to accept and implement a TOD beneficiary designation like the one just suggested. If offered, such a registration form should be implemented by registering entity terms and conditions providing for disposition of the share of a beneficiary who predeceases the owner when two or more of a group of multiple beneficiaries survive the owner. For example, the terms might direct the share of the predeceased beneficiary to the survivors in the proportion that their original shares bore to each other. Unless unequal shares are specified in a registration in beneficiary form designating multiple beneficiaries, the shares of the beneficiaries would, of course, be equal.

The statement that a security registered in beneficiary form is in the deceased owner's estate when no beneficiary survives the owner is not intended to prevent application of any anti-lapse statute that might direct a nonprobate transfer on death to the surviving issue of a beneficiary who failed to survive the owner. Rather, the statement is intended only to indicate that the registering entity involved should transfer or reregister the security as directed by the decedent's personal representative.

See the Comment to Section 6–301 regarding the meaning of "survive" for purposes of this part.

§ 6–308. Protection of Registering Entity.

(a) A registering entity is not required to offer or to accept a request for security registration in beneficiary form. If a registration in beneficiary form is offered by a registering entity, the owner requesting registration in beneficiary form assents to the protections given to the registering entity by this part.

(b) By accepting a request for registration of a security in beneficiary form, the registering entity agrees that the registration will be implemented on death of the deceased owner as provided in this part.

(c) A registering entity is discharged from all claims to a security by the estate, creditors, heirs, or devisees of a deceased owner if it registers a transfer of the security in accordance with Section 6–307 and does so in good faith reliance (i) on the registration, (ii) on this part, and (iii) on information provided to it by affidavit of the personal representative of the deceased owner, or by the surviving beneficiary or by the surviving beneficiary's representatives, or other information available to the registering entity. The protections of this part do not extend to a reregistration or payment made after a registering entity has received written notice from any claimant to any interest in the security objecting to implementation of a registration in beneficiary form. No other notice or other information available to the registering entity affects its right to protection under this part.

(d) The protection provided by this part to the registering entity of a security does not affect the rights of beneficiaries in disputes between themselves and other claimants to ownership of the security transferred or its value or proceeds.

COMMENT

It is to be noted that the "request" for a registration in beneficiary form may be in any form chosen by a registering entity. This part does not prescribe a particular form and does not impose record-keeping requirements. Registering entities' business practices, including any industry standards or rules of transfer agent associations, will control.

The written notice referred to in subsection (c) would qualify as a notice under UCC § 8–403.

"Good faith" as used in this section is intended to mean "honesty in fact and the observance of reasonable commercial standards of fair dealing in the trade," as specified in UCC § 2–103(1)(b).

The protections described in this section are designed to meet any questions regarding registering entity protection that may not be foreclosed by issuer protections provided in the Uniform Commercial Code. Because persons interested in this part may wish to be reminded of relevant UCC provisions, a brief summary follows.

"U.C.C. § 8–403, 'Issuer's Duty as to Adverse Claims' contains detailed provisions regarding duties of inquiry by an issuer of a certificated or uncertificated security who is requested to effect a transfer, and the availability and use of 30 day notices to force adverse claimants to start litigation if further delay in transfer is desired. U.C.C. § 8–201's definition of 'issuer' for purposes of 'registration of transfer....' is simply 'a person on whose behalf transfer books are maintained'. U.C.C. § 8–403 is among the sections dealing with registration of transfers.

"U.C.C. sections 8–308 and 8–404(1) appear to exonerate an issuer who acts in response to transfer directions signalled by the 'necessary indorsement' on or with a certificated security or in response to 'an instruction originated by an appropriate person' in the case of an uncertificated security. Section 8–308 describes the meaning of 'appropriate person' in the case of a certificated security as 'the person specified by the certificated security ... to be entitled to the security.' U.C.C. § 8–308(6) (1978). In the case of an uncertificated security, 'appropriate person' means the 'registered owner.' *Id.* § 8–308(7). The survivor of owners listed as joint tenants with right of survivorship is specifically defined as an authorized person. *Id.* § 8–308(8)(d). The U.C.C. aspect of the problem could be met by an additional sub-paragraph to section 8–308(8) that would include a TOD beneficiary as an 'appropriate person' when the beneficiary has survived the owner.

"No U.C.C. addition would be necessary if a TOD beneficiary designation were viewed as a contingent order for transfer at the owner's death that may be safely implemented as a direction from the owner as an 'authorized person.' The owner's death before completion of the transfer would not pose U.C.C. problems because section 8–308(10) provides: 'Whether the person signing is appropriate is determined as of the date of signing and an indorsement made by or an instruction originated by him does not become unauthorized for the purposes of this Article by virtue of any subsequent change of circumstances.'

"It might be questioned whether a TOD direction, which may be revoked before it is carried into effect and is also contingent on the beneficiary's survival of the registrant, is within the transfer directions contemplated by the U.C.C. framers for purposes of issuer protection. However, since section 8–202 explicitly protects issuers against problems arising because of restrictions or conditions on transfers, only the novelty of revocable directions for transfer on death gives pause.

"In general, article 8 of the U.C.C. reflects a careful attempt to protect implementation of a wide range of transfer instructions so long as the signatures are genuine and are those of owners acting in conformity with duly imposed rules of the issuer organization ... Hence, existing U.C.C. protections should be adequate, ..."

Wellman, Transfer-On-Death Securities Registration: A New Title Form, 21 Ga.L.Rev. 789, 823 n. 90 (1987).

§ 6–309. Nontestamentary Transfer on Death.

(a) A transfer on death resulting from a registration in beneficiary form is effective by reason of the contract regarding the registration between the owner and the registering entity and this part and is not testamentary.

(b) This part does not limit the rights of creditors of security owners against beneficiaries and other transferees under other laws of this State.

COMMENT

Subsection (a) is comparable to UPC § 6–214. Subsection (b) is similar to UPC § 6–101(b).

§ 6–310. Terms, Conditions, and Forms for Registration.

(a) A registering entity offering to accept registrations in beneficiary form may establish the terms and conditions under which it will receive requests (i) for registrations in beneficiary form, and (ii) for implementation of registrations in beneficiary form, including requests for cancellation of previously registered TOD beneficiary designations and requests for reregistration to effect a change of beneficiary. The terms and conditions so established may provide for proving death, avoiding or resolving any problems concerning fractional shares, designating primary and contingent beneficiaries, and substituting a named beneficiary's descendants to take in the place of the named beneficiary in the event of the beneficiary's death. Substitution may be indicated by appending to the name of the primary beneficiary the letters LDPS, standing for "lineal descendants per stripes." This designation substitutes a deceased beneficiary's descendants who survive the owner for a beneficiary who fails to so survive, the descendants to be identified and to share in accordance with the law of the beneficiary's domicile at the owner's death governing inheritance by descendants of an intestate. Other forms of identifying beneficiaries who are to take on one or more contingencies, and rules for providing proofs and assurances needed to satisfy reasonable concerns by registering entities regarding conditions and identities relevant to accurate implementation of registrations in beneficiary form, may be contained in a registering entity's terms and conditions.

(b) The following are illustrations of registrations in beneficiary form which a registering entity may authorize:

(1) Sole owner-sole beneficiary: John S Brown TOD (or POD) John S Brown Jr.

(2) Multiple owners-sole beneficiary: John S Brown Mary B Brown JT TEN TOD John S Brown Jr.

(3) Multiple owners-primary and secondary (substituted) beneficiaries: John S Brown Mary B Brown JT TEN TOD John S Brown Jr SUB BENE Peter Q Brown *or* John S Brown Mary B Brown JT TEN TOD John S Brown Jr LDPS.

COMMENT

Use of "and" or "or" between the names of persons registered as co-owners is unnecessary under this part and should be discouraged. If used, the two words should have the same meaning insofar as concerns a title form; *i.e.*, that of "and" to indicate that both namedpersons own the asset.

Descendants of a named beneficiary who take by virtue of a "LDPS" designation appended to a beneficiary's name take as TOD beneficiaries rather than as intestate successors. If no descendant of a predeceased primary beneficiary survives the owner, the security passes as a part of the owner's estate as provided in Section 6–307.

[§ 6–311. Application of Part.

This part applies to registrations of securities in beneficiary form made before or after [effective date], by decedents dying on or after [effective date].]

COMMENT

Section 6–311 is an optional provision that may be particularly useful in a state that has previously enacted the Uniform Probate Code, since the general effective date and transitional provisions of UPC § 8–101 are not expressly adapted for the addition of this part. A state newly enacting the Uniform Probate Code, including this part, may find that general Section 8–101 is adequate for this purpose and addition of optional Section 6–311 unnecessary.

ARTICLE VII

TRUST ADMINISTRATION

PART 1

TRUST REGISTRATION

PART 2

JURISDICTION OF COURT CONCERNING TRUSTS

PART 3

DUTIES AND LIABILITIES OF TRUSTEES

PART 4

POWERS OF TRUSTEES

[GENERAL COMMENT ONLY]

COMMENT

Several considerations explain the presence in the Uniform Probate Code of procedures applicable to inter vivos and testamentary trusts. The most important is that the Court assumed by the Code is a full power court which appropriately may receive jurisdiction over trustees. Another is that personal representatives under Articles III and IV and conservators under Article V, have the status of trustees. It follows naturally that these fiduciaries and regular trustees should bear a similar relationship to the Court. Also, the general move of the Code away from the concept of supervisory jurisdiction over any fiduciary is compatible with the kinds of procedural provisions which are believed to be desirable for trustees.

The relevance of trust procedures to those relating to settlement of decedents' estates is apparent in many situations. Many trusts are created by will. In a substantial number of states, statutes now extend probate court control over decedents' estates to testamentary trustees, but the same procedures rarely apply to inter vivos trusts. For example, eleven states appear to require testamentary trustees to qualify and account in much the same manner as executors, though quite different requirements relate to trustees of inter vivos trusts in these same states. Twenty-four states impose some form of mandatory court accountings on testamentary trustees, while only three seem to have comparable requirements for inter vivos trustees.

From an estate planning viewpoint, probate court supervision of testamentary trustees causes many problems. In some states, testamentary trusts cannot be released to be administered in another state. This requires complicated planning if inconvenience to interested persons is to be avoided when the beneficiaries move elsewhere. Also, some states preclude foreign trust companies from serving as trustees of local testamentary trusts without complying with onerous or prohibitive qualification requirements. Regular accountings in court have proved to be more expensive than useful in relation to the vast majori-

ty of trusts and sometimes have led to the ill-advised use of legal life estates to avoid these burdens.

The various restrictions applicable to testamentary trusts have caused many planners to recommend use of revocable inter vivos trusts. The widely adopted Uniform Testamentary Addition to Trusts Act has accelerated this tendency by permitting testators to devise estates to trustees of previously established receptacle trusts which have and retain the characteristics of inter vivos trusts for purpose of procedural requirements.

The popularity of this legislation and the widespread use of pour-over wills indicates rather vividly the obsolescence and irrelevance of statutes contemplating supervisory jurisdiction.

One of the problems with inter vivos and receptacle trusts at the present time, however, is that persons interested in these arrangements as trustees or beneficiaries frequently discover that there are no simple and efficient statutory or judicial remedies available to them to meet the special needs of the trust relationship. Proceedings in equity before courts of general jurisdiction are possible, of course, but the difficulties of obtaining jurisdiction over all interested persons on each occasion when a judicial order may be necessary or desirable are commonly formidable. A few states offer simplified procedures on a voluntary basis for inter vivos as well as testamentary trusts. In some of these, however, the legislation forces inter vivos trusts into unpopular patterns involving supervisory control. Nevertheless, it remains true of the legislation in most states that there is too little for inter vivos trusts and too much for trusts created by will.

Other developments suggest that enactment of useful, uniform legislation on trust procedures is a matter of considerable social importance. For one thing, accelerating mobility of persons and estates is steadily increasing the pressure on locally oriented property institutions. The drafting and technical problems created by lack of uniformity of trust procedures in the several states are quite serious. If people cannot obtain efficient trust service to preserve and direct wealth because of state property rules, they will turn in time to national arrangements that eliminate property law problems. A general shift away from local management of trusteed wealth and increased reliance on various contractual claims against national funds seems the most likely consequence if the local law of trusts remains nonuniform and provincial.

Modestly endowed persons who are turning to inter vivos trusts to avoid probate are of more immediate concern. Lawyers in all parts of the country are aware of the trend toward reliance on revocable trusts as total substitutes for wills which recent controversies about probate procedures have stimulated. There would be little need for concern about this development if it could be assumed also that the people involved are seeking and getting competent advice and fiduciary assistance. But there are indications that many people are neither seeking nor receiving adequate information about trusts they are using. Moreover, professional fiduciaries are often not available as trustees for small estates. Consequently, neither settlors nor trustees of "do-it-yourself" trusts have much idea of what they are getting into. As a result, there are corresponding dangers to beneficiaries who are frequently uninformed or baffled by formidable difficulties in obtaining relief or information.

Enactment of clear statutory procedures creating simple remedies for persons involved in trust problems will not prevent disappointment for many of these persons but should help minimize their losses.

Several objectives of the Code are suggested by the preceding discussion. They may be summarized as follows:

1. To eliminate procedural distinctions between testamentary and inter vivos trusts.

2. To strengthen the ability of owners to select trustees by eliminating formal qualification of trustees and restrictions on the place of administration.

3. To locate nonmandatory judicial proceedings for trustees and beneficiaries in a convenient court fully competent to handle all problems that may arise.

4. To facilitate judicial proceedings concerning trusts by comprehensive provisions for obtaining jurisdiction over interested persons by notice.

5. To protect beneficiaries by having trustees file written statements of acceptance of trusts with suitable courts, thereby acknowledging jurisdiction and providing some evidence of the trust's existence for future beneficiaries.

6. To eliminate routinely required court accountings, substituting clear remedies and statutory duties to inform beneficiaries.

PART 1

TRUST REGISTRATION

GENERAL COMMENT

Registration of trusts is a new concept and differs importantly from common arrangements for retained supervisory jurisdiction of courts of probate over testamentary trusts. It applies alike to inter vivos and testamentary trusts, and is available to foreign-created trusts as well as those locally created. The place of registration is related not to the place where the trust was created, which may lose its significance to the parties concerned, but is related to the place where the trust is primarily administered, which in turn is required (Section 7–305) to be at a location appropriate to the purposes of the trust and the interests of its beneficiaries. Sections 7–102 and 7–305 provide for transfer of registration. The procedure is more flexible than the typical retained jurisdiction in that it permits registration or submission to other appropriate procedures at another place, even in another state, in order to accommodate relocation of the trust at a place which becomes more convenient for its administration. (Cf. 20 [Purdon's] Pa.Stat. § 2080.309.) In addition, the registration acknowledges that a particular court will be accessible to the parties on a permissive basis without subjecting the trust to compulsory, continuing supervision by the court.

The process of registration requires no judicial action or determination but is accomplished routinely by simple acts on the part of the trustee which will place certain information on file with the court (Section 7–102). Although proceedings involving a registered trust will not be continuous but will be separate each time an interested party initiates a proceeding, it is contemplated that a court will maintain a single file for each registered trust as a record available to interested persons. Proceedings are facilitated by the broad jurisdiction of the court (Section 7–201) and the Code's representation and notice provisions (Section 1–403).

Section 7–201 provides complete jurisdiction over trust proceedings in the court of registration. Section 7–103 above provides for jurisdiction over parties. Section 7–104 should facilitate use of trusts involving assets in several states by providing for a single principal place of administration and reducing concern about qualification of foreign trust companies.

Section 7–101. [Duty to Register Trusts.]

The trustee of a trust having its principal place of administration in this state shall register the trust in the Court of this state at the principal place of administration. Unless otherwise designated in the trust instrument, the principal place of administration of a trust is the trustee's usual place of business where the records pertaining to the trust are kept, or at the trustee's residence if he has no such place of business. In the case of co-trustees, the principal place of administration, if not otherwise designated in the trust instrument, is (1) the usual place of business of the corporate trustee if there is but one corporate co-trustee, or (2) the usual place of business or residence of the individual trustee who is a professional fiduciary if there is but one such person and no corporate co-trustee, and otherwise (3) the usual place of business or residence of any of the co-trustees as agreed upon by them. The duty to register under this Part does not apply to the trustee of a trust if registration would be inconsistent with the retained jurisdiction of a foreign court from which the trustee cannot obtain release.

COMMENT

This section rests on the assumption that a central "filing office" will be designated in each county where the Court may sit in more than one place.

The scope of this section and of Article VII is tied to the definition of "trustee" in Section 1–201. It was suggested that the definition should be expanded to include "land trusts." It was concluded, however that the inclusion of this term which has special meaning principally in Illinois, should be left for decision by enacting states. Under the definition of "trust" in this Code, custodial arrangements as contemplated by legislation dealing with gifts to minors, are excluded, as are "trust accounts" as defined in Article VI.

Section 7–102. [Registration Procedures.]

Registration shall be accomplished by filing a statement indicating the name and address of the trustee in which it acknowledges the trusteeship. The statement shall indicate whether the trust has been registered elsewhere. The statement shall identify the trust: (1) in the case of a testamentary trust, by the name of the testator and the date and place of domiciliary probate; (2) in the case of a written inter vivos trust, by the name of each settlor and the original trustee and the date of the trust instrument; or (3) in the case of an oral trust, by information identifying the settlor or other source of funds and describing the time and manner of the trust's creation and the terms of the trust, including the subject matter, beneficiaries and time of performance. If a trust has been registered elsewhere, registration in this state is ineffective until the earlier registration is released by order of the Court where prior registration occurred, or an instrument executed by the trustee and all beneficiaries, filed with the registration in this state.

Additional duties of the clerk of the Court are provided in Section 1–305. The duty to register trusts is stated in Section 7–101.

Section 7–103. [Effect of Registration.]

(a) By registering a trust, or accepting the trusteeship of a registered trust, the trustee submits personally to the jurisdiction of the Court in any proceeding under Section 7–201 of this Code relating to the trust that may be initiated by any interested person while the trust remains registered. Notice of any proceeding shall be delivered to the trustee, or mailed to him by ordinary first class mail at his address as listed in the registration or as thereafter reported to the Court and to his address as then known to the petitioner.

(b) To the extent of their interests in the trust, all beneficiaries of a trust properly registered in this state are subject to the jurisdiction of the court of registration for the purposes of proceedings under Section 7–201, provided notice is given pursuant to Section 1–401.

This section provides for jurisdiction over the parties. Subject matter jurisdiction for proceedings involving trusts is described in Sections 7–201 and 7–202. The basic jurisdictional concept in Section 7–103 is that reflected in widely adopted long-arm statutes, that a state may properly entertain proceedings when it is a reasonable forum under all the circumstances, provided adequate notice is given. Clearly the trustee can be deemed to consent to jurisdiction by virtue of registration. This basis for consent jurisdiction is in addition to and not in lieu of other bases of jurisdiction during or after registration. Also, incident to an order releasing registration under Section 7–305, the Court could condition the release on registration of the trust in another state or court. It also seems reasonable to require beneficiaries to go to the seat of the trust when litigation has been initiated there concerning a trust in which they claim beneficial interests, much as the rights of shareholders of a corporation can be determined at a corporate seat. The settlor has indicated a principal place of administration by his selection of a trustee or otherwise, and it is reasonable to subject rights under the trust to the jurisdiction of the Court where the trust is properly administered. Although most cases will fit within traditional concepts of jurisdiction, this section goes beyond established doctrines of in personam or quasi in rem jurisdiction as regards a nonresident beneficiary's interests in foreign land of chattels, but the National Conference believes the section affords due process and represents a worthwhile step forward in trust proceedings.

Section 7–104. [Effect of Failure to Register.]

A trustee who fails to register a trust in a proper place as required by this Part, for purposes of any proceedings initiated by a beneficiary of the trust prior to registration, is subject to the personal jurisdiction of any Court in which the trust could have been registered. In addition, any trustee who, within 30 days after receipt of a written demand by a settlor or beneficiary of the trust, fails to register a trust as required by this Part is subject to removal and denial of compensation or to surcharge as the Court may direct. A provision in the terms of the trust purporting to excuse the trustee from the duty to register, or directing that the trust or trustee shall not be subject to the jurisdiction of the Court, is ineffective.

COMMENT

Under Section 1-108, the holder of a presently exercisable general power of appointment can control all duties of a fiduciary to beneficiaries who may be changed by exercise of the power. Hence, if the settlor of a revocable inter vivos trust directs the trustee to refrain from registering a trust, no liability would follow even though another beneficiary demanded registration. The ability of the general power holder to control the trustee ends when the power is terminated.

Section 7-105. [Registration, Qualification of Foreign Trustee.]

A foreign corporate trustee is required to qualify as a foreign corporation doing business in this state if it maintains the principal place of administration of any trust within the state. A foreign co-trustee is not required to qualify in this state solely because its co-trustee maintains the principal place of administration in this state. Unless otherwise doing business in this state, local qualification by a foreign trustee, corporate or individual, is not required in order for the trustee to receive distribution from a local estate or to hold, invest in, manage or acquire property located in this state, or maintain litigation. Nothing in this section affects a determination of what other acts require qualification as doing business in this state.

COMMENT

Section 7-105 deals with non-resident trustees in a fashion which should correct a widespread deficiency in present regulation of trust activity. Provisions limiting business of foreign corporate trustees constitute an unnecessary limitation on the ability of a trustee to function away from its principal place of business. These restrictions properly relate more to continuous pursuit of general trust business by foreign corporations than to isolated instances of litigation and management of the assets of a particular trust. The ease of avoiding foreign corporation qualification statutes by the common use of local nominees or subtrustees, and the acceptance of these practices, are evidence of the futility and undesirability of more restrictive legislation of the sort commonly existing today. The position embodied in this section has been recommended by important segments of the banking and trust industry through a proposed model statute, and the failure to adopt this reform has been characterized as unfortunate by a leading trust authority. See 5 Scott on Trusts § 558 (3rd ed. 1967).

PART 2

JURISDICTION OF COURT CONCERNING TRUSTS

Section 7–201. [Court; Exclusive Jurisdiction of Trusts.]

(a) The Court has exclusive jurisdiction of proceedings initiated by interested parties concerning the internal affairs of trusts. Proceedings which may be maintained under this section are those concerning the administration and distribution of trusts, the declaration of rights and the determination of other matters involving trustees and beneficiaries of trusts. These include, but are not limited to, proceedings to:

(1) appoint or remove a trustee;

(2) review trustees' fees and to review and settle interim or final accounts;

(3) ascertain beneficiaries, determine any question arising in the administration or distribution of any trust including questions of construction of trust instruments, to instruct trustees, and determine the existence or nonexistence of any immunity, power, privilege, duty or right; and

(4) release registration of a trust.

(b) Neither registration of a trust nor a proceeding under this section result in continuing supervisory proceedings. The management and distribution of a trust estate, submission of accounts and reports to beneficiaries, payment of trustee's fees and other obligations of a trust, acceptance and change of trusteeship, and other aspects of the administration of a trust shall proceed expeditiously consistent with the terms of the trust, free of judicial intervention and without order, approval or other action of any court, subject to the jurisdiction of the Court as invoked by interested parties or as otherwise exercised as provided by law.

COMMENT

Derived in small part from Florida Statutes, 1965, Chapters 737 and 87, and Title 20, Penna.Statutes, (Purdon) 32080.101 et seq.

Section 7–202. [Trust Proceedings; Venue.]

Venue for proceedings under Section 7–201 involving registered trusts is in the place of registration. Venue for proceedings under Section 7–201 involving trusts not registered in this state is in any place where the trust properly could have been registered, and otherwise by the rules of civil procedure.

Section 7–203. [Trust Proceedings; Dismissal of Matters Relating to Foreign Trusts.]

The Court will not, over the objection of a party, entertain proceedings under Section 7–201 involving a trust registered or having its principal place of administration in another state, unless (1) when all appropriate parties could not be bound by litigation in the courts of the state where the trust is registered or has its principal place of administration or (2) when the interests of justice otherwise would seriously be impaired. The Court may condition a stay or dismissal of a proceeding under this section on the consent of any party to jurisdiction of the state in which the trust is registered or has its principal place of business, or the Court may grant a continuance or enter any other appropriate order.

COMMENT

While recognizing that trusts which are essentially foreign can be the subject of proceedings in this state, this section employs the concept of forum non conveniens to center litigation involving the trustee and beneficiaries at the principal place of administration of the trust but leaves open the possibility of suit elsewhere when necessary in the interests of justice. It is assumed that under this section a court would refuse to entertain litigation involving the foreign registered trust unless for jurisdictional or other reasons, such as the nature and location of the property or unusual interests of the parties, it is manifest that substantial injustice would result if the parties were referred to the court of registration. As regards litigation involving third parties, the trustee may sue and be sued as any owner and manager of property under the usually applicable rules of civil procedure and also as provided in Section 7–203.

The concepts of res judicata and full faith and credit applicable to any managing owner of property have generally been applicable to trustees. Consequently, litigation by trustees has not involved the artificial problems historically found when personal representatives maintain litigation away from the state of their appointment, and a prior adjudication for or against a trustee rendered in a foreign court having jurisdiction is viewed as conclusive and entitled to full faith and credit. Because of this, provisions changing the law, analogous to those relating to personal representatives in Section 4–401 do not appear necessary. See also Section 3–408. In light of the foregoing, the issue is essentially only one of forum non conveniens in having litigation proceed in the most appropriate forum. This is the function of this section.

Section 7-204. [Court; Concurrent Jurisdiction of Litigation Involving Trusts and Third Parties.]

The Court of the place in which the trust is registered has concurrent jurisdiction with other courts of this state of actions and proceedings to determine the existence or nonexistence of trusts created other than by will, of actions by or against creditors or debtors of trusts, and of other actions and proceedings involving trustees and third parties. Venue is determined by the rules generally applicable to civil actions.

Section 7-205. [Proceedings for Review of Employment of Agents and Review of Compensation of Trustee and Employees of Trust.]

On petition of an interested person, after notice to all interested persons, the Court may review the propriety of employment of any person by a trustee including any attorney, auditor, investment advisor or other specialized agent or assistant, and the reasonableness of the compensation of any person so employed, and the reasonableness of the compensation determined by the trustee for his own services. Any person who has received excessive compensation from a trust may be ordered to make appropriate refunds.

COMMENT

In view of the broad jurisdiction conferred on the probate court, description of the special proceeding authorized by this section might be unnecessary. But the Code's theory that trustees may fix their own fees *and* those of their attorneys marks an important departure from much existing practice under which fees are determined by the Court in the first instance. Hence, it seems wise to emphasize that any interested person can get judicial review of fees if he desires it. Also, if excessive fees have been paid, this section provides a quick and efficient remedy. This review would meet in part the criticism of the broad powers given in the Uniform Trustees' Powers Act.

Section 7-206. [Trust Proceedings; Initiation by Notice; Necessary Parties.]

Proceedings under Section 7-201 are initiated by filing a petition in the Court and giving notice pursuant to Section 1-401 to interested parties. The Court may order notification of additional persons. A decree is valid as to all who are given notice of the proceeding though fewer than all interested parties are notified.

PART 3

DUTIES AND LIABILITIES OF TRUSTEES

Section 7–301. [General Duties Not Limited.]

Except as specifically provided, the general duty of the trustee to administer a trust expeditiously for the benefit of the beneficiaries is not altered by this Code.

Section 7–302. [Trustee's Standard of Care and Performance.]

Except as otherwise provided by the terms of the trust, the trustee shall observe the standards in dealing with the trust assets that would be observed by a prudent man dealing with the property of another, and if the trustee has special skills or is named trustee on the basis of representations of special skills or expertise, he is under a duty to use those skills.

COMMENT

This is a new general provision designed to make clear the standard of skill expected from trustees, both individual and corporate, nonprofessional and professional. It differs somewhat from the standard stated in § 174 of the Restatement of Trusts, Second, which is as follows:

"The trustee is under a duty to the beneficiary in administering the trust to exercise such care and skill as a man of ordinary prudence would exercise in dealing with his own property; and if the trustee has or procures his appointment as trustee by representing that he has greater skill than that of a reasonable man of ordinary prudence, he is under a duty to exercise such skill."

By making the basic standard align to that observed by a prudent man in dealing with the property of another, the section accepts a standard as it has been articulated in some decisions regarding the duty of a trustee concerning investments. See Estate of Cook, (Del.Chanc. 1934) 20 Del. Ch. 123, 171 A. 730. Also, the duty as described by the above section more clearly conveys the idea that a trustee must comply with an external, rather than with a personal, standard of care.

Section 7–303. [Duty to Inform and Account to Beneficiaries.]

The trustee shall keep the beneficiaries of the trust reasonably informed of the trust and its administration. In addition:

(a) Within 30 days after his acceptance of the trust, the trustee shall inform in writing the current beneficiaries and if possible, one or more persons who under Section 1–403 may represent beneficiaries with future interests, of the Court in which the trust is registered and of his name and address.

(b) Upon reasonable request, the trustee shall provide the beneficiary with a copy of the terms of the trust which describe or affect his interest and with relevant information about the assets of the trust and the particulars relating to the administration.

(c) Upon reasonable request, a beneficiary is entitled to a statement of the accounts of the trust annually and on termination of the trust or change of the trustee.

COMMENT

Analogous provisions are found in Section 3–705.

This provision does not require regular accounting to the Court nor are copies of statements furnished beneficiaries required to be filed with the Court. The parties are expected to assume the usual ownership responsibility for their interests including their own record keeping. Under Section 1–108, the holder of a general power of appointment or of revocation can negate the trustee's duties to any other person.

This section requires that a reasonable selection of beneficiaries is entitled to information so that the interests of the future beneficiaries may adequately be protected. After mandatory notification of registration by the trustee to the beneficiaries, further information may be obtained by the beneficiary upon request. This is to avoid extensive mandatory formal accounts and yet provide the beneficiary with adequate protection and sources of information. In most instances, the trustee will provide beneficiaries with copies of annual tax returns or tax statements that must be filed. Usually this will be accompanied by a narrative explanation by the trustee. In the case of the charitable trust, notice need be given only to the attorney general or other state officer supervising charitable trusts and in the event that the charitable trust has, as its primary beneficiary, a charitable corporation or institution, notice should be given to that charitable corporation or institution. It is not contemplated that all of the individuals who may receive some benefit as a result of a charitable trust be informed.

In any circumstance in which a fiduciary accounting is to be prepared, preparation of an accounting in conformity with the Uniform Principles and Model Account Formats promulgated by the National Fiduciary Accounting Project shall be considered as an appropriate manner of presenting a fiduciary account. See ALI–ABA Monograph, Whitman, Brown and Kramer, Fiduciary Accounting Guide (2nd edition 1990).

Section 7–304. [Duty to Provide Bond.]

A trustee need not provide bond to secure performance of his duties unless required by the terms of the trust, reasonably requested by a beneficiary or found by the Court to be necessary to protect the interests of the beneficiaries who are not able to protect themselves and whose interests otherwise are not adequately represented. On petition of the trustee or other interested person the Court may excuse a requirement of bond, reduce the amount of the bond, release the surety, or permit the substitution of another bond with the same or different sureties. If bond is required, it shall be filed in the Court of registration or other appropriate Court in amounts and with sureties and liabilities as provided in Sections 3–604 and 3–606 relating to bonds of personal representatives.

COMMENT

See Sections 3–603 and 3–604; 60 Okla.Stats.1961, § 175.24 [60 Okl.St. Ann. § 175.24]; Pa.Fid. Act, 1949, § 390.911(b) [20 Purdon's Pa.Stat. § 390.911(b)]; cf. Tenn.Code Ann. § 35–113.

Section 7–305. [Trustee's Duties; Appropriate Place of Administration; Deviation.]

A trustee is under a continuing duty to administer the trust at a place appropriate to the purposes of the trust and to its sound, efficient management. If the principal place of administration becomes inappropriate for any reason, the Court may enter any order furthering efficient administration and the interests of beneficiaries, including, if appropriate, release of registration, removal of the trustee and appointment of a trustee in another state. Trust provisions relating to the place of administration and to changes in the place of administration or of trustee control unless compliance would be contrary to efficient administration or the purposes of the trust. Views of adult beneficiaries shall be given weight in determining the suitability of the trustee and the place of administration.

COMMENT

This section and 7–102 are related. The latter section makes it clear that registration may be released without Court order if the trustee and beneficiaries can agree on the matter. Section 1–108 may be relevant, also.

The primary thrust of Article VII is to relate trust administration to the jurisdiction of courts, rather than to deal with substantive matters of trust law. An aspect of deviation, however, is touched here.

Section 7–306. [Personal Liability of Trustee to Third Parties.]

(a) Unless otherwise provided in the contract, a trustee is not personally liable on contracts properly entered into in his fiduciary capacity in the course of administration of the trust estate unless he fails to reveal his representative capacity and identify the trust estate in the contract.

(b) A trustee is personally liable for obligations arising from ownership or control of property of the trust estate or for torts committed in the course of administration of the trust estate only if he is personally at fault.

(c) Claims based on contracts entered into by a trustee in his fiduciary capacity, on obligations arising from ownership or control of the trust estate, or on torts committed in the course of trust administration may be asserted against the trust estate by proceeding against the trustee in his fiduciary capacity, whether or not the trustee is personally liable therefor.

(d) The question of liability as between the trust estate and the trustee individually may be determined in a proceeding for accounting, surcharge or indemnification or other appropriate proceeding.

COMMENT

The purpose of this section is to make the liability of the trust and trustee the same as that of the decedent's estate and personal representative.

Ultimate liability as between the estate and the fiduciary need not necessarily be determined whenever there is doubt about this question. It should be permissible, and often it will be preferable, for judgment to be entered, for example, against the trustee individually for purposes of determining the claimant's rights without the trustee placing that matter into controversy. The question of his right of reimbursement may be settled informally with beneficiaries or in a separate proceeding in the probate court involving reimbursement. The section does not preclude the possibility, however, that beneficiaries might be permitted to intervene in litigation between the trustee and a claimant and that all questions might be resolved in that action.

Section 7–307. [Limitations on Proceedings Against Trustees After Final Account.]

Unless previously barred by adjudication, consent or limitation, any claim against a trustee for breach of trust is barred as to any beneficiary who has received a final account or other statement fully disclosing the matter and showing termination of the trust relationship between the trustee and the beneficiary unless a proceeding to assert the claim is commenced within [6 months] after receipt of the final account or statement. In any event and notwithstanding lack of full disclosure a trustee who has issued a final account or statement received by the beneficiary and has informed the beneficiary of the location and availability of records for his examination is protected after 3 years. A beneficiary is deemed to

481

have received a final account or statement if, being an adult, it is received by him personally or if, being a minor or disabled person, it is received by his representative as described in Section 1–403(1) and (2).

COMMENT

Final accounts terminating the trustee's obligations to the trust beneficiaries may be formal or informal. Formal judicial accountings may be initiated by the petition of any trustee or beneficiary. Informal accounts may be conclusive by consent or by limitation. This section provides a special limitation supporting informal accounts. With regard to facilitating distribution see Section 5–103.

Section 1–108 makes approval of an informal account or settlement with a trustee by the holder of a presently exercisable general power of appointment binding on all beneficiaries. In addition, the equitable principles of estoppel and laches, as well as general statutes of limitation, will apply in many cases to terminate trust liabilities.

PART 4

POWERS OF TRUSTEES

GENERAL COMMENT

There has been considerable interest in recent years in legislation giving trustees extensive powers. The Uniform Trustees' Powers Act, approved by the National Conference in 1964 has been adopted in Idaho, Kansas, Mississippi and Wyoming. New York and New Jersey have adopted similar statutes which differ somewhat from the Uniform Trustees' Powers Act, and Arkansas, California, Colorado, Florida, Iowa, Louisiana, Oklahoma, Pennsylvania, Virginia and Washington have comprehensive legislation which differ in various respects from other models. The legislation in Connecticut, North Carolina and Tennessee provides lists of powers to be incorporated by reference as draftsmen wish.

Comprehensive legislation dealing with trustees' powers appropriately may be included in the Code package at this point.

*

ARTICLE VIII

EFFECTIVE DATE AND REPEALER

Section
8–101. [Time of Taking Effect; Provisions for Transition.]
8–102. [Specific Repealer and Amendments.]

Section 8–101. [Time of Taking Effect; Provisions for Transition.]

(a) This Code takes effect on January 1, 19____.

(b) Except as provided elsewhere in this Code, on the effective date of this Code:

(1) the Code applies to any wills of decedents dying thereafter;

(2) the Code applies to any proceedings in Court then pending or thereafter commenced regardless of the time of the death of decedent except to the extent that in the opinion of the Court the former procedure should be made applicable in a particular case in the interest of justice or because of infeasibility of application of the procedure of this Code;

(3) every personal representative including a person administering an estate of a minor or incompetent holding an appointment on that date, continues to hold the appointment but has only the powers conferred by this Code and is subject to the duties imposed with respect to any act occurring or done thereafter;

(4) an act done before the effective date in any proceeding and any accrued right is not impaired by this Code. If a right is acquired, extinguished or barred upon the expiration of a prescribed period of time which has commenced to run by the provisions of any statute before the effective date, the provisions shall remain in force with respect to that right;

(5) any rule of construction or presumption provided in this Code applies to instruments executed and multiple party accounts opened before the effective date unless there is a clear indication of a contrary intent;

(6) a person holding office as judge of the Court on the effective date of this Act may continue the office of judge of this Court and may be selected for additional terms after the effective date of this Act even though he does not meet the qualifications of a judge as provided in Article I.

485

Section 8–102. [Specific Repealer and Amendments.]

(a) The following Acts and parts of Acts are repealed:

   (1)

   (2)

   (3)

(b) The following Acts and parts of Acts are amended:

   (1)

   (2)

   (3)

APPENDIX I

AMENDMENTS TO UNIFORM PROBATE CODE
AND CORRESPONDING SECTIONS OF UNIFORM GUARDIANSHIP AND PROTEC- TIVE PROCEEDINGS ACT
AND UNIFORM DURABLE POWER OF AT- TORNEY ACT

JULY 1, 1987

AMENDMENT 1

Section 1–107 of the Code is amended to read:

SECTION 1–107. [Evidence as to Death or Status.]

In proceedings under this Code the rules of evidence in courts of general jurisdiction including any relating to simultaneous deaths, are applicable unless specifically displaced by the Code. In addition, the following rules relating to determination of death and status are applicable:

(1) a certified or authenticated copy of a death certificate purporting to be issued by an official or agency of the place where the death purportedly occurred is prima facie proof of the fact, place, date and time of death and the identity of the decedent;

(2) a certified or authenticated copy of any record or report of a governmental agency, domestic or foreign, that a person is missing, detained, dead, or alive is prima facie evidence of the status and of the dates, circumstances and places disclosed by the record or report;

(3) in the absence of prima facie evidence of death under (1) or (2) above, the fact of death may be established by clear and convincing evidence, including circumstantial evidence;

(3) (4) a person whose death is not established under the preceding subparagraphs who is absent for a continuous period of 5 years, during which he has not been heard from, and whose absence is not satisfactorily explained after diligent search or inquiry is presumed to be dead. His death is presumed to have

487

occurred at the end of the period unless there is sufficient evidence for determining that death occurred earlier.

Comment

As reported to JEB–UPC, some lawyers and judges read the Section so narrowly as to permit proof of death only by any evidence specified in the three numbered subparagraphs. So read, proof of disappearance under circumstances tending to establish death, such as disappearance following departure by airplane or boat in an area hit shortly thereafter by hurricane force winds, has been ruled inadmissible prior to five years following the disappearance. To remedy the situation and clarify the sense originally intended by the Conference, the JEB recommends Amendment 1.

AMENDMENT 2

Section 2–607 of the Code is amended to read:

SECTION 2–607. [Change in Securities; Accessions; Nonademption.]

(a) If the testator intended a specific devise of certain securities rather than the equivalent value thereof, the specific devisee is entitled only to:

(1) as much of the devised securities as is a part of the estate at time of the testator's death;

(2) any additional or other securities of the same entity owned by the testator by reason of action initiated by the entity excluding any acquired by exercise of purchase options;

(3) securities of another entity owned by the testator as a result of a merger, consolidation, reorganization or other similar action initiated by the entity; and

(4) any additional securities of the entity owned by the testator as a result of a plan of reinvestment if it is a regulated investment company.

(b) Distributions prior to death with respect to a specifically devised security not provided for in subsection (a) are not part of the specific devise.

Comment

Many entities other than regulated investment companies now offer dividend reinvestment plans. The limitation is obsolete. The JEB–UPC recommends Amendment 2.

488

AMENDMENT 3

Section 2–608 of the Code is amended to read:

SECTION 2–608. [Nonademption of Specific Devises in Certain Cases; Unpaid Proceeds of Sale, Condemnation or Insurance; Sale by Conservator.]

(a) A specific devisee has the right to the remaining specifically devised property and:

(1) any balance of the purchase price (together with any security interest) owing from a purchaser to the testator at death by reason of sale of the property;

(2) any amount of a condemnation award for the taking of the property unpaid at death;

(3) any proceeds unpaid at death on fire or casualty insurance on the property; and

(4) property owned by testator at his death as a result of foreclosure, or obtained in lieu of foreclosure, of the security for a specifically devised obligation.

(b) If specifically devised property is sold by a conservator or an agent acting within the authority of a durable power of attorney for a principal who is under a disability, or if a condemnation award or insurance proceeds are paid to a conservator or an agent acting within the authority of a durable power of attorney for a principal who is under a disability as a result of condemnation, fire, or casualty, the specific devisee has the right to a general pecuniary devise equal to the net sale price, the condemnation award, or the insurance proceeds. This subsection does not apply if after the sale, condemnation or casualty, it is adjudicated that the disability of the testator has ceased and the testator survives the adjudication by one year. The right of the specific devisee under this subsection is reduced by any right he has under subsection (a).

Comment

The recommendation of Amendment 3 reflects increased use of durable powers of attorney. The problem of one now incompetent and under the protection of a conservator or an agent operating under a durable power is the same. His gift of specific property by a previously executed will should not be adeemed by a sale of the asset of which he is unaware.

489

AMENDMENT 4

Section 3–108 of the Code is amended to read:

SECTION 3–108. [Probate, Testacy and Appointment Proceedings; Ultimate Time Limit.]

No informal probate or appointment proceeding or formal testacy or appointment proceeding, other than a proceeding to probate a will previously probated at the testator's domicile and appointment proceedings relating to an estate in which there has been a prior appointment, may be commenced more than 3 years after the decedent's death, except (1) if a previous proceeding was dismissed because of doubt about the fact of the decedent's death, appropriate probate, appointment or testacy proceedings may be maintained at any time thereafter upon a finding that the decedent's death occurred prior to the initiation of the previous proceeding and the applicant or petitioner has not delayed unduly in initiating the subsequent proceeding; (2) appropriate probate, appointment or testacy proceedings may be maintained in relation to the estate of an absent, disappeared or missing person for whose estate a conservator has been appointed, at any time within three years after the conservator becomes able to establish the death of the protected person; and (3) a proceeding to contest an informally probated will and to secure appointment of the person with legal priority for appointment in the event the contest is successful, may be commenced within the later of twelve months from the informal probate or three years from the decedent's death; and (4) if no proceeding concerning the succession or administration of the estate has occurred within 3 years after decedent's death, a formal testacy proceeding may be commenced at any time thereafter for the sole purpose of establishing a devise of property which the devisee or his successors and assigns possessed in accordance with the will or property which was not possessed or claimed by anyone by virtue of the decedent's title during the 3–year period, and the order of the Court shall be limited to that property. These limitations do not apply to proceedings to construe probated wills or determine heirs of an intestate. In cases under (1) or (2) above, the date on which a testacy or appointment proceeding is properly commenced shall be deemed to be the date of the decedent's death for purposes of other limitations provisions of this Code which relate to the date of death.

Comment

The purpose of the addition is to provide a black-letter procedure for obtaining a court order confirming a devise of property by an unprobated will after the time limited for probating a will and opening an administration has passed. The possibility of a valid devise by an unprobated will arises because of exceptions provided in Section 3–102. The proposed amendment merely supplies a specific procedural opportunity to replace the general jurisdictional grant found in the first sentence of Section 3–105. The recommended addition also makes it clear that a devise by an unprobated will is subject to the same requirements and proofs vis a vis the validity of the devise as would apply if the will were offered for probate in a formal testacy proceeding.

AMENDMENT 5

Section 3–304 of the Code is amended to read:

SECTION 3–304. [Informal Probate; Unavailable in Certain Cases.]

Applications for informal probate which relate to one or more of a known series of testamentary instruments (other than a will and ~~its codicil~~ one or more codicils thereto), the latest of which does not expressly revoke the earlier, shall be declined.

Comment

The present text is confusing. JEB–UPC has concluded that Amendment 5 should be substituted. No change of meaning is intended.

AMENDMENT 6

Section 3–705 of the Code is amended to read:

SECTION 3–705. [Duty of Personal Representative; Information to Heirs and Devisees.]

Not later than 30 days after his appointment every personal representative, except any special administrator, shall give information of his appointment to the heirs and devisees, including, if there has been no formal testacy proceeding and if the personal representative was appointed on the assumption that the decedent died intestate, the devisees in any will mentioned in the application for appointment of a personal representative. The information shall be delivered or sent by ordinary mail to each of the heirs and devisees whose address is reasonably available to the personal representative. The duty does not extend to require information to persons who have been adjudicated in a prior formal testacy proceeding to have no interest in the estate. The information shall include the name and address of the personal representative, indicate that it is being sent to persons who have or may have some interest in the estate being administered, indicate whether bond has been filed, and describe the court where papers relating to the estate are on file. The information shall state that the estate is being administered by the personal representative under the [State] Probate Code without supervision by the Court but that recipients are entitled to information regarding the administration from the personal representative and can petition the Court in any matter relating to the estate, including distribution of assets and expenses of administration. The personal representative's failure to give this information is a breach of his duty to the persons concerned but does not affect the validity of his appointment, his powers or other duties. A personal representative may inform other persons of his appointment by delivery or ordinary first class mail.

Comment

The addition serves to improve the likelihood that persons interested in an estate that is being administered in UPC's "unsupervised estate" mode will realize certain information from the personal representative may be expected and that the probate court, though unlikely to intervene on its own motion, is the appropriate place to file petitions for any desired relief by the court.

AMENDMENT 7

Section 3–806 of the Code is amended to read:

SECTION 3–806. [Allowance of Claims.]

(a) As to claims presented in the manner described in Section 3–804 within the time limit prescribed in 3–803, the personal representative may mail a notice to any claimant stating that the claim has been disallowed. If, after allowing or disallowing a claim, the personal representative changes his decision concerning the claim, he shall notify the claimant. The personal representative may not change a disallowance of a claim after the time for the claimant to file a petition for allowance or to commence a proceeding on the claim has run and the claim has been barred. Every claim which is disallowed in whole or in part by the personal representative is barred so far as not allowed unless the claimant files a petition for allowance in the Court or commences a proceeding against the personal representative not later than 60 days after the mailing of the notice of disallowance or partial allowance if the notice warns the claimant of the impending bar. Failure of the personal representative to mail notice to a claimant of action on his claim for 60 days after the time for original presentation of the claim has expired has the effect of a notice of allowance.

(b) After allowing or disallowing a claim the personal representative may change the allowance or disallowance as hereafter provided. The personal representative may prior to payment change the allowance to a disallowance in whole or in part, but not after allowance by a court order or judgment or an order directing payment of the claim. He shall notify the claimant of the change to disallowance, and the disallowed claim is then subject to bar as provided in subsection (a). The personal representative may change a disallowance to an allowance, in whole or in part, until it is barred under subsection (a); after it is barred, it may be allowed and paid only if the estate is solvent and all successors whose interests would be affected consent.

(b) (c) Upon the petition of the personal representative or of a claimant in a proceeding for the purpose, the Court may allow in whole or in part any claim or claims presented to the personal representative or filed with the clerk of the Court in due time and not barred by subsection (a) of this section. Notice in this proceeding shall be given to the claimant, the personal representative and those other persons interested in the estate as the Court may direct by order entered at the time the proceeding is commenced.

(c) (d) A judgment in a proceeding in another court against a personal representative to enforce a claim against a decedent's estate is an allowance of the claim.

(d) (e) Unless otherwise provided in any judgment in another court entered against the personal representative, allowed claims bear interest at the legal rate for the period commencing 60 days after the time for original presentation of the claim has expired unless based on a contract making a provision for interest, in which case they bear interest in accordance with that provision.

Comment

Courts and lawyers in UPC states have differed regarding the ability of a personal representative to change an allowed claim to a disallowed claim after 60 days from the original presentation of the claim. The intention of the drafters was to permit a personal representative to change his position regarding an allowed claim, thereby starting the 60–day period within which the claimant may protest the claim classification by commencing a court proceeding on the claim. The drafters considered that the allowance by inaction called for by the last sentence of (a), like an allowance by written notice, could be changed as is clearly stated by the second and third sentences. Otherwise, allowance by inaction can serve as a terrible trap for a personal representative.

AMENDMENT 8

Section 3–906 of the Code is amended to read:

SECTION 3–906. [Distribution in Kind; Valuation; Method.]

(a) Unless a contrary intention is indicated by the will, the distributable assets of a decedent's estate shall be distributed in kind to the extent possible through application of the following provisions:

(1) A specific devisee is entitled to distribution of the thing devised to him, and a spouse or child who has selected particular assets of an estate as provided in Section 2–402 shall receive the items selected.

(2) Any homestead or family allowance or devise ~~payable in~~ of a stated sum of money may be satisfied ~~by value~~ in kind provided

(i) the person entitled to the payment has not demanded payment in cash;

(ii) the property distributed in kind is valued at fair market value as of the date of its distribution, and

(iii) no residuary devisee has requested that the asset in question remain a part of the residue of the estate.

(3) For the purpose of valuation under paragraph (2) securities regularly traded on recognized exchanges, if distributed in kind, are valued at the price for the last sale of like securities traded on the business day prior to distribution, or if there was no sale on that day, at the median between amounts bid and offered at the close of that day. Assets consisting of sums owed the decedent or the estate by solvent debtors as to which there is no known dispute or defense are valued at the sum due with accrued interest or discounted to the date of distribution. For assets which do not have readily ascertainable values, a valuation as of a date not more than 30 days prior to the date of distribution, if otherwise reasonable, controls. For purposes of facilitating distribution, the personal representative may ascertain the value of the assets as of the time of the proposed distribution in any reasonable way, including the employment of qualified appraisers, even if the assets may have been previously appraised.

(4) The residuary estate shall be distributed in ~~kind if there is no objection to the proposed distribution and it is practicable to distribute undivided interests. In other cases, residuary property may be converted into cash for distribution~~ any equitable manner.

(b) After the probable charges against the estate are known, the personal representative may mail or deliver a proposal for distribution to all persons who have a right to object to the proposed distribution. The right of any distributee to object to the proposed distribution on the basis of the kind or value of asset he is to receive, if not waived earlier in writing, terminates if he fails to object in writing received by the personal representative within 30 days after mailing or delivery of the proposal.

Comment

Responding to criticisms of the original text by New York City estate planning expert Richard Covey that serious administrative and tax complications attend the notion that estate beneficiaries are tenants in common of residuary assets, the Joint Editorial Board agreed to changes in the section at its meeting in 1979.

AMENDMENT 9

Section 3–915 of the Code is amended to read:

SECTION 3–915. [Distribution to Person Under Disability.]

(a) A personal representative may discharge his obligation to distribute to any person under legal disability by distributing ~~to his conservator or any other person authorized by this Code or otherwise to give a valid receipt and discharge for the distribution~~ in a manner expressly provided in the will.

(b) Unless contrary to an express provision in the will, the personal representative may discharge his obligation to distribute to a minor or person under other disability as authorized by Section 5–101 or any other statute. If the personal representative knows that a conservator has been appointed or that a proceeding for appointment of a conservator is pending, the personal representative is authorized to distribute only to the conservator.

(c) If the heir or devisee is under disability other than minority, the personal representative is authorized to distribute to:

(1) an attorney in fact who has authority under a power of attorney to receive property for that person; or

(2) the spouse, parent or other close relative with whom the person under disability resides if the distribution is of amounts not exceeding [$10,000] a year, or property not exceeding [$10,000] in value, unless the court authorizes a larger amount or greater value.

Persons receiving money or property for the disabled person are obligated to apply the money or property to the support of that person, but may not pay themselves except by way of reimbursement for out-of-pocket expenses for goods and services necessary for the support of the disabled person. Excess sums must be preserved for future support of the disabled person. The personal representative is not responsible for the proper application of money or property distributed pursuant to this subsection.

Comment

Reflecting a number of concerns, the JEB–UPC recommends that a more comprehensive and useful "facility of payment" provision be substituted.

AMENDMENT 10

Section 5–301 of the Uniform Probate Code and corresponding Section 2–201 of Uniform Guardianship and Protective Proceedings Act are amended to read:

[Uniform Probate Code SECTION 5–301.] [Uniform Guardianship and Protective Proceedings Act SECTION 2–201.] [Appointment of Guardian for Incapacitated Person by Will or Other Writing.]

(a) The parent of an unmarried incapacitated person may appoint by will, or other writing signed by the parent and attested by at least 2 witnesses, a guardian of the incapacitated person. If both parents are dead or the surviving parent is adjudged incapacitated, a parental appointment becomes effective when, after having given 7 days prior written notice of intention to do so to the incapacitated person and to the person having the care of the person or to the nearest adult relative, the guardian files acceptance of appointment in the court in which the will is [informally or formally] probated, or in the case of a non-testamentary nominating instrument, in the Court at the place where the incapacitated person resides or is present. The notice shall state that the appointment may be terminated by filing a written objection in the Court, as provided by subsection (d). If both parents are dead, an effective appointment by the parent who died later has priority.

(b) The spouse of a married incapacitated person may appoint by will, or other writing signed by the spouse and attested by at least 2 witnesses, a guardian of the incapacitated person. The appointment becomes effective when, after having given 7 days prior written notice of intention to do so to the incapacitated person and to the person having care of the incapacitated person or to the nearest adult relative, the guardian files acceptance of appointment in the Court in which the will is informally or formally probated or, in the case of non-testamentary nominating instrument, in the Court at the place where the incapacitated person resides or is present. The notice shall state that the appointment may be terminated by filing a written objection in the Court, as provided by subsection (d). An effective appointment by a spouse has priority over an appointment by a parent.

496

(c) An appointment effected by filing the guardian's acceptance under a will probated in the state of the decedent's domicile is effective in this State.

(d) Upon the filing in the Court in which the will was probated or, in the case of a non-testamentary nominating instrument, in the Court at the place where the incapacitated person resides or is present, of written objection to the appointment by the incapacitated person for whom a parental or spousal appointment of guardian has been made, the appointment is terminated. An objection does not prevent appointment by the Court in a proper proceeding of the parental or spousal nominee or any other suitable person upon an adjudication of incapacity in proceedings under the succeeding sections of this Part.

Comment

This change meets a recommendation of the ABA Commission on the Mentally Disabled.

AMENDMENT 11

Section 5–311 of the Uniform Probate Code and corresponding Section 2–211 of Uniform Guardianship and Protective Proceedings Act are amended to read:

[Uniform Probate Code SECTION 5–311.] [Uniform Guardianship and Protective Proceedings Act SECTION 2–211.] [Removal or Resignation of Guardian; Termination of Incapacity.]

(a) On petition of the ward or any person interested in the ward's welfare, the Court, after hearing, may remove a guardian if in the best interest of the ward. On petition of the guardian, the Court, after hearing, may accept a resignation.

(b) An order adjudicating incapacity may specify a minimum period, not exceeding ~~one year~~ six months, during which a petition for an adjudication that the ward is no longer incapacitated may not be filed without special leave. Subject to that restriction, the ward or any person interested in the welfare of the ward may petition for an order that the ward is no longer incapacitated and for termination of the guardianship. A request for an order may also be made informally to the Court and any person who knowingly interferes with transmission of the request may be adjudged guilty of contempt of court.

(c) Upon removal, resignation, or death of the guardian, or if the guardian is determined to be incapacitated, the Court may appoint a successor guardian and make any other appropriate order. Before appointing a successor guardian, or ordering that a ward's incapacity has terminated, the Court shall follow the same procedures to safeguard the rights of the ward that apply to a petition for appointment of a guardian.

Comment

This change meets a recommendation of the ABA Commission on the Mentally Disabled.

AMENDMENT 12

Section 5–418 of the Uniform Probate Code and corresponding Section 2–318 of Uniform Guardianship and Protective Proceedings Act are amended to read:

[Uniform Probate Code SECTION 5–418.] [Uniform Guardianship and Protective Proceedings Act SECTION 2–318.] [Accounts.]

Each conservator shall account to the Court for administration of the trust not less than annually unless the Court directs otherwise, upon resignation or removal and at other times as the Court may direct. On termination of the protected person's minority or disability, a conservator shall account to the Court or to the formerly protected person or the successors of that person. Subject to appeal or vacation within the time permitted, an order after notice and hearing allowing an intermediate account of a conservator adjudicates as to liabilities concerning the matters considered in connection therewith; and an order, following notice and hearing, allowing a final account adjudicates as to all previously unsettled liabilities of the conservator to the protected person or the protected person's successors relating to the conservatorship. In connection with any account, the Court may require a conservator to submit to a physical check of the estate, to be made in any manner the Court specifies.

Comment

This change meets a recommendation of the ABA Commission on the Mentally Disabled.

AMENDMENT 13

Section 5–502 of the Uniform Probate Code and corresponding Section 2 of Uniform Durable Power of Attorney Act are amended to read:

[Uniform Probate Code SECTION 5–502.] [Uniform Durable Power of Attorney Act SECTION 2.] [Durable Power of Attorney Not Affected By Lapse of Time, Disability or Incapacity.]

All acts done by an attorney in fact pursuant to a durable power of attorney during any period of disability or incapacity of the principal have the same effect and inure to the benefit of and bind the principal and his successors in interest as if the principal were competent and not disabled. Unless the instrument states a time of termination, the power is exercisable notwithstanding the lapse of time since the execution of the instrument.

*

APPENDIX II

UNIFORM DURABLE POWER OF ATTORNEY ACT

1984 AMENDMENTS

The following technical changes to the Uniform Durable Power of Attorney Act were approved by the National Conference in 1984— additions are underlined, deletions are stricken:

SECTION 1. [Definition.]

A durable power of attorney is a power of attorney by which a principal designates another his attorney in fact in writing and the writing contains the words "This power of attorney shall not be affected by subsequent disability or incapacity of the principal, or lapse of time," or "This power of attorney shall become effective upon the disability or incapacity of the principal," or similar words showing the intent of the principal that the authority conferred shall be exercisable notwithstanding the principal's subsequent disability or incapacity, and, unless it states a time of termination, notwithstanding the lapse of time since the execution of the instrument.

*

APPENDIX III

1988 AMENDMENTS

AMENDMENTS TO UNIFORM PROBATE CODE AND UNIFORM GUARDIANSHIP AND PROTECTIVE PROCEEDINGS ACT

July 28, 1988

AMENDMENT 1

Section 5–401 of the Code and corresponding Section 2–301 of the Act are amended to read:

[SECTION 5–401.] [SECTION 2–301.] [Protective Proceedings.]

(a) Upon petition and after notice and hearing in accordance with the provisions of this Part, the Court may appoint a conservator or make any other protective order for cause as provided in this section.

(b) Appointment of a conservator or other protective order may be made in relation to the estate and affairs of a minor if the Court determines that a minor owns money or property requiring management or protection that cannot otherwise be provided or has or may have business affairs that may be jeopardized or prevented by minority, or that funds are needed for support and education and that protection is necessary or desirable to obtain or provide funds.

(c) Appointment of a conservator or other protective order may be made in relation to the estate and affairs of a person if the Court determines that (i) the person is unable to manage property and business affairs effectively for such reasons as mental illness, mental deficiency, physical illness or disability, ~~advanced age,~~ chronic use of drugs, chronic intoxication, confinement, detention by a foreign power, or disappearance; and (ii) the person has property that will be wasted or dissipated unless property management is provided or money is needed for the support, care, and welfare of

503

the person or those entitled to the person's support and that protection is necessary or desirable to obtain or provide money.

AMENDMENT 2

Section 5–406 of the Code and corresponding Section 2–306 of the Act are amended to read:

[SECTION 5–406.] [SECTION 2–306.] [Procedure Concerning Hearing and Order on Original Petition.]

(a) Upon receipt of a petition for appointment of a conservator or other protective order because of minority, the Court shall set a date for hearing. If the Court determines at any time in the proceeding that the interests of the minor are or may be inadequately represented, it may appoint an attorney to represent the minor, giving consideration to the choice of the minor if 14 or more years of age. An attorney appointed by the Court to represent a minor may be granted the powers and duties of a guardian ad litem.

(b) Upon receipt of a petition for appointment of a conservator or other protective order for reasons other than minority, the Court shall set a date for hearing. Unless the person to be protected has chosen counsel, the Court shall appoint an attorney to represent the person who may be granted the powers and duties of a guardian ad litem. If the alleged disability is mental illness, mental deficiency, physical illness or disability, ~~advanced age,~~ chronic use of drugs, or chronic intoxication, the Court may direct that the person to be protected be examined by a physician designated by the Court, preferably a physician who is not connected with any institution in which the person is a patient or is detained. The Court may send a visitor to interview the person to be protected. The visitor may be a guardian ad litem or an officer or employee of the Court.

(c) The Court may utilize, as an additional visitor, the service of any public or charitable agency to evaluate the condition of the person to be protected and make appropriate recommendations to the Court.

(d) The person to be protected is entitled to be present at the hearing in person. The person is entitled to be represented by counsel, to present evidence, to cross-examine witnesses, including any Court-appointed physician or other qualified person and any visitor [, and to trial by jury]. The issue may be determined at a closed hearing [or without a jury] if the person to be protected or counsel for the person so requests.

(e) Any person may apply for permission to participate in the proceeding and the Court may grant the request, with or without hearing, upon determining that the best interest of the person to be protected will be served thereby. The Court may attach appropriate conditions to the permission.

(f) After hearing, upon finding that a basis for the appointment of a conservator or other protective order has been established, the Court shall make an appointment or other appropriate protective order.

*

APPENDIX IV

1989 AMENDMENTS

AMENDMENTS TO UNIFORM PROBATE CODE

As Approved by the Executive Committee of the National Conference of Commissioners on Uniform State Laws

February 4, 1989

Background

In *Tulsa Professional Collection Services v. Pope*, 108 S.Ct. 1340, 485 U.S. 478 (1988), the U.S. Supreme Court, in an 8 to 1 decision, ruled that notice to creditors by publication, made as part of a court-supervised probate administration of a decedent's estate as directed by Oklahoma legislation, was ineffective, under the principle of *Mullane v. Central Hanover Bank & Trust Co.*, 339 U.S. 306 (1950), to subject known or reasonably ascertainable creditors of the decedent to a statutory bar on claims not presented within two months of the publication.

The decision jeopardized the functioning of probate administrations in a large number of states, for reliance on publication of notice to creditors to trigger non-claim bars expediting administrations has been a common feature of state probate laws.

The explicit basis of the *Pope* decision is that the Oklahoma probate court, as an agency of the state, was intimately involved in the publication of notice and implementation of the bar against creditors who failed to respond to the publication. Hence, state action was involved and the *Mullane* precedent governed.

Unless supervised administration under UPC Sections 3–501 et seq. is involved (a rare occurrence in states that have enacted UPC Article III), it is arguable that UPC's Sections 3–801 (describing notice by publication to creditors) and 3–803(a)(1) read with 3–806(a) (barring claims not presented within four months of first publication) describe a self-implementing statute of limitations that functions solely by force of statute and described statutory events. A UPC personal representative (UPC) operates independently of any supervision by, or need to report to, the probate office that issues letters of authority (3–703, 3–704). The "informal proceeding" leading to issuance of letters creating a p.r. is explicitly "concluded by an order making or declining the appointment" meaning that the public office connection incident to opening of an estate is necessarily over before publication may occur (3–107). The Code purports to require publication of notice to creditors by every p.r. (3–801), but other provisions of the Code recognize and provide for the possibility that no notice to creditors by publication may have occurred (3–803(a)(1); 3–1004; 3–1006). Closing of an estate is optional (3–1001, 3–1002, 3–1003).

Under a majority of state probate codes, assurance that all known creditors have been satisfied or barred is vitally important to the complete effectiveness of distributive orders by supervising courts of probate. Titles to inherited real estate may be flawed if applicable statutes as affected by *Pope* leave open a possibility that a known or reasonably ascertainable creditor of the decedent may still perfect a claim against estate assets. By invalidating non-claim statutes keyed to creditor failure to present claims before the expiration of a set period following publication of general notice to creditors, *Pope* forces probate lawmakers in many states to add new procedures and duties for executors and administrators designed to eliminate risks of known or knowable unbarred claims.

Even if *Pope* applies to UPC, the problems in a UPC state flowing from failure to bar a known creditor are of a much smaller magnitude. The Code is designed to enable p.r.'s to administer and distribute estate assets without the benefit of any binding court order. Unbarred claims do not jeopardize inherited titles for marketability of assets by distributees is accomplished via purchaser protection devices derived from commercial law (3–714, 3–910). Distributees of estate assets incur liability to make pro rata restitution for the benefit of late-discovered and possibly unbarred claims (3–1004), but such claims are subject to being barred by limitations running prior to the decedent's death which are merely suspended for a four month period following death (3–802) and are barred in any event three years from death except where distribution occurred more than two years from death (3–1006).

It remains true, however, that prior to *Pope* persons in UPC states operated under the assumption that known, possibly known and unknown claims were barred by publication of notice and claimant-failure to get a written statement of claim to the personal representative within four months thereafter. Now, it can be argued that *Pope* applies to UPC since published notice under UPC can only occur following state acts creating a personal representative. Attorneys in UPC states are likely to reject the prospect of claims pass-through as an acceptable fall-back position even though pass-through of unsatisfied claims had long been a trouble-free feature of probate law in some states, including Georgia, New York and Pennsylvania. Understandably, perhaps, attorneys want their estate clients to be free of worries regarding possibly unbarred claims.

Also, UPC has become the standard by which probate laws in general are assessed and revised when some need for change develops. Hence, many believe that UPC should reflect careful attention to the World of Probate's most recent calamity, the *Pope* case.

JEB–UPC's response, which we recommend for approval by the Executive Committee and the National Conference, affects the UPC sections listed below. As previously reported to the Executive Committee by Chairman Straus: "There is strong feeling among some members of the Board that the principle of the *Pope* decision does not affect the Uniform Probate Code insofar as unsupervised administration of estates is concerned. This position is based primarily on the view that unsupervised or informal administration under the Code does not trigger 'state action' in such a manner as to invoke the protection of Article 14. However, it is the view of the majority of the Board that the Executive Committee should review these suggestions which are so drafted as not to change the basic approach of the Code on notice, but do provide a method of meeting the requirements of the *Pope* decision in those jurisdictions which have concerns over the application of *Pope*."

Not all of the amendments recommended relate to the *Pope* case problem. Those affecting subsections (b) and (c) of Section 3–803 were agreed upon by the JEB–UPC some time ago, but were removed from the list of technical amendments presented to the National Conference in June, 1987, because a decision in a case like *Pope* was anticipated at the time and it was decided that all changes likely to affect 3–803 should be perfected and approved at the same time. Also, the clarification of Section 3–802 by subdivision is unrelated to *Pope*.

Sections Affected

The sections affected by the changes here recommended are Sections 3–801, 3–802, 3–803, 3–807, 3–1003 and 3–1006.

Recommendations

The suggested changes in text and commentary are indicated below by underline for new language and strikeout of language to be removed.

Section 3–801. [Notice to Creditors.]

(a) Unless notice has already been given under this section, a personal representative upon his appointment [may] [shall] publish a notice to creditors once a week for three successive weeks in a newspaper of general circulation in the [county] announcing his the appointment and the personal representative's address and notifying creditors of the estate to present their claims within four months after the date of the first publication of the notice or be forever barred.

(b) A personal representative may give written notice by mail or other delivery to a creditor, notifying the creditor to present his [or her] claim within four months after the published notice, if given as provided in subsection (a), or within 60 days after the mailing or other delivery of the notice, whichever is later, or be forever barred. Written notice must be the notice described in subsection (a) above or a similar notice.

(c) The personal representative is not liable to a creditor or to a successor of the decedent for giving or failing to give notice under this section.

COMMENT

Section 3–1203, relating to small estates, contains an important qualification on the duty created by this section.

In 1989, the Joint Editorial Board recommended replacement of the word "shall" with "[may] [shall]" in (a) to signal its approval of a choice between mandatory publication and optional publication of notice to creditors to be made by the legislature in an enacting state. Publication of notice to creditors is quite expensive in some populous areas of the country and, if *Tulsa Professional Collection Services v. Pope,* 108 S.Ct. 1340, 485 U.S. 478 (1988) applies to this code, is useless, except to bar unknown creditors. Even if *Pope* does not apply, personal representatives for estates involving successors willing to assume the risk of unbarred claims should have (and have had under the code as a practical consequence of absence of court supervision and mandatory closings) the option of failing to publish.

Additional discussion of the impact of *Pope* on the Code appears in the Comment to Section 3–803, infra.

~~Failure~~ If a state elects to make publication of notice to creditors a duty for personal representatives, failure to advertise for claims would involve a breach of duty on the part of the personal representative. If, as a result of such breach, a claim is later asserted against a distributee under Section 3–1004, the personal representative may be liable to the distributee for costs related to discharge of the claim and the recovery of contribution from other distributees. The protection afforded personal representatives under Section 3–1003 would not be available, for that section applies only if the personal representative truthfully recites that ~~he has advertised for~~ the time limit for presentation of claims ~~as required by this section~~ has expired.

~~It would~~ Putting aside *Pope* case concerns regarding state action under this code, it might be appropriate, by ~~court rule~~ legislation, to channel publications through the personnel of the probate court. See Section 1–401. If notices are controlled by a centralized authority, some assurance could be gained against publication in newspapers of small circulation. Also, the form of notices could be made uniform and certain efficiencies could be achieved. For example, it would be compatible with this section for the Court to publish a single notice each day or each week listing the names of personal representatives appointed since the last publication, with addresses and dates of non-claim.

Section 3–802. [Statutes of Limitations.]

(a) Unless an estate is insolvent, the personal representative, with the consent of all successors whose interests would be affected, may waive any defense of limitations available to the estate. If the defense is not waived, no claim ~~which was~~ barred by ~~any~~ a statute of limitations at the time of the decedent's death ~~shall~~ may be allowed or paid. ~~The running of any statute of limitations measured from some other event than death and advertisement for claims against a decedent is suspended during the 4 months following the decedent's death but resumes thereafter as to claims not~~

510

~~barred pursuant to the sections which follow. For purposes of any statute of limitations, the proper presentation of a claim under Section 3-804 is equivalent to commencement of a proceeding on the claims.~~

<u>(b) The running of a statute of limitations measured from an event other than death or the giving of notice to creditors is suspended for four months after the decedent's death, but resumes thereafter as to claims not barred by other sections.</u>

<u>(c) For purposes of a statute of limitations, the presentation of a claim pursuant to Section 3-804 is equivalent to commencement of a proceeding on the claim.</u>

COMMENT

This section means that four months is added to the normal period of limitations by reason of a debtor's death before a debt is barred. It implies also that after the expiration of four months from death, the normal statute of limitations may run and bar a claim even though the non-claim provisions of Section 3-803 have not been triggered. Hence, the non-claim and limitation provisions of Section 3-803 are not <u>mutually</u> exclusive.

It should be noted that under Sections 3-803 and 3-804 it is possible for a claim to be barred by the process of claim, disallowance and failure by the creditor to commence a proceeding to enforce his claim prior to the end of the four month suspension period. Thus, the regular statute of limitations applicable during the debtor's lifetime, the non-claim provisions of Sections 3-803 and 3-804, and the three-year limitation of Section 3-803 all have potential application to a claim. The first of the three to accomplish a bar controls.

In 1975, the Joint Editorial Board recommended a change that makes it clear that only those successors who would be affected thereby, must agree to a waiver of a defense of limitations available to an estate. As the original text stood, the section appeared to require the consent of "all successors," even though this would include some who, under the rules of abatement, could not possibly be affected by allowance and payment of the claim in question.

<u>In 1989, in connection with other amendments recommended in sequel to *Tulsa Professional Collection Services v. Pope*, 108 S.Ct. 1340, 485 U.S. 478 (1988), the Joint Editorial Board recommended the splitting out, into Subsections (b) and (c), of the last two sentences of what formerly was a four-sentence section. The first two sentences now appear as Subsection (a). The rearrangement aids understanding that the section deals with three separable ideas. No other change in language is involved, and the timing of the changes to coincide with *Pope* case amendments is purely coincidental.</u>

Section 3-803. [Limitations on Presentation of Claims.]

(a) All claims against a decedent's estate which arose before the death of the decedent, including claims of the state and any subdivision thereof, whether due or to become due, absolute or contingent, liquidated or unliquidated, founded on contract, tort, or other legal basis, if not barred earlier by ~~other~~ another statute of limitations or non-claim statute, are barred against the estate, the personal representative, and the heirs and devisees of the decedent, unless presented ~~as follows~~ within the earlier of the following:

(1) ~~within 4 months after the date of the first publication of notice to creditors if notice is given in compliance with Section 3–801, provided, claims barred by the non-claim statute at the decedent's domicile before the first publication for claims in this state are also barred in this state.~~ one year after the decedent's death; or

(2) ~~within [3] years after the decedent's death, if notice to creditors has not been published~~ the time provided by Section 3–801(b) for creditors who are given actual notice, and the time provided in 3–801(a) for all creditors barred by publication.

(b) A claim described in subsection (a) which is barred by the non-claim statute of the decedent's domicile before the giving of notice to creditors in this State is barred in this State.

~~(b)~~(c) All claims against a decedent's estate which arise at or after the death of the decedent, including claims of the state and any subdivision thereof, whether due or to become due, absolute or contingent, liquidated or unliquidated, founded on contract, tort, or other legal basis, are barred against the estate, the personal representative, and the heirs and devisees of the decedent, unless presented as follows:

(1) a claim based on a contract with the personal representative, within four months after performance by the personal representative is due; or

(2) any other claim, within 4 the later of four months after it arises, or the time specified in subsection (a)(1).

~~(c)~~(d) Nothing in this section affects or prevents:

(1) any proceeding to enforce any mortgage, pledge, or other lien upon property of the estate; ~~or~~

(2) to the limits of the insurance protection only, any proceeding to establish liability of the decedent or the personal representative for which he is protected by liability insurance~~.~~; or

(3) collection of compensation for services rendered and reimbursement for expenses advanced by the personal representative or by the attorney or accountant for the personal representative of the estate.

512

COMMENT

There was some disagreement among the Reporters over whether a short period of limitations, or of non-claim, should be provided for claims arising at or after death. Sub-paragraph (b) was finally inserted because most felt it was desirable to accelerate the time when unadjudicated distributions would be final. The time limits stated would not, of course, affect any personal liability in contract, tort, or by statute, of the personal representative. Under Section 3–808 a personal representative is not liable on transactions entered into on behalf of the estate unless he agrees to be personally liable or unless he breaches a duty by making the contract. Creditors of the estate and not of the personal representative thus face a special limitation that runs four months after performance is due from the personal representative. Tort claims normally will involve casualty insurance of the decedent or of the personal representative, and so will fall within the exception of sub-paragraph ~~(c)~~(d). If a personal representative is personally at fault in respect to a tort claim arising after the decedent's death, his personal liability would not be affected by the running of the special short period provided here.

~~The limitation stated in sub-paragraph (2) of (a) dove-tails with the three-year-limitation provided in Section 3–108 to eliminate most questions of succession that are controlled by state law after 3 years from death have elapsed. Questions of interpretation of any will probated within such period, or of the identity of heirs in intestacy are not barred, however.~~

In 1989, the Joint Editorial Board recommended amendments to Subsection (a). The change in (1) shortens the ultimate limitations period on claims against a decedent from 3 years after death to 1 year after death. Corresponding amendments were recommended for Sections 3–1003(a)(1) and 3–1006. The new one-year from death limitation (which applies without regard to whether or when an estate is opened for administration) is designed to prevent concerns stemming from the possible applicability to this Code of *Tulsa Professional Collection Services v. Pope*, 108 S.Ct. 1340, 485 U.S 478 (1988) from unduly prolonging estate settlements and closings;

Subsection (a)(2), by reference to 3–801(a) and 3–801(b), adds an additional method of barring a prospective claimant of whom the personal representative is aware. The new bar is available when it is appropriate, under all of the circumstances, to send a mailed warning to one or more known claimants who have not presented claims that the recipient's claim will be barred if not presented within 60 days from the notice. This optional, mailed notice, described in accompanying new text in Section 3–801(b), is designed to enhance the ability of personal representatives to protect distributees against pass-through liability (under Section 3–1004) to possibly unbarred claimants. Personal representatives acting in the best interests of successors to the estate (see Section 3–703(a) and the definition of "successors" in Section 1–201(42)) may determine that successors are willing to assume risks (i) that *Pope*, supra, will be held to apply to this Code in spite of absence of any significant contact between an agency of the state and the acts of a personal representative operating independently of court supervision; and (ii) that a possibly unbarred claim is valid and will be pursued by its owner against estate distributees in time to avoid bar via the earliest to run of its own limitation period (which, under Section 3–802(b), resumes running four months after death), or the one-year from death limitation now provided

513

by § 3–803(a)(1). If publication of notice as provided in Section 3–801 has occurred and if *Pope* either is inapplicable to this Code or is applicable but the late-arising claim in question is judged to have been unknown to the personal representative and unlikely to have been discovered by reasonable effort, an earlier, four months from first publication bar will apply.

The Joint Editorial Board recognized that the new bar running one year after death may be used by some sets of successors to avoid payment of claims against their decedents of which they are aware. Successors who are willing to delay receipt and enjoyment of inheritances may consider waiting out the non-claim period running from death simply to avoid any public record of an administration that might alert known and unknown creditors to pursue their claims. The scenario was deemed to be unlikely, however, for unpaid creditors of a decedent are interested persons (Section 1–201(20)) who are qualified to force the opening of an estate for purposes of presenting and enforcing claims. Further, successors who delay opening an administration will suffer from lack of proof of title to estate assets and attendant inability to enjoy their inheritances. Finally, the odds that holders of important claims against the decedent will need help in learning of the death and proper place of administration is rather small. Any benefit to such claimants of additional procedures designed to compel administrations and to locate and warn claimants of an impending non-claim bar, is quite likely to be heavily outweighed by the costs such procedures would impose on all estates, the vast majority of which are routinely applied to quick payment of the decedents' bills and distributed without any creditor controversy.

Note that the new bar described by Section 3–801(b) and Section 3–803(a)(2) is the earlier of one year from death or the period described by reference to § 3–801(b) and § 3–801(a) in § 3–803(a)(2). If publication of notice is made under § 3–801(a), and the personal representative thereafter gives actual notice to a known creditor, when is the creditor barred? If the actual notice is given less than 60 days prior to the expiration of the four months from first publication period, the claim will not be barred four months after first publication because the actual notice given by § 3–801(b) advises the creditor that it has no less than 60 days to present the claim. It is as if the personal representative gave the claimant a written waiver of any benefit the estate may have had by reason of the four month bar following published notice. (c.f., the ability of a personal representative, under § 3–802 to change claims from allowed to disallowed, and vice versa, and the 60 day period given by § 3–806(a) within which a claimant may contest a disallowance). The period ending with the running of 60 days from actual notice replaces the four month from publication period as the "time for original presentation" referred to in Section 3–806(a).

Note, too, that if there is no publication of notice as provided in Section 3–801(a), the giving of actual notice to known creditors establishes separate, 60 days from time of notice, non-claim periods for those so notified. The failure to publish also means that no general non-claim period, other than the one year period running from death, will be working for the estate. If an actual notice to a creditor is given before notice by publication is given, a question arises as to whether the 60 day period from actual notice, or the longer, four-month from publication applies. Subsections 3–

514

801(a) and (b), which are pulled into Section 3–803(a)(2) by reference, make no distinction between actual notices given before publication and those given after publication. Hence, it would seem that the later time bar would control in either case. This reading also fits more satisfactorily with Section 3–806(a) and other code language referring in various contexts to "the time limit prescribed in § 3–803."

The proviso, formerly appended to 3–803(a)(1), regarding the effect in this state of the prior running of a non-claim statute of the decedent's domicile, has been restated as 3–803(b), and former subsections (b) and (c) have been redesignated as (c) and (d). The relocation of the proviso was made to improve the style of the section. No change of meaning is intended.

The second paragraph of the original comment has been deleted because of inconsistency with amended § 3–803(a).

The 1989 changes recommended by the Joint Editorial Board relating to former § 3–803(b) now designated as 3–803(c) are unrelated to the *Pope* case problem. The original text failed to describe a satisfactory non-claim period for claims arising at or after the decedent's death other than claims based on contract. The four months "after [any other claim] arises" period worked unjustly as to tort claims stemming from accidents causing the decedent's death by snuffing out claims too quickly, sometimes before an estate had been opened. The language added by the 1989 amendment assures such claimants against any bar working prior to the later of one year after death or four months from the time the claim arises.

The other change affecting what is now § 3–803(d) is the addition of a third class of items which are not barred by any time bar running from death, publication of notice to creditors, or any actual notice given to an estate creditor. The addition resembles a modification to the Code as enacted in Arizona.

Section 3–807. [Payment of Claims.]

(a) Upon the expiration of ~~4 months from the date of the first publication of the notice to creditors~~ the earlier of the time limitations provided in Section 3–803 for the presentation of claims, the personal representative shall proceed to pay the claims allowed against the estate in the order of priority prescribed, after making provision for homestead, family and support allowances, for claims already presented ~~which~~ that have not yet been allowed or whose allowance has been appealed, and for unbarred claims ~~which~~ that may yet be presented, including costs and expenses of administration. By petition to the Court in a proceeding for the purpose, or by appropriate motion if the administration is supervised, a claimant whose claim has been allowed but not paid ~~as provided herein~~ may secure an order directing the personal representative to pay the claim to the extent ~~that~~ funds of the estate are available ~~for the payment~~ to pay it.

(b) The personal representative at any time may pay any just claim ~~which~~ that has not been barred, with or without formal

515

presentation, but is personally liable to any other claimant whose claim is allowed and who is injured by ~~such~~ its payment if:

(1) ~~the~~ payment was made before the expiration of the time limit stated in subsection (a) and the personal representative failed to require the payee to give adequate security for the refund of any of the payment necessary to pay other claimants; or

(2) ~~the~~ payment was made, due to ~~the~~ negligence or ~~wilful~~ willful fault of the personal representative, in such manner as to deprive the injured claimant of ~~his~~ priority.

COMMENT

As recommended for amendment in 1989 by the Joint Editorial Board, the section directs the personal representative to pay allowed claims at the earlier of one year from death or the expiration of 4 months from first publication. This interpretation reflects that distribution need not be delayed further on account of creditors' claims once a time bar running from death or publication has run, for known creditors who have failed to present claims by such time may have received an actual notice leading to a bar 60 days thereafter and in any event can and should be the occasion for withholding or the making of other provision by the personal representative to cover the possibility of later presentation and allowance of such claims. Distribution would also be appropriate whenever competent and solvent distributees expressly agree to indemnify the estate for any claims remaining unbarred and undischarged after the distribution.

Section 3–1003. [Closing Estates; By Sworn Statement of Personal Representative.]

(a) Unless prohibited by order of the Court and except for estates being administered in supervised administration proceedings, a personal representative may close an estate by filing with the court no earlier than ~~6~~ six months after the date of original appointment of a general personal representative for the estate, a verified statement stating that ~~he~~ the personal representative, or a ~~prior~~ previous personal representative ~~whom he has succeeded~~, has ~~or have~~:

(1) ~~published notice to creditors as provided by Section 3–801 and that the first publication occurred more than 6 months prior to the date of the statement.~~ determined that the time limited for presentation of creditors' claims has expired;

(2) fully administered the estate of the decedent by making payment, settlement, or other disposition of all claims ~~which~~ that were presented, expenses of administration and estate, inheritance and other death taxes, except as specified in the statement, and that the assets of the estate have been distributed to the

516

persons entitled. If any claims remain undischarged, the statement ~~shall~~ must state whether the personal representative has distributed the estate subject to possible liability with the agreement of the distributees or ~~it shall~~ state in detail other arrangements ~~which~~ that have been made to accommodate outstanding liabilities; and

(3) sent a copy ~~thereof~~ of the statement to all distributees of the estate and to all creditors or other claimants of whom ~~he~~ the personal representative is aware whose claims are neither paid nor barred and has furnished a full account in writing of ~~his~~ the personal representative's administration to the distributees whose interests are affected thereby.

(b) If no proceedings involving the personal representative are pending in the Court one year after the closing statement is filed, the appointment of the personal representative terminates.

COMMENT

Add new paragraph to existing Comment as follows:

In 1989 the Joint Editorial Board recommended changing sub-paragraph (a)(1) to make the time reference correspond to changes recommended for Section 3–803.

Section 3–1006. [Limitations on Actions and Proceedings Against Distributees.]

Unless previously adjudicated in a formal testacy proceeding or in a proceeding settling the accounts of a personal representative or otherwise barred, the claim of ~~any~~ a claimant to recover from a distributee who is liable to pay the claim, and the right of ~~any~~ an heir or devisee, or of a successor personal representative acting in their behalf, to recover property improperly distributed or ~~the~~ its value ~~thereof~~ from any distributee is forever barred at the later of ~~(1)~~ three years after the decedent's death~~;~~ or ~~(2)~~ one year after the time of its distribution thereof, but all claims of creditors of the decedent are barred one year after the decedent's death. This section does not bar an action to recover property or value received as a result of fraud.

COMMENT

Add new paragraph to existing Comment as follows:

In 1989, the Joint Editorial Board recommended changing the section so as to separate proceedings involving claims by claimants barred one year after decedent's death by Section 3–803(a)(1); and other proceedings by unbarred claimants or by omitted heirs or devisees.

*

517

APPENDIX V

PRE–1989 ARTICLE VI

*The Official Text and Comments of Article VI, as it existed
prior to the 1989 Revision of that Article, are set forth below.*

ARTICLE VI

NON–PROBATE TRANSFERS

PART 1

MULTIPLE–PARTY ACCOUNTS

PART 2

PROVISIONS RELATING TO EFFECT OF DEATH

PART 1

MULTIPLE–PARTY ACCOUNTS

Section 6–101. [Definitions.]

In this part, unless the context otherwise requires:

(1) "account" means a contract of deposit of funds between a
depositor and a financial institution, and includes a checking ac-

count, savings account, certificate of deposit, share account and other like arrangement;

(2) "beneficiary" means a person named in a trust account as one for whom a party to the account is named as trustee;

(3) "financial institution" means any organization authorized to do business under state or federal laws relating to financial institutions, including, without limitation, banks and trust companies, savings banks, building and loan associations, savings and loan companies or associations, and credit unions;

(4) "joint account" means an account payable on request to one or more of two or more parties whether or not mention is made of any right of survivorship;

(5) a "multiple-party account" is any of the following types of account: (i) a joint account, (ii) a P.O.D. account, or (iii) a trust account. It does not include accounts established for deposit of funds of a partnership, joint venture, or other association for business purposes, or accounts controlled by one or more persons as the duly authorized agent or trustee for a corporation, unincorporated association, charitable or civic organization or a regular fiduciary or trust account where the relationship is established other than by deposit agreement;

(6) "net contribution" of a party to a joint account as of any given time is the sum of all deposits thereto made by or for him, less all withdrawals made by or for him which have not been paid to or applied to the use of any other party, plus a pro rata share of any interest or dividends included in the current balance. The term includes, in addition, any proceeds of deposit life insurance added to the account by reason of the death of the party whose net contribution is in question;

(7) "party" means a person who, by the terms of the account, has a present right, subject to request, to payment from a multiple-party account. A P.O.D. payee or beneficiary of a trust account is a party only after the account becomes payable to him by reason of his surviving the original payee or trustee. Unless the context otherwise requires, it includes a guardian, conservator, personal representative, or assignee, including an attaching creditor, of a party. It also includes a person identified as a trustee of an account for another whether or not a beneficiary is named, but it does not include any named beneficiary unless he has a present right of withdrawal;

(8) "payment" of sums on deposit includes withdrawal, payment on check or other directive of a party, and any pledge of sums on

deposit by a party and any set-off, or reduction or other disposition of all or part of an account pursuant to a pledge;

(9) "proof of death" includes a death certificate or record or report which is prima facie proof of death under Section 1–107;

(10) "P.O.D. account" means an account payable on request to one person during his lifetime and on his death to one or more P.O.D. payees, or to one or more persons during their lifetimes and on the death of all of them to one or more P.O.D. payees;

(11) "P.O.D. payee" means a person designated on a P.O.D. account as one to whom the account is payable on request after the death of one or more persons;

(12) "request" means a proper request for withdrawal, or a check or order for payment, which complies with all conditions of the account, including special requirements concerning necessary signatures and regulations of the financial institution; but if the financial institution conditions withdrawal or payment on advance notice, for purposes of this part the request for withdrawal or payment is treated as immediately effective and a notice of intent to withdraw is treated as a request for withdrawal;

(13) "sums on deposit" means the balance payable on a multiple-party account including interest, dividends, and in addition any deposit life insurance proceeds added to the account by reason of the death of a party;

(14) "trust account" means an account in the name of one or more parties as trustee for one or more beneficiaries where the relationship is established by the form of the account and the deposit agreement with the financial institution and there is no subject of the trust other than the sums on deposit in the account; it is not essential that payment to the beneficiary be mentioned in the deposit agreement. A trust account does not include a regular trust account under a testamentary trust or a trust agreement which has significance apart from the account, or a fiduciary account arising from a fiduciary relation such as attorney-client;

(15) "withdrawal" includes payment to a third person pursuant to check or other directive of a party.

COMMENT

This and the sections which follow are designed to reduce certain questions concerning many forms of joint accounts and the so-called Totten trust account. An account "payable on death" is also authorized.

As may be seen from examination of the sections that follow, "net contribution" as defined by subsection (f) has no application to the financial institution-depositor relationship. Rather, it is relevant only to controversies that may arise between parties to a multiple-party account.

Various signature requirements may be involved in order to meet the withdrawal requirements of the account. A "request" involves compliance with these requirements. A "party" is one to whom an account is presently payable without regard for whose signature may be required for a "request."

Section 6–102. [Ownership As Between Parties, and Others; Protection of Financial Institutions.]

The provisions of Sections 6–103 to 6–105 concerning beneficial ownership as between parties, or as between parties and P.O.D. payees or beneficiaries of multiple-party accounts, are relevant only to controversies between these persons and their creditors and other successors, and have no bearing on the power of withdrawal of these persons as determined by the terms of account contracts. The provisions of Sections 6–108 to 6–113 govern the liability of financial institutions who make payments pursuant thereto, and their set-off rights.

COMMENT

This section organizes the sections which follow into those dealing with the relationship between parties to multiple-party accounts, on the one hand, and those relating to the financial institution-depositor (or party) relationship, on the other. By keeping these relationships separate, it is possible to achieve the degree of definiteness that financial institutions must have in order to be induced to offer multiple-party accounts for use by their customers, while preserving the opportunity for individuals involved in multiple-party accounts to show various intentions that may have attended the original deposit, or any unusual transactions affecting the account thereafter. The separation thus permits individuals using accounts of the type dealt with by these sections to avoid unconsidered and unwanted definiteness in regard to their relationship with each other. In a sense, the approach is to implement a layman's wish to "trust" a co-depositor by leaving questions that may arise between them essentially unaffected by the form of the account.

Section 6–103. [Ownership During Lifetime.]

(a) A joint account belongs, during the lifetime of all parties, to the parties in proportion to the net contributions by each to the sums on deposit, unless there is clear and convincing evidence of a different intent.

(b) A P.O.D. account belongs to the original payee during his lifetime and not to the P.O.D. payee or payees; if two or more parties are named as original payees, during their lifetimes rights as between them are governed by subsection (a) of this section.

(c) Unless a contrary intent is manifested by the terms of the account or the deposit agreement or there is other clear and convincing evidence of an irrevocable trust, a trust account belongs beneficially to the trustee during his lifetime, and if two or more parties are named as trustee on the account, during their lifetimes beneficial rights as between them are governed by subsection (a) of this section. If there is an irrevocable trust, the account belongs beneficially to the beneficiary.

COMMENT

This section reflects the assumption that a person who deposits funds in a multiple-party account normally does not intend to make an irrevocable gift of all or any part of the funds represented by the deposit. Rather, he usually intends no present change of beneficial ownership. The assumption may be disproved by proof that a gift was intended. Read with Section 6–101(6) which defines "net contributions," the section permits parties to certain kinds of multiple-party accounts to be as definite, or as indefinite, as they wish in respect to the matter of how beneficial ownership should be apportioned between them. It is important to note that the section is limited to describe ownership of an account while original parties are alive. Section 6–104 prescribes what happens to beneficial ownership on the death of a party. The section does not undertake to describe the situation between parties if one withdraws more than he is then entitled to as against the other party. Sections 6–108 and 6–112 protect a financial institution in such circumstances without reference to whether a withdrawing party may be entitled to less than he withdraws as against another party. Presumably, overwithdrawal leaves the party making the excessive withdrawal liable to

the beneficial owner as a debtor or trustee. Of course, evidence of intention by one to make a gift to the other of any sums withdrawn by the other in excess of his ownership should be effective.

The final Code contains no provision dealing with division of the account when the parties fail to prove net contributions. The omission is deliberate. Undoubtedly a court would divide the account equally among the parties to the extent that net contributions cannot be proven; but a statutory section explicitly embodying the rule might undesirably narrow the possibility of proof of partial contributions and might suggest that gift tax consequences applicable to creation of a joint tenancy should attach to a joint account. The theory of these sections is that the basic relationship of the parties is that of individual ownership of values attributable to their respective deposits and withdrawals; the right of survivorship which attaches unless negated by the form of the account really is a right to the values theretofore owned by another which the survivor receives for the first time at the death of the owner. That is to say, the account operates as a valid disposition at death rather than as a present joint tenancy.

Section 6–104. [Right of Survivorship.]

(a) Sums remaining on deposit at the death of a party to a joint account belong to the surviving party or parties as against the estate of the decedent unless there is clear and convincing evidence of a different intention at the time the account is created. If there are 2 or more surviving parties, their respective ownerships during lifetime shall be in proportion to their previous ownership interests under Section 6–103 augmented by an equal share for each survivor of any interest the decedent may have owned in the account immediately before his death; and the right of survivorship continues between the surviving parties.

(b) if the account is a P.O.D. account;

(1) on death of one of 2 or more original payees the rights to any sums remaining on deposit are governed by subsection (a);

(2) on death of the sole original payee or of the survivor of two or more original payees, any sums remaining on deposit belong to the P.O.D. payee or payees if surviving, or to the survivor of them if one or more die before the original payee; if 2 or more P.O.D. payees survive, there is no right of survivorship in the event of death of a P.O.D. payee thereafter unless the terms of the account or deposit agreement expressly provide for survivorship between them.

(c) if the account is a trust account;

(1) on death of one of 2 or more trustees, the rights to any sums remaining on deposit are governed by subsection (a);

(2) on death of the sole trustee or the survivor of 2 or more trustees, any sums remaining on deposit belong to the person or persons named as beneficiaries, if surviving, or to the survivor of them if one or more die before the trustee, unless there is clear evidence of a contrary intent; if 2 or more beneficiaries survive, there is no right of survivorship in event of death of any beneficiary thereafter unless the terms of the account or deposit agreement expressly provide for survivorship between them.

(d) In other cases, the death of any party to a multiple-party account has no effect on beneficial ownership of the account other than to transfer the rights of the decedent as part of his estate.

(e) A right of survivorship arising from the express terms of the account or under this section, a beneficiary designation in a trust account, or a P.O.D. payee designation, cannot be changed by will.

COMMENT

The effect of (a) of this section, when read with the definition of "joint account" in 6–101(4), is to make an account payable to one or more of two or more parties a survivorship arrangement unless "clear and convincing evidence of a different contention" is offered.

The underlying assumption is that most persons who use joint accounts want the survivor or survivors to have all balances remaining at death. This assumption may be questioned in states like Michigan where existing statutes and decisions do not provide any safe and wholly practical method of establishing a joint account which is not survivorship. See Leib v. Genesee Merchants Bank, 371 Mich. 89, 123 N.W.(2d) 140 (1962). But, use of a form negating survivorship would make (d) of this section applicable. Still, the financial institution which paid after the death of a party would be protected by 6–108 and 6–109. Thus, a safe nonsurvivorship account form is provided. Consequently, the presumption stated by this section should become increasingly defensible.

The section also is designed to apply to various forms of multiple-party accounts which may be in use at the effective date of the legislation. The risk that it may turn nonsurvivorship accounts into unwanted survivorship arrangements is meliorated by various considerations. First of all, there is doubt that many persons using any form of multiple name account would not want survivorship rights to attach. Secondly, the survivorship incidents described by this section may be shown to have been against the intention of the parties. Finally, it would be wholly consistent with the purpose of the legislation to provide for a delayed effective date so that financial institutions could get notices to customers warning them of possible review of accounts which may be desirable because of the legislation.

Subsection (c) accepts the New York view that an account opened by "A" in his name as "trustee for B" usually is intended by A to be an informal will of any balance remaining on deposit at his death. The section is framed so that accounts with more than one "trustee," or more than one "beneficiary" can be accommodated. Section 6–103(c) would apply to such an account during the lifetimes of "all parties." "Party" is defined by 6–101(7) so as to exclude a beneficiary who is not described by the account as having a present right or withdrawal.

In the case of a trust account for two or more beneficiaries, the section prescribes a presumption that all beneficiaries who survive the last "trustee" to die own equal and undivided interests in the account. This dovetails with Sections 6–111 and 6–112 which give the financial institution protection only if it pays to all beneficiaries who show a right to withdraw by presenting appropriate proof of death. No further survivorship between surviving beneficiaries of a trust account is presumed because these persons probably have had no control over the form of the account prior to the death of the trustee. The situation concerning further survivorship between two or more surviving parties to a joint account is different.

In 1975, the Joint Editorial Board recommended expansion of subsections (b) and (c) so that the subsections now deal explicitly with cases involving multiple original payees in P.O.D. accounts, and multiple trustees in trust accounts. These changes were conceived to clarify, rather than to change, the text.

Section 6–105. [Effect of Written Notice to Financial Institution.]

The provisions of Section 6–104 as to rights of survivorship are determined by the form of the account at the death of a party. This form may be altered by written order given by a party to the financial institution to change the form of the account or to stop or vary payment under the terms of the account. The order or request must be signed by a party, received by the financial institution during the party's lifetime, and not countermanded by other written order of the same party during his lifetime.

COMMENT

It is to be noted that only a "party" may issue an order blocking the provisions of Section 6-104. "Party" is defined by Section 6-101(7). Thus if there is a trust account in the name of A or B in trust for C, C cannot change the right of survivorship because he has no present right of withdrawal and hence is not a party.

Section 6–106. [Accounts and Transfers Nontestamentary.]

Any transfers resulting from the application of Section 6-104 are effective by reason of the account contracts involved and this statute and are not to be considered as testamentary or subject to Articles I through IV, except as provided in Sections 2-201 through 2-207, and except as a consequence of, and to the extent directed by, Section 6-107.

COMMENT

The purpose of classifying the transactions contemplated by Article VI as nontestamentary is to bolster the explicit statement that their validity as effective modes of transfers at death is not to be determined by the requirements for wills. The section is consistent with Part 2 of Article VI.

The closing reference to Article II, Part 2, and to 6-107 was added in 1975 at the recommendation of the Joint Editorial Board to clarify the intention of the original text.

Section 6–107. [Rights of Creditors.]

No multiple-party account will be effective against an estate of a deceased party to transfer to a survivor sums needed to pay debts, taxes, and expenses of administration, including statutory allowances to the surviving spouse, minor children and dependent children, if other assets of the estate are insufficient. A surviving party, P.O.D. payee, or beneficiary who receives payment from a multiple-party account after the death of a deceased party shall be liable to account to his personal representative for amounts the decedent owned beneficially immediately before his death to the extent necessary to discharge the claims and charges mentioned above remaining unpaid after application of the decedent's estate. No proceeding to assert this liability shall be commenced unless the personal representative has received a written demand by a surviving spouse, a creditor or one acting for a minor or dependent child of the decedent, and no proceeding shall be commenced later than two years following the death of the decedent. Sums recovered by the personal representative shall be administered as part of the decedent's estate. This section shall not affect the right of a financial institution to make payment on multiple-party accounts according to the terms thereof, or make it liable to the estate of a deceased party unless before payment the institution has been served with process in a proceeding by the personal representative.

COMMENT

The sections of this Article authorize transfers at death which reduce the estate to which the surviving spouse, creditors and minor children normally must look for protection against a decedent's gifts by will. Accordingly, it seemed desirable to provide a remedy to these classes of persons which should assure them that multiple-party accounts cannot be used to reduce the essential protection they would be entitled to if such accounts were deemed to permit a special form of specific devise. Under this Section a surviving spouse is automatically assured of some protection against a multiple-party account if the probate estate is insolvent; rights are limited, however, to sums needed for statutory allowances. The phrase "statutory allowances" includes the homestead allowance under Section 2–401, the family allowance under Section 2–403, and any allowance needed to make up the deficiency in exempt property under Section 2–402. In any case (including a solvent estate) the surviving spouse could proceed under Section 2–201 et seq. to claim an elective share in the account if the deposits by the decedent satisfy the requirements of Section 2–202 so that the account falls within the augmented net estate concept. In the latter situation the spouse is not proceeding as a creditor under this section.

Section 6–108. [Financial Institution Protection; Payment on Signature of One Party.]

Financial institutions may enter into multiple-party accounts to the same extent that they may enter into single-party accounts. Any multiple-party account may be paid, on request, to any one or more of the parties. A financial institution shall not be required to inquire as to the source of funds received for deposit to a multiple-party account, or to inquire as to the proposed application of any sum withdrawn from an account, for purposes of establishing net contributions.

Section 6–109. [Financial Institution Protection; Payment After Death or Disability; Joint Account.]

Any sums in a joint account may be paid, on request, to any party without regard to whether any other party is incapacitated or deceased at the time the payment is demanded; but payment may not be made to the personal representative or heirs of a deceased party unless proofs of death are presented to the financial institution showing that the decedent was the last surviving party or unless there is no right of survivorship under Section 6–104.

Section 6–110. [Financial Institution Protection; Payment of P.O.D. Account.]

Any P.O.D. account may be paid, on request, to any original party to the account. Payment may be made, on request, to the P.O.D. payee or to the personal representative or heirs of a deceased P.O.D. payee upon presentation to the financial institution of proof of death showing that the P.O.D. payee survived all persons named as original payees. Payment may be made to the personal representative or heirs of a deceased original payee if proof of death is presented to the financial institution showing that his decedent was the survivor of all other persons named on the account either as an original payee or as P.O.D. payee.

Section 6–111. [Financial Institution Protection; Payment of Trust Account.]

Any trust account may be paid, on request, to any trustee. Unless the financial institution has received written notice that the beneficiary has a vested interest not dependent upon his surviving the trustee, payment may be made to the personal representative or heirs of a deceased trustee if proof of death is presented to the financial institution showing that his decedent was the survivor of all other persons named on the account either as trustee or beneficiary. Payment may be made, on request, to the beneficiary upon presentation to the financial institution of proof of death showing that the beneficiary or beneficiaries survived all persons named as trustees.

Section 6–112. [Financial Institution Protection; Discharge.]

Payment made pursuant to Sections 6–108, 6–109, 6–110 or 6–111 discharges the financial institution from all claims for amounts so paid whether or not the payment is consistent with the beneficial ownership of the account as between parties, P.O.D. payees, or beneficiaries, or their successors. The protection here given does not extend to payments made after a financial institution has received written notice from any party able to request present payment to the effect that withdrawals in accordance with the terms of the account should not be permitted. Unless the notice is withdrawn by the person giving it, the successor of any deceased party must concur in any demand for withdrawal if the financial institution is to be protected under this section. No other notice or any other information shown to have been available to a financial institution shall affect its right to the protection provided here. The protection here provided shall have no bearing on the rights of parties in disputes between themselves or their successors concerning the beneficial ownership of funds in, or withdrawn from, multiple-party accounts.

Section 6–113. [Financial Institution Protection; Set-off.]

Without qualifying any other statutory right to set-off or lien and subject to any contractual provision, if a party to a multiple-party account is indebted to a financial institution, the financial institution has a right to set-off against the account in which the party has or had immediately before his death a present right of withdrawal. The amount of the account subject to set-off is that proportion to which the debtor is, or was immediately before his death, beneficially entitled, and in the absence of proof of net contributions, to an equal share with all parties having present rights of withdrawal.

PART 2

PROVISIONS RELATING TO EFFECT OF DEATH

Section 6–201. [Provisions for Payment or Transfer at Death.]

(a) Any of the following provisions in an insurance policy, contract of employment, bond, mortgage, promissory note, deposit agreement, pension plan, trust agreement, conveyance or any other written instrument effective as a contract, gift, conveyance, or trust is deemed to be nontestamentary, and this Code does not invalidate the instrument or any provision:

(1) that money or other benefits theretofore due to, controlled or owned by a decedent shall be paid after his death to a person designated by the decedent in either the instrument or a separate writing, including a will, executed at the same time as the instrument or subsequently;

(2) that any money due or to become due under the instrument shall cease to be payable in event of the death of the promisee or the promissor before payment or demand; or

(3) that any property which is the subject of the instrument shall pass to a person designated by the decedent in either the instrument or a separate writing, including a will, executed at the same time as the instrument or subsequently.

(b) Nothing in this section limits the rights of creditors under other laws of this state.

COMMENT

This section authorizes a variety of contractual arrangements which have in the past been treated as testamentary. For example most courts treat as testamentary a provision in a promissory note that if the payee dies before payment is made the note shall be paid to another named person, or a provision in a land contract that if the seller dies before payment is completed the balance shall be cancelled and the property shall belong to the vendee. These provisions often occur in family arrangements. The result of holding the provisions testamentary is usually to invalidate them because not executed in accordance with the statute of wills. On the other hand the same courts have for years upheld beneficiary designations in life insurance contracts. Similar kinds of problems are arising in regard to beneficiary designations in pension funds and under annuity contracts. The analogy of the power of appointment provides some historical base for solving some of these problems aside from a validating statute. However, there appear to be no policy reasons for continuing to treat these varied arrangements as testamentary. The revocable living trust and the multi-ple-party bank accounts, as well as the experience with United States government bonds payable on death to named beneficiaries, have demonstrated that the evils envisioned if the statute of wills is not rigidly enforced simply do not materialize. The fact that these provisions often are part of a business transaction and in any event are evidenced by a writing eliminate the danger of "fraud."

Because the types of provisions described in the statute are characterized as nontestamentary, the instrument does not have to be executed in compliance with Section 2–502; nor does it have to be probated, nor does the personal representative have any power or duty with respect to the assets involved.

The sole purpose of this section is to eliminate the testamentary characterization from the arrangements falling within the terms of the section. It does not invalidate other arrangements by negative implication. Thus it is not intended by this section to embrace oral trusts to hold property at death for named persons; such arrangements are already generally enforceable under trust law.

APPENDIX VI

PRE-1990 SECTION 1-201

The Official Text and Comment of Section 1-201, as it existed prior to revision in 1990 in conjunction with the approval of Revised II, are set forth below.

Section 1-201. [General Definitions.]

Subject to additional definitions contained in the subsequent Articles which are applicable to specific Articles or parts, and unless the context otherwise requires, in this Code:

(1) "Application" means a written request to the Registrar for an order of informal probate or appointment under Part 3 of Article III.

(2) "Beneficiary", as it relates to trust beneficiaries, includes a person who has any present or future interest, vested or contingent, and also includes the owner of an interest by assignment or other transfer and as it relates to a charitable trust, includes any person entitled to enforce the trust.

(3) "Child" includes any individual entitled to take as a child under this Code by intestate succession from the parent whose relationship is involved and excludes any person who is only a stepchild, a foster child, a grandchild or any more remote descendant.

(4) "Claims", in respect to estates of decedents and protected persons, includes liabilities of the decedent or protected person whether arising in contract, in tort or otherwise, and liabilities of the estate which arise at or after the death of the decedent or after the appointment of a conservator, including funeral expenses and expenses of administration. The term does not include estate or inheritance taxes, or demands or disputes regarding title of a decedent or protected person to specific assets alleged to be included in the estate.

(5) "Court" means the Court or branch having jurisdiction in matters relating to the affairs of decedents. This Court in this state is known as [..........].

(6) "Conservator" means a person who is appointed by a Court to manage the estate of a protected person.

(7) "Devise", when used as a noun, means a testamentary disposition of real or personal property and when used as a verb, means to dispose of real or personal property by will.

(8) "Devisee" means any person designated in a will to receive a devise. In the case of a devise to an existing trust or trustee, or to a trustee on trust described by will, the trust or trustee is the devisee and the beneficiaries are not devisees.

(9) "Disability" means cause for a protective order as described by Section 5–401.

(10) "Distributee" means any person who has received property of a decedent from his personal representative other than as creditor or purchaser. A testamentary trustee is a distributee only to the extent of distributed assets or increment thereto remaining in his hands. A beneficiary of a testamentary trust to whom the trustee has distributed property received from a personal representative is a distributee of the personal representative. For purposes of this provision, "testamentary trustee" includes a trustee to whom assets are transferred by will, to the extent of the devised assets.

(11) "Estate" includes the property of the decedent, trust, or other person whose affairs are subject to this Code as originally constituted and as it exists from time to time during administration.

(12) "Exempt property" means that property of a decedent's estate which is described in Section 2–402.

(13) "Fiduciary" includes personal representative, guardian, conservator and trustee.

(14) "Foreign personal representative" means a personal representative of another jurisdiction.

(15) "Formal proceedings" means those conducted before a judge with notice to interested persons.

(16) "Guardian" means a person who has qualified as a guardian of a minor or incapacitated person pursuant to testamentary or court appointment, but excludes one who is merely a guardian ad litem.

(17) "Heirs" means those persons, including the surviving spouse, who are entitled under the statutes of intestate succession to the property of a decedent.

(18) "Incapacitated person" is as defined in Section 5–101.

(19) "Informal proceedings" mean those conducted without notice to interested persons by an officer of the Court acting as a registrar for probate of a will or appointment of a personal representative.

(20) "Interested person" includes heirs, devisees, children, spouses, creditors, beneficiaries and any others having a property right in or claim against a trust estate or the estate of a decedent, ward or protected person which may be affected by the proceeding. It also includes persons having priority for appointment as personal representative, and other fiduciaries representing interested persons. The meaning as it relates to particular persons may vary from time to time and must be determined according to the particular purposes of, and matter involved in, any proceeding.

(21) "Issue" of a person means all his lineal descendants of all generations, with the relationship of parent and child at each generation being determined by the definitions of child and parent contained in this Code.

(22) "Lease" includes an oil, gas, or other mineral lease.

(23) "Letters" includes letters testamentary, letters of guardianship, letters of administration, and letters of conservatorship.

(24) "Minor" means a person who is under [21] years of age.

(25) "Mortgage" means any conveyance, agreement or arrangement in which property is used as security.

(26) "Nonresident decedent" means a decedent who was domiciled in another jurisdiction at the time of his death.

(27) "Organization" includes a corporation, government or governmental subdivision or agency, business trust, estate, trust, partnership or association, 2 or more persons having a joint or common interest, or any other legal entity.

(28) "Parent" includes any person entitled to take, or who would be entitled to take if the child died without a will, as a parent under this Code by intestate succession from the child whose relationship is in question and excludes any person who is only a stepparent, foster parent, or grandparent.

(29) "Person" means an individual, a corporation, an organization, or other legal entity.

(30) "Personal representative" includes executor, administrator, successor personal representative, special administrator, and persons who perform substantially the same function under the law governing their status. "General personal representative" excludes special administrator.

(31) "Petition" means a written request to the Court for an order after notice.

(32) "Proceeding" includes action at law and suit in equity.

(33) "Property" includes both real and personal property or any interest therein and means anything that may be the subject of ownership.

(34) "Protected person" is as defined in Section 5–101.

(35) "Protective proceeding" is as defined in Section 5–101.

(36) "Registrar" refers to the official of the Court designated to perform the functions of Registrar as provided in Section 1–307.

(37) "Security" includes any note, stock, treasury stock, bond, debenture, evidence of indebtedness, certificate of interest or participation in an oil, gas or mining title or lease or in payments out of production under such a title or lease, collateral trust certificate, transferable share, voting trust certificate or, in general, any interest or instrument commonly known as a security, or any certificate of interest or participation, any temporary or interim certificate, receipt or certificate of deposit for, or any warrant or right to subscribe to or purchase, any of the foregoing.

(38) "Settlement," in reference to a decedent's estate, includes the full process of administration, distribution and closing.

(39) "Special administrator" means a personal representative as described by Sections 3–614 through 3–618.

(40) "State" includes any state of the United States, the District of Columbia, the Commonwealth of Puerto Rico, and any territory or possession subject to the legislative authority of the United States.

(41) "Successor personal representative" means a personal representative, other than a special administrator, who is appointed to succeed a previously appointed personal representative.

(42) "Successors" means those persons, other than creditors, who are entitled to property of a decedent under his will or this Code.

(43) "Supervised administration" refers to the proceedings described in Article III, Part 5.

(44) "Testacy proceeding" means a proceeding to establish a will or determine intestacy.

(45) "Trust" includes any express trust, private or charitable, with additions thereto, wherever and however created. It also includes a trust created or determined by judgment or decree under which the trust is to be administered in the manner of an express trust. "Trust" excludes other constructive trusts, and it excludes resulting trusts, conservatorships, personal representatives, trust accounts as defined in Article VI, custodial arrangements pursuant to [each state should list its legislation, including that relating to gifts to minors, dealing with special custodial situations], business trusts

534

providing for certificates to be issued to beneficiaries, common trust funds, voting trusts, security arrangements, liquidation trusts, and trusts for the primary purpose of paying debts, dividends, interest, salaries, wages, profits, pensions, or employee benefits of any kind, and any arrangement under which a person is nominee or escrowee for another.

(46) "Trustee" includes an original, additional, or successor trustee, whether or not appointed or confirmed by court.

(47) "Ward" is as defined in Section 5–101.

(48) "Will" includes codicil and any testamentary instrument which merely appoints an executor or revokes or revises another will.

[FOR ADOPTION IN COMMUNITY PROPERTY STATES]

[(49) "Separate property" (if necessary, to be defined locally in accordance with existing concept in adopting state).

(50) "Community property" (if necessary, to be defined locally in accordance with existing concept in adopting state).]

COMMENT

Additional sections with special definitions for Articles V and VI are 5–101 and 6–101. Except as controlled by special definitions applicable to these particular Articles, the definitions in 1–201 apply to the entire Code.

The definition of "trust" and the use of the term in Article VII eliminate procedural distinctions between testamentary and inter vivos trusts. Article VII does not deal with questions of substantive validity of trusts where a difference between inter vivos and testamentary trusts will continue to be important.

The exclusions from the definition of "trust" are modelled basically after those in Section 1, Uniform Trustees' Powers Act. The exclusions in the Act for "a trust created in deposits in any financial institution, or other trust the nature of which does not admit of general trust administration" are omitted above. The first of these is inappropriate because of Article VI's treatment of "Totten Trusts". Moreover,

the probate court remedies and procedures being established by Article VII would seem suitable to unclassified trustee-beneficiary relationships that are in the nature of express trusts. Perhaps many controversies involving "hold and deliver" trusts or other dubious arrangements will involve the issue of whether there is a trust, but there would seem to be no harm in conferring jurisdiction on the probate court for these controversies.

The meanings of "child", "issue" and "parent" are related to Section 2–109.

See Comment, Section 7–101, concerning the definition of "trustee".

No definition of "community property" and "separate property" is made here because these are defined in other statutes in every community property state.

In 1975, the Joint Editorial Board recommended the addition of the last sentence to the definition of "distributee" in Paragraph (10).

The purpose of the addition is to extend to trustees of inter vivos, receptacle trusts, the same power to act as distributees of devised assets that is given to testamentary trustees. "Distributees" are enabled, by Section 3–910, to create a good title to devised assets in purchasers, even though possibilities remain open that the devised assets or the proceeds from any sale thereof may be reclaimed for some other person interested in the estate. Also, Sections 3–1004 and 3–1006 relate to "distributees".

APPENDIX VII

PRE–1990 ARTICLE II

The Official Text and Comments of Article II, as it existed prior to the 1990 Revision of that Article, are set forth below.

ARTICLE II

INTESTATE SUCCESSION AND WILLS

PART 1

INTESTATE SUCCESSION

PART 2

ELECTIVE SHARE OF SURVIVING SPOUSE

PART 3

SPOUSE AND CHILDREN UNPROVIDED FOR IN WILLS

537

PART 8

GENERAL PROVISIONS

PART 9

CUSTODY AND DEPOSIT OF WILLS

PART 10

UNIFORM INTERNATIONAL WILLS ACT [INTERNATIONAL WILL; INFORMATION REGISTRATION]

PART 1

INTESTATE SUCCESSION

COMMENT

Part 1 of Article II contains the basic pattern of intestate succession historically called descent and distribution. It is no longer meaningful to have different patterns for real and personal property, and under the proposed statute all property not disposed of by a decedent's will passes to his heirs in the same manner. The existing statutes on descent and distribution in the United States vary from state to state. The most common pattern for the immediate family retains the imprint of history, giving the widow a third of realty (sometimes only for life by her dower right) and a third of the personalty, with the balance passing to issue. Where the decedent is survived by no issue, but leaves a spouse and collateral blood relatives, there is wide variation in disposition of the intestate estate, some states giving all to the surviving spouse, some giving substantial shares to the blood relatives. The Code attempts to reflect the normal desire of the owner of wealth as to disposition of his property at death, and for this purpose the prevailing patterns in wills are useful in determining what the owner who fails to execute a will would probably want.

A principal purpose of this Article and Article III of the Code is to provide suitable rules and procedures for the person of modest means who relies on the estate plan provided by law. For a discussion of this important aspect of the Code, see 3 Real Property, Probate and Trust Journal (Fall 1968) p. 199.

The principal features of Part 1 are:

(1) A larger share is given to the surviving spouse, if there are issue, and the whole estate if there are no issue or parent.

(2) Inheritance by collateral relatives is limited to grandparents and those descended from grandparents. This simplifies proof of heirship and eliminates will contests by remote relatives.

(3) An heir must survive the decedent for five days in order to take under the statute. This is an extension of the reasoning behind the Uniform Simultaneous Death Act and is similar to provisions found in many wills.

(4) Adopted children are treated as children of the adopting parents for all inheritance purposes and cease to be children of natural parents; this reflects modern policy of recent statutes and court decisions.

(5) In an era when inter vivos gifts are frequently made within the family, it is unrealistic to preserve concepts of advancement developed when such gifts were rare. The statute provides that gifts during lifetime are not advancements unless declared or acknowledged in writing.

While the prescribed patterns may strike some as rules of law which may in some cases defeat intent of a decedent, this is true of every statute of this type. In assessing the changes it must therefore be borne in mind that the decedent may always choose a different rule by executing a will.

Section 2–101. [Intestate Estate.]

Any part of the estate of a decedent not effectively disposed of by his will passes to his heirs as prescribed in the following sections of this Code.

Section 2–102. [Share of the Spouse.]

The intestate share of the surviving spouse is:

(1) if there is no surviving issue or parent of the decedent, the entire intestate estate;

(2) if there is no surviving issue but the decedent is survived by a parent or parents, the first [$50,000], plus one-half of the balance of the intestate estate;

(3) if there are surviving issue all of whom are issue of the surviving spouse also, the first [$50,000], plus one-half of the balance of the intestate estate;

(4) if there are surviving issue one or more of whom are not issue of the surviving spouse, one-half of the intestate estate.

COMMENT

This section gives the surviving spouse a larger share than most existing statutes on descent and distribution. In doing so, it reflects the desires of most married persons, who almost always leave all of a moderate estate or at least one-half of a larger estate to the surviving spouse when a will is executed. A husband or wife who desires to leave the surviving spouse less than the share provided by this section may do so by executing a will, subject of course to possible election by the surviving spouse to take an elective share of one-third under Part 2 of this Article. Moreover, in the small estate (less than $50,000 after homestead allowance, exempt property, and allowances) the surviving spouse is given the entire estate if there are only children who are issue of both the decedent and the surviving spouse; the result is to avoid protective proceedings as to property otherwise passing to their minor children.

See Section 2–802 for the definition of spouse which controls for purposes of intestate succession.

ALTERNATIVE PROVISION FOR COMMUNITY PROPERTY STATES

[Section 2–102A. [Share of the Spouse.]

The intestate share of the surviving spouse is as follows:

(1) as to separate property

(i) if there is no surviving issue or parent of the decedent, the entire intestate estate;

(ii) if there is no surviving issue but the decedent is survived by a parent or parents, the first [$50,000], plus one-half of the balance of the intestate estate;

(iii) if there are surviving issue all of whom are issue of the surviving spouse also, the first [$50,000], plus one-half of the balance of the intestate estate;

(iv) if there are surviving issue one or more of whom are not issue of the surviving spouse, one-half of the intestate estate.

(2) as to community property

(i) the one-half of community property which belongs to the decedent passes to the [surviving spouse].]

Section 2–103. [Shares of Heirs Other Than Surviving Spouse.]

The part of the intestate estate not passing to the surviving spouse under Section 2–102, or the entire intestate estate if there is no surviving spouse, passes as follows:

(1) to the issue of the decedent; if they are all of the same degree of kinship to the decedent they take equally, but if of unequal degree, then those of more remote degree take by representation;

(2) if there is no surviving issue, to his parent or parents equally;

(3) if there is no surviving issue or parent, to the issue of the parents or either of them by representation;

(4) if there is no surviving issue, parent or issue of a parent, but the decedent is survived by one or more grandparents or issue of grandparents, half of the estate passes to the paternal grandparents if both survive, or to the surviving paternal grandparent, or to the issue of the paternal grandparents if both are deceased, the issue taking equally if they are all of the same degree of kinship to the decedent, but if of unequal degree those of more remote degree take by representation; and the other half passes to the maternal relatives in the same manner; but if there be no surviving grandparent or issue of grandparent on either the paternal or the maternal side, the entire estate passes to the relatives on the other side in the same manner as the half.

COMMENT

This section provides for inheritance by lineal descendants of the decedent, parents and their descendants, and grandparents and collateral relatives descended from grandparents; in line with modern policy, it eliminates more remote relatives tracing through great-grandparents.

In general the principle of representation (which is defined in Section 2–106) is adopted as the pattern which most decedents would prefer.

If the pattern of this section is not desired, it may be avoided by a properly executed will or, after the decedent's death, by renunciation by particular heirs under Section 2–801.

In 1975, the Joint Editorial Board recommended replacement of the original text of subsection (3) which referred to "brothers and sisters" of the decedent, and to their issue. The new language is much simpler, and it avoids the problem that "brother" and "sister" are not defined terms. "Issue" by contrast is defined in Section 1–201(21). The

definition refers to other defined terms, "parent" and "child", both of which refer to Section 2–109 where the effect of illegitimacy and adoption on relationships for inheritance purposes is spelled out.

The Joint Editorial Board gave careful consideration to a change in the Code's system for distribution among issue as recommended in Waggoner, "A Proposed Alternative to the Uniform Probate Code's System for Intestate Distribution Among Descendants," 66 Nw.U.L. Rev. 626 (1971). Though favored as a recommended change in the Code by a majority of the Board, others opposed on the ground that the original text had been enacted already in several states, and that a change in this basic section of the Code would weaken the case for uniformity of probate law in all states. Nonetheless, since some states as of 1975 had adopted versions of the Code containing deviations from the original text of this and related sections, it was the consensus that Prof. Waggoner's recommendation and the statutory changes that would be necessary to implement it, should be described in Code commentary.

The changes involved would appear in this section and in Section 2–106. The old and the revised text of these sections would be as follows if the Waggoner recommendation is accepted by an enacting state which decides that uniformity of the substantive rules of intestate succession is not vital:

Change Section 2–103(1), (3) and (4) by altering, in each instance, the language referring to taking per capita or by representation, as follows:

2–103 . . .

(1) to the issue of the decedent; *to be distributed per capita at each generation as defined in Section 2–106;* ~~if they are all of the same degree of kinship to the decedent they take equally, but if of unequal degree then those of more remote degree take by representation;~~

(3) if there is no surviving issue or parent, to the issue of the parents or either of them *to be distributed per capita at each generation as defined in Section 2–106;* ~~by representation;~~

(4) . . . or to the issue of the paternal grandparents if both are deceased *to be distributed per capita at each generation as defined in Section 2–106;* ~~the issue taking equally if they are all of the same degree of kinship to the decedent, but if of unequal degree those of more remote degree take by representation.~~

Also, alter 2–106 as follows:

SECTION 2–106. [*Per Capita at Each Generation.*]

If per capita at each generation representation is called for by this Code, the estate is divided into as many shares as there are surviving heirs in the nearest degree of kinship *which contains any surviving heirs* and deceased persons in the same degree who left issue who survive the decedent,~~.~~ ~~e~~*E*ach surviving heir in the nearest degree *which contains any surviving heir is allocated one share and the remainder of the estate is divided in the same manner as if the heirs already allocated a share and their issue had predeceased the decedent.* ~~receiving one share and the share of each deceased person in the same degree being divided among his issue in the same manner.~~

Section 2–104. [Requirement That Heir Survive Decedent For 120 Hours.]

Any person who fails to survive the decedent by 120 hours is deemed to have predeceased the decedent for purposes of homestead allowance, exempt property and intestate succession, and the decedent's heirs are determined accordingly. If the time of death of the decedent or of the person who would otherwise be an heir, or the times of death of both, cannot be determined, and it cannot be established that the person who would otherwise be an heir has survived the decedent by 120 hours, it is deemed that the person failed to survive for the required period. This section is not to be applied where its application would result in a taking of intestate estate by the state under Section 2–105.

COMMENT

This section is a limited version of the type of clause frequently found in wills to take care of the common accident situation, in which several members of the same family are injured and die within a few days of each other. The Uniform Simultaneous Death Act provides only a partial solution, since it applies only if there is no proof that the parties died otherwise than simultaneously. This section requires an heir to survive by five days in order to succeed to decedent's intestate property; for a comparable provision as to wills, see Section 2–601. This section avoids multiple administrations and in some instances prevents the property from passing to persons not desired by the decedent. The five-day period will not hold up administration of a decedent's estate because sections 3–302 and 3–307 prevent informal probate of a will or informal issuance of letters for a period of five days from death. The last sentence prevents the survivorship requirement from affecting inheritances by the last eligible relative of the intestate who survives him for any period.

I.R.C. § 2056(b)(3) makes it clear that an interest passing to a surviving spouse is *not* made a "terminable interest" and thereby disqualified for inclusion in the marital deduction by its being conditioned on failure of the spouse to survive a period not exceeding six months after the decedent's death, if the spouse in fact lives for the required period. Thus, the intestate share of a spouse who survives the decedent by five days is available for the marital deduction. To assure a marital deduction in cases where one spouse fails to survive the other by the required period, the decedent must leave a will. The marital deduction is not a problem in the typical intestate estate. The draftsmen and Special Committee concluded that the statute should accommodate the typical estate to which it applies, rather than the unusual case of an unplanned estate involving large sums of money.

Section 2–105. [No Taker.]

If there is no taker under the provisions of this Article, the intestate estate passes to the [state].

Section 2–106. [Representation.]

If representation is called for by this Code, the estate is divided into as many shares as there are surviving heirs in the nearest degree of kinship and deceased persons in the same degree who left issue who survive the decedent, each surviving heir in the nearest degree receiving one share and the share of each deceased person in the same degree being divided among his issue in the same manner.

COMMENT

Under the system of intestate succession in effect in some states, property is directed to be divided "per stirpes" among issue or descendants of identified ancestors. Applying a meaning commonly associated with the quoted words, the estate is first divided into the number indicated by the number of children of the ancestor who survive, *or* who leave issue who survive. If, for example, the property is directed to issue "per stirpes" of the intestate's parents, the first division would be by the number of children of parents (other than the intestate) who left issue surviving even though no person of this generation survives. Thus, if the survivors are a child and a grandchild of a deceased brother of the intestate and five children of his deceased sister, the brother's descendants would divide one-half and the five children of the sister would divide the other half. Yet, if the parent of the brother's grandchild also had survived, most statutes would give the seven nephews and nieces equal shares because it is commonly provided that if all surviving kin are in equal degree, they take per capita.

The draft rejects this pattern and keys to a system which assures that the first and principal division of the estate will be with reference to a generation which includes one or more living members.

Section 2–107. [Kindred of Half Blood.]

Relatives of the half blood inherit the same share they would inherit if they were of the whole blood.

Section 2–108. [Afterborn Heirs.]

Relatives of the decedent conceived before his death but born thereafter inherit as if they had been born in the lifetime of the decedent.

Section 2–109. [Meaning of Child and Related Terms.]

If, for purposes of intestate succession, a relationship of parent and child must be established to determine succession by, through, or from a person,

(1) an adopted person is the child of an adopting parent and not of the natural parents except that adoption of a child by the spouse of a natural parent has no effect on the relationship between the child and either natural parent.

(2) In cases not covered by Paragraph (1), a person is the child of its parents regardless of the marital status of its parents and the parent and child relationship may be established under the [Uniform Parentage Act].

Alternative subsection (2) for states that have not adopted the Uniform Parentage Act.

[(2) In cases not covered by Paragraph (1), a person born out of wedlock is a child of the mother. That person is also a child of the father, if:

545

(i) the natural parents participated in a marriage ceremony before or after the birth of the child, even though the attempted marriage is void; or

(ii) the paternity is established by an adjudication before the death of the father or is established thereafter by clear and convincing proof, but the paternity established under this sub-paragraph is ineffective to qualify the father or his kindred to inherit from or through the child unless the father has openly treated the child as his, and has not refused to support the child.]

COMMENT

The definition of "child" and "parent" in Section 1–201 incorporates the meanings established by this section, thus extending them for all purposes of the Code. See Section 2–802 for the definition of "spouse" for purposes of intestate succession.

The change in 1975 from "that" to "either" as the third from the last word in subsection (1) was recommended by the Joint Editorial Board so that children would not be detached from any natural relatives for inheritance purposes because of adoption by the spouse of one of its natural parents. The change in this section, which is referred to by the definitions in Section 1–201 of "child", "issue" and "parent", affects, inter alia, the meaning of Sections 2–102, 2–103, 2–106, 2–302, 2–401, 2–402, 2–403, 2–404 and 2–605. As one consequence, the child of a deceased father who has been adopted by the mother's new spouse does not cease to be "issue" of his father and his parents, and so, under Section 2–605, would take a devise from one of his natural, paternal grandparents in favor of the child's deceased father who predeceased the testator. This situation is sug-gested by In re Estate of Bissell, 342 N.Y.S.(2d) 718.

The recommended addition of a new section, Section 2–114, dealing with the possibility of double inheritance where a person establishes relationships to a decedent through two lines of relatives is attributable, in part, to the change recommended in Section 2–109(1).

The approval in 1973 by the National Conference of Commissioners on Uniform State Laws of the Uniform Parentage Act reflects a change of policy by the Conference regarding the status of children born out of wedlock to one which is inconsistent with Section 2–109(2) of the Code as approved in 1969. The new language of 2–109(2) conforms the Uniform Probate Code to the Uniform Parentage Act. In view of the fact that eight states [as of 1975] have enacted the 1969 version of 2–109(2), the former language is retained, in brackets, to indicate that states, consistently with enactment of the Uniform Probate Code, may accept either form of approved language.

Section 2–110. [Advancements.]

If a person dies intestate as to all his estate, property which he gave in his lifetime to an heir is treated as an advancement against the latter's share of the estate only if declared in a contemporaneous writing by the decedent or acknowledged in writing by the heir to be an advancement. For this purpose the property advanced is valued as of the time the heir came into possession or enjoyment of the property or as of the time of death of the decedent, whichever first occurs. If the recipient of the property fails to survive the decedent, the property is not taken into account in computing the intestate share to be received by the recipient's issue, unless the declaration or acknowledgment provides otherwise.

COMMENT

This section alters the common law relating to advancements by requiring written evidence of the intent that an inter vivos gift be an advancement. The statute is phrased in terms of the donee being an "heir" because the transaction is regarded as of decedent's death; of course, the donee is only a prospective heir at the time of the transfer during lifetime. Most inter vivos transfers today are intended to be absolute gifts or are carefully integrated into a total estate plan. If the donor intends that any transfer during lifetime be deducted from the donee's share of his estate, the donor may either execute a will so providing or, if he intends to die intestate, charge the gift as an advance by a writing within the present section. The present section applies only when the decedent died intestate and not when he leaves a will.

This section applies to advances to collaterals (such as nephews and nieces) as well as to lineal descendants. The statute does not spell out the method of taking account in the advance, since this process is well settled by the common law and is not a source of litigation.

Section 2–111. [Debts to Decedent.]

A debt owed to the decedent is not charged against the intestate share of any person except the debtor. If the debtor fails to survive the decedent, the debt is not taken into account in computing the intestate share of the debtor's issue.

COMMENT

This supplements the content of Section 3–903, *infra*.

Section 2–112. [Alienage.]

No person is disqualified to take as an heir because he or a person through whom he claims is or has been an alien.

COMMENT

The purpose of this section is to eliminate the ancient rule that an alien cannot acquire or transmit land by descent, a rule based on the feudal notions of the obligations of the tenant to the King. Although there never was a corresponding rule as to personalty, the present section is phrased in light of the basic premise of the Code that distinctions between real and personal property should be abolished.

This section has broader vitality in light of the recent decision of the United States Supreme Court in Zschernig v. Miller, 88 S.Ct. 664, 389 U.S. 429, 19 L.Ed.2d 683 (1968) holding unconstitutional a state statute providing for escheat if a non-resident alien cannot meet three requirements: the existence of a reciprocal right of a United States citizen to take property on the same terms as a citizen or inhabitant of the foreign country, the right of United States citizens to receive payment here of funds from estates in the foreign country, and the right of the foreign heirs to receive the proceeds of the local estate without confiscation by the foreign government. The rationale was that such a statute involved the local probate court in matters which essentially involve United States foreign policy, whether or not there is a governing treaty with the foreign country. Hence, the statute is "an intrusion by the State into the field of foreign affairs which the Constitution entrusts to the President and the Congress".

[Section 2–113. [Dower and Curtesy Abolished.]

The estates of dower and curtesy are abolished.]

COMMENT

The provisions of this Code replace the common law concepts of dower and curtesy and their statutory counterparts. Those estates provided both a share in intestacy and a protection against disinheritance.

In states which have previously abolished dower and curtesy, or where those estates have never existed, the above section should be omitted.

Section 2–114. [Persons Related to Decedent Through Two Lines.]

A person who is related to the decedent through 2 lines of relationship is entitled to only a single share based on the relationship which would entitle him to the larger share.

COMMENT

This section was added in 1975. The language is identical to that appearing as Section 2–112 in U.P.C. Working Drafts 3 and 4, and as Section 2–110 in Working Draft 5. The section was dropped because, with adoptions serving to transplant adopted children from all natural relationships to full relationship with adoptive relatives, and inheritance eliminated as between persons more distantly related than descendants of a common grandparent, the prospects of double inheritance seemed too remote to warrant the burden of an extra section. The changes recommended in Section 2–109(1) increase the prospects of double inheritance to the point where the addition of Section 2–114 seemed desirable. The section would have potential application in the not uncommon case where a deceased person's brother or sister marries the spouse of the decedent and adopts a child of the former marriage; it would block inheritance through two lines if the adopting parent died thereafter leaving the child as a natural and adopted grandchild of its grandparents.

PART 2

ELECTIVE SHARE OF SURVIVING SPOUSE

GENERAL COMMENT

The sections of this Part describe a system for common law states designed to protect a spouse of a decedent who was a domiciliary against donative transfers by will and will substitutes which would deprive the survivor of a "fair share" of the decedent's estate. Optional sections adapting the elective share system to community property jurisdictions were contained in preliminary drafts, but were dropped from the final Code. Problems of disherison of spouses in community states are limited to situations involving assets acquired by domiciliaries of common law states who later become domiciliaries of a community property state, and to instances where substantially all of a deceased spouse's property is separate property. Representatives of community property states differ in regard to whether either of these problem areas warrant statutory solution.

Almost every feature of the system described herein is or may be controversial. Some have questioned the need for any legislation checking the power of married persons to transfer their property as they please. See Plager, "The Spouse's Nonbarrable Share: A Solution in Search of a Problem", 33 Chi.L.Rev. 681 (1966). Still, virtually all common law states impose some restriction on the power of a spouse to disinherit the other. In some, the ancient concept of dower continues to prevent free transfer of land by a married person. In most states, including many which have abolished dower, a spouse's protection is found in statutes which give a surviving spouse the power to take a share of the decedent's probate estate upon election rejecting the provisions of the decedent's will. These statutes expand the spouse's protection to all real and personal assets owned by the decedent at death, but usually take no account of various will substitutes which permit an owner to transfer ownership at his death without use of a will. Judicial doctrines identifying certain transfers to be "illusory" or to be in "fraud" of the spouse's share have been evolved in some jurisdictions to offset the problems caused by will substitutes, and in New York and Pennsylvania, statutes have extended the elective share of a surviving spouse to certain non-testamentary transfers.

Questions relating to the proper size of a spouse's protected interest may be raised in addition to those concerning the need for, and method of assuring, any protection. The traditions in both common law and community property states point toward some capital sum related to the size of the deceased spouse's holdings rather than to the needs of the surviving spouse. The community property pattern produces one-half for the surviving spouse, but is somewhat misleading as an analogy, for it takes no account of the decedent's separate property. The fraction of one-third, which is stated in Section 2–201, has the advantage of familiarity, for it is used in many forced share statutes.

Although the system described herein may seem complex, it should not complicate administration of a married person's estate in any but very unusual cases. The surviving spouse rather than the executor or the probate court has the burden of asserting an election, as well as the burden of proving the matters which must be shown in order to make a successful claim to more than he or she has received. Some of the apparent complexity arises

from Section 2–202, which has the effect of compelling an electing spouse to allow credit for all funds attributable to the decedent when the spouse, by electing, is claiming that more is due. This feature should serve to reduce the number of instances in which an elective share will be asserted. Finally, Section 2–204 expands the effectiveness of attempted waivers and releases of rights to claim an elective share. Thus, means by which estate planners can assure clients that their estates will not become embroiled in election litigation are provided.

Uniformity of law on the problems covered by this Part is much to be desired. It is especially important that states limit the applicability of rules protecting spouses so that only estates of domiciliary decedents are involved.

Section 2–201. [Right to Elective Share.]

(a) If a married person domiciled in this state dies, the surviving spouse has a right of election to take an elective share of one-third of the augmented estate under the limitations and conditions hereinafter stated.

(b) If a married person not domiciled in this state dies, the right, if any, of the surviving spouse to take an elective share in property in this state is governed by the law of the decedent's domicile at death.

COMMENT

See Section 2–802 for the definition of "spouse" which controls in this Part.

Under the common law a widow was entitled to dower, which was a life estate in a fraction of lands of which her husband was seized of an estate of inheritance at any time during the marriage. Dower encumbers titles and provides inadequate protection for widows in a society which classifies most wealth as personal property. Hence the states have tended to substitute a

forced share in the whole estate for dower and the widower's comparable common law right of curtesy. Few existing forced share statutes make adequate provisions for transfers by means other than succession to the surviving spouse and others. This and the following sections are designed to do so. The theory of these sections is discussed in Fratcher, "Toward Uniform Succession Legislation," 41 N.Y.U.L.Rev. 1037, 1050–1064 (1966). The existing law is discussed in MacDonald, Fraud on the Widow's Share (1960). Legislation comparable to that suggested here became effective in New York on Sept. 1, 1966. See Decedent Estate Law, § 18.

Section 2–202. [Augmented Estate.]

The augmented estate means the estate reduced by funeral and administration expenses, homestead allowance, family allowances and exemptions, and enforceable claims, to which is added the sum of the following amounts:

(1) The value of property transferred to anyone other than a bona fide purchaser by the decedent at any time during marriage, to or for the benefit of any person other than the surviving spouse, to the extent that the decedent did not receive adequate and full consideration in money or money's worth for the transfer, if the transfer is of any of the following types:

(i) any transfer under which the decedent retained at the time of his death the possession or enjoyment of, or right to income from, the property;

(ii) any transfer to the extent that the decedent detained at the time of his death a power, either alone or in conjunction with any other person, to revoke or to consume, invade or dispose of the principal for his own benefit;

(iii) any transfer whereby property is held at the time of decedent's death by decedent and another with right of survivorship;

(iv) any transfer made to a donee within two years of death of the decedent to the extent that the aggregate transfers to any one donee in either of the years exceed $3,000.00.

Any transfer is excluded if made with the written consent or joinder of the surviving spouse. Property is valued as of the decedent's death except that property given irrevocably to a donee during lifetime of the decedent is valued as of the date the donee came into possession or enjoyment if that occurs first. Nothing herein shall cause to be included in the augmented estate any life insurance, accident insurance, joint annuity, or pension payable to a person other than the surviving spouse.

(2) The value of property owned by the surviving spouse at the decedent's death, plus the value of property transferred by the spouse at any time during marriage to any person other than the decedent which would have been includible in the spouse's augmented estate if the surviving spouse had predeceased the decedent to the extent the owned or transferred property is derived from the decedent by any means other than testate or intestate succession

551

without a full consideration in money or money's worth. For purposes of this paragraph:

(i) Property derived from the decedent includes, but is not limited to, any beneficial interest of the surviving spouse in a trust created by the decedent during his lifetime, any property appointed to the spouse by the decedent's exercise of a general or special power of appointment also exercisable in favor of others than the spouse, any proceeds of insurance (including accidental death benefits) on the life of the decedent attributable to premiums paid by him, any lump sum immediately payable and the commuted value of the proceeds of annuity contracts under which the decedent was the primary annuitant attributable to premiums paid by him, the commuted value of amounts payable after the decedent's death under any public or private pension, disability compensation, death benefit or retirement plan, exclusive of the Federal Social Security system, by reason of service performed or disabilities incurred by the decedent, any property held at the time of decedent's death by decedent and the surviving spouse with right of survivorship, any property held by decedent and transferred by contract to the surviving spouse by reason of the decedent's death and the value of the share of the surviving spouse resulting from rights in community property in this or any other state formerly owned with the decedent. Premiums paid by the decedent's employer, his partner, a partnership of which he was a member, or his creditors, are deemed to have been paid by the decedent.

(ii) Property owned by the spouse at the decedent's death is valued as of the date of death. Property transferred by the spouse is valued at the time the transfer became irrevocable, or at the decedent's death, whichever occurred first. Income earned by included property prior to the decedent's death is not treated as property derived from the decedent.

(iii) Property owned by the surviving spouse as of the decedent's death, or previously transferred by the surviving spouse, is presumed to have been derived from the decedent except to the extent that the surviving spouse establishes that it was derived from another source.

(3) For purposes of this section a bona fide purchaser is a purchaser for value in good faith and without notice of any adverse claim. Any recorded instrument on which a state documentary fee is noted pursuant to [insert appropriate reference] is prima facie evidence that the transfer described therein was made to a bona fide purchaser.

COMMENT

The purpose of the concept of augmenting the probate estate in computing the elective share is two-fold: (1) to prevent the owner of wealth from making arrangements which transmit his property to others by means other than probate deliberately to defeat the right of the surviving spouse to a share, and (2) to prevent the surviving spouse from electing a share of the probate estate when the spouse has received a fair share of the total wealth of the decedent either during the lifetime of the decedent or at death by life insurance, joint tenancy assets and other nonprobate arrangements. Thus essentially two separate groups of property are added to the net probate estate to arrive at the augmented net estate which is the basis for computing the one-third share of the surviving spouse. In the first category are transfers by the decedent during his lifetime which are essentially will substitutes, arrangements which give him continued benefits or controls over the property. However, only transfers during the marriage are included in this category. This makes it possible for a person to provide for children by a prior marriage, as by a revocable living trust, without concern that such provisions will be upset by later marriage. The limitation to transfers during marriage reflects some of the policy underlying community property. What kinds of transfers should be included here is a matter of reasonable difference of opinion. The finespun tests of the Federal Estate Tax Law might be utilized, of course. However, the objectives of a tax law are different from those involved here in the Probate Code, and the present section is therefore more limited. It is intended to reach the kinds of transfers readily usable to defeat an elective share in only the probate estate.

In the second category of assets, property of the surviving spouse derived from the decedent and property derived from the decedent which the spouse has, in turn, given away in a transaction that is will-like in effect or purpose, the scope is much broader. Thus a person can during his lifetime make outright gifts to relatives and they are not included in this first category unless they are made within two years of death (the exception being designed to prevent a person from depleting his estate in contemplation of death). But the time when the surviving spouse derives her wealth from the decedent is immaterial; thus if a husband has purchased a home in the wife's name and made systematic gifts to the wife over many years, the home and accumulated wealth she owns at his death as a result of such gifts ought to, and under this section do, reduce her share of the augmented estate. Likewise, for policy reasons life insurance is not included in the first category of transfers to other persons, because it is not ordinarily purchased as a way of depleting the probate estate and avoiding the elective share of the spouse; but life insurance proceeds payable to the surviving spouse are included in the second category, because it seems unfair to allow a surviving spouse to disturb the decedent's estate plan if the spouse has received ample provision from life insurance. In this category no distinction is drawn as to whether the transfers are made before or after marriage.

Depending on the circumstances it is obvious that this section will operate in the long run to decrease substantially the number of elections. This is because the statute will encourage and provide a legal base for counseling of testators against schemes to disinherit the spouse, and because the spouse can no longer elect in cases where substantial provision is made by joint tenancy, life insurance, lifetime gifts, living trusts set up by the decedent, and the other numerous nonprobate arrangements by which wealth is today transferred. On the other hand the section should provide realistic protection against disinheritance of the spouse in the rare case where decedent tries to achieve that purpose by depleting his probate estate.

The augmented net estate approach embodied in this section is relatively complex and assumes that litigation may be required in cases in which the right to an elective share is asserted. The proposed scheme should not complicate administration in well-planned or routine cases, however, because the spouse's rights are freely releasable under Section 2–204 and because of the time limits in Section 2–205. Some legislatures may wish to consider a simpler approach along the lines of the Pennsylvania Estates Act provision reading:

"A conveyance of assets by a person who retains a power of appointment by will, or a power of revocation or consumption over the principal thereof, shall at the election of his surviving spouse, be treated as a testamentary disposition so far as the surviving spouse is concerned to the extent to which the power has been reserved, but the right of the surviving spouse shall be subject to the rights of any income beneficiary whose interest in income becomes vested in enjoyment prior to the death of the conveyor. The provisions of this subsection shall not apply to any contract of life insurance purchased by a decedent, whether payable in trust or otherwise."

In passing, it is to be noted that a Pennsylvania widow apparently may claim against a revocable trust or will even though she has been amply provided for by life insurance or other means arranged by the decedent. Penn.Stats.Annot. title 20, § 301.11(a).

The New York Estates, Powers and Trusts Law § 5–1.1(b) also may be suggested as a model. It treats as testamentary dispositions all gifts causa mortis, money on deposit by the decedent in trust for another, money deposited in the decedent's name payable on death to another, joint tenancy property, and transfers by decedent over which he has a power to revoke or invade. The New York law also expressly excludes life insurance, pension plans, and United States savings bonds payable to a designated person. One of the drawbacks of the New York legislation is its complexity, much of which is attributable to the effort to prevent a spouse from taking an elective share when the deceased spouse has followed certain prescribed procedures. The scheme described by Sections 2–201 et seq. of this draft, like that of all states except New York, leaves the question of whether a spouse may or may not elect to be controlled by the economics of the situation, rather than by conditions on the statutory right. Further, the New York system gives the spouse election rights in spite of the possibility that the spouse has been well provided for by insurance or other gifts from the decedent.

In 1975, the Joint Editorial Board recommended the addition of reference to bona fide purchaser in paragraph (1), "to a donee" in paragraph (1)(iv) and the addition of paragraph (3) to the above section to reflect recommendations evolved in discussions by committees of the Colorado Bar Association to meet title problems that had been identified under the Code as originally enacted. One problem that should be cured by the amendments arose when real property experts in Colorado took the position that, since any transfer might be found to be for less than "adequate and full consideration in money or money's worth," the language of the original text, all deeds from married persons had to be joined in by the spouse, lest the grantor die within two years and the grantee be subjected to the claim that the value involved was a part of the augmented estate.

Also, the Joint Editorial Board in 1975 recommended the addition in Section 2–202(2)(i) of language referring to property moving to the surviving spouse via joint and survivorship holdings with the decedent. The addition would not, in all probability, change the meaning of the subsection, but it would clarify it in relation to jointly held property which will be present in a great number of cases.

Section 2–203. [Right of Election Personal to Surviving Spouse.]

The right of election of the surviving spouse may be exercised only during his lifetime by him. In the case of a protected person, the right of election may be exercised only by order of the court in which protective proceedings as to his property are pending, after finding that exercise is necessary to provide adequate support for the protected person during his probable life expectancy.

COMMENT

See Section 5–101 for definitions of protected person and protective proceedings.

Section 2–204. [Waiver of Right to Elect and of Other Rights.]

The right of election of a surviving spouse and the rights of the surviving spouse to homestead allowance, exempt property and family allowance, or any of them, may be waived, wholly or partially, before or after marriage, by a written contract, agreement or waiver signed by the party waiving after fair disclosure. Unless it provides to the contrary, a waiver of "all rights" (or equivalent language) in the property or estate of a present or prospective spouse or a complete property settlement entered into after or in anticipation of separation or divorce is a waiver of all rights to elective share, homestead allowance, exempt property and family allowance by each spouse in the property of the other and a renunciation by each of all benefits which would otherwise pass to him from the other by intestate succession or by virtue of the provisions of any will executed before the waiver or property settlement.

555

COMMENT

The right to homestead allowance is conferred by Section 2–401, that to exempt property by Section 2–402, and that to family allowance by Section 2–403. The right to renounce interests passing by testate or intestate succession is recognized by Section 2–801. The provisions of this section, permitting a spouse or prospective spouse to waive all statutory rights in the other spouse's property seem desirable in view of the common and commendable desire of parties to second and later marriages to insure that property derived from prior spouses passes at death to the issue of the prior spouses instead of to the newly acquired spouse. The operation of a property settlement as a waiver and renunciation takes care of the situation which arises when a spouse dies while a divorce suit is pending.

Section 2–205. [Proceeding for Elective Share; Time Limit.]

(a) The surviving spouse may elect to take his elective share in the augmented estate by filing in the Court and mailing or delivering to the personal representative, if any, a petition for the elective share within 9 months after the date of death, or within 6 months after the probate of the decedent's will, whichever limitation last expires. However, non-probate transfers, described in Section 2–202(1), shall not be included within the augmented estate for the purpose of computing the elective share, if the petition is filed later than 9 months after death.

The Court may extend the time for election as it sees fit for cause shown by the surviving spouse before the time for election has expired.

(b) The surviving spouse shall give notice of the time and place set for hearing to persons interested in the estate and to the distributees and recipients of portions of the augmented net estate whose interests will be adversely affected by the taking of the elective share.

(c) The surviving spouse may withdraw his demand for an elective share at any time before entry of a final determination by the Court.

(d) After notice and hearing, the Court shall determine the amount of the elective share and shall order its payment from the assets of the augmented net estate or by contribution as appears appropriate under Section 2–207. If it appears that a fund or property included in the augmented net estate has not come into the possession of the personal representative, or has been distributed by the personal representative, the Court nevertheless shall fix the liability of any person who has any interest in the fund or property or who has possession thereof, whether as trustee or otherwise. The proceeding may be maintained against fewer than all persons against whom relief could be sought, but no person is subject to contribution in any greater amount than he would have been if relief had been secured against all persons subject to contribution.

(e) The order or judgment of the Court may be enforced as necessary in suit for contribution or payment in other courts of this state or other jurisdictions.

COMMENT

In 1975, the Joint Editorial Board recommended changes in subsection (a) that were designed to meet a question, arising under the original text, of whether the right to an elective share was ever barred in cases of unadministered estates. The new language also has the effect of clearing included, non-probate transfers to persons other than the surviving spouse of the lien of any possible elective share proceeding unless the spouse's action is commenced within nine months after death. This bar on efforts to recapture nonprobate assets for an elective share does not apply to probate assets. Probate assets may be controlled by a will that may not be offered for probate until as late as three years from death. As to these, the limitation on the surviving spouse's proceeding is six months after the probate.

Section 2-206. [Effect of Election on Benefits by Will or Statute.]

A surviving spouse is entitled to homestead allowance, exempt property, and family allowance, whether or not he elects to take an elective share.

COMMENT

The election does not result in a loss of benefits under the will (in the absence of renunciation) because those benefits are charged against the elective share under Sections 2-201, 2-202 and 2-207(a).

In 1975, the Joint Editorial Board recommended changes in this and the following section that reverse the position of the original text which permitted an electing spouse to accept or reject particular benefits as provided him by the decedent without reducing the dollar value of his elective share. The new language in this section, replacing former Section 2-206(a) and (b), does not mention renunciation of transfers which is now dealt with in Section 2-207. The remaining content of this section is restricted to a simple statement indicating that the family exemptions described by Article II, Part 4 may be distributed from the probate estate without reference to whether an elective share right is asserted, and without being charged to the electing spouse as a part of the elective share. In the view of the Board, deletion of language in the original form of Section 2-206(b), dealing with devises that are intended to be in lieu of family exemptions, does not alter the ability of a testator, by express provision in the will, from putting a surviving spouse to an election between accepting the devises provided or accepting the family exemptions provided by law. This matter is dealt with in Sections 2–401, 2–402, 2–403 and 2–404.

Section 2–207. [Charging Spouse With Gifts Received; Liability of Others For Balance of Elective Share.]

(a) In the proceeding for an elective share, values included in the augmented estate which pass or have passed to the surviving spouse, or which would have passed to the spouse but were renounced, are applied first to satisfy the elective share and to reduce any contributions due from other recipients of transfers included in the augmented estate. For purposes of this subsection, the electing spouse's beneficial interest in any life estate or in any trust shall be computed as if worth one half of the total value of the property subject to the life estate, or of the trust estate, unless higher or lower values for these interests are established by proof.

(b) Remaining property of the augmented estate is so applied that liability for the balance of the elective share of the surviving spouse is equitably apportioned among the recipients of the augmented estate in proportion to the value of their interests therein.

(c) Only original transferees from, or appointees of, the decedent and their donees, to the extent the donees have the property or its proceeds, are subject to the contribution to make up the elective share of the surviving spouse. A person liable to contribution may choose to give up the property transferred to him or to pay its value as of the time it is considered in computing the augmented estate.

COMMENT

Sections 2–401, 2–402 and 2–403 have the effect of giving a spouse certain exempt property and allowances in addition to the amount of the elective share.

In 1975, the Joint Editorial Board recommended changes in Section 2–206 and subsection (a) of this section which have the effect of protecting a decedent's plan as far as it provides values for the surviving spouse. The spouse is not compelled to accept the benefits devised by the decedent, but if these benefits are rejected, the values involved are charged to the electing spouse as if the devises were accepted. The second sentence of new subsection (a) provides a rebuttable presumption of the value of a life estate or an interest in a trust, when this form of benefit is provided for an electing spouse by the decedent's plan.

PART 3

SPOUSE AND CHILDREN UNPROVIDED FOR IN WILLS

Section 2–301. [Omitted Spouse.]

(a) If a testator fails to provide by will for his surviving spouse who married the testator after the execution of the will, the omitted spouse shall receive the same share of the estate he would have received if the decedent left no will unless it appears from the will that the omission was intentional or the testator provided for the spouse by transfer outside the will and the intent that the transfer be in lieu of a testamentary provision is shown by statements of the testator or from the amount of the transfer or other evidence.

(b) In satisfying a share provided by this section, the devises made by the will abate as provided in Section 3–902.

COMMENT

Section 2–508 provides that a will is not revoked by a change of circumstances occurring subsequent to its execution other than as described by that section. This section reflects the view that the intestate share of the spouse is what the decedent would want the spouse to have if he had thought about the relationship of his old will to the new situation. One effect of this section should be to reduce the number of instances where a spouse will claim an elective share.

Section 2–302. [Pretermitted Children.]

(a) If a testator fails to provide in his will for any of his children born or adopted after the execution of his will, the omitted child receives a share in the estate equal in value to that which he would have received if the testator had died intestate unless:

(1) it appears from the will that the omission was intentional;

(2) when the will was executed the testator had one or more children and devised substantially all his estate to the other parent of the omitted child; or

(3) the testator provided for the child by transfer outside the will and the intent that the transfer be in lieu of a testamentary provision is shown by statements of the testator or from the amount of the transfer or other evidence.

(b) If at the time of execution of the will the testator fails to provide in his will for a living child solely because he believes the child to be dead, the child receives a share in the estate equal in value to that which he would have received if the testator had died intestate.

559

(c) In satisfying a share provided by this section, the devises made by the will abate as provided in Section 3–902.

COMMENT

This section provides for both the case where a child was born or adopted after the execution of the will and not foreseen at the time and thus not provided for in the will, and the rare case where a testator omits one of his existing children because of mistaken belief that the child is dead.

Although the sections dealing with advancement and ademption by satisfaction (2–110 and 2–612) provide that a gift during lifetime is not an advancement or satisfaction unless the testator's intent is evidenced in writing, this section permits oral evidence to establish a testator's intent that lifetime gifts or nonprobate transfers such as life insurance or joint accounts are in lieu of a testamentary provision for a child born or adopted after the will.

Here there is no real contradiction of testamentary intent, since there is no provision in the will itself for the omitted child.

To preclude operation of this section it is not necessary to make any provision, even nominal in amount, for a testator's present or future children; a simple recital in the will that the testator intends to make no provision for then living children or any the testator thereafter may have would meet the requirement of (a)(1).

Under subsection (c) and Section 3–902, any intestate estate would first be applied to satisfy the share of a pretermitted child.

This section is not intended to alter the rules of evidence applicable to statements of a decedent.

PART 4

EXEMPT PROPERTY AND ALLOWANCES

GENERAL COMMENT

This part describes certain rights and values to which a surviving spouse and certain children of a deceased domiciliary are entitled in preference over unsecured creditors of the estate and persons to whom the estate may be devised by will. If there is a surviving spouse, all of the values described in this Part, which total $8,500 plus whatever is allowed to the spouse for support during administration, pass to the spouse. Minor or dependent children become entitled to the homestead exemption of $5,000 and to support allowances if there is no spouse, and may receive some of the support allowance if they live apart

from the surviving spouse. The exempt property section confers rights on the spouse, if any, or on all children, to $3,500 in certain chattels, or funds if the unencumbered value of chattels is below the $3,500 level. This provision is designed in part to relieve a personal representative of the duty to sell household chattels when there are children who will have them.

These family protection provisions supply the basis for the important small estate provisions of Article III, Part 12.

States adopting the Code may see fit to alter the dollar amounts suggested in these sections, or to vary the terms and conditions in other ways so as to accommodate existing traditions. Although creditors of estates would be aided somewhat if all family exemption provisions relating to probate estates were the same throughout the country, there is probably less need for uniformity of law regarding these provisions than for any of the other parts of this article. Still, it is quite important for all states to limit their homestead, support allowance and exempt property provisions, if any, so that they apply only to estates of decedents who were domiciliaries of the state.

Notice that Section 2–104 imposes a requirement of survival of the decedent for 120 hours on any spouse or child claiming under this Part.

Section 2–401. [Homestead Allowance.]

A surviving spouse of a decedent who was domiciled in this state is entitled to a homestead allowance of [$5,000]. If there is no surviving spouse, each minor child and each dependent child of the decedent is entitled to a homestead allowance amounting to [$5,000] divided by the number of minor and dependent children of the decedent. The homestead allowance is exempt from and has priority over all claims against the estate. Homestead allowance is in addition to any share passing to the surviving spouse or minor or dependent child by the will of the decedent unless otherwise provided, by intestate succession or by way of elective share.

COMMENT

See Section 2–802 for the definition of "spouse" which controls in this Part. Also, see Section 2–104. Waiver of homestead is covered by Section 2–204. "Election" between a provision of a will and homestead is not required unless the will so provides.

A set dollar amount for homestead allowance was dictated by the desirability of having a certain level below which administration may be dispensed with or be handled summarily, without regard to the size of allowances under Section 2–402. The "small estate" line is controlled largely, though not entirely by the size of the homestead allowance. This is because Part 12 of Article III dealing with small estates rests on the assumption that the only justification for keeping a decedent's assets from his creditors is to benefit the decedent's spouse and children.

Another reason for a set amount is related to the fact that homestead allowance may prefer a decedent's minor or dependent children over his other children. It was felt desirable to minimize the consequence of application of an arbitrary age line among children of the testator.

[Section 2–401A. [Constitutional Homestead.]

The value of any constitutional right of homestead in the family home received by a surviving spouse or child shall be charged against that spouse or child's homestead allowance to the extent

that the family home is part of the decedent's estate or would have
been but for the homestead provision of the constitution.]

COMMENT

This optional section is designed
for adoption only in states with a
constitutional homestead provision.
The value of the surviving spouse's
constitutional right of homestead
may be considerably less than the
full value of the family home if the
constitution gives her only a terminable life estate enjoyable in common with minor children.

Section 2–402. [Exempt Property.]

In addition to the homestead allowance, the surviving spouse of a
decedent who was domiciled in this state is entitled from the estate
to value not exceeding $3,500 in excess of any security interests
therein in household furniture, automobiles, furnishings, appliances
and personal effects. If there is no surviving spouse, children of
the decedent are entitled jointly to the same value. If encumbered
chattels are selected and if the value in excess of security interests,
plus that of other exempt property, is less than $3,500, or if there is
not $3,500 worth of exempt property in the estate, the spouse or
children are entitled to other assets of the estate, if any, to the
extent necessary to make up the $3,500 value. Rights to exempt
property and assets needed to make up a deficiency of exempt
property have priority over all claims against the estate, except that
the right to any assets to make up a deficiency of exempt property
shall abate as necessary to permit prior payment of homestead
allowance and family allowance. These rights are in addition to
any benefit or share passing to the surviving spouse or children by
the will of the decedent unless otherwise provided, by intestate
succession, or by way of elective share.

COMMENT

Unlike the exempt values described in Sections 2–401 and 2–403,
the exempt values described in this
section are available in a case where
the decedent left no spouse but left
only adult children. The possible
difference between beneficiaries of
the exemptions described by Sections 2–401 and 2–403, and this section, explain the provision in this
section which establishes priorities.

Section 2–204 covers waiver of exempt property rights. This section
indicates that a decedent's will may
put a spouse to an election with
reference to exemptions, but that no
election is presumed to be required.

Section 2–403. [Family Allowance.]

In addition to the right to homestead allowance and exempt
property, if the decedent was domiciled in this state, the surviving

spouse and minor children whom the decedent was obligated to support and children who were in fact being supported by him are entitled to a reasonable allowance in money out of the estate for their maintenance during the period of administration, which allowance may not continue for longer than one year if the estate is inadequate to discharge allowed claims. The allowance may be paid as a lump sum or in periodic installments. It is payable to the surviving spouse, if living, for the use of the surviving spouse and minor and dependent children; otherwise to the children, or persons having their care and custody; but in case any minor child or dependent child is not living with the surviving spouse, the allowance may be made partially to the child or his guardian or other person having his care and custody, and partially to the spouse, as their needs may appear. The family allowance is exempt from and has priority over all claims but not over the homestead allowance.

The family allowance is not chargeable against any benefit or share passing to the surviving spouse or children by the will of the decedent unless otherwise provided, by intestate succession, or by way of elective share. The death of any person entitled to family allowance terminates his right to allowances not yet paid.

COMMENT

The allowance provided by this section does not qualify for the marital deduction under the Federal Estate Tax Act because the interest is terminable. A broad code must be drafted to provide the best possible protection for the family in all cases, even though this may not provide desired tax advantages for certain larger estates. In the estates falling in the federal estate tax bracket where careful planning may be expected, it is important to the operation of formula clauses that the family allowance be clearly terminable or clearly nonterminable. With the proposed section clearly creating a terminable interest, estate planners can create a plan which will operate with certainty. Finally, in order to facilitate administration of this allowance without court supervision it is necessary to provide a fairly simple and definite framework.

In determining the amount of the family allowance, account should be taken of both the previous standard of living and the nature of other resources available to the family to meet current living expenses until the estate can be administered and assets distributed. While the death of the principal income producer may necessitate some change in the standard of living, there must also be a period of adjustment. If the surviving spouse has a substantial income, this may be taken into account. Whether life insurance proceeds payable in a lump sum or periodic installments were intended by the decedent to be used for the period of adjustment or to be conserved as capital may be considered. A living trust may provide the needed income without resorting to the probate estate. If a husband has been the principal source of family support, a wife should not be expected to use her capital to support the family.

Obviously, need is relative to the circumstances, and what is reasonable must be decided on the basis of the facts of each individual case. Note, however, that under the next section the personal representative may not determine an allowance of more than $500 per month for one year; a Court order would be necessary if a greater allowance is reasonably necessary.

Section 2–404. [Source, Determination and Documentation.]

If the estate is otherwise sufficient, property specifically devised is not used to satisfy rights to homestead and exempt property. Subject to this restriction, the surviving spouse, the guardians of the minor children, or children who are adults may select property of the estate as homestead allowance and exempt property. The personal representative may make these selections if the surviving spouse, the children or the guardians of the minor children are unable or fail to do so within a reasonable time or if there are no guardians of the minor children. The personal representative may execute an instrument or deed of distribution to establish the ownership of property taken as homestead allowance or exempt property. He may determine the family allowance in a lump sum not exceeding $6,000 or periodic installments not exceeding $500 per month for one year, and may disburse funds of the estate in payment of the family allowance and any part of the homestead allowance payable in cash. The personal representative or any interested person aggrieved by any selection, determination, payment, proposed payment, or failure to act under this section may petition the Court for appropriate relief, which relief may provide a family allowance larger or smaller than that which the personal representative determined or could have determined.

COMMENT

See Sections 3–902, 3–906 and 3–907.

PART 5

WILLS

GENERAL COMMENT

Part 5 of Article II deals with capacity and formalities for execution and revocation of wills. If the will is to be restored to its role as the major instrument for disposition of wealth at death, its execution must be kept simple. The basic intent of these sections is to validate the will whenever possible. To this end, the age for making wills is lowered to eighteen, formalities for a written and attested will are kept to a minimum, holographic wills written and signed by the testator are authorized, choice of law as to validity of execution is broadened, and revocation by operation of law is limited to divorce or annulment. However, the statute also provides for a more formal method of execution with acknowledgment before a public officer (the self-proved will).

Section 2–501. [Who May Make a Will.]

Any person 18 or more years of age who is of sound mind may make a will.

COMMENT

This section states a uniform minimum age of eighteen for capacity to execute a will. "Minor" is defined in Section 1–201, and may involve a different age than that prescribed here.

Section 2–502. [Execution.]

Except as provided for holographic wills, writings within Section 2–513, and wills within Section 2–506, every will shall be in writing signed by the testator or in the testator's name by some other person in the testator's presence and by his direction, and shall be signed by at least 2 persons each of whom witnessed either the signing or the testator's acknowledgment of the signature or of the will.

COMMENT

The formalities for execution of a witnessed will have been reduced to a minimum. Execution under this section normally would be accomplished by signature of the testator and of two witnesses; each of the persons signing as witnesses must "witness" any of the following: the signing of the will by the testator, an acknowledgment by the testator that the signature is his, or an acknowledgment by the testator that the document is his will. Signing by the testator may be by mark under general rules relating to what constitutes a signature; or the will may be signed on behalf of the testator by another person signing the testator's name at his direction and in his presence. There is no requirement that the testator publish the document as his will, or that he request the witnesses to sign, or that the witnesses sign in the presence of the testator or of each other. The testator may sign the will outside the presence of the witnesses if he later acknowledges to the witnesses that the signature is his or that the document is his will, and they sign as witnesses. There is no requirement that the testator's signature be at the end of the will; thus, if he writes his name in the body of the will and intends it to be his signature, this would satisfy the statute. The intent is to validate wills which meet the minimal formalities of the statute.

A will which does not meet these requirements may be valid under Section 2–503 as a holograph.

Section 2-503. [Holographic Will.]

A will which does not comply with Section 2-502 is valid as a holographic will, whether or not witnessed, if the signature and the material provisions are in the handwriting of the testator.

COMMENT

This section enables a testator to write his own will in his handwriting. There need be no witnesses. The only requirement is that the signature and the material provisions of the will be in the testator's handwriting. By requiring only the "material provisions" to be in the testator's handwriting (rather than requiring, as some existing statutes do, that the will be "entirely" in the testator's handwriting) a holograph may be valid even though immaterial parts such as date or introductory wording be printed or stamped. A valid holograph might even be executed on some printed will forms if the printed portion could be eliminated and the handwritten portion could evidence the testator's will. For persons unable to obtain legal assistance, the holographic will may be adequate.

Section 2-504. [Self-proved Will.]

(a) Any will may be simultaneously executed, attested, and made self-proved, by acknowledgment thereof by the testator and affidavits of the witnesses, each made before an officer authorized to administer oaths under the laws of the state where execution occurs and evidenced by the officer's certificate, under official seal, in substantially the following form:

I, _____, the testator, sign my name to this instrument this _____ day of _____, 19___, and being first duly sworn, do hereby declare to the undersigned authority that I sign and execute this instrument as my last will and that I sign it willingly (or willingly direct another to sign for me), that I execute it as my free and voluntary act for the purposes therein expressed, and that I am eighteen years of age or older, of sound mind, and under no constraint or undue influence.

_____
Testator

We, _____, _____, the witnesses, sign our names to this instrument, being first duly sworn, and do hereby declare to the undersigned authority that the testator signs and executes this instrument as his last will and that he signs it willingly (or willingly directs another to sign for him), and that each of us, in the presence and hearing of the testator, hereby signs this will as witness to the testator's signing, and that to the best of our knowledge the testator is eighteen years of age or older, of sound mind, and under no constraint or undue influence.

Witness
Witness

The State of _____

County of _____

Subscribed, sworn to and acknowledged before me by _____, the testator, and subscribed and sworn to before me by _____, and _____, witnesses, this _____ day of _____.

(Seal)

(Signed)   _____

_____
(Official capacity of officer)

(b) An attested will may at any time subsequent to its execution be made self-proved by the acknowledgment thereof by the testator and the affidavits of the witnesses, each made before an officer authorized to administer oaths under the laws of the state where the acknowledgment occurs and evidenced by the officer's certificate, under the official seal, attached or annexed to the will in substantially the following form:

The State of _____

County of _____

We, _____, _____, and _____, the testator and the witnesses, respectively, whose names are signed to the attached or foregoing instrument, being first duly sworn, do hereby declare to the undersigned authority that the testator signed and executed the instrument as his last will and that he had signed willingly (or willingly directed another to sign for him), and that he executed it as his free and voluntary act for the purposes therein expressed, and that each of the witnesses, in the presence and hearing of the testator, signed the will as witness and that to the best of his knowledge the testator was at that time eighteen years of age or older, of sound mind and under no constraint or undue influence.

Testator
Witness
Witness

Subscribed, sworn to and acknowledged before me by ———,
the testator, and subscribed and sworn to before me by ———, and
———, witnesses, this ——— day of ———.

(*Seal*)

(*Signed*) ——————————————

——————————————
(Official capacity of officer)

COMMENT

A self-proved will may be admitted to probate as provided in Sections 3–303, 3–405 and 3–406 without the testimony of any subscribing witness, but otherwise it is treated no differently than a will not self-proved. Thus, a self-proved will may be contested (except in regard to signature requirements), revoked, or amended by a codicil in exactly the same fashion as a will not self-proved. The significance of the procedural advantage for a self-proved will is limited to formal testacy proceedings because Section 3–303 dealing with informal probate dispenses with the necessity of testimony of witnesses even though the instrument is not self-proved under this section.

The original text of this section directed that the officer who assisted the execution of a self-proved will be authorized to act by virtue of the laws of "this State", thereby restricting this mode of execution to wills offered for probate in the state where they were executed. Also, the original text authorized only the addition to an already signed and witnessed will, of an acknowledgment of the testator and affidavits of the witnesses, thereby requiring testator and witnesses, to sign twice even though the entire execution ceremony occurred in the presence of a notary or other official. In 1975, the Joint Editorial Board recommended the substitution of new text that eliminates these problems.

Section 2–505. [Who May Witness.]

(a) Any person generally competent to be a witness may act as a witness to a will.

(b) A will or any provision thereof is not invalid because the will is signed by an interested witness.

COMMENT

This section simplifies the law relating to interested witnesses. Interest no longer disqualifies a person as a witness, nor does it invalidate or forfeit a gift under the will. Of course, the purpose of this change is not to foster use of interested witnesses, and attorneys will continue to use disinterested witnesses in execution of wills. But the rare and innocent use of a member of the testator's family on a home-drawn will would no longer be penalized. This change does not increase appreciably the opportunity for fraud or undue influence. A substantial gift by will to a person who is one of the witnesses to the execution of the will would itself be a suspicious circumstance, and the gift could be challenged on grounds of undue influence. The requirement of disinterested witnesses has not succeeded in preventing fraud and undue influence; and in most cases of undue influence, the influencer is careful not to sign as witness but to use disinterested witnesses.

An interested witness is competent to testify to prove execution of the will, under Section 3–406.

Section 2-506. [Choice of Law as to Execution.]

A written will is valid if executed in compliance with Section 2–502 or 2–503 or if its execution complies with the law at the time of execution of the place where the will is executed, or of the law of the place where at the time of execution or at the time of death the testator is domiciled, has a place of abode or is a national.

COMMENT

This section permits probate of wills in this state under certain conditions even if they are not executed in accordance with the formalities of Section 2–502. Such wills must be in writing but otherwise are valid if they meet the requirements for execution of the law of the place where the will is executed (when it is executed in another state or country) or the law of testator's domicile, abode or nationality at either the time of execution or at the time of death. Thus, if testator is domiciled in state 1 and executes a typed will merely by signing it without witnesses in state 2 while on vacation there, the Court of this state would recognize the will as valid if the law of either state 1 or state 2 permits execution by signature alone. Or if a national of Mexico executes a written will in this state which does not meet the requirements of Section 2–502 but meets the requirements of Mexican law, the will would be recognized as validly executed under this section. The purpose of this section is to provide a wide opportunity for validation of expectations of testators. When the Uniform Probate Code is widely adopted, the impact of this section will become minimal.

A similar provision relating to choice of law as to revocation was considered but was not included. Revocation by subsequent instruments are covered. Revocations by act, other than partial revocations, do not cause much difficulty in regard to choice of laws.

Section 2-507. [Revocation by Writing or by Act.]

A will or any part thereof is revoked

(1) by a subsequent will which revokes the prior will or part expressly or by inconsistency; or

(2) by being burned, torn, canceled, obliterated, or destroyed, with the intent and for the purpose of revoking it by the testator or by another person in his presence and by his direction.

COMMENT

Revocation of a will may be by either a subsequent will or an act done to the document. If revocation is by a subsequent will, it must be properly executed. This section employs the traditional language which has been interpreted by the courts in many cases. It leaves to the Court the determination of whether a subsequent will which has no express revocation clause is inconsistent with the prior will so as to revoke it wholly or partially, and in the case of an act done to the document the determination of whether the act is a sufficient burn-ing, tearing, canceling, obliteration or destruction and was done with the intent and for the purpose of revoking. The latter necessarily involves exploration of extrinsic evidence, including statements of testator as to intent.

The section specifically permits partial revocation. Each Court is free to apply its own doctrine of dependent relative revocation.

The section does not affect present law in regard to the case of accidental destruction which is later confirmed by revocatory intention.

Section 2–508. [Revocation by Divorce; No Revocation by Other Changes of Circumstances.]

If after executing a will the testator is divorced or his marriage annulled, the divorce or annulment revokes any disposition or appointment of property made by the will to the former spouse, any provision conferring a general or special power of appointment on the former spouse, and any nomination of the former spouse as executor, trustee, conservator, or guardian, unless the will expressly provides otherwise. Property prevented from passing to a former spouse because of revocation by divorce or annulment passes as if the former spouse failed to survive the decedent, and other provisions conferring some power or office on the former spouse are interpreted as if the spouse failed to survive the decedent. If provisions are revoked solely by this section, they are revived by testator's remarriage to the former spouse. For purposes of this section, divorce or annulment means any divorce or annulment which would exclude the spouse as a surviving spouse within the meaning of Section 2–802(b). A decree of separation which does not terminate the status of husband and wife is not a divorce for purposes of this section. No change of circumstances other than as described in this section revokes a will.

COMMENT

The section deals with what is sometimes called revocation by operation of law. It provides for revocation by a divorce or annulment only. No other change in circumstances operate to revoke the will; this is intended to change the rule in some states that subsequent marriage or marriage plus birth of issue operate to revoke a will. Of course, a specific devise may be adeemed by transfer of the property during the testator's lifetime except as otherwise provided in this Code; although this is occasionally called revocation, it is not within the present section. The provisions with regard to invalid divorce decrees parallel those in Section 2–802. Neither this section nor 2–802 includes "divorce from bed and board" as an event which affects devises or marital rights on death.

But see Section 2–204 providing that a complete property settlement entered into after or in anticipation of separation or divorce constitutes a renunciation of all benefits under a prior will, unless the settlement provides otherwise.

Although this Section does not provide for revocation of a will by subsequent marriage of the testator, the spouse may be protected by Section 2–301 or an elective share under Section 2–201.

Section 2–509. [Revival of Revoked Will.]

(a) If a second will which, had it remained effective at death, would have revoked the first will in whole or in part, is thereafter revoked by acts under Section 2–507, the first will is revoked in whole or in part unless it is evident from the circumstances of the revocation of the second will or from testator's contemporary or subsequent declarations that he intended the first will to take effect as executed.

(b) If a second will which, had it remained effective at death, would have revoked the first will in whole or in part, is thereafter revoked by a third will, the first will is revoked in whole or in part, except to the extent it appears from the terms of the third will that the testator intended the first will to take effect.

COMMENT

This section adopts a limited revival doctrine. If testator executes will no. 1 and later executes will no. 2, revoking will no. 1 and still later revokes will no. 2 by act such as destruction, there is a question as to whether testator intended to die intestate or have will no. 1 revived as his last will. Under this section will no. 1 can be probated as testator's last will if his intent to that effect can be established. For this purpose testimony as to his statements at the time he revokes will no. 2 or at a later date can be admitted. If will no. 2 is revoked by a third will, will no. 1 would remain revoked except to the extent that will no. 3 showed an intent to have will no. 1 effective.

Section 2–510. [Incorporation by Reference.]

Any writing in existence when a will is executed may be incorporated by reference if the language of the will manifests this intent and describes the writing sufficiently to permit its identification.

Section 2–511. [Testamentary Additions to Trusts.]

A devise or bequest, the validity of which is determinable by the law of this state, may be made by a will to the trustee of a trust established or to be established by the testator or by the testator and some other person or by some other person (including a funded or unfunded life insurance trust, although the trustor has reserved any or all rights of ownership of the insurance contracts) if the trust is identified in the testator's will and its terms are set forth in a written instrument (other than a will) executed before or concurrently with the execution of the testator's will or in the valid last will of a person who has predeceased the testator (regardless of the existence, size, or character of the corpus of the trust). The devise is not invalid because the trust is amendable or revocable, or because the trust was amended after the execution of the will or after the death of the testator. Unless the testator's will provides otherwise, the property so devised (1) is not deemed to be held under a testatmentary trust of the testator but becomes a part of the trust to which it is given and (2) shall be administered and disposed of in accordance with the provisions of the instrument or will setting forth the terms of the trust, including any amendments thereto made before the death of the testator (regardless of whether made before or after the execution of the testator's will), and, if the testator's will so provides, including any amendments to the trust made after the death of the testator. A revocation or termination of the trust before the death of the testator causes the devise to lapse.

COMMENT

This is Section 1 of the Uniform Testamentary Additions to Trusts Act.

Section 2–512. [Events of Independent Significance.]

A will may dispose of property by reference to acts and events which have significance apart from their effect upon the dispositions made by the will, whether they occur before or after the execution of the will or before or after the testator's death. The execution or revocation of a will of another person is such an event.

Section 2–513. [Separate Writing Identifying Bequest of Tangible Property.]

Whether or not the provisions relating to holographic wills apply, a will may refer to a written statement or list to dispose of items of tangible personal property not otherwise specifically disposed of by the will, other than money, evidences of indebtedness, documents of title, and securities, and property used in trade or business. To be admissible under this section as evidence of the intended disposition, the writing must either be in the handwriting of the testator or be signed by him and must describe the items and the devisees with reasonable certainty. The writing may be referred to as one to be in existence at the time of the testator's death; it may be prepared before or after the execution of the will; it may be altered by the testator after its preparation; and it may be a writing which has no significance apart from its effect upon the dispositions made by the will.

COMMENT

As part of the broader policy of effectuating a testator's intent and of relaxing formalities of execution, this section permits a testator to refer in his will to a separate document disposing of certain tangible personalty. The separate document may be prepared after execution of the will, so would not come within Section 2–510 on incorporation by reference. It may even be altered from time to time. It need only be either in the testator's handwriting or signed by him. The typical case would be a list of personal effects and the persons whom the testator desired to take specified items.

PART 6

RULES OF CONSTRUCTION

GENERAL COMMENT

Part 6 deals with a variety of construction problems which commonly occur in wills. All of the "rules" set forth in this part yield to a contrary intent expressed in the will and are therefore merely presumptions. Some of the sections are found in all states, with some variation in wording; others are relatively new. The sections deal with such problems as death before the testator (lapse), the inclusiveness of the will as to property of the testator, effect of failure of a gift in the will, change in form of securities specifically devised, ademption by reason of fire, sale and the like, exoneration, exercise of power of appointment by general language in the will, and the kinds of persons deemed to be included within various class gifts which are expressed in terms of family relationships.

Section 2–601. [Requirement That Devisee Survive Testator by 120 Hours.]

A devisee who does not survive the testator by 120 hours is treated as if he predeceased the testator, unless the will of decedent

573

contains some language dealing explicitly with simultaneous deaths or deaths in a common disaster, or requiring that the devisee survive the testator or survive the testator for a stated period in order to take under the will.

COMMENT

This parallels Section 2–104 requiring an heir to survive by 120 hours in order to inherit.

Section 2–602. [Choice of Law as to Meaning and Effect of Wills.]

The meaning and legal effect of a disposition in a will shall be determined by the local law of a particular state selected by the testator in his instrument unless the application of that law is contrary to the provisions relating to the elective share described in Part 2 of this Article, the provisions relating to exempt property and allowances described in Part 4 of this Article, or any other public policy of this State otherwise applicable to the disposition.

COMMENT

New York Estates, Powers & Trusts Law Sec. 3–5.1(h) and Illinois Probate Act Sec. 896(b) direct respect for a testator's choice of local law with reference to personal and intangible property situated in the enacting state. This provision goes further and enables a testator to select the law of a particular state for purposes of interpreting his will without regard to the location of property covered thereby. So long as local public policy is accommodated, the section should be accept-

ed as necessary and desirable to add to the utility of wills. Choice of law regarding formal validity of a will is in Sec. 2–506. See also Sections 3–202 and 3–408.

In 1975, the Joint Editorial Board recommended the addition of explicit reference to the elective share described in Article II, Part 2, and the exemptions and allowances described in Article II, Part 4, as embodying policies of this state which may not be circumvented by a testator's choice of applicable law.

Section 2–603. [Rules of Construction and Intention.]

The intention of a testator as expressed in his will controls the legal effect of his dispositions. The rules of construction expressed in the succeeding sections of this Part apply unless a contrary intention is indicated by the will.

Section 2–604. [Construction That Will Passes All Property; After–Acquired Property.]

A will is construed to pass all property which the testator owns at his death including property acquired after the execution of the will.

Section 2–605. [Anti-lapse; Deceased Devisee; Class Gifts.]

If a devisee who is a grandparent or a lineal descendant of a grandparent of the testator is dead at the time of execution of the will, fails to survive the testator, or is treated as if he predeceased the testator, the issue of the deceased devisee who survive the testator by 120 hours take in place of the deceased devisee and if they are all of the same degree of kinship to the devisee they take equally, but if of unequal degree than those of more remote degree take by representation. One who would have been a devisee under a class gift if he had survived the testator is treated as a devisee for purposes of this section whether his death occurred before or after the execution of the will.

COMMENT

This section prevents lapse by death of a devisee before the testator if the devisee is a relative and leaves issue who survives the testator. A relative is one related to the testator by kinship and is limited to those who can inherit under Section 2–103 (through grandparents); it does not include persons related by marriage. Issue include adopted persons and illegitimates to the extent they would inherit from the devisee; see Sections 1–201 and 2–109. Note that the section is broader than some existing anti-lapse statutes which apply only to devises to children and other descendants, but is narrower than those which apply to devises to any person. The section is expressly applicable to class gifts, thereby eliminating a frequent source of litigation. It also applies to the so-called "void" gift, where the devisee is dead at the time of execution of the will. This, though contrary to some decisions, seems justified. It still seems likely that the testator would want the issue of a person included in a class term but dead when the will is made to be treated like the issue of another member of the class who was alive at the time the will was executed but who died before the testator.

The five day survival requirement stated in Section 2–601 does not require issue who would be substituted for their parent by this section to survive their parent by any set period.

Section 2–106 describes the method of division when a taking by representation is directed by the Code.

Section 2–606. [Failure of Testamentary Provision.]

(a) Except as provided in Section 2–605 if a devise other than a residuary devise fails for any reason, it becomes a part of the residue.

(b) Except as provided in Section 2–605 if the residue is devised to two or more persons and the share of one of the residuary devisees fails for any reason, his share passes to the other residuary devisee, or to other residuary devisees in proportion to their interests in the residue.

COMMENT

If a devise fails by reason of lapse and the conditions of Section 2–605 are met, the latter section governs rather than this section. There is also a special rule for renunciation contained in Section 2–801; a renounced devise may be governed by either Section 8–605 or the present section, depending on the circumstances.

Section 2–607. [Change in Securities; Accessions; Nonademption.]

(a) If the testator intended a specific devise of certain securities rather than the equivalent value thereof, the specific devisee is entitled only to:

(1) as much of the devised securities as is a part of the estate at time of the testator's death;

(2) any additional or other securities of the same entity owned by the testator by reason of action initiated by the entity excluding any acquired by exercise of purchase options;

(3) securities of another entity owned by the testator as a result of a merger, consolidation, reorganization or other similar action initiated by the entity; and

(4) any additional securities of the entity owned by the testator as a result of a plan of reinvestment.

(b) Distributions prior to death with respect to a specifically devised security not provided for in subsection (a) are not part of the specific devise.

As amended in 1987.

For material relating to the 1987 amendment, see Appendix I, infra.

COMMENT

The Joint Editorial Board considered amending Subsection (a)(2) so as to exclude additional securities of the same entity that were not acquired by testator as a result of his ownership of the devised securities. It concluded that, in context, the present language is clear enough to make the proposed amendment unnecessary.

Subsection (b) is intended to codify existing law to the effect that cash dividends declared and payable as of a record date occurring before the testator's death do not pass as a part of the specific devise even though paid after death. See Section 4, Revised Uniform Principal and Income Act.

Section 2–608. [Nonademption of Specific Devises in Certain Cases; Unpaid Proceeds of Sale, Condemnation or Insurance; Sale by Conservator.]

(a) A specific devisee has the right to the remaining specifically devised property and:

(1) any balance of the purchase price (together with any security interest) owing from a purchaser to the testator at death by reason of sale of the property;

(2) any amount of a condemnation award for the taking of the property unpaid at death;

(3) any proceeds unpaid at death on fire or casualty insurance on the property; and

(4) property owned by testator at his death as a result of foreclosure, or obtained in lieu of foreclosure, of the security for a specifically devised obligation.

(b) If specifically devised property is sold by a conservator or an agent acting within the authority of a durable power of attorney for a principal who is under a disability, or if a condemnation award or insurance proceeds are paid to a conservator or an agent acting within the authority of a durable power of attorney for a principal who is under a disability as a result of condemnation, fire, or casualty, the specific devisee has the right to a general pecuniary devise equal to the net sale price, the condemnation award, or the insurance proceeds. This subsection does not apply if after the sale, condemnation or casualty, it is adjudicated that the disability of the testator has ceased and the testator survives the adjudication by one year. The right of the specific devisee under this subsection is reduced by any right he has under subsection (a).

As amended in 1987.

For material relating to the 1987 amendment, see Appendix I, infra.

COMMENT

In 1975, the Joint Editorial Board recommended a re-ordering of the title of this section and a reversal of the original order of the subsections. This recommendation was designed to correct an unintended interpretation of the section to the effect that all of the events described in subsections (a) and (b) had relevance only when the testa- tor was under a conservatorship. The original intent of the section, made more apparent by this re-or- dering, was to prevent ademption in all cases involving sale, condemna- tion or destruction of specifically devised assets where testator's death occurred before the proceeds of the sale, condemnation or any insur- ance, had been paid to the testator.

Section 2–609.　[Non–Exoneration.]

A specific devise passes subject to any mortgage interest existing at the date of death, without right of exoneration, regardless of a general directive in the will to pay debts.

COMMENT

See Section 3–814 empowering the personal representative to pay an encumbrance under some cir- cumstances; the last sentence of that section makes it clear that such payment does not increase the right of the specific devisee. The present section governs the substantive rights of the devisee. The common law rule of exoneration of the spe- cific devise is abolished by this sec- tion, and the contrary rule is adopted.

For the rule as to exempt proper- ty, see Section 2–402.

Section 2–610.　[Exercise of Power of Appointment.]

A general residuary clause in a will, or a will making general disposition of all of the testator's property, does not exercise a power of appointment held by the testator unless specific reference is made to the power or there is some other indication of intention to include the property subject to the power.

COMMENT

Although there is some indication that more states will adopt special legislation on powers of appoint- ment, and this Code has therefore generally avoided any provisions re- lating to powers of appointment, there is great need for uniformity on the subject of exercise by a will purporting to dispose of all of the donee's property, whether by a stan- dard residuary clause or a general recital of property passing under the will. Although a substantial num- ber of states have legislation to the effect that a will with a general re- siduary clause does manifest an in- tent to exercise a power, the con- trary rule is stated in the present section for two reasons: (1) this is still the majority rule in the United States, and (2) most powers of ap- pointment are created in marital deduction trusts and the donor would prefer to have the property pass under his trust instrument unless the donee affirmatively manifests an intent to exercise the power.

Under this section and Section 2–603 the intent to exercise the power is effective if it is "indicated by the will." This wording permits a Court to find the manifest intent if the language of the will interpreted in light of all the surrounding circumstances shows that the donee intended an exercise, except, of course, if the donor has conditioned exercise on an express reference to the original creating instrument. In other words, the modern liberal rule on interpretation of the donee's will would be available.

Section 2–611. [Construction of Generic Terms to Accord with Relationships as Defined for Intestate Succession.]

Halfbloods, adopted persons, and persons born out of wedlock are included in class gift terminology and terms of relationship in accordance with rules for determining relationships for purposes of intestate succession. [However, a person born out of wedlock is not treated as the child of the father unless the person is openly and notoriously so treated by the father.]

COMMENT

The purpose of this section is to facilitate a modern construction of gifts, usually class gifts, in wills.

In 1975, the Joint Editorial Board recommended that the section end with the words, "of intestate succession", in order to align the section with the Uniform Parentage Act of 1973. The Board also recommended retention, as a bracketed alternative form for states that do not enact the Uniform Parentage Act, of the language of the 1969 text beginning with "but a person born out of wedlock", and continuing through to the end of the original section.

Section 2–612. [Ademption by Satisfaction.]

Property which a testator gave in his lifetime to a person is treated as a satisfaction of a devise to that person in whole or in part, only if the will provides for deduction of the lifetime gift, or the testator declares in a contemporaneous writing that the gift is to be deducted from the devise or is in satisfaction of the devise, or the devisee acknowledges in writing that the gift is in satisfaction. For purpose of partial satisfaction, property given during lifetime is valued as of the time the devisee came into possession or enjoyment of the property or as of the time of death of the testator, whichever occurs first.

COMMENT

This section parallels Section 2–110 on advancements and follows the same policy of requiring written evidence that lifetime gifts are to be taken into account in distribution of an estate, whether testate or intestate. Although Courts traditionally call this "ademption by satisfaction" when a will is involved, and "advancement" when the estate is intestate, the difference in terminology is not significant. Some wills expressly provide for lifetime advances by a hotchpot clause. Where the will is silent, the above section would require either the testator to declare in writing that the gift is an advance or satisfaction or the devisee to acknowledge the same in writing. The second sentence on value accords with Section 2–110 and would apply if property such as stock is given. If the devise is specific, a gift of the specific property during lifetime would adeem the devise by extinction rather than by satisfaction, and this section would be inapplicable. If a devisee to whom an advancement is made predeceases the testator and his issue take under 2–605, they take the same devise as their ancestor; if the devise is reduced by reason of this section as to the ancestor, it is automatically reduced as to his issue. In this respect the rule in testacy differs from that in intestacy; see Section 2–110.

PART 7

CONTRACTUAL ARRANGEMENTS RELATING TO DEATH

(See, also, Article VI, Non–Probate Transfers)

Section 2–701. [Contracts Concerning Succession.]

A contract to make a will or devise, or not to revoke a will or devise, or to die intestate, if executed after the effective date of this Act, can be established only by (1) provisions of a will stating material provisions of the contract; (2) an express reference in a will to a contract and extrinsic evidence proving the terms of the contract; or (3) a writing signed by the decedent evidencing the contract. The execution of a joint will or mutual wills does not create a presumption of a contract not to revoke the will or wills.

COMMENT

It is the purpose of this section to tighten the methods by which contracts concerning succession may be proved. Oral contracts not to revoke wills have given rise to much litigation in a number of states; and in many states if two persons execute a single document as their joint will, this gives rise to a presumption that the parties had contracted not to revoke the will except by consent of both. This section requires that either the will must set forth the material provisions of the contract, or the will must make express reference to the contract and extrinsic evidence prove the terms of the contract, or there must be a separate writing signed by the decedent evidencing the contract. Oral testimony regarding the contract is permitted if the will makes reference to the contract, but this provision of the statute is not intended to affect normal rules regarding admissibility of evidence.

PART 8

GENERAL PROVISIONS

GENERAL COMMENT

Part 8 contains three general provisions which cut across both testate and intestate succession. The first section permits renunciation; the existing law in most states permits renunciation of gifts by will but not by intestate succession, a distinction which cannot be defended on policy grounds. The second section deals with the effect of divorce and separation on the right to elect against a will, exempt property and allowances, and an intestate share. The last section, an optional provision, spells out the legal consequence of murder on the right of the murderer to take as heir, devisee, joint tenant or life insurance beneficiary.

Section 2–801. [Renunciation of Succession.]

(a) A person or the representative of an incapacitated or protected person, who is an heir, devisee, person succeeding to a renounced interest, beneficiary under a testamentary instrument, or appointee under a power of appointment exercised by a testamentary instrument, may renounce in whole or in part the right of succession to any property or interest therein, including a future interest, by filing a written renunciation under this Section. The right to renounce does not survive the death of the person having it. The instrument shall (1) describe the property or interest renounced, (2) declare the renunciation and extent thereof, and (3) be signed by the person renouncing.

Comment to Subsection (a)

Who May Disclaim: At common law it was settled that the taker of property under a will had the right to accept or reject a legacy or devise (per Abbott, C.J. in *Townson v. Tickell,* 3 B & Ald 3, 136, 106 Eng.Rep. 575, 576). The same rule prevails in the United States (*Peter v. Peter,* 343 Ill. 493, 175 N.E. 846 (1931) 75 ALR 890). It is said that no one can make another an owner of an estate against his consent by devising it to him. See, for example, *People v.* *Flanagin,* 331 Ill. 203, 162 N.E. 848, (1928) 60 ALR 305:

"The law is clear that a legatee or devisee is under no obligation to accept a testamentary gift . . . and he may renounce the gift, by which act the estate will descend to the heir or pass in some other direction under the will . . ."

Under the rule permitting the disclaimer of testate successions, the disclaimed interest related back to the date of the testator's death so

581

that the interest did not vest in the grantee but remained in the original owner as if the will had never been executed (*People v. Flanagin,* supra).

Unlike the devisee or legatee, an heir had no common law power to prevent passage of title to himself by disclaimer. "An heir at law is the only person in whom the law of England vests property, whether he will or not," declares Williams on Real Property, and adds, "No disclaimer that he may make will have any effect, though, of course, he may as soon as he pleases dispose of the property by ordinary conveyance." (Williams on Law of Real Property 75 [2d Am.Ed.1857]. See also 6 Page on Wills [Bowe–Parker Revision] Section 49.1.)

The difference between testate and intestate successions in respect to the right to disclaim, has produced a number of illogical and undesirable consequences. An heir who sought to reject his inheritance was subjected to the Federal gift tax on the theory that since he could not prevent the passage of title to himself, any act done to rid himself of the interest necessarily involved a transfer subject to gift tax liability [*Hardenberg v. Com'r,* 198 F.2d 63 (8th Cir.) cert. denied, 344 U.S. 863, (1952) aff'g 17 T.C. 166 (1951); *Maxwell v. Com'r,* 17 T.C. 1589 (1952). See Lauritzen, Only God Can Make an Heir, 48 NWL Rev. 568; Annotation 170 ALR 435]. On the other hand, a legatee or devisee who rejected a legacy or devise under the will incurred no such tax consequences [*Brown v. Routzahn,* 63 F.2d 914 (6th Cir.) cert. denied, 290 U.S. 641 (1933)].

Subsection (a) places an heir on the same basis as a devisee or legatee and provides that he and others upon whom successions may devolve, have the full right to disclaim in whole or in part the passage of property to them, with the same legal consequences applying in all such cases.

Successive disclaimers are permitted by the express inclusion of "person succeeding to a disclaimed interest" among those who may disclaim.

Beneficiary: The term beneficiary is used in a broad sense to include any person entitled, but for his disclaimer, to possess or enjoy an equitable or legal interest, present or future, in the property or interest, including a power to consume, appoint, or apply it for any purpose or to enforce the transfer in any respect.

Subsection (a) extends the right to disclaim to the representative of an incapacitated or protected person. This accords with the general rule that the probate or surrogate court in the exercise of its traditional jurisdiction over the person and estate of a minor or incompetent may authorize or direct the guardian, conservator or committee to exercise the right on behalf of his ward when it is in the ward's interest to do so. *Davis v. Mather,* 309 Ill. 284, 141 N.E. 209 (1923).

On the other hand, absent a statute, the general rule is that the right to disclaim is personal to the person entitled to exercise it, and dies with him in the absence of fraud or concealment or conflict of interest of his representative, even though the time within which the right might have been utilized has not expired and even though he may be incompetent. *Rock Island Bank & Trust Co. v. First Nat. Bank of Rock Island,* 26 Ill.2d 47, 185 N.E.2d 890, (1962), 3 ALR 3d 114. Subsection (a) adopts this position by stating that the right to disclaim does not survive the death of the person having it.

The Act makes no provision here or elsewhere, for an extension of time to disclaim or other relief from a strict observance of the statutory requirements for disclaimer and the time limitations for expressing the right of disclaimer apply to persons under disability as well as to others.

What May be Disclaimed: Subsection (a) specifies that the "succession" to any property, real or personal or interest therein, may be disclaimed, and it is immaterial whether it derives by way of will, intestacy, exercise of a power of appointment or disclaimer. It would include the right to renounce any survivorship interest in the community in a community property state. Cf. *U.S. v. Mitchell*, 403 U.S. 190 (1971), rev'g 430 F.2d (5th Cir.1970), aff'g 51 T.C. 641 (1969).

Future Interests: Subsection (a) contemplates the disclaimer of future interests by reference to "beneficiary under a testamentary instrument" and "appointee under a power of appointment." The time for making such a disclaimer is dealt with in Subsection (b).

Partial Disclaimer: The status of partial disclaimers has been uncertain in many states. The result has often turned on whether the gift is "severable" or constitutes a "sin-gle, aggregate" gift [*Olgesby v. Springfield Marine Bank*, 395 Ill. 37, 69 N.E.2d 269 (1946); *Brown v. Routzahn*, supra]. Subsection (a) makes it clear that a partial, as well as a total, disclaimer is permitted.

Discretionary administrative and investment powers under a trust have been held to constitute a "severable" interest and subject to partial disclaimer. *Estate of Harry C. Jaecker*, 58 T.C. 166, CCH Dec. 31,-356 (1972).

Method of Disclaiming: Ir many states no satisfactory case law has existed as to the form and manner of making disclaimers of devises or legacies under wills. See Annotation 93 ALR 2d 8—What Constitutes or Establishes Beneficiary's Acceptance or Renunciation of Bequest or Devise. Because certainty of titles and the expeditious administration of estates makes definiteness desirable in this area. Subsection (a) requires a disclaimer to (i) describe the property or interest disclaimed; (ii) declare the disclaimer and the extent thereof; and (iii) be signed by the disclaimant.

(b)(1) An instrument renouncing a present interest shall be filed not later than [9] months after the death of the decedent or the donee of the power.

(2) An instrument renouncing a future interest may be filed not later than [9] months after the event determining that the taker of the property or interest is finally ascertained and his interest is indefeasibly vested.

(3) The renunciation shall be filed in the [probate] court of the county in which proceedings have been commenced for the administration of the estate of the deceased owner or deceased donee of the power or, if they have not been commenced, in which they could be commenced. A copy of the renunciation shall be delivered in person or mailed by registered or certified mail to any personal representative, or other fiduciary of the decedent or donee of the power. If real property or an interest therein is renounced, a copy of the renunciation may be recorded in the office of the

[Recorder of Deeds] of the county in which the real estate is situated.*

If Torrens system is in effect, add provisions to comply with local law.

Comment to Subsection (b)

Time for Making Disclaimer: At common law, no specific time evolved within which disclaimer had to be made. The only requirement was that it be within a "reasonable" time (*In re Wilson's Estate*, 298 N.Y. 398, 83 N.E.2d 852 (1949); *Ewing v. Rountree*, 228 F.Supp. 137 (D.C.Tenn.1964)). As a result, divergent holdings were reached by the courts (*Brown v. Routzahn*, 63 F.2d 914, (6th Cir.), cert. denied, 290 U.S. 641 (1933)). Subsection (b) fixes a definite time for filing of disclaimers. This approach follows the pattern of the Federal estate tax law which prescribed the time for filing estate tax returns in terms of the decedent's death. The time allowed should overlast the time for filing claims and contesting the will and enable the executor or administrator to know with certainty who the takers of the estate will be. On the other hand, it should not be so long as to work against an early determination of the acceptance or rejection of succession to an estate, or increase the risk of inadvertent acceptance of the benefits of the property, creating an estoppel. In the case of future interests the disclaimer period should run from the time the takers of the interest are finally ascertained and their interest indefeasibly fixed. *Seifner v. Weller*, 171 S.W.2d 617 (Mo., 1943). For the consequence of selecting too short a period, see *Brodhag v. U.S.*, 319 F.Supp. 747 (S.D.W.Va., 1970) involving a 2–month period fixed by West Virginia law.

In the case of future interests it should be noted that the person need not wait until the occurrence of the determinative event before filing a disclaimer, but may do so at any time after the death of the decedent or donee, so long as it is made "not later than" the prescribed period.

Federal Gift Tax Implications: Disclaimers have significance under the Federal gift tax law. Section 2511(a) of the Internal Revenue Code imposes a gift tax upon the transfer of property by gift whether the transfer is in trust or otherwise, and whether the gift is direct or indirect. The Treasury regulations under this section state that where local law gives the beneficiary, heir or next-of-kin an unqualified right to refuse to accept ownership of property transferred from a decedent, whether by will or by intestacy, a refusal to accept ownership does not constitute the making of a gift if the refusal is made within a "reasonable time" after knowledge of the existence of the transfer.

A "reasonable time" for gift tax purposes is not defined in the Code or regulations. It has been held that the courts will look to the law of the states in determining the question. (*Brown v. Routzahn*, 63 F.2d 914 (6th Cir.) cert. denied 290 U.S. 641 (1933)), not conclusively, but as relevant and having probative value (*Keinath v. C.I.R.*, 480 F.2d 57, (8th Cir.,1973), rev'g 58 T.C. 352, (1972)), and that an unequivocal disclaimer filed within 6 months of the determinative event is made within a "reasonable time." It has been held, further, that as regards future interests, the "reasonable time" period runs from the termination of the preceding estate or interest, and not from the time the transfer was made, *Keinath v. C.I.R.*, supra.

Place of Filing Disclaimer: Subsection (b) requires a disclaimer to be filed in the probate court. If real property or an interest therein is involved, a copy of the disclaimer may also be recorded in the office of the recorder of deeds or other appropriate office in the county in which the real estate is situated. If the Torrens system is in effect, appropriate provisions should be added to comply with local law.

Notice: A copy of the disclaimer is required to be delivered in person or mailed by registered or certified mail to the personal representative or other fiduciary of the decedent or of the donee of the power as the case may be.

(c) Unless the decedent or donee of the power has otherwise provided, the property or interest renounced devolves as though the person renouncing had predeceased the decedent or, if the person renouncing is designated to take under a power of appointment exercised by a testamentary instrument, as though the person renouncing had predeceased the donee of the power. A future interest that takes effect in possession or enjoyment after the termination of the estate or interest renounced takes effect as though the person renouncing had predeceased the decedent or the donee of the power. A renunciation relates back for all purposes to the date of the death of the decedent or the donee of the power.

Comment to Subsection (c)

Devolution of Disclaimed Property: When a beneficiary disclaims his interest under a will, the question arises as to what happens to the rejected interest. In *People v. Flanagin*, 331 Ill. 203, 162 N.E. 848 (1928), 60 ALR 305, the court, quoting the New York case of *Burritt v. Sillman*, 13 N.Y. 93 (1855) said that the disclaimed property will "descend to the heir or pass in some other direction under the will." From this, it may be assumed that the court meant that if the decedent left no will, the renounced interest passed according to the rules of descent, but if he left a will, it passed according to its terms.

It has been generally thought that devolution in the case of disclaimer should be the same as in the case of lapse, which is controlled by sections of the probate law. Subsection (c) takes this approach. It provides that unless the will of the decedent or the donee of the power has otherwise provided, the disclaimed interest devolves as if the disclaimant had predeceased the decedent or the donee of the power. In every case the disclaimer relates back to the date of the death of the decedent or of the donee. The provision that the disclaimer "relates back", codifies the rule that a renunciation of a devise or legacy relates to the date of death of the decedent or donee and prevents the succession from becoming operative in favor of the disclaimant. See *In re Wilson's Estate*, 298 N.Y. 398, 83 N.E.2d 852 (1949). Also, *Bouse, for use of State v. Hull*, 168 Md. 1, 176 A. 645 (1935).

Acceleration of Future Interests: If a life estate or other future interest is disclaimed, the problem is raised of whether succeeding interests or estates accelerate in possession or enjoyment or whether the disclaimed interest must be marshalled to await the actual happening of the

585

contingency. Subsection (c) provides that remainder interests are accelerated, the second sentence specifically stating that any future interest which is to take effect in possession or enjoyment after the termination of the estate or interest disclaimed, takes effect as if the disclaimant had predeceased the deceased owner or deceased donee of the power. Thus, if T leaves his estate in trust to pay the income to his son for life, remainder to his son's children who survive him, and S disclaims with two children then living, the remainder in the children accelerates; the trust terminates and the children receive possession and enjoyment, even though the son may subsequently have other children or that one or more of the living children may die during their father's lifetime.

Effect of Death or Disability of Person Entitled to Disclaim: The effect of death of a person entitled to disclaim, including one under disability, is discussed under Subsection (a). A guardian or conservator of the estate of an incapacitated or protected person may disclaim for the ward. Subsection (b) makes no provision for an extension of time or for other relief in case of disability for the observance of the statutory requirements for effective disclaimer. The intent is that the period for disclaimer applies to a person under disability as well as to others, and includes a court which purports to act on behalf of one under disability in the absence of fraud, misconduct or other unusual circumstances. *Pratt v. Baker,* 48 Ill.App.2d 442, 199 N.E.2d 307 (1964).

Rights of Creditors and Others: As regards creditors, taxing authorities and others, the provision for "relation back" has the legal effect of preventing a succession from becoming operative in favor of the disclaimant. The relation back is "for all purposes" which would include, among others for the purpose of rights of creditors, taxing authorities and assertion of dower. It is immaterial that the effect is to avoid the imposition of a higher death tax than would be the case if the interest had been accepted: *Estate of Aylsworth,* 74 Ill.App.2d 375, 219 N.E.2d 779 (1966) [motive for the disclaimer is immaterial]; *People v. Flanagin,* 331 Ill. 203, 162 N.E. 848 (1928), 60 ALR 305; *Cook v. Dove,* 32 Ill.2d 109, 203 N.E.2d 892 (1965) [upholding for inheritance tax the right of appointees to take by default rather than under the powerholder's exercise of power]; *Matter of Wolfe's Estate,* 179 N.Y. 599, 72 N.E. 1152 (1904); aff'g 89 App.Div. 349, 83 N.Y.Supp. 949 (1903); *Brown v. Routzahn,* 63 F.2d 914 (6th Cir.), cert. denied 290 U.S. 641 (1933); *In re Stone's Estate,* 132 Ia. 136, 109 N.W. 455 (1906); *Tax Commission v. Glass,* 119 Ohio St. 389, 164 N.E. 425 (1929); *U.S. v. McCrackin,* 189 F.Supp. 632 (S.D.Ohio 1960).

Similarly, numerous cases have held that a devisee or legatee can disclaim a devise or legacy despite the claims of creditors: *Hoecker v. United Bank of Boulder,* 476 F.2d 838 (CA 10, 1973) aff'g 334 F.Supp. 1080 (D.Colo.1971) (bankruptcy); *U.S. v. McCrackin,* supra (Federal income tax liens); *Shoonover v. Osborne,* 193 Ia. 474, 187 N.W. 20 (1922); *Bradford v. Calhoun,* 120 Tenn. 53, 109 S.W. 502 (1908); *Carter v. Carter,* 63 N.J.Eq. 726, 53 A. 160 (1902); *Estate of Hansen,* 109 Ill.App.2d 283, 248 N.E.2d 709 (1969) (judgment creditor); 37 Mich.L.Rev. 1168; 43 Yale L.J. 1030; 27 ALR 477; 133 ALR 1428. A creditor is not entitled to notice of the disclaimer (*In re Estate of Hansen,* 109 Ill.App.2d 283, 248 N.E.2d 709 (1969)).

(d)(1) The right to renounce property or an interest therein is barred by (i) an assignment, conveyance, encumbrance, pledge, or transfer of the property or interest, or a contract therefor, (ii) a written waiver of the right to renounce, (iii) an acceptance of the property or interest or benefit thereunder, or (iv) a sale of the property or interest under judicial sale made before the renunciation is effected.

(2) The right to renounce exists notwithstanding any limitation on the interest of the person renouncing in the nature of a spendthrift provision or similar restriction.

(3) A renunciation or a written waiver of the right to renounce is binding upon the person renouncing or person waiving and all persons claiming through or under him.

Comment to Subsection (d)

Bars to Disclaimer—Waiver—Estoppel: It may be necessary or advisable to sell real estate in a decedent's estate before the expiration of the period permitted for disclaimer. In such case, the possibility of a disclaimer being filed within the period, could be a deterrent to sale and delivery of good title. Subsection (d) expressly authorizes an heir, devisee, legatee or other person entitled to disclaim, to indicate in writing his intention to "waive" his right of disclaimer, and thus avoid any delay in the completion of a sale or other disposition of estate assets. The written waiver bars the right of the person subsequently to disclaim the property or interest therein and is binding on persons claiming through or under him.

Similarly, Subsection (d) provides that various acts of a person entitled to disclaim in regard to property or an interest therein, such as making an assignment, conveyance, encumbrance, pledge or transfer of the property or interest, or a contract therefor, bars the right of the person to disclaim and is binding on all persons claiming through or under him.

Spendthrift Provisions: The existence of a limitation on the interest of an heir, legatee, devisee or other disclaimant in the nature of a spendthrift provision or similar restriction is expressly declared not to affect the right to disclaim. Without this provision, there might be a question as to whether the beneficiary of a spendthrift trust can disclaim under the statute (Griswold, Spendthrift Trust [2d Ed] Section 524, p. 603). If a person who is under no legal disability wishes to refuse a beneficial interest under a trust, he should not be powerless to make an effective disclaimer even though the intended interest once accepted by him would be inalienable. (Scott on Trusts, Section 337.-7, p. 2683, 3d Ed.)

When a beneficial interest is accepted by a beneficiary, he cannot thereafter disclaim or release it (Griswold, supra, Section 534, p. 603 note 48). As to what conduct amounts to an acceptance, see *In Re Wilson's Estate,* 298 N.Y. 398, 83 N.E.2d 852 (1949).

Judicial Sale: The section provides that the right to disclaim is barred by a sale of the property or interest under a judicial sale. Judicial sales are ordered in many different types of proceeding such as foreclosure of mortgage or trust deed, enforcement of lien, partition proceedings and proceedings for the sale of real property of a decedent or ward for certain purposes. Probate laws frequently permit a representative to mortgage or pledge property of the decedent or ward in certain circumstances. Execution sales are made pursuant to a writ to satisfy a money judgment. Subsection (d) has the effect of providing that the making of a judicial sale for the account of the heir, devisee, or beneficiary, bars him from renouncing the property or interest. To be distinguished from a judicial sale, is a taking pursuant to eminent domain, which is considered to be a taking of property without the owner's consent and unrelated to his obligations or commitments. The right to disclaim the proceeds of a condemnation action if otherwise timely and in accordance with this Section, should not, therefore, be barred under Subsection (d).

(e) This Section does not abridge the right of a person to waive, release, disclaim, or renounce property or an interest therein under any other statute.

Comment to Subsection (e)

Subsection (e) provides that the right to disclaim under the law does not abridge the right of any person to waive, release, disclaim or renounce any property or interest therein under any other statute. The principal statutes to which this provision is pointed are those dealing with spousal renunciations and release of powers.

Being a codification of the common law in regard to the renunciation of the property, this Section is intended to constitute an *exclusive remedy* for the disclaimer of testamentary successions apart from those provided by other statutes, and supplants the common law right to disclaim.

(f) An interest in property existing on the effective date of this Section as to which the time for filing a renunciation under this Section would have begun to run were this Section in effect when the interest was created, may be renounced within [9] months after the effective date of this Section.

Comment to Subsection (f)

Subsection (f) deals with the application of this Section to property interests under instruments or in estates in existence on the effective date. If the interest is a present one and the filing time has not expired, the holder is given a full period after enactment within which to disclaim the interest. If the interest is a future one, the holder is given a full period after the interest becomes indefeasibly vested or the takers finally ascertained, after enactment in which to disclaim it. If T dies in 1960 trusteeing his estate to W for life, remainder to such of T's sons as are living at W's death and W dies in 1975, this Section permits a son to disclaim his remainder interest after it ripens even though it arises under an instrument predating the effective date of this Section. The application of statute to pre-existing instruments in like situations finds support in cases such as *Will of Allis*, 6 Wis.2d 1, 94 N.W.2d 226, (1959) 69 ALR2d 1128.

Comment to Section 2–801

The above text, consists of Sections 1 through 6 of Uniform Disclaimer of Transfers By Will, Intestacy or Appointment Act of 1973, redesignated as subsections (a) through (f).

The Comments following each subsection are the Official Comments to the 1973 statute. The word "renunciation" has been substituted for "disclaimer" because the original Section 2–801 used the term "renunciation" and several cross-references to this term appear in other sections of this Code. It is the view of the Joint Editorial Board that the terms "renunciation" and "disclaimer" have the same meaning.

The principal substantive difference between original Section 2–801 and the 1973 replacement therefor is that the former permitted renunciation by the personal representative of a person who might have renounced during his lifetime. Under the new uniform act, which is now the official text of Section 2–801, the right to renounce terminates upon the death of the person who might have renounced during his lifetime. Also, the original version was less precise than the present version in the important provisions of subsection (b) which govern the time for renunciation.

This Section is designed to facilitate renunciation in order to aid postmortem planning. Although present law in all states permits renunciation of a devise under a will, the common law did not permit renunciation of an intestate share.

There is no reason for such a distinction, and some states have already adopted legislation permitting renunciation of an intestate share. Renunciation may be made for a variety of reasons, including carrying out the decedent's wishes not expressed in a properly executed will.

Under the rule of this Section, renounced property passes as if the renouncing person had failed to survive the decedent. In the case of intestate property, the heir who would be next in line in succession would take; often this will be the issue of the renouncing person, taking by representation. For consistency the same rule is adopted for renunciation by a devisee; if the devisee is a relative who leaves issue surviving the testator, the issue will take under Section 2–605; otherwise disposition will be governed by Section 2–606 and general rules of law.

The Section limits renunciation to nine months after the death of the decedent or if the taker of the property is not ascertained at that time, then nine months after he is ascertained. If the personal representative is concerned about closing the estate within that nine months period in order to make distribution, he can obtain a waiver of the right to renounce. Normally this should be no problem, since the heir or devisee cannot renounce once he has taken possession of the property.

The presence of a spendthrift clause does not prevent renunciation under this Section.

Section 2–802. [Effect of Divorce, Annulment, and Decree of Separation.]

(a) A person who is divorced from the decedent or whose marriage to the decedent has been annulled is not a surviving spouse unless, by virtue of a subsequent marriage, he is married to the decedent at the time of death. A decree of separation which does not terminate the status of husband and wife is not a divorce for purposes of this section.

(b) For purposes of Parts 1, 2, 3 & 4 of this Article, and of Section 3–203, a surviving spouse does not include:

(1) a person who obtains or consents to a final decree or judgment of divorce from the decedent or an annulment of their marriage, which decree or judgment is not recognized as valid in this state, unless they subsequently participate in a marriage ceremony purporting to marry each to the other, or subsequently live together as man and wife;

(2) a person who, following a decree or judgment of divorce or annulment obtained by the decedent, participates in a marriage ceremony with a third person; or

(3) a person who was a party to a valid proceeding concluded by an order purporting to terminate all marital property rights.

COMMENT

See Section 2–508 for similar provisions relating to the effect of divorce to revoke devises to a spouse.

Although some existing statutes bar the surviving spouse for desertion or adultery, the present section requires some definitive legal act to bar the surviving spouse. Normally, this is divorce. Subsection (a) states an obvious proposition, but subsection (b) deals with the difficult problem of invalid divorce or annulment, which is particularly frequent as to foreign divorce decrees but may arise as to a local decree where there is some defect in jurisdiction; the basic principle underlying these provisions is estoppel against the surviving spouse. Where there is only a legal separation, rather than a divorce, succession patterns are not affected; but if the separation is accompanied by a complete property settlement, this may operate under Section 2–204 as a renunciation of benefits under a prior will and by intestate succession.

In 1975, the Joint Editorial Board recommended the addition, in the preliminary statement of subsection (b), of explicit reference to Section 3–203 which controls priorities for appointment as personal representative.

[Section 2–803. [Effect of Homicide on Intestate Succession, Wills, Joint Assets, Life Insurance and Beneficiary Designations.]

(a) A surviving spouse, heir or devisee who feloniously and intentionally kills the decedent is not entitled to any benefits under the will or under this Article, and the estate of decedent passes as if the killer had predeceased the decedent. Property appointed by the will of the decedent to or for the benefit of the killer passes as if the killer had predeceased the decedent.

(b) Any joint tenant who feloniously and intentionally kills another joint tenant thereby effects a severance of the interest of the decedent so that the share of the decedent passes as his property and the killer has no rights by survivorship. This provision applies to joint tenancies [and tenancies by the entirety] in real and personal property, joint and multiple-party accounts in banks, savings and loan associations, credit unions and other institutions, and any other form of co-ownership with survivorship incidents.

(c) A named beneficiary of a bond, life insurance policy, or other contractual arrangement who feloniously and intentionally kills the principal obligee or the person upon whose life the policy is issued is not entitled to any benefit under the bond, policy or other contractual arrangement, and it becomes payable as though the killer had predeceased the decedent.

(d) Any other acquisition of property or interest by the killer shall be treated in accordance with the principles of this section.

(e) A final judgment of conviction of felonious and intentional killing is conclusive for purposes of this section. In the absence of a conviction of felonious and intentional killing the Court may determine by a preponderance of evidence whether the killing was felonious and intentional for purposes of this section.

(f) This section does not affect the rights of any person who, before rights under this section have been adjudicated, purchases from the killer for value and without notice property which the killer would have acquired except for this section, but the killer is liable for the amount of the proceeds or the value of the property. Any insurance company, bank, or other obligor making payment according to the terms of its policy or obligation is not liable by reason of this section unless prior to payment it has received at its home office or principal address written notice of a claim under this section.]

COMMENT

This section is bracketed to indicate that it may be omitted by an enacting state without difficulty.

A growing group of states have enacted statutes dealing with the problems covered by this section, and uniformity appears desirable. The section is confined to intentional and felonious homicide and excludes the accidental manslaughter killing.

At first it may appear that the matter dealt with is criminal in nature and not a proper matter for probate courts. However, the concept that a wrongdoer may not profit by his own wrong is a civil concept, and the probate court is the

591

proper forum to determine the effect of killing on succession to property of the decedent. There are numerous situations where the same conduct gives rise to both criminal and civil consequences. A killing may result in criminal prosecution for murder and civil litigation by the murdered person's family under wrongful death statutes. While conviction in the criminal prosecution under this section is treated as conclusive on the matter of succession to the murdered person's property, acquittal does not have the same consequences. This is because different considerations as well as a different burden of proof enter into the finding of guilty in the criminal prosecution. Hence it is possible that the defendant on a murder charge may be found not guilty and acquitted, but if the same person claims as an heir or devisee of the decedent, he may in the probate court be found to have feloniously and intentionally killed the decedent and thus be barred under this section from sharing in the estate. An analogy exists in the tax field, where a taxpayer may be acquitted of tax fraud in a criminal prosecution but found to have committed the fraud in a civil proceeding. In many of the cases arising under this section there may be no criminal prosecution because the murderer has committed suicide.

PART 9

CUSTODY AND DEPOSIT OF WILLS

Section 2–901. [Deposit of Will With Court in Testator's Lifetime.]

A will may be deposited by the testator or his agent with any Court for safekeeping, under rules of the Court. The will shall be kept confidential. During the testator's lifetime a deposited will shall be delivered only to him or to a person authorized in writing signed by him to receive the will. A conservator may be allowed to examine a deposited will of a protected testator under procedures designed to maintain the confidential character of the document to the extent possible, and to assure that it will be resealed and left on deposit after the examination. Upon being informed of the testator's death, the Court shall notify any person designated to receive the will and deliver it to him on request; or the Court may deliver the will to the appropriate Court.

COMMENT

Many states already have statutes permitting deposit of wills during a testator's lifetime. Most of these statutes have elaborate provisions governing purely administrative matters: how the will is to be enclosed in a sealed wrapper, what is to be endorsed on the wrapper, the form of receipt or certificate given to the testator, the fee to be charged, how the will is to be opened after testator's death and who is to be notified. Under this section, details have been left to Court rule, except as other relevant statutes such as one governing fees may apply.

It is, of course, vital to maintain the confidential nature of deposited wills. However, this obviously does not prevent the opening of the will after the death of the testator if necessary in order to determine the executor or other interested persons to be notified. Nor should it prevent opening the will to microfilm for confidential record storage, for example. These matters could again be regulated by Court rule.

It is suggested that in the near future it may be desirable to develop a central filing system regarding the presence of deposited wills, because the mobility of our modern population makes it probable that the testator will not die in the county where his will is deposited. Thus a statute might require that the local registrar notify an appropriate official, that the will is on file; the state official would in effect provide a clearing-house for information on location of deposited wills without disrupting the local administration.

The provision permitting examination of a will of a protected person by the conservator supplements Section 5–427.

Section 2–902. [Duty of Custodian of Will; Liability.]

After the death of a testator and on request of an interested person, any person having custody of a will of the testator shall deliver it with reasonable promptness to a person able to secure its probate and if none is known, to an appropriate Court. Any person who wilfully fails to deliver a will is liable to any person aggrieved for the damages which may be sustained by the failure. Any person who wilfully refuses or fails to deliver a will after being ordered by the Court in a proceeding brought for the purpose of compelling delivery is subject to penalty for contempt of Court.

COMMENT

Model Probate Code Section 63, slightly changed. A person authorized by a Court to accept delivery of a will from a custodian may, in addition to a registrar or clerk, be a universal successor or other person authorized under the law of another nation to carry out the terms of a will.

PART 10

UNIFORM INTERNATIONAL WILLS ACT [INTERNATIONAL WILL; INFORMATION REGISTRATION]

The Board that acted for the National Conference of Commissioners on Uniform State Laws in preparing the Uniform International Wills Act was as follows:

JOINT EDITORIAL BOARD FOR
UNIFORM PROBATE CODE

Conference Representatives:

CHARLES HOROWITZ, Supreme Court, Temple of Justice, Olympia, WA 98504, *Co–Chairman*

CLARKE A. GRAVEL, 109 South Winooski Avenue, Burlington, VT 05401

BERT McELROY, 205 Denver Building, Tulsa, OK 74119

EUGENE F. SCOLES, University of Oregon, School of Law, Eugene, OR 97403

ALLAN D. VESTAL, University of Iowa, College of Law, Iowa City, IA 52242

DON J. McCLENAHAN, 310 Simplot Building, Boise, ID 83702, *Chairman, Division A, Ex Officio*

JAMES M. BUSH, 363 North First Avenue, Phoenix, AZ 85003, *President, Ex Officio*

RICHARD V. WELLMAN, University of Georgia, School of Law, Athens, GA 30602, *Reporter*

American Bar Association Representatives:

J. PENNINGTON STRAUS, 1719 Packard Building, Philadelphia, PA 19102, *Co–Chairman*

PETER J. BRENNAN, 111 West Monroe Street, Chicago, IL 60603

HARRISON F. DURAND, 250 Park Avenue, New York, NY 10017

J. THOMAS EUBANK, JR., 3000 One Shell Plaza, Houston, TX 77002

MALCOLM A. MOORE, 4200 Seattle First National Bank Building, Seattle, WA 98154

ADVISORS TO JOINT EDITORIAL BOARD
FOR UNIFORM PROBATE CODE

ROBERT E. DALTON, Department of State, Washington, DC 20520

RICHARD KEARNEY, Department of State, Washington, DC 20520

PREFATORY NOTE

Introduction

The purpose of the Washington Convention of 1973 concerning international wills is to provide testators with a way of making wills that will be valid as to form in all countries joining the Convention. As proposed by the Convention, the objective would be achieved through uniform local rules of form, rather than through local or international law that makes recognition of foreign wills turn on choice of law rules involving possible application of foreign law. The international will provisions, prepared for the National Conference of Commissioners on Uniform State Laws by the Joint Editorial Board for the Uniform Probate Code which has functioned as a special committee of the Conference for the project, should be enacted by all states, including those that have not accepted the Uniform Probate Code. To that end, this statute is framed both as a freestanding act and as an added part of the Uniform Probate Code.

The bracketed headings and numbers fit the proposal into UPC; the others present the proposal as a free-standing act.

Uniform state enactment of these provisions will permit the Washington Convention of 1973 to be implemented through state legislation familiar to will draftsmen. Thus, local proof of foreign law and reliance on federal legislation regarding wills can be avoided when foreign wills come into our states to be implemented. Also, the citizens of all states will have a will form available that should greatly reduce perils of proof and risks of invalidity that attend proof of American wills abroad.

History of the International Will

Discussions about possible international accord on an acceptable form of will led the Governing Council of UNIDROIT (International Institute for the Unification of Private Law) in 1960 to appoint a small committee of experts from several countries to develop proposals. Following week-long meetings at the Institute's quarters in Rome in 1963, and on two occasions in 1965, the Institute published and circulated a Draft Convention of December 1966 with an annexed uniform law that would be required to be enacted locally by those countries agreeing to the convention. The package and accompanying explanations were reviewed in this country by the Secretary of State's Advisory Committee on Private International Law. In turn, it referred the proposal to a special committee of American probate specialists drawn from members of NCCUSL's Special Committee on the Uniform Probate Code and its advisers and reporters. The resulting reports and recommendations were affirmative and urged the State Department to cooperate in continuing efforts to develop the 1966 Draft Convention, and to endeavor to interest other countries in the subject.

Encouraged by support for the project from this country and several others, UNIDROIT served as host for a 1971 meeting in Rome of an expanded group that included some of the original panel of experts and others from several countries that were not represented in the early drafting sessions. The result of this meeting was a revised draft of the proposed convention and annexed uniform law and this, in turn, was the subject of study and discussion by many more persons in this country. In mid–1973, the proposal from UNIDROIT was discussed in a joint program of the Real Property Probate and Trust Law Section, and the Section of International Law at the American Bar Association's annual meeting held that year in Washington, D.C. By late 1973, the list of published, scholarly discussions of the International Will proposals included Fratcher, "The Uniform Probate Code and the International Will", 66 Mich.L.Rev. 469 (1968); Wellman, "Recent Unidroit

Drafts on the International Will", 6 The International Lawyer 205 (1973); and Wellman, "Proposed International Convention Concerning Wills", 8/4 Real Property, Probate and Trust Journal 622 (1973).

In October 1973, pursuant to a commitment made earlier to UNIDROIT representatives that it would provide leadership for the international will proposal if sufficient interest from other countries became evident, the United States served as host for the diplomatic Conference on Wills which met in Washington from October 10 to 26, 1973. 42 governments were represented by delegations, 6 by observers. The United States delegation of 8 persons plus 2 Congressional advisers and 2 staff advisers, was headed by Ambassador Richard D. Kearney, Chairman of the Secretary of State's Advisory Committee on Private International Law who also was selected president of the Conference. The result of the Conference was the Convention of October 26, 1973 Providing a Uniform Law on the Form of an International Will, an appended Annex, Uniform Law on the Form of an International Will, and a Resolution recommending establishment of state assisted systems for the safekeeping and discovery of wills. These three documents are reproduced at the end of these preliminary comments.

A more detailed account of the UNIDROIT project and the 1973 Convention, together with recommendations regarding United States implementation of the Convention, appears in Nadelmann, "The Formal Validity of Wills and the Washington Convention 1973 Providing the Form of an International Will", XXII The American Journal of Comparative Law, 365 (1974).

Description of the Proposal

The 1973 Convention obligates countries becoming parties to make the annexed uniform law a part of their local law. The proposed uniform law contemplates the involvement in will executions under this law of a state recognized expert who is referred to throughout the proposals as the "authorized person". Hence, the local law called for by the Convention must designate authorized persons, and prescribe the formalities for an international will and the role of authorized persons relating thereto. The Convention binds parties to respect the authority of another party's authorized persons and this obligation, coupled with local enactment of the common statute prescribing the role of such persons and according finality to their certificates regarding due execution of wills, assures recognition of international wills under local law in all countries joining the Convention.

The Convention and the annexed uniform law deal only with the formal validity of wills. Thus, the proposal is entirely neutral in relation to local laws dealing with revocation of wills, or those defining the scope of testamentary power, or regulating the probate, interpretation, and construction of wills, and the administration of decedents' estates. The proposal describes a highly formal mode of will execution; one that is sufficiently protective against imposition and mistake to command international approval as being safe enough. However, failure to meet the requirements of an international will does not necessarily result in invalidity, for the mode of execution described for an international will does not pre-empt or exclude other standards of testamentary validity.

The details of the prescribed mode of execution reflect a blend of common and civil law elements. Two attesting witnesses are required in the tradition of the English Statute of Wills of 1837 and its American counterparts. The authorized person whose participation in the ceremony of execution is required, and whose certificate makes the will self-proved, plays a role not unlike that of the civil law notary, though he is not required to retain custody of the will as is customary with European notaries.

The question of who should be given state recognition as authorized persons was resolved by designation of all licensed attorneys. The reasons for this can be seen in the observations about the role of Kurt H. Nadelmann, writing in The American Journal of Comparative Law:

The duties imposed by the Uniform Law upon the person doing the certifying go beyond legalization of signatures, the domain of the notary public. At least paralegal training is a necessity. Abroad, in countries with the law trained notary, the designation is likely to go to this class or at least to include it. Similarly, in countries with a closely supervised class of solicitors, their designation may be expected.

Attorneys are subject to training and licensing requirements everywhere in this country. The degree to which they are supervised after qualification varies considerably from state to state, but the trend is definitely in the direction of more rather than less supervision. Designation of attorneys in the uniform law permits a state to bring the statute into its local law books without undue delay.

Roles for Federal and State Law in Relation to International Will

Several alternatives are available for arranging federal and state laws on the subject of international wills. The 1973 Convention obligates nations becoming parties to introduce the annexed uniform law into their local law, and to recognize the authority, *vis a vis* will executions and certificates relating to wills, of persons designated as authorized by other parties to the Convention. But, the Convention includes a clause for federal states that may be used by the United States as it moves, through the process of Senate Advice and Consent, to accept the international compact. Through it, the federal government may limit the areas in this country to which the Convention will be applicable. Thus, Article XIV of the 1973 Convention provides:

1. If a state has two or more territorial units in which different systems of law apply in relation to matters respecting the form of wills, it may at the time of signature, ratification, or accession, declare that this Convention shall extend to all its territorial units or only to one or more of them, and may modify its declaration by submitting another declaration at any time.

2. These declarations shall be notified to the Depositary Government and shall state expressly the territorial units to which the Convention applies.

One alternative would be for the federal government to refrain from use of Article XIV and to accept the Convention as applicable to all areas of the country. The obligation to introduce the uniform law into local law then could be met by passage of a federal statute incorporating the uniform law and designating authorized persons who can assist testators desiring to use the international format, possibly leaving it open for state legislatures, if they wish, to designate other or additional groups of authorized persons. As to constitutionality, the federal statute on wills could be rested on the power of the federal government to bind the states by treaty and to implement a treaty obligation to bring agreed upon rules into local law by any appropriate method. Missouri v. Holland, 252 U.S. 416 (1920); Nadelmann, "The Formal Validity of Wills and the Washington Convention 1973 Providing the Form of An International Will", XXII The Am. Jn'l of Comp.L. 365, 375 (1974). Prof. Nadelmann favors this approach, arguing that new risks of invalidity of wills would arise if the treaty were limited so as to be applicable only in designated areas of the country, presumably those where state enactment of the uniform law already had occurred.

One disadvantage of this approach is that it would place a potentially important method for validating wills in federal statutes where probate practitioners, long accustomed to finding the statutes pertinent to their specialty in state compilations, simply would not discover it. Another, of course, relates to more generalized concerns that would attend any move by the federal government into an area of law traditionally reserved to the states.

Alternatively, the federal government might accept the Convention and uniform law as applicable throughout the land, so that international wills executed with the aid of authorized persons of other countries would be good anywhere in this country, but refrain from any designation of authorized persons, other than possibly of some minimum federal cadre, or of those who could function within the District of Columbia, leaving the selection of more useful groups of authorized persons entirely to the states. One result would be to greatly narrow the advantage of international wills to American testators who wanted to execute their instruments at home. In probable consequence, there would be pressure on state legislatures to enact the uniform law so as to make the advantages of the system available to local testators. Assuming some state legislatures respond to the pressure affirmatively and others negatively, a crazyquilt pattern of international will states would develop, leading possibly to some of the confusion and risk of illegality feared by Prof. Nadelmann. On the other hand, since execution of an international will involves use of an authorized person who derives authority from (on this assumption) state legislation, it seems somewhat unlikely that testators in states which have not designated authorized persons will be led to believe that they can make an international will unless they go to a state where authorized persons have been designated. Hence, the confusion may not be as great as if the Convention were inapplicable to portions of the country.

Finally, the federal government might use Article XIV as suggested earlier, and designate some but not all states as areas of the country in which the Convention applied. This seems the least desirable of all alternatives because it subjects international wills from abroad to the risk of non-recognition in some states, and offers the risk of confusion of American testators regarding the areas of the country where they can execute a will that will be received outside this country as an international will.

Under any of the approaches, the desirability of widespread enactment of state statutes embodying the uniform law and designating authorized persons, seems clear, as does the necessity for this project of the National Conference of Commissioners on Uniform State Laws.

Style

In preparing the International Will proposal, the special committee, after considerable discussion and consideration of alternatives, decided to stick as closely as possible to the wording of the Annex to the Convention of October 26, 1973. The Convention and its Annex were written in the English, French, Russian and Spanish languages, each version, as declared by Article XVI of the Convention, being equally authentic. Not surprisingly, the English version of the Annex has a style that is somewhat different than that to which the National Conference is accustomed. Nonetheless, from the view of those using languages other than English who may be reviewing our state statutes on the International Will to see if they adhere to the Annex, it is more important to stick with the agreed formulations than it is to re-style these expressions to suit our traditions. However, some changes from the Annex were made in the interests of clarity, and because some of the language of the Annex is plainly inappropriate in a local enactment. These changes are explained in the Comments.

Will Registration

A bracketed section 10[2–1010], is included in the International Will proposal to aid survivors in locating international and other wills that have been kept secret by testators during their lives. Differing from the section 2–901 of the Uniform Probate Code and the many existing statutes from which section 2–901 was derived which constitute the probate court as an agency for the safekeeping of wills deposited by living testators, the bracketed proposal is for a system of registering certain minimum information about wills, including where the instrument will be kept pending the death of the testator. It can be separated or omitted from the rest of the Act.

This provision for a state will registration system is derived from recommendations by the Council of Europe for common market countries. These recommendations were urged on the group that assembled in Rome in 1971, and were received with interest by representatives of United Kingdom, Canada and United States, where will-making laws and customs have not included any officially sanctioned system for safekeeping of wills or for locating information about wills, other than occasional statutes providing for ante-mortem deposit of wills with probate courts. Interest was expressed also by the notaries from civil law countries who have traditionally aided will-making both by formalizing execution and by being the source thereafter of official certificates about wills, the originals of which are retained with the official records of the notary and carefully protected and regulated by settled customs of the profession. All recognized that acceptance of the international will would tend to increase the frequency with which owners of property in several different countries relied on a single will to control all of their properties. This prospect, plus increasing mobility of persons between countries, indicates that new methods for safekeeping and locating wills after death should be developed. The Resolution adopted as the final act of the 1973 Conference on

Wills shows that the problem also attracted the interest and attention of that assembly.

Apart from problems of wills that may have effect in more than one country, Americans are moving from state to state with increasing frequency. As the international will statute becomes enacted in most if not all states, our laws will tend to induce persons to rely on a single will as sufficient even though they may own land in two or more states, and to refrain from making new wills when they change domicile from one state to another. The spread of the Uniform Probate Code, tending as it does to give wills the same meaning and procedural status in all states, will have a similar effect.

General enactment of the will registration section should lead to development of new state and interstate systems to meet the predictable needs of testators and survivors that will follow as the law of wills is detached from provincial restraints. It is offered with the international will provisions because both meet obvious needs of the times.

Documents from 1973 Convention

Three documents representing the work of the 1973 Convention are reproduced here for the convenience of members of the Conference.

CONVENTION PROVIDING A UNIFORM LAW ON THE FORM OF AN INTERNATIONAL WILL

The States signatory to the present Convention,

DESIRING to provide to a greater extent for the respecting of last wills by establishing an additional form of will hereinafter to be called an "international will" which, if employed, would dispense to some extent with the search for the applicable law;

HAVE RESOLVED to conclude a Convention for this purpose and have agreed upon the following provisions:

Article I 1. Each Contracting Party undertakes that not later than six months after the date of entry into force of this Convention in respect of that Party it shall introduce into its law the rules regarding an international will set out in the Annex to this Convention.

2. Each Contracting Party may introduce the provisions of the Annex into its law either by reproducing the actual text, or by translating it into its official language or languages.

3. Each Contracting Party may introduce into its law such further provisions as are necessary to give the provisions of the Annex full effect in its territory.

4. Each Contracting Party shall submit to the Depositary Government the text of the rules introduced into its national law in order to implement the provisions of this Convention.

Article II 1. Each Contracting Party shall implement the provisions of the Annex in its law, within the period provided for in the preceding article, by designating the persons who, in its territory, shall be authorized to act in connection with international wills. It may also designate as a person authorized to act with regard to its nationals its diplomatic or consular agents abroad insofar as the local law does not prohibit it.

2. The Party shall notify such designation, as well as any modifications thereof, to the Depositary Government.

Article III The capacity of the authorized person to act in connection with an international will, if conferred in accordance with the law of a Contracting Party, shall be recognized in the territory of the other Contracting Parties.

Article IV The effectiveness of the certificate provided for in Article 10 of the Annex shall be recognized in the territories of all Contracting Parties.

Article V 1. The conditions requisite to acting as a witness of an international will shall be governed by the law under which the authorized person was designated. The same rule shall apply as regards an interpreter who is called upon to act.

2. Nonetheless no one shall be disqualified to act as a witness of an international will solely because he is an alien.

Article VI 1. The signature of the testator, of the authorized person, and of the witnesses to an international will, whether on the will or on the certificate, shall be exempt from any legalization or like formality.

2. Nonetheless, the competent authorities of any Contracting Party may, if necessary, satisfy themselves as to the authenticity of the signature of the authorized person.

Article VII The safekeeping of an international will shall be governed by the law under which the authorized person was designated.

Article VIII No reservation shall be admitted to this Convention or to its Annex.

Article IX 1. The present Convention shall be open for signature at Washington from October 26, 1973, until December 31, 1974.

2. The Convention shall be subject to ratification.

3. Instruments of ratification shall be deposited with the Government of the United States of America, which shall be the Depositary Government.

Article X 1. The Convention shall be open indefinitely for accession.

2. Instruments of accession shall be deposited with the Depositary Government.

Article XI 1. The present Convention shall enter into force six months after the date of deposit of the fifth instrument of ratification or accession with the Depositary Government.

2. In the case of each State which ratifies this Convention or accedes to it after the fifth instrument of ratification or accession has been deposited, this Convention shall enter into force six months after the deposit of its own instrument of ratification or accession.

Article XII 1. Any Contracting Party may denounce this Convention by written notification to the Depositary Government.

2. Such denunciation shall take effect twelve months from the date on which the Depositary Government has received the notification, but such denunciation shall not affect the validity of any will made during the period that the Convention was in effect for the denouncing State.

Article XIII 1. Any State may, when it deposits its instrument of ratification or accession or at any time thereafter, declare, by a notice addressed to the Depositary Government, that this Convention shall apply to all or part of the territories for the international relations of which it is responsible.

2. Such declaration shall have effect six months after the date on which the Depositary Government shall have received notice thereof or, if at the end of such period the Convention has not yet come into force, from the date of its entry into force.

3. Each Contracting Party which has made a declaration in accordance with paragraph 1 of this Article may, in accordance with Article XII, denounce this Convention in relation to all or part of the territories concerned.

Article XIV 1. If a State has two or more territorial units in which different systems of law apply in relation to matters respecting the form of wills, it may at the time of signature, ratification, or accession, declare that this Convention shall extend to all its territorial units or only to one or more of them, and may modify its declaration by submitting another declaration at any time.

2. These declarations shall be notified to the Depositary Government and shall state expressly the territorial units to which the Convention applies.

Article XV If a Contracting Party has two or more territorial units in which different systems of law apply in relation to matters respecting the form of wills, any reference to the internal law of the place where the will is made or to the law under which the authorized person has been appointed to act in connection with international wills shall be construed in accordance with the constitutional system of the Party concerned.

Article XVI 1. The original of the present Convention, in the English, French, Russian and Spanish languages, each version being equally authentic, shall be deposited with the Government of the United States of America, which shall transmit certified copies thereof to each of the signatory and acceding States and to the International Institute for the Unification of Private Law.

2. The Depositary Government shall give notice to the signatory and acceding States, and to the International Institute for the Unification of Private Law, of:

(a) any signature;

(b) the deposit of any instrument of ratification or accession;

(c) any date on which this Convention enters into force in accordance with Article XI;

(d) any communication received in accordance with Article I, paragraph 4;

(e) any notice received in accordance with Article II, paragraph 2;

(f) any declaration received in accordance with Article XIII, paragraph 2, and the date on which such declaration takes effect;

(g) any denunciation received in accordance with Article XII, paragraph 1, or Article XIII, paragraph 3, and the date on which the denunciation takes effect;

(h) any declaration received in accordance with Article XIV, paragraph 2, and the date on which the declaration takes effect.

IN WITNESS WHEREOF, the undersigned Plenipotentiaries, being duly authorized to that effect, have signed the present Convention.

604

DONE at Washington this twenty-sixth day of October, one thousand nine hundred and seventy-three.

Annex

UNIFORM LAW ON THE FORM OF AN INTERNATIONAL WILL

Article 1 1. A will shall be valid as regards form, irrespective particularly of the place where it is made, of the location of the assets and of the nationality, domicile or residence of the testator, if it is made in the form of an international will complying with the provisions set out in Articles 2 to 5 hereinafter.

2. The invalidity of the will as an international will shall not affect its formal validity as a will of another kind.

Article 2 This law shall not apply to the form of testamentary dispositions made by two or more persons in one instrument.

Article 3 1. The will shall be made in writing.

2. It need not be written by the testator himself.

3. It may be written in any language, by hand or by any other means.

Article 4 1. The testator shall declare in the presence of two witnesses and of a person authorized to act in connection with international wills that the document is his will and that he knows the contents thereof.

2. The testator need not inform the witnesses, or the authorized person, of the contents of the will.

Article 5 1. In the presence of the witnesses and of the authorized person, the testator shall sign the will or, if he has previously signed it, shall acknowledge his signature.

2. When the testator is unable to sign, he shall indicate the reason therefor to the authorized person who shall make note of this on the will. Moreover, the testator may be authorized by the law under which the authorized person was designated to direct another person to sign on his behalf.

3. The witnesses and the authorized person shall there and then attest the will by signing in the presence of the testator.

Article 6 1. The signatures shall be placed at the end of the will.

2. If the will consists of several sheets, each sheet shall be signed by the testator or, if he is unable to sign, by the person signing on his behalf or, if there is no such person, by the authorized person. In addition, each sheet shall be numbered.

605

Article 7 1. The date of the will shall be the date of its signature by the authorized person.

2. This date shall be noted at the end of the will by the authorized person.

Article 8 In the absence of any mandatory rule pertaining to the safekeeping of the will, the authorized person shall ask the testator whether he wishes to make a declaration concerning the safekeeping of his will. If so and at the express request of the testator the place where he intends to have his will kept shall be mentioned in the certificate provided for in Article 9.

Article 9 The authorized person shall attach to the will a certificate in the form prescribed in Article 10 establishing that the obligations of this law have been complied with.

Article 10 The certificate drawn up by the authorized person shall be in the following form or in a substantially similar form:

CERTIFICATE

(Convention of October 26, 1973)

1. I, _____ (name, address and capacity), a person authorized to act in connection with international wills
2. Certify that on _____ (date) at _____ (place)
3. (testator) _____ (name, address, date and place of birth) in my presence and that of the witnesses
4.   (a) _____ (name, address, date and place of birth)
     (b) _____ (name, address, date and place of birth) has declared that the attached document is his will and that he knows the contents thereof.
5. I furthermore certify that:
6.   (a) in my presence and in that of the witnesses
     (1) the testator has signed the will or has acknowledged his signature previously affixed.
    *(2) following a declaration of the testator stating that he was unable to sign his will for the following reason

        –I have mentioned this declaration on the will
        * –the signature has been affixed by _____
        (name, address)
7.   (b) the witnesses and I have signed the will;
8. * (c) each page of the will has been signed by _____ and numbered;
9.   (d) I have satisfied myself as to the identity of the testator and of the witnesses as designated above;
10.   (e) the witnesses met the conditions requisite to act as such according to the law under which I am acting;

11.   * (f)   the testator has requested me to include the following
statement concerning the safekeeping of his will:

_____

_____

12.   PLACE
13.   DATE
14.   SIGNATURE and, if necessary, SEAL
*To be completed if appropriate

Article 11   The authorized person shall keep a copy of the certificate and deliver another to the testator.

Article 12   In the absence of evidence to the contrary, the certificate of the authorized person shall be conclusive of the formal validity of the instrument as a will under this Law.

Article 13   The absence or irregularity of a certificate shall not affect the formal validity of a will under this Law.

Article 14   The international will shall be subject to the ordinary rules of revocation of wills.

Article 15   In interpreting and applying the provisions of this law, regard shall be had to its international origin and to the need for uniformity in its interpretation.

RESOLUTION

The Conference

Considering the importance of measures to permit the safeguarding of wills and to find them after the death of the testator;

Emphasizing the special interest in such measures with respect to the international will, which is often made by the testator far from his home;

RECOMMENDS to the States that participated in the present Conference

—that they establish an internal system, centralized or not, to facilitate the safekeeping, search and discovery of an international will as well as the accompanying certificate, for example, along the lines of the Convention on the Establishment of a Scheme of Registration of Wills, concluded at Basel on May 16, 1972;

—that they facilitate the international exchange of information in these matters and, to this effect, that they designate in each state an authority or a service to handle such exchanges.

NUMBERING SECTIONS OF ACT

The Uniform International Wills Act may be adopted as a separate act or as part of the Uniform Probate Code. If

adopted as a separate act, the unbracketed section numbers would govern. If adopted as part of the Probate Code, i.e., as Part 10 of Article 2, the section numbers in brackets would govern.

Section 1. [2–1001.] [Definitions.]

In this Act: [Part:]

(1) "International will" means a will executed in conformity with sections 2 [2–1002] through 5 [2–1005].

(2) "Authorized person" and "person authorized to act in connection with international wills" mean a person who by section 9 [2–1009], or by the laws of the United States including members of the diplomatic and consular service of the United States designated by Foreign Service Regulations, is empowered to supervise the execution of international wills.

COMMENT

The term "international will" connotes only that a will has been executed in conformity with this act. It does not indicate that the will was planned for implementation in more than one country, or that it relates to an estate that has or may have international implications. Thus, it will be entirely appropriate to use an "international will" whenever a will is desired.

The reference in subsection (2) to persons who derive their authority to act from federal law, including Foreign Service Regulations, anticipates that the United States will become a party to the 1973 Convention, and that Congress, pursuant to the obligation of the Convention, will enact the annexed uniform law and include therein some designation, possibly of a cadre only, of authorized persons. See the discussion under "Roles for Federal and State Law in Relation to International Will", in the Prefatory Note, *supra.* If all states enact similar laws and designate all attorneys as authorized persons, the need for testators to resort to those designated by federal law may be minimal. It

seems desirable, nonetheless, to associate whoever may be designated by federal law as suitable authorized persons for purposes of implementing state enactments of the uniform act. The resulting "borrowing" of those designated federally should minimize any difficulties that might arise from variances in the details of execution of international wills that may develop in the state and federal enactment process.

In the Explanatory Report of the 1973 Convention prepared by Mr. Jean–Pierre Plantard, Deputy Secretary–General of the International Institute for the Unification of Private Law (UNIDROIT) as published by the Institute in 1974, the following paragraphs that are relevant to this section appear:

"The Uniform Law gives no definition of the term will. The preamble of the Convention also uses the expression 'last wills'. The material contents of the document are of little importance as the Uniform Law governs only its form. There is, therefore, nothing to prevent this form being used to register last wishes that do not involve the naming of an heir and which in some legal systems are called by a special name, such as 'Kodizill' in Austrian Law (ABGB § 553).

"Although it is given the qualification 'international', the will dealt with by the Uniform Law can easily be used for a situation without any international element, for example, by a testator disposing in his own country of his assets, all of which are situated in that same country. The adjective 'international', therefore, only indicates what was had in mind at the time when this new will was conceived. Moreover, it would have been practically impossible to define a satisfactory sphere of application, had one intended to restrict its use to certain situations with an international element. Such an element could only be assessed by reference to several factors (nationality, residence, domicile of the testator, place where the will was drawn up, place where the assets are situated) and, moreover, these might vary considerably between when the will was drawn up and the beginning of the inheritance proceedings.

"Use of the international will should, therefore, be open to all testators who decide they want to use it. Nothing should prevent it from competing with the traditional forms if it offers advantages of convenience and simplicity over the other forms and guarantees the necessary certainty."

Section 2. [2–1002.] [International Will; Validity.]

(a) A will shall be valid as regards form, irrespective particularly of the place where it is made, of the location of the assets and of the nationality, domicile, or residence of the testator, if it is made in the form of an international will complying with the requirements of this Act. [Part.]

(b) The invalidity of the will as an international will shall not affect its formal validity as a will of another kind.

(c) This Act [Part] shall not apply to the form of testamentary dispositions made by two or more persons in one instrument.

COMMENT

This section combines what appears in Articles 1 and 2 of the Annex into a single section. Except for the reference to later sections, the first sentence is identical to Article 1, section 1 of the Annex, the second sentence is identical to Article 1, section 2, and the third is identical to Article 2.

Mr. Plantard's commentary that is pertinent to this section is as follows:

"The Uniform Law is intended to be introduced into the legal system of each Contracting State. Article 1, therefore, introduces into the internal law of each Contracting State the new, basic principle according to which the international will is valid irrespective of the country in which it was made, the nationality, domicile or residence of the testator and the place where the assets forming the estate are located.

"The scope of the Uniform Law is thus defined in the first sentence. As was mentioned above, the idea behind it was to establish a new type of will, the form of which would be the same in all countries. The Law obviously does not affect the subsistence of all the other forms of will known under each national law. . . .

"Some of the provisions relating to form laid down by the Uniform Law are considered essential. Violation of these provisions is sanctioned by the invalidity of the will as an international will. These are: that the will must be made in writing, the presence of two witnesses and of the authorised person, signature by the testator and by the persons involved (witnesses and authorised person) and the prohibition of joint wills. The other formalities, such as the position of the signature and date, the delivery and form of the certificate, are laid down for reasons of convenience and uniformity but do not affect the validity of the international will.

"Lastly, even when the international will is declared invalid because one of the essential provisions contained in Articles 2 to 5 has not been observed, it is not necessarily deprived of all effect. Paragraph 2 of Article 1 specifies that it may still be valid as a will of another kind, if it conforms with the requirements of the applicable national law. Thus, for example, a will written, dated and signed by the testator but handed over to an authorised person in the absence of witnesses or without the signature of the witnesses and the authorised person could

quite easily be considered a valid holograph will. Similarly, an international will produced in the presence of a person who is not duly authorised might be valid as a will witnessed in accordance with Common law rules.

"However, in these circumstances, one could no longer speak of an international will and the validity of the document would have to be assessed on the basis of the rules of internal law or of private international law.

"A joint will cannot be drawn up in the form of an international will. This is the meaning of Article 2 of the Uniform Law which does not give an opinion as to whether this prohibition on joint wills, which exists in many legal systems, is connected with its form or its substance.

"A will made in this international form by several people together in the same document would, therefore, be invalid as an international will but could possibly be valid as another kind of will, in accordance with Article 1, paragraph 2 of the Uniform Law.

"The terminology used in Article 2 is in harmony with that used in Article 4 of The Hague Convention on the Conflicts of Laws Relating to the Form of Testamentary Dispositions."

Section 3. [2–1003.] [International Will; Requirements.]

(a) The will shall be made in writing. It need not be written by the testator himself. It may be written in any language, by hand or by any other means.

(b) The testator shall declare in the presence of two witnesses and of a person authorized to act in connection with international wills that the document is his will and that he knows the contents thereof. The testator need not inform the witnesses, or the authorized person, of the contents of the will.

(c) In the presence of the witnesses, and of the authorized person, the testator shall sign the will or, if he has previously signed it, shall acknowledge his signature.

(d) When the testator is unable to sign, the absence of his signature does not affect the validity of the international will if the testator indicates the reason for his inability to sign and the authorized person makes note thereof on the will. In these cases, it is permissible for any other person present, including the authorized person or one of the witnesses, at the direction of the testator to sign the testator's name for him, if the authorized person makes note of this also on the will, but it is not required that any person sign the testator's name for him.

(e) The witnesses and the authorized person shall there and then attest the will by signing in the presence of the testator.

COMMENT

The five subsections of this section correspond in content to Articles 3 through 5 of the Annex to the 1973 Convention. Article 1, section 1 makes it clear that compliance with all requirements listed in Articles 3 through 5 is necessary in order to achieve an international will. As re-organized for enactment in the United States, all mandatory requirements have been grouped in this section. Except for subsection (d), each of the sentences in the subsections corresponds exactly with a sentence in the Annex. Subsection (d), derived from Article 5, section 2 of the Annex, was re-worded for the sake of clarity.

Mr. Plantard's comments on the requirements are as follows:

"Paragraph 1 of Article 3 lays down an essential condition for a will's validity as an international will: it must be made in writing.

"The Uniform Law does not explain what is meant by 'writing'. This is a word of everday language which, in the opinion of the Law's authors, does not call for any definition but which covers any form of expression made by signs on a durable substance.

"Paragraphs 2 and 3 show the very liberal approach of the draft.

"Under paragraph 2, the will does not necessarily have to be written by the testator himself. This provision marks a moving away from the holograph will toward the other types of will: the public will or the mystic will and especially the Common law will. The latter, which is often very long, is only in exceptional cases written in the hand of the testator, who is virtually obliged to use a lawyer, in order to use the technical formulae necessary to give effect to his wishes. This is all the more so as wills frequently involve inter vivos family arrangements, and fiscal considerations play a very important part in this matter.

"This provision also allows for the will of illiterate persons, or persons who, for some other reason, cannot write themselves, for example paralysed or blind persons.

"According to paragraph 3 a will may be written in any language. This provision is in contrast with the rules accepted in various countries as regards public wills. It will be noted that the Uniform Law does not even require the will to be written in a language known by the testator. The latter is, therefore, quite free to choose according to whichever suits him best: it is to be expected that he will usually choose his own language but, if he thinks it is better, he will sometimes also choose the language of the place where the will is drawn up or that of the place where the will is mainly to be carried out. The important point is that he have full knowledge of the contents of his will, as is guaranteed by Articles 4 and 10.

"Lastly, a will may be written by hand or by any other method. This provision is the corollary of paragraph 2. What is mainly had in mind is a typewriter, especially in the case of a will drawn up by a lawyer advising the testator.

"The liberal nature of the principles set out in Article 3 calls for certain guarantees on the other hand. These are provided by the presence of three persons, already referred to in the context of Articles III and V of the Convention, that is to say, the authorised person and the two witnesses. It is evident that these three persons must all be simultaneously present with the testator during the carrying out of the formalities laid down in Articles 4 and 5.

"Paragraph 1 of Article 4 requires, first of all, that the testator declare, in the presence of these persons, that the document produced by him is his will and that he knows the contents thereof. The word 'declares' covers any unequivocal expression of intention, by way of words as well as by gestures or signs, as, for example, in the case of a testator who is dumb. This declaration must be made on pain of the international will being invalid. This is justified by the fact that the will produced by the testator might have been materially drawn up by a person other than the testator and even, in theory, in a language which is not his own.

"Paragraph 2 of the article specifies that this declaration is sufficient: the testator does not need to 'inform' the witnesses or the authorised person 'of the contents of the will'. This rule makes the international will differ from the public will and brings it closer to the other types of will: the holograph will and especially the mystic will and the Common law will.

"The testator can, of course, always ask for the will to be read, a precaution which can be particularly useful if the testator is unable to read himself. The paragraph under consideration does not in any way prohibit this; it only aims at ensuring respect for secrecy, if the testator should so wish. The international will can therefore be a secret will without being a closed will.

"The declaration made by the testator under Article 4 is not sufficient: under Article 5, paragraph 1, he must also sign his will. However, the authors of the Uniform Law presumed that, in certain cases, the testator might already have signed the document forming his will before producing it. To require a second signature would be evidence of an exaggerated formalism and a will containing two signatures by the testator would be rather strange. That is why the same paragraph provides that, when he has already signed the will, the testator can merely acknowledge it. This acknowledgement is completely informal and is normally done by a simple declaration in the presence of the authorised person and witnesses.

"The Uniform Law does not explain what is meant by 'signature'. This is once more a word drawn from everyday language, the meaning of which is usually the same in the various legal systems. The presence of the authorised person, who will necessarily be a practising lawyer will certainly guarantee that there is a genuine signature correctly affixed.

"Paragraph 2 was designed to give persons incapable of signing the possibility of making an international will. All they have to do is indicate their incapacity and the reason therefor to the authorised person. The authorised person must then note this declaration on the will which will then be valid, even though it has not been signed by the testator. Indication of the reason for incapacity is an additional guarantee as it can be checked. The certificate drawn up by the authorised person in the form prescribed in Article 10 again reproduces this declaration.

"The authors of the Uniform Law were also conscious of the fact that in some legal systems—for example, English law—persons who are incapable of signing can name someone to sign in their place. Although this procedure is completely unknown to other systems in which a signature is exclusively personal, it was accepted that the testator can ask another person to sign in his name, if this is permitted under the law from which the authorised person derives his authority. This amounts to nothing more than giving satisfaction to the practice of certain legal systems, as the authorised person must, in any case, indicate on the will that the testator declared that he could not sign, and give the reason therefor. This indication is sufficient to make the will valid. There will, therefore simply be a signature affixed by a third person instead of that of the testator. Although there is nothing stipulating this in the Uniform Law, one can expect the authorised person to explain the source of this signature on the document, all the more so as the signature of this substitute for the testator must also appear on the other pages of the will, by virtue of Article 6.

"This method over which there were some differences of opinion at the Diplomatic Conference, should not however interfere in any way with the legal systems which do not admit a signature in the name of someone else. Besides, its use is limited to the legal systems which admit it already and it is now implicitly accepted by the others when they recognise the validity of a foreign document drawn up according to this method. However, this situation can be expected to arise but rarely, as an international will made by a person who is incapable of signing it will certainly be a rare event.

"Lastly, Article 5 requires that the witnesses and authorised person also sign the will there and then in the presence of the testator. By using the words 'attest the will by signing', when only the word 'sign' had been used when referring to the testator, the authors of the Uniform Law intended to make a distinction between the person acknowledging the contents of a document and those who have only to affix their signature in order to certify their participation and presence.

"In conclusion, the international will will normally contain four signatures: that of the testator, that of the authorised person and those of the two witnesses. The signature of the testator might be missing: in this case, the will must contain a note made by the authorised person indicating that the testator was incapable of signing, adding his reason. All these signatures and notes must be made on pain of invalidity. Finally, if the signature of the testator is missing, the will could contain the signature of a person designated by the testator to sign in his name, in addition to the above-mentioned note made by the authorised person."

Section 4. [2–1004.] [International Will; Other Points of Form.]

(a) The signatures shall be placed at the end of the will. If the will consists of several sheets, each sheet will be signed by the testator or, if he is unable to sign, by the person signing on his behalf or, if there is no such person, by the authorized person. In addition, each sheet shall be numbered.

(b) The date of the will shall be the date of its signature by the authorized person. That date shall be noted at the end of the will by the authorized person.

(c) The authorized person shall ask the testator whether he wishes to make a declaration concerning the safekeeping of his will. If so and at the express request of the testator the place where he intends to have his will kept shall be mentioned in the certificate provided for in Section 5.

(d) A will executed in compliance with Section 3 shall not be invalid merely because it does not comply with this section.

COMMENT

Mr. Plantard's commentary about Articles 6, 7 and 8 of the Annex [supra] relate to subsections (a), (b) and (c) respectively of this section. Subsections (a) and (b) are identical to Articles 6 and 7; subsection (c) is the same as Article 8 of the Annex except that the prefatory language "In the absence of any mandatory rule pertaining to the safekeeping of the will …" has been deleted because it is inappropriate for inclusion in a local statute designed for enactment by a state that has had no tradition or familiarity with mandatory rules regarding the safekeeping of the wills. Subsection (d) embodies the sense of Article 1, section 1 of the Annex which states that compliance with Articles 2 to 5 is necessary and so indicates that compliance with the remaining articles prescribing formal steps is not necessary.

Mr. Plantard's commentary is as follows:

"The provisions of Article 6 and those of the following articles are not imposed on pain of invalidity. They are nevertheless compulsory legal provisions which can involve sanctions, for example, the professional, civil and even criminal liability of the authorised person, according to the provisions of the law from which he derives his authority.

"The first paragraph, to guarantee a uniform presentation for international wills, simply indicates that signatures shall be placed at the end of international wills, that is, at the end of the text.

"Paragraph 2 provides for the frequent case in which the will consists of several sheets. Each sheet has to be signed by the testator, to guarantee its authenticity and to avoid substitutions. The use of the word 'signed' seems to imply that the signature must be in the same form as that at the end of the will. However, in the legal systems which merely require that the individual sheets be paraphed, usually by means of initials, this would certainly have the same value as signature, as a signature itself could simply consist of initials.

"The need for a signature on each sheet, for the purpose of authentifying each such sheet, led to the introduction of a special system for the case when the testator is incapable of signing. In this case it will generally be the authorised person who will sign each sheet in his place, unless, in accordance with Article 5, paragraph 2, the testator has designated another person to sign in his name. In this case, it will of course be this person who will sign each sheet.

"Lastly, it is prescribed that the sheets shall be numbered. Although no further details are given on this subject, it will in practice be up to the authorised person to check if they have already been numbered and, if not, to number them or ask the testator to do so.

"The aim of this provision is obviously to guarantee the orderliness of the document and to avoid losses, subtractions or substitutions.

"The date is an essential element of the will and its importance is quite clear in the case of successive wills. Paragraph 1 of Article 7 indicates that the date of the will in the case of an international will is the date on which it was signed by the authorised person, this being the last of the formalities prescribed by the Uniform Law on pain of invalidity (Article 5, paragraph 3). It is, therefore, from the moment of this signature that the international will is valid.

"Paragraph 2 stipulates that the date shall be noted at the end of the will by the authorised person. Although this is compulsory for the authorised person, this formality is not sanctioned by the invalidity of the will which, as is the case in many legal systems such as English, German and Austrian law, remains fully valid even if it is not dated or is wrongly dated. The date will then have to be proved by some other means. It can happen that the will has two dates, that of its drawing up and the date on which it was signed by the authorised person as a result of which it became an international will. Evidently only this last date is to be taken into consideration.

"During the preparatory work it had been intended to organise the safekeeping of the international will and to entrust its care to the authorised person. This plan caused serious difficulties both for the countries which do not have the notary as he is known in Civil law systems and for the countries in which wills must be deposited with a public authority, as is the case, for example, in the Federal Republic of Germany, where wills must be deposited with a court.

"The authors of the Uniform Law therefore abandoned the idea of introducing a unified system for the safekeeping of international wills. However, where a legal system already has rules on this subject, these rules of course also apply to the international will as well as to other types of will. Finally, the Washington Conference adopted, at the same time as the Convention, a resolution recommending States, in particular, to organise a system facilitating the safekeeping of international wills (see the commentary on this resolution, at the end of this Report). It should lastly be underlined that States desiring to give testators an additional guarantee as regards the international will will organise its safekeeping by providing, for example, that it shall be deposited with the authorised person or with a public officer. Complementary legislation of this kind could be admitted within the framework of paragraph 3 of Article 1 of the Convention, as was mentioned in our commentary on that article.

"These considerations explain why Article 8 starts by stipulating that it only applies 'in the absence of any mandatory rule pertaining to the safekeeping of the will'. If there happens to be such a rule in the national law from which the authorised person derives his authority this rule shall govern the safekeeping of the will. If there is no such rule, Article 8 requires the authorised person to ask the testator whether he wishes to make a declaration in this regard. In this way, the authors of the Uniform Law sought to reconcile the advantage of exact information so as to facilitate the discovery of the will after the death of the testator, on the one hand, and respect for the secrecy which the testator may want as regards the place where his will is kept, on the other hand. The testator is therefore quite free to make or not to make a declaration in this regard, but his attention is nevertheless drawn to the possibility left open to him, and particularly to the opportunity he has, if he expressly asks for it, to have the details he thinks appropriate in this regard mentioned on the certificate provided for in Article 9. It will thus be easier to find the will again at the proper time, by means of the certificate made out in three copies, one of which remains in the hands of the authorised person."

Section 5. [2–1005.] [International Will; Certificate.]

The authorized person shall attach to the will a certificate to be signed by him establishing that the requirements of this Act [Part] for valid execution of an international will have been complied with. The authorized person shall keep a copy of the certificate and deliver another to the testator. The certificate shall be substantially in the following form:

CERTIFICATE

(Convention of October 26, 1973)

1. I, _____ (name, address and capacity), a person authorized to act in connection with international wills
2. Certify that on _____ (date) at _____ (place)
3. (testator) _____
   (name, address, date and place of birth) in my presence and that of the witnesses
4. (a) _____ (name, address, date and place of birth)
   (b) _____ (name, address, date and place of birth)
   has declared that the attached document is his will and that he knows the contents thereof.
5. I furthermore certify that:
6. (a) in my presence and in that of the witnesses
      (1) the testator has signed the will or has acknowledged his signature previously affixed.
    * (2) following a declaration of the testator stating that he was unable to sign his will for the following

reason _____, I have mentioned this declaration on the will

* and the signature has been affixed by _____ (name and address)

7.   (b)   the witnesses and I have signed the will;

8.   * (c)   each page of the will has been signed by _____ and numbered;

9.   (d)   I have satisfied myself as to the identity of the testator and of the witnesses as designated above;

10.   (e)   the witnesses met the conditions requisite to act as such according to the law under which I am acting;

11.   * (f)   the testator has requested me to include the following statement concerning the safekeeping of his will:

_____ _____

12.   PLACE OF EXECUTION
13.   DATE
14.   SIGNATURE and, if necessary, SEAL
    * to be completed if appropriate

COMMENT

This section embodies the content of Articles 9, 10 and 11 of the Annex with only minor, clarifying changes. Those familiar with the pre-proved will authorized by Uniform Probate Code § 2–504 should be comfortable with sections 5 and 6 of this act. Indeed, inclusion of these provisions in the Annex was the result of a concession by those familiar with civil law approaches to problems of execution and proof of wills, to the English speaking countries where will ceremonies are divided between those occurring as testator acts, and those occurring later when the will is probated. Further, since English and Canadian practices reduce post-mortem probate procedures down to little more than the presentation of the will to an appropriate registry and so, approach civil law customs, the concession was largely to accommodate American states where post-mortem probate procedures are very involved. Thus, the primary purpose of the certificate, which provides conclusive proof of the formal validity of the will, is to put wills executed before a civil law notary and wills executed in the American tradition on a par; with the certificate, both are good without question insofar as formal requirements are concerned.

It should be noted that Article III of the Convention binds countries becoming parties to recognize the capacity of an authorized person to act in relation to an international will, as conferred by the law of another country that is a party. This means that an international will coming into one of our states that has enacted the uniform law will be entirely good under local law, and that the certificate from abroad will provide conclusive proof of its validity.

May an international will be contested? The answer is clearly affirmative as to contests based on lack of capacity, fraud, undue influence, revocation or ineffectiveness based on the contents of the will or substantive restraints on testamentary power. Contests based on failure to follow mandatory requirements of execution are not precluded because the next section provides that the certificate is conclusive only "in the absence of evidence to the contrary". However, the Convention becomes relevant when one asks whether a probate court may require additional proof of the genuineness of signatures by testators and witnesses. It provides:

Article VI 1. The signature of the testator, of the authorized person, and of the witnesses to an international will, whether on the will or on the certificate, shall be exempt from any legalization or like formality.

2. Nonetheless, the competent authorities of any Contracting Party may, if necessary, satisfy themselves as to the authenticity of the signature of the authorized person. Presumably, the prohibition against legalization would not preclude additional proof of genuineness if evidence tending to show forgery is introduced, but without contrary proof, the certificate proves the will.

Mr. Plantard's commentary on the articles of the Annex that are pertinent to section 5, are as follows:

"This provision specifies that the authorised person must attach to the international will a certificate drawn up in accordance with the form set out in Article 10, establishing that the Uniform Law's provisions have been complied with. The term 'joint au testament' means that the certificate must be added to the will, that is, fixed thereto. The English text which uses the word 'attach' is perfectly clear on this point. Furthermore, it results from Article 11 that the certificate must be made out in three copies. This document, the contents of which are detailed in Article 10, is proof that the formalities required for the validity of the international will have been complied with. It also reveals the identity of the persons who participated in drawing up the document and may, in addition, contain a declaration by the testator as to the place where he intends his will to be kept. It should be

stressed that the certificate is drawn up under the entire responsibility of the authorised person who is the only person to sign it.

"Article 10 sets out the form for the certificate. The authorised person must abide by it, in accordance with the provisions of Article 10 itself, laying down this or a substantially similar form. This last phrase could not be taken as authorising him to depart from this form: it only serves to allow for small changes of detail which might be useful in the interests of improving its comprehensibility or presentation, for example, the omission of the particulars marked with an asterisk indicating that they are to be completed where appropriate when in fact they do not need to be completed and thus become useless.

"Including the form of a certificate in one of the articles of a Uniform Law is unusual. Normally these appear in the annexes to Conventions. However, in this way, the authors of the Uniform Law underlined the importance of the certificate and its contents. Moreover, the Uniform Law already forms the Annex to the Convention itself.

"The 14 particulars indicated on the certificate are numbered. These numbers must be reproduced on each certificate, so as to facilitate its reading, especially when the reader speaks a foreign language, as they will help him to find the relevant details more easily: the name of the authorised person and the testator, addresses, etc.

"The certificate contains all the elements necessary for the identification of the authorised person, testator and witnesses. It expressly mentions all the formalities which have to be carried out in accordance with the provisions of the Uniform Law. Furthermore, the certificate contains all the information required for the will's registration according to the system introduced by the Council of Europe Convention on the Establishment of a Scheme of Registration of Wills, signed at Basle on 16 May 1972.

"The authorised person must keep a copy of the certificate and deliver one to the testator. Seeing that another copy has to be attached to the will in accordance with Article 9, it may be deduced that the authorised person must make out altogether three copies of the certificate. These cannot be simple copies but have to be three signed originals. This provision is useful for a number of reasons. The fact that the testator keeps a copy of the certificate is a useful reminder for him, especially when his will is being kept by the authorised person or deposited with someone designated by national law. Moreover, discovery of the certificate among the testators' papers will inform his heirs of the existence of a will and will enable them to find it more easily. The fact that the authorised person keeps a copy of the certificate enables him to inform the heirs as well, if necessary. Lastly, the fact that there are several copies of the certificate is a guarantee against changes being made to one of them and even, to a certain extent, against certain changes to the will itself, for example as regards its date."

Section 6. [2–1006.] [International Will; Effect of Certificate.]

In the absence of evidence to the contrary, the certificate of the authorized person shall be conclusive of the formal validity of the instrument as a will under this Act. [Part.] The absence or irregularity of a certificate shall not affect the formal validity of a will under this Act. [Part.]

COMMENT

This section, which corresponds to Articles 11 and 12 of the Annex, must be read with the definition of "authorized person" in section 1, and Articles III and IV of the 1973 Convention which will become binding on all states if and when the United States joins that treaty. Articles III and IV of the Convention provide:

Article III The capacity of the authorized person to act in connection with an international will, if conferred in accordance with the law of a Contracting Party, shall be recognized in the territory of the other Contracting Parties.

Article IV The effectiveness of the certificate provided for in Article 10 of the Annex shall be recognized in the territories of all Contracting Parties.

In effect, the state enacting this law will be recognizing certificates by authorized persons designated, not only by this state, but by the United States and other parties to the 1973 Convention. Once the identity of one making a certificate on an international will is established, the will may be proved without more, assuming the presence of the recommended form of certificate. Article IX (3) of the 1973 Convention constitutes the United States as the Depositary under the Convention, and Article II obligates each country joining the Convention to notify the Depositary Government of the persons designated by its law as authorized to act in connection with international wills. Hence, persons interested in local probate of an international will from another country will be enabled to determine from the Department of State whether the official making the certificate in which they are interested had the requisite authority.

In this connection, it should be noted that under Article II of the Convention, each contracting country may designate its diplomatic or consular representatives abroad as authorized persons insofar as the local law does not prohibit it. Since the Uniform Act will be the law locally, and since it does not prohibit persons designated by foreign states that are parties to the Convention from acting locally in respect to international wills, there should be a considerable amount of latitude in selecting authorized persons to assist with wills and a correlative reduction in the chances of local non-recognition of an authorized person from abroad. Also, it should be noted that the Uniform Act does not restrict the persons which it constitutes as authorized persons in relation to the places where they can so function. This supports the view that local law as embodied in this statute should not be construed as restrictive in relation to local activities concerning international wills of foreign diplomatic and consular representatives who are resident here.

The certificate requires the authorized person to state that the witnesses had the requisite capacity. If the authorized person derives his authority from the law of a state other than that where he is acting, it would be advisable to have the certificate identify the applicable law.

The Uniform Act is silent in regard to methods of meeting local probate requirements contemplating deposit of the original will with the court. Section 3–409 of the Uni-

form Probate Code, or its counterpart in a state that has not adopted the uniform law on the point, becomes pertinent. The last sentence of UPC 3–409 provides:

A will from a place which does not provide for probate of a will after death, may be proved for probate in this state by a duly authenticated certificate of its legal custodian that the copy introduced is a true copy and that the will has become effective under the law of the other place.

One final matter warrants mention. Implicit in local proof of an instrument by means of authentication provided by a foreign official, is the problem of proving the authority of the official. The traditional, exceedingly formalistic, method of accomplishing this has been through what has been known as "legalization", a process that involves a number of certificates. The capacity of the official who authenticates the signature of the party to the document, if derived from his status as a county official, is proved by the certificate of a high county official. In turn, the county official's status is proved by the certificate of the area's secretary of state, whose status is established by another and so on until, ultimately, the Department of State certifies to the identity of the highest state official in a format that will be persuasive to the receiving country's foreign relations representative.

Article VI of the 1973 Convention forbids legalization of the signature of testators and witnesses. It provides:

1. The signature of the testator, of the authorized person, and of the witnesses to an international will, whether on the will or on the certificate, shall be exempt from any legalization or like formality.

2. Nonetheless, the competent authorities of any Contracting Party may, if necessary, satisfy themselves as to the authenticity of the signature of the authorized person.

Thus, it would appear that if the United States, as contracting party, satisfies itself that the signature of a foreign authorized person is authentic, and so indicates to those interested in local probate of the document, the local court, though presumably able to receive and to act upon evidence to the contrary, cannot reject an international will for lack of proof. This is not to say, of course, that the authenticity of the signature of the foreign authorized person must be shown through the aid of the State Department; plainly, the point may be implied from the face of the document unless and until challenged.

Mr. Plantard's commentary on this portion of the uniform law is as follows:

"Article 12 states that the certificate is conclusive of the formal validity of the international will. It is therefore a kind of proof supplied in advance.

"This provision is only really understandable in those legal systems, like the United States, where a will can only take effect after it has been subjected to a preliminary procedure of verification ('Probate') designed to check on its validity. The mere presentation of the certificate should suffice to satisfy the requirements of this procedure.

"However, the certificate is not always irrefutable as proof, as is indicated by the words 'in the absence of evidence to the contrary'. If it is challenged, then the ensuing litigation will be solved in accordance with the legal procedure applicable in the Contracting State where the will and certificate are presented.

"The principle set out in Article 13 is already implied by Article 1, as only the provisions of Articles 2 to 5 are prescribed on pain of invalidity. Besides, it is perfectly logical that the absence of or irregularities in a certificate should not affect the formal validity of the will, as the certificate is a document serving essentially for purposes of proof drawn up by the authorised person, without the testator taking any part either in drawing it up or in checking it. This provision is in perfect harmony with Article 12 which by the terms 'in the absence of evidence to the contrary' means that one can challenge what is stated in the certificate.

"In consideration of the fact that the authorised person will be a practising lawyer officially designated by each Contracting State, it is difficult to imagine him omitting or neglecting to draw up the certificate provided for by the national law to which he is subject. Besides, he would lay himself open to an action based on his professional and civil liability. He could even expose himself to sanctions laid down by his national law.

"However, the international will subsists, even if, by some quirk, the certificate which is a means of proof but not necessarily the only one, should be missing, be incomplete or contain particulars which are manifestly erroneous. In these undoubtedly very rare circumstances, proof that the formalities prescribed on pain of invalidity have been carried out will have to be produced in accordance with the legal procedures applicable in each State which has adopted the Uniform Law."

Section 7. [2–1007.] [International Will; Revocation.]

The international will shall be subject to the ordinary rules of revocation of wills.

COMMENT

Mr. Plantard's commentary on this portion of the uniform law is as follows:

"The authors of the Uniform Law did not intend to deal with the subject of the revocation of wills. There is indeed no reason why the international will should be submitted to a regime different from that of other kinds of will. Article 14 therefore merely gives expression to this idea. Whether or not there has been revocation—for example, by a subsequent will—is to be assessed in accordance with the law of each State which has adopted the Uniform Law, by virtue of Article 14. Besides, this is a question mainly concerning rules of substance which would thus overstep the scope of the Uniform Law."

Section 8. [2–1008.] [Source and Construction.]

Sections 1 [2–1001] through 7 [2–1007] derive from Annex to Convention of October 26, 1973, Providing a Uniform Law on the Form of an International Will. In interpreting and applying this Act [Part], regard shall be had to its international origin and to the need for uniformity in its interpretation.

COMMENT

Mr. Plantard's commentary on this portion of the uniform law is as follows:

"This Article contains a provision which is to be found in a similar form in several conventions or draft Uniform Laws. It seeks to avoid practising lawyers interpreting the Uniform Law solely in terms of the principles of their respective internal law, as this would prejudice the international unification being sought after. It requests judges to take the international character of the Uniform Law into consideration and to work towards elaborating a sort of common caselaw, taking account of the foreign legal systems which provided the foundation for the Uniform Law and the decisions handed down on the same text by the courts of other countries. The effort toward unification must not be limited to just bringing about the Law's adoption, but should be carried on into the process of putting it into operation."

Section 9. [2–1009.] [Persons Authorized to Act in Relation to International Will; Eligibility; Recognition by Authorizing Agency.]

Individuals who have been admitted to practice law before the courts of this state and who are in good standing as active law practitioners in this state, are hereby declared to be authorized persons in relation to international wills.

COMMENT

The subject of who should be designated to be authorized persons under the Uniform Law is discussed under the heading "Description of the Proposal" in the Prefatory Note.

The first draft of the Uniform Law presented to the National Conference at its 1975 meeting in Quebec City included provision for a special new licensing procedure through which others than attorneys might become qualified. The ensu-ing discussion resulted in rejection of this approach in favor of the simpler approach of section 9. Among other difficulties with the special licensee approach, representatives of the State Department expressed concern about the attendant burden on the U.S. as Depositary Government, of receiving, keeping up to date, and interpreting to foreign governments the results of fifty different state licensing systems.

[Section 10. [2–1010.] [International Will Information Registration.]

The [Secretary of State] shall establish a registry system by which authorized persons may register in a central information center, information regarding the execution of international wills, keeping that information in strictest confidence until the death of the maker and then making it available to any person desiring information about any will who presents a death certificate or other satisfactory evidence of the testator's death to the center. Information that may be received, preserved in confidence until death, and reported as indicated is limited to the name, social-security or any other individual-identifying number established by law, address, and date and place of birth of the testator, and the intended place of deposit or safekeeping of the instrument pending the death of the maker. The [Secretary of State], at the request of the authorized person, may cause the information it receives about execution of any international will to be transmitted to the registry system of another jurisdiction as identified by the testator, if that other system adheres to rules protecting the confidentiality of the information similar to those established in this state.]

COMMENT

The relevance of this optional, bracketed section to the other sections constituting the uniform law concerning international wills is explained in the Prefatory Note. Also, Mr. Plantard's observations regarding the Resolution attached to the 1973 Convention are pertinent. He writes:

"The Resolution adopted by the Washington Conference and annexed to its Final Act encourages States which adopt the Uniform Law to make additional provisions for the registering and safekeeping of the international will. The authors of the Uniform Law considered that it was not possible to lay down uniform rules on this subject on account of the differences in tradition and outlook, but several times, both during the preparatory work and during the final diplomatic phase, they underlined the importance of States making such provisions.

"The Resolution recommends organising a system enabling ... 'the safekeeping, search and discovery of an international will as well as the accompanying certificate' ...

"Indeed lawyers know that many wills are never carried out because the very existence of the will itself remains unknown or because the will is never found or is never produced. It would be quite possible to organise a register or index which would enable one to know after the death of a person whether he had drawn up a will. Some countries have already done something in this field, for example, Quebec, Spain, the Federal Republic of Germany, where this service is connected with the Registry of Births, Marriages and Deaths. Such a system could perfectly well be fashioned so as to ensure respect for the legitimate wish of testators to keep the very existence of their will secret.

"The Washington Conference also underlined that there is already an International Convention on this subject, namely the Council of Europe Convention on the Establishment of a Scheme of Registration of Wills, concluded at Basle on 16 May 1972, to which States which are not members of the Council of Europe may accede.

"In this Convention the Contracting States simply undertake to create an internal system for registering wills. The Convention stipulates the categories of will which should be registered, in terms which include the international will. Apart from national bodies in charge of registration, the Convention also provides for the designation by each Contracting State of a national body which must remain in contact with the national bodies of other States and communicate registrations and any information asked for. The Convention specifies that registration must remain secret during the life of the testator. This system, which will come into force between a number of European States in the near future, interested the authors of the Convention, even if they do not accede to it. The last paragraph of the Resolution follows the pattern of the Basle Convention by recommending, in the interests of facilitating an international exchange of information on this matter, the designation in each State of authorities or services to handle such exchanges.

"As for the organisation of the safekeeping of international wills, the resolution merely underlies the importance of this, without making any specific suggestions in this regard. This problem has already been discussed in connection with Article 8 of the Uniform Law.

"The Council of Europe Convention on the Establishment of a Scheme of Registration of Wills of May 16, 1972 and related documents were available to the reporter and provided the guidelines for section 10 of this Act."

APPENDIX VIII

ORIGINAL 1969 APPROVAL OF ARTICLE V

The Official Text and Comments of Article V, as originally approved in 1969, are set forth below.

ARTICLE V

PROTECTION OF PERSONS UNDER DISABILITY AND THEIR PROPERTY

PART 1
GENERAL PROVISIONS

PART 2
GUARDIANS OF MINORS

PART 3
GUARDIANS OF INCAPACITATED PERSONS

PART 4

PROTECTION OF PROPERTY OF PERSONS UNDER DISABILITY AND MINORS

PART 5

POWERS OF ATTORNEY

Section

5-501. [When Power of Attorney Not Affected by Disability.]
5-502. [Other Powers of Attorney Not Revoked Until Notice of Death or Disability.]

GENERAL COMMENT

Article V, entitled "Protection of Persons Under Disability and Their Property" embodies separate systems of guardianship to protect persons of minors and mental incompetents. It also includes provisions for a type of power of attorney that does not terminate on disability of the principal which may be used by adults approaching senility or incompetence to avoid the necessity for other kinds of protective regimes. Finally, Part 4 of the Article offers a system of protective proceedings, including conservatorships, to provide for the management of substantial aggregations of property of persons who are, for one reason or another, including minority and mental incompetence, unable to manage their own property.

It should be emphasized that the Article contains many provisions designed to minimize or avoid the necessity of guardianship and protective proceedings, as well as provisions designed to simplify and minimize arrangements which become necessary for care of persons or their property. The power of attorney which confers authority notwithstanding later incompetence is one example of the former. Another is a facility of payment provision which permits relatively small sums owed to a minor to be paid whether or not there is a guardian or other official who has been designated to act for the minor. A new device tending to simplify necessary protective proceedings, is found in provisions in Part 4 which permit a judge to make appropriate orders concerning the property of a disabled person without appointing a fiduciary.

The highspots of the several parts of Article V, considered in somewhat more detail, include the following:

(a) The facility of payment clause, which is Section 5-103 in Part 1, permits one owing up to $5,000 per year to a minor to be validly discharged by payment to the minor, if he is over eighteen or married, to the minor's parent or grandparent or other adult with whom the minor resides, to a guardian, or by deposit in an account in the name of the minor.

(b) A provision in Part 2 permits the surviving parent of a minor to designate a guardian by will. A similar provision in Part 3 authorizes a parent or spouse to designate a guardian for an incapacitated person by will. Such designation becomes effective upon probate of the will and the filing of an acceptance by the guardian. Thereafter the status of guardian and ward arises. It is like guardianship *of the person*, rather than *of estate*. It is described as a parental relationship without the parental obligation of support. The relationship follows the guardian and ward and is properly recognized and implemented, as and when necessary, by the courts of any jurisdiction where these persons may be located. No requirement of periodic reports or accounts is imposed on a testamentary guardian. The question of his proper expenditure of the small sums which he may receive for the ward is left to be settled by the guardian and ward after the ward attains full age. If the amounts involved become more than the guardian cares to be responsible for on this basis, he or any other interested person may seek the appointment of a property manager who is called a "conservator" by the Code. The guardian may be eligible to be appointed to this position.

Part 2 also permits a testamentary guardian of a minor to receive and expend sums payable to the minor for the minor's support and education without court order. He may not pay himself for services, however, and is under a duty to deposit excess funds, or to seek a suitable property-protection order if other management is needed.

(c) A parent or guardian is permitted to delegate his authority for short periods as necessitated by anticipated absence or incapacity.

(d) As previously mentioned, Part 4 of the Article deals with protective proceedings designed to permit substantial property interests of minors and others unable properly to manage their own affairs to be controlled by court order or managed by a conservator appointed by the court. The causes for inability of owner-management that are listed by the statute are quite broad. Technical incompetency is but one of several reasons why one may be unable to manage his affairs. See Section 5–401(2). The draftsmen's view was that reliance should be placed on the fact that the court applying the statute would be a full power court and on the various procedural safeguards, including a right to jury trial, to protect against unwise use of the proceedings, rather than to attempt to state and rely upon a narrow or technical test of lack of ability.

Section 5–409 is important, for it makes it clear that a court entertaining a protective proceeding has full power, through its orders, to do anything the protected person himself might have done if not disabled. Another provision broadens the form of relief so that the court may handle a single transaction, like renewal of a mortgage, or a sale and related investment of proceeds, which is recommended in respect to the affairs of a protected person directly by its orders rather than through the appointment of a conservator.

(e) If a conservator is appointed, provisions in Part 4 of the draft give him broad powers of management that may be exercised without a court order. On the other hand, provision is made for restricting the managerial or distribution powers of a conservator, provided notation of the restriction appears on his letters of appointment. Unless restricted, the fiduciary may be able to distribute and end the arrangement without court order if he can meet the terms of the Act. Among other kinds of expenditures and disbursements authorized, payments for the support and education of the protected person as determined by a guardian of the protected person, if any, or by the conservator, if there is no guardian, are approved. Also, certain payments for the support of dependents of the protected person are approved by the Code and hence would require no special approval.

(f) Other provisions in Part 4 round out the relationship of protective proceedings to creditors of the protected person and persons who deal with a conservator. Claims are handled by the conservator who is given a fiduciary responsibility to claimants and suitable discretion concerning allowance. If questions arise, the appointing court has all needed power to deal with disputes with creditors. The draft changes the common law rule that contracts of a guardian are his personal responsibility. A conservator is not liable personally on contracts made for the estate unless he agrees to such liability. A section buttresses the managerial powers given to conservator by protecting all persons who deal with them.

(g) Another section seeks to reduce the importance of state lines in respect to the authority of conservators by permitting appointees of foreign courts to act locally. Also, it follows the pattern of Article III dealing with ancillary administration of decedents' estates by giving the conservator appointed at the domicile of the protected person priority for appointment locally in case local administration of a protected person's assets becomes necessary.

(h) The many states which have adopted the Uniform Veterans Guardianship Act now have two systems for protection of the property of minors and mental incompetents, one of which applies *if* the property was derived, in whole or in part,

from benefits paid by the Veterans Administration *and* its minor or incompetent owner is or has been a beneficiary of the Veterans Administration, and the other of which applies to all other property. It is sometimes difficult to ascertain whether a person has ever received a benefit from the Veterans Administration and commonly impossible to determine whether property was derived in part from benefits paid by the Veterans Administration. Part 4 would provide a single system for the protection of property of minors and others unable to manage their own property, thus superseding the Uniform Veterans Guardianship Act. It would preserve the right of the Veterans Administration to appear in protective proceedings involving the property of its beneficiaries and would permit the imposition of the same safeguards provided by the superseded Uniform Veterans Guardianship Act.

PART 1

GENERAL PROVISIONS

Section 5–101. [Definitions and Use of Terms.]

Unless otherwise apparent from the context, in this Code:

(1) "incapacitated person" means any person who is impaired by reason of mental illness, mental deficiency, physical illness or disability, advanced age, chronic use of drugs, chronic intoxication, or other cause (except minority) to the extent that he lacks sufficient understanding or capacity to make or communicate responsible decisions concerning his person;

(2) a "protective proceeding" is a proceeding under the provisions of Section 5–401 to determine that a person cannot effectively manage or apply his estate to necessary ends, either because he lacks the ability or is otherwise inconvenienced, or because he is a minor, and to secure administration of his estate by a conservator or other appropriate relief;

(3) a "protected person" is a minor or other person for whom a conservator has been appointed or other protective order has been made;

(4) a "ward" is a person for whom a guardian has been appointed. A "minor ward" is a minor for whom a guardian has been appointed solely because of minority.

COMMENT

"Conservator," "estate," "guardian" and "minor," and other terms having relevance to Article V, are defined in 1–201. "Disability" as defined in Section 1–201(9) keys to an adjudication for the causes listed in Section 5–401. The definition of "incapacitated" on the other hand contains the bases for appointment of a guardian under Section 5–303.

Section 5–102. [Jurisdiction of Subject Matter; Consolidation of Proceedings.]

(a) The Court has jurisdiction over protective proceedings and guardianship proceedings.

(b) When both guardianship and protective proceedings as to the same person are commenced or pending in the same court, the proceedings may be consolidated.

Section 5–103. [Facility of Payment or Delivery.]

Any person under a duty to pay or deliver money or personal property to a minor may perform this duty, in amounts not exceeding $5,000 per annum, by paying or delivering the money or property to, (1) the minor, if he has attained the age of 18 years or is married; (2) any person having the care and custody of the minor with whom the minor resides; (3) a guardian of the minor; or (4) a financial institution incident to a deposit in a federally insured savings account in the sole name of the minor and giving notice of the deposit to the minor. This section does not apply if the person making payment or delivery has actual knowledge that a conservator has been appointed or proceedings for appointment of a conservator of the estate of the minor are pending. The persons, other than the minor or any financial institution under (4) above, receiving money or property for a minor, are obligated to apply the money to the support and education of the minor, but may not pay themselves except by way of reimbursement for out-of-pocket expenses for goods and services necessary for the minor's support. Any excess sums shall be preserved for future support of the minor and any balance not so used and any property received for the minor must be turned over to the minor when he attains majority.

Persons who pay or deliver in accordance with provisions of this section are not responsible for the proper application thereof.

COMMENT

Where a minor has only a small amount of property, it would be wasteful to require protective proceedings to deal with the property. This section makes it possible for other persons, such as the guardian, to handle the less complicated property affairs of the ward. Protective proceedings, including the possible establishment of a conservatorship, will be sought where substantial property is involved.

This section does not go as far as many facility of payment provisions found in trust instrument which usually permit application of sums due minor beneficiary to any expense or charge for the minor. It was felt that a grant of so large an area of discretion to any category of person who might owe funds to a minor would be unwise. Nonetheless, the section as drafted should reduce the need for trust facility of payment provision somewhat, while extending opportunities to insurance companies and other debtors to minors for relatively simple methods of gaining discharge.

Section 5–104. [Delegation of Powers by Parent or Guardian.]

A parent or a guardian of a minor or incapacitated person, by a properly executed power of attorney, may delegate to another person, for a period not exceeding 6 months, any of his powers regarding care, custody, or property of the minor child or ward, except his power to consent to marriage or adoption of a minor ward.

COMMENT

This section permits a temporary delegation of parental powers. For example, parents (or guardian) of a minor plan to be out of the country for several months. They wish to empower a close relative (an uncle, e.g.) to take any necessary action regarding the child while they are away. Using this section, they could execute an appropriate power of attorney giving the uncle custody and power to consent. Then if an emergency operation were required, the uncle could consent on behalf of the child; as a practical matter he would of course attempt to communicate with the parents before acting. The section is designed to reduce problems relating to consents for emergency treatment.

PART 2

GUARDIANS OF MINORS

Section 5–201. [Status of Guardian of Minor; General.]

A person becomes a guardian of a minor by acceptance of a testamentary appointment or upon appointment by the Court. The guardianship status continues until terminated, without regard to the location from time to time of the guardian and minor ward.

Section 5–202. [Testamentary Appointment of Guardian of Minor.]

The parent of a minor may appoint by will a guardian of an unmarried minor. Subject to the right of the minor under Section 5–203, a testamentary appointment becomes effective upon filing the guardian's acceptance in the Court in which the will is probated, if before acceptance, both parents are dead or the surviving parent is adjudged incapacitated. If both parents are dead, an effective appointment by the parent who died later has priority. This state recognizes a testamentary appointment effected by filing the guardian's acceptance under a will probated in another state which is the testator's domicile.

Section 5–203. [Objection by Minor of Fourteen or Older to Testamentary Appointment.]

A minor of 14 or more years may prevent an appointment of his testamentary guardian from becoming effective, or may cause a previously accepted appointment to terminate, by filing with the Court in which the will is probated a written objection to the appointment before it is accepted or within 30 days after its acceptance. An objection may be withdrawn. An objection does not preclude appointment by the Court in a proper proceeding of the testamentary nominee, or any other suitable person.

Section 5–204. [Court Appointment of Guardian of Minor; Conditions for Appointment.]

The Court may appoint a guardian for an unmarried minor if all parental rights of custody have been terminated or suspended by circumstances or prior Court order. A guardian appointed by will as provided in Section 5–202 whose appointment has not been prevented or nullified under 5–203 has priority over any guardian who may be appointed by the Court but the Court may proceed with an appointment upon a finding that the testamentary guardian has failed to accept the testamentary appointment within 30 days after notice of the guardianship proceeding.

COMMENT

The words "all parental rights of custody" are to be read with Sections 5–201 and 5–209 which give testamentary and court-appointed guardians of minors certain parental rights respecting the minor. Hence, no authority to appoint a guardian for a minor exists if a testamentary guardian has accepted an effective appointment by will. The purpose of this restriction is to support and encourage testamentary appointments which may occur without judicial act. If a testamentary guardian proves to be unsatisfactory, removal proceedings as provided in Section 5–211 may be used if the objection device of Section 5–203 is unavailable.

Section 5–205. [Court Appointment of Guardian of Minor; Venue.]

The venue for guardianship proceedings for a minor is in the place where the minor resides or is present.

COMMENT

Section 1–303 provides for conflicts of venue and for transfer of venue.

Section 5–206. [Court Appointment of Guardian of Minor; Qualifications; Priority of Minor's Nominee.]

The Court may appoint as guardian any person whose appointment would be in the best interests of the minor. The Court shall appoint a person nominated by the minor, if the minor is 14 years of age or older, unless the Court finds the appointment contrary to the best interests of the minor.

COMMENT

Rather than provide for priorities among various classes of relatives, it was felt that the only priority should be for the person nominated by the minor. The important point is to locate someone whose appointment will be in the best interests of the minor. If there is contention among relatives over who should be named, it is not likely that a statutory priority keyed to degrees of kinship would help resolve the matter. For example, if the argument involved a squabble between relatives of the child's father and relatives of its mother, priority in terms of degrees of kinship would be useless.

Guardianships under this Code are not likely to be attractive positions for persons who are more interested in handling a minor's estate than in his personal well being. An order of a court having equity power is necessary if the guardian is to receive payment for services where there is no conservator for the minor's estate. Also, the powers of management of a ward's estate conferred on a guardian are restricted so that if a substantial estate is involved, a conservator will be needed to handle the financial matters.

Section 5–207. [Court Appointment of Guardian of Minor; Procedure.]

(a) Notice of the time and place of hearing of a petition for the appointment of a guardian of a minor is to be given by the petitioner in the manner prescribed by Section 1–401 to:

(1) the minor, if he is 14 or more years of age;

(2) the person who has had the principal care and custody of the minor during the 60 days preceding the date of the petition; and

(3) any living parent of the minor.

(b) Upon hearing, if the Court finds that a qualified person seeks appointment, venue is proper, the required notices have been given, the requirements of Section 5–204 have been met, and the welfare and best interests of the minor will be served by the requested appointment, it shall make the appointment. In other cases the Court may dismiss the proceedings, or make any other disposition of the matter that will best serve the interest of the minor.

(c) If necessary, the Court may appoint a temporary guardian, with the status of an ordinary guardian of a minor, but the authority of a temporary guardian shall not last longer than six months.

(d) If, at any time in the proceeding, the Court determines that the interests of the minor are or may be inadequately represented, it may appoint an attorney to represent the minor, giving consideration to the preference of the minor if the minor is fourteen years of age or older.

Section 5–208. [Consent to Service by Acceptance of Appointment; Notice.]

By accepting a testamentary or court appointment as guardian, a guardian submits personally to the jurisdiction of the Court in any proceeding relating to the guardianship that may be instituted by any interested person. Notice of any proceeding shall be delivered to the guardian, or mailed to him by ordinary mail at his address as listed in the Court records and to his address as then known to the petitioner. Letters of guardianship must indicate whether the guardian was appointed by will or by court order.

COMMENT

The "long-arm" principle behind this section is well established. It seems desirable that the Court in which acceptance is filed be able to serve its process on the guardian wherever he has moved. The continuing interest of that court in the welfare of the minor is ample to justify this provision. The consent to service is real rather than fictional in the guardianship situation, where the guardian acts voluntarily in filing acceptance. It is probable that the form of acceptance will expressly embody the provisions of this section, although the statute does not expressly require this.

Section 5–209. [Powers and Duties of Guardian of Minor.]

A guardian of a minor has the powers and responsibilities of a parent who has not been deprived of custody of his minor and unemancipated child, except that a guardian is not legally obligated to provide from his own funds for the ward and is not liable to third persons by reason of the parental relationship for acts of the ward. In particular, and without qualifying the foregoing, a guardian has the following powers and duties:

(a) He must take reasonable care of his ward's personal effects and commence protective proceedings if necessary to protect other property of the ward.

(b) He may receive money payable for the support of the ward to the ward's parent, guardian or custodian under the terms of any statutory benefit or insurance system, or any private contract, devise, trust, conservatorship or custodianship. He also may receive money or property of the ward paid or delivered by virtue of Section 5–103. Any sums so received shall be applied to the ward's current needs for support, care and education. He must exercise due care to conserve any excess for the ward's future needs unless a conservator has been appointed for the estate of the ward, in which case excess shall be paid over at least annually to the conservator. Sums so received by the guardian are not to be used for compensation for his services except as approved by order of court or as determined by a duly appointed conservator other than the guardian. A guardian may institute proceedings to compel the performance by any person of a duty to support the ward or to pay sums for the welfare of the ward.

(c) The guardian is empowered to facilitate the ward's education, social, or other activities and to authorize medical or other professional care, treatment, or advice. A guardian is not liable by reason of this consent for injury to the ward resulting from the negligence or acts of third persons unless it would have been illegal for a parent to have consented. A guardian may consent to the marriage or adoption of his ward.

(d) A guardian must report the condition of his ward and of the ward's estate which has been subject to his possession or control, as ordered by Court on petition of any person interested in the minor's welfare or as required by Court rule.

COMMENT

See Section 5–212. See, also, Section 5–424(a) which confers the powers of a guardian on a conservator who is responsible for the estate of a minor under 18 for whom no guardian has been named.

Section 5–210. [Termination of Appointment of Guardian; General.]

A guardian's authority and responsibility terminates upon the death, resignation or removal of the guardian or upon the minor's death, adoption, marriage or attainment of majority, but termination does not affect his liability for prior acts, nor his obligation to account for funds and assets of his ward. Resignation of a guardian does not terminate the guardianship until it has been approved by the Court. A testamentary appointment under an informally probated will terminates if the will is later denied probate in a formal proceeding.

Section 5–211. [Proceedings Subsequent to Appointment; Venue.]

(a) The Court where the ward resides has concurrent jurisdiction with the Court which appointed the guardian, or in which acceptance of a testamentary appointment was filed, over resignation, removal, accounting and other proceedings relating to the guardianship.

(b) If the Court located where the ward resides is not the Court in which acceptance of appointment is filed, the Court in which proceedings subsequent to appointment are commenced shall in all appropriate cases notify the other Court, in this or another state, and after consultation with that Court determine whether to retain jurisdiction or transfer the proceedings to the other Court, whichever is in the best interest of the ward. A copy of any order accepting a resignation or removing a guardian shall be sent to the Court in which acceptance of appointment is filed.

COMMENT

Under Section 1–302, the Court is designated as the proper court to handle matters relating to guardianship. The present section is intended to give jurisdiction to the forum where the ward resides as well as to the one where appointment initiated. This has primary importance where the ward's residence has been moved from the appointing state. Because the Court where acceptance of appointment is filed may as a practical matter be the only forum where jurisdiction over the person of the guardian may be obtained (by reason of Section 5–208), that Court is given concurrent jurisdiction.

Section 5–212. [Resignation or Removal Proceedings.]

(a) Any person interested in the welfare of a ward, or the ward, if 14 or more years of age, may petition for removal of a guardian on the ground that removal would be in the best interest of the ward. A guardian may petition for permission to resign. A petition for removal or for permission to resign may, but need not, include a request for appointment of a successor guardian.

(b) After notice and hearing on a petition for removal or for permission to resign, the Court may terminate the guardianship and make any further order that may be appropriate.

(c) If, at any time in the proceeding, the Court determines that the interests of the ward are, or may be, inadequately represented, it may appoint an attorney to represent the minor, giving consideration to the preference of the minor if the minor is 14 or more years of age.

PART 3

GUARDIANS OF INCAPACITATED PERSONS

Section 5–301. [Testamentary Appointment of Guardian For Incapacitated Person.]

(a) The parent of an incapacitated person may by will appoint a guardian of the incapacitated person. A testamentary appointment by a parent becomes effective when, after having given 7 days prior written notice of his intention to do so to the incapacitated person and to the person having his care or to his nearest adult relative, the guardian files acceptance of appointment in the court in which the will is informally or formally probated, if prior thereto, both parents are dead or the surviving parent is adjudged incapacitated. If both parents are dead, an effective appointment by the parent who died later has priority unless it is terminated by the denial of probate in formal proceedings.

(b) The spouse of a married incapacitated person may by will appoint a guardian of the incapacitated person. The appointment becomes effective when, after having given 7 days prior written notice of his intention to do so to the incapacitated person and to the person having his care or to his nearest adult relative, the guardian files acceptance of appointment in the Court in which the will is informally or formally probated. An effective appointment by a spouse has priority over an appointment by a parent unless it is terminated by the denial of probate in formal proceedings.

(c) This state shall recognize a testamentary appointment effected by filing acceptance under a will probated at the testator's domicile in another state.

(d) On the filing with the Court in which the will was probated of written objection to the appointment by the person for whom a testamentary appointment of guardian has been made, the appointment is terminated. An objection does not prevent appointment by the Court in a proper proceeding of the testamentary nominee or any other suitable person upon an adjudication of incapacity in proceedings under the succeeding sections of this Part.

COMMENT

This section, modelled after Section 5–205, is designed to give the surviving parent, or the spouse, of an incapacitated person, the ability to confer the authority of a guardian on a person designated by will. This opportunity may be most useful in cases where parents, during their lifetime, have arranged an informal or voluntary commitment of an incompetent child, and are anxious to designate another who can maintain contact with the patient and act on his behalf without the necessity of a sanity hearing. The person designated by will must act by filing acceptance of the appointment. This provides a check against will directions which might prove to be unwise or unnecessary after the parents' death. Moreover, the testamentary designee will have the risk of the possibility that the ward is not in fact incapacitated to prevent him from using the authority conferred to restrain the liberty of the ward. In cases of doubt, the testamentary appointee should petition for a Court appointment under Section 5–303.

Section 5–302. [Venue.]

The venue for guardianship proceedings for an incapacitated person is in the place where the incapacitated person resides or is present. If the incapacitated person is admitted to an institution pursuant to order of a Court of competent jurisdiction, venue is also in the county in which that Court sits.

Venue in guardianship proceedings lies in the county where the incapacitated person is present, as well as where he resides. Thus, if the person is temporarily away from his county of usual abode, the Court of the county where he happens to be may handle requests for guardianship proceedings relating to him. In protective proceedings, venue is normally in the county of residence. See Section 5–403. See Section 1–303 for disposition when venue is in two counties, and for transfer of venue.

Section 5–303. [Procedure For Court Appointment of a Guardian of an Incapacitated Person.]

(a) The incapacitated person or any person interested in his welfare may petition for a finding of incapacity and appointment of a guardian.

(b) Upon the filing of a petition, the Court shall set a date for hearing on the issues of incapacity and unless the allegedly incapacitated person has counsel of his own choice, it shall appoint an appropriate official or attorney to represent him in the proceeding, who shall have the powers and duties of a guardian ad litem. The person alleged to be incapacitated shall be examined by a physician appointed by the Court who shall submit his report in writing to the Court and be interviewed by a visitor sent by the Court. The visitor also shall interview the person seeking appointment as guardian, and visit the present place of abode of the person alleged to be incapacitated and the place it is proposed that he will be detained or reside if the requested appointment is made and submit his report in writing to the Court. The person alleged to be incapacitated is entitled to be present at the hearing in person, and to see or hear all evidence bearing upon his condition. He is entitled to be present by counsel, to present evidence, to cross-examine witnesses, including the Court-appointed physician and the visitor [, and to trial by jury]. The issue may be determined at a closed hearing [without a jury] if the person alleged to be incapacitated or his counsel so requests.

The procedure here is similar to, but not precisely the same as, protective proceedings for certain disabled persons. It is not required that the visitor be a lawyer. In urban areas, the visitor may be a social worker capable of determining the needs of the person for whom the appointment is sought. By brackets, the National Conference indicates that enacting states should decide whether it is appropriate to create a right to jury trial.

Section 5–304. [Findings; Order of Appointment.]

The Court may appoint a guardian as requested if it is satisfied that the person for whom a guardian is sought is incapacitated and that the appointment is necessary or desirable as a means of providing continuing care and supervision of the person of the incapacitated person. Alternatively, the Court may dismiss the proceeding or enter any other appropriate order.

COMMENT

The purpose of guardianship is to provide for the care of a person who is unable to care for himself. There is no reason to seek a guardian in those situations where the problems to be dealt with center around the property of a disabled person. In that event, a protective proceeding under Part 4 may be in order.

It is assumed that the standards suggested by the definition in Section 5–101 for the "incapacitated" person are different from those which will determine when a person may be committed as mentally ill. For example, involuntary commitment proceedings may well be inappropriate unless it is determined that the patient is or probably will become *dangerous* to himself or the person or property of others. As indicated in 5–101, the meaning of "incapacitated" turns on whether the subject lacks "understanding or capacity to make or communicate responsible decisions concerning his person." There is overlap between the two sets of standards, but they *are* different. Hence, a finding that a person is "incapacitated" does not amount to a finding that he is mentally ill, or can be committed. In the reverse situation, if a person has been committed to institutional care and custody because of mental illness, it may be unnecessary to appoint a guardian for him. Nonetheless, it may be desirable to have a personal guardian for one who is or may be committed or who will be cared for by an institution. For one thing, a guardian, having custody, might arrange for a voluntary care arrangement like that which a parent for a minor and incapacitated child could establish. Moreover, the limited authority of a guardian over property of his ward may be appropriate in cases where the ward is committed. Because of the relationship between existing guardianship legislation and the handling of committed persons appears to vary considerably from state to state, the Code was deliberately left rather general on points relevant to the relationship. Section 5–312 qualifies the power of a guardian to determine the place of residence of a ward who has been committed.

Section 5–305. [Acceptance of Appointment; Consent to Jurisdiction.]

By accepting appointment, a guardian submits personally to the jurisdiction of the Court in any proceeding relating to the guardianship that may be instituted by any interested person. Notice of any proceeding shall be delivered to the guardian or mailed to him by ordinary mail at his address as listed in the Court records and to his address as then known to the petitioner.

COMMENT

The proceedings under Article V are flexible. The Court should not appoint a guardian unless one is necessary or desirable for the care of the person. If it develops that the needs of the person who is alleged to be incapacitated are not those which would call for a guardian, the Court may adjust the proceeding accordingly. By acceptance of the appointment, the guardian submits to the Court's jurisdiction in much the same way as a personal representative. Cf. Sec. 3–602.

Section 5–306. [Termination of Guardianship for Incapacitated Person.]

The authority and responsibility of a guardian for an incapacitated person terminates upon the death of the guardian or ward, the determination of incapacity of the guardian, or upon removal or resignation as provided in Section 5–307. Testamentary appointment under an informally probated will terminates if the will is later denied probate in a formal proceeding.

Section 5–307. [Removal or Resignation of Guardian; Termination of Incapacity.]

(a) On petition of the ward or any person interested in his welfare, the Court may remove a guardian and appoint a successor if in the best interests of the ward. On petition of the guardian, the Court may accept his resignation and make any other order which may be appropriate.

(b) An order adjudicating incapacity may specify a minimum period, not exceeding one year, during which no petition for an adjudication that the ward is no longer incapacitated may be filed without special leave. Subject to this restriction, the ward or any person interested in his welfare may petition for an order that he is no longer incapacitated, and for removal or resignation of the guardian. A request for this order may be made by informal letter to the Court or judge and any person who knowingly interferes with transmission of this kind of request to the Court or judge may be adjudged guilty of contempt of Court.

(c) Before removing a guardian, accepting the resignation of a guardian, or ordering that a ward's incapacity has terminated, the Court, following the same procedures to safeguard the rights of the ward as apply to a petition for appointment of a guardian, may send a visitor to the residence of the present guardian and to the place where the ward resides or is detained, to observe conditions and report in writing to the Court.

The ward's incapacity is a question that may usually be reviewed at any time. However, provision is made for a discretionary restriction on review. In all review proceedings, the welfare of the ward is paramount.

Section 5–308. [Visitor in Guardianship Proceeding.]

A visitor is, with respect to guardianship proceedings, a person who is trained in law, nursing or social work and is an officer, employee or special appointee of the Court with no personal interest in the proceedings.

The visitor should have professional training and should not have a personal interest in the outcome of the guardianship proceedings.

Section 5–309. [Notices in Guardianship Proceedings.]

(a) In a proceeding for the appointment or removal of a guardian of an incapacitated person other than the appointment of a temporary guardian or temporary suspension of a guardian, notice of hearing shall be given to each of the following:

(1) the ward or the person alleged to be incapacitated and his spouse, parents and adult children;

(2) any person who is serving as his guardian, conservator or who has his care and custody; and

(3) in case no other person is notified under (1), at least one of his closest adult relatives, if any can be found.

(b) Notice shall be served personally on the alleged incapacitated person, and his spouse and parents if they can be found within the state. Notice to the spouse and parents, if they cannot be found within the state, and to all other persons except the alleged incapacitated person shall be given as provided in Section 1–401. Waiver of notice by the person alleged to be incapacitated is not effective unless he attends the hearing or his waiver of notice is confirmed in an interview with the visitor. Representation of the alleged incapacitated person by a guardian ad litem is not necessary.

The persons entitled to notice in guardianship proceeding are usually fewer in number than those in a protective proceeding. Cf. Sec. 5–405. Required notice shall be given in accordance with the general notice provision of the Code. See Section 1–401.

Section 5–310. [Temporary Guardians.]

If an incapacitated person has no guardian and an emergency exists, the Court may exercise the power of a guardian pending notice and hearing. If an appointed guardian is not effectively performing his duties and the Court further finds that the welfare of the incapacitated person requires immediate action, it may, with or without notice, appoint a temporary guardian for the incapacitated person for a specified period not to exceed 6 months. A temporary guardian is entitled to the care and custody of the ward and the authority of any permanent guardian previously appointed by the Court is suspended so long as a temporary guardian has authority. A temporary guardian may be removed at any time. A temporary guardian shall make any report the Court requires. In other respects the provisions of this Code concerning guardians apply to temporary guardians.

COMMENT

The temporary guardian is analogous to a special administrator under Sections 3–614 through 3–618. His appointment would be obtained in emergency situations or as a protective device against default by a guardian. The temporary guardian has all the powers of a guardian, except as the order appointing him may provide otherwise.

Section 5–311. [Who May Be Guardian; Priorities.]

(a) Any competent person or a suitable institution may be appointed guardian of an incapacitated person.

(b) Persons who are not disqualified have priority for appointment as guardian in the following order:

(1) the spouse of the incapacitated person;

(2) an adult child of the incapacitated person;

(3) a parent of the incapacitated person, including a person nominated by will or other writing signed by a deceased parent;

(4) any relative of the incapacitated person with whom he has resided for more than 6 months prior to the filing of the petition;

(5) a person nominated by the person who is caring for him or paying benefits to him.

Section 5–312. [General Powers and Duties of Guardian.]

(a) A guardian of an incapacitated person has the same powers, rights and duties respecting his ward that a parent has respecting his unemancipated minor child except that a guardian is not liable to third persons for acts of the ward solely by reason of the parental relationship. In particular, and without qualifying the foregoing, a guardian has the following powers and duties, except as modified by order of the Court:

(1) To the extent that it is consistent with the terms of any order by a court of competent jurisdiction relating to detention or commitment of the ward, he is entitled to custody of the person of his ward and may establish the ward's place of abode within or without this state.

(2) If entitled to custody of his ward he shall make provision for the care, comfort and maintenance of his ward and, whenever appropriate, arrange for his training and education. Without regard to custodial rights of the ward's person, he shall take reasonable care of his ward's clothing, furniture, vehicles and other personal effects and commence protective proceedings if other property of his ward is in need of protection.

(3) A guardian may give any consents or approvals that may be necessary to enable the ward to receive medical or other professional care, counsel, treatment or service.

(4) If no conservator for the estate of the ward has been appointed, he may:

(i) institute proceedings to compel any person under a duty to support the ward or to pay sums for the welfare of the ward to perform his duty;

(ii) receive money and tangible property deliverable to the ward and apply the money and property for support, care and education of the ward; but, he may not use funds from his ward's estate for room and board which he, his spouse, parent, or child have furnished the ward unless a charge for the service is approved by order of the Court made upon notice to at least one of the next of kin of the incompetent ward, if notice is possible. He must exercise care to conserve any excess for the ward's needs.

(5) A guardian is required to report the condition of his ward and of the estate which has been subject to his possession or control, as required by the Court or court rule.

(6) If a conservator has been appointed, all of the ward's estate received by the guardian in excess of those funds expended to meet current expenses for support, care, and education of the ward must be paid to the conservator for management as provided in this Code, and the guardian must account to the conservator for funds expended.

(b) Any guardian of one for whom a conservator also has been appointed shall control the custody and care of the ward, and is entitled to receive reasonable sums for his services and for room and board furnished to the ward as agreed upon between him and the conservator, provided the amounts agreed upon are reasonable under the circumstances. The guardian may request the conservator to expend the ward's estate by payment to third persons or institutions for the ward's care and maintenance.

COMMENT

The guardian is responsible for the care of the person of his ward. This section gives him the powers necessary to carry out this responsibility. Where there are no protective proceedings, the guardian also has limited authority over the property of the ward. Where the ward has substantial property, it may be desirable to have protective proceedings to handle his property problems. The same person, of course, may serve as guardian and conservator. Section 5-408 authorizes the Court to make preliminary orders protecting the estate once a petition for appointment of a conservator is filed.

Section 5–313. [Proceedings Subsequent to Appointment; Venue.]

(a) The Court where the ward resides has concurrent jurisdiction with the Court which appointed the guardian, or in which acceptance of a testamentary appointment was filed, over resignation, removal, accounting and other proceedings relating to the guardianship.

(b) If the Court located where the ward resides is not the Court in which acceptance of appointment is filed, the Court in which proceedings subsequent to appointment are commenced shall in all appropriate cases notify the other Court, in this or another state, and after consultation with that Court determine whether to retain jurisdiction or transfer the proceedings to the other Court, whichever may be in the best interest of the ward. A copy of any order accepting a resignation or removing a guardian shall be sent to the Court in which acceptance of appointment is filed.

PART 4

PROTECTION OF PROPERTY OF PERSONS UNDER DISABILITY AND MINORS

Section 5–401. [Protective Proceedings.]

Upon petition and after notice and hearing in accordance with the provisions of this Part, the Court may appoint a conservator or make other protective order for cause as follows:

(1) Appointment of a conservator or other protective order may be made in relation to the estate and affairs of a minor if the Court determines that a minor owns money or property that requires management or protection which cannot otherwise be provided, has or may have business affairs which may be jeopardized or prevented by his minority, or that funds are needed for his support and education and that protection is necessary or desirable to obtain or provide funds.

(2) Appointment of a conservator or other protective order may be made in relation to the estate and affairs of a person if the court determines that (i) the person is unable to manage his property and affairs effectively for reasons such as mental illness, mental deficiency, physical illness or disability, advanced age, chronic use of drugs, chronic intoxication, confinement, detention by a foreign power, or disappearance; and (ii) the person has property which will be wasted or dissipated unless proper management is provided, or that funds are needed for the support, care and welfare of the person or those entitled to be supported by him and that protection is necessary or desirable to obtain or provide funds.

COMMENT

This is the basic section of this part providing for protective proceedings for minors and disabled persons. "Protective proceedings" is a generic term used to describe proceedings to establish conservatorships and obtain protective orders. "Disabled persons" is used in this section to include a broad category of persons who, for a variety of different reasons, may be unable to manage their own property.

Since the problems of property management are generally the same for minors and disabled persons, it was thought undesirable to treat these problems in two separate parts. Where there are differences, these have been separately treated in specific sections.

The Comment to Section 5–304, *supra*, points up the different meanings of *incapacity* (warranting guardianship), and *disability*.

Section 5–402. [Protective Proceedings; Jurisdiction of Affairs of Protected Persons.]

After the service of notice in a proceeding seeking the appointment of a conservator or other protective order and until termination of the proceeding, the Court in which the petition is filed has:

(1) exclusive jurisdiction to determine the need for a conservator or other protective order until the proceedings are terminated;

(2) exclusive jurisdiction to determine how the estate of the protected person which is subject to the laws of this state shall be managed, expended or distributed to or for the use of the protected person or any of his dependents;

(3) concurrent jurisdiction to determine the validity of claims against the person or estate of the protected person and his title to any property or claim.

COMMENT

While the bulk of all judicial proceedings involving the conservator will be in the court supervising the conservatorship third parties may bring suit against the conservator or the protected person on some matters in other courts. Claims against the conservator after his appointment are dealt with by Section 5–428.

Section 5–403. [Venue.]

Venue for proceedings under this Part is:

(1) In the place in this state where the person to be protected resides whether or not a guardian has been appointed in another place; or

(2) If the person to be protected does not reside in this state, in any place where he has property.

COMMENT

Venue for protective proceedings lies in the county of residence (rather than domicile) or, in the case of the non-resident, where his property is located. Unitary management of the property is obtainable through easy transfer of proceedings (Section 1–303(b)) and easy collection of assets by foreign conservators (Section 5–431).

Section 5–404. [Original Petition for Appointment or Protective Order.]

(a) The person to be protected, any person who is interested in his estate, affairs or welfare including his parent, guardian, or custodian, or any person who would be adversely affected by lack of effective management of his property and affairs may petition for the appointment of a conservator or for other appropriate protective order.

(b) The petition shall set forth to the extent known, the interest of the petitioner; the name, age, residence and address of the person to be protected; the name and address of his guardian, if any; the name and address of his nearest relative known to the petitioner; a general statement of his property with an estimate of the value thereof, including any compensation, insurance, pension or allowance to which he is entitled; and the reason why appointment of a conservator or other protective order is necessary. If the appointment of a conservator is requested, the petition also shall set forth the name and address of the person whose appointment is sought and the basis of his priority for appointment.

Section 5–405. [Notice.]

(a) On a petition for appointment of a conservator or other protective order, the person to be protected and his spouse or, if none, his parents, must be served personally with notice of the proceeding at least 14 days before the date of hearing if they can be found within the state, or, if they cannot be found within the state, they must be given notice in accordance with Section 1–401. Waiver by the person to be protected is not effective unless he attends the hearing or, unless minority is the reason for the proceeding, waiver is confirmed in an interview with the visitor.

(b) Notice of a petition for appointment of a conservator or other initial protective order, and of any subsequent hearing, must be given to any person who has filed a request for notice under Section 5–406 and to interested persons and other persons as the Court may direct. Except as otherwise provided in (a), notice shall be given in accordance with Section 1–401.

Section 5–406. [Protective Proceedings; Request for Notice; Interested Person.]

Any interested person who desires to be notified before any order is made in a protective proceeding may file with the Registrar a request for notice subsequent to payment of any fee required by statute or Court rule. The clerk shall mail a copy of the demand to the conservator if one has been appointed. A request is not effective unless it contains a statement showing the interest of the person making it and his address, or that of his attorney, and is effective only as to matters occurring after the filing. Any governmental agency paying or planning to pay benefits to the person to be protected is an interested person in protective proceedings.

Section 5–407. [Procedure Concerning Hearing and Order on Original Petition.]

(a) Upon receipt of a petition for appointment of a conservator or other protective order because of minority, the Court shall set a date for hearing on the matters alleged in the petition. If, at any time in the proceeding, the Court determines that the interests of the minor are or may be inadequately represented, it may appoint an attorney to represent the minor, giving consideration to the choice of the minor if fourteen years of age or older. A lawyer appointed by the Court to represent a minor has the powers and duties of a guardian ad litem. After hearing, upon finding that a basis for the appointment of a conservator or other protective order has been established, the Court shall make an appointment or other appropriate protective order.

(b) Upon receipt of a petition for appointment of a conservator or other protective order for reasons other than minority, the Court shall set a date for hearing.

(c) Unless the person to be protected has counsel of his own choice, the Court must appoint a lawyer to represent him who then has the powers and duties of a guardian ad litem. If the alleged disability is mental illness, mental deficiency, physical illness or disability, advanced age, chronic use of drugs, or chronic intoxication, the Court may direct that the person to be protected be examined by a physician designated by the Court, preferably a physician who is not connected with any institution in which the person is a patient or is detained. The Court may send a visitor to interview the person to be protected. The visitor may be a guardian ad litem or an officer or employee of the Court.

COMMENT

The section establishes a framework within which professionals, including the judge, attorney and physician, if any, may be expected to exercise good judgment in regard to the minor or disabled person who is the subject of the proceeding. The National Conference accepts that it is desirable to rely on profes-

sionals rather than to attempt to
draft detailed standards or conditions for appointment.

Section 5–408. [Permissible Court Orders.]

The Court has the following powers which may be exercised directly or through a conservator in respect to the estate and affairs of protected persons;

(1) While a petition for appointment of a conservator or other protective order is pending and after preliminary hearing and without notice to others, the Court has power to preserve and apply the property of the person to be protected as may be required for his benefit or the benefit of his dependents.

(2) After hearing and upon determining that a basis for an appointment or other protective order exists with respect to a minor without other disability, the Court has all those powers over the estate and affairs of the minor which are or might be necessary for the best interests of the minor, his family and members of his household.

(3) After hearing and upon determining that a basis for an appointment or other protective order exists with respect to a person for reasons other than minority, the Court has, for the benefit of the person and members of his household, all the powers over his estate and affairs which he could exercise if present and not under disability, except the power to make a will. These powers include, but are not limited to power to make gifts, to convey or release his contingent and expectant interests in property including marital property rights and any right of survivorship incident to joint tenancy or tenancy by the entirety, to exercise or release his powers as trustee, personal representative, custodian for minors, conservator, or donee of a power of appointment, to enter into contracts, to create revocable or irrevocable trusts of property of the estate which may extend beyond his disability or life, to exercise options of the disabled person to purchase securities or other property, to exercise his rights to elect options and change beneficiaries under insurance and annuity policies and to surrender the policies for their cash value, to exercise his right to an elective share in the estate of his deceased spouse and to renounce any interest by testate or intestate succession or by inter vivos transfer.

(4) The Court may exercise or direct the exercise of, its authority to exercise or release powers of appointment of which the protected person is donee, to renounce interests, to make gifts in trust or otherwise exceeding 20 percent of any year's income of the estate or

to change beneficiaries under insurance and annuity policies, only if satisfied, after notice and hearing, that it is in the best interests of the protected person, and that he either is incapable of consenting or has consented to the proposed exercise of power.

(5) An order made pursuant to this section determining that a basis for appointment of a conservator or other protective order exists, has no effect on the capacity of the protected person.

COMMENT

The Court, which is supervising a conservatorship, is given all the powers which the individual would have if he were of full capacity. These powers are given to the Court that is managing the protected person's property since the exercise of these powers have important consequences with respect to the protected person's property.

Section 5–409. [Protective Arrangements and Single Transactions Authorized.]

(a) If it is established in a proper proceeding that a basis exists as described in Section 5–401 for affecting the property and affairs of a person the Court, without appointing a conservator, may authorize, direct or ratify any transaction necessary or desirable to achieve any security, service, or care arrangement meeting the foreseeable needs of the protected person. Protective arrangements include, but are not limited to, payment, delivery, deposit or retention of funds or property, sale, mortgage, lease or other transfer of property, entry into an annuity contract, a contract for life care, a deposit contract, a contract for training and education, or addition to or establishment of a suitable trust.

(b) When it has been established in a proper proceeding that a basis exists as described in Section 5–401 for affecting the property and affairs of a person the Court, without appointing a conservator, may authorize, direct or ratify any contract, trust or other transaction relating to the protected person's financial affairs or involving his estate if the Court determines that the transaction is in the best interests of the protected person.

(c) Before approving a protective arrangement or other transaction under this section, the Court shall consider the interests of creditors and dependents of the protected person and, in view of his disability, whether the protected person needs the continuing protection of a conservator. The Court may appoint a special conservator to assist in the accomplishment of any protective arrangement or other transaction authorized under this section who shall have the authority conferred by the order and serve until discharged by order after report to the Court of all matters done pursuant to the order of appointment.

COMMENT

It is important that the provision be made for the approval of single transactions or the establishment of protective arrangements as alternatives to full conservatorship. Under present law, a guardianship often must be established simply to make possible a valid transfer of land or securities. This section eliminates the necessity of the establishment of long-term arrangements in this situation.

Section 5–410. [Who May Be Appointed Conservator; Priorities.]

(a) The Court may appoint an individual, or a corporation with general power to serve as trustee, as conservator of the estate of a protected person. The following are entitled to consideration for appointment in the order listed:

(1) a conservator, guardian of property or other like fiduciary appointed or recognized by the appropriate court of any other jurisdiction in which the protected person resides;

(2) an individual or corporation nominated by the protected person if he is 14 or more years of age and has, in the opinion of the Court, sufficient mental capacity to make an intelligent choice;

(3) the spouse of the protected person;

(4) an adult child of the protected person;

(5) a parent of the protected person, or a person nominated by the will of a deceased parent;

(6) any relative of the protected person with whom he has resided for more than 6 months prior to the filing of the petition;

(7) a person nominated by the person who is caring for him or paying benefits to him.

(b) A person in priorities (1), (3), (4), (5), or (6) may nominate in writing a person to serve in his stead. With respect to persons having equal priority, the Court is to select the one who is best qualified of those willing to serve. The Court, for good cause, may pass over a person having priority and appoint a person having less priority or no priority.

COMMENT

A flexible system of priorities for appointment as conservator has been provided. A parent may name

a conservator for his minor children
in his will if he deems this desirable.

Section 5–411. [Bond.]

The Court may require a conservator to furnish a bond conditioned upon faithful discharge of all duties of the trust according to
law, with sureties as it shall specify. Unless otherwise directed, the
bond shall be in the amount of the aggregate capital value of the
property of the estate in his control plus one year's estimated
income minus the value of securities deposited under arrangements
requiring an order of the Court for their removal and the value of
any land which the fiduciary, by express limitation of power, lacks
power to sell or convey without Court authorization. The Court in
lieu of sureties on a bond, may accept other security for the
performance of the bond, including a pledge of securities or a
mortgage of land.

COMMENT

The bond requirements for conservators are somewhat more strict
than the requirements for personal
representatives. Cf. Section 3–603.

Section 5–412. [Terms and Requirements of Bonds.]

(a) The following requirements and provisions apply to any bond
required under Section 5–411:

(1) Unless otherwise provided by the terms of the approved
bond, sureties are jointly and severally liable with the conservator
and with each other;

(2) By executing an approved bond of a conservator, the surety
consents to the jurisdiction of the Court which issued letters to
the primary obligor in any proceeding pertaining to the fiduciary
duties of the conservator and naming the surety as a party
defendant. Notice of any proceeding shall be delivered to the
surety or mailed to him by registered or certified mail at his
address as listed with the court where the bond is filed and to his
address as then known to the petitioner;

(3) On petition of a successor conservator or any interested
person, a proceeding may be initiated against a surety for breach
of the obligation of the bond of the conservator;

(4) The bond of the conservator is not void after the first
recovery but may be proceeded against from time to time until
the whole penalty is exhausted.

(b) No proceeding may be commenced against the surety on any matter as to which an action or proceeding against the primary obligor is barred by adjudication or limitation.

Section 5–413. [Acceptance of Appointment; Consent to Jurisdiction.]

By accepting appointment, a conservator submits personally to the jurisdiction of the Court in any proceeding relating to the estate that may be instituted by any interested person. Notice of any proceeding shall be delivered to the conservator, or mailed to him by registered or certified mail at his address as listed in the petition for appointment or as thereafter reported to the Court and to his address as then known to the petitioner.

Section 5–414. [Compensation and Expenses.]

If not otherwise compensated for services rendered, any visitor, lawyer, physician, conservator or special conservator appointed in a protective proceeding is entitled to reasonable compensation from the estate.

Section 5–415. [Death, Resignation or Removal of Conservator.]

The Court may remove a conservator for good cause, upon notice and hearing, or accept the resignation of a conservator. After his death, resignation or removal, the Court may appoint another conservator. A conservator so appointed succeeds to the title and powers of his predecessor.

Section 5–416. [Petitions for Orders Subsequent to Appointment.]

(a) Any person interested in the welfare of a person for whom a conservator has been appointed may file a petition in the appointing court for an order (1) requiring bond or security or additional bond or security, or reducing bond, (2) requiring an accounting for the administration of the trust, (3) directing distribution, (4) removing the conservator and appointing a temporary or successor conservator, or (5) granting other appropriate relief.

(b) A conservator may petition the appointing court for instructions concerning his fiduciary responsibility.

(c) Upon notice and hearing, the Court may give appropriate instructions or make any appropriate order.

Once a conservator has been appointed, the Court supervising the trust acts only upon the request of some moving party.

Section 5–417. [General Duty of Conservator.]

In the exercise of his powers, a conservator is to act as a fiduciary and shall observe the standards of care applicable to trustees as described by Section 7–302.

Section 5–418. [Inventory and Records.]

Within 90 days after his appointment, every conservator shall prepare and file with the appointing Court a complete inventory of the estate of the protected person together with his oath or affirmation that it is complete and accurate so far as he is informed. The conservator shall provide a copy thereof to the protected person if he can be located, has attained the age of 14 years, and has sufficient mental capacity to understand these matters, and to any parent or guardian with whom the protected person resides. The conservator shall keep suitable records of his administration and exhibit the same on request of any interested person.

Section 5–419. [Accounts.]

Every conservator must account to the Court for his administration of the trust upon his resignation or removal, and at other times as the Court may direct. On termination of the protected person's minority or disability, a conservator may account to the Court, or he may account to the former protected person or his personal representative. Subject to appeal or vacation within the time permitted, an order, made upon notice and hearing, allowing an intermediate account of a conservator, adjudicates as to his liabilities concerning the matters considered in connection therewith; and an order, made upon notice and hearing, allowing a final account adjudicates as to all previously unsettled liabilities of the conservator to the protected person or his successors relating to the conservatorship. In connection with any account, the Court may require a conservator to submit to a physical check of the estate in his control, to be made in any manner the Court may specify.

The persons who are to receive notice of intermediate and final accounts will be identified by Court order as provided in Section 5–405(b). Notice is given as described in 1–401. In other respects, procedures applicable to accountings will be as provided in court rule.

Section 5–420. [Conservators; Title by Appointment.]

The appointment of a conservator vests in him title as trustee to all property of the protected person, presently held or thereafter acquired, including title to any property theretofore held for the protected person by custodians or attorneys in fact. The appointment of a conservator is not a transfer or alienation within the meaning of general provisions of any federal or state statute or regulation, insurance policy, pension plan, contract, will or trust instrument, imposing restrictions upon or penalties for transfer or alienation by the protected person of his rights or interest, but this section does not restrict the ability of persons to make specific provision by contract or dispositive instrument relating to a conservator.

COMMENT

This section permits independent administration of the property of protected persons once the appointment of a conservator had been obtained. Any interested person may require the conservator to account in accordance with Section 5–419. As a trustee, a conservator holds title to the property of the protected person. The appointment of a conservator is a serious matter and the Court must select him with great care. Once appointed, he is free to carry on his fiduciary responsibilities. If he should default in these in any way, he may be made to account to the Court.

Unlike a situation involving appointment of a guardian, the appointment of a conservator has no bearing on the capacity of the disabled person to contract or engage in other transactions.

Section 5–421. [Recording of Conservator's Letters.]

Letters of conservatorship are evidence of transfer of all assets of a protected person to the conservator. An order terminating a conservatorship is evidence of transfer of all assets of the estate from the conservator to the protected person, or his successors. Subject to the requirements of general statutes governing the filing or recordation of documents of title to land or other property, letters of conservatorship, and orders terminating conservatorships, may be filed or recorded to give record notice of title as between the conservator and the protected person.

Section 5–422. [Sale, Encumbrance or Transaction Involving Conflict of Interest; Voidable; Exceptions.]

Any sale or encumbrance to a conservator, his spouse, agent or attorney, or any corporation or trust in which he has a substantial beneficial interest, or any transaction which is affected by a substantial conflict of interest is voidable unless the transaction is approved by the Court after notice to interested persons and others as directed by the Court.

Section 5–423. [Persons Dealing with Conservators; Protection.]

A person who in good faith either assists a conservator or deals with him for value in any transaction other than those requiring a Court order as provided in Section 5–408, is protected as if the conservator properly exercised the power. The fact that a person knowingly deals with a conservator does not alone require the person to inquire into the existence of a power or the propriety of its exercise, except that restrictions on powers of conservators which are endorsed on letters as provided in Section 5–426 are effective as to third persons. A person is not bound to see to the proper application of estate assets paid or delivered to a conservator. The protection here expressed extends to instances in which some procedural irregularity or jurisdictional defect occurred in proceedings leading to the issuance of letters. The protection here expressed is not by substitution for that provided by comparable provisions of the laws relating to commercial transactions and laws simplifying transfers of securities by fiduciaries.

Section 5–424. [Powers of Conservator in Administration.]

(a) A conservator has all of the powers conferred herein and any additional powers conferred by law on trustees in this state. In addition, a conservator of the estate of an unmarried minor under the age of 18 years, as to whom no one has parental rights, has the duties and powers of a guardian of a minor described in Section 5–209 until the minor attains the age of 18 or marries, but the parental rights so conferred on a conservator do not preclude appointment of a guardian as provided by Part 2.

(b) A conservator has power without Court authorization or confirmation, to invest and reinvest funds of the estate as would a trustee.

(c) A conservator, acting reasonably in efforts to accomplish the purpose for which he was appointed, may act without Court authorization or confirmation, to

(1) collect, hold and retain assets of the estate including land in another state, until, in his judgment, disposition of the assets should be made, and the assets may be retained even though they include an asset in which he is personally interested;

657

(2) receive additions to the estate;

(3) continue or participate in the operation of any business or other enterprise;

(4) acquire an undivided interest in an estate asset in which the conservator, in any fiduciary capacity, holds an undivided interest;

(5) invest and reinvest estate assets in accordance with subsection (b);

(6) deposit estate funds in a bank including a bank operated by the conservator;

(7) acquire or dispose of an estate asset including land in another state for cash or on credit, at public or private sale; and to manage, develop, improve, exchange, partition, change the character of, or abandon an estate asset for a term within or extending beyond the term of the conservatorship in connection with the exercise of any power vested in the conservator;

(8) make ordinary or extraordinary repairs or alterations in buildings or other structures, to demolish any improvements, to raze existing or erect new party walls or buildings;

(9) subdivide, develop, or dedicate land to public use; to make or obtain the vacation of plats and adjust boundaries; to adjust differences in valuation on exchange or to partition by giving or receiving considerations; and to dedicate easements to public use without consideration;

(10) enter for any purpose into a lease as lessor or lessee with or without option to purchase or renew for a term within or extending beyond the term of the conservatorship;

(11) enter into a lease or arrangement for exploration and removal of minerals or other natural resources or enter into a pooling or unitization agreement;

(12) grant an option involving disposition of an estate asset, to take an option for the acquisition of any asset;

(13) vote a security, in person or by general or limited proxy;

(14) pay calls, assessments, and any other sums chargeable or accruing against or on account of securities;

(15) sell or exercise stock subscription or conversion rights; to consent, directly or through a committee or other agent, to the reorganization, consolidation, merger, dissolution, or liquidation of a corporation or other business enterprise;

(16) hold a security in the name of a nominee or in other form without disclosure of the conservatorship so that title to the

security may pass by delivery, but the conservator is liable for any act of the nominee in connection with the stock so held;

(17) insure the assets of the estate against damage or loss, and the conservator against liability with respect to third persons;

(18) borrow money to be repaid from estate assets or otherwise; to advance money for the protection of the estate or the protected person, and for all expenses, losses, and liability sustained in the administration of the estate or because of the holding or ownership of any estate assets and the conservator has a lien on the estate as against the protected person for advances so made;

(19) pay or contest any claim; to settle a claim by or against the estate or the protected person by compromise, arbitration, or otherwise; and to release, in whole or in part, any claim belonging to the estate to the extent that the claim is uncollectible;

(20) pay taxes, assessments, compensation of the conservator, and other expenses incurred in the collection, care, administration and protection of the estate;

(21) allocate items of income or expense to either estate income or principal, as provided by law, including creation of reserves out of income for depreciation, obsolescence, or amortization, or for depletion in mineral or timber properties;

(22) pay any sum distributable to a protected person or a dependent of the person who is a minor or incompetent, without liability to the conservator, by paying the sum to the distributee or by paying the sum for the use of the distributee either to his guardian or if none, to a relative or other person with custody of his person;

(23) employ persons, including attorneys, auditors, investment advisors, or agents, even though they are associated with the conservator to advise or assist him in the performance of his administrative duties; to act upon their recommendation without independent investigation; and instead of acting personally, to employ one or more agents to perform any act of administration, whether or not discretionary;

(24) prosecute or defend actions, claims or proceedings in any jurisdiction for the protection of estate assets and of the conservator in the performance of his duties; and

(25) execute and deliver all instruments which will accomplish or facilitate the exercise of the powers vested in the conservator.

Section 5–425. [Distributive Duties and Powers of Conservator.]

(a) A conservator may expend or distribute income or principal of the estate without Court authorization or confirmation for the support, education, care or benefit of the protected person and his dependents in accordance with the following principles:

(1) The conservator is to consider recommendations relating to the appropriate standard of support, education and benefit for the protected person made by a parent or guardian, if any. He may not be surcharged for sums paid to persons or organizations actually furnishing support, education or care to the protected person pursuant to the recommendations of a parent or guardian of the protected person unless he knows that the parent or guardian is deriving personal financial benefit therefrom, including relief from any personal duty of support, or unless the recommendations are clearly not in the best interests of the protected person.

(2) The conservator is to expend or distribute sums reasonably necessary for the support, education, care or benefit of the protected person with due regard to (i) the size of the estate, the probable duration of the conservatorship and the likelihood that the protected person, at some future time, may be fully able to manage his affairs and the estate which has been conserved for him; (ii) the accustomed standard of living of the protected person and members of his household; (iii) other funds or sources used for the support of the protected person.

(3) The conservator may expend funds of the estate for the support of persons legally dependent on the protected person and others who are members of the protected person's household who are unable to support themselves, and who are in need of support.

(4) Funds expended under this subsection may be paid by the conservator to any person, including the protected person to reimburse for expenditures which the conservator might have made, or in advance for services to be rendered to the protected person when it is reasonable to expect that they will be performed and where advance payments are customary or reasonably necessary under the circumstances.

(b) If the estate is ample to provide for the purposes implicit in the distributions authorized by the preceding subsections, a conservator for a protected person other than a minor has power to make gifts to charity and other objects as the protected person might have been expected to make, in amounts which do not exceed in total for any year 20 percent of the income from the estate.

(c) When a minor who has not been adjudged disabled under Section 5–401(2) attains his majority, his conservator, after meeting all prior claims and expenses of administration, shall pay over and distribute all funds and properties to the former protected person as soon as possible.

(d) When the conservator is satisfied that a protected person's disability (other than minority) has ceased, the conservator, after meeting all prior claims and expenses of administration, shall pay over and distribute all funds and properties to the former protected person as soon as possible.

(e) If a protected person dies, the conservator shall deliver to the Court for safekeeping any will of the deceased protected person which may have come into his possession, inform the executor or a beneficiary named therein that he has done so, and retain the estate for delivery to a duly appointed personal representative of the decedent or other persons entitled thereto. If after [40] days from the death of the protected person no other person has been appointed personal representative and no application or petition for appointment is before the Court, the conservator may apply to exercise the powers and duties of a personal representative so that he may proceed to administer and distribute the decedent's estate without additional or further appointment. Upon application for an order granting the powers of a personal representative to a conservator, after notice to any person demanding notice under Section 3–204 and to any person nominated executor in any will of which the applicant is aware, the Court may order the conferral of the power upon determining that there is no objection, and endorse the letters of the conservator to note that the formerly protected person is deceased and that the conservator has acquired all of the powers and duties of a personal representative. The making and entry of an order under this section shall have the effect of an order of appointment of a personal representative as provided in Section 3–308 and Parts 6 through 10 of Article III except that estate in the name of the conservator, after administration, may be distributed to the decedent's successors without prior re-transfer to the conservator as personal representative.

COMMENT

This section sets out those situations wherein the conservator may distribute property or disburse funds during the continuance of or on termination of the trust. Section 5–416(b) makes it clear that a conservator may seek instructions from the Court on questions arising under this section. Subsection (e) is derived in part from § 11.80.150 Revised Code of Washington [RCWA 11.80.150].

Section 5–426. [Enlargement or Limitation of Powers of Conservator.]

Subject to the restrictions in Section 5–408(4), the Court may confer on a conservator at the time of appointment or later, in addition to the powers conferred on him by Sections 5–424 and 5–425, any power which the Court itself could exercise under Sections 5–408(2) and 5–408(3). The Court may, at the time of appointment or later, limit the powers of a conservator otherwise conferred by Sections 5–424 and 5–425, or previously conferred by the Court, and may at any time relieve him of any limitation. If the Court limits any power conferred on the conservator by Section 5–424 or Section 5–425, the limitation shall be endorsed upon his letters of appointment.

COMMENT

This section makes it possible to appoint a fiduciary whose powers are limited to part of the estate or who may conduct important transactions, such as sales and mortgages of land, only with special Court authorization. In the latter case, a conservator would be in much the position of a guardian of property under the law currently in force in most states, except that he would have title to the property. The purpose of giving conservators title as trustees is to ensure that the provisions for protection of third parties have full effect. The Veterans Administration may insist that, when it is paying benefits to a minor or disabled, the letters of conservatorship limit powers to those of a guardian under the Uniform Veteran's Guardianship Act and require the conservator to file annual accounts.

The Court may not only limit the powers of the conservator but may expand his powers so as to make it possible for him to act as the Court itself might act.

Section 5–427. [Preservation of Estate Plan.]

In investing the estate, and in selecting assets of the estate for distribution under subsections (a) and (b) of Section 5–425, in utilizing powers of revocation or withdrawal available for the support of the protected person, and exercisable by the conservator or the Court, the conservator and the Court should take into account any known estate plan of the protected person, including his will, any revocable trust of which he is settlor, and any contract, transfer or joint ownership arrangement with provisions for payment or transfer of benefits or interests at his death to another or others which he may have originated. The conservator may examine the will of the protected person.

Section 5–428. [Claims Against Protected Person; Enforcement.]

(a) A conservator must pay from the estate all just claims against the estate and against the protected person arising before or after the conservatorship upon their presentation and allowance. A claim may be presented by either of the following methods: (1) the claimant may deliver or mail to the conservator a written statement of the claim indicating its basis, the name and address of the claimant and the amount claimed; (2) the claimant may file a written statement of the claim, in the form prescribed by rule, with the clerk of the Court and deliver or mail a copy of the statement to the conservator. A presented claim is allowed if it is not disallowed by written statement mailed by the conservator to the claimant within 60 days after its presentation. The presentation of a claim tolls any statute of limitation relating to the claim until thirty days after its disallowance.

(b) A claimant whose claim has not been paid may petition the Court for determination of his claim at any time before it is barred by the applicable statute of limitation, and, upon due proof, procure an order for its allowance and payment from the estate. If a proceeding is pending against a protected person at the time of appointment of a conservator or is initiated against the protected person thereafter, the moving party must give notice of the proceeding to the conservator if the outcome is to constitute a claim against the estate.

(c) If it appears that the estate in conservatorship is likely to be exhausted before all existing claims are paid, preference is to be given to prior claims for the care, maintenance and education of the protected person or his dependents and existing claims for expenses of administration.

Section 5–429. [Individual Liability of Conservator.]

(a) Unless otherwise provided in the contract, a conservator is not individually liable on a contract properly entered into in his fiduciary capacity in the course of administration of the estate unless he fails to reveal his representative capacity and identify the estate in the contract.

(b) The conservator is individually liable for obligations arising from ownership or control of property of the estate or for torts committed in the course of administration of the estate only if he is personally at fault.

(c) Claims based on contracts entered into by a conservator in his fiduciary capacity, on obligations arising from ownership or control of the estate, or on torts committed in the course of administration of the estate may be asserted against the estate by proceeding against the conservator in his fiduciary capacity, whether or not the conservator is individually liable therefor.

(d) Any question of liability between the estate and the conservator individually may be determined in a proceeding for accounting, surcharge, or indemnification, or other appropriate proceeding or action.

Section 5–430. [Termination of Proceeding.]

The protected person, his personal representative, the conservator or any other interested person may petition the Court to terminate the conservatorship. A protected person seeking termination is entitled to the same rights and procedures as in an original proceeding for a protective order. The Court, upon determining after notice and hearing that the minority or disability of the protected person has ceased, may terminate the conservatorship. Upon termination, title to assets of the estate passes to the former protected person or to his successors subject to provision in the order for expenses of administration or to conveyances from the conservator to the former protected persons or his successors, to evidence the transfer.

COMMENT

The persons entitled to notice of a petition to terminate a conservatorship are identified by Section 5–405.

Any interested person may seek the termination of a conservatorship when there is some question as to whether the trust is still needed. In some situations (e.g., the individual who returns after being missing) it may be perfectly clear that he is no longer in need of a conservatorship.

An order terminating a conservatorship may be recorded as evidence of the transfer of title from the estate. See 5–421.

Section 5–431. [Payment of Debt and Delivery of Property to Foreign Conservator Without Local Proceedings.]

Any person indebted to a protected person, or having possession of property or of an instrument evidencing a debt, stock, or chose in action belonging to a protected person may pay or deliver to a conservator, guardian of the estate or other like fiduciary appointed by a court of the state or residence of the protected person, upon being presented with proof of his appointment and an affidavit made by him or on his behalf stating:

(1) that no protective proceeding relating to the protected person is pending in this state; and

(2) that the foreign conservator is entitled to payment or to receive delivery.

If the person to whom the affidavit is presented is not aware of any protective proceeding pending in this state, payment or delivery in response to the demand and affidavit discharges the debtor or possessor.

COMMENT

Section 5–410(a)(1) gives a foreign conservator or guardian of property, appointed by the state where the disabled person resides, first priority for appointment as conservator in this state. A foreign conservator may easily obtain any property in this state and take it to the residence of the protected person for management.

*

INDEX TO
UNIFORM PROBATE CODE

References are to sections of Code

INDEX

CLOSING ESTATES—Cont'd

Borrowing, personal representative transactions authorized, § 3–715.

Boundaries, personal representative transactions authorized, § 3–715.

Breach of duty, § 3–712.

Failure of personal representative to give information of appointment to devisees and heirs, § 3–705.

Limitations on proceedings against personal representatives, § 3–1005.

Buildings, personal representative transactions authorized, § 3–715.

Burial arrangements, power of executor named in will to carry out instructions prior to appointment, § 3–701.

Business transactions, personal representative transactions authorized, § 3–715.

Calls against securities, personal representative transactions authorized, § 3–715.

Care, standards applicable to personal representatives, § 3–703.

Cash,

Deposit or investment, personal representative transactions authorized, § 3–715.

Payments, personal representative transactions authorized, § 3–715.

Casualty insurance, personal representative transactions authorized, § 3–715.

Charitable pledges, satisfaction, personal representative transactions authorized, § 3–715.

Children, duty of personal representative to administer and distribute estate to dependent minor or pretermitted child, § 3–703.

Claimants' rights, duty of personal representative to administer and distribute estate, § 3–703.

Closing statements,

Limitations, proceedings against personal representative, § 3–1005.

Personal representatives, § 3–1003.

Small estates, summary administration, §§ 3–1203, 3–1204.

Collection of personal property by affidavit, small estates, successors, §§ 3–1201, 3–1202.

Commencement of powers and duties of personal representative, time, § 3–701.

Commercial paper, personal representative transactions authorized, § 3–715.

CLOSING ESTATES—Cont'd

Community property, devolution of estate at death, § 3–101A.

Compensation and salaries,

Authorized personal representative transactions, § 3–715.

Personal representatives, §§ 3–718, 3–719.

Proceedings for review, § 3–721.

Refunds, excessive compensation to personal representatives and employees of estate, § 3–721.

Compromise and settlement, personal representative transactions authorized, § 3–715.

Concurrence in acts of personal representatives, co-representatives, § 3–717.

Conduct, general duties of personal representatives, § 3–703.

Conflict of interest, personal representative's transactions, § 3–713.

Consolidation and merger of corporations, personal representative transactions authorized, § 3–715.

Formal proceedings terminating administration, §§ 3–1001, 3–1002.

Contracts,

Compensation of personal representative, § 3–719.

Personal representative transactions authorized, § 3–715.

Rights of purchasers and others dealing with personal representative, § 3–712 et seq.

Contribution, distributees' liability for undischarged claims, § 3–1004.

Control of decedent's property, personal representative's duty, § 3–709.

Conversion rights, stock, authorized personal representative transactions, § 3–715.

Conveyances,

Personal representative transactions authorized, § 3–715.

Personal representative's power to avoid transfers, § 3–710.

Inventory, personal representative's duty to interested persons, § 3–706.

Copies of,

Supplementary inventory, personal representatives' duties, § 3–708.

Sworn closing statement of personal representative, sending to distributees of estate, etc., § 3–1003.

Co-representatives, personal representative powers and duties, § 3–717.

Surviving personal representative powers, § 3–718.

INDEX

INDEX

687

INDEX

INDEX

DEEDS AND CONVEYANCES—Cont'd
Personal representative's power to avoid transfers, § 3–710.
Rights of purchasers and others, dealing with personal representatives, § 3–712 et seq.
Rules of construction regarding donative dispositions. Donative Dispositions, generally, this index.
Supervised Administration of Estates, this index.

DEEDS OF DISTRIBUTION
Distribution of Estates, this index.

DEFECTS
Informal probate, applications or procedures, § 3–302.

DEFENSES
Expenses of personal representative in estate litigation, § 3–720.
Personal representatives, power to prosecute or defend claims, § 3–715.

DEFINITIONS
Words and Phrases, generally, this index.

DELEGATION OF AUTHORITY
Co-representative powers and duties, § 3–717.
Personal representatives, transactions authorized, § 3–715.

DELIVERY
Conservators, generally, this index.
Creditors' Claims Against Estates, this index.
Deed or conveyance, personal representative transactions authorized, § 3–715.
Foreign personal representatives, delivery of property without local administration, § 4–201.
Notice, mail, acceptance of appointment, personal representative, § 3–602.
Property, request, personal representative's duty, § 3–709.
Protective Proceedings for Minors and Disabled Persons, generally, this index.

DEMOLITION
Buildings, personal representative transactions authorized, § 3–715.

DENIAL
Informal probate and appointment proceedings,
Application, § 3–303 et seq.

DENIAL—Cont'd
Informal probate and appointment proceedings—Cont'd
Informal appointment, §§ 3–308, 3–311.
Supervised administration of estate, request, § 3–502.

DEPENDENT CHILDREN AND MINORS
Children and Minors, generally, this index.

DEPOSITS
Agreements. Nonprobate Transfers on Death, generally, this index.
Authorized transactions, personal representative, § 3–715.
Bank Deposits and Accounts, generally, this index.
Certificates of deposit, security, defined, general provision, § 1–201.
Informal probate and appointment proceedings, deposit of copy of previously probated will, § 3–303.
Liquid assets of estate, personal representative transactions authorized, § 3–715.
Personal representatives, cash in lieu of bond, § 3–603.

DEPOSITS IN COURT
Will, in testator's lifetime, § 2–515.

DESCENDANT
Defined, general provisions, § 1–201.

DESCENT AND DISTRIBUTION
Intestate Succession, generally, this index.

DETECTIVES
Notice, formal testacy and appointment proceedings, hearing on petition, § 3–403.

DETENTION BY FOREIGN POWER
Conservators, generally, this index.
Guardianship and Protective Proceedings, generally, this index.

DEVELOPMENT OF PROPERTY
Personal representative transactions authorized, § 3–715.

DEVISEES
Defined, general provisions, wills, § 1–201.
Interested person, defined, general provisions, § 1–201.
Multiple-person accounts. See Nonprobate Transfers on Death, generally, this index.
Wills, deceased devisee, construction of wills, § 2–603.

705

INDEX

INDEX

INDEX

INDEX

727

730

INDEX

INDEX

INDEX

753

INDEX

INDEX

INDEX

INDEX

772

INDEX

INSURANCE

Annuities, generally, this index.

Creditors' claims against estate, limitation on claims presentation, § 3–803.

Casualty insurance, personal representatives, insuring assets of estates, § 3–715.

Guardianship and Protective Proceedings, generally, this index.

Life Insurance, generally, this index.

Personal representatives, insuring assets of estates, § 3–715.

Policies. Nonprobate Transfers on Death, generally, this index.

Unpaid proceeds on specifically devised property, nonademption, § 2–606.

INTER VIVOS TRUSTS

Trusts and Trustees, generally, this index.

INTEREST

Accounts, deposits, personal representative transactions authorized, § 3–715.

Creditors' claims against estates, allowance of claims, § 3–806.

Distribution of Estates, this index.

Multiple-person accounts. See Nonprobate Transfers on Death, generally, this index.

INTERESTED PARTIES

Defined, general provisions, § 1–201.

Informal probate, findings required, § 3–303.

Personal representative's power over title to property of estate, § 3–711.

Personal representatives' powers and duties, §§ 3–703, 3–704.

INTERIM ACCOUNTS

Trusts and Trustees, this index.

INTERIM ORDERS

Supervised administration of estates, §§ 3–504, 3–505.

INTERLOCUTORY APPEAL

Generally, § 1–308.

INTERNATIONAL WILLS ACT

Wills, generally, this index.

INTESTATE SUCCESSION

Generally, §§ 2–101 et seq., 3–101.

Abandoned or unclaimed property, personal representative transactions authorized, § 3–715.

Abatement and revival of actions, personal representatives' powers and duties, § 3–703.

INTESTATE SUCCESSION—Cont'd

Absolute ownership, personal representative's power over title to property of estate, § 3–711.

Acceptance, power of personal representative to ratify act on behalf of estate, § 3–701.

Acquisition of assets, personal representative transactions authorized, § 3–715.

Actions and proceedings,

Expenses, § 3–720.

Independent nature, § 3–107.

Jurisdiction, § 3–105.

Notice, § 3–106.

Personal representatives' powers and duties, § 3–703.

Petition for orders, § 3–107.

Recover possession of property of estate, personal representative's duty, § 3–709.

Surviving death of decedent, personal representatives' powers and duties, § 3–703.

Adjudication of no will, § 3–107.

Advancements, § 2–109.

Funds for protection of estate, personal representative transactions authorized, § 3–715.

Adverse or pecuniary interest, personal representative's transactions, § 3–713.

Affidavit for collection of personal property, small estate, §§ 3–1201, 3–1202.

Afterborn heirs, § 2–108.

Agents and agencies,

Appeal and review, employment of agents and compensation by personal representative, § 3–721.

Authorized personal representative, § 3–715.

Conflict of interest, transactions involving personal representative's agent, § 3–713.

Alienage, § 2–111.

Alleged decedent found alive, protection of good faith personal representative and third party transactions, § 3–714.

Allocations to income or principal, personal representative transactions authorized, § 3–715.

Alterations in buildings, personal representative transactions authorized, § 3–715.

Amendments, supplementary inventory, personal representatives' duties, § 3–708.

Ancillary Administration of Estates, generally, this index.

INDEX

INDEX

INDEX

INDEX

INDEX

INDEX

INDEX

INDEX

†